The Birth of a Consumer Society
The Commercialization of Eighteenth-Century England

The Birth of a Consumer Society

The Commercialization of Eighteenth-Century England

Neil McKendrick, John Brewer
and J.H. Plumb

Second Expanded Edition with new Introduction

EER
Edward Everett Root Publishers, Brighton, 2018

EER
Edward Everett Root Publishers Co. Ltd.,
30 New Road, Brighton, Sussex, BN1 1BN, England.
www.eerpublishing.com

edwardeverettroot@yahoo.co.uk

The Birth of a Consumer Society
The Commercialization of Eighteenth-Century England
Neil McKendrick, John Brewer and J.H. Plumb

First published in England 1982. This expanded edition 2018.

Neil McKendrick, John Brewer and the estate of J.H. Plumb

© 1982, 2018.

This edition © Edward Everett Root Publishers 2018.

ISBN: 978-1-912224-26-5 Paperback
ISBN: 978-1-912224-27-2 Hardback

Neil McKendrick, John Brewer, and the executors of the estate of J.H. Plumb have asserted their right to be identified as the author of this Work in accordance with the Copyright, Designs and Patents Act 1988 as the owner of this Work. All rights reserved. No part of this publication may be reproduced, stored in a retrieval system or transmitted in any form or by any means, electronic, mechanical, photocopying, recording or otherwise, without the prior permission of the copyright owner.

Cover designed by Pageset Limited, High Wycombe.

Contents

Notes on the Authors · vi

Preface *Neil McKendrick* · vii

Introduction to 2018 edition *Neil McKendrick* · ix

Introduction. The Birth of a Consumer Society: the Commercialization of Eighteenth-century England *Neil McKendrick* · 1

PART I: COMMERCIALIZATION AND THE ECONOMY
Neil McKendrick

1. The Consumer Revolution of Eighteenth-Century England · 9
2. The Commercialization of Fashion · 34
3. Josiah Wedgwood and the Commercialization of the Potteries · 100
4. George Packwood and the Commercialization of Shaving: The Art of Eighteenth-Century Advertising or "The Way to Get Money and be Happy" · 146

PART II: COMMERCIALIZATION AND POLITICS
John Brewer

5. Commercialization and Politics · 197

PART III: COMMERCIALIZATION AND SOCIETY
J. H. Plumb

6. The Commercialization of Leisure · 265
7. The New World of Children · 286
8. The Acceptance of Modernity · 316

PART IV: COMMERCIALIZATION OF LEISURE
Neil McKendrick

9. Botany, Gardening and the Birth of a Consumer Society · 337

Index · 379

Notes on the Authors in 2018

Neil McKendrick graduated with a 'starred' First in History at Cambridge in 1956. He was elected into a Research Fellowship at Christ's College in March 1958 and elected as Fellow, College Lecturer and Director of Studies in History at Gonville & Caius College in October 1958. He was appointed Chairman of the History Faculty in 1985 and Master of Caius in 1996. His publications include *Historical Perspectives: Studies in English Thought and Society* (1974), *The Birth of a Consumer Society: the Commercialization of Eighteenth-Century England* (1983), *The Birth of Foreign & Colonial: the World's First Investment Trust* (1993), and *F & C: a History of Foreign & Colonial Investment Trust* (1999). He was general editor of the *Europa Library of Business Biography* and the *Europa History of Human Experience*. He is, perhaps, best known for his work on Josiah Wedgwood and the Industrial Revolution. He is currently a Life Fellow and former Master of Caius College and an Honorary Fellow of Christ's College.

John Brewer graduated with a 'starred First' in History at Cambridge in 1968. He was elected into a Research Fellowship at Sidney Sussex College in 1969 and then into a Fellowship at Corpus Christi and his first university post in Cambridge. He has held many professorships including chairs at Washington University in St Louis, Yale and Harvard. In 1987 he left Harvard to become the Director of the Clark Library and the Center for Seventeenth and Eighteenth Century Studies at UCLA, where he directed a three year research programme funded by the National Endowment of the Humanities, entitled 'Culture and Consumption in the 17th and 18th Centuries'. He became Professor of Cultural History at the European University Institute. In 1999 he returned to the United States as Professor in English and History at the University of Chicago, but moved to the California Institute of Technology in 2002 where he held the Eli and Edye Broad Professorship in Humanities and Social Science.

J. H. Plumb graduated with the first 'First' in History achieved as an external London degree from University College Leicester in 1933. He was elected into a Research Fellowship at King's College, Cambridge in 1939, and then into a Fellowship at Christ's College in 1946. He was successively Lecturer, Reader and Professor at Cambridge. He was elected Master of Christ's in 1978 and was knighted on his retirement in 1982. He held five American professorships and was awarded seven Honorary Degrees (five of them in the States). He published *England in the Eighteenth Century* (1950), *Chatham* (1953), *The First Four Georges* (1956), *Sir Robert Walpole*, vol. i (1956) and vol. ii (1960), *Men and Places* (1962), *The Growth of Political Stability in England, 1675–1725* (1967), *The Death of the Past* (1969), *In the Light of History* (1972), *Royal Heritage* (1977), *Georgian Delights* (1980) and many other works. Sir John died in 2001 aged ninety.

Preface

This book was conceived at a meeting of the Caius historical society—a body sometimes more noted for its critical rigour than for its creative vigour—when after a paper by Professor Brewer, it became clear that the three authors of this book had all, at different times, been working separately in Cambridge on different aspects of the commercialization of eighteenth-century England.

Neil McKendrick's work on Wedgwood had drawn attention in the early 1960s to the commercial revolution which Wedgwood and Bentley had achieved in their own industry;[1] Professor Plumb in the early 1970s had drawn attention to the commercialization of leisure in his Stenton Lecture;[2] and finally Professor Brewer's work on Wilkes had revealed parallel developments in the political world.[3]

To draw together the work of three scholars—one working primarily in economic history, one (on this occasion) in social history, and one in political history—is more unusual than it should be. To do so in a monograph which hopes to stimulate more research in an exciting but little publicized field, and which is inevitably more speculative than definitive in some areas, is possibly more adventurous than it should be. But all three contributors have done further recent work in this field[4] and are convinced that they have jointly identified an important and neglected historical phenomenon. They feel that it deserves both greater recognition and more detailed attention. If by jointly publishing some of the results of their past and recent research they can establish the former and encourage the latter they will be more than satisfied.

Even if they fail to achieve either of these modest ambitions, there are consolations to be found in this essay in co-operation. For it is comforting to note how much of the work of scholars operating within ostensibly separate (and all too often mutually hostile) historical disciplines can fruitfully overlap. And it is difficult to deny that when the authors' three separate and tentative

---

[1] Neil McKendrick, 'Josiah Wedgwood: An Eighteenth Century Entrepreneur in Salesmanship and Marketing Techniques', *Economic History Review*, 2nd series, XII, no. 3 (April 1960), pp. 408– 33. (Reprinted in *Essays in Economic History*, ed. E. M. Carus-Wilson, vol. III (1962), pp. 353–70; 'The Discovery of Pompeii and Herculaneum and the Neo-Classical Revival', *Horizon*, vol. IV, no. 4, March 1962, pp. 42–75; 'Josiah Wedgwood and Thomas Bentley: An Inventor-Entrepreneur Partnership in the Industrial Revolution', *Transactions of the Royal Historical Society*, 5th series, vol. 14 (1964), pp. 1–33.
[2] J. H. Plumb, *The Commercialization of Leisure in Eighteenth Century England* (The Stenton Lecture). The University of Reading, 1973.
[3] John Brewer, *Party Ideology and Popular Politics at the Accession of George III.* (Cambridge, 1976).
[4] Neil McKendrick, 'Home Demand and Economic Growth: A New View of the Role of Women and Children in the Industrial Revolution', *Historical Perspectives: Studies in English Thought and Society*, ed. Neil McKendrick (London, 1974), pp. 152– 210; J. H. Plumb, 'The New World of Children in Eighteenth Century England', *Past and Present*, no. 67, (1975), pp. 64–95, *The Pursuit of Happiness* (Yale, 1977), and *Georgian Delights* (London, 1980).

probes into the darkness of the past are brought together, the spotlight they produce illuminates the problem more brightly and throws the whole subject into sharper relief than their individual beams of light could ever have done alone. This is not to suggest that the authors have attempted to focus exclusively on a single aspect of their chosen century. The individual spotlights dance away to reveal, if only partially, other problems lying slightly off-centre on the academic stage, and to offer glimpses of yet others even deeper in the shadows of ignorance and unexplored archives. Individually at least (and outside the confines of this book) efforts are being made to bring them into focus and into the spotlight too.

Some of what is offered here is admittedly in the nature of preliminary studies. As is so often the case, the English critic can offer a more elegant guide to the art of the disarming preface than the historian can, and it is with gratitude that I borrow from Professor Steiner his definition of 'working papers' or 'position papers', as exercises in which scholars 'put forward a point of view, analysis or proposition' in a form which while it attempts to be inclusive and is certainly assertive, is nonetheless 'explicitly provisional'.[5] Some parts of this book have some claim to be authoritative, others are published specifically to solicit 'correction, modification, and that collaborative disagreement on which the hopes of rational discourse depend'.[5]

NEIL McKENDRICK

Gonville &- Caius College, Cambridge.

---

[5] George Steiner, *On Difficulty* (Oxford, 1978). Preface.

Introduction to 2018 edition

My interest in consumer behaviour started very early in my academic career. One of the first papers I ever gave, some sixty years ago, was rather clumsily entitled *The Purchase of Delight: The Pursuit of Happiness through the Treasured Possessions of Material Goods*. The reaction to it was not encouraging.

In the late 1950s such a subject was thought to be at best better confined to one's leisure hours – a harmless hobby but not a subject to be taken seriously in the Cambridge History Faculty. In those days even social and economic history played very little part in the Cambridge History Tripos – the history of material culture played virtually no part at all.

The Cambridge historians of power and influence and patronage were preoccupied with what were then regarded as altogether more serious concerns – with constitutional history, political history, ecclesiastical history, military history and the history of political thought. The big beasts in Cambridge were almost all historians of such traditional subjects. They were to end their careers as Sir Herbert Butterfield, Dom David Knowles, (Sir) Owen Chadwick, Sir Geoffrey Elton, Sir John Plumb, Sir Harry Hinsley, and Sir Moses Finley. The two great outliers – Joseph Needham and E. H. Carr, who were working in Cambridge but outside the History faculty – had little or no interest in business history or the history of consumption.

It was much the same outside Cambridge – in Oxford the two most influential historians were A. J. P. Taylor and Hugh Trevor Roper (later Lord Dacre) who dazzled in their work on the traditional subjects. Outside Oxbridge, J. E. Neale (later Sir John Neale) and L. B. Namier (later Sir Lewis Namier) also wielded their great power and influence as political historians. Of this generation of high fliers, Asa Briggs (later Lord Briggs) was the notable exception. The Cambridge stars of the next generation such as Sir John Elliott and Denis Mack Smith were also mainly political historians – Sir Tony Wrigley, who came from outside the History faculty, being a distinguished exception.

So dominant were these traditional areas of study that I was solemnly warned by several of these senior scholars that even to embark on research as a business historian was to endanger my future career prospects.

To be fair to my senior advisors, I took much the same view when counseling my own pupils. Certainly those who I taught very early in my career in the early 1960s (stars such as Quentin Skinner, future Regius professor at Cambridge, and Norman Stone, future Professor of Modern History at Oxford) chose the safer traditional routes to future distinction. Indeed revealingly, of all the distinguished Caian historians that I taught and helped to launch on their academic careers in the twentieth century very few chose to follow my lead in the choice of their research topic. There were more than fifty of them; more than half of them became professors (two of them Regius professors); eight of them are Fellows of the British Academy; three were offered knighthoods (two of them accepted them) and one became Master of a Cambridge college. But of that constellation of talent and achievement, only one devoted his career to business history.

Admittedly Geoff Crossick co-authored a book on *Palaces of Consumption* in 1999 and more recently Melissa Calaresu co-edited *Treasured Possessions* in 2015. Fortunately, too, pupils that I taught from other Cambridge colleges, such as Roy Porter, Simon Schama, James Raven and Mary Laven, have made important contributions to the history of consumption, but I think the subject choices of most of those I have supervised demonstrate how very far the history of consumption was from being a leading brand in Cambridge.

For if working on business history in general was very far from being fashionable, publishing work on retailing, marketing and advertising was even less so. The dominant view was that in the hierarchy of historical studies the status of business history ranked very lowly indeed; and the prevailing view, even amongst business historians themselves, was that respectability was far more easily to be found in the study of production than in the study of selling.

They were right in one thing. Economic historians in general were much more interested in supply than in demand. Producers were seen as of more central importance than consumers. The lives of factory workers were ranked as far more worthy of study than lives of shopkeepers. Industrial inventions in manufacturing ranked far higher than entrepreneurial brilliance in marketing and retailing.

These were not views that I shared.

Fortunately for me my first research subject was Josiah Wedgwood and the Industrial Revolution and I soon realized than his career required as much attention to consumers as it did to producers, as much to marketing as it did to manufacturing, as much to his advertising campaigns as it did to his discipline of his labour force, as much to his London showrooms as to his factory at Etruria. I was, of course, always keen to stress the symbiotic relationship between supply and demand, and much of my research was inevitably and very properly devoted to the supply side of the economic equation – to Wedgwood's ceramic inventions, his factory and his labour force, his scientific research programmes, his factory discipline, his debt collecting, his cost accountancy and his promotion of canal building – to all of which he brought outstanding new ideas and brilliant new levels of invention and innovation.

However, since the existing Wedgwood historiography centred so powerfully on the production side of the equation, I decided in 1960, as a corrective rebalancing exercise, to publish my first significant scholarly article on his marketing and salesmanship. I followed this up in 1964 with an article on his partner Thomas Bentley which stressed the importance of Bentley's role in London, as he and Wedgwood together plotted to manipulate the market and cultivate new levels of demand for their products with a series of brilliantly inventive sales campaigns.

To press home my conviction that the supply side of the economic equation was still enjoying a too little challenged dominance and to attempt to correct the prevailing pessimistic interpretation of the Industrial Revolution so influentially promoted by historians such as Eric Hobsbawm and E. P. Thompson, I published in 1974 a more general piece on "Home Demand and Economic Growth: A New View of the Role of Women and Children in the Industrial Revolution".

By the early 1980s the tide of opinion had begun to change and I was very keen to take advantage of the newly favourable currents. In 1982, in his hugely influential *The Wheels of Commerce*, Fernand Braudel had declared that demand was "the right string to start the engine of capitalism". By now J.H.Plumb was moving decisively away from his earlier devotion to political history. It was also in 1982 that I confidently asserted that:

"There was a consumer boom in England in the eighteenth century. In the third quarter of the century that boom reached revolutionary proportions. Men, and in particular women, bought as never before. Even their children enjoyed access to a greater number of goods than ever before. In fact, the later eighteenth century saw such a convulsion of getting and spending, such an eruption of new prosperity, and such an explosion of new production and marketing techniques, that a greater proportion of the population than in any previous society in human history was able to enjoy the pleasures of buying consumer goods. They bought not only necessities, but decencies, and even luxuries. The roots of such a development reach back, of course, into previous centuries but the eighteenth century marked a major watershed. Whatever popular metaphor is preferred – whether revolution or take-off or lift-off or the achievement of critical mass – the same unmistakable breakthrough occurred in consumption as occurred in production. Just as the Industrial Revolution of the eighteenth century marks one of the great discontinuities in history, one of the great turning points in the history of human experience, so, in my view, does the matching revolution in consumption. For the consumer revolution was the necessary analogue to the industrial revolution, the necessary convulsion on the demand side of the equation to match the convulsion on the supply side.

We are only just beginning to realize how pervasive were the social and economic effects of that change, and how considerable were the pressures needed to bring it about. For the results were such as to bring about as great a change in the lifestyle of the population as was brought about by the Neolithic revolution in agriculture which began some eight thousand years before the birth of Christ."

These were bold and novel claims. So, not surprisingly, I prefaced the confident assertion that the authors of *The Birth of a Consumer Society* "are convinced that they have jointly identified an important and neglected historical phenomenon that deserves both greater recognition and more detailed attention" with the proviso that some parts of the book were "explicitly provisional". While "some parts of this book have some claim to be authoritative, others are published specifically to solicit correction, modification and that collaborative disagreement on which hopes of rational discourse depend".

Our hopes for greater recognition and more detailed attention were not disappointed. The reviews were overwhelmingly encouraging. They recognized the novelty and significance of the publication but they stressed that this was pioneering work. It was "something new" which "contains work in progress that will eventually reshape our view of the century". Many scholars took up the challenge to provide more detailed attention to our claims. Amongst many influential works, Colin Campbell published *The Romantic Movement and the Spirit of Modern Consumerism* in 1987; Robert Bocock published *Consumption* in 1993; and John Brewer and Roy Porter organized annual conferences in Los Angeles that led to their publication in 1993 of *Consumption and the World of Goods*.

By 1995, in a plea for more attention to the rich literary evidence heralding the arrival of a consumer society, I felt able to sum up some of the progress that had been made since the early 1980s on the nature and timing of new levels of consumption. I argued that:

"Economic historians have been accused of excessive fertility in spawning a whole family of consumer revolutions in recent years. This is a parody of reality. What has actually happened is that the embryonic beginnings of consumerism in the seventeenth century have been identified by Joan Thirsk, the much heralded birth of a consumer society in the eighteenth century has been announced by Neil McKendrick, the further growth of popular consumption in the late nineteenth century has been described by Peter Mathias, Hamish Fraser and Asa Briggs, and the development into a mature mass consumer society in the twentieth century has been confirmed by historians such as David Aldcroft and many others. The emergence and development of consumerism has been widely observed elsewhere, notably in Holland by Jan de Vries and in France and America by Michael Miller, Rosalind Williams and Ronald Edsforth. In the last ten years or so there has been an explosion of new work on the subject – both theoretical and empirical, both authoritative and speculative."

INTRODUCTION TO 2018 EDITION

The Birth of a Consumer Society: The Commercialization of Eighteenth-Century England alone seems to have spawned a host of major international conferences and to have inspired a mass of important new research, which has built on and refined its initial claims. For, since the later stages of consumerism were already well recognized (even if inadequately researched and understood), much attention has been concentrated on the more novel and exciting claims made about the seventeenth and eighteenth centuries. In recent years important work by historians such as Chandra Mukerji, Margaret Spufford, Lorna Weatherill, Hoh-Cheung and Lorna Mui, Carole Shammas, Timothy Breen and Beverley Lemire has done much to consolidate and refine our knowledge of early consumerism and the birth of modern materialism.

Particular attention has been given to probate records, to inventories, to advertisements, to pedlars and to shops. There has been an entirely appropriate concern to measure whatever economic data can be found. Some important corrections have been made. As a result a sharper quantitative picture has emerged. But there is a danger that a proper concern to quantify may degenerate into what one of my Cambridge colleagues calls "the mere counting of chamber-pots".

Unfair though that verdict might be, there was a warning worth heeding here. Mere enumeration of household inventories is not the only aspect of a consumer society worth studying. It is worth lifting one's eyes from the gritty fundamentals of the eighteenth-century economy to some of the more qualitative responses which can teach us as much as the aggregate statistics can.

There were many other neglected sources to enrich our understanding of the consumer revolution. In the mid-1990s I was eager to explore their potential. At the Datini Institute in Prato I lectured on "The Commercialization of Leisure and the Birth of a Consumer Society" and chose to limit myself almost exclusively to the wonderfully vivid and woefully neglected visual evidence of early consumerism. When I lectured at the Louvre in Paris I concentrated exclusively on the ceramic evidence. When I lectured in Berlin I restricted myself to the equally vivid (and until recently the sadly neglected) resources of eighteenth-century English literature.

As necessary corrective exercises, these lectures in the mid-1990s may have concentrated on one source rather than another, but they were, in fact, intended as a plea for fruitful symbiosis. As Brewer and Porter have recently pointed out there are many approaches and many evidential seams still to be exploited. Some of those seams faithfully reflect the fact and nature of novel consumer behaviour, some of them revealingly explain it. The literary evidence does both.

It has been reasonably asked "If consumption is such an important component of modern industrial society, then surely it should be revealingly reflected in our literary culture?" It is. The more meaningful historical question should be "Why was its significance for so long overlooked?"

If historians had listened to the voices of novelists, poets, playwrights, to the words of critics, reviewers, and journalists, to the message of sermons, magazines and newspapers, they would never have doubted that contemporary writers witnessed and recorded the birth of a consumer society and the commercialization of eighteenth-century England. Together such writers made up "The Luxury Debate of Georgian England". The debate not only records the fact of emerging consumerism; it charts its chronology and its geography; and it mirrors its social stages (first aristocratic luxury, then the luxury of the monied interests, then the luxury of the middling ranks, then the luxury of the labouring classes, and finally and paradoxically the luxury of the poor).

Even more interestingly it proposes its own diagnosis of the social motivations involved. It explains the social causes of consumerism. It tells us why "self-image" was so important to eighteenth-century men and women, why fashion was so pre-eminent, why the hunger for new possessions was so powerful, why the need to possess consumer goods was so potent, why contemporary entrepreneurs exploited particular social values and appealed to particular social weaknesses in their marketing and advertising campaigns. All this and more is to be found in eighteenth-century English literature.

I wanted to stress that the idea of luxury was as central to the eighteenth century as the idea of poverty was to the nineteenth. As Paul Langford wrote in 1989, "a history of luxury and attitudes to luxury would come close to being a history of the eighteenth century". It preoccupied the leading commentators of the day and has left an extraordinary rich seam of evidence of how English society and its most articulate observers reacted to rapid economic change.

Few records give a better insight into the nature of the emerging consumer society than these cultural sources. They reflect the delight in, and the doubts over what contemporaries called "this torrent of luxury", this "all consuming opulence", this "rage to consume", this "fever of getting and spending", this "purchase of delight", this "universal luxury". The very language used to condemn or commend it is revealing. For what excited both its admirers and its detractors was not only that it was novel, astonishing and unprecedented in any previous society or century, but also that it was spreading. To its opponents the repeated metaphor of a fever, a sickness, an infection, a contagion, an insidious distemper, a pestilence, even a plague, reveals how very powerful an adversary they felt that they faced. To many eighteenth-century writers the democratization of consumption was an evil to be fought, as well as an established fact to be faced up to. "Universal luxury" and "unprecedented opulence" were widely recognized but not universally welcomed.

INTRODUCTION TO 2018 EDITION

My aim was to draw attention to the way in which scholars of English literature had revealed how eighteenth-century writers exploited the powerful metaphor of fashion and luxurious consumption. Louis Landa on Pope, Geoffrey Vichert on Swift, Maurice Goldsmith on Mandeville, Maximilian Novak on Defoe, Martin Battestin on Fielding, John Sekora on Smollet, Jim Clifford on Johnson have all made invaluable contributions. More recently cultural historians such as James Raven and Gerald Newman have attempted more general and thematic treatments. Of these John Sekora's and James Raven's work is the most substantial and important in explaining the literary significance of luxury in the eighteenth century. Other historians, preeminently Joyce Appleby and A. W. Coats, have charted the changes in contemporary economic thought in the eighteenth century. Professor Appleby has shown how marked a change in economic thinking emerged from the 1690s onwards. For much of the seventeenth century domestic consumption, or home demand, was seen as, at best, a necessary evil, which grew, if at all, in response to population growth. To the mercantilist writers total demand was seen as inelastic. The rich were expected to buy their luxuries, the poor to have enough to subsist. The possibility that consumers at all social levels might acquire new wants and find new means to enhance their purchasing power, which would in turn generate new spending and produce habits capable of destroying all traditional limits to the wealth of nations, was un-thought of, if not unthinkable.

All this was to change in the course of the long eighteenth century. How and why it changed was vividly revealed in eighteenth century literature.

I first became fully aware of the full potential of literary evidence as a remarkably rich source for both charting and explaining the character of consumer history when I was invited by Stanley Kubrick to act as a historical advisor for his film version of Thackeray's novel, *The Luck of Barry Lyndon*, which was explicitly set in the eighteenth century. Spending ten hours a day being remorselessly grilled by Kubrick about how to turn Thackeray's words on the page into accurate and authentic visual images on the screen made me increasingly conscious of Thackeray's obsession with fashionable consumption. As I wrote in 1995:

"It is worth remembering that Thackeray (writing when the Condition-of-England novelists were insistently preoccupied with poverty, immiseration, squalor and exploitation) was compulsively preoccupied with luxury and indulgent consumption.

Thackeray revelled in consumption, wallowed in a world of commodities, and mirrored (in all its rich diversity) a world of heady materialism. Critics may differ radically on his verdict on luxurious consumption, but none denies his preoccupation with it. "Thackeray", wrote Barbara Hardy in *The Exposure of Luxury*, "is the great sociologist of nineteenth century fiction, the great accumulator of social symbols of class and money. To read him is to read a fictional form of Veblen's *The Theory of the Leisure Class*, or Marcel Mauss's *Essai sur le Don*, or Galbraith's *The Affluent Society*". Thackeray's portrait of nineteenth-century England is the portrait of rampant consumption and unrestrained self-indulgence in material possessions. His characters sit in carriages "rolling the street from mercer to toy shop – from goldsmith to laceman". The antechambers to their homes are crowded with obsequious salesmen offering them everything from "jewels, salvers and tankards" to "hangings and velvets and brocades". They bear names like Lord Squanderfield. Their moral standing is defined by their possessions. In Lady Kew's words, "they belonged to their belongings".

Thackeray, to John Carey, is not only "the novelist of commodities", but also "of people apprehended through" their commodities. Bonnets and boots and buttons, gloves and hats and shoes, these are not incidental to, but pivotal to, Thackeray's writing. His three great social novels (*Vanity Fair* (1847–8), *Pendennis* (1849–50), and *The Newcomes* (1853–55)) are sustained hymns to prodigality. All the protean delights of a growing consumer society are listed and labelled, identified and priced. The advertisements which promoted them, the shops which sold them, are recorded with a loving precision.

Here, at the peak of literary concern with poverty, is a major novelist obsessed with the details of a consumer society.

The character of his obsession is not without significance. For although commodities were an unfailing stimulant to his imagination, he was not much interested in their manufacture. He was a novelist of demand not supply, of consumption not production. "Tracing the resplendent window display of Victorian wealth to its sources in mills and factories and mean streets of disease-stricken dwellings was not an enterprise that impressed him as at all enticing", writes Carey. His imagination was stirred by commodities and advertisements and shops, with brand names and trade names, with details of the possessions that clothed his characters and filled their rooms. Thackeray is prepared to entertain the possibility that to regard a person as a bundle of commodities could be an enriching idea rather than an impoverishing delusion. His characters' innermost feelings are shown as being enmeshed in commodity standards. He even wanted to create a religion which depended wholly on commodities.

As significant as his general preoccupations with consumption were, it was the specific details of it that obsessed him. First he was obsessed with buttons. He believed that the course of human history could be observed through the history of buttons. Indeed the details of his characters' clothes were a central concern of his descriptive method and his moral judgement. Of those clothes, hats, gloves and boots (with of course their accompanying buttons and buckles) mattered most. They, he believed, were "the best barometers of social change". In his view poverty always attacks the extremities first: "the coverings of head, feet and hands are its first prey". To Thackeray, opulence and prosperity were equally well signalled by such commodities.

It is no accident that such apparently insignificant consumer goods were the basis of England's industrial revolution. Birmingham's wealth was built on buttons and buckles, Lancashire's fortunes were dependent on cottons, London's commercial dominance was heavily dependent on the fashion industries of clothing accessories. Thackeray's preoccupation with the advertisements which promoted such goods and his rapturous accounts of the shop windows that displayed them were as relevant to England's economy as were Dickens' factories at Coketown. Thackeray's concern with luxury was, and is, as significant as Dickens' concern with poverty. He was as much a poet of urban consumption as Dickens was a poet of urban pollution.

His verdict was not without ambivalence any more than Dickens' verdict was. But Thackeray's ambivalence, and his moral ambiguities, are to be found in his treatment of Palaces of Consumption not Dark Satanic Mills. The largest display of commodities in Victorian England – the Great Exhibition of 1851 at Crystal Palace – inspired him to write two poems: one is a celebration of consumer goods under a "blazing arch of lucid glass": the other, in comic Irish, presents it all "as meaningless heaps of teapots, coffins and suits of clothes in a palace made of windows". The point is that whether treated to grandiose celebration or heavy-handed satire, the subjects of the poems are consumer goods.

It is worth asking why historians so rarely quote Thackeray on the pleasures of consumption, and so ubiquitously quote Dickens on the perils of production. It is worth asking why the reality of the consumer society has been so traditionally neglected in the historical record (until recently almost wholly effaced), whilst the grim reality of production – the world of factories, machinery and exploited labour – has been so enthusiastically explored. For Thackeray was not alone in his interest in the "Ornamental Classes" and it is worth asking why the influence of the "Condition of England and Hard Times" school of moralists has not been more equitably balanced by the "Silver Fork and Vanity Fair" school of writers.

For the purposes of this argument it is even more worth asking why the rich literary evidence of the eighteenth century has been so little studied by historians of social and economic change.

For although the literary and moral response to the coming of industrialization in England has left us a wonderfully rich cultural legacy, it has been very unevenly appreciated; some parts of it are universally recognized and are studied almost to the point of satiety; others are neglected to the point of almost being effaced from the common memory, and barely recognized even by the educated elite.

The mid-Victorian debate is of the first kind – kept vividly alive through the words of Carlyle, Engels, Ruskin, Arnold, Morris and Smiles, continually re-read in the novels of Dickens, Disraeli, Kingsley, Mrs. Gaskell and Charlotte Bronte, and further reinforced by the works of writers such as Mrs. Tonna, Mrs. Trollope, Mrs. Craik, Charles Pimlico, Charles Reade and William Lever. It is indelibly imprinted on our cultural consciousness by both our literary and historiographical traditions.

The mid-eighteenth debate is of the second kind — little studied, less read and hardly known outside the confines of academic scholarship. It is not that it did not attract writers of stature. On the contrary, Bernard Mandeville, David Hume, Adam Smith and Dr. Johnson all produced weighty contributions to the argument, and Swift, Defoe, Fielding and Smollett all left a decided literary imprint on the controversy. One cannot easily dismiss a debate which played such an important role in works of the order of *The Fable of the Bees*, *The Great Law of Subordination Consider'd*, *The Decline and Fall of the Roman Empire* and *The Wealth of Nations*; which left its impact on works as influential as *Robinson Crusoe*, *Gulliver's Travels* and *Sandford and Merton*; which so centrally concerned novels of the quality of *Tom Jones*, *Joseph Andrews*, *The Man of Feeling* or *Humphrey Clinker*; which inspired poems such as Pope's *The Rape of the Lock* in 1712 and Oliver Goldsmith's *The Deserted Village* in 1770; which was polemically debated in some forty eighteenth-century journals, from *The Female Tatler* and Addison's *Spectator* to the *Annual Register* and the *Gentleman's Magazine*; and which has left 460 books and pamphlets still extant on the subject published in the half century which ran from the 1720s to the 1770s.

Contemporaries spoke of 500 pamphlets on the subject in the 1760s alone. If one includes published sermons, the list of titles becomes almost endless.

More revealing than the differences in the literary and intellectual quality of these two great controversies were their very different content and concerns and their very different posthumous receptions. For the popular posthumous success of one helps to explain posterity's neglect of the other. It is as if the emotional and historical impact of the "Condition of England" debate had blocked out the historical significance of the Luxury debate of the eighteenth century.

Both debates were preoccupied with the consequences (both real and imagined) of dramatic social and economic change. But whilst the "Condition of England" question was dominated by a preoccupation with poverty, exploitation, squalor and immiseration — all seen as the consequences of industrialisation — the debate over the State of the Nation in the eighteenth century was cast in a dramatically different form. It was dominated by a preoccupation with luxury, conspicuous consumption, self-indulgence, fashionable excess and new levels of prosperity — all seen as the consequences of commerce and manufacture.

Both debates could and did envisage the direst consequences for the nation, but they did so for dramatically different reasons. The "Condition of England" debate was conducted in the shadow of economic crisis (commercial collapse and widespread unemployment as experienced in the depression of 1839–42), and was discussed in terms of social upheaval, class confrontation, environmental squalor and aesthetic distaste. In dramatic contrast, the Luxury debate of the eighteenth century contemplated national decline as a consequence of over-indulgence, as a result of excessive consumption of fashionable luxuries and novelties, as the effects of unwonted prosperity led to weakness, decadence and effeminacy; and as the effects of social emulation threatened to subvert the social and political status quo.

The positive case for the endorsement, approval and acceptance of change did not, of course, go unstated. The negative responses are stressed here merely to show how very different the main causes for national pessimism were thought to be in the two centuries. Almost polar opposites were being debated as a cause for national concern. The idea of luxury was as central to the eighteenth century as the idea of poverty was to the nineteenth. Yet the discussions of the dangers of luxury and, of course, its benefits (as expounded in the doctrine of the utility of beneficial luxury) have been culturally overshadowed almost to the point of total eclipse by the response to the crisis of the 1840s. It is difficult to overstate the contrast between the cultural impact of the two controversies. In both critical, literary and historiographical traditions the image of poverty and the malign consequences of industry have remained vividly clear. The image of luxury and the beneficial consequences of commerce have rarely been more than shadowy and vaguely perceived in the popular mind.

Fortunately it is now more readily accepted in the academic mind that in the eighteenth century a powerful and influential literary tradition in favour of luxury had emerged to counteract the popular cry against it.

At the beginning of the century, in Mandeville's provocative and highly controversial equation of "Private Vices" and "Publick Benefits", he argued that "the very Poor lived better than the Rich before" as a direct result of "Their darling Folly, Fickleness in Diet, Furniture and Dress, That strange ridic'lous Vice, was made The very wheel that turn'd the Trade". In Mandeville's metaphor for society the entire population was addicted to luxury, and its prosperity stemmed directly from its self-indulgence. Not surprisingly his *The Fable of the Bees* provoked a violent reaction.

The outraged response was predictable and sustained. It has been estimated that the number responding ran to several thousands for the eighteenth century alone, and some have seen the whole luxury debate as a prolonged attempt to come to terms with his arguments. It was hardly likely that they would win immediate acceptance. For many at this time the idea that "consumption was the sole end of production", that the "latent consuming capacity of the public at large might become an engine for sustained growth", that "society was an aggregation of self-interested individuals tied to one another by the tenuous bonds of envy, exploitation and competition" were too alarmingly novel to be easily accepted". As Joyce Appleby argued, "Dangerous leveling tendencies lurked beneath the idea of personal improvement through imitative buying." Socially exclusive luxury was one thing; "bare-fac'd luxury, the spreading Contagion of which is the greatest Corrupter of Publick Manners" was very different, and there was an urgent demand for its "immediate suppression". Jonathan Swift, for instance, argued that to prevent "all Excesses in Cloathing, Furniture and the Like" it would be necessary to "enact and enforce sumptuary Laws against Luxury".

It was to take the next half a century until in 1776 Adam Smith in *The Wealth of Nations* could signal that the idea of the increased propensity to consume had now taken its rightful place in the orthodox part of the explanation of economic growth. By then he could pronounce with authority and certainty that "consumption is the sole end and purpose of all production; and the interest of the producer ought to be attended to, only as far it may be necessary for promoting that of the consumer. The maxim is....perfectly self-evident".

By then attitudes to luxury had decisively changed. Dr Johnson left unequivocal evidence of his acceptance of the doctrine of beneficial luxury. He explicitly rejected the teaching of his literary predecessors when he said to Boswell in 1776, "Many things which are false are transmitted from book to book and gain credit in the world. One of them is the cry against the evil of luxury. Now the truth is, that luxury produces much good". Lest there be any doubt about it he made clear that he included the democratization of consumption amongst the benefits. His trenchant comments are splendidly unambiguous: "Depend upon it, Sir, every state of society is as luxurious as it can be"; or again, "You cannot spend on luxury without doing good to the poor"; or again, "Luxury, as far as it reaches the poor, will do good to the race of the people; it will strengthen and multiply them. Sir, no nation was ever hurt by luxury".

By then writers of the stature of David Hume, Malachy Postlethwaite, Nathaniel Forster, James Steuart, Soame Jenyns, Adam Ferguson and Adam Smith had all recognized and applauded the beneficial consequences of luxury, particularly in terms of the consuming habits of the poor. Dr. Johnson summed up with suitable certainty and finality: "To entail irreversible poverty upon generation after generation only because the ancestor happened to be poor, is in itself cruel, if not unjust, and is wholly contrary to the maxims of a commercial nation."

English writers seemed to feel a particular compulsion to offer some explanation of the consumer boom they felt themselves to be living through. Foreign observers were usually content simply to record their amazed responses. Awe, admiration and astonishment were the characteristic keynotes of foreign eye-witness commentators. Pehr Kalm from Sweden, de Saussure from Switzerland, Karamzin from Russia, de Saint Fond from France, Count Pecchio from Italy, Lichtenberg and von Archenholz from Germany – these and many others such as Sophie von la Roche, Carl Moritz and Francois de la Rochefoucauld produced a multi-lingual chorus of praise of the spread of luxury and the unprecedented democratization of consumption. By the 1770s the luxury and extravagance of the English lower and middling ranks were thought to have "risen to such a pitch as never before seen in the world"; by the 1780s it was said of England, "Everything presented an aspect of…plenty. Not one object from Dover to London reminded me of poverty"; by the 1790s it was argued that "England surpasses all the other nations in Europe in luxury…and the luxury is increasing daily!…All classes enjoy the accumulation of riches, luxury and pleasure". Even the labourers in the fields were held to be dressed in the height of fashion. If one is looking for evidence of the fact of the birth of a consumer society (or at least an ecstatic announcement of the delivery and the flourishing infancy) then a trawl though the diaries of eighteenth-century foreign visitors is a richly rewarding exercise. If one is seeking an explanation for its arrival (or at least seeking to understand why contemporaries thought it had occurred) then English writers offer a far more profitable source.

For although many English reporters recorded the same "UNIVERSAL" luxury (even indulging in capital letters for emphasis) and described the same prevailing "opulence" of all classes, it was not enough for them simply to describe "the inveterate national habit of luxury of the English"; they felt that they had to account for it.

These explanations – the mechanics of change offered by eye-witness commentators – deserve our close attention. If economic historians are to avoid the charge of economic reductionism they cannot afford to ignore the wealth of cultural evidence which complements and so often confirms the findings of their aggregate statistics, their detailed class and regional studies, their business case studies, and indeed their economic logic. The evidence of attitudinal change is too important to neglect but it plays a surprisingly small part in most accounts of eighteenth-century social and economic change.

In 1767 Nathaniel Forster approvingly identified the emulative motives that lay behind the need to possess the fashionable symbols of social status. "In England", he wrote, "the several ranks of men slide into each other almost imperceptibly, and a spirit of equality runs through every part of their constitution. Hence arises a strong emulation in all the several stations and conditions to vie with each other; and the perpetual restless ambition in each of the inferior ranks to raise themselves to the level of those immediately above them. In such a state as this fashion must have uncontrolled sway. And a fashionable luxury must spread through it like a contagion". By then he was one amongst many identifying the same process.

These characteristics – the closely stratified nature of English society (what sociologists call "the compression of the socio-economic spectrum"), the striving for vertical social mobility, the emulative spending bred by social emulation, and the compulsive power of fashion bred by social competition – were increasingly recognized as part of a benign economic circle. The role of economic factors was not forgotten. It was not enough for the new consumer goods to be wanted. They had to be advertised, marketed and efficiently distributed. They had to be available, accessible and affordable. The value of higher wages to a consumer-oriented society was increasingly recognized. The "doctrine of the utility of beneficial luxury" had by 1770 taken over from the "doctrine of the utility of poverty".

I wrote my plea for the place of literary evidence in enriching our understanding of the nature of consumer behaviour in Georgian England in 1995. Since then there has been a flood of work on the history of consumption – most of which sees the 1980s as the turning point in the approach of social and economic historians. As Hamish Fraser wrote, in the 2017 edition of *The Coming of the Mass Market*, "Economic historians until the 1980s were largely concerned with the "supply" side of the market equation. Production was generally the analytical starting point. Studies focused on industrial workers and labour politics", and then added the trenchant comment "Things began to change in the 1980s". The influence of *The Birth of a Consumer Society* in helping to bring about those changes has been widely and generously acknowledged, but there was still much work that needed to be done as I conceded in 1995. It was in that year that I was elected into the Mastership of Gonville & Caius College and effectively lured away from any further research on consumption. Fortunately the baton was successfully passed on to many other scholars.

In the best recent bibliography of the history of consumption, (in the 2017 edition of *The Coming of the Mass Market*), Hamish Fraser comprehensively and authoritatively lists, among many others, the significant work of scholars such as Nicholas Alexander and Gary Akehurst, *The Emergence of Modern Retailing, 1750–1950* (1999); John Benson and Laura Ugolini, *A Nation of Shopkeepers: Five Centuries of British Retailing* (2003); Deborah Cohen, *Household Gods: The British and their Possessions* (2006); Woodruff D. Smith, *Consumption and the Making of Respectability, 1600–1800* (2002); and Frank Trentman (ed.), *The Oxford Handbook of the History of Consumption* (2012). The history of consumption is clearly now a thriving subject.

Perhaps the most elegant indicator of the progress that the study of consumption has made in Cambridge, since *The Birth of a Consumer Society* was published in 1982, is the publication of *Treasured Possessions* in 2015. This multi-authored, multi-edited, magnificently illustrated volume began, in the words of Tim Knox, the Director of the Fitzwilliam Museum in Cambridge, "as an unprecedented collaboration between the Applied Arts Department of the Fitzwilliam Museum and staff and students from the

INTRODUCTION TO 2018 EDITION

History Faculty of Cambridge University. Over a period of three years, undergraduates who opted to do a final year paper in 'The Material Culture of the Early Modern World' were encouraged to get to know the artefacts on display in the Museum. It was a process of discovery that neither they nor their tutors would ever forget; just as the students were given a taste of how curatorial expertise could expand their understanding of the past, so the curators were challenged by the interpretive questions posed by historians as they worked together." The transformation in attitudes to material culture since I was an undergraduate in the early 1950s could hardly be more dramatic. Few things better highlight the change in attitudes to consumer history than the number and quality of historians involved in this project, and few things better contextualize the pioneering significance of the publication of *The Birth of a Consumer Society* in 1982.

As perhaps befits a historian now in his ninth decade of life, my role in this splendid publication was largely that of an observer, but I was very happy to be involved in raising the very considerable sums needed for a work of this scope, and even happier that I was able to persuade two of my former pupils (Sir Douglas Myers and Adrian Binks) to give so handsomely towards it. I also took some comfort from the fact that, of the two of historians most responsible for editing *Treasured Possessions*, I had taught one, Mary Laven, as an undergraduate, and the other, Melissa Calaresu, is currently the Neil McKendrick Lecturer in History at Caius – a post funded by the £1 million raised by 93 of my pupils.

Neil McKendrick

INTRODUCTION

The Birth of a Consumer Society
The Commercialization of Eighteenth-century England

by

Neil McKendrick

'The English of those several denominations [Peasants and Mechanics, Farmers, Freeholders, Tradesmen and Manufacturers in Middling Life, Wholesale Dealers, Merchants and all persons of Landed Estates] have better Conveniences in their Houses and affect to have more in Quantity of clean, neat Furniture, and a greater variety, such as Carpets, Screens, Window Curtains, Chamber Bells, polished Brass Locks, Fenders etc., (Things Hardly known abroad among persons of such Rank) than are to be found in any other Country of Europe ... were an inventory to be taken of Household Goods and Furniture of a Peasant, or Mechanic, in France, and of a Peasant, or Mechanic in England, the latter would be found on average to Exceed the former in Value by at least three to one.'

JOSIAH TUCKER

PART I

Commercialization and the Economy

by

Neil McKendrick

Luxury

      Employ'd a Million of the Poor,
(M.) And odious Pride a Million more.
(N.) Envy it self and Vanity
      Were Ministers of Industry;
      Their darling Folly, Fickleness
      In Diet, Furniture and Dress,
      That strange ridic'lous Vice, was made
      The very Wheel, that turn'd the Trade.
      Their Laws and Cloaths were equally
      Objects of Mutability;

      Thus Vice nursed Ingenuity,
      Which join'd with Time, and Industry
      Had carry'd Life's Conveniencies,
(O.) It's real Pleasures, Comforts, Ease,
(P.) To such a Height, the very Poor
      Lived better than the Rich before;
      And nothing could be added more:

                      Mandeville, *The Fable of the Bees*, 1714.

CHAPTER ONE

The Consumer Revolution of Eighteenth-century England

There was a consumer boom in England in the eighteenth century. In the third quarter of the century that boom reached revolutionary proportions. Men, and in particular women, bought as never before. Even their children enjoyed access to a greater number of goods than ever before. In fact, the later eighteenth century saw such a convulsion of getting and spending, such an eruption of new prosperity, and such an explosion of new production and marketing techniques, that a greater proportion of the population than in any previous society in human history was able to enjoy the pleasures of buying consumer goods. They bought not only necessities, but decencies, and even luxuries. The roots of such a development reach back, of course, into previous centuries but the eighteenth century marked a major watershed. Whatever popular metaphor is preferred—whether revolution or take-off or lift-off or the achievement of critical mass—the same unmistakable breakthrough occurred in consumption as occurred in production. Just as the Industrial Revolution of the eighteenth century marks one of the great discontinuities in history, one of the great turning points in the history of human experience, so, in my view, does the matching revolution in consumption. For the consumer revolution was the necessary analogue to the industrial revolution, the necessary convulsion on the demand side of the equation to match the convulsion on the supply side.

We are only just beginning to realize how pervasive were the social and economic effects of that change, and how considerable were the pressures needed to bring it about. For the results were such as to bring about as great a change in the lifestyle of the population as was brought about by the neolithic revolution in agriculture which began some eight thousand years before the birth of Christ.

Changes of that order do not occur without comment, and contemporaries were eloquent in their descriptions and explanations of what Arthur Young in 1771 called this 'UNIVERSAL' luxury, and what Dibden in 1801 described as the prevailing 'opulence' of all classes.[1] Foreign commentators were astounded by what one called 'the inveterate national habit of luxury

---

[1] See in Neil McKendrick, 'Home Demand and Economic Growth. A New View of the Role of Women and Children in the Industrial Revolution', *Historical Perspectives. Studies in English Thought and Society,* ed. by Neil McKendrick (London, 1974), p. 193.

of the English', and almost invariably recorded their amazed reactions to it. The Göttingen professor Lichtenberg said of England in the 1770s that the luxury and extravagance of the lower and middling classes had 'risen to such a pitch as never before seen in the world';[2] the Russian writer Karamzin said of England in the 1780s 'Everything presented an aspect of ... plenty. Not one object from Dover to London reminded me of poverty';[3] the historian von Archenholz said of the 1790s 'England surpasses all the other nations of Europe in ... luxury ... and the luxury is increasing daily!' 'All classes', he concluded, 'enjoy the accumulation of riches, luxury and pleasure.'[4] One does not have to take all such hyperbole literally to realize that something momentous was thought to be happening. By the end of the eighteenth century there was a deafening chorus of comment—full of wonder or, more often, complaint at the manifold signs of this great change in consumer behaviour.

The rich, of course, led the way. They indulged in an orgy of spending. Magnificent houses were built reaching a crescendo of building in the 1760s and 1770s when the brothers Adam designed so many memorable Georgian houses to replace Elizabethan and Jacobean mansions ruthlessly demolished to make space for them. Superlative furniture was commissioned from the published directories of Chippendale, Hepplewhite and Sheraton. Porcelain and pottery of a quality unparalleled in English history appeared, including Chelsea, Bow, Worcester and Derby for the few, and Wedgwood for the many. Silver ranged from the sturdy mastery of the early Huguenot silversmiths to the characteristic elegance of a Schofield candlestick to the feminine delicacy of Hester Bateman. Mirrors came from the great master Linnell; cutlery from the master smiths of Sheffield; 'toys' in protean variety, from the costly 'exclusives' of Matthew Boulton to the cheap buttons for the mass market. Wonderful new gardens were created with orangeries bursting with the latest 'exotiques' like pineapples and camellias. Whole estates were replanted for posterity with trees chosen from nurseries offering an unprecedented number and variety of species. Collections of aristocratic pets resembled menageries or private zoos. In all these areas there flourished the unmistakable signs of conspicuous consumption. In all a desire for novelty—so all-consuming that Dr. Johnson complained that men were even 'to be hanged in a new way'. In fashion novelty became an irresistible drug. In possessions for the home, new fashions were insisted on—in pottery, furniture, fabrics, cutlery, even wallpaper. Even their animals must be new, and improved breeds of horses, cattle and sheep, dogs, fishes, birds and plants, were all deliberately pursued with a new intensity and a matching success.

[2] G. C. Lichtenberg, *Lichtenberg's Visits to England,* translated and edited by M. L. Marc and W. H. Quarrel (1938).
[3] N. M. Karamzin, *Letters of a Russian Traveller 1789-90* (1957), trans. and abridged by F. Jonas, p. 261.
[4] J. W. von Archenholz, *A Picture of England* (1791), pp. 75-83.

It is alarming to think of how many trees, flowers and animals which we take for granted they bred or imported for the first time.[5]

In imitation of the rich the middle ranks spent more frenziedly than ever before, and in imitation of them the rest of society joined in as best they might—and that best was unprecedented in the importance of its impact on aggregate demand. Spurred on by social emulation and class competition, men and women surrendered eagerly to the pursuit of novelty, the hypnotic effects of fashion, and the enticements of persuasive commercial propaganda. As a result many objects, once the prized possessions of the rich, reached further than ever before down the social scale.

Forster in 1767 neatly encapsulated all the features of the new demand stressed by modern historians when he wrote

> In England the several ranks of men slide into each other almost imperceptibly, and a spirit of equality runs through every part of their constitution. Hence arises a strong emulation in all the several stations and conditions to vie with each other; and the perpetual restless ambition in each of the inferior ranks to raise themselves to the level of those immediately above them. In such a state as this fashion must have uncontrolled sway. And a fashionable luxury must spread through it like a contagion.[6]

These characteristics—the closely stratified nature of English society, the striving for vertical social mobility, the emulative spending bred by social emulation, the compulsive power of fashion begotten by social competition—combined with the widespread ability to spend (offered by novel levels of prosperity) to produce an unprecedented propensity to consume: unprecedented in the depth to which it penetrated the lower reaches of society and unprecedented in its impact on the economy.

Both commercial activity and the consumer response to it were feverish. Uncontrolled by any sense of commercial decorum men advertised in unprecedented numbers—whole newspapers were taken over by advertisements, and a very large proportion of all newspapers was filled with advertising. And the customer had plenty to choose from. For, spurred on by rampant demand, designers produced both fashions of outrageous absurdity and styles of lasting elegance. Fashion in hats and hairstyles, dresses and shoes and wigs and such like, arguably reached even greater extremes than ever before and certainly changed more rapidly and influenced a greater proportion of society.

As early as 1711 we find Addison writing ironically of 'the ladies' that 'the whole sex is now dwarfed and shrunk into a race of beauties that seems almost another species. I remember several ladies who were once near seven foot high that at present want some inches of five.' He comforts himself that 'most are of the opinion that they are at present like trees lopped and pruned that will certainly sprout up and flourish with greater heads than before'.

[5] See J. H. Plumb below, pp. 316–34.
[6] N. Forster, *An Enquiry into the Present High Price of Provisions* (1767), p. 41.

They did. Men and women's wigs were caricatured as needing special openings in the roofs of their carriages in the 1770s. Women with enormous swollen hoops found it difficult to negotiate narrow doorways, and announced their presence through wide ones with several feet of swollen skirt before they arrived themselves. Hats sprouted upwards and sideways, and such was the rage to follow fashion that even labourers in the fields were recorded by Stubbs and Blake in graceful wide-brimmed picture hats.[7]

Styles in furniture, silver and pottery and the like were (by the nature of their market and the nature of its demand structure) less susceptible to annual or even monthly change in taste, and they achieved an enviable serenity which we still cherish two centuries later. Despite the conflicting claims of Gothic, Chinoiserie and Neo-Classical, some designers managed to impose a remarkable uniformity of style on all classes in the last decade of the century—the rich had Adam and the rest had Adamesque. Even Gothic and Chinoiserie were adapted to classical proportions (apart from occasional extravaganzas like Beckford's Fonthill or the Pagoda at Kew). But within those limits objects of the most marvellous quality and variety were produced for the higher ranks of society. Unworried by any sense of the impropriety of ample profits, manufacturers were able to exploit what they called this 'epidemical madness' to consume, this sickness to buy even at inflated prices, this 'universal' contagion to spend. They felt such 'infections should be cherished'. They felt that the compulsive power of fashion should be pandered to. They made sure that this obsessive need to consume was constantly titillated and encouraged.

So although the dominant style was neo-classical, the designers produced endless fashionable variations on the prevailing theme. Prolific inventiveness found an encouraging market response. So long as the inventor could make his new product fashionable, make it accessible, and could disperse it through a wide enough 'secret army' of commercial agents, it would sell. Given those helpful 'introductions' and 'distributions', unprecedentedly large sales to an unprecedentedly large market were both possible and achieved. Temporary infidelities to the prevailing 'Greek' style allowed the market to be refreshed with such novelties as the sphinxes and crocodiles of the Egyptian style, as well as the variations on the Chinese and the Gothic; but in the main the neo-classic would suffice for the English market. In clothes the kaleidoscope of fashion almost obliterates any prevailing style in a confetti-coloured snowstorm of rapidly changing costume. But the neo-classical dominated pottery, brass, silver, furniture, cutlery, glass and so much more which made up the incidentals of Georgian consumption—clocks and door furniture, window frames and fanlights, cameos and cuff buttons, wallpaper and ink wells, and all those myriad other productions whose style still proclaims their late Georgian origins.

[7] See below, pp. 60–3.

Many needed 'a proper and noble introduction'. Many were made fashionable through judiciously placed presents. Many others were announced to the public through exhibitions, auctions and special sales, directed initially at the 'taste makers who led the fashion'. Even more were heavily advertised in the press, and heavily 'sold' by shopkeepers, pedlars, hawkers, scotch drapers and the like. Traditional outlets were multiplied in number, new sales techniques developed to reinforce the old, and amongst the leading élite a remarkable battery of commercial skills was deployed to capture and expand the market for consumer goods.

It is with the methods being used, and the attitudes being inculcated and exploited, that much of the following chapters will be concerned. But before one explains the growth of consumer behaviour and describes the many influences which brought it to such a pitch of excitement, one should first, perhaps, justify one's initial claims of the importance of the phenomenon being explained; and explain some of the barriers which have stood in the way of that importance being fully recognized.

* * *

It will be one of the major burdens of this book to show that consumer behaviour was so rampant and the acceptance of commercial attitudes so pervasive that no one in the future should doubt that the first of the world's consumer societies had unmistakably emerged by 1800. But to claim that the eighteenth century saw the birth of a consumer society or that many aspects of that society were imbued with a new commercial attitude should not be misinterpreted as a belief that by 1800 England had achieved *all* the features of modern consumer society. Nor should it be assumed that the birth occurred without a long period of gestation.

Events of this kind of magnitude do not happen without long periods of preparation, development and growth. The consumer revolution, like most revolutions had its roots deep in the past. It occurred in eighteenth-century England because of a happy combination of many circumstances. Like the industrial revolution, it was a multi-causal phenomenon, and many of the causes were shared by the twin industrial and commercial developments. But it could not have occurred without the pre-existence of many preparatory conditions dating back to the seventeenth century, and some even deeper into the past.

Intellectually, for instance, the eighteenth century was well prepared for a consumer boom, but once again the foundations for that advance were laid during the seventeenth century. If we seek the intellectual origins of the revolution in consumption we will find them in the 1690s. If we seek the widespread acceptance and application of these ideas we have to move into the second half of the eighteenth century.

At the beginning of the seventeenth century prevailing economic idioms were trapped in the mercantilist balance-of-payments explanation of how a nation's wealth grew. Writers like Mun, Malynes, Misselden and Vaughan remained largely blind to the benefits of increased spending. Luxuries were equated with foreign 'exotiques' and were therefore a danger to the balance of trade. Domestic consumption, or home demand, was at best a necessary evil, which grew, if at all, in response to population growth. To them 'total demand appeared inelastic. The rich were expected to buy their luxuries, the poor to have enough to subsist. The possibility that at all levels of society consumers might acquire new wants and find new means to enhance their purchasing power which would generate new spending and produce habits capable of destroying all traditional limits to the wealth of nations was unthought of, if not unthinkable.'[8] It was not until the 1690s that what had been for so much of the century 'mere consumption'[9] lost its pejorative meaning.

But as the range and variety and amount of English manufacturing developed, as the evidence for increased domestic consumption of the products of these manufacturers grew, so some writers 'responding to the obvious, if uneven economic growth, began to speculate upon the dynamic effect of increased demand. The word "markets" in their pamphlets subtly changed from a reference to the point of sales to the more elusive concept of expandable spending.'[10]

It was, in fact, one of the first examples of the unleashing of latent home demand (in the face of suddenly prolific cheap calico and muslins from India) which stimulated the new recognition of both the elastic nature of domestic consumption and its benefits.[11] As a result many of the underlying causes of the consumer revolution of the eighteenth century were explicitly recognized for the first time. For in the 1690s the taste for the cheap, colourful fabrics imported by the East India Company reached 'epidemic proportions'. It was then 'when the maverick spirit of fashion revealed itself in the craze over printed calicoes [that] the potential market power of previously unfelt wants came clearly into view. Here was a revolutionary force. Under the sway of new consuming tastes, people had spent more, and in spending more the elasticity of demand had become apparent. In this elasticity, the defenders of domestic spending discovered the propulsive power (and the economic advantages to the nation) of envy, emulation, love of luxury, vanity and vaulting ambition.'[12]

By the turn of the century it is possible to marshal an impressive array of contemporary writers who now saw the constructive and beneficial aspects

---

[8] Joyce Appleby, 'Ideology and Theory: The Tension between Political and Economic Liberalism in Seventeenth Century England'. *The American Historical Review*, vol. 81, no. 3 (June 1976), pp. 500-1.
[9] The pejorative view can be found in the writings of Culpeper, Petty and Cary.
[10] Appleby, op. cit., p. 532.
[11] P. J. Thomas, *Mercantilism in the East India Trade* (1963), p. 30; Bruno and Suviranta, *The Theory of the Balance of Trade in England* (1923), p. 7.
[12] Appleby, op. cit., p. 505.

of progressive levels of spending. The increased propensity to consume, what modern economists call 'the Veblen effect' of emulative spending, the indulgence in fashionable consumption, all found their theoretical justification.[13]

Dudley North wrote in 1691 that 'the main spur to Trade, or rather to Industry and Ingenuity, is the exorbitant Appetites of Men, which they will take pains to gratifie, and so be disposed to work, when nothing else will incline them to it; for did Men content themselves with bare Necessaries, we should have a poor World'.[14] Even earlier John Houghton wrote that 'our High-Living so far from Prejudicing the Nation, it enriches it', and anticipated Mandeville in finding economic virtues in the sins of the moralists. For in his view pride, finery, vanity, and luxury, caused 'more Wealth to the Kingdom than loss to private estates'.[15] Nicholas Barbon was even more explicit, writing that it 'is not Necessity that causeth the Consumption. Nature may be Satisfied with little; but it is the wants of the Mind, Fashion and the desire of Novelties and Things Scarce that causeth Trade.'[16] These paeans in praise of prodigality were not of course universal. The standard disapproval of self indulgence was still the prevailing orthodoxy, but it was being vigorously challenged for the first time.

The economic advantages of competition, envy, emulation, vanity and fashion were more and more explicitly stated: fashion, said Barbon, 'occasions the Expence of Cloaths before the Old ones are worn out'; envy, said North, is a goad to industry and ingenuity even among the meaner sort who 'are spurred up to imitate this Industry' by the example of the rich; the man who ruined himself, even to the point of bankruptcy in pursuit of social emulation added to the national good by 'the extraordinary Application he made, to support his Vanity'.[17] As Professor Appleby has demonstrated 'The idea of man as a consuming animal with boundless appetites, capable of driving the economy to new levels of prosperity, arrived with the economic literature of the 1690s',[18] but the idea presented too many political as well as moral threats to gain immediate widespread acceptance. Not until the 1770s did the idea of the increased propensity to consume assume its rightful place in models of economic growth which recognized the vital contribution of the elasticity of demand. In 1776 Adam Smith could state 'Consumption is the sole end and purpose of all production; and the interest of the producer ought to be attended to, only so far as it may be necessary for promoting that of the consumer. The maxim is ... perfectly self-evident'.[19]

---

[13] Gordon Vichert 'The Theory of Conspicuous Consumption in the 18th Century' in *The Varied Pattern: Studies in the 18th Century* (Toronto, 1971) ed. Peter Hughes and David Williams, pp. 253-69.
[14] [Sir Dudley North], *Discourses upon Trade*, (1691), p. 14.
[15] John Houghton, *A Collection of Letters for the Improvement of Husbandry and Trade*, (1681), p. 60.
[16] Nicholas Barbon, *A Discourse of Trade* (1690).
[17] See Appleby, p. 506.
[18] Appleby, op. cit., p. 509.
[19] Adam Smith, *An Inquiry into the Nature and Causes of the Wealth of Nations* (1776).

Such views were not acceptable at the beginning of the eighteenth century. The unleashing of the acquisitive instincts of all classes still posed too great a threat: 'the idea of self-improvement through spending implied genuine social mobility. The assertion that "the meaner sort" could and should emulate their betters suggested that class distinctions were based on little more than purchasing power. The moral implications of growth through popular spending were even more suspect. Unlike the work ethic which called upon powerful longings for self-discipline and purposeful activity, the ethic of consumption . . . offered nothing more than a calculating hedonism'.[20] What Professor Appleby calls 'the democratization of consumption'[20] threatened to undermine a class discipline and a system of social control previously bolstered up by the patriotic and ascetic elements in orthodox mercantilist theory.

The remarkably hostile reception of the economic rationalism and moral cynicism of Mandeville's *Fable of the Bees* gives some indication of how great the threat was held to be.

Few read Mandeville now. But in the early eighteenth century the effects of his famous insect allegory of English society could hardly have been greater if he had tipped his 'grumbling hive' straight into the pulpits and libraries of educated England. The sting in his subtitle—*Private Vices, Publick Benefits*—was alone sufficient to provoke moral outrage. For it presented in epigrammatic form his argument stressing the national, social and economic benefits that could, and in his view did, spring from luxury, avarice, prodigality, pride, envy and vanity. And for saying this he was held to rival Machiavelli and Hobbes as the Father of Lies. To John Brown, Hobbes and Mandeville were 'Detested Names! yet sentenc'd ne'er to die; Snatched from Oblivion's Grave by Infamy.'[21] Until John Wesley read *The Fable of the Bees* he had 'imagined there had never appeared in the world such a book as the works of Machiaval. But de Mandeville goes far beyond them in wickedness'.[22] To an anonymous contemporary poet Mandeville was Anti-Christ himself

> And, if GOD-MAN Vice to abolish came,
> Who Vice commends, MAN-DEVIL be his Name[23]

He was the target of a furious onslaught[24] in the press, the pulpit and the courts, as incensed moralists competed to denounce him. In the five years after the appearance in 1724 of his final version of *The Fable*, which included 'A Vindication of the Book', no less than ten books attacking it were

---

[20] Appleby, op. cit., p. 515.
[21] John Brown, *Humour, a Poem* (1743).
[22] *The Journal of the Rev. John Wesley*, ed. Nehemiah Curnock, (1909–16), IV, p. 157 (entry in the diary for 14 April 1756).
[23] Anon., *The Character of the Times Delineated* (1732).
[24] See Philip Harth's introduction to the Penguin edition (1970) of *The Fable of the Bees*, pp. 7–50.

published.[25] In France the book was ordered to be hanged by the common hangman, and Mandeville was burned in effigy.

What gave most immediate offence was the apparent championship of luxury, the cynical justification of the benefits which accrued from vice. In *Vice and Luxury, Publick Mischiefs,* John Dennis wrote in outrage in 1724 that 'a Champion for Vice and Luxury, a serious, a cool, a deliberate Champion, *that* is a Creature intirely new, and has never been heard of before in any Nation, or any Age of the World'.[26] Such hyperbole was typical of Dennis, but it was common to many others who read with fury Mandeville's description of the luxurious hive in which

> These Insects lived like Men, and all
> Our Actions they perform'd in small.[27]

For in Mandeville's metaphor for society, the entire population is addicted to luxury, and its prosperity stemmed directly from its self indulgence—

> '... every Part was full of Vice,
> Yet the whole Mass a Paradise.'

The whole hive was

> 'Slave to Prodigality,
> (K.) That Noble Sin; (L.) whilst Luxury
> Employ'd a Million of the Poor,
> (M.) And odious Pride a Million More.
> (N.) Envy it self, and Vanity
> Were Ministers of Industry;
> Their darling Folly, Fickleness
> In Diet, Furniture and Dress,
> That strange ridic'lous Vice, was made
> The very Wheel, that turn'd the Trade.
> Their Laws and Cloaths were equally
> Objects of Mutability;
> For what was well done for a Time,
> In half a Year became a Crime;
> . . .
> Thus Vice nursed Ingenuity,
> Which join'd with Time, and Industry
> Had carry'd Life's Conveniences,
> (O.) It's real Pleasures, Comforts, Ease,
> To such a Height, the very Poor
> Lived better than the Rich before;'[28]

The alphabetic accompaniment to Mandeville's barbed doggerel referred to his Prose remarks in *An Enquiry into the Origin of Moral Virtue* which

---

[25] William Law, John Dennis, Frances Hutcheson, Archibald Campbell and Isaac Watts all wrote books in criticism.
[26] John Dennis, *Vice and Luxury, Publick Mischiefs* (1724), pp. xvi–xvii.
[27] Bernard Mandeville, *The Grumbling Hive: or, Knaves Turn'd Honest* included in *The Fable of the Bees* (1970 edition with an introduction by Philip Harth), p. 63.
[28] Ibid., pp. 67–9.

acted as explication of the text of the poem. His explication was intended to explain and to justify his '*Moral*'.[29] In it he spelt out the economic logic of his moral message. Here he pointed out that 'Mercers, Upholsterers, Taylors and many others . . . would be starv'd in half a Year's time, if *Pride* and *Luxury* were at once to be banish'd the nation.'[30] Here he asked what use is 'a Plumb' (by which he meant 'a man worth £100,000') if he did not lavishly spend his wealth and stimulate the economy through employment and consumption? Here he argues that even highwaymen encourage trade by spending lavishly what they have stolen; and since even 'a poor common Harlot . . . must have Shoes and Stockings, Gloves, the Stay and Mantua-maker, the Sempstress, the Linnen-draper, all must get something by her, and a hundred different Tradesmen dependent on those she laid her Money out with, may touch part of it before a Month is at an end'.[31] Here he sings the praises of conspicuous consumption and emulative spending, writing 'the Labour of Millions would soon be at an end if there were not other Millions . . . Employ'd, To see their Handy-works destroy'd'.[32]

The 'Prodigal' he writes, 'is a Blessing to the whole Society';[33] whereas 'Frugality is, like Honesty, *a mean starving Virtue*, that is only fit for small Societies of good peaceable Men, who are contented to be poor so they may be easy; but in a large stirring Nation you may have soon enough of it. '*Tis an idling dreaming Virtue that employs no Hands,* and therefore very useless in a trading Country, where there are vast numbers that one way or other must be all set to Work'.[34]

It was hardly to be expected that such ideas would be accepted without controversy. The ideas that 'consumption was the logical end of production', that the 'latent consuming capacity of the public at large might become an engine for sustained growth', that 'society was an aggregation of self-interested individuals tied to one another by the tenuous bonds of envy,

[29] It concluded that to 'live in Ease' and
'T'enjoy the World's Conveniences,
. . .
Without great Vices, is a vain
Eutopia seated in the Brain.
Fraud, Luxury, and Pride must live
Whilst we the Benefits receive.'
Ibid. p. 76.

[30] Ibid., p. 118.

[31] Ibid., pp. 118–120. Remark (G.) 'The Worst of all the Multitude Did Something for the Common Good'.

[32] Ibid., p. 119.

[33] Ibid., p. 133. 'Prodigality has a thousand Inventions to keep People from sitting still that Frugality would never think of'. Ibid., p. 135.

[34] Ibid., pp. 134–35. My italics. Mandeville touched a sensitive nerve with *The Fable of the Bees*. Most of his writing evoked no such response which is perhaps not surprising when his major work has been described as having 'all the intimate charm to be expected of a four hundred page transcript of consultations between a family doctor and an ailing couple whose teenage daughter exhibits the most unpleasant symptoms of gastric disorder'. See J. Noxon, 'Dr. Mandeville: A Thinking Man', *The Varied Pattern* (Toronto, 1971), ed. P. Hughes and D. Williams, p. 235.

exploitation and competition' were new and, to many, alarming. 'Dangerous levelling tendencies lurked behind the idea of personal improvement through imitative buying'.[35]

Inevitably those, like the merchants, who espoused these novel views of the nature of heightened domestic consumption were sharply attacked. The Tory landowners and their allies even demanded new sumptuary laws for 'the immediate suppression of bare-fac'd Luxury, the spreading Contagion of which is the greatest Corrupter of Publick Manners and the greatest Extinguisher of *Public Spirit*'.[36] Jonathan Swift, for instance, argued that to prevent 'all Excesses in Cloathing, Furniture and the Like' it would be necessary to 'enact and enforce sumptuary Laws against Luxury'.[37] Others, however, increasingly accepted the 'necessary Evil',[38] and by the late eighteenth century the value of a heightened propensity to consume was widely accepted—it was the linchpin of *The Wealth of Nations*. The 'doctrine of beneficial luxury' had taken over from the doctrine of the 'utility of poverty'. It was increasingly admitted that the increased '*availability* of the comforts and conveniences of life as well as the necessities of life could operate as a powerful stimulus to industry by all ranks of society'.[38a] The pursuit of luxury could now be seen as socially desirable, for as the growth of new wants stimulated increased effort and output, improved consumption by all ranks of society would further stimulate economic progress.[39]

Such views had been accompanied by a changing attitude to the wages of labour: 'the doctrine of the social utility of hard times'[40] gave way to the view that high wages were both socially and economically desirable. As a contribution to greater equality in the distribution of wealth, and more specifically as a stimulus to increasing effective demand, a raised standard of living for the mass of the population found increasing justification. Higher real wages would act as an incentive to greater effort for the workforce, and would allow the workers to benefit from the growing output of consumer goods. Their increased consumption would further boost demand and the results of this 'benign circle' would be in the interests of the workforce, the entrepreneurs and the economy.

Socially England was as well prepared for a consumer boom as it was intellectually. Indeed English society provided an ideal breeding ground for

---

[35] These phrases are used by Professor Appleby, loc. cit., pp. 507–11.
[36] John Dennis, *An Essay upon Publick Spirit: being a Satyr in Prose upon the Manners and Luxuries of the Times....* (1711), p. v.
[37] Jonathan Swift, *Prose Works*, ed. H. Davis (Oxford, 1951), VII, p. 95.
[38] [Charles Davenant.] *An essay upon the Probable Methods of making People Gainers in the Balance of Trade*, 2nd edn. (1700), p. 152.
[38a] A. W. Coats, 'Changing Attitudes to Labour in the Mid-Eighteenth Century', *Economic History Review*, 2nd. series, vol. XI, (1958–9), p. 49.
[39] See Coats, loc. cit., p. 30, citing the contemporary views of Sir James Steuart, *Inquiry into the Principles of Political Economy* (1767).
[40] E. Furness, *The Position of the Labourer in a System of Nationalism* (New York, 1920), p. 127.

those commercially intent on exploiting new consumer wants. The structure of English society, the potential it offered for social mobility, the social competition bred by its closely packed layers, all offered exciting opportunities for the entrepreneur. For England had experienced more markedly than anywhere else in Europe what has been called 'the compression of the socio-economic spectrum' or 'the narrowing of social distance'.[41] When Adam Smith wrote that 'the accommodation of a European prince does not always so much exceed that of an industrious and frugal peasant as the accommodation of the latter exceeds that of many an African King, the absolute master of the lives and liberties of ten thousand naked savages',[42] his generalization must have been heavily influenced by his knowledge of English society. French society, in which in Arthur Young's words 'you go at once from beggary to profusion'[43] or, in Harold Perkin's words, from 'a large mass of consumption-resisting peasants' to 'a small class of luxury consumers',[44] was held to be very different from English society with its closely packed social strata—many observers, like Joseph Harris in 1757, referring in England to 'that gradual and easy transition from rank to rank'.[45] From Gregory King to Patrick Colquhoun, the social analysts had depicted a multi-layered society in which vertical mobility was both possible and greatly coveted. Malthus had specifically identified 'the hope to rise or the fear to fall in society' as the cause of 'that animated activity in bettering our own condition which now forms *the master spring of public prosperity*'.[46]

The importance of such a social structure for the rapid transmission of new wants, for the rapid spread of new fashions, for class competition, social emulation and emulative spending is obvious. In a society in which the social distance between the classes is *too great to bridge,* as say between a landed aristocracy and a landless peasantry, or in which the distance is *unbridgeable,* as in a caste society, then new patterns of increased expenditure on consumer goods are extremely difficult if not impossible to induce. In such societies the consumption of luxuries is limited to an exclusive market at the apex of society, beyond the reach or the interest of the mass market and, therefore, of very limited economic significance. In England where there was a constant restless striving to clamber from one rank to the next, and where possessions, and especially clothes, both symbolized and signalled each step in the social

---

[41] Harold Perkin has done more than anyone else to stress the importance of these features of English society. See his *The Origins of Modern English Society, 1780–1880,* (1969). See also E. L. Jones, 'The Fashion Manipulators: Consumer Tastes and British Industries, 1660–1800', in L. P. Cain and P. J. Uselding (eds.), *Business Enterprise and Economic Change* (Ohio, 1973), pp. 198–226.

[42] Adam Smith, *The Wealth of Nations,* (1910 edn.), I, p. 33.

[43] *Arthur Young's Travels in France, 1787–89.*

[44] Harold Perkin, *The Origins of Modern English Society* (1969), p. 91.

[45] Joseph Harris, *An Essay upon Money and Coins* (1757), pt. I, p. 70. A. W. Coats, loc. cit., p. 49, indicates how widespread such comments were.

[46] T. R. Malthus, *Essay on the Principles of Population* (1798). My italics.

promotion, the economic potentialities of such social needs could, if properly harnessed, be immense.

England possessed another prime advantage for the creation of a consumer society in the size and character of its capital city. The remarkable growth of London from some 200,000 inhabitants in 1600 to 900,000 in 1800 was unique in Europe. Towards the end of the seventeenth century London had already become the biggest European city and had, of course, no serious rival in England. Paris was the only comparable capital city but there were important differences, for where the proportion of Frenchmen living in Paris remained at about 2.5 per cent—the same proportion in 1750 as in 1650—London housed 7 per cent of the population of England in 1650 and 11 per cent in 1750. No other city in Europe could match that proportion (only Amsterdam came close to it). In addition, Professor Wrigley has estimated that when one allows for the effects of population movement in and out of the metropolis and for the effect of the London season, one in six of the total adult population of England had experience of living in London at some stage of their lives.[47] With 16 per cent of the total adult population being exposed to the influence of London's shops, London's lifestyle and the prevailing London fashions, its potential for influencing consumer behaviour was enormous. It served as the shopwindow for the whole country, the centre of forms of conspicuous consumption which would be eagerly mimicked elsewhere, the place which set the style for the season and saw the hordes of provincial visitors and their retinues of servants carry back those styles to the rest of the country. There were many important allies in this process (as the next chapter will show) but without the existence of London it would have been much more difficult for commercial manipulation to achieve the ephemeral conformity of taste which so suited the standardized production of the new factory system. Entrepreneurs needed to ring the fashion changes in order to keep up and inflate even further the buoyant home demand of the late eighteenth century, but having set their production machines to meet its fickle needs, they needed to be able to control and 'fix' its fugitive character for long enough to profit fully from its potentialities before its successors were, in turn, allowed their fleeting fashion life-cycle. All those tiny London satellites to the Lancashire cotton mills—the tailors, dressmakers, milliners and mantuamakers—would produce enough minor variations on the prevailing fashions to satisfy the market, keep its interest alive and allow the factories to churn out stripes or muslins or whatever was required—whether prevailing material or dominant colour—until the next major change was introduced—if possible, carefully stage managed and timed to suit the needs of commerce.

The domestic servant class was a further vital link in this chain of fashion and social emulation and increased spending. Domestic service was probably

[47] E. A. Wrigley, 'A Simple Model of London's Importance in Changing English Society and Economy, 1650-1750', *Past and Present*, 37 (1967), pp. 44-60.

still the largest single employment for women at the turn of the century and as the group closest to the spending habits and life style of the upper and middle classes it acted as a very important channel of communication for transmitting the latest styles and spreading a desire for new commodities.[48]

One of the weaknesses, however, in arguments drawing attention to the domestic servant class, or the role of London, or the character, structure and mobility of English society as explanations of increasing home demand and rising levels of spending is that critics can promptly point out that none of them were new to the eighteenth century. Servants mimicking their masters are an age-old phenomenon, one rank in society being eager to join a higher group is just as old, and London as a centre of conspicuous consumption was by no means new. Giovanni Botero had written of great cities as early as 1606 that

> Experience teacheth that the residence of noblemen in cities makes them to be more glorious and more populous, not onely by cause they bring their people and their families into it, but also by cause a nobleman dispendeth much more largely through the accesse of friends unto him and through the emulation of others in a Citie where he is abiding and visited continually by honourable personages than he spendeth in the country where he liveth amongst the brute beasts of the field and converseth with plaine country people and goes apparelled among them in plain and simple garments.[49]

London certainly produced all of Botero's effects long before the eighteenth century and, as to its disproportionate size, every schoolchild knows James I's opinion that 'Soon London will be all England'.

The answer to such criticism is partly the change of scale—London had swollen to an even more disproportionate dominance, English society permitted greater social mobility, domestic servants were even more given to emulation. But more is needed to convince one of the distinctive change in the quality of English habits of consumption. And something more was required to turn a potential for change into achieved change. London needed to develop the commercial capacity to exploit its fashionable dominance more fully, its shops needed to develop commercial techniques to exploit its custom more regularly and systematically, its marketing, distribution and advertising had to grow in sophistication to export the consuming behaviour of the capital to the rest of the country. The long-felt desire of so many members of English society to ape their superiors had to be given a fresh impetus to do so, a new spending ability to enable them to do so, and easier access to a greater variety of amply available new commodities. A mass consumer market awaited those products of the industrial revolution which skilful sales promotion could make fashionably desirable, heavy advertisement could

---

[48] See J. J. Hecht, *The Domestic Servant Class in Eighteenth Century England* (1956).
[49] G. Botero, *A Treatise Concerning the Causes of the Magnificence and Greatness of Cities* (trans. R, Pearson, 1606), p. 63. Quoted in F. J. Fisher, 'The Development of London as a Centre of Conspicuous Consumption', *Trans. Roy. Hist. Soc.*, 4th series, XXX(1948), pp. 39–40.

make widely known, and whole batteries of salesmen could make easily accessible.

The process of commercialization is described in the following chapters, but the process would not have achieved such significant results without some important accompanying changes. For although advertisement, sales promotion and the exploitation of fashion can influence the market's propensity to consume, can intensify its need to possess new products, can make its desire to ape its betters more insistently felt, that process will be greatly eased if the increased *desire* to spend is accompanied by an increased *ability* to do so. Fortunately this too occurred in the eighteenth century.

Different historians have advanced a variety of reasons why sufficient sections of the working classes could enjoy the substantial increases in income which would explain the growing democratization of consumption which, together with the spending of the middle ranks, could usher in a mass consumer market. Elizabeth Gilboy showed that wage *rates* increased gradually for much of the century, more rapidly between 1760 and 1780, and most rapidly in the industrializing areas where the demand for labour was strongest.[50] A. H. John has suggested that *money* wages rose as a result of the fall in food prices during the extraordinary run of good harvests in the second quarter of the century;[51] and it has also been suggested that family unit earnings rose substantially when wives and children joined the wage earning labour force employed in industry.[52] Those family earnings could be further inflated as a result of the long hours of work insisted on by the new factory discipline.[53] Where whole families were employed for long hours at rising wage rates in the rapid growth sectors of the economy, the increased take-home earnings could increase dramatically—easily carrying working class families into the class of consumers willing and able to afford not just the necessities but the decencies of life.[54] With more wives employed, there would be an increase in demand for goods previously made at home (clothes, beer, candles instead of rush lights, manufactured cutlery and pottery instead of home made treen, furniture etc.). With women having command of earnings of their own and access to a greater total family income, one would expect a greater demand for goods dominated by female consumer choice—clothes, curtains, linens, pottery, cutlery, furniture, brass and copper for the home; buckles, buttons and fashion accessories for the person. With more income in cash and less in kind (for those who gave up living-in as agricultural workers, and for those in domestic service who received higher

---

[50] E. W. Gilboy, *Wages in Eighteenth Century England* (Cambridge, Mass., 1934).
[51] A. H. John, 'Agricultural Productivity and Economic Growth in England, 1700–1760', *Journal of Economic History*, XXV (1965).
[52] Neil McKendrick, 'Home Demand and Economic Growth', loc. cit.
[53] Neil McKendrick, 'Josiah Wedgwood and Factory Discipline', *Historical Journal*, IV (1961).
[54] D. E. C. Eversley, 'The Home Market and Home Demand, 1750–1780', in *Land Labour and Population in the Industrial Revolution* (1967), ed. E. L. Jones and A. H. John.

money wages as a result in the rising competition for labour) working class consumers would have greater personal choice and a greater opportunity to follow their own tastes—spending on those inessential fripperies, so condemned by middle-class moralists, if they so wished.

There is not space here to do justice to the scholarship which supports those arguments, nor to the criticisms which have refined and qualified them.[55] But it is not unreasonable to suggest that there was an agriculturally-induced increase in home demand before 1750; that between 1750 and 1780 the proportion of the population with family incomes in the £50 to £400 per annum range increased from something like 15 per cent to something approaching 25 per cent; and that these extra households made a major contribution to the market for the mass consumer products of the early Industrial Revolution.[56]

There are many assumptions built into this model of explanation. There are many regional variations (in some areas a far higher proportion of the population would have joined the new consumer market, in other areas far fewer would have done so), but this model is consistent with the commercial development described elsewhere in this volume, it is consistent with the best available aggregate statistics, and it is certainly consistent with contemporary reactions to the growth of the home market. For contemporaries were by now convinced of the value and importance of the home market. David Macpherson in his *Annals of Commerce* wrote at the beginning of the nineteenth century 'The home trade is with good reason believed to be a vast deal greater in value than the whole of the foreign trade, the people of Great Britain being the best customers to the manufacturers and traders of Great Britain'.[57] By 1805 he was merely echoing the views of a whole catalogue of contemporary commentators making the same point. As early as 1750 Fielding had spelt out the impact on society.

> Nothing has wrought such an alteration in this order of people, as the introduction of trade. This hath indeed given a new face to the whole nation, hath in great measure subverted the former state of affairs, and hath almost totally changed the manners, customs, and habits of the people, more especially of the lower sort. The narrowness of their future is changed into wealth; their frugality into luxury, their humility into pride, and their subjection into equality.[58]

---

[55] See especially M. W. Flinn, 'Agricultural Productivity and Economic Growth: A Comment', *Journal of Economic History*, XXVI (1966), and A. H. John's reply, ibid.; E. L. Jones (ed.) *Agricultural and Economic Growth, 1650–1815* (1967); and A. J. Little, *Deceleration in the Eighteenth Century British Economy* (1967).

[56] Eversley suggests the figure of 150,000 households spending between £50 and £400 per annum. I would suggest more households with a lower upper limit, but the effect on demand would be much the same.

[57] Vol. III, p. 340. Quoted in T. S. Ashton, *An Economic History of England. The 18th Century* (1955), p. 63. Macpherson reported the over-enthusiastic calculation that 'the home consumption of this country is two and thirty times as much as the exports to foreign countries'.

[58] Henry Fielding, *Enquiry into the Causes of the Late Increase of Robbers* (1750).

The motive in Fielding's view was social emulation. As he wrote in 1750 'while the Noblemen will emulate the Grandeur of a Prince and the Gentleman will aspire to the proper state of a Nobleman; the Tradesman steps from behind his Counter into the vacant place of the Gentleman. Nor doth the confusion end there: It reaches the very Dregs of the People. who aspire still to a degree beyond that which belongs to them.'[59] By 1763 the *British Magazine* felt that the process had proceeded so far and so fast that 'The present rage of imitating the manners of high life hath spread itself so far among the gentlefolks of lower life, that in a few years we shall probably have no common folk at all'.[60]

The process which Mandeville had so controversially prophesied at the beginning of the century was increasingly accepted as being undeniably underway. Some parts of Mandeville's arguments remained unacceptable, but as the behaviour of English society was seen to come more and more to resemble that described in *The Fable of the Bees,* many were forced, however reluctantly, to concede that Mandeville's intellectual justification of emulative spending and the elasticity of home demand had 'very much' opened their eyes to the behaviour of 'real life'.[61] It was increasingly accepted that man was a consuming animal with boundless appetites to follow fashion, to emulate his betters, to seek social advance through spending, to achieve vertical social mobility through possessions. To enjoy the act of purchase was no longer seen as the prerogative of the rich.

This was not simply an intellectual recognition of the constructive and beneficial aspects of progressive levels of spending. The intellectual justification of materialism was matched by a recognition that the democratization of consumption was actually taking place. When Dr. Johnson wrote 'Depend on it, sir, every state of society is as luxurious as it can be. Men always take the best they can', or argued that 'you cannot spend in luxury without doing good to the poor',[62] he had seen ample practical evidence to that effect in the society around him.

What Mandeville described in predictive allegory in the first quarter of the century was being described in detailed fact in the last quarter. Compared with previous generations the English were said to be buying more than ever before, compared with other nations they were said to own more than anyone else, compared with both a greater proportion of English society was said to be involved in buying an unprecedented range of household goods. 'Were an inventory to be taken' wrote Josiah Tucker, 'of Household Goods and Furniture of a Peasant, or Mechanic, in France, and of a Peasant or

---

[59] Fielding, op. cit. See Fielding's *Works,* II, p. 783.
[60] *British Magazine,* IV (1763), p. 417.
[61] Dr. Johnson quoted in 'Dr Johnson and the Business World' in Peter Mathias, *The Transformation of England* (1980), p. 302.
[62] ditto.

Mechanic in England, the latter would be found on average to Exceed the former in Value by at least three to one'.[63]

Tucker spelt out the implications for English consumption patterns and for the demand for particular goods, when he went on to say that English manufacturers

> are more adapted for the demands of Peasants and Mechanics, in order to appear in warm circumstances, for Farmers, Freeholders, Tradesmen and Manufacturers in Middling Life; and for Wholesale Dealers, Merchants, and for all persons of Landed Estates to appear in genteel life; than for the Magnificence of Palaces or the Cabinets of Princes. Thus it is ... that the English of those several denominations have better Conveniences in their Houses, and affect to have more in Quantity of Clean, neat Furniture, and a greater variety, such as Carpets, Screens, Window Curtains, Chamber Bells, polished Brass Locks, Fenders etc. (Things Hardly known abroad among Persons of such Rank) than are to be found in any other country of Europe.[64]

Without the detailed quantitative work that is required on English and European inventories, such judgements cannot yet be confirmed.[65] What work has been done suggests that whereas the pre-industrial world was characterized by extremely modest possessions, the people of late eighteenth-century England welcomed an increasing flow of 'blankets, linens, pillows, rugs, curtains and cloths'; along with 'pewter, glass and china; and brass, copper and ironware' into their homes.[66]

The decencies owned by the poorest man who figures in the probate inventories of Sedgley in Staffordshire included the following:

> fireshovel, coal hammer, toasting iron, house bellows, a copper can, wooden furniture, a tun dish, scissors, a warming pan, a brass kettle, two iron pots, one pail, a search (sieve), two old candlesticks, glass bottles and earthenware, linen of all sorts in a chamber, a pair of bedsteads, a 'coverlid', a rug, a blanket, a kneading tub, two barrels, two coffers, a box, some trenchers, pewter, a brass skimmer, a brass basting spoon, an iron flesh fork, a tin calender, and so on.[67]

---

[63] Significantly Tucker allowed the possible exception of Holland. Recent work on peasant demand patterns in Friesland suggests that he was right to do: see Jan de Vries, 'Peasant Demand Patterns and Economic Development: Friesland 1550–1750', *European Peasants and their Markets: Essays in Agrarian Economic History*, ed. William N. Parker and Eric L. Jones (Princeton 1976), pp. 205–38.

[64] *Josiah Tucker: A Selection from his Economic and Political Writings*, ed. R. L. Schuyler (1931).

[65] The admirable work of de Vries is an example. The records exist and could be made to yield invaluable evidence on consumption patterns. Much local work of value has been done by Owen Ashmore, P. Brears, F. G. Emmison, W. G. Hoskins, J. A. Johnson, P. A. Kennedy, G. H. Kenyon, J. D. Marshall, J. S. Moore, T. Munckton, F. W. Steer, J. Thirsk. As de Vries says 'No effort has yet been made to use inventories for interregional or international comparison', and English historians have chiefly used probated inventories to describe farm production methods and trends.

[66] See D. E. C. Eversley, 'The Home Market and Home Demand, 1750–1780' in *Land, Labour and Population in the Industrial Revolution* (1967), ed. E. L. Jones and C. E. Mingay, pp. 237–9.

[67] See J. S. Roper, *Sedgley Probate Inventories* (Dudley, 1965), p. 1. Richard Wainwright's inventory, No. 130, 27 August 1739. Quoted Eversley, loc. cit., p. 237.

Wainwright's total possessions were valued at £10. When one moved up to £20, the value that John Atwood left, there were more imposing decencies—a clock and case, four brass pans, table linen, even books to the value of 25s. In the more prosperous wills the appearance of new products—obviously the result of personal purchase not inheritance—is striking, and when one reaches a victualler worth £284 the evidence of personal consumption of newly manufactured goods becomes unmistakable. As household possessions became more commonplace in the eighteenth century the practice grew of giving only a generalized account of all goods, and a total value, but there are many examples of families at the end of the century owning immense lists of varied household goods in dramatic contrast to those left by their forefathers.[68] The pre-industrial home was marked for most men and women by a simplicity, an austerity, a sheer lack of possessions, which can still startle one when one reads the probate inventories. John Demos gave a vivid picture of the possessions of pre-industrial society in his *Little Commonwealth*. The chilling picture of poverty evoked by the inventory of one James Cushman in 1648 can be conveyed by the contents of his kitchen: 'one small iron pott', 'a small scillite' and 'one small brass scimer'. The poorest families owned no table linen, little pottery and less cutlery. Spoons were the one essential, knives turned up more rarely, forks were non-existent. Furniture was sparse and simple: 'a single fully fledged chair' seems to have sufficed for many families. Feather beds were a mark of wealth, and bedspreads too appear only in the inventories of the wealthy. Even for the more prosperous members of the community who mustered a more impressive inventory, few of the possessions were new and 'much of the crudely made cookware ... served a family through two or three generations'.[69]

It is important to distinguish between new purchases and prized possessions, however humble, which are passed on by inheritance, because inherited goods obviously do not register as effective demand. What was distinctive about the consumer behaviour of the late eighteenth century was that those who had possessed little bought more, those who had inherited ample possessions bought new ones, and those born to superfluity seemed eager to add to the excess with every passing fashion.

One of the things which critics like Cobbett most disliked about the new middle-class patterns of consumption was the fact that their households were now monuments to novelty and fashion in the sense that where once they had inherited their furniture, now they bought it new:

> Everything about the farmhouse was formerly the scene of *plain manners* and *plentiful living*. Oak clothes-chests, oak bed-steads, oak chests of drawers, and oak tables to eat on, long, strong and well supplied with joint stools. Some of the things were many hundred of years old.

---

[68] See for example John S. Moore, ed., *The Goods and Chattels of our Forefathers* (1976), Inventory 409, p. 269.
[69] John Demos, *A Little Commonwealth* (New York, 1970), pp. 37–48.

Now everything was new: 'some showy chairs and a sofa (a *sofa* by all means): half a dozen prints in gilt frames hanging up: some swinging book-shelves with novels ... many *wine decanters* and *wine glasses* and '*a dinner set*' and '*a breakfast set*' and '*desert knives*' ... and worst of all a *parlour*! Aye, and a *carpet* and a *bell-pull* too! One end of the front of this once plain and substantial house had been moulded into a 'parlour'; and there was the mahogany table, the fine chairs, and the fine glass.'

Cobbett was appalled by the social competition in 'show and luxury', the new 'consumption' and 'carryings on', the 'constant anxiety to make a show'.[70] But here was proof of the persuasive power of the new commercial arts. Such families had long been in command of income sufficient to acquire new possessions, but now they felt compelled to do so. Fashionable mahogany must replace traditional oak, showy chairs must replace well jointed stools, whole sets of pottery—a different set for each meal or even each course—must be acquired, together with changes of cutlery for dessert, new decanters, new glasses, new prints, new book shelves, new novels—all of which betokens a whole new approach to buying by a part of the traditional prosperous middle class. Those farmers' wives who had so startled Pehr Kalm in 1748 by being dressed like 'ladies of quality' were now responding just as surely to the wiles of those selling pottery and glass and carpets and cutlery and furniture as they had first done to those selling fashionable clothes.[71] When John Foster used the Countess of Bective to give snob appeal to his carpets or Wedgwood used the Duchess of Devonshire to give social cachet to his pottery, this was the kind of latent demand they were attempting to release. These were the customers who caught 'from example the contagion of desire'.[72]

Here is one explanation of the spectacular success of the Gillows of Lancaster and the Seddons of London with their massive furniture stocks. They produced and sold furniture on an unprecedented scale: Seddon and Son of Aldersgate Street had stock worth more than £100,000 in 1790, and in 1796 the firm had over 400 employees—gilders, mirror workers, locksmiths, carvers, seamstresses as well as the sawyers and joiners.[73]

The same pattern of increased consumption can be seen in a whole array of commodities. Tea was 'singled out by such as Jonas Hanway as the apotheosis of luxury spending on needless extravagance by the poor. He was shocked to find that even labourers mending the road demanded their daily tea'.[74] Hanway blamed this habit, too, on the downward spiral of fashion and social emulation, 'it took its rise by Example, and by Example it is

---

[70] W. Cobbett, *Rural Rides,* entry for 25 October 1825, p. 226.
[71] Pehr Kalm, *Account of his Visit to England ... in 1748* (London 1892).
[72] See below, Chapter 3.
[73] Donald Wintersgill, *Book of Antiques, 1700–1830* (1975), pp. 50–1.
[74] Peter Mathias, 'Leisure and Wages in Theory and Practice', ch. 8 of his *The Transformation of England* (1979), p. 162.

supported'.[75] And such contemporary views were born out by the statistics—during the course of the eighteenth century[76] the per capita consumption of tea increased fifteenfold.[77]

Such statistics are likely for many to be the ultimate proof of the growth of demand, the democratization of consumption and the arrival of a consumer society. The fact that during the last fifteen years of the century the consumption of excised commodities in mass demand, such as tobacco, soap, candles, printed fabrics, spirits, and beer, was increasing more than twice as fast as the population, makes acceptance of rising patterns of consumption difficult to avoid.[78] While the population increased by 14 per cent in this period, tea consumption increased by 97.7 per cent and that of printed fabrics by 141.9 per cent. 'After a period of rising money wage rates', says Professor Mathias, such figures 'surely tell their own story'.[79]

In fact the figures provided by Schumpeter, Deane and Cole, and Mitchell and Deane[80] provide the statistical underpinning for the growth of a new consumer market. Obviously there are great regional differences, but if we accept that industrial output trebled in the course of the eighteenth century, if, as Mrs. Schumpeter's figures suggest, export of manufactured goods account for only a small proportion of the total, and if the bulk of manufactured products were of the mass consumption type, then the acceptance of a substantially larger market is difficult to avoid. The rich simply cannot have drunk all the beer, worn all the cheap cottons, bought all the cheap pottery, buckles, buttons and so on. If too, as Eversley suggests, the home market accounted for about £10 million or a notional £10 per household per annum at the end of the seventeenth century, by 1770 it accounted for more than £30 million or perhaps £25 per household, and by 1801 it accounted for about £90 million or about £40 a household. Even allowing for inflation this suggests a significant increase in per capita consumption of home products, and although obviously all householders did not reach this average, it is extremely improbable that all this extra consumption could be absorbed by the top layers of income.[81] In view of the handsome margin between income and expenditure for minimum subsistence indicated by contemporary family budget estimates, this seems even more improbable.[82]

With so much evidence and so many arguments in favour of a consumer

---

[75] J. Hanway, 'Essay on Tea' printed in *A Journal of Eight Days' Journey* (1756), pp. 215–16.
[76] Actually between the decade from 1715–24, and the period 1785–1800.
[77] E. B. Schumpeter, *English Overseas Statistics, 1697–1808* (Oxford, 1960). Table XVIII.
[78] Peter Mathias, *The Transformation of England* (1979), p. 162.
[79] Ibid.
[80] E. B. Schumpeter, op. cit.; P. Deane and W. A. Cole, *British Economic Growth 1688–1959* (Cambridge, 1962) and B. R. Mitchell and P. Deane, *Abstract of British Historical Statistics* (Cambridge, 1962).
[81] See Eversley, loc. cit., pp. 226–31.
[82] See, for example, J. Trusler, *The Economist* (1777) with his 'variety of estimates of how comfortable a family can live ... for little money', or *Practical Estimates for Household Expenses* in *A New System of Practical Domestic Economy* (1825).

revolution and the role of commercialization in producing it, one has to ask why so many historians have been so reluctant to proclaim their importance. The simple answer is that 'economic history is a supply side subject'[83] which takes market expansion to be a straightforward reflection of, and automatic response to, increased supply. But there are deeper-seated reasons which help to explain the traditional historian's lack of appreciation of the expansion of the consumer market and the role of commerce in expanding it. There are deeply influential beliefs incorporated in the prelapsarian myth (the idea that once there was a just and organic society in which men lived comfortable lives, athrob with job satisfaction and supported by a sufficiency uncorrupted by commerce and industry); in the pessimistic interpretation of the Industrial Revolution (the fact that many suffered during the late eighteenth century, and even more in the later stages of industrialization, has prevented some historians from recognizing those who gained); in the adverse literary verdict on industrialists and all their works (which produces a mental block in many which prevents them, for instance, seeing *any* benefits in the employment of women and children in the factories);[84] in the low status of men involved in selling ('It would be next to impossible to apply to a well dressed man in the street a more offensive appelation than 'shopman', it was said in 1843), which placed them at the bottom of the business hierarchy and caused them to be further underestimated and understudied.[85]

Even theory has seemed against the recognition of the importance of the expansion of the home market. Economists like Berrill defy one to find an example of rapid economic growth produced by a sharp increase in home demand, on the grounds that home demand is insufficiently elastic to do so and that one must seek the explanation in exports.[86] Here the effect of the empirical evidence has almost swung opinion too far in the opposite direction, so that exports are now in danger of being dismissed as 'a mere reverberation of home demand'[87] in the eighteenth century.

The prelapsarian myth has been shaken, too, by our increasing appreciation of the texture of poverty in the pre-industrial world. When we read that 'the poor in the towns and countryside ... lived in almost complete

---

[83] Eric L. Jones, loc. cit., in *Business History and Economic Change*, p. 198.

[84] See for a fuller discussion of this point Neil McKendrick, 'A New View of the Role of Women and Children in the Industrial Revolution', *Historical Perspectives* (1974), ed. N. McKendrick, pp. 152-210.

[85] See Neil McKendrick, 'The Enemies of Technology and the Self-Made Man', the General Introduction to Roy Church, *Herbert Austin: The British Motor Industry to 1941* (1979), pp. ix-lii; 'Literary Luddism and the Businessman', the General Introduction to P. N. Davies, *Sir Alfred Jones: Shipping Entrepreneur Par Excellence* (1978), pp. ix-lvi; 'In Search of a Secular Ideal', the General Introduction to Clive Trebilcock, *The Vickers Brothers: Armaments and Enterprise 1854-1914* (1977). pp. ix-xxxiv; and 'General Introduction' to R. J. Overy, *William Morris, Viscount Nuffield* (1976), pp. vii-xliv.

[86] K. Berrill, 'Industrial Trade and the Rate of Economic Growth', *Economic History Review*, XII (1959-60).

[87] See M. W. Flinn, *The Origins of the Industrial Revolution* (1960), especially ch. iv.

THE CONSUMER REVOLUTION

deprivation';[88] or that 'the average man's income was so low that even a poor man's diet absorbed 60 to 80 per cent of that income ... in good times.... After having bought their food, the mass of the people had little left for their wants, no matter how elementary they were. In pre-industrial Europe the purchase of a garment, or the cloth for a garment, remained a luxury the common people could only afford a few times in their lives';[89] when we hear that even the clothes of plague victims were eagerly sought by their relatives; and when we learn of the low expectation of life, the high infant mortality, the sickness which threaded their lives, the poor diet and few comforts they had to sustain them, then the gains made in the eighteenth century look all the more impressive.

If there is, then, some evidence of the tide beginning to turn in favour of a willingness to accept the extension of the market in the eighteenth century, there is still too little appreciation of the richness of the commercial response, the fertility and ingenuity of entrepreneurial ideas, the extent to which society accepted consumer attitudes. The consumerism and commercialism had not, of course, yet reached the mature stage of a modern consumer society. It already had many elements in common with that later stage of economic development, but what strikes one most as one leafs through the advertisements of provincial newspapers, or reads the correspondence of eighteenth-century manufacturers, or reads the contemporary descriptions of their consumer purchases, is the variety of small scale enterprise. The lesser tradesman, who have been forgotten, are even more apparent there than the giants whose entrepreneurial brilliance has glittered brightly enough for them still to be remembered. There were profits—even small fortunes—to be made from very modest artefacts indeed. It is no accident that Adam Smith's famous exemplar of the division of labour was taken from the manufacture of pins, or that T. S. Ashton founded the modern study of business with his work on Peter Stubs the nail maker, or that Birmingham's prosperity was built on the manufacture of buttons and buckles and candlesticks, or that Sheffield grew on the profits of cutlery, or that Staffordshire owed its prosperity to crockery, or that Manchester mushroomed on the cotton that provided the mass market for fashionable prodigality at the end of the eighteenth century. Other areas thrived on hats and gloves, and belts, and wigs, and shoes and dresses, and saucepans and brass and copper, and chairs and tables and cloth.

All of these small items of household consumption offered the lure of profit for those who flocked to make and sell them. There was a vast and growing market clamouring to buy. For those with the skills to manufacture and to market, the opportunities were legion. It was not for nothing that the first

---

[88] F. Braudel, op. cit., p. 202.
[89] Carlo Cipolla, *Before the Industrial Revolution* (1976), pp. 29-33. Little wonder in such a deprived society that dress should acquire such important symbolic values and that men and women should develop such powerful if at that stage unsatisfied desires to acquire them.

industries to blossom in the Industrial Revolution were more characteristically to be found in the consumer sector than in the heavy industrial sector. The beauty of smallness had not been recognized as such in the eighteenth century, but the profitability of such unconsidered trifles as pins and nails, buttons and forks, knobs and knockers, pots and pans, hats and coats, gloves and shoes certainly had.

The market opportunities were protean, the possibility of profit high, the fortunes made legion. The names of those who made them are so famous that it has sometimes concealed how modest were the consumer objects they made: Joseph Bramah and locks, Josiah Wedgwood and pots, Matthew Boulton and buckles and buttons, the Pilkingtons and glass, not to mention the great cotton magnates who built their fortunes on the clothes and underclothes of our Georgian predecessors. And for every Wedgwood there were hundreds of lesser potmakers crowding the potbanks of the five towns, and surviving only in the contemporary lists of commercial directories and the collections of trade cards—the production of which fuelled further demand for ephemera from printers and booksellers and print makers and the like.

One should, however, resist the facile assumption that success was in any way assured even in such favourable long-term demand conditions. The eighteenth-century economy saw its full share of failures. Even the boom *periods* encompassed years of black depression, and even the boom *years* saw disaster for some. The eighteenth-century bankruptcy courts kept their grim count of those who responded to economic opportunity and met only financial disaster there. Spectacular success for the few must be measured against relative failure of the many, and complete collapse of an uncomfortably large number of business enterprises. The prospect of profit attracts the feckless, the inadequate, the over-confident and the unlucky, just as it attracts the bold, the gifted and the fortunate. Three hundred and ninety eight bankruptcies in the depression year of 1772 shows what a bad year could do in the midst of rampant demand; six hundred and twenty three bankruptcies in 1773, when the market for some was already picking up, shows what the post depression year could do when the creditors insisted on their bills being finally met. As T. S. Ashton once wrote it was not for nothing that November became known as the month for suicides because that was the time of year when men's debts were finally called in. It was the annual peak for bankruptcies.

The mortality rate in business fluctuated with the irregular ebb and flow of demand—surging up from 471 in 1777 to 623 in 1778 as depression struck late that year and reaching 634 in 1779—but even in 1761 and 1762 the *Gentleman's Magazine* recorded 184 and 171 failures which reached the bankruptcy courts.[90] There were many reasons for failure. Not even buoyant

---

[90] T. S. Ashton, *Economic Fluctuations in England, 1700–1800* (1959), pp. 125–30.

demand was proof against some businessmen's incompetence, and in the years of black depression it required a very considerable range of skills to survive. The level of commercial skill needed to *excel* was very much higher than is often realized.[91]

So the commercial hierarchy at the customer's service was long and varied. It led from pedlar to packman, from the higgler to small shopkeeper, from market to fair, from auctions to seasonal sales and exhibitions. The experience of buying could vary from haggling at one's doorstep to helping oneself from a self-service counter in London, from hiring a dress for a Saturday night dance from a Georgian forerunner of Moss Bros. in the 1760s to buying from international showrooms or sharing the company of the gentry, the aristocracy and even royalty at the elegant showrooms of one of the great manufacturers. The great chain of enterprise included a vast range of ability, ingenuity, profitability and magnitude. They were all competing for the custom of a newly affluent society, eager to consume the (by the standards of the time) uniquely wide range of products, and, for the first time in their history for most of them, possessing the wherewithal to do so.

The hierarchical metaphor is apt not only for stressing, in terms of the commercial response, the different layers of expertise and achievement, the different levels of success and failure, but also for stressing on the consumer side the fact that there were those who gorged on material objects (the lords of the social jungle), those who got more than they needed in the middling ranks of society, those who enjoyed a decent sufficiency (a large and multi-layered section of society), those who scraped a bare sufficiency, and those who just survived.

* * *

By 1700 the embryonic development of a consumer society had certainly begun, but the pregnancy had still had some way to go. By 1700 the barriers to retail trade were certainly coming down, but there were still too many in place to prevent the protracted birth pangs of a nation giving birth to a consumer society from being seen to be over.

By 1800, however, those barriers had given way and the consumer society had been announced by so many observers (not all of them wishing it well) with such a wealth of eye witness reports, such a mass of supporting evidence, that its arrival should no longer be doubted. In Braudel's words 'the future belonged to societies which were trifling enough, but also rich and inventive enough, to bother about changing colours, materials and styles of costume'.[92]

The next chapter endeavours to show that England was just such a society.

---

[91] See below, pp. 100–194, and N. McKendrick, 'Josiah Wedgwood and Cost Accounting in the Industrial Revolution', *Economic History Review* (1970).
[92] F. Braudel, op. cit., pp. 235–6.

CHAPTER TWO

The Commercialization of Fashion

> In England the several ranks of men slide into each other almost imperceptibly, and a spirit of equality runs through every part of their constitution. Hence arises a strong emulation in all the several stations and conditions to vie with each other; and the perpetual ambition in each of the inferior ranks to raise themselves to the level of those immediately above them. In such a state as this fashion must have uncontrolled sway. And a fashionable luxury must spread through it like a contagion.
>
> N. Forster, 1767

> Is Fashion in fact such a trifling thing? Or, as we think, do these signs constitute evidence in depth concerning the energies, possibilities, demands and *joie de vivre* of a given society, economy and civilization?
>
> Costume is a language. It is no more misleading than the graphs drawn by demographers and price historians.
>
> Ferdinand Braudel, 1973

The concept of fashion is now deeply embedded in Western European society, and its importance in modern industrialized economies is difficult to overlook. Whole industries are built around, and dependent upon, design changes and the public reaction to them. There are even explicitly named *fashion industries* which exploit man's—and more particularly, in some societies, woman's—constant need for variety and change. But it would be a mistake to think—as so many moralists have done—that the importance of fashion is a constant of the human condition. Man has not always hungered for fashionable change, and even in those societies in which they *have* hungered they have often been unable to satisfy their appetites.

An anthology of quotations concerning fashion might seem to point to both its age and its universal influence. Proverbial wisdom was recorded in classical Latin to the effect that 'Fashion is more powerful than any tyrant', and the poets of antiquity were as specific as they were prolific on the subject. Ovid, as early as the year 8 A.D., wrote in *The Art of Love,*

> I cannot keep track of all the vagaries of fashion,
> Every day, so it seems, brings in a different style.

The Bible and Homer can take one even further into the past with variations on the same theme. Even English literature can provide a respectably antique pedigree. Chaucer in 'The Knight's Tale' confirmed the truism that 'There's never a new fashion but its old'; Shakespeare in *Much Ado About Nothing* affirmed that 'The fashion wears out more apparel than the man', and in *Henry VIII* complained that 'new customs, Though they be never so ridiculous (Nay, let 'em be unmanly), yet are followed.' But such quotations do not encompass all societies and, even in those they do include, they are often more relevant to a history of attitudes than to a history of material possessions.

It may be a constant of the human condition to want to be in fashion. It is certainly not a constant of that condition to be able to be so. Nor has being in fashion entailed frequent changes for many societies and most classes.

For if one takes a long enough view and a sufficiently international one, the history of costume is a remarkably stable one. Fashion, in the clothes worn by most men and women in most societies, has been remarkably static. 'The general rule', to quote Braudel, 'was changelessness'.[1] The fashionable tumult over the last two hundred years or so is the chronological exception not the rule; and geographically, until very recently, only the West experienced the full frenzy of fashionable excess. For much of human history most people have been virtually immune to the effect of fashion. Most were born to immunity through poverty; some acquired immunity through the scarcity of objects to indulge their fashionable whims upon—in such a consumer vacuum the propensity to spend is effectively held in check; some had immunity thrust upon them by royal edict or sumptuary laws.

Recent work in social history has reminded us forcibly that there are fewer constants in the human condition than we have usually imagined, or has often been assumed. The sex drive, for instance, was not constant. It could be severely repressed by hunger, hard work or an inadequate diet (not to mention the effect of changing cultural norms and expectations); it could be intensified by leisure, prosperity and ample nutrition. The age of marriage is not constant either. The average age at first marriage—or the proportions of any given society who marry at all—can vary remarkably in the face of varying social and economic restraints and inducements: from the child brides of the extended families of some Eastern societies, who marry soon after puberty, to the much higher age of the characteristic Western European marriage pattern, to the extremes of the middle-aged husbands of Irish farming society in the twentieth century who marry on average at the age of 38. The marriage *rate* can also fluctuate alarmingly with changing opportunities: ranging from the modest choice of marriage partners offered by eighteenth-century Lisbon where one-third of the women were nuns, to the ubiquitous marriage of prosperous twentieth-century America where some 90 per cent of women marry. Illegitimacy rates can vary from the

---

[1] Fernand Braudel, *Capitalism and Material Life, 1400–1800*, (1973) p. 231.

remarkably low average of one or two per cent in the face-to-face society of pre-industrial Europe to 73 per cent in some parts of the West Indies of the mid-twentieth century. The age at which different societies characteristically give birth to their children is also more flexible than many historians have imagined. All such phenomena have proved to be very sensitive to economic circumstance and cultural expectations.

When the basic human drives to marry, to make love and to raise a family can vary so markedly in the face of social, cultural and economic restraints, so *a fortiori* can the less basic but nonetheless pressing human need to be dressed in the latest fashion.

It is not difficult to recognize the importance of diet, housing and medical breakthroughs in allowing so many more people to live to the full the age-old assumed life-potential of three score years and ten. It is not difficult to grasp that as a result the average expectation of life at birth has risen in Europe from less than thirty to nearly seventy in little more than three hundred years. It has not so far been so readily realized and accepted that man's potential to consume has also only very recently undergone a revolution of similar dimensions.

The historical forces working against fashion were many. Poverty was the most important. Custom and tradition were powerful allies. A stable society was a further buttress against change: established hierarchies, which prevented or severely restricted vertical social mobility, remained remarkably faithful to the costumes which distinguished men's place in that hierarchy.

In Japan the *kimono* and the *jinbaori* remained virtually unchanged for centuries: so much so, that in the early seventeenth century the Shogun's secretary at Yedo could claim to show 'by the evidence of traditions and old papers that his nation had not changed in costume for over a thousand years'.[2] In China, eighteenth-century engravers were still copying details of the same style of dress which had been drawn by Father de las Cortes in 1626; and in 1793, a traveller confirmed the lack of change when he wrote 'In China, the form of clothing is rarely changed by fashion or whim. . . . Even the women have scarcely any new fashions.'[3] In Algiers, the detailed descriptions of female fashions provided by Father Haedo in 1590 'could be used with very little correction as a caption to engravings of 1830'.[4] In Peru, the peasants were faithful to the *poncho* for centuries; in India the *dhoti* has enjoyed similar popularity and longevity as the prevailing fashion; in North Africa and the Middle East, the *jelabi* has a long and barely disturbed history; and amongst many Muslim countries the *pyjama* and the *chapkar* reigned for long unchallenged. Indeed as Mouradj d'Osson wrote in 1741, 'Fashions which tyrannize European women hardly disturb the fair sex in

[2] Quoted Braudel, op. cit., p. 235.
[3] Quoted Neil McKendrick, op. cit., p. 204–5.
[4] Braudel, op. cit., p. 228.

the East: hair styles, cut of clothing and type of fabric are almost always the same'.[5]

Museums of costume can be deceptive. Richness and grandeur which strike us as strange, even 'fantastical' may have been the unchanging costume of kings and priests for centuries: splendour and variety in the dress of a queen may well have been the result of conspicuous consumption by a single individual operating within the bounds of a single hardly varying fashionable mode.

Power often needs display and ornament. The divinity which 'doth hedge about a king' has usually needed more tangible expression to impress most of his subjects. The 'Emperor's clothes' would be seen through by more than the innocent eye of a child, unless they were of a splendour and magnificence which could not be overlooked. Clothes in the past were 'used to set apart men and women, enhance their glory, touch them with a divinity to which these men who toiled and worked, or bought and sold, could never hope to aspire'.[6]

Sumptuary laws forbidding imitation were designed to reinforce their élite status, to restrict the grandeur to the few, and to guarantee their sense of separateness. In its simplest but most extreme form, the great simply monopolized a single colour. The Sons of Heaven, the Chinese Emperors, wore yellow, reserved to them alone: the Roman emperors wore the imperial purple preserved for them and their immediate family. In societies in which such restrictive devices could not be enforced, separateness has been insisted on by wealth. The famous extravagance of Queen Elizabeth's wardrobe fulfilled a very political need. It was the visible external proof of her divinity; it buttressed her political power; and her courtiers were expected to buttress it further with a spectacular display of satellite finery. Professor Plumb has described the situation in characteristically vivid terms.

> Her clothes, of course, marked her divinity. She wore ruffs and lace of almost inconceivable complexity; her hair elaborately adorned with pearls and jewels, her vast and ornate dresses alive with rubies, sapphires and diamonds. And nor were these clothes kept for portraits only: so bedecked, she was carried in a litter through London and through the countryside on her famous progresses, like some monstrous painted but living idol. Naturally this divine monarch was surrounded by her high priests and priestesses, whose clothing, too, marked them off from the common herd: aristocrats with velvet breeches studded with elaborate emblems in gold thread, sporting codpieces that proclaimed their more than mortal manliness, and ladies-in-waiting whose beflowered skirts and intricate ruffs were the result of years of patient embroidery that no mere mortal could afford. The cost was prodigious, for gods and goddesses must never appear old-fashioned and their clothes always had to be radiant and new. Viscount Montague spent £1,500 on two dresses for his daughters. Sir Edmund Bacon wore 138 gold buttons on one suit which was no sooner worn than discarded. As one puritanically inclined member of the House of Commons burst out, women 'carry manors and thousands of oak trees about their necks'.

[5] Mouradj d'Osson, *Tableau général de l'Empire Ottoman* (1941).
[6] J. H. Plumb, 'Clothes', *In the Light of History*, (1972) p. 190.

This was the last age of human gods, marked out by wanton exhibitionism, in Western Europe. And so one should not dismiss the rich furs, the costly velvets, the golden gleaming silks of Rembrandt's pictures as mere visual delight on Rembrandt's part. They proclaimed grandeur, nobility, *virtù*.[7]

But such a picture, accurate as it is, should not deceive us into thinking that the eighteenth century, by the end of which monarchs were much more soberly dressed, saw a decline of the power of fashionable excess. For where in the sixteenth century men longed to be able to follow fashion and ape the nobility and gentry, in the eighteenth century they were able to do so. Of course, the attractions of fashion were not new to the eighteenth century. 'Since in every age fashions beguile all ages and classes in varying degrees, ordinary folks lower down the social scale were susceptible too, and strained their resources to ape their betters. As the proclamation of 1562 bewailed "such as be of the meaner sort, and be least able with their livings to maintain the same" felt that they must follow the fashion'.[8]

Dr. Thirsk has shown that sixteenth-century fashion is 'full of baleful comment upon the dictates of fashion, which first seized the rich in thrall and then their servants'.[9] 'No other nations take such pride in apparel as England', wrote Philip Stubbs in 1595, 'No people in the world are so curious in new fangles as they of England be'. 'I have known divers [serving men]', wrote William Vaughan in 1600, 'who would bestow all the money they had in the world on sumptuous garments'.[10] But that pride, that curiosity, that desire to 'bestow their money' and strain their resources was not allowed its full expression until the eighteenth century. Just as some individuals lived their natural span to the full in previous centuries, so some succumbed happily to the tyranny of fashion. But just as the evidence of geriatric Elizabethans is no evidence of a high expectation of life in the late sixteenth century, so these quotations prove only the existence of the desire to follow fashion and the ability of a few to do so. It is only in the last two centuries that the 'Veblen effect' has spread throughout society, only since the eighteenth century that fashion approached its full potential and was accepted by contemporaries as exercising 'uncontrolled sway'.[11]

The historian should be chary of reading too much into the unsupported views of the poets. After all John Donne was rhyming 'shops of fashions' with 'changeable Camelions' long before the eighteenth century.[12] And at first sight there might seem to be widespread evidence of similar isolated

---

[7] Ibid., pp. 192-3.
[8] Joan Thirsk, 'The Fantastical Folly of Fashion: The English Stocking Knitting Industry, 1500-1700', *Textile History and Economic History* (Manchester 1973), ed. N. B. Harte and K. G. Ponting, p. 50.
[9] Ibid. See also W. Hooper, 'Tudor Sumptuary Laws', *English Historical Review*, XXX, (1915), p. 439.
[10] Thirsk, op. cit., pp. 50-1.
[11] N. Forster, *'An Enquiry into the Present High Prices of Provisions'* (1767), p. 41.
[12] John Donne's 'Elegie: On his Mistris'. *Poems* (1635) but probably written between 1595 and 1598.

contemporary views. One can span the eighteenth century with such famous comments on fashion as Colley Cibber's 'One had as good be out of the world as out of fashion'[13] which he wrote in 1696; through Lord Chesterfield's 'If you are not in fashion, you are nobody' which he wrote in 1750;[14] to Charles Caleb Colton's rather laboured 'Ladies of Fashion starve their happiness to feed their vanity, and their love to feed their pride' of 1825;[15] or William Hazlitt's more socially perceptive 'Fashion is gentility running away from vulgarity and afraid of being overtaken' of 1830.[16]

Such quotations—and the list could be effortlessly extended—are typical more for their brevity and their economy (and occasionally their perception and wit) than they are specially revealing of their time. They can be prefaced by Burton's view in *The Anatomy of Melancholy* that 'he is only fantastical that is *not* in fashion',[17] and followed by Ambrose Bierce's definition of fashion from *The Devil's Dictionary*, 'a despot whom the wise ridicule and obey',[18] or George Bernard Shaw's briefer definition—'only induced epidemics'.[19]

All such comments are a better index to the incidence of wit or the taste for attempted aphorisms, than an index to consumer behaviour or the strength of the grip of fashion. They do, of course, reflect in particularly well expressed form, the truisms of their day, and, therefore, inevitably tell us something about the attitudes and activities of their time, but they are hardly more relevant as a measure of the incidence of those activities than are the comments of Aeschylus, or Aretino, or Bion or Sir Thomas Browne on old age or on the span of human life. Old age simply had to exist to elicit comments from Euripides, to be ensconced in ancient proverbs, to find expression in the Bible. It did not have to be common. The same is true of fashion.

In one sense, of course, the poets and the proverbs are right. Such is the biological display function of clothes, such are the possibilities for displaying status, rank, wealth and class, that some form of costume differentiation can be found in most societies and most ages. But fashion in the sense of rapid change in shape, material and style is something quite different.

So the prudent historian does well to pause before translating the proverbial wisdom of the poets into the assumed behaviour of society. Just as he does well to check the comments of contemporaries for substantial independent evidential support. Much, for instance, might be made of the often quoted comments of Emmanuel van Meteren that in Elizabethan England 'they are

---

[13] Colley Cibber. *Love's Last Shift* (1696), p. 2.
[14] Lord Chesterfield, *Letters to his Son*, 30 April 1750.
[15] Charles Caleb Colton, *Lacon* (1825), 2, p. 217.
[16] William Hazlitt, *The Conversations of James Northcote* (1830).
[17] Robert Burton, *The Anatomy of Melancholy* (1621).
[18] Ambrose Bierce, *The Devil's Dictionary* (1881-1911).
[19] George Bernard Shaw, 'Doctors, Fashions and Epidemics', preface to *The Doctor's Dilemma* (1913).

very inconsistent and desirous of novelties changing their fashions every year, both men and women'.[20] But the history of costume does not support him. There is no evidence of annual fashion in Tudor England: indeed fashions remained remarkably stable and spread very slowly, men in 1596 being reported as still wearing the fashions of the reign of Henry VIII.[21] Moreover sharply rising prices and falling real wages in late Elizabethan England would make reading any great significance into van Meteren's remark highly suspect. The looked-for statistical support of rapidly rising consumption is not there, the looked-for costume changes to suggest annual fashion are not there, there is no supporting evidence of how fashions could have been rapidly and widely transmitted through Elizabethan England, no substantial biographical evidence of industrialists and merchants manipulating and profiting from fashionable innovations.

Such are the social and sexual potentialities of fine costume that there will always be examples to be found of inventive exploitation of it. Such is the perverse nature of mankind that sumptuary laws will always intensify the desire of some of those legally deprived in this way to wear the banned material.[22] Such is the ingenuity of men and women that even in the most inauspicious circumstances some will contrive to indulge themselves in fashion. But more than that is needed to bring about the revolutionary commitment to fashion, the commercial hold over fashion and the widespread social dispersion of fashion which I want to describe and explain. It was no longer a matter of the aspiring few wanting to be in fashion. In the late eighteenth century large numbers in society felt that they *must* be in fashion, whether they liked it or not, even to the point of ridicule. It was no longer forbidden fruit or an atypical social need. It was now *de rigueur*, socially required of one to be in fashion. As the *Town and Country Magazine* asked plaintively in 1785, 'What can a man do?'

> Banyans are worn in every part of town from Wapping to Westminster, and if a sword is occasionally put on it sticks out of the middle behind. This however is the fashion, the ton, and what can a man do? He *must* wear a banyan.

By the end of the eighteenth century the first signs of a surfeit of fashion can be seen, as commerce increasingly took over the manipulation and direction of fashion. Men and women increasingly *had* to wear what commerce dictated, had to raise or lower their hems and their heels at the

---

[20] Emmanuel van Meteren, *Nederlandtche Historie* (1575), quoted Elizabeth Burton, *The Pageant of Elizabethan England* (New York, 1958), pp. 119-22. Also see C. W. and P. Cunnington, *Handbook of English Costume in the 16th Century* (1954), p. 179.

[21] See Cunnington, op. cit., p. 53, p. 193 and *passim*.

[22] When they were required 'to wear white Knit Caps of wollen yearn ... for three or four years...unless their husbands...could prove themselves gentlemen' they had a clear incentive to wear something else. See Cunnington, op. cit., p. 199. See also N. B. Harte, 'State Control of Dress and Social Change in Pre-Industrial England', ch. 8 of *Trade, Government and Economy in Pre-Industrial England*, ed. D. C. Coleman and A. H. John, (1976), pp. 132-65.

dictates of the cloth manufacturers and the shoe sellers. So that one finds Jane Austen describing the wife of an undistinguished colonel living in the depths of rural Hampshire turning up for a family dinner, on a freezing night in the first week of January 1801, dressed 'nakedly in white muslin' as London fashion decreed she should, 'a devotion to fashion bordering on the frenetic'.[23]

In my view the Western European fashion pattern (and indeed the more general Western European consumer pattern) is as marked, as important and as worthy of attention as the much studied 'European Marriage Pattern'.[24] If and when they are both recognized, the well advised historians will eventually wish to look back to the sixteenth century at least, just as they will certainly need to look at Holland in the early eighteenth century and France in the later, but for the first full efflorescence of the new fashion and consumer patterns they will need to concentrate on eighteenth-century England. There they will find not just one or two isolated comments on annual fashion but a multiplicity, not just the occasional foreign visitor describing his admiring reactions to English fashion but dozens expressing their astonishment, not just a few burgesses' wives desirous of following fashion but virtually all the middle class, many of the tradesmen, mechanics and more prosperous working classes. There too, they will find the statistical backing of rising aggregate demand, there they will find that before 1780 most of the increased demand came from the home consumption of manufactured goods. The other necessary supporting evidence will also be found there: the well-evidenced cases of commercial manipulation of fashion and the well-substantiated cases of major industrialists building their fortunes on fashionable goods. The vital agents in the spread of fashion can be found too: not only the traditional fairs and pedlars, but the Manchester Men, the Scotch Drapers, Scotch Hawkers and the provincial shopkeepers. The vital agents in the transmission of accurate fashion intelligence were also for the first time available—the fashion magazines, the fashion plates and the English fashion doll. In addition there were the advertising columns of the press, both of the provinces and London. The role of London, indeed, swelled to a quite new significance as the radiant centre of the fashion world and conspicuous consumption, transmitting through its season, its exhibitions, its shops and their trade cards, new patterns of consumption more widely than ever before. They were transmitted along the new turnpike roads, by the more efficient coaching system, along the new canals, and through the new satellite centres of fashion and commerce in the province. The process was by 1800 unmistakable, the evidence overwhelming.

---

[23] Jane Austen to her sister Cassandra, 8 January 1801. Quoted by Alison Adburgham, *Shops and Shopping, 1800–1914* (1964), pp. 1–2.

[24] See for the classic exposition of this important concept H. J. Hajnal, 'European Marriage Pattern in Perspective', *Population in History* (1965), ed. D. V. Glass and D. E. C. Eversley, pp. 101–43.

Where in the sixteenth century, for instance, we have a composite image of the Tudors—and one not due simply to the massive imprint of Holbein—for the eighteenth century it would be difficult to confuse the products of one reign with another. The accelerating pace of fashion change can only be accommodated by referring to the styles of George I, George II, the 1760s, the 1770s, the 1780s and 1790s, and with many fashion goods even that is insufficient and anyone with scholarship worthy of the name would have to refer to individual years.

One could not possibly confuse Wedgwood jasper with the pottery made under George II or confuse the classical simplicity of Schofield's silver with the rococo confections of the 1740s and 50s; nor, as the pace speeded up, confuse the furniture of Chippendale, Hepplewhite and Sheraton. Hepplewhite's *Guide,* published in 1788, claimed to follow the 'latest ... most prevailing fashions', but as Sheraton happily wrote of it in 1791, when he began to publish his *Guide* 'if we compare some of the designs, particularly the chairs, with the newest taste, we shall find his work has already caught the decline, and perhaps in a little time, will suddenly die of the disorder'. In lesser fashion accessories the speed of change was even greater. Such was the fugitive conformity of taste that while the meanest tyro can distinguish between the dress fashion of the 1780s and 1790s, a trained eye can do better and place *most* fashion goods of the eighteenth century in their decade and, with real expertise, place many, like hats, in their year of production.

This fashion revolution did not happen by accident. The social and economic circumstances were immensely favourable, but fully to realize its great economic potential required careful guidance and skilful exploitation. The role played in this by the process of commercialization was of vital importance. Many different experts have described many parts of it, many specialist scholars have assembled the raw materials, but the process has yet to be satisfactorily explained as a whole.[25]

* * *

[25] The historians of costume, pre-eminently the Cunningtons, have provided the detailed scholarship of the minutiae of fashion change. The theoretical implications of fashion for economics and business history have been discussed by H. Leibenstein, 'Bandwaggon, Snob and Veblen Effects in the Theory of Consumers' Demand', *Quarterly Journal of Economics,* 64 (1950), and D. E. Robinson 'The Importance of Fashions in Taste to Business History', *Business History Review,* 37 (1963) and 'The Styling and Transmission of Fashions Historically Considered', *Journal of Economic History,* 20 (1960). The history of shopping has been illuminated by the work of Dorothy Davis, *A History of Shopping* (1966), and the history of retailing and distribution by such as R. B. Westerfield, 'Middlemen in English Business 1660–1760', *Transactions of the Connecticut Academy of Arts and Sciences,* 19 (New Haven, 1915) and D. Alexander, *Retailing in England during the industrial revolution* (1970). Individual case studies of Wedgwood by N. McKendrick and Boulton by Eric Robinson have shown how important fashion could be to major industrialists. But the interlocking relationships of these different developments (and the new explanations of the rise in home demand) have rarely been studied as a whole.

The commercialization of fashion in eighteenth-century England can be encapsulated in the history of the fashion doll. The doll may seem, to some, to be a curious, even a trivial, expression of the commercial techniques and the emergent consumer demand which underlay the Industrial Revolution. But as a vivid symbol of both the extension of the market and the means by which that market was extended, it dramatically exemplifies the change from fashion which was expensive, exclusive and Paris-based, to a fashion which was cheap, popular and London-based. Most dramatically of all it exemplifies the change from a fashion which was royal in origin, limited (essentially aristocratic) in its immediate influence, and very slow to filter through to the rest of society, to a fashion which was directly aimed at the popular market, indeed which was specifically intended to extend it further into a *mass* one. This fashion promoter was not only immediately available to the new consumer market, it was also capable of responding very rapidly to its needs, its growth, and its fluctuations. Where the French fashion doll of the first decades of the century served only an *élite*, the English fashion doll of the last decades of that century served a mass consumer market. Perhaps even more significantly, where the former was court controlled the latter was controlled by business. Entrepreneurs had taken over the fashion doll and committed it to the service of commerce. Its role was now the manipulation and extension of consumer demand. Its dramatic metamorphosis in the course of the century nicely confirms the change from a world where fashion was not only designed to serve the few but was designed to mark them off from the rest of society, to a world where fashion was being deliberately designed to encourage social imitation, social emulation and emulative spending, a world which blurred rather than reinforced class divisions and allowed the conspicuous lead of the fashion leaders to be quickly copied by the rest of society. By the end of the eighteenth century the competitive, socially emulative aspect of fashion was being consciously manipulated by commerce in pursuit of increased consumption. This new fashion world was one in which entrepreneurs were trying deliberately to induce fashionable change, to make it rapidly available to as many as possible and yet to keep it so firmly under their control that the consuming public could be sufficiently influenced to buy at the dictate of *their* fashion decisions, at the convenience of *their* production lines. Those fashion decisions were increasingly based on economic grounds rather than aesthetic ones, on the basis of what the factories could produce and what the salesmen could sell rather than on what the French court dictated. Commerce was now pulling the strings in control of the fashion doll. They still needed the co-operation of the exclusive world of the fashionable aristocracy. The fashionable few remained what Wedgwood called 'the legislators of taste', but they were no longer the sole beneficiaries of its pleasures, and the fashionable lead they provided was increasingly under the manipulative control of entrepreneurs seeking a quicker access to a mass market.

BIRTH OF A CONSUMER SOCIETY

The changing face of the fashion doll reveals the extent to which this change occurred in the course of the eighteenth century.

At the beginning of the eighteenth century the fashion doll came over every year from Paris. Even war could not hinder its progress. For as the Abbé Prevost wrote in 1704 'by an act of gallantry, which is worthy of being noted in the chronicle of history, for the benefit of the ladies the ministers of both Courts granted a special pass to the mannequin; that pass was always respected, and during the times of greatest enmity experienced on both sides the mannequin was the one object which remained unmolested'. Addison was outraged at the import of 'the wooden Mademoiselle' at the height of war, and in his anger claimed that one came carrying the French fashions every month.[26] Other evidence suggests that one a year was the normal ration. It also makes clear that the doll was sent first to the English court[27] and then, when the Queen and the ladies of the court had absorbed its fashionable lessons, it made its way to the leading London fashion makers.[28] Advertisements announcing that 'Last Saturday the *French doll for the year 1712* arrived at my house in King Street, Covent Garden', suggests that those who believed that 'for a twelvemonths this remained the dressmakers' model' were right.[29]

Variously known as 'pandoras', 'mannequins', 'dolls of the Rue St. Honoré' (the centre of French fashion) and 'grand courriers de la mode'[30] the fashion dolls could be extremely elaborate and very expensive. Many were made 'lifesize in order that the clothes with which they were dressed might immediately be worn';[31] they were to be models for hairstyles, head gear, and all the accessories of fashion—even down to the details of 'how they wore their underclothing'.[32]

Such was their influence that after the Queen, her ladies-in-waiting, and the London fashion shops had had their fill, the dolls spread further abroad. One was advertised in *The New England Weekly Journal* in 1733 where

---

[26] Addison in the *Spectator*, quoted in R. Bayne-Powell, *Eighteenth-Century London Life* (New York, 1938), pp. 178–9.
[27] In his trade lexicon of 1723, Savary describes the elaborately coiffeured and richly dressed mannequins which were sent each year to foreign courts, and in the 1750s Risbeck described them as still ruling 'despotically' in Vienna.
[28] In 1727 Lady Lansdowne sent to Queen Caroline's ladies-in-waiting the mannequin for that year with the request that, after it had circulated amongst them, they should dispatch it to Mrs. Tempest the dressmaker. It was, of course, in full Court dress.
[29] There are many contemporary comments suggesting that the fashion doll was an annual event. See Antonia Fraser, *Dolls* (1973), p. 31, and Max von Boehn. *Dolls* (1972) translated by J. Nicoll from the original *Puppen* (1929). p. 140.
[30] They were invoiced under that title when they were imported at Dover in 1764.
[31] Madame Eloffe supplied the Comtesse Bombelles with a life-size mannequin in Court dress on August 18, 1788, which cost 409 francs, 12 centimes. Marie-Antoinette used the furniture designer Röntgu to transport the Paris fashion by this method to her mother and sisters.
[32] Alice K. Early, *English Dolls, Effigies and Puppets* (1955); Max von Boehn, *Dolls and Puppets* (1932); Eleanor St George, *Dolls of Three Centuries* (1951); G. White, *Dolls of the World* (1962).

it was announced that for two shillings you could look at it, and for seven shillings take it away.[33]

Eventually the geographical spread of the fashion doll's influence was very great.[34] But its immediate social impact was small, and it was too expensive to influence directly the mass market. To transmit fashions in quantity (cheaply and quickly, and yet accurately) something less ponderous was needed than the life size, fully dressed, elaborately coiffured French mannequin. The answer was the English fashion doll which has been described as 'a revolutionary invention conquering the market from 1790 onwards'. It was a flat fashion model cut out of cardboard. It cost only three shillings in 1790 and later only a few pence. It was printed by the thousand. It was, in the words of a contemporary commentator in 1791, 'about eight inches high', with 'simply dressed hair', and 'complete with underclothing and corset'. With it went

> six complete sets of tastefully coloured, cut-out dresses and coiffures, which means summer—and winter—clothing, complete dresses and négligés, caracos, chemises, furs, hats, bonnets, poufs, etc. Each dress and hat is made in such a way that the doll can easily be dressed in it, giving a fully dressed or décolleté effect while the dress fits perfectly in either case. Hat or bonnet can be adjusted freely to be pulled over the face or set back. They can be put straight or at an angle, suiting the hairstyle in a tasteful manner or otherwise. In short: dress and coiffure can be varied, and by trying, each given its particular 'air'. This dressing and undressing, being able to set up and change again, makes for the uniqueness of the English doll. One might obtain even more changes by having some extra dresses designed and painted. The whole is packed in a neat paper envelope, and can easily be carried in portfolio or working bag.[35]

In 1791 it was described in Germany as 'a new and pretty invention' from England from which 'mothers and grown women' could observe and even study 'good or bad taste in dress or coiffure'.[36] Very soon hundreds of different sheets of the dolls were available, specifically aimed at different classes and professions, as it was realized how quickly it could spread new fashion ideas.

It was original, cheap and effective. It was capable of almost endless

---

[33] *The New England Weekly Journal*, 2 July 1733: 'At Mrs. Hannah Teatt's dressmaker at the top of Sumner Street, Boston, is to be seen a mannequin in the latest fashion with articles of dress, night dress, and everything appertaining to women's attire. It had been brought from London by Captain White. Ladies who choose to see it may come or send for it. It is always ready to serve you. If you come, it will cost you two shillings, but if you send for it, seven shillings.' A New York advertisement of 1757 also announced the arrival of the latest mannequin from London; and in 1796 the 'mannequin which had just come from England to give us an idea of the latest fashions' was still eagerly awaited and visited. See Max von Boehn, op. cit., pp. 147–8.

[34] Sébastien Mercier in his *Tableau de Paris* (1771) could congratulate himself that French fashion 'is imitated by all nations who obediently submit to the taste of the Rue Saint-Honoré'.

[35] *Journal des Luxus und der Moden* (1791), published by Friedrich Justin Bertuch. See M. Bachmann and C. Handmann, *Dolls* (1973), p. 107.

[36] Ibid.

variety. It could penetrate many different social levels. As an advertisement it had good survival value, for even when discarded by mothers it was taken up by children as a toy, and so could begin the indoctrination of the next generation of fashion consumers—teaching even in infancy the importance and intricacies of fashion awareness. Those who produced the English fashion doll did not rely simply on the accidents of parental dispersal—they marketed the fashion doll separately as a toy aimed specifically at children.

The original fashion doll continued to serve the upper end of the market, while the English one publicized the latest fashions to the rest of society, until Napoleon finally ordered that the export of French dolls should cease.

After over four hundred years the French fashion doll was dethroned by a popular usurper. The first record of the fashion doll dates back to 1396 and the English royal court. The purpose it had so expensively, so exclusively and so ponderously served was now to pass to a mere paper cut-out—so humble and so ephemeral as to be beneath the notice of most historians but symptomatic of the rapid changes in the diffusion of fashion views which had occurred in the eighteenth century. For by the time of its appearance, the fashion manipulators had a host of other means by which they could spread the latest fashions down through the ranks of English society.[37]

Some of them have fortunately proved more durable than the little paper cutouts. For few English fashion dolls have survived to offer us visible proof of the extension of the market. Their more imposing, more impressive, more collectable ancestors have displayed a greater ability to survive, and in doing so have helped to obscure the popular influence of their ephemeral, if popular, descendants. Like so many of the commercial techniques of the eighteenth century, the fashion doll has a tradition which long predates its commercial apotheosis. Its use by the French as a popular means of propaganda for centuries has long been recognized: 'At a time when as yet the press was non-existent, long before the invention of such mechanical means of reproduction as the woodcut and the copper plate, . . . the doll was given the task of popularizing French fashions abroad'.[38] The English version of this means of spreading their fashions has received less attention, but it was certainly effective. Its almost infinite variety deservedly earned it the contemporary description of 'the protean figure'. It provided a direct channel to those who wished to be in fashion. It offered an effective means by which artisans, craftsmen and even labourers—and more especially the wives of all of them—could be sucked into the thrall of fashion. The wives of the newly

---

[37] The royal tradition was an international one and the costs were usually very high. The wardrobe for what was said to be a lifesize dummy with the measurements of the English queen cost 450 francs in 1396. In 1496 Queen Isabella of Spain received a doll which was dressed twice over to meet her exacting fashion requirements. When Henry IV of France was about to marry Marie de Medici he sent her several model dolls 'as samples of our fashions'. See Alice K. Early, op. cit., and Antonia Fraser, op. cit., p. 103.

[38] Max von Boehn, *Puppen und Puppenspiele* (1929), translated as *Dolls and Puppets* (1932). The first volume was published as *Dolls* (1972).

prosperous artisans (those who in Moll Flanders' words had 'lived like a tradesman but spent like a lord') now knew what to spend their money on.

* * *

Fortunately there were other sources of fashion intelligence to satisfy the growing appetite for accurate information which grew in step with the rising demand for consumer goods. The fashion plate and the fashion magazine and the advertisements of fashions in the newspapers were effective allies of the fashion doll, and have survived in sufficient numbers to demonstrate clearly both their quality and the period in which they revealed their importance.

For although the first fashion magazine appeared in France in the 1670s, and even fashion drawings have been found as early as 1677 in *Le Mercure Galant,* 'it was in England that the systematic and ... widespread production of fashion prints began'.[39] The time was the last three decades of the eighteenth century.

The Lady's Magazine brought out its first fashion print in 1770, and it was at this time that an enterprising advertiser started to insert a page of the latest hats and dresses into ladies pocket books and almanacs. These were specifically devised for the guidance of 'ordinary young gentlewomen, not the extravagant few'. Between 1771 and 1800 the following ladies' almanacks and annuals, carrying such fashion details, have been identified: *The Annual Present for the Ladies or a New and Fashionable Pocket Book, Carnan's Ladies' Complete Pocket Book, The Court and Royal Ladies' Pocket Book, The General Companion to the Ladies or Useful Memorandum Book, The Ladies' Companion or Complete Pocket Book, The Ladies' Compleat Pocket Book, The Ladies' Mirror or Mental Companion, The Ladies' Miscellany or Entertaining Companion, The Ladies' Museum or Pocket Memorandum Book, The Ladies' New and Elegant Pocket Book, The Lady's Own Memorandum Book, The Ladies' Pocket Journal or Toilet Assistant, Lane's Ladies' Museum, Lane's Pocket Book, The London Fashionable and Polite Repository, The Polite and Fashionable Ladies' Companion.*[40]

The first coloured fashion print is dated 1771 and appeared in *The Lady's Magazine* described as 'à fine Copper-plate beautifully coloured',[41] but within a few years,[42] 'when much greater elaboration had been attained and

---

[39] D. Langley Moore, *Fashion through Fashion Plates 1771–1970,* (1971), p. 12.
[40] Ibid., p. 13. Where the cost is known it was one shilling for each of these productions.
[41] *The Lady's Magazine,* 1771.
[42] Sufficient research has been done to date and identify the work and style of individual artists working in this field—men such as E. F. Burney (nephew of Dr. Burney and cousin of Fanny), Henry Moses, a designer who did his own engraving, and the prolific J. Stevenson. Thomas Stothard, whose anonymous work can be identified from *The Lady's Magazine* to *La Belle Assemblée,* was a Royal Academician and charged a guinea a piece for his accomplished sketches. Stothard also provided a further service in advertising the prevailing fashions in the periodicals like the *Novelists' Magazine* where the novels, short stories and contemporary dramas were illustrated with sketches of fashionable life-styles,

the circulation of such journals was far larger', whole teams of colourists (each member handling only a single colour) worked on assembly line principles passing the page along until it reached its multi-coloured completion.[43]

These fashion plates were, in fact, trade plates, designed as commercial propaganda. Their intention was to stimulate demand, to spread new fashions, to encourage imitation of the 'taste-makers'. As the earliest editors assured their subscribers, they would no longer have to rely on the French fashion dolls, those 'puppets always inadequate and yet extremely dear, which give at best merely a hint of our new modes.'[44]

At the top end of the market was the flagship of them all, *The Gallery of Fashion* which ran from 1794 to 1803. It was deliberately exclusive, it cost three guineas a year to subscribe, and it offered only two plates a month. Vyvyan Holland has estimated that the total number circulated could never have been more than 450 copies.[45]

Such was its quality that Heideloff's *The Gallery of Fashion* is inevitably celebrated in all histories of fashion, but although it played its role (so characteristic of the late eighteenth century as Josiah Wedgwood's promotional campaigns show, and Matthew Boulton's, and indeed George Packwood's,[46] and those of many others less well-known) in encouraging imitation and emulation from below, the provincial newspapers and the fashion advertisements were of far greater significance in effectively spreading the word further afield. Mary Ann Bell kept 'the Nobility and Gentry' supplied with a succession of novelties at her premises in Upper King Street called 'The Fashionable Millinery and Dress Rooms', and advertised her triumphs to a wider audience in *La Belle Assemblée* every month.

La Belle Assemblée carried not only exclusive fashion news but a mass of other trade notices. Like Mrs. Bell, the advertisers might invoke the patronage of the great, but they were increasingly aiming at the rest of society. *The World of Fashion* which took over, in 1824, the right to publish Mrs. Bell's exclusive models claimed a circulation of 20,000 by the 1830s, and those advertising straw hats, artificial flowers, and paper patterns were in Doris Langley Moore's words 'assuredly not addressing themselves to the Nobility and Gentry'.[47]

Mrs. Bell held a fashion show for her novelties on 'THE FIRST DAY OF EVERY MONTH' as the banner headlines of *La Belle Assemblée* announced it. Some mention of her approach is made in a later chapter,[48]

---

but this was incidental rather than direct advertisement. See D. Langley Moore, op. cit., pp. 13–14.
[43] D. Langley Moore. op. cit., p. 14.
[44] Quoted Langley Moore, op. cit., p. 11.
[45] *The Gallery of Fashion* was started by a German artist, Nicolaus von Heideloff.
[46] See below for a discussion of Boulton, Wedgwood and Packwood.
[47] Langley Moore, op. cit., p. 22.
[48] See below 'The Art of Eighteenth Century Advertising', pp. 146–94.

but as the London source of a flow of monthly fashions which were taken up and celebrated in the provinces she was merely the culmination of a process typical of the eighteenth century. The stay maker of North Walsham who advertised in the *Norwich Mercury* of 1788 'that he is *just returned from Town with* the newest Fashions... in Stays, Corsetts and Riding Stays' knew what his customers wanted to hear. His assurance that 'their Orders [will be] executed in a Height of Taste not inferior to *the first Shops in London*' offered to his female customers the confidence that even the least displayed part of their clothing would be in the latest fashion. What was invisible to the world at large would be seen by her maid, and, in the closely stratified society of provincial England, demonstrating the modishness of even one's underwear to one's maidservant was a sufficiently desirable event for the local tradesman to insist on the fashionability of each and every undergarment. And Mrs. Bell played a vital role in keeping the provincial world supplied with a constant flow of such London prototypes to copy.

In the last thirty years of the eighteenth century the fashion plate and the fashion magazine offered wholly new means of spreading fashionable contagions. Unprecedentedly accurate, they and the fashion doll in the last ten years, marked the culmination of the commercialization of fashion which had been developing so rapidly in the rest of the century. But their novelty at the end of the century must not distract us from other agents of commercialization and other manipulators of fashion which had been effectively at work earlier in the century.

* * *

There were many traditional agents of fashionable change operating throughout the eighteenth century, and even earlier. Many had been highly effective, and there is ample contemporary comment to testify to their powers. According to *The London Tradesman* of 1747 such was the power of the fashionable tailor that 'to some he not only makes their Dress, but ... may be said to make themselves'.[49] Richard Campbell mockingly described fashionable Londoners' dependence on, what he called, their 'Shape Merchant'[50] in mid-eighteenth-century England:

> There are Numbers of Beings in about this Metropolis who have no other identical Existence than what the Taylor, Milliner, and Perriwig-Maker bestow upon them: Strip them of these Distinctions, and they are quite a different Species of Beings; have no more Relation to their dressed selves, than they have to the Great *Mogul,* and are as insignificant in Society as Punch, deprived of his moving Wires, and hung up upon a Peg.[51]

Such was the power of those who controlled fashionable dress that to some, '*Prometheus* ... was really no more than a Taylor, who, by his Art metamorphosed Mankind so, that they appeared a new Species of Beings'.

---

[49] Richard Campbell, *The London Tradesman* (1747), p. 191.
[50] Ibid., p. 192.
[51] Ibid., p. 191.

In fact by 1747 *The London Tradesman* in its catalogue of 'all the TRADES' had already recognized the pervasive impact of fashion on the most diverse employment. Trade after trade was said to require 'a fruitful Fancy, to invent new Whims, to please the Changeable Foible of the Ladies'; or 'a quick Invention for new Patterns ... to create Trade'; or the ability to create 'a new Fashion' since 'he that can furnish them oftenest with the newest Whim has the best Chance for their Custom'.[52] A Tradesman's 'Fancy must always be on the Wing, and his Wit ... a Fashion-hunting': he must be 'a Perfect *Proteus*, change Shapes as often as the Moon, and still find something new';[53] for 'the continual Flux and Reflux of Fashion, obliges him to learn something new almost every day'.[54] He must be 'a perfect Connoiseur in Dress and Fashion'.[55]

Campbell recognized not only the whimsical advantages of the introduction of the hooped-petticoat.

> They are the Friends of Men, for they let us into all the Secrets of the Ladies Legs, which we might have been ignorant of to Eternity without their Help

but also their real advantages to the economy as a new fashion which will

> encourage the Consumption of our Manufacturers in a prodigious Degree.[56]

By mid-century most of the commercial benefit of fashion was felt to accrue to London: the shoes made in the provinces sold in the London 'Saleshops',[57] the cutlery of Birmingham and Sheffield furnished the 'great Demand' for cutlery sold in the London shops who 'put their own Marks upon them and sell them as *London* made';[58] and yet London was still regarded as being heavily dependent on Paris for new fashions in 'Wigs, Perukes and Fans'.

It was to take longer for London to take over from Paris, for the provinces to adopt the fashions of London, and for the full battery of commercial practices designed to exploit fashion to be developed. Thirty years after Campbell wrote, Trusler was convinced that the fashionable contagion, or what he called 'the infection of the metropolis',[59] had spread. In his view, published in 1777, 'The great degree of luxury to which this country has arrived, within a few years, is not only astonishing but almost dreadful to think of. Time was, when those articles of indulgence, which now every mechanic aims to be in possession of, were enjoyed only by the Lord or Baron of a district.'[60] As the result of the increase of trade and riches 'men

---

[52] Ibid., p. 143.
[53] Campbell, op. cit., p. 192.
[54] Campbell, op. cit., p. 204.
[55] Campbell, p. 207.
[56] Campbell, p. 212.
[57] Ibid., p. 219.
[58] Ibid., p. 239.
[59] John Trusler, *The Way to be Rich and Respectable*, (London 1777), p. 6.
[60] Trusler, op. cit., p. 1.

began to feel new wants'. They 'sighed for indulgences they never dreamed of before'. The 'wish to be thought opulent ... led them into luxury of dress. The homespun garb then gave way to more costly attire, and respectable plainness was soon transformed into laughable frippery' and 'every succeeding year gave way to fresh wants and new expences'.[61]

The spread down the social scale was explicitly described: 'the infection of the first class soon spread among the second', 'a taste for elegancies spread itself through all ranks and degrees of men'. The influence of London was explicitly blamed: 'The several cities and large towns of this island catch the manners of the metropolis ... the notions of splendour that prevail in the Capital are eagerly adopted; the various changes of the fashion exactly copied'.[62]

The ever increasing speed of change was also widely noted. Mandeville had actually supplied a convenient contemporary index by which to measure the spread of fashionable change in the early eighteenth century. For he wrote in 1723 that 'Experience has taught us, that these Modes seldom last above Ten or Twelve Years, and a Man of Threescore must have observ'd five or six Revolutions of 'em at least.'[63] By the 1770s contemporary observers found the pace of change so accelerated that they regarded fashions as annual, and amongst the super-fashionable as monthly. As the pace of fashionable change stepped up, not everyone could keep up. The costume museums of eighteenth-century dress are very revealing as to the skilful feminine subterfuges that were employed to keep a single dress in line with the demands of fashion. For even the museum pieces show repeated signs of alterations as their wearers struggled to keep up with the short-lived modes of the eighteenth century. Not even the fashionable could always afford to buy new clothes when the whirligig of fashion was spinning as rapidly as it did in the reign of George III, and the rest of society had to make constant use of the needle and their own ingenuity. But however ingenious the changes they devised, the evidence of increased spending suggests that the eighteenth-century fashion manipulators made them buy more than ever before.

Fortunately, contemporary comment has left a uniquely rich record of the chronology and nature of changes in fashion in the eighteenth century. Not surprisingly, those comments are dominated by a concern with contemporary costume. Fashion and dress are often used almost interchangeably. From Mandeville onwards special attention was given to the role of clothes in this process of social and economic change.

---

[61] Trusler, op. cit., pp. 1–3.

[62] Trusler, op. cit., pp. 4–6. Trusler was very opposed to fashionable extravagance in dress and produced family budgets to show how prudently a family could live by avoiding them. Whether the family income was £80 p.a. or £800 he advised spending no more than 15 per cent on clothes if they wished 'to live with Frugality': see J. Trusler, *The Economist*, (Dublin 1777), pp. 1–31.

[63] Mandeville, 'A Search into the Nature of Society' which was added to the 1723 edition of *The Fable of the Bees*. See 1970 edition, ed. by P. Harth, p. 333.

Fashion was the key used by many commentators to explain the forces of social imitation, social emulation, class competition and emulative spending. These were the motive forces which made fashion such a potent commercial weapon in the eighteenth century. Mandeville had specifically identified them as such in *The Fable of the Bees*. He knew that consumption occurred for motives very different from everyday utility. He knew that consumption could serve as the visible evidence of wealth. He knew that fashionable clothes could serve as, what Veblen later called, 'the insignia of leisure'.[64] He recognized that elegant clothes could serve as an overt statement of social superiority.

In this he anticipated Veblen. For if, in Veblen's language, good repute rested on pecuniary strength, then one of the best means of displaying that strength, and thereby retaining or enhancing one's social standing, would be to indulge in conspicuous consumption of goods. The most obvious, the most socially visible way of doing this in early eighteenth-century society lay in displaying the clothes one wore. As Mandeville wrote, 'People ... are generally honour'd according to their Clothes ... from the richness of them we judge their Wealth ... It is this which encourages every Body, who is conscious of his little Merit, if he is any ways able, to wear Clothes above his Rank.'[65] He even recognizes the way in which a growing and more mobile population, either congregating in, or merely visiting, more 'Populous cities', would intensify 'the Veblen effect'. The desire to dress above one's rank would operate, he argued, 'especially in large and populous Cities, where obscure men may hourly meet with fifty Strangers to one Acquaintance, and consequently have the pleasure of being esteem'd by a vast Majority, not as what they are, but what they appear to be'.[66]

Many other early eighteenth-century writers recognized, and made good use of, the powerful metaphor of fashion and consumption. Professor Landa has shown how literary form could be shaped by the climate of current economic opinion: Pope's Belinda, in her role as a consumer of imported luxuries, being seen as peculiarly a child of her time.[67] And Professor Vichert, writing on conspicuous consumption, has drawn attention to the clothing metaphor which dominates *A Tale of a Tub,* and the glittering artifice of Belinda's dress in *The Rape of the Lock*.[68] But Mandeville made brilliantly

[64] Thorstein Veblen *The Theory of the Leisure Classes*, (New York, 1926), p. 171.
[65] Bernard Mandeville, *The Fable of the Bees; or, Private Vices, Publick Benefits*, ed. F. B. Kaye (Oxford, 1924), I, p. 127.
[66] Ibid., p. 127.
[67] Louis Landa, *Essays in Eighteenth-Century English Literature* (Princeton, 1980).
[68] Gordon Vichert, 'The Theory of Conspicuous Consumption in the Eighteenth Century' in *The Varied Pattern: Studies in the Eighteenth Century* (Toronto, 1971), ed. P. Hughes and D. Williams, p. 254. The social and economic potentialities of clothes had a powerful hold over some of the more influential writers of the day. It was one of Defoe's recurring fantasies that civilization in the form of English clothes would sweep through Africa: 'Millions of Africans, now ashamed of their nakedness, would regularly demand suit of bays and English stocking'. See Peter Earle, 'The Economics of Stability: The Views of Daniel Defoe', *Trade, Government and Economy in Pre-Industrial England* (1976), p. 280.

explicit the force which many later in the century were to see as the master springs of conspicuous consumption and fashionable excess. Much of what Mandeville so controversially described in *The Fable of the Bees* was to be played out in *many* areas of public consumption later in the century. But the process was inevitably demonstrated most obviously in the world of clothes.

Clothes were the first mass consumer products to be noticed by contemporary observers. It is often forgotten that the industrial revolution was, to a large extent, founded on the sales of humble products to very large markets—the beer of London, the buckles and buttons of Birmingham, the knives and forks of Sheffield, the cups and saucers of Staffordshire, the cheap cottons of Lancashire. Beer was arguably the first mass consumer product to be mass produced under factory conditions and sold to the public for cash at fixed prices by pure retailers.[69] But the sales of mass-produced cheap clothes understandably excited more attention. When *The British Magazine* of 1763 wrote that 'The present rage of imitating the manners of high life hath spread itself so far among the gentle folks of lower life, that in a few years we shall probably have no common folks at all', it was the imitation of fashionable dress that it was complaining of.

Dress was the most public manifestation of the blurring of class divisions which was so much commented on. Social expectations rose with family income. The standards of what Veblen later called 'pecuniary decency'[70] rose too as succeeding layers of English society joined the consuming ranks. The effects excited much comment, 'It is the curse of this nation that the labourer and the mechanic will ape the lord', wrote Hanway;[71] 'the different ranks of people are too much confounded: the lower orders press so hard on the heels of the higher, if some remedy is not used the Lord will be in danger of becoming the valet of his Gentleman'.[72] Dibdin complained that 'the Tradesman vies with my Lord'.[73] Tucker made the same point when he wrote that 'the different stations of Life so run into and mix with each other, that it is hard to say, where the one ends, and the other begins'.[74] The *London Magazine* for 1772 reported that the classes were imitating one another so closely that 'the lower orders of the people (if there are any, for distinctions are now confounded) are equally immerged in their fashionable vices'.[75] In 1775 it complained more specifically that 'whenever a thing becomes the mode it is universally and absurdly adopted from the garret to the kitchen, when it is only intended for some very few Belles in the first floor'.[76]

---

[69] See Peter Mathias, *The Brewing Industry in England 1700–1830*, (1959) and D. Davis, *A History of Shopping* (1966), p. 213.
[70] Veblen, op. cit., p. 113.
[71] Hanway, 'Essay on Tea', printed in *A Journal of Eight Days' Journey* (1756), p. 224.
[72] Ibid, pp. 282–3.
[73] Dibdin, op. cit., I, 34–5.
[74] *Josiah Tucker: A Selection from his Economic and Political Writings*, p. 264.
[75] *London Magazine or Gentleman's Monthly Intelligencer*, 1772.
[76] Ibid., 1775. Quoted C. W. and P. Cunnington, op. cit., p. 16.

BIRTH OF A CONSUMER SOCIETY

Writer after writer notes the 'absence of those outward distinctions which formerly characterized different classes'. Somerville, writing in the early nineteenth century, reflects on the changes which had taken place in his lifetime. 'At that time various modes of dress indicated at first sight the rank, profession and the age of every individual. Now even the servants are hardly distinguishable in their equipment from their masters and mistresses.'[77] Davis, in his *Friendly Advice to Industrious and Frugal Persons,* drew attention to the same phenomenon: 'a fondness for Dress may be said to be the folly of the age, and it is to be lamented that it has nearly destroyed those becoming marks whereby the several classes of society were formerly distinguished'.[78]

All the historians of fashion record the change in fashion tempo in the middle of the eighteenth century. Significantly the books written by those invaluable and indefatigable recorders of the minutiae of fashion—the Cunningtons—suddenly double in size when they reach the eighteenth century.[79] This, of course, is partly a reflection of the availability of evidence. The fashion prints, fashion magazines and newspaper advertisements inform the twentieth-century historian as well as they informed the buying public of the eighteenth. But this change of pace was real as well as better recorded. Most authorities place the turning point in the reign of George II and see the culmination of fashion frenzy early in the reign of George III. Fashion from this time has been described as 'such a varying goddess, that neither history, tradition nor painting has been able to preserve all her mimic forms; like Proteus struggling in the arms of Telemachus, on the Phanic coasts, she passes from shape to shape with the rapidity of thought.'[80] All agree that fashion for the first thirty years of the century 'moved with deliberation'. All agree that by the first two decades of the reign of George III a revolutionary increase in pace had occurred.

On every side contemporaries rushed into print to explain the phenomenon. It was the result, they all agreed, of the downward spread of fashion, and of the imitation by the poor of their social superiors. As early as 1750 Fielding complained that 'an infinite number of lower people aspire to the pleasures of the fashionable'. In 1755 *The World* complained of 'this foolish vanity that prompts us to imitate our superiors ... we have no such thing as common people among us ... Attorneys' clerks and city prentices dress like cornets of dragoons ... every commoner ... treads hard on the heels of the quality in dress'.[81]

But whereas Fielding was full of admiration for the way the fashion leaders used their arts 'to deceive and dodge their imitators ... when they

---

[77] T. Somerville, *My Own Life and Times, 1741–1814* (1861), pp. 376–7.
[78] 1817, p. 23.
[79] *The Handbook of Fashion for the Seventeenth Century* ran to 229 pages; *The Handbook of Fashion for the Eighteenth Century* ran to 453.
[80] Quoted by C. W. and P. Cunnington, *British Costume of the Eighteenth Century,* (1960), p. 349.
[81] Quoted C. W. and P. Cunnington, p. 21.

are hunted out in any favourable mode',[82] *The World,* writing five years later, saw the result of the 'perpetual warfare' as defeat for 'the nobility'. For they 'who can aim no higher, plunge themselves into debt to preserve their rank'. They were 'beaten out of all their resources for superior distinction; out of innumerable fashions in dress, every one of which they have been obliged to abandon as soon as occupied by their impertinent rivals. In vain have they armed themselves with lace and embroidery and intrenched themselves in hoops and furbelows; in vain have they had recourse to full-bottomed perriwigs and toupees; to high heads and low heads and no heads at all.

'Trade has bestowed riches on the competitors and riches have procured them equal finery. Hair has curled as genteely on one side of Temple Bar as on the other and hoops have grown to as prodigious a magnitude in the foggy air of Cheapside as in the purer regions of Grosvenor Square and Hill street.'[83]

Part of the increased consumption of the eighteenth century was the result not only of new levels of spending in the lower ranks, but also new levels of spending by those in the higher ranks who felt for the first time threatened by the loss of their distinctive badge of identity. At the beginning of the century Steele had written 'each by some particular in their dress shows to what class they belong';[83] at the end of the century Wenderborne, in contrast, declared 'Dress is carried to the very utmost, and the changes it undergoes are more frequent than those of the moon . . . this rage for finery and fashion spreads from the highest to the lowest; and in public places . . . it is very difficult to guess at [people's] rank in society or at the heaviness of their purse'.[84]

The situation was unique as well as novel. It had never happened before in Britain. It had not yet happened anywhere else in the world. As von Archenholz wrote, 'in other countries the vulgar imitate the higher ranks, [in England] on the contrary, the great are solicitous to distinguish themselves from the mob'.[85]

Finally, as the pace of fashion changes accelerated ever more rapidly, we find the rich moving into subtleties of cut rather than competing (as they did in the 1750s and 1760s and even more so in the 1770s and 1780s) in ever greater extremes of fashion. And finally a kind of fashion truce was called. 'For the first time in our history the Gentleman began to adopt the styles of dress and the actual garments of the working man.'[86] It was, in fact, part of the change from 'a crude to a subtle method of expressing social superior-

---

[82] Fielding, Works II, p. 239-40.
[83] Quoted by C. W. and P. Cunnington, op. cit., p. 21-2.
[84] F. A. Wenderborne, *A View of England towards the End of the Eighteenth Century,* p. 314.
[85] J. W. von Archenholz, *A Picture of England* (1791), pp. 75-83. For fuller discussion of this point see Neil McKendrick, 'Home Demand and Economic Growth', loc. cit., pp. 195-211.
[86] Cunnington, op. cit., p. 14.

ity'—a change which finally triumphed in Beau Brummel's doctrine that 'a gentleman's clothes should be inconspicuous in material and exquisite only in cut'. This process still had a long way to go. Distinctions in dress, of course, survived—very marked ones to our eyes—but they were much less obvious, particularly in male costume, in the eyes of contemporary observers.[87]

Although fashions changed rapidly, there was greater social uniformity in the changes. All of which, of course, suited those producing and selling fashion. Demand could be controlled to suit their needs. A larger and more homogeneous market was the basis of mass-produced factory output.

As a result of this increased homogeneity, each year is seen as having a distinctive stamp, and experts can date fashion prints with almost the same certainty that one can read the hallmarks of Georgian silver. 'Fashion in hats and hair dressing changed so rapidly in the last quarter of the eighteenth century that ... dating offers no great difficulty'.[88] The changes in colour, shape, material and style were immensely various, but the changes were sufficiently marked and sufficiently widespread to be dateable. Contemporaries even referred to the in-colour of each year. In 1753 purple was the in-colour—'all colours were neglected for that purple: in purple we glowed from the hat to the shoe'. In 1757 the fashion was for white linen with a pink pattern. In the 1770s the changes were rung even more rapidly—in 1776 the fashionable colour was 'couleur de Noisette', in 1777 dove grey, in 1779 'the fashionable dress was laycock satin trimmed with fur'. By 1781 'stripes in silk or very fine cambric-muslin' were in; by 1785 steel embroidery on dress was all the rage; by 1790 'the fashionable colours were lilac and yellow and brown and pale green'.[89] So although at the end of the century men complained that 'fashions alter in these days so much, that a man can hardly wear a coat two months before it is out of fashion',[90] the pattern of change was now more uniform, and more than ever at the behest, and for the convenience, of commerce.

* * *

One does not need to rely solely on contemporary writers to illustrate the story of a society in thrall to fashion and exhibiting an unprecedented capacity to pursue and to purchase consumer goods.

The pictorial evidence is as vivid and revealing as the literary evidence. Much of it tells the same story of social imitation and emulative spending penetrating deeper than ever before through the closely packed ranks of eighteenth-century society. Fashionable excess amongst the rich has long been minutely recorded by fashionable artists, and few satirized more

---

[87] There were many who remained far below the reach of these changes and remained wholly distinct as the abject poor.
[88] D. Langley Moore, *Fashion through Fashion Plates, 1771–1970* (1971), p. 13.
[89] C. W. and P. Cunnington op. cit., pp. 320–4.
[90] Wenderborne, op. cit., pp. 160–1.

effectively or more often than Hogarth. Even the pictures *in* his pictures mock fashionable excess. In *Taste à la Mode* the paintings on the walls underline the message of the foreground, being mostly devoted to caps, hoops, solitaires, wigs, muffs and high-heeled shoes and the other emblems of eighteenth-century fashion. Both the contents and the narrative message are the same: in one painting while a cupid makes a fire of discarded fashions, the Venus de Medici is made to submit to a voluminous hoop and high-heeled shoes! Even the firescreen shows the absurdity of trying to fit current feminine fashions into a sedan chair. Hogarth even published engravings in the form of advertisements mocking the scholarship of the fashionable 'taste makers' with their rigid rules and orders as in his *Five Orders of Periwigs* of 1761, which not only mocked the headdresses worn at the coronation but satirized the exclusive and expensive imprint which men like 'Athenian' Stewart tried to impose on current taste.

Rarely, if ever, has the fashionable imitation of so much of the rest of society been so frequently mocked, so accurately recorded and so pointedly revealed in so many different art forms. Cartoons are always quick to mock contemporary habits and it comes as no surprise to find, along with those satirizing the excesses of the rich, cartoons which mock those who so assiduously aped their social superiors. Sometimes they managed to do both at the same time. Gillray's cartoon of a nursing mother of 1796, not only sends up his major target—the nursing mother dressed in the height of *Directoire* fashion with two huge ostrich plumes two feet high, long drop earrings and slits in her elegant gown through which an eager baby grasps a breast and suckles; but he also more subtly depicts the flower buckle, the shapely slipper and the elegantly puffed-up mob cap of the maid who holds the baby to the breast. This insight is an incidental one, for the maid's dress is essentially homely in deliberate contrast to the exaggerated finery and extreme fashionability of her mistress, but verisimilitude made Gillray include, nonetheless, the odd give-away fashionable details in *her* dress too.[91]

More pointed and more deliberate was the engraving by Woodward of 1800 which shows a cook-maid dressed in a high mob cap with green ribbon, yellow neckerchief, and white dress with pink stripes in direct and obvious imitation of her mistress's clothes with whom she stands, the one almost a mirror image of the other. There are small differences in detail but the essentials are remarkably similar. It makes it easy to understand the common eighteenth-century failure to distinguish mistress from maid.[92]

Little wonder that foreign visitors were so startled by this lack of social distinctions. Typical of many was J. W. von Archenholz who recorded his amazement in 1787, writing 'The appearance of the female domestics will perhaps astonish a foreign visitor more than anything in London'. It was not

---

[91] James Gillray engraving of 1796. Reproduced in *The Costume of Birth and Death* by C. W. and P. Cunnington (1972).
[92] British Museum George Catalogue, No. 9646.

simply that they were 'well!' and 'tastefully' clothed, and that they were 'clad in gowns well adjusted to their shapes' and in 'hats adorned with ribbons', but that they 'even wear silk and satin' dresses.[93]

Even more revealing are the engravings seeking to make no social point and free, therefore, of exaggeration. Straight descriptive prints attempting accurately to portray the different stations and positions of contemporary life record, even more precisely, how far highly fashionable costume could reach down the social scale. To take the cook-maid example again, there is a 1772 engraving by Caldwell, after a painting by Brandoin, of a cook-maid selecting her day's supply of vegetables. She wears a stunningly fashionable black hat over a white coif, an apron over a fashionable polonaise dress (i.e. with an overskirt bunched up behind), ankle-length under-skirt, and dainty high-heeled shoes. Her blouse is prettily gathered and ruched in the sleeves. Around her neck she wears a velvet ribbon. She is a picture of fashionable elegance as she fingers her leeks, and looks over her cabbages and carrots. Significantly the social limits of fashion are indicated in the engraving by the man selling the vegetables—for although he is sturdily dressed with well buttoned coat cuffs, wide-brimmed hat and leather boots, there are no hints of high fashion about him; no hint of finery either. He is dressed in shabby adequacy.

Domestic servants will be suspect evidence to some since they might be taken more as an advertisement of their employer's property than their own. Those richly-dressed negro page boys in Hogarth's *Harlot's Progress* with their fancy turbans, fine feathers, silver collars and elaborate shoulder knots are obviously not evidence of negro prosperity in the mid eighteenth century. They are evidence (in a very pure form) of what Veblen labelled 'vicarious consumption'—consumption by the poor on behalf of the rich.[94] Servants are suspect as evidence, too, because they were notoriously the recipient of their employer's cast-offs. Such suspicions are understandable when one sees the 1772 engraving of 'High Life below Stairs', showing the footman in a very stylish frock coat with a 'solitaire' of black ribbon round his neck; the housemaid in a day cap known as a 'dormeuse' which was all the rage in the 1770s and also wearing a 'solitaire' of black velvet; the cook in her beribboned mob cap; the lady's maid most spectacular of all in a protective shoulder negligée, dainty high-heeled shoes, with a fan and a bergere hat with elaborately ruffled ribbons lying casually at her feet; the valet smartly dressed and complete with wig; and the humbly dressed laundry woman in a jacket bodice and modest mob cap.[95] But nevertheless the frequency of

---

[93] J. W. von Archenholz, *A Picture of England* (1787) translated in 1791. Quoted in the chapter on 'Lower ranks of women servants' in Phyllis Cunnington, *Costume of Household Servants* (1974), p. 135. Von Archenholz also complained that he could not 'distinguish between guests and servants' when he visited the Duke of Newcastle, and was particularly thrown by the fact that the butler dressed like his master.

[94] Thorstein Veblen, *The Theory of the Leisure Class* (New York 1926). p. 78.

[95] George Paston, *Social Caricatures of the Eighteenth Century* (1905), Plate 1.

comment at the time and the insistence that the extravagance is novel eventually carries conviction: 'Now so fantastical is the age grown that it is common to see a puppy at an Assembly, perhaps who gets £50 or £60 a year, dress'd in his bag [i.e. his wig] and *sword* and the next morning you'll see him sweeping his master's doorway and taking down the shutters'.[96]

That conviction is strengthened by the evidence of similar sartorial finery in other members of what contemporaries called 'the lower ranks'. For the pictorial evidence suggests that it was not just the increased money wages of domestic servants, with their access to passed down finery from their mistresses, which allowed fashionable costume to filter down the social hierarchy. The print of the 'POT FAIR, CAMBRIDGE' published 25 June 1777, shows (against the backdrop of King's Chapel and a sprinkling of dons) the common pot sellers and their customers and the pottery they are selling. The pottery alone is a revealing comment on the many and the modest outlets through which even fashionable pottery reached the mass consumer market, for the pottery being sold on the open stalls is in the latest neo-classical style of Wedgwood's creamware with elegant sauce boats and handsome soup tureens mixed in with the cache pots, chamber pots and everyday tea ware; but the clothes on view are just as fashionable: elaborate mob caps are worn by seller and customer alike, as are the decorative ribbons, the high heeled shoes, the buckles, and bows. There is no suggestion here that the *classes* are indistinguishable—the female potseller has the musculature of a Neanderthal wrestler and the facial expression of a ferocious fish wife; the buyer is refined in both feature and bearing. But the refinement is facial, the distinction one of bearing, for the clothes of the two classes are virtually identical in style, materials and fashionability.[97]

There can be no doubt, however, that servant girls were an important channel for spreading the new fashions. They provided a direct link between the upper and lower classes. They saw new fashions at first hand being worn by their employers, they brought word to the provinces of what was being worn in London; they quickly copied what their mistresses wore ('she had not liv'd with me three weeks before she sew'd three penny canes round the bottom of her shift instead of a hoop-petticoat')[98] even when they did not inherit it from her second-hand. Early in the century Defoe complained that when 'requir'd ... to salute the Ladies, I kis'd the chamber jade into the bargain for she was as well dress'd as the rest.'[99] She wore according to him

---

[96] The Diary of John Crozier (unpublished). The Holly Trees Museum, Colchester. Quoted Phillis Cunnington, op. cit., p. 65. See also D. E. C. Eversley, op. cit., pp. 226-7 for the significance of the effective demand generated by domestic servants.
[97] 'The Pot Fair, Cambridge'. Published 25 June 1777 by Mr. Bunbury and J. Bretherton. Another curious point, among the objects in the foreground is a wig-stand complete with wig: an unexpected object to be sold in the open air at a pot fair.
[98] Mrs. Centlivre, *The Artifice* (1722).
[99] Defoe, *Everybody's Business is Nobody's Business* (1725).

high heels, silk stockings, silk skirt 'four or five yards wide' and of course, 'she must have her Hoop too' to turn 'plain Country Joan into a fine London Madam'. Others agreed with him, writing

> Our servant wenches are so puffed up with pride nowadays that they never think they go fine enough. It is a hard matter to know the mistress from the maid by their dress; nay very often, the maid shall be much the finer of the two . . . it seems as if the whole business of the Female Sex were nothing but excess of Pride and extravagance in Dress.[100]

The same comments continued through the rest of the eighteenth century growing more frequent, more generalized and testifying to an even quicker turn round in the fashions worn. Increasingly servant girls are cited as symbolic illustrations of society's *general* addiction to fashion rather than as deplorable exceptions to their class and station. In 1782 C. P. Moritz marvelled that 'Fashion is *so generally attended among Englishwomen* that the poorest servant is careful to be in the fashion, particularly in their hats and bonnets which they all wear'.[101]

The expansion of the market, revealed in the literary evidence, occurred first among the domestic-servant class, then among the industrial workers, and finally among the agricultural workers. The servants were the most readily observed group seen by the articulate middle and upper class observers who dominate our records, but from the 1750s and 1760s onwards

> the accounts of increasing luxury among the labourers—both urban and rural—were becoming much more frequent. These continued through the next thirty years and by the end of the century what had previously been looked on as a luxury for the worker was thought of in terms of being a decency or even a necessity.[102]

Contemporaries complained that more and more classes and more and more occupations were being sucked into the pursuit of fashion. Even the watermen of London were described as wearing silk stockings. Even the women labouring in the fields were described as succumbing to fashionable hats and other accessories. So surprising were some of the fashions that one contemporary complained 'After-ages, who perhaps may see this contrivance only in the painting of some great masters, shall with pain believe what the justness of the pencil presents.'[103] This has certainly been the case with six of the finest paintings of late eighteenth-century England—the superb series of agricultural labourers by George Stubbs on the theme of haymaking and harvesting, called simply *The Reapers* and *Haymakers* first painted in 1783.

These paintings have greatly puzzled art historians who have both seen them as treating 'the everyday activities of the ordinary working men with

---

[100] *A Trip through the Town* (1735). Reprint of 18th century Tracts, ed. by Ralph Strauss.
[101] *Travels of C. P. Moritz in England.*
[102] Richard Kent, 'Home Demand as a Factor in 18th Century English Economic Growth' (unpublished M. Litt. Thesis, Cambridge 1969).
[103] *Whitehall Evening Post,* 1744.

a dispassionate objectivity which is unique in English Art',[104] and also as the 'most artificial images of the rural labourer that the century produced'.[105] What particularly troubles many critics is that the women seem to be 'dressed well above their station'. So grand is their dress, so fashionable their hats that to deny that they are idealized seems 'incomprehensible'[106] to some. A simple solution to the problem is to argue that the painting 'far from being ... masterpieces of realism, are pictures of fancy ... the equivalent of the pastoralism of Marie Antoinette'.[107]

Rather than accept the evidence that the fashionable picture hats of the female farmworkers might be accurately portrayed, rather than accept the fact that their long skirts, their aprons and neckerchiefs, their frilled sleeves, even the rakish angle at which their hats are worn, fits so snugly with so many other contemporary sources both pictorial and literary, a great master of realism has to become a fantasist. It is a marvellous irony that Stubbs, who laboured so long to master exactly the musculature of the horse, should be so misdescribed. It shows how reluctant historians can be to recognize the significance of so much evidence, that they prefer so to misrepresent Stubbs' genius rather than accept it. Such was his undeviating pursuit of clinical accuracy that Stubbs started his experiences at the age of twenty-two on the corpse of a pregnant woman provided by graverobbers and finished by embarking at the age of eighty on a study of comparative anatomy which would have taken at least thirty years to complete.[108] Such was his devotion to realism that his pictures could be dated from their depiction of female fashion alone. Whether painting the hats of grooms or jockeys or hunters or servants or ladies of fashion, he is always precise and accurate. In fact he painted *three* pairs of pictures on the haymaking and reaping themes, the first pair in 1783, the second pair in 1784 and 1785, the third pair on Wedgwood creamware plaques in 1794 and 1795. Far from being idealized objects of social fantasy they are exact representations of the fashions of the years in which they were painted. The hats in the *Haymakers* of 1783 are strikingly different from those in the *Haymakers* of 1785, and even more strikingly different from that worn by the central figure in the *Haymakers* of 1795—and all are exactly in line with the prevailing hat fashions of those years: the sharp forward tilt of 1783,[109] the immensely high soft crown worn over the mob cap of 1785,[110] the enormous picture hat swept up at one side

---

[104] Tate Gallery Press Release of 25 July 1977.
[105] John Barrell, *The dark side of the landscape: The rural poor in English painting 1730–1840*, (1980), p. 25.
[106] Barrell, op. cit., p. 25.
[107] Denys Sutton, *Financial Times*, 6 September 1977. Quoted Barrell, op. cit., p. 27.
[108] See Neil McKendrick, 'Josiah Wedgwood and George Stubbs', *History Today*, (1957), pp. 504-14; and Basil Taylor, *Stubbs* (1971).
[109] 'Hats of the 1780s ... a sharp tilt down over the forehead and up behind until 1783, less so until 1785, then unfashionable'. C. W. and P. Cunnington, *Handbook of English Costume in the Eighteenth Century* (1957), p. 357. See the left hand figure in the 1783 Stubbs.
[110] See Hilda Amphlett, *Hats: A History of Fashion in Headwear* (1974), pp. 119-20, fig. 376.

which was made ultra-fashionable by Gainsborough's portrait of the Duchess of Devonshire and which, in simpler forms, spread in popularity through the later eighties and early 1790s.[111] In *The Reapers,* too, the hat on the central figure changes as fashion dictated that it should between the 1783 version and the 1784 version. As a fantasist Stubbs would seem to have limitations. As a precise observer of the social scene he scores very high marks for accuracy. Many foreign visitors had commented that in Britain knee breeches and perukes, bonnets and panniered dresses could be seen on the very labourers in the fields.[112] Historians can be forgiven for overlooking obscure contemporaries, but it seems ungrateful to reject the evidence which Stubbs so famously and so superbly immortalized for them.

This is not, of course, to suggest that all agricultural labourers dressed in the height of fashion. Patently they did not. Most were still poor—many wretchedly so. Many of the poorer sort must have dressed like Rowlandson's *Hedger and Ditcher.* But one must remember that at harvest time many extra female workers joined the men. Women who earned their major income elsewhere were drafted in to join in the seasonal work and it would be entirely consistent with contemporary comment if they appeared in the clothes they had grown accustomed to as domestic servants or textile workers. The male workers in Stubbs' paintings who were far more likely to work in the fields the whole year present no such problems. Their pattern of dress is essentially that of the reaper in Blake's watercolour to Gray's 'Elegy', but it should be noted that the woman bringing *his* refreshment is also dressed in the latest fashion with picture hat and neo-classical silhouette.[113]

Stubbs was reflecting the popular fashion of these limited parts of the working class who were enjoying the benefits of rapid economic progress. He was not alone. Other pictorial sources of fashion intelligence of the same period tell the same story. Take the popular Staffordshire pottery plaques by Ralph Wood. These are earthy, rumbustious rollicking pieces, full of a coarse sense of humour, quite unlike the frieze-like precision of the Stubbs pictures. A typical example entitled *Patricia and her Lover* or *Jack on a Cruise*[114] shows a young sailor in pursuit of a young woman dressed in the height of fashion. Jack's pop-eyes are firmly fixed on Patricia's fashionably padded buttocks, over which her blue dress is drawn up over her green underskirt in the prevailing short Polonaise style which revealed the ankle, emphasized the rump, and allowed the neckline to be worn encouragingly low. Jack seems oblivious to her ochre parasol, her velvet neckband, her

---

[111] No fashion was uniform or universal. Stubbs re-used one hat in almost exactly the same form between 1785 and 1795.

[112] P. Kalm, *'An Account of his Visit to England . . . in 1748'* (translated J. Lucas, 1892), p. 52.

[113] Illustrated in John Barrell, op. cit., pp. 28–9. It is no. 109 of William Blake's watercolour illustrations to the *Works of Thomas Gray* (Chicago 1972), ed. Sir Geoffrey Keynes.

[114] Recently sold at Sotheby's for £2,600 (cracked). See illustrations in *Country Life,* 20 November 1980, p. 1887.

spectacular hat piled high with ribbons, bows and padded flaps, but as a burlesque on extravagant popular fashions Patricia is a splendid example of the current vogue. Jack, too, in his plumed hat, his ochre waistcoat, his striped trousers, his wig, his casually knotted cravat and his short sword, is hardly an advertisement for sartorial restraint.

There are many such tributes to fashionable excess in the cartoons and prints of late eighteenth-century England. They offer further evidence in support of the potent power of fashion and the effectiveness with which it was promoted and spread by the many agents of the process of commercialization. For potent as the force of fashion was, it needed to be released and mobilized and exploited before it could significantly add to aggregate demand. The conditions making this possible grew steadily more favourable. Rising real incomes gave many families more to spend on consumables. Rising population constantly expanded the market. Rising production meant that the industrialists had more to sell. Improving transport meant that entrepreneurs could reach a wider range of buyers. But it still required active and aggressive selling to reach that market and exploit its full potential.

There were many minor satellites circulating round the great industrial centres and helping to keep up and extend the demand for their products. What contemporaries called 'miniature manias' were induced and exploited with consummate skill by the hordes of fashion makers operating in the sale of hats and gloves, hairstyles and wigs, shoes and stockings. Annual fashion was insufficient to satisfy some markets. Every passing whim and every notable event (from a victory in battle to a royal wedding, from the triumph of vaccine to the Montgolfier brothers' balloon exploits) were gleefully pounced upon and incorporated into the ephemeral designs of high fashion. As a result the tempo of fashion reached such a pitch that in 1772 the *London Magazine* announced that 'there are at present three or four hundred methods of dressing the hair of a man in fashion',[115] and some professional hairdressers claimed to be master of two hundred of them. Where for so much of human history a hairstyle would be 'good for centuries',[116] suddenly it could be out of fashion within months. The ultra fashionable went to prodigious lengths to keep ahead of the pack in the 1770s and 1780s. Live flowers—with concealed bottles of water to keep them fresh—large butterflies, baskets of fruit, caterpillars in blown glass, even models of coaches and horses sprouted from, or galloped across, or merely inhabited the mountainous hairstyles then in vogue. In 1778 even vegetables were in fashion as hair accessories. As one historian has written, when one reads the trade descriptions one begins to doubt whether the cartoons of the reign of George III were caricatures at all.[117] Hannah More wrote in 1777 of the hairstyles of eleven young women who had just visited her, 'I protest I can hardly do them

[115] *London Magazine,* July 1772.
[116] Richard Corson, *Fashions in Hair* (1965), p. 19.
[117] Corson, Chapter 10, pp. 327-98.

justice when I pronounce that they had amongst them, on their heads, an acre and a half of shrubbery, besides slopes, garden plots, tulip beds, clumps of peonies, kitchen gardens, and greenhouses'.[118]

To judge from what one fashionable London hairdresser offered, even *they* had not exhausted the possibilities available to them. Ivan Peter Alexis Knoutschoffschlerwitz offered to 'change their locks into a fine chestnut, blue, crimson or green according to the mode which might prevail'. He claimed to 'dress hair in every mode, and engages to make any lady's head appear like the head of a lion, a wolf, a tiger, a bear, a fox or any exotic beast which she should choose to resemble. He does not, however, confine himself to beasts, for anyone who happened to prefer the form of a peacock, a swan, a goose, a Friesland hen, or any other bird, he engaged to give a perfect likeness'.[119]

This was the fantasy land of the rich and the ultra fashionable. Its significance for other members of society is that they were now being publicly appealed to by professional hairdressers who publicly advertised their success with the nobility and gentry and the fashionable few. The extreme fashions are, of course, symptomatic of the lengths to which the rich were prepared to go to proclaim their wealth, their rank, their 'insignia of leisure', but to those advertising them their significance lay elsewhere. They used these extreme fashions, and the exclusive clientele who adopted them, as promotional publicity to attract the custom of the less extreme, the more timid who wanted to be in fashion but needed a 'lead' even to try a watered-down version of the current vogue. Like Mary Quant's famous recommendation of heart-shaped pubic hair in the 1960s, the value of these 'exotics' lay in their publicity not in the numbers adopting the fashion. Most never seriously caught on, others never strayed beyond the tiny, exclusive nucleus of the most fashion-conscious of the London rich. But many others were widely enough adopted to give further openings for the inventive and adroit entrepreneurs in the fashion world. When the elaborate styles of the 1770s were at their peak and the mountainous structures required pads, wire and false hair mingled with lard and whiting, they could not be taken down every night (some sources quote some surviving for a month or more 'unopened'). The *Salisbury Journal* of 1777 not only tells of 'the many melancholy accidents which have lately happened as a consequence of mice getting into ladies hair at night time' but advertises the proposed solution: a New Bond Street silversmith had promptly invented 'night caps made of silver wire so strong that no mouse or even a rat can gnaw through them'. With self-congratulation typical of eighteenth-century advertisements it was claimed that 'the present demand for these articles is incredible. Sold at 3 guineas each, but the ton have them of gilt wire from 6 to 10 guineas'.[120]

[118] Corson, p. 348.   [119] Corson, p. 352.
[120] *Salisbury Journal*, 1777, quoted in C. W. and P. Cunnington, *Handbook of English Costume in the Eighteenth Century* (1957), p. 28.

Even the three-guinea market must have been tiny, but the commercial response of those involved in selling fashion did not like to neglect even the most restricted opening—especially when it gave them the opportunity to advertise all their more mundane goods at the same time. Such articles were analogous with Wedgwood's 'uniques': not necessarily very profitable in themselves, not capable of ever becoming a worthwhile line of production, but worth it for their advertising value. There was always the possibility that a 'sleeper' would catch on, like a scholarly book published for prestige purpose which suddenly takes off. Some seemingly small openings were to yield surprisingly rich pickings. Take the victory of the handbag over women's pockets. The pocket was a traditional part of feminine costume, worn under the skirt. So traditional that some thieves specialized in picking them—and taking a justifiable pride in their manual dexterity: 'My chief dexterity was in robbing the ladies. There is a peculiar delicacy required in whipping one's hand up a lady's petticoats and carrying off her pockets'.[121] But in the 1760s handbags were introduced as an extra receptacle to carry fans, purses and the ever-increasing tide of fashionable knick-knacks. By 1799 we read in *The Times* of 'the total abjuration of the female pocket', and the popularity of the handbag can be judged not only from the fashion prints of 1799, but also from the fact that they were now called 'Indispensables'. A whole new fashion industry had been successfully launched.

Dozens of such tiny fashion decisions kept the market alive and its demand buoyant. Each one could have repercussions elsewhere. When the fashionable advertisements announced the 'in colour' for stockings each year, the news sent tiny ripples through all the fashion-based industries—from the dye industry and the textile industries to all those making, co-ordinating and selling fashion accessories. Their trade cards still survive as evidence of the hundreds and hundreds of shops in central London alone dedicated to just such activities. The industrialist who told his spinners to devise methods of spinning ever-finer thread did so because he needed to satisfy the demand of this market and the needs of the mass market which trailed imitatively in its wake.[122]

As Braudel says, those who see the history of fashion as mere antiquarianism, or fail to read the significance of fashion changes can miss 'evidence in depth concerning the energies, possibilities and demands of . . . a given society, economy and civilization'.[123] The history of fashion is more than a history of anecdote. Its fluctuations can be as significant as those in production, supply and price. A sharp break in trend can be of even greater importance. For as long as the pursuit of luxury was limited to the few, it was more like an engine 'running in neutral than an element of growth'.[124] Once this

[121] Francis Coventry, *Pompey the Little* (1751). Quoted in Cunnington, op. cit., p. 399.
[122] See Charles Wilson, 'The Entrepreneur in the Industrial Revolution in Britain', *Explorations in Entrepreneurial History*, vii, 3 (1955).
[123] F. Braudel, *Capitalism and Material Life 1400–1800* (1973), p. 235.
[124] Braudel, op. cit., p. 124.

pursuit was made possible for an ever-widening proportion of the population, then its potential was released, and it became an engine for growth, a motive power for mass production. Explaining the release of that power, in terms of the release of a latent desire for new consumption patterns, goes a long way towards explaining the coming of the Industrial Revolution and the birth of a consumer society.

* * *

This process was not limited to clothes, and there is ample evidence of the increasing commercial importance of fashion outside the world of eighteenth-century dress. Some of these areas may seem surprising at first sight. But one can show that even flowers had to submit to the tyranny of fashion. Nature itself had to conform to the lust for novelty.

'How Whimsical is the Florist in his Choice! Sometimes the Tulip, sometimes the Auricula, and at other times the Carnation shall engross his Esteems, and every Year a new Flower in his Judgement beats all the old ones, tho' it is much inferior to them both in Colour and Shape.'[125] The seedsmen, nurserymen and bulb growers (with their printed, illustrated, fixed-price catalogues, their free offers, their immense range of stock, all well advertised) successfully adapted the commercial techniques of other salesmen to the needs of flowers and bulbs and fruits. Such was the potent force of fashion that it was even mobilized here. Imported exotics were quickly fed to the market and used to keep up consumer interest. The introduction of both the camellia and the fuchsia was later stage-managed as artfully as Boulton's ormolu or Wedgwood's jasper. Both were at first expensive (the fuchsia deliberately made so to make it more desirable), for both aimed to gain the esteem of being exclusive, but were later successfully popularized through auctions, lotteries and promotional campaigns. For the humbler end of the market the pansy, the pink and the auricula served a similar purpose. But the successful promotion of popular gardening is treated elsewhere.[126] There are, in any case, much more important industries with which to illustrate the commercialization of fashion. Even the metal industries could be revolutionized by fashion in the eighteenth century. As William Hutton, the historian of contemporary Birmingham, wrote in 1781 'the fashion of today is thrown into the casting pot tomorrow'.[127] And by 1801

---

[125] Bernard Mandeville, 'A Search into the Nature of Society' added to *The Fable of the Bees: or, Private Vices, Publick Benefits* in the 1723 edition. See the Penguin edition for 1970, ed. Philip Harth, p. 332. Not only the flowers but the gardens which contained them were subject to fashionable upheaval. ['The many ways of laying out a Garden Judiciously are almost Innumerable, and what is call'd Beautiful in them varies according to the different Taste', ibid., p. 333] but here the labour involved meant that the rate of change was slower. The publications of John Harvey have made accessible the detailed evidence with which to demonstrate the remarkable size and spread of English nurseries. Their catalogues are testimony to their range of product and their ability to sell.

[126] See J. H. Plumb, below, p. 323; and John Harvey. *Early Gardening Catalogues* (1972), and *Early Nurserymen* (1974).

[127] William Hutton, *History of Birmingham* (1781).

COMMERCIALIZATION OF FASHION

Birmingham was regarded as being dependent on 'the moods of fashion'.[128] Other historians of Birmingham were equally clear that the commercial exploitation of fashion was essentially the product of the mid-eighteenth century. Samuel Timmins wrote that 'the position of the brass trade between 1689 and 1760 was that of *making only*'. They had not yet started positively to sell. 'The manufacturers remained at home and let the orders come to them. . . . The era of travellers and blue bags had not then arrived. Oak brass-bound boxes, filled with pattern cards on which are displayed samples of the articles made by the houses represented had not then been called into existence; and of pattern books, folio in size, with representations of the articles there were none.'[129] Timmins exaggerated slightly the novelty of aggressive selling, and certainly drew too sharp a line at 1760,[130] but his verdict is right in spirit, if not in detail, and contemporaries drew attention to the same dramatic change in commercial attitudes. Admittedly in 1744 (when carriers with instructions to collect their orders from Birmingham received directions no more specific than 'in Warwickshire. N. B. Turn at Coleshill'[131]) Birmingham was still 'protected' by ruinous roads, but its industrial expansion was also restricted by its lack of any adequate commercial organization. As Hutton wrote in 1780 'The practice of the Birmingham manufacturer for perhaps *a hundred generations* was to *keep within the warmth of his own forge*'.[132] This did not prevent him selling his products, did not prevent even foreign customers buying from him by dint of twice yearly applications. But by 1780 this age-old mode of business, although 'not totally extinguished', had given way to 'a very different one'. The energetic commercial extrovert had taken over from the forge-bound manufacturing introvert; or, as Hutton put it: '*The merchant stands at the head of the manufacturer*, purchases his produce, and *travels the whole island to promote the sale*; a practice which would have *astounded our forefathers*'.[133]

They sought to satisfy not just home demand, but foreign demand as well. 'The commercial spirit of the age has penetrated beyond the confines of Britain, and explored the whole Continent of Europe; nor does it stop there, for the West Indies and the American world are infinitely acquainted with the Birmingham Merchant.'[133] Timmins confirmed that Germany, Holland, France, Portugal and America were 'all in favour of Brummagen buttons'.[134] By 1770 there were 'Eighty Three Button Makers . . . (producing) . . . an Infinite Variety', plus Forty-Three Buckle Makers, Seven Candlestick

[128] Eric Svedenstierna, *Svedenstierna's Tour, 1802-3* (1973), p. 79.
[129] Samuel Timmins (ed.), *The Resources, Products and Industrial History of Birmingham and Midland Hardware District* (1865).
[130] John Taylor was extremely active in the 1750s.
[131] *Birmingham Gazette*, 6 February and 28 May 1744. Quoted in Rupert Gentle and Rachel Feild, *English Domestic Brass 1680-1810* (1975), p. 52.
[132] W. Hutton, *History of Birmingham*, quoted Gentle and Feild, p. 52. My italics.
[133] Ibid. My italics.
[134] Timmins, op. cit.,

67

Makers, Ten Braziers, Three Brass Founders.[135] Other centres of the brass industry in Bristol, Bridgwater, Chester and St. Albans produced objects of equal quality, but Birmingham eclipsed them all. It was hailed as 'the toyshop of Europe'.[136]

Many things had contributed to its success. The new canal opened in 1769; the technical advances, between 1769 and 1779, of John Pickering, Richard Ford, John Smith, Marston and Bellamy, and William Bell, opened the way for massively improved productions, but the wares still needed selling. To speak of the pattern cards and pattern books which tempted Dutch, Italian and French buyers in their own languages, and, of course tempted British and American buyers in theirs, is to take note of the spread of the market; to note that there was a special range of brass made exclusively for Holland, and pages in the pattern books devoted to fittings to suit the particular needs of the American market, indicates that different national tastes were accommodated (the ornate Rococo designs still produced for Dutch cabinet makers were wholly unsuited to the prevailing English aesthetic, dominated after 1770 by the pure, simple lines of the neo-classic); to recognize that most English brass was unmarked so that it could enter, anonymously and therefore more easily, hostile markets at war with England, underlines the commercial desire to export widely; to quote Hutton on John Taylor reminds one that sales to the nobility could be combined with the mass sales which allowed Taylor to amass a fortune of £200,000: 'To this uncommon genius we owe the gilt button.... In his shop were weekly manufactured buttons to the amount of £800 exclusive of other valuable products. One of the present nobility, of distinguished taste, examining the work with the master, purchased some of the articles, amongst others a toy of 80 guineas value, and while paying for them observed with a smile "he plainly could not affort to reside in Birmingham for less than £200 a day".'[137]

To quote the contemporary complaints that 'tradesmen were aping their betters with myriads of gold buttons and loops, high gaiters, shoes and overgrown hats' reminds one that the products of brass were as much part of the market for fashion goods which was spreading down the social scale as were new fashions in clothes. That fashion was attended to is also made clear by the pattern books, for although they were usually undated, their watermarks show that brass could quickly respond to changes in styles even if those aimed at provincial or overseas markets often carried styles which would long have lost their selling power in London.[138]

All this is evidence of a new willingness assiduously to attend to fashion, accurately to inform the customer, actively to extend one's sales. It is also

---

[135] *Tradesman's True Guide, an Universal Dictionary for the towns of Birmingham, Walsall* etc. (1770).
[136] See Gentle and Feild, op. cit., p. 45.
[137] Hutton, op. cit., Earlier, in 1773, Fothergill had reported that Taylor got 'a neat profit of £40 p. week' on buttons. J. Fothergill to Matthew Boulton, 7 April 1773.
[138] Gentle and Feild, op. cit., pp. 60-3.

evidence that the new commercial attitudes were succeeding. But it does little justice to the *quality* of the new commercial approach which deliberately and consciously aimed at controlling the market, sustaining consumer interest, and creating new demand.

Yet the evidence of this qualitative change is as rich and as accessible for the Birmingham brass trade, and the Birmingham toy trade in general, as it is for women's fashions or Staffordshire pottery. For the Birmingham toy trade boasted the first great 'Brass Baron'—Matthew Boulton—and his archive is a marvellously well stocked source from which to study the commercialization of fashion. It rivals Wedgwood's records of the commercial achievements of Etruria.

And yet just as in the traditional historiography, Wedgwood has been presented first as an artist, second as an industrialist (a master of division of labour and new methods of production), and finally as a man who having laboured to produce work of outstanding beauty and unquestioned quality was largely unconcerned with its methods of sale, so Boulton has been presented first and foremost as the manufacturer of steam engines, the great master of power, and hardly at all as the manipulator of fashion, the 'huckster extraordinary of the button trade'.[139]

Yet to ignore Wedgwood and Boulton's contribution to selling and to the commercialization of fashion is about as fair a reflection of what preoccupied their minds for much of their lives as it would be to ignore the concern with theology of John Donne and Isaac Newton. Such distortions produce biographical absurdities, and when the biographies are cited to illustrate the characteristic preoccupations of their day it produces an even greater historical absurdity. No one would wish to ignore Newton's science or Donne's poetry, and no one *could* understand Boulton and Wedgwood's marketing campaigns without understanding Boulton's contribution to steam power or Wedgwood's to ceramic invention and production, but to ignore the other concerns which dominated most of their lives—how to sell and how to extend the sales of their products—is to erect just as serious a barrier to our historical understanding of them and their achievements. Most historians have, alas, been content to leave that barrier in place.

Posterity's opinion of Matthew Boulton is typical of the way in which the production side of the industrial revolution has won out in the traditional economic orthodoxies at the expense of the consumer and commercial revolution. Matthew Boulton is largely remembered for his role in the production of steam engines—*the* characteristic invention of the industrial revolution. He is largely forgotten for his role in the Birmingham toy trade—arguably *the* characteristic consumer industry of the commercial revolution. And although in this case posterity's verdict is understandable and indeed justifiable in the sense that, in the long run, the importance of

---

[139] There are honourable exceptions to the traditional orthodoxies. See below, pp. 70–7 and 100–45.

steam far outweighed the significance of toys, it has by largely forgetting the latter seriously distorted the historical record and unfairly diminished the role of the consumer revolution in the early industrial revolution. For Boulton was a major figure in the process of commercialization, a major example of how consumer demand was manipulated and satisfied with a range of commercial devices either unknown to previous centuries, or unused on anything like the same scale. As a salesman Boulton, the toymaker and toy seller, can stand comparison with Wedgwood, 'vase maker general to the universe', and potseller extraordinary.

It is usually forgotten that to Boulton the choice between his two callings was not an easy one. As late as September 1778 he was still not certain 'how far it may be prudent in me to stick to Engines or Buttons for I can consider Buttons as a Sheet Anchor'.[140] Contemporaries like Mrs. Montague found it equally difficult to decide which was the more important side of this 'doubly endowed ... Genius' who combined 'a happy turn for things of use' *and* 'for matters of ornament'. As she wrote to him in 1778 'I shall owe to you the richest and most beautiful part of my Furniture, and by a Fire Engine of your improved construction shall in time save money equivalent to the expence of these articles of elegant luxury'.[141]

Posterity has no such doubts, but by neglecting Boulton the manufacturer of fashion goods, most historians have deprived themselves of important insights into the nature and importance of contemporary economic change, and ignored a revealing case study into the role of fashion in the commercial life of one of the eighteenth-century economy's great figures.

Boulton, like his major rivals in Birmingham John Taylor, John Gimblett and the firm of Ingram and Duncomb, was operating in a highly competitive mass production industry which was the basis of Birmingham's spectacular growth and prosperity. It is not often realized how much of the new consumer market was satisfied by the products of Birmingham 'small arms'. The Birmingham 'toy' trade belittles itself by its very name. For although as Robinson says 'the foundation of Boulton's greatness was the button trade',[142] the range of his products, and those of his rivals, was immense. His pattern books contain some 1,470 designs of cut steel buttons, buckles, chatelaines, watch-guards, sword hilts and suchlike,[143] but to appreciate more fully the

---

[140] Matthew Boulton to J. Scale, 18 September 1778. Quoted in E. Robinson, 'Eighteenth Century Commerce and Fashion: Matthew Boulton's Marketing Techniques', *Economic History Review*, 2nd series, XVI, no. 1, 1963, p. 39. Robinson's articles confirmed many of the findings of how major eighteenth-century entrepreneurs manipulated fashion to market their goods which I had described in my article on Wedgwood's marketing campaign, published in the *Economic History Review* in 1960. My debt to Robinson's article in the pages that follow on Boulton will be obvious, and I gratefully acknowledge it.

[141] Mrs. E. Montague to Matthew Boulton, 1 October 1778. This, and the references which follow, are mainly culled from E. Robinson, op. cit., pp. 39-60.

[142] Robinson, op. cit., p. 42.

[143] W. A. Seaby and R. S. Hetherington, 'The Matthew Boulton Pattern Books', *Apollo*, 1950, pp. 48-50.

number of goods Boulton and Fothergill manufactured, one needs to quote from the firm's correspondence of 1772, which listed

> Men's and Women's Steel, pinchbeck, and Gilt Watch Chains—Steel pinchbeck Gilt and Teutenague, and Silver Buttons—platina, Sterling Gilt and plated Steel, Bath Metal and filligree plated Buttons on Box and on Box Moulds—gilt, Silver, plated Shagreen Tortoise plain and inlaid with Silver and Gold in 4 Colours, Snuff Boxes, Instrument Cases, toothpick Cases—gilt, glass and steel Trinkets, Silver filligree Boxes, Needle Books etc. etc.—All manner of plated Goods, as Tea Kitchens, Tankards, Cups, Coffee potts, Cream Jugs, Candlesticks—sauce boats, Terrines etc etc—Bronz'd Tea Kitchens and Tea Kettles as well plated as Tin'd inside, Saucepans, Cheese Toasters etc etc etc—Buckle Chapes of all Qualitys—platina, inlaid and Steel Links—Candlestick Vases with 2 to 6 Branches, Girandoles, Sugar Basons, Essence pots Clock Cases etc etc—and all manner of Chimney piece Ornaments, intirely gilt in Or Moulu, or of Radix Amethysti mounted in Or Moulu, such as we sell annually great quantities of to the Nobility and Trades men—plated Bottle stands Cruet frames Inkstands Teutenague Candlesticks—and a number of other Articles.[144]

The trade in these fashion goods was so highly competitive, that a London shopkeeper reported in 1762 that 'Taylor, Gimblett, Ward and Rabone had been with him like so many wolves for orders'. To keep ahead of the pack required careful manipulation of the market.

Boulton like the others realized that there were favourable conditions to exploit. The potentialities of home demand were great, but it required skilful manipulation to take full advantage of that *existing* demand, to release the potentiality of *latent* demand, and by creating new wants and provoking new needs, to create *new* demand which would not have become economically operational without the requisite entrepreneurial skills to conjure it into existence. As Boulton said to Mrs. Montagu 'Fashion has much to do in these things'.[145] Like Wedgwood, Boulton sought royal and aristocratic patronage to give a lead to the rest of society in the confident knowledge that social emulation would ensure emulative spending in the rest of society. Like Wedgwood, he knew that a product made fashionable at the apex of the social pyramid would rapidly spread through the closely packed layers of English society to the wider social base where the mass market he sought was to be found. This process brought an ever growing market to men like Boulton and Wedgwood, and their many imitators, who used the social effects of snobbery to their own commercial advantage.

Just as Wedgwood schemed to become 'Potter to Her Majesty', sought out what he called 'the Legislators of Taste' like 'Athenian' Stewart and Sir William Hamilton, courted ambassadorial introductions to foreign markets, and constantly attended to the needs of the fashionable social élite; so Boulton cultivated (in the pursuit of royal patronage) the King's architect, Sir William Chambers, the King's clockmaker, Thomas Wright, the King's physician,

---

[144] Quoted Robinson, op. cit., pp. 44–5.
[145] Matthew Boulton to Mrs. Montagu, 18 January 1772.

Dr. Lind, as well as the King's cutler, Nathaniel Jeffreys, and the Prince of Wales' shoemaker. The cutler's role was to push Boulton buttons, the shoemaker was to push Boulton buckles within the palace, and so on.[146] Like Wedgwood, Boulton, too, sent presents to Lady Hamilton, and assiduously cultivated the diplomatic service in order to have the advantage of their 'puffing' their wares in foreign courts, and setting the fashion by wearing their presents.

Any possible openings for special productions were eagerly anticipated. Royal birthdays, for instance, were carefully prepared for: 'In future we shall take care to have something new in the Button way against every Birth Day of our Sovereign and shall present to such of the Nobility as we can make so free with ... some Setts to garnish their Cloaths with on that Day'.[147] To extend the idea further, Lady Claremont was asked to persuade the men in her fashionable circle to wear new buttons on *Her* Majesty's Birthday, and so create another new opportunity for selling. The *Gentleman's Magazine* was giving special publicity to royal birthdays in the 1760s, just as *La Belle Assemblée* was publicizing seasonal sales and special gift days (like New Year's Day) in the first decade of the nineteenth century.[148] It was all part of the spread of the process of commercialization, the increasing attention to keeping consumer demand alive and buoyant.

Like many manufacturers in the eighteenth century Boulton used spectacular London sales to boost demand and to win the attention of the fashion leaders. The release of Boulton's newly acquired skill in the manufacture of ormolu (a technique which had cost him great difficulty, and even bribery, to acquire) paralleled very closely Wedgwood's release of his new inventions in pottery. When Boulton was ready for the world of fashion to see his new product he took elaborate care to ensure that it was appropriately publicized. Christie's were to conduct the sales in their auction rooms in Pall Mall, and Boulton told Christie 'I would have the Advertisement continued for a week together and in about 6 days after we will publish something else, and so soon as the day is fix'd for the Sale we will publish that: for tis necessary the Town should talk a little upon the Subject before the important week, and be brought into proper tune'. The advertisement was to be lavish, precisely timed, and to include all the familiar references to royal patronage of the manufacturers in order to milk the effects of social emulation and emulative spending. Boulton personally monitored the effects of his advertising campaign, and, not satisfied with the results, ordered the campaign to be stepped up. He ordered 'the advertisement to be inserted in some paper on every other day',[149] saying firmly that he would 'rather have it appear in too many papers than too few'.[150]

[146] E. Robinson, op. cit., p. 50.
[147] Boulton and Fothergill to John Perchard, 6 August 1771.
[148] See below, chapter 3.
[149] Robinson, op. cit., p. 51.
[150] Matthew Boulton to W. Matthews, 16 March 1771.

COMMERCIALIZATION OF FASHION

His trust in advertisement never faltered. He and Wedgwood kept an eagle eye on the other to prevent one stealing an advertising march. In 1770 Wedgwood complained of 'a most famous puff for Boulton' in the *St James's Chronicle* and told Bentley to get a 'spontaneous article in praise of Wedgwood' placed in the next issue.[151] Wedgwood later denied that he ever advertised without affixing his name,[152] but the puffs in contemporary newspapers tell a different story. As late as 1789 Boulton and Wedgwood were still competing and Boulton's correspondence reveals that his agents were not above bribery (in this as in other commercial activities) to keep ahead in this race. In 1789 he was informed by his London agent Richard Chippendall 'I have got Copys of the Advertisements out to 3 papers—the *World—Herald* and *Diary*—some of which will appear on Monday, Tuesday and Wednesday—but I much fear their meeting them in time without *a Bribe* on Account of so much Advertising about this Confounded procession. I am the more anxious too on account of Wedgwood having something of the same sort to appear on Monday next.'[153]

Advertisement alone was not enough to ensure the success of his sales. Boulton wrote separate specimen letters for dukes, duchesses and the gentry and sat up until the early hours of the morning dispatching them 'to the nobility'. Like a modern couturier Boulton and Fothergill insisted, as did Wedgwood and Bentley, that their major sales were initially to be socially exclusive. They issued tickets for 'the Nobility and gentry' and took special steps 'to keep the common folks out'.[154] Boulton insisted that his exhibitions should 'be continued for 2 or 3 weeks for inspection and sale to the Nobility and Gentry only, as care will be taken to expell that class who do not come to purchase but expressly to incommode those who do'.[155]

But the mistake must not be made, as by some historians it unfortunately has, of assuming that Boulton and Wedgwood, in confining their attention to the fashionable social élite, were also intent on confining their ultimate sales campaign to them alone.

Just as Wedgwood took elaborate steps to develop and adjust his pricing strategy so that the high prices 'necessary' to make his goods 'esteemed as ornaments in palaces' did not become a barrier to sales to a mass market,[156] so Boulton's exclusive approach was merely the necessary prelude to gaining the custom of a mass market. Boulton's price policy was different from Wedgwood's. Boulton's choice was 'to make great quantities with small profits',[157] but he was equally intent on using the patronage of the famous

---

[151] WMSS. E. 18325-25. Josiah Wedgwood to Thomas Bentley, 13 October 1770.
[152] Leith Hill Place MSS. Josiah Wedgwood to Thomas Bentley, 11 February 1771.
[153] R. Chippendall to Matthew Boulton, 19 April 1789.
[154] See below, pp. 118-20.
[155] Boulton and Fothergill to the Duchess of Portland, 6 November 1771.
[156] This is discussed in detail in 'Prices and Profit in the Industrial Revolution: A Study of Josiah Wedgwood's Pricing Policy', a paper which I have delivered at a conference but not yet published.
[157] See Robinson, op. cit., p. 43.

and the fashionable to draw attention to his goods, to make them seem more desirable by buying them. Having once made them fashionable in an exclusive circle, and therefore made them desirable to a socially emulative market, he then pressed home his advantage by making them accessible in price and place of sale to a mass market.

Boulton chose to have his sales at Easter, for example, for the same reason that many other astute manufacturers chose to have their most influential sales then. The London season lasted from October to Easter, and at Easter 'People of Fashion [were] preparing for their transmigration to the Countrey [sic]'.[158] The great exhibitions would not only catch the attention of fashionable London (so much so that in Boulton's words to his wife in April 1771, 'I had made so great a bussle [sic] amongst the Nobility even to such a degree as to stop up Pall Mall with coaches'), but also ensure that those up for the season (and their retinues of servants) carried back to the provinces exciting news of the new fashions.

They needed to be exclusive to make them fashionable, they needed to be dispersed as widely as possible to make them sell. The arrival of the fashion leaders back from the London season with the latest news from the capital was the signal for provincial England of what was in fashion. Just as newspapers spread the word of how an exclusive new fashion idea had been received in the capital, so those who had actually seen it or better still bought it, could proudly display or excitedly describe its novelty, and its social impact. According to a writer in *The Connoisseur* of 1756 fashion in dress spread so quickly that 'I could trace their gradations in their dress according to . . . the distance from London'. The return from a mere visit to London could bring novelties which stunned the locals and excited their eager desire to compete: 'At church in a populous city in the North the mace-bearer cleared the way for Mrs Mayoress who came sidling after him in an enormous fan-hoop of a pattern that had never been seen in those parts. At another church I saw several negligees with furbelowed aprons . . . but these were woefully eclipsed by a burgess' daughter, just come from London who appeared in a Trolloppee of Slammerkin with treble ruffles to the cuffs, pinked and gymped, and the sides of the petticoats drawn up in festoons.'[159]

When he was fully in command of the situation, the manufacturer had introduced the fashion idea himself, made it desirable, and easily accessible, first in London, then heavily advertised it, and flooded his provincial outlets. The whole process had to be carefully monitored. Adjustments to design, like adjustments to price, were part of the successful businessman's constant effort to trim his sails to meet the slightest variation in the winds of change. The most ephemeral gust in fashion's fickle requirements could influence the demand for his goods—such as, for instance, a court mourning suddenly spoiling 'for a time our Button business'[160] for Boulton in 1765.

[158] Quoted Robinson, op. cit., p. 52.   [159] *The Connoisseur,* 1756.
[160] J. Fothergill to Matthew Boulton, 3 Nov. 1765. Quoted Robinson, op. cit., p. 47.

Other changes were of more significance. Throughout the 1770s and 1780s watches were the height of fashion. Source after source tells us that two watches, or one watch and one miniature, suspended from ribbons or watch chains, were the prevailing mode. 'Two watches *were universal* unless a picture was substituted for one of them' said the *Ipswich Journal* of 1788. But by 1792 the *Lady's Magazine* firmly pronounced their death knell: 'Watches, trinkets, etc. quite mauvais ton'.[161] To the Birmingham toy trade advance warnings of such changes were vital. With that advantage production could be switched, and the favourable trade wind of the demand for the new fashion could be successfully exploited. With time for preparation it could be further puffed along by newspaper advertisements, new pattern books and eye-catching displays all fulsomely promoting the new fashion; while the products of the old production lines 'much seen and blown upon' could be rapidly switched to the distant provinces, or better still dumped abroad.

Wedgwood constantly begged Bentley for news of any new opening—'Ise [sic] make you new Vases like lightning when you think we may do it with safety'[162]—and thanked him warmly when it arrived—'since your wants have been made known to us we have been at work night and day'.[163] Bentley not only had to decide 'the time & way of ushering in the Grecian vases'.[164] he also had to warn Wedgwood when a new fashion was imminent. He had to act as both social oracle and the barometer of fashion. Accurate social judgements and accurate fashion readings were both necessary if the correct decisions were to be made about the numbers that could be sold, and the price at which they would sell, and the designs chosen first to please the few and then to attract many. Such accurate fashion decisions were vital to prevent even the highest quality goods failing to sell, or remaining the concern of merely an exclusive aristocratic *cul-de-sac* which offered no opening into the beckoning mass market—and that alone could sustain the demand which could make full use of the assembly line production at Etruria. One reason why Boulton failed to prosper in fashion goods to the same extent as Wedgwood is that he lacked a partner of Bentley's commercial acumen and fine judgement of the potential of a given market.

It was Bentley who passed on to Wedgwood Sir William Hamilton's warning that the new taste for the antique amongst the fashionable aristocracy would make gilding increasingly unacceptable on his pottery. And although Wedgwood complained that he did 'not find it an easy matter to make a Vase with the colouring so Natural ... & the shape so delicate ... seem worth a great deal of money, without the additional trappings of ... ornaments & Gilding', Sir William, from the source of the revival in Naples,

---

[161] See C. W. and P. Cunnington, op. cit., p. 404.
[162] WMSS. JW to TB, 22 March 1772. Another example of the vogue for imitation negro speech.
[163] WMSS. JW to TB, 10 April (1775).
[164] WMSS. JW to TB, 22 March 1772.

had deemed such decoration 'offensive', and so Wedgwood had to obey and much to his dislike banish gilding from his vases—and the gilders from his workshops.[165] Indeed he took the advice so seriously that he wrote 'as I shall expect the Golden Surfeit will rage with you higher than ever this Spring I shall almost tremble even for a gilt listel amongst your Vases, & would advise you by *all means* to provide a Curtain immediately for your Pebble ware shelves, which you may open or shut, (to) inlarge or diminish the shew of gilding as you find your Customs affected'.[166]

Wedgwood needed immediate information about *any* changes in consumer demand. He needed prompt news of market saturation lest Etruria's highly efficient assembly line should churn out more than could be sold, and thereby build up 'an enormous old stock [which would] Gorgon like, stir [sic] me in the face & chill me into activity'.[167] He needed prompt news of any new fashion like women's craze for bleaching their hands with arsenic which gave such a boost to black basalt tea ware during the general down-turn in home demand in late 1772.[168] Few knew better than Wedgwood that he could not rely simply on quality as a guide to what would sell. After one of their rare failures to read the needs of the market correctly, he sadly rehearsed the reasons for their failure with Bentley: 'We will make no more Gorgons Heads—But *these things being some of the finest things we have, & not knowing they did not sell,* we ventur'd to make a few more of them when we did not know what to make. We stand in need of *Negative* as well as *Positive* orders, & it is always of the first consequence to us to know what *does not,* as well as what *does* sell.'[169]

But once men like Wedgwood and Boulton had got first wind of a new fashion, or by careful stage management had whipped up a powerful demand for a new product of their own, they needed to push home their advantage if it was not to be wasted. When 'a violent Vase madness broke out amongst the Irish' Wedgwood took decisive measures to cherish the disorder and to encourage the contagion to spread. Wedgwood developed a whole battery of commercial techniques to exploit such openings. Boulton was the master of a similar array of aggressive selling devices. Like Wedgwood Boulton accepted special individual orders for the sake of prestige and publicity, offered free carriage of goods to London, and made flexible use of credit facilities. He too used a London showroom, spectacular sales and exhibitions, widespread advertisement and judiciously placed puffs, he too sought royal patronage and the support of the fashionable. He too gave gifts to ambassadors and their wives in the hope that 'the prejudice of the Italian Ladies' to

---

[165] WMSS. JW to TB, 11 April 1772.
[166] Ditto.
[167] WMSS. JW to TB, 28 March 1778.
[168] WMSS. JW to TB, 20 December 1772. 'Thank you for your discovery in favour of the black Teapots. I hope *white* hands will continue in fashion and then we may continue to make black Teapots.'
[169] WMSS. JW to TB, 23 November 1776. My italics.

buckles would collapse 'at the feet of Lady Hamilton' if her ladyship were *'to set the Example'*.[170] He too built a display room to attract aristocratic visitors to Soho where they could buy his latest inventions direct just as Wedgwood did at Etruria. The parallels are endless.

This is scarcely surprising since they faced so many similar problems in reaching out to the mass market they both sought for their goods. Sales to the exclusive tip of the social iceberg must be followed up with mass sales to that hidden part of the market, socially anonymous and not accessible to personal charm and individual attention. The unfashionable and the provincial markets needed to be actively pursued. They could not be bribed or flattered into buying, but they could be made to react to the prompting of fashion.

Boulton, like Wedgwood, had to tread a delicate path between supplying high quality introductions for the few which had of necessity to be expensive, and yet cashing in on the emulative spending those exclusive sales excited amongst the rest of society. Boulton was quite explicit that he wanted to sell to a mass market. His famous boast to James Watt that 'It would not be worth my while to make for three countries only; but I find it well worth my while to make for all the world'[171] is symptomatic of his commercial intentions. More informative about his commercial *technique* was his letter, written a quarter of a century later, stating authoritatively his reliance on a host of lesser allies to reach the mass market which was always his ambition:

> We think it of far more consequence to supply the People than the Nobility only; and though you speak contemptuously of Hawkers, Pedlars and those who supply *Petty Shops,* yet we must own that we think they will do more towards supporting a great Manufactory, than all the Lords in the Nation, and however lofty your notions may be, we assure you we have no objection against pulling off our Hats and thanking them 4 times a Year and must beg you will allow us to do it, without dictating when it should be done.[172]

This letter to his agent in London went on to spell out the message even more explicitly:

> It is certain that Buckles of Gold, Silver, Plated, Steel, Pinchbeck, Gilt etc. etc. will sell, and therefore let it be understood, once for all, that we mean to follow the fashions of all Countries...
> We have Agents in most parts of Europe, as well as in most of the great Towns in England, and we have considered London and its environs as your province; provided you take pains to supply every safe and reputable Dealer in Buckles from St James Street down to Wapping.[173]

---

[170] Matthew Boulton to Sir William Hamilton, 21 October 1795. Quoted Robinson, loc. cit., p. 49.
[171] Matthew Boulton to James Watt, 7 Feb. 1769.
[172] Matthew Boulton to R. Chippendall, 9 Aug. 1794. Quoted in Robinson, loc. cit., p. 59.
[173] Ditto.

This was no inconsiderable shopping area to cover. A contemporary guide book for visitors to London gives us a simple description of the main shopping streets:

> There are two sets of streets, running nearly parallel, almost from the Eastern extremity of the town to the Western, forming (with the exceptions of a very few houses), a line of shops. One, lying to the South, nearer the river, extends from Mile End to Parliament Street, including Whitechapel, Leadenhall Street, Cornhill, Cheapside, St Paul's Churchyard, Ludgate Street, Fleet Street, the Strand and Charing Cross. The other, to the North, reaches from Shoreditch Church almost to the end of Oxford Street, including Shoreditch, Bishopsgate Street, Threadneedle Street, Cheapside, Newgate Street, Snow-hill, Holborn, Broad Street, St Giles, and Oxford Street.
>
> The Southern Line, which is the most splendid, is more than three miles in length; the other is about four miles. There are several large streets also occupied by the retail trade, that run parallel to parts of the two grand lines, or intersect them, among the most fashionable of which are Fenchurch Street and Gracechurch Street in the City of London; and Cockspur Street, Pall Mall, St James's Street, Piccadilly, King's Street, Covent Garden, and New Bond Street, at the West end of the town.[174]

I have quoted this *in extenso* to give some impression of the commercial extent of retail London. To reinforce that impression another near contemporary source tells us that Oxford Street shops alone included 153 catering solely for 'the whim-whams and fribble-frabble of fashion'.[175] This was the commercial shop window of England. Here fashion reached its apotheosis in splendour and variety. It was this which moved Robert Southey to enthuse 'If I were to pass the remainder of my life in London I think the shops would always continue to amuse me. Something extraordinary or beautiful is for ever to be seen in them ... There is a perpetual exhibition of whatever is curious in nature or art, exquisite in workmanship, or singular in costume; and the display is perpetually varying as the ingenuity of trade and the absurdity of fashion are ever producing something new.'[176] According to Southey the shops were furnished with everything which would 'tempt' the passer-by who would be irresistibly lured to what another contemporary called 'the great windows of large panes exhibiting the richest manufactures'.[177] On those windows were trained outside lights which were 'of infinite service to the rest of the inhabitants by their Liberal use of the Patent Lamp, to shew their commodities during the long evenings of winter'.[178]

Examples chosen from 1807 show to what extent London shopping had developed through the eighteenth century. Southey reminds us in that year that the great glass windows 'were seldom used in shops before the present

---

[174] *The Picture of London* (1803) quoted in Alison Adburgham, *Shops and Shopping, 1800–1914* (1964), p. 5.
[175] *Johnstone's London Commercial Guide* (1817).
[176] Robert Southey, *Letters from England* (1807), quoted Adburgham, op. cit., p. vi.
[177] James Peller Malcolm, *Anecdotes of the Manner and Customs of London during the 18th Century, with a Review of the State of Society in 1807* (1810), Vol. II, p. 402.
[178] Ibid, Vol. II, p. 383.

COMMERCIALIZATION OF FASHION

reign' and even then they had not 'universally come into fashion';[179] and gas lighting was not invented until 1792. But by the reign of George III, the impact of London shops on foreign visitors was powerful enough to demonstrate that a dramatic transformation had taken place during the century. Compared with the rest of Europe the commercialization of London had moved at a revolutionary pace.

Take the ecstatic reactions of Sophie von la Roche in 1786:

> Behind the great glass windows absolutely everything one can think of is neatly, attractively displayed, in such abundance of choice as almost to make one greedy. Now large slipper and shoe shops for anything from adults down to dolls, can be seen; now fashion-articles or silver or brass shops, books, guns, glasses, the confectioner's goodies, the pewterer's wares, fans etc. . . . There is a cunning device for showing women's materials. Whether they are silks, chintzes, or muslins, they hang down in folds behind the fine, high windows so that the effect of this or that material, as it would be in the ordinary folds of a woman's dress, can be studied.[180]

Sophie von la Roche was enthralled by what she called 'lovely Oxford Street' and she, too, confirmed that by 1786 the shops were brilliantly lit by oil lamps which illuminated the shops until ten in the evening. Her portrait of Oxford Street confirms the attractions which shops offered to the passer-by. Impulse buyers were surely tempted as

> First one passes a watch-making, then a silk or fan store, now a silversmith's, a china or glass shop. The spirit booths are particularly tempting . . . here crystal flasks of every shape and form are exhibited: each one has a light behind which makes all the different coloured spirits sparkle. Just as alluring are the confectioners and fruiterers, where, behind the handsome glass windows pyramids of pink apples, figs, grapes, oranges and all manner of fruits are on show. We enquired the price of a pineapple and did not think it too dear at 6s. Most of all we admired a stall with Argand lamps situated in a corner house and forming a really dazzling spectacle. Every variety of lamp, crystal, lacquer and metal ones, silver and brass in every possible shape.[181]

Many others confirmed this dazzling impression made by London and its shops. When the Russian writer, Nikolai Mikhailovitch Karamzin arrived in 1789 he felt he was entering a new world. He was astonished by the pervasive evidence of prosperity: 'everywhere there are stone pavements for pedestrians'; 'everywhere great numbers of coaches, chaises and horsemen': everywhere 'crowds of well dressed people'; and everywhere 'beautiful shops' and the wares exhibited in the shops 'as in a continuous fair'.[182] What struck Karamzin was not splendour but general prosperity. The contrast with Paris

---

[179] Robert Southey, *Letters from England* (1807), quoted Adburgham, p. 6.
[180] *The Diary of Sophie von La Roche* (1786), published as S. von La Roche, *Sophie in London (1786)* ed. Clare Williams (1933), p. 87.
[181] Sophie von la Roche, op. cit., p. 141.
[182] N. M. Karamzin, *Letters of a Russian Traveller, 1789–90*, Translated and abridged by Florence Jonas (New York, 1957), pp. 261–77.

was very striking: 'How different this is from Paris! There vastness and filth, here simplicity and astonishing cleanliness; there wealth and poverty in continued contrast, here a general appearance of sufficiency; there palaces out of which crawls poverty, here tiny brick cottages out of which health and contentment walk with an air of dignity and tranquillity—lord and artisan almost indistinguishable in their immaculate dress'.[183] Karamzin attributed such benefits to the life-enhancing consequences of trade—'To the right, between green banks, lay the glistening Thames where countless shipmasts rose like a forest seared by lightning. This is the foremost port in the world, the focus of world commerce!'[184] His pages are full of the praises of commerce; of 'the richly stocked shops ... in which you can see, through glass doors, an abundance of wares of every sort'; of the lamps which lit up the shopping streets of London;[185] at the ease of travel, 'the consequences of ... widespread wealth'; at the ubiquity of the press, 'Here newspapers and magazines are in everyone's hands, not only in town but in small villages as well.'[186]

Karamzin's hymn of praise to commercial prosperity stretched from the country houses of the rich where 'attached to each house are vast greenhouses, where fruit and plants have been gathered from all parts of the world, and huge stables, where horses live better than many human beings', to 'housemaids in all their finery, in long dresses and bonnets, carrying fans'. But he admitted that beneath the 'decency' of 'servants, artisans, salesmen, chemists' apprentices' and suchlike, there lurked 'a vile rabble'. In Karamzin's eyes English society was 'good on the surface and in the middle, but do not look underneath'.[187] And although Karamzin admired the 'general spirit of trade' of the English, he did not admire their attitude to those who failed to prosper—'If you wish to oppress still more someone oppressed by poverty, let him come to England. Here in the midst of wealth, of thriving abundance and heaps of guineas, he will come to know the agony of Tantalus.'[188]

Critics of English society often stressed the same point. The anglophobes drew attention to the same opulent display, the same excesses of fashionable change, the same spread of luxurious living but they interpreted it very differently from the admiring majority. At one end of the scale was the anglophile novelist and blue stocking Sophie von la Roche who was so impressed by the sight of Wedgwood's pottery that she felt moved to write 'It is not partiality but the simple truth that the Briton is born for all that

[183] Ibid., pp. 265-7.
[184] Ditto.
[185] 'Never having seen anything like this I did not wonder at the error of a certain German prince who, upon entering London at night and seeing the streets brilliantly lighted, believed that the city had been illuminated for his arrival. The English people like light, and they give the government millions to replace the sun artificially. What a striking indication of a nation's wealth'. op. cit., p. 268.
[186] Karamzin, op. cit., pp. 266, 327, 329.
[187] Karamzin, op. cit., p. 325. 'The lees of the finest and the poorest wine taste equally disgusting.'
[188] Karamzin, op cit., p. 331.

is noble. For as soon as his spirit can go its own way and act independently it pursues in everything the path of greatness, simplicity and beauty.'[189]

At the other end of the spectrum is the Prussian preacher Andreas Riem, whose *Travels*, written between 1796 and 1801, found nothing to commend about the English but their landscape. He has been called 'the best example we possess of a good hater of this country'.[190] He saw 'the basic evil of the English character as materialism and the commercial spirit'.[191] He, too, could not miss the signs of heightened commercial activity, the heightened wish to possess material possessions.

* * *

One type of evidence alone—the tradesmen's cards of eighteenth-century London[192]—allows us to do some justice to the charm and variety and commercial endeavour of the London shops. They show us that the visitor to London could satisfy a remarkable range of wants. If he wanted 'Venice treacle' or 'elephants' teeth', a backgammon table or 'artificial' eyes, then the trade cards would lead him to the specialist supplier. If he wanted asses' milk, Thomas Edwards' charming trade card advertised his service at the *Ass and Foal* at the bottom of Wigmore Street; while from James Jones, at the *Ass and Foal* in Wood's Cross, he could buy the milk or even rent the ass (offered at monthly rates).

Other specialist services were equally well advertised. If he needed a ratcatcher or, more bizarrely, a sow gelder, the appropriate experts were all at hand. Should he require fans, feather beds, fountain pens, fireworks or fishing tackle, all were easily available from a multiplicity of outlets. Should he want pineapples, perukes or pewter, they too were on sale. Should he want tea, tobacco or jewellery, there was massive competition to serve him. Should he want a trunk, he could have a hair one, a sumpter one, a portmanteau one, a gilded leather one, or a peruke box or a leather container to hold liquors, or a case for his plate: the trunkmakers offered all—and more—for his custom. Should he want to buy a toy for his children, he faced an embarassment of choice: at the cheap end of the market he could get a jigsaw puzzle from the original inventor, John Spilsbury, whose trade card of the early 1760s describes him as a 'Map Dissector in Wood';[193] if he wanted to go up market he could buy a portable printing press made for children of the rich by J. Sutter of St. Martin's Lane.[194]

---

[189] Sophie von la Roche, *Sophie in London 1786*, ed. C. Williams (1933).
[190] W. D. Robson-Scott, 'Foreign Impressions of England in the Eighteenth Century', in *Silver Renaissance* (1961), ed. Alex Naton, p. 203.
[191] Ibid., p. 204. He found the English materially more advanced, but morally inferior to the rest of Europe, 'they are little better than coarse crude, uncouth, arrogant, half savage barbarians'.
[192] Ambrose Heal, *London Tradesmen's Cards of the XVIII Century* (1925). Unless otherwise stated, most of the detail on tradesmen's cards comes from this work.
[193] Linda Hannas, *The English Jigsaw Puzzle 1760–1890* (1972), pp. 18–19.
[194] J. Sutter also advertised his portable printing press in the *Reading Mercury and Oxford Gazette*, 30 October 1769. See J. Moran, *Printing Presses* (1973), p. 230.

Should a lady want her own honey supply, 'The Honey Warehouse' sold 'glass beehives contriv'd so the lady may have them on their dressing tables without the least danger of being stung'. Should she wish to restock with patches or cosmetics or hair shampoos or hair dye or toothpaste, should she need a new cork rump, or false breasts or false hips, they too were on sale. If she wished to promise even greater pneumatic bliss, there were spring-loaded false bodices on sale and even sprung rumps. The market in what were called 'artificials' or 'bosom friends' was as well developed as one would expect of the fashions prevailing in the 1770s and 1780s. To stay in fashion a man could require false calves, and a woman could even require a 'false front' when in 1783 the Duchess of Devonshire's pregnancy made that condition fashionable; while, of course, 'artificial teeth', 'fictitious hair' and 'false eyebrows' were widely available. A charming caricature of a shop front of 1782 advertised ivory teeth and mouse eyebrows as two of its main lines, and many sources made fun of both fashions: the eyebrows were made from strips of mouse skin and inevitably attracted as much attention from the satirists as they apparently did from the cats. There were even more extreme fashion devices on sale: even cheeks could be restored to a youthful roundness with 'cork plumpers'—'Mrs Button wears cork plumpers in each cheek and never hazards more than six words for fear of shewing them'.[195]

More straightforwardly, makers of clogs, clocks and coach springs, of cricket balls, rocking horses, fish hooks, and bows and arrows were eager to satisfy the 'most discriminating needs' and 'all in the latest fashion'. A man could be purged, perfumed and taught by a prize fighter within the space of a few hundred yards. Food sellers tempted him with everything from 'portable soup' to 'icecream whip'. And, of course, clothes sellers proliferated everywhere. Hatters, haberdashers, hosiers, drapers and tailors offered a bewildering variety of garments in an astonishing variety of materials: 'Duffel Cloaks' and 'Jeans' may have a reassuring ring for modern ears, and 'real-nine-times-dyed blue flannel for the Gout and rhumatism' explains itself; 'mecklenbergs' present no difficulty for those who know the details of Queen Charlotte's family; and ALLAMODES might seem obvious (in fact alamode was a light, glossy silk); but a knowledge of eighteenth century fashion is needed to decipher ALLOPEENS and FIGURED AMENS, BARRAGONS and CHERRY DERRYS, GARUCKS and HUGA-BACKS, PEELINGS and PELLICOATS, ROCCELOES, RASDEMOR-RAS, SHALLOONS, SAGATHYS and SHAGGS, or TIFFANYS, TABBIES and TABBYNETS—and these are only a sample. To the eighteenth-century market, familiarized with trade cards and newspaper advertisements and illustrated prints, the message of MANCHESTER COTTON (a textile with stripes of cotton and wool) or PARAGON or NORWICH CREPE was as clear as gingham, poplin, plush, mohair and hessian (all widely advertised then) are to us today.

[195] Mrs. Cowley, *The Belle's Stratagem* (1780).

And, as many trade cards made absolutely clear, many of these were now sold ready-made. The message informing the market of the ready availability of these goods 'ready made, for ready money, and at a fixed price' was being loudly proclaimed. Source after source tells us that it was a rare exception to bargain in a London shop by the end of the century. A greater commercial uniformity spread as commercial practice grew more sophisticated, and as the scale of sales increased the fixed price inevitably established itself.[196]

The Londoner could now be clothed from birth to death at a fixed price in ready-made clothes: even the shrouds were advertised ready-made. In this the dead were as well served as the living, with ready-made coffins to match the ready-made shrouds and 'all the other conveniences belonging to funerals'. Even the dead's more specialist needs could be satisfied from a variety of sources: one undertaker advertised with splendid economy 'SAFETY FOR THE DEAD . . . THE RIGHT TO INTER IN IRON (a fashion which Wilkinson, the great ironmaster, had tried so hard to popularize); while another more wordily offered

> IMPROVED COFFINS—THE FASTENINGS OF THESE IMPROVED RECEPTACLES BEING ON SUCH PRINCIPLES AS TO RENDER IT IMPRACTICABLE FOR THE GRAVE ROBBERS TO OPEN THEM. THIS SECURITY MUST AFFORD GREAT CONSOLATION AT AN AERA WHEN IT IS A WELL AUTHENTICATED FACT THAT NEARLY ONE THOUSAND BODIES ARE ANNUALLY APPROPRIATED FOR THE PURPOSE OF DISSECTION.

If those in search of anatomical knowledge were thwarted by the improved coffins there was a skeleton seller advertising a simpler substitute.

London commerce in the shape of its shopkeepers had ensured that most of the easily imaginable wants of a consumer society could be met. Those wanting to use the services of an archill (a man who sold dyes made from lichens) or an aquarellist (a man who sold aquatints) would find one; and since Paul Sandby was the aquarellist it is not easy to disparage the quality. Those whose trade cards also survive include Hogarth, who advertised his engravings, Sheraton, his designs for cabinets, and Wedgwood, his pottery. The trade cards were not simple statements of place of sale—they informed the public of the chimney sweeps who operated a satisfaction-or-money-back policy, crisply advertised as 'NO CURE, NO PAY'; and they informed it that Josiah Wedgwood 'delivers his goods safe and carriage free . . . as he sells for ready money only'. The second part of this was not true for his fashionable customers, who were allowed credit, but it was true for the market he wished to reach with his trade cards. He eventually banned them from his really fashionable showrooms in London and Bath—their role was to attract a much wider public.

Their purpose was unequivocally to advertise; to draw attention to any

---

[196] See, for a typical reaction, *Svedenstierna's Tour of Great Britain 1802-3* (1973), p. 20.

special quality or any distinctive patronage, even if it were only inherited like Eleanor Brainiff's, who advertised herself as 'Daughter and Successor to her late father George Bridges, BUGG DESTROYER TO HIS MAJESTY' and even if the patronage was only to 'the lesser royals' or even more humbly to 'several of His Majesty's offices', or not royal at all—'the only maker of Sir Hans Sloane's Milk Chocolates'.

The historian's understandable predilection for the picturesque must not mislead one into thinking that the market was solely one in fashionable fripperies. The demand for such accessories was, of course, amply met, but there are endless examples of the sales promotion of more mundane household goods as well: advertisements for pots and pans, pins and needles, copper kettles and brass scuttles, knives and forks, candles and candlesticks, curtains and blankets, lanterns and firegrates, shoes and stockings, spades and garden forks, prints and picture frames, books and wallpapers, baskets and bedcovers, razors and scissors, buckets and brushes, flower pots and dog collars, and, of course, chairs and tables and stools and boxes in their infinite variety. Even shops offering to match curtains with wallpapers and upholstery were not uncommon.

And although much fun has been had by historians quoting Addison's mockery of inappropriate shop signs inherited by newly moved shopkeepers—'A cook should not live at the *Boot*, nor a Shoemaker at the *Roasted Pig*'—the trade cards make clear that such incongruity was shortlived and rare. In fact when in 1762 the elaborate shopsigns were ordered to be removed, having become too numerous and too dangerous, the trade cards advertised their new street numbers *and* the old signs,[197] which they incorporated into the advertisements. They were designed to imprint their commercial message and the signs served as a valuable mnemonic; so that musical instruments were sold at the sign of the 'Horn and Trumpet', brass and copper at the sign of the 'Frying Pan', upholstery at the sign of the 'Three Covered Chairs', breeches at the 'Boot and Breeches', perukes at the 'White Peruke', and so on. Long after the signs were gone such trademarks were used to advertise the place of sale and the distinctive character of a well known product. Some were even used in national chains of provincial shops, as Packwood's use of the 'Naked Truth' as *the* name for the provincial shops which sold his wares makes clear.[198]

The trade cards backed up by newspaper advertisements were to the shopkeepers what the fashion doll and the fashion print were to the fashion designers. It is no accident that trade cards had hardly come into existence before the eighteenth century, that specimens dating from 1700 to 1730 are exceedingly rare, that their peak of collectable elegance was reached between 1730 and 1770, although they continued to proliferate after that date. It is

---

[197] See Ambrose Heal, *The Signboards of Old London Shops* (1947).
[198] See below, pp. 146–94.

no accident either that they were known to contemporaries as 'shopkeepers' bills'.[199]

In an increasingly competitive market the cards were an important part of the shopkeepers' promotional efforts. Aggregate demand might be rising but to keep it growing, and to keep and increase one's share of it, required both commercial vigilance and ingenuity. Above all it was felt to require advertisement, and the trade cards allowed the shopkeeper to advertise the quality of his shop as well as his goods. The booksellers Lackington Allen and Co., boasted on their trade card that their premises constituted 'the finest shop in the world being 140 feet in front', and they displayed their fourteen, tall, round-headed windows on one card and their 'Lounging Rooms', where buyers could comfortably browse, on another. Other trade cards reveal in marvellously precise detail the methods of display which filled Sophie von la Roche with delight, and which, as Dr. Johnson and Southey realized, made impulse buying so hard to resist even for one 'who is resolved to buy no more'.[200]

They also draw attention to the distinctive architectural forms which historians have seen as 'part of the new aggressive attitude to business'[201] and to methods of selling. Indeed, the 'rectilinear simplicity' of shop fronts of the 1790s has been described as 'surprisingly prophetic of the typical shop front in today's cities'.[202] The modern note was a real one, the break with the past was very apparent. These new shops were in size, in appearance, and in scale of operations, the true precursors of their commercial descendents which serve our present society of high mass consumption. These were not the mere hutches or mere stalls which so many contemporaries described as shops in the seventeenth century. The contrast between the spacious elegance of George Dance's plans for shops in Leadenhall Street in the 1790s, and Inigo Jones' plans for the New Exchange in the early seventeenth century is a stark and revealing one. When one first reads of the plans for the New Exchange with its hundred new shops arranged on two floors, it sounds immensely impressive, but when one learns that many were little more than booths five and a half feet deep and described by their tenants as suffering from 'a want of Stowage for their wares ... the shopps being, as it were, small chests rather than shopps',[203] one is considerably less impressed.

When one reads of the takings of London shopkeepers one is forcibly reminded again that there are shops and shops. Five years after the opening of the New Exchange, for instance, a contemporary offered this estimate of

[199] A mixture of possible confusion over the word 'bill' and a genteel dislike of the word 'shopkeeper' led collectors to rename them tradesmen's cards.
[200] Dr. Johnson, *Idler*, no. 56.
[201] H. Kalman, 'The Architecture of Mercantilism: Commercial Buildings by George Dance the Younger', *The Triumph of Culture: 18th Century Perspectives* (Toronto, 1972), pp. 69–96.
[202] Ibid., p. 79.
[203] L. Stone, 'Inigo Jones and the New Exchange', *Archaeological Journal*, CXIV, (1957), p. 117.

a shopkeeper's turnover: 'It may well be supposed but an ill-customed shop that taketh not five shillings a day, one day with another throughout the whole year'.[204] It is this kind of evidence which casts doubt on the economic significance of the 'Mighty Torrent' of shopkeepers said to be pouring over the kingdom in 1684, and on the view, from the same source, that 'every country village' with ten houses has a shopkeeper dealing 'in many substantial commodities'.[205] Even if some of them did have, as *The Compleat Tradesman* claimed, a stock worth 'no less than one thousand pounds', it pales into insignificance compared with the developments at the end of the eighteenth century. Commercial practice was moving so rapidly then and the scale of change was so dramatic, that what James Lackington had tried to introduce in 1780[206]—fixed prices and no credit—was regarded as being established by 1800,[207] and by 1821 a single fixed price 'NO ABATEMENT' linen draper was reported to be taking £500 a day and employing up to thirty assistants.[208] All these figures are of course open to doubt, but the change of scale is unmistakable. London had long been regarded as the centre of conspicuous consumption but such was the qualitative change in the nature of commercial enterprise in the eighteenth century that London was now the centre of a new scale of commerce, the undisputed leader in the commercialization of fashion which had helped to bring about unprecedentedly high levels of spending. The watershed is nicely symbolized by the arrival of many commercial names still famous in London retailing. Fortnum and Mason arrived in Piccadilly early in the eighteenth century, Flint and Clark (later Clark and Debenham) arrived in 1778, Dickins and Smith (later Dickins and Jones) arrived in 1790, Heal's arrived in 1810, and although it was not until 1812 that Swan and Edgar opened their shop in Piccadilly, they had both been selling separately in London before that date.

In stressing London's importance, one must not forget that there were many other unsung heroes in the spread of fashion to a new market of consumers—the new class of itinerant salesmen and the provincial shopkeepers. It is hardly surprising that historians have so largely overlooked the lesser agents of the commercializing process—the pedlars, the 'Scotch drapers', the 'Scotch hawkers' or the 'Manchester Men'. They did not serve the gentry or the more literate middle class. They operated in the depths of the provinces. They were not seen by visiting foreigners doing their Great Tours of England (to London, the great houses and the great industrial

[204] Barnaby Rich, *The Honestie of The Age* (1614). Little wonder that Dorothy Davis concludes that 'all the evidence on seventeenth-century retailers points to a general acceptance of a very slow turn over ... and with a few notable exceptions, to a poor and precarious livelihood'. Davis, op. cit., p. 102.
[205] N. H., *The Compleat Tradesman* (1684), p. 26.
[206] 'It was thought I might as well attempt to rebuild the Tower of Babel as to establish a large business without giving credit'. James Lackington, writing of the year 1780, in *Memoirs of the First Forty-five Years* (1830), p. 214.
[207] See above, p. 83
[208] See Davis, op. cit., p. 259.

centres). And as Hoskins said of them they have 'no annals', not even 'that sad passport to immortality' a tax assessment. In consequence, as Dorothy Davis has written, 'Among so many obscurities and uncertainties in the history of retail trade, nothing is so obscure and uncertain as the role of the pedlar'.

Yet they served a vital if often concealed role in the further spread of consumer goods through provincial society. Some indication of *how* vital came in the 1780s when the Exchequer proposed first a Shops Tax to raise money from an obviously growing and prosperous source, then, to soften the blow to the shopkeepers, a Bill proposing to make all peddling illegal. The Bill was revoked as a result of a storm of protest, not from the customers, who were too poor to have any effective voice, not from pedlars themselves, who were equally insignificant politically, but from 'the manufacturers of linen, wool and cotton, the millowners of Glasgow and Lancashire and Yorkshire, many of whom objected that they would be driven to close down their mills without pedlars—and in particular Scotch drapers—to market their goods'.[209] They raised a storm of protest. The petitions to the Commons all stressed the absolute necessity to the major manufacturers of the hawkers, pedlars and Scotch drapers. They all stressed their role in extending the market for their goods and 'introducing them into Parts of the Country where they could not otherwise have been sold'. They all stressed the important part these men played in developing new markets among the working class: one petition to the Commons claimed that the Scotch Drapers in the neighbourhood of Halifax were owed about £40,000 by 'labouring Mechanics and manufacturers in the small villages of the West Riding'. They stressed, too, that the total trade conducted by the itinerants was far greater than 'may have been apprehended'.[210]

The case stating 'the many great and important Advantages' which derived from this 'useful and industrious Class of Tradesmen' was set out very clearly in a petition from Whitehaven, that pointed out that

> the Quantity of goods bought and disposed of by them was considerably more extensive than had been generally conceived, and the Mode of Sale which is wholly confined to small Villages and Places remote from general Markets tends very greatly to diffuse the Manufacturers of the Kingdom in general and is a source of great convenience to those Inhabitants who live at a Distance from the principal Towns, great Quantities of goods of almost every description being vended in detail, which the remote Inhabitants could not find leisure to seek and when Necessity might compel them to go from Home, the Expense of the Journey would frequently be as great as the Object of his Purchase.[211]

Exactly how many of these itinerant salesmen there were we do not know. When they were said to be declining in Victorian England, the 1851 Census

---

[209] Davis, op. cit., p. 245.   [210] Ibid., pp. 1026 and 1007.
[211] Ibid., p. 1072. Just how important the cost of a journey could be is made clear in some seventeenth-century accounts quoted by Davis, op. cit., p. 134: 'Shrimps 8d, Bringing it 7d'; 'A Sturgen 3s 4d, Bringing it 2s'; 'For a seale [!] 20d, Bringing it 3s 4d'. For these three items the total cost of transport was greater than the total cost of the goods purchased.

gives a figure of some 30,000, while in the eighteenth century, when they were at the height of their importance, only 2,000 licences were taken out each year. But since the country pedlars were said to 'avoid the plate', this tells us little, compared with those urgent petitions from so many manufacturers in the 1780s.

The pedlars they were defending were not the pedlars of the traditional sort. These Scotch Drapers, or Scotch Hawkers, were not like the pedlar who had tramped England for centuries bringing delight to distant hamlets with his purses, points, gloves and ribbons as he travelled from fair to fair with his small pack of goods. The contents of Autolycus's pack as painted by Shakespeare in *The Winter's Tale* (1611) sound beguiling enough but the contents of an actual pedlar's pack when he was arrested in 1657 were pathetically small—'3 hankes and 4 bolts of yarn, 1 candlestick, 1 measure, an old pistol and some tobacco'.[212] The total value was six shillings. According to Samuel Bamford the Scotch Hawkers carried huge and weighty packs 'four feet in length and two or more in depth'[213] but the more significant difference from the traditional pedlar was his method of sale. First, he specialized in the products of the new industrial centres; second, he sold on credit; third, he had his special area in which he called on his customers every week for cash by instalments.[214] He offered the ideal service for the families of factory hands he typically served. He brought direct to their door the latest products of the mills and factories, he would accept a small weekly sum on account, and as soon as the total was paid off he was ready to interest them in something new. The prevailing fashions announced in the advertising columns of the provincial press—or at least an adequate approximation to them—could be produced for his remote customers by the Scotch Draper. He was a new kind of genuine retailer—a cross between the London tallyman and the traditional pedlar.

The manufacturers had another major new ally in the spread of consumer goods to the country at large. For the Manchester Man was a genuinely new type of wholesaler. The Manchester Man dealt not with individual households, but with individual shops. He was the wholesale version for provincial shopkeepers of what the Scotch Draper was for the working-class housewife. He too brought his goods direct to the retailers' doorstep where they could judge and choose their stock for themselves. He too sold often on credit. He too brought a range of goods previously obtainable only from London. But the scale was altogether bigger. For although some had only a single pack animal, others had long trains of several laden packhorses and stock valued

---

[212] James Jackson, *The Diary of a Cumberland Farmer 1650–83. Trans. of the Cumberland and Westmorland Antiq. Society*, n.s. XXI, p. 109. Quoted Davis, op. cit., p. 239. Admittedly some carried more than this. See Thirsk. op. cit., p. 123.

[213] Samuel Bamford, *Early Days* (1849), quoted in A. P. Wadsworth and J. de L. Mann, *The Cotton Trade and Industrial Manchester* (1931), p. 240.

[214] He in turn obtained his stock on credit. Some firms employed them to sell their goods direct to the new industrial working class.

at thousands of pounds. As a type they signalled the arrival of an early version of the commercial traveller, and they 'gradually transformed the resources of the provincial shops'.[215] They speeded up the process of distribution and smoothed the way for a quicker transmission of the prevailing fashions.

There can be little doubt that without the service of these new itinerant salesmen much of the provincial market would have been stifled for want of opportunity to buy. Its latent demands could not have been satisfied. National aggregate demand would have been the loser. There was still, of course, no truly national market. Regional consumption could still be dominated by a local producer, which is 'why in the normal way you had to go to Burton-on-Trent if you wanted a tankard of Bass or Worthington, and had to limit yourself in London to brands like Truman's or Whitbread's'.[216] One could still be cut off from luxuries in the provinces. Sydney Smith characterized his banishment to a remote country parish in Yorkshire with the immortal description that it was 'so out of the way that it was actually 12 miles from a lemon'. A century earlier he could have faced more serious problems. The daughter of Judge Fell who lived near Ulverston was 278 miles from a lemon! And the same distance from an orange! And the same even from a larding needle! Perhaps even more telling than the fact that she had to send to London for these goods is the fact that she had to travel 18 miles to Kendal or 25 miles over the sands of the tidal estuary to Lancaster for *any* manufactured goods. She made these arduous journeys every few weeks, for bellows, pans, soap, shoes, nails and garden tools. That she sent to Newcastle for her cheese might simply be the result of personal preference, but that can hardly explain the fact that she had to send ten miles in another direction for salt![217]

The solution to the problem of consumer isolation was the provincial shop. Where the Scotch draper brought his goods to the door of the working class home, the provincial shop was to offer a permanent outlet for the whole of provincial society. Where the traditional pedlar offered an unpredictable, if welcome, opportunity to spend, and the annual fair a regular, but all too brief, opportunity to see a larger range of goods, the provincial shop could offer a permanent, regular outlet which, if well served by London and the major industrialists, could satisfy the provincial appetite for fashion.

Fairs, of course, continued. In some parts of the country they even increased,[218] but in the words of Eric Jones 'shops were really the coming

---

[215] Davis, op. cit., p. 243. There were Sheffield Men and Shrewsbury Men as well as Manchester Men.
[216] E. N. Williams, *Life in Georgian England* (1962), p. 6.
[217] *The Household Account Book of Sarah Fell*, 1673–78, ed. Norman Penney (1921). p. 123 and p. 155.
[218] Although there was a steeply falling trend for most of the country they increased between 1792 and 1888 in Cheshire, Cornwall, Cumberland, Durham, Lancashire and Westmorland.

thing'.[219] They offered fixed premises, with fixed prices. Backed by the services of newspaper advertisements informing the public of its latest attractions, its array of fashions and its links with London, its ultimate victory as the main retail outlet was assured. Even some village shopkeepers could afford to be philosophical about the 'hurt to trade' caused by the arrival of an itinerant salesman. As Thomas Turner wrote in 1764, 'This day came to Jones's a man with a cartload of millinery, mercery, linen-drapery, silver, &c., to keep sale for two days, which must undoubtedly be some hurt to trade; for the novelty of the thing (and novelty is surely the predominant passion of the English nation, and of Sussex in particular) will catch the ignorant multitude, and perhaps not them only, but people of sense, who are not judges of goods and trade, as indeed few are; but, however, as it is it must pass'.[220] With booming demand there was trade for all, and the town shopkeeper with his special offers, seasonal sales, the latest fashions, and the promotion of particular manufactured goods found their own ways of appealing to the prevailing 'passion for novelty'. Mr. Parsons and Mr. Price of Leicester advertised in the press the latest line in Wedgwood & Bentley's Fountain Ink-pots on 16 October 1779;[221] and Mr. East advertised not only a full selection of Wedgwood's wares in 1796, but also advertised his ability to supply the country shops.[222]

Individual studies of provincial shopkeepers are rare. We know that the great industrialists like Wedgwood built provincial warehouses and supplied hundreds of provincial shops. We know that men like Packwood kept many provincial outlets supplied with his distinctively advertised products. We know from the newspaper advertisements that thousand upon thousand of such provincial shopkeepers advertised their ability to provide the latest fashion. But the few detailed case studies which are known to us support the sense of marked commercial change. For if one compares the commercial techniques and scale of operation of Roger Lowe, who ran a village shop in Leigh, and William Stout the famous Quaker grocer of Lancaster (and one has little other choice in the seventeenth century) with, say, Mr. McGuffog of Stamford in the 1770s or Elizabeth Towsey of Chester in the 1780s or John Watt's Manchester Bazaar of 1819, then the qualitative change is undeniable.

Roger Lowe's village shop was little more than a shed. If he 'kept shop all day'[223] he thought it worth special mention, for day after day he left the shop shut up while he went off to try to buy some stock to sell, or collect in some debts to buy it with. The conclusion is unavoidable that Roger Lowe's shop was 'a lock-up premises of negligible value, stocked with a hetereoge-

---

[219] E. L. Jones, op. cit., p. 215.
[220] Thomas Turner, *The Diary of a Georgian Shopkeeper*, ed. G. H. Jennings (Oxford, 1979), p. 67. Jones's was one of the two village pubs in East Hoathly.
[221] *The Leicester & Nottingham Journal*, 16 October 1779.
[222] *The Salisbury & Winchester Journal*, 31 October 1796.
[223] W. L. Sachse (ed.), *Diary of Roger Lowe 1663–74*, (1938).

neous collection of any cheap goods the man could lay his hands on, open for trade intermittently and unpredictably, granting credit as a matter of course to all and sundry, and run by a man heavily dependent upon a sideline ... to make a bare living'.[224]

Compared with Roger Lowe and his like the much quoted operations of William Stout look more impressive, but the scale and methods of operation were still very primitive. He still lost between one third and one half his profits in bad debts, and he still had difficulty in getting an adequate supply of goods: cheese for funerals and smuggled tobacco and brandy being notable highlights in his sales. Again in Dorothy Davis's words 'to get the goods and to get the money, those were the arts of shopkeeping. Merely selling the stuff was child's play, and very often children, or at least young apprentices were left to do it'.[225]

The contrast with Robert Owen's early master Mr. McGuffog is immediately apparent. He made a considerable fortune from his fine shop in Stamford. According to Owen's enthusiastic account 'The articles dealt with were the best, the finest and most choice qualities that could be procured from all the markets of the world'.[226] The shop became a meeting place for the local nobility in the 1770s with some six or seven carriages at a time often waiting outside.

Browns of Chester provides further detailed support for the ability of eighteenth-century shops to provide provincial England with the latest fashions. These shops still depended on London for high fashion and contemporaries claimed that they could trace the 'gradation of dress in distant parts of the country according to the distance from London'. In the middle of the century the outward spread of fashion was still limited to the squire's wife and the vicar's wife in the villages, but 'in the larger cities and towns, where the newest fashions are brought down weekly by the stage-coach or waggon, all the wives and daughters of the most topping tradesmen vie with each other every Sunday in the elegance of their apparel'. At this date in the mid-fifties the fashion contest lay between mercers' daughters and grocers' wives, and a burgess's daughter could 'eclipse' the local competition by appearing in the latest London fashion—'a Trolloppee or Slammerkin' or a 'Nun's Hood' or 'a new fashion'd cap called a Joan'.[227]

In the next few decades the competition increased, as the provincial shops with the support of the provincial press spread such behaviour both geographically and socially.

The provincial newspapers of the eighteenth century which carried fashion news—such as *Boston Newsletter, Cambridge Journal and Flying Post, Chelmsford Chronicle, Chester Chronicle, Ipswich Journal, Leeds Mercury,*

---

[224] Davis, op. cit., p. 151.
[225] Davis, op. cit., p. 113.
[226] *Life of Robert Owen. Written by Himself* (1879), p. 16.
[227] Quoted in C. W. and P. Cunnington, op. cit., p. 20-2.

Northampton Post, Salisbury Journal, York Chronicle and Weekly Advertiser, York Courant—make it clear that every detail of London fashion was eagerly reported to the readers throughout the country. Gloves, hats, shoes, pockets, parasols, buckles, buttons and all the paraphernalia of fashion were described in detail. When bosom bottles came in mid-century—small containers to hold water to keep flowers worn in women's cleavages fresh—the *Boston Evening Post* carried an advertisement announcing 'Bosom bottles, pear shaped, flat, 4 inches long, of ribbed glass for bouqets'.[228] For those who liked extra reassurance that their bottles would not spill, the same paper carried an advertisement for both gold 'Breast hooks' and plain stay hooks.[229]

Fashions changed with kaleidoscopic speed—'high heels are much more the rage' announced *The Times* in 1796, when only a year or two before flat heels had been in. But it was not only the unmistakable changes from the high heels of the mid 1750s, or the flat heels of the early 1780s and back to high in the mid 1790s; there were endless other adjustments to colour, shape, material, and accessories. Toes went from sharp pointed to round pointed to square toed, as remorselessly as they do in the twentieth century, and at roughly the same speed. The size of buckles could change dramatically almost overnight: she used 'to fasten her shoe with a circle scarcely larger than a bird's eye, and since, she has fastened it with a parallelogram as large as the buckle of a crack-spring'.[230] And there were moments of fashion indecision, such as when the *London Chronicle* reported in 1762 that 'as to their shoe-heels, ladies go just as they did, some as broad as a teacup's brim, some as narrow as the china circle the cup stands on'.

As the provincial press now kept the country so accurately informed, the provincial shopkeeper had to keep in touch. Such rapid changes did wonders for sales and constantly boosted demand. What hard work did too slowly, fashionable obsolescence could do in a trice. It could turn over stock more quickly, extend sales more widely and create demand which would otherwise not have existed. Women trembled for news of a changing hemline, a change in the shape of a shoe or the style of a bonnet. A prized garment could become unwearable almost overnight and the provincial shopkeepers, if up to date with the latest fashion and provided with a suitable stock, could replenish their suddenly outmoded wardrobes.

It was for this reason that Jane Austen expected even her village shopkeeper to 'go to town' to lay in fresh stocks of the materials then in fashion to satisfy the local customers.[231] It was for this reason that Mrs. Gaskell's shopkeeper in *Cranford*—a mere cheesemonger-cum-milliner—claimed that he always went straight to London to buy the latest fashions. While in the early 1780s

---

[228] *Boston Evening Post*, 1770.
[229] See C. Cunnington and P. Cunnington, *Handbook of English Costume in the Eighteenth Century* (1957), p. 402.
[230] *Ipswich Journal*, 1787.
[231] A. Adburgham, *Shops and Shopping, 1800–1914* (1964), pp. 5–9.

Elizabeth Towsey, who kept a little millinery and haberdashery shop in Chester, travelled regularly to London to buy the very latest fashions and immediately announced their arrival in the local newspaper. Since the journey took six days each way it shows an impressive belief in the hold of fashion even over distant Chester. Mrs. Towsey's letters and bills survive to show how widely and discriminatingly she shopped in London, with different suppliers for gloves, ribbons and 'modes of all sorts'; her forewoman had to sample the goods on sale in dozens of London suppliers just to get something 'particularly pretty in the ribbon way'.[232]

For want of the required research little is known about the individual techniques of the smaller shopkeepers. We know of course that many advertised their royal patronage as eagerly and prominently as Wedgwood and Bentley. Many used local newspaper advertisements, others used their own colourful personalities as an advertisement to attract trade. Martin von Butchell, one time pupil of John Hunter, earned himself an 'enormously lucrative' practice (as a doctor-turned-dentist and seller of medicine) by advertising *himself*—the eccentricity of his manners and his extraordinary costume. We are told by contemporaries that he 'astonished all beholders' by his methods of self advertisement. It was 'his custom to ride on a white pony which he sometimes painted all purple and sometimes with spots'.[233] In Hogarth's *Execution of an Idle Apprentice* of 1747 one can see another individual salesman who used his own extreme of fashion to advertise his wares. To attract attention to the gingerbread he was selling he appeared in an imitation of court dress, lace ruffled shirt, gold-laced and feathered hat. These were little more than individual exploitation of the traditional street cries or the public advertisement of age old skills—like the ratcatchers and itinerant gelders who advertised their services with special shoulder sashes (ornamented with rats for one and horseshoes for the other)[234] to make sure they were not overlooked.

Many shopkeepers did better than this, inundating their customers with specially printed trade cards, shop bills and individual advertisements of surprising ingenuity and imaginative quality.[235] Not all sales techniques were as obvious as the use of a purple pony. Some of the more subtle ones were meant to be concealed from their customers and have as a result all too often remained hidden from historians—even those which were practised very widely. Even the humble eighteenth-century shopkeeper can be shown to have been the master of methods of boosting sales which are, all too often, confidently attributed to the ingenuity of twentieth-century commerce.

The concept of the loss leader, for example, was well established amongst

[232] See M. D. Willcock (ed.), *Browns and Chester: Portrait of a Shop 1780–1946* (1947).
[233] R. S. Kirby, *Wonderful and Scientific Museum* (1893). Quoted in P. Cunnington and C. Lucas, *Occupational Costume* (1967), pp. 380–1.
[234] Contemporary illustrations show a ratcatcher of 1803 carrying a ferret in one and a cage of rats in the other; while the gelder announced his presence by blowing a horn.
[235] See below, Packwood, pp. 146–94.

eighteenth-century shopkeepers. As Campbell wrote in 1747 'A custom has prevailed among Grocers to sell Sugars for the Prime Cost, and [they] are out of Pocket by the Sale'. The losses were not inconsiderable: 'The Expence for some Shops in *London* for the single Article of Paper and Pack-Thread for Sugars amounts to Sixty or Seventy Pounds *per Annum*', and there was also the cost of 'their Labour in breaking and weighing it out'.[236] The intention (as it still is today) was to attract customers with this loss leader and then induce them to buy 'other Commodities' (thereby boosting the shop keeper's turnover) on which they would have to 'pay extravagant Prices'[237] (thereby boosting the shopkeeper's profits). Many of the lesser known advertisers used money-back-if-not-satisfied policies which was for long attributed to the commercial ingenuity of American businessmen in the nineteenth century.

The greatest entrepreneurs were, of course, the masters of a greater range of commercial techniques. But the fact that self-service schemes, inertia-selling campaigns, product-differentiation policies, market segmentation and massive advertising schemes are primarily associated with the entrepreneurial élite does not mean that the mass of eighteenth-century traders had not mastered some surprisingly modern commercial techniques themselves. When one recalls for how long the salesmanship and the marketing techniques of even the great much-studied masters of eighteenth-century business were neglected, and even denied, there is little room for complacent dismissal of the likely skills of what Defoe called 'merchants, shopkeepers, employers of others in trades', a group which Defoe regarded as far larger than those employed in actual manufacturing. England was already a commercialized society by 1800. But like its twin the consumer society, which was born and recognized (if not formally christened) in the eighteenth century, it was to continue to grow and expand in the nineteenth century. The actual number of shops in the provinces was to grow dramatically between 1820 and 1850, as Dr. Alexander has shown, but the pattern of retailing methods for a consumer society was already established.[238]

* * *

The *results* of their commercial endeavours were easier to recognize than the commercial techniques they used to bring those results about. When von Archenholz argued that no other nation in Europe could match the English in 'luxury of dress and apparel'[239] he was voicing a common opinion. The tumult of late eighteenth-century fashion was difficult to miss. Contemporaries were in no doubt that 'a fondness for Dress' was the characteristic

---

[236] R. Campbell, *The London Tradesman* (1747), pp. 188-9.
[237] Ibid., p. 189.
[238] David Alexander, *Retailing in England during the Industrial Revolution* (1970), pp. 89-109.
[239] J. W. von Archenholz, op. cit., pp. 75-83.

'folly of the age'.[240] This 'Folly' was described as 'so epidemic' that many spent all they earned on 'Ribbands, Ruffles, Necklaces, Fans, Hoop-Petticoats and all those Superfluities in Dress'.[241] As the century progressed such accounts became more and more numerous. Whether they complained of fashions being *'retailed out'* to industrious tradesmen in 1773, or of 'a spirit of extravagance' being *'diffused* among the lower orders' in 1782, or of 'the contagion of luxury' being *'spread* by example among the lower ranks of society' in 1785;[242] they all agreed that a process of ever-widening social diffusion was spreading the ability to follow the latest fashions. 'Apeing the fashions' of the social elite was held to be 'as infectious by Example, as the Plague itself by Contact'.[243]

Arcadius described the general process in 1773 as 'even the lower class, both in town and country are so much infected with this preposterous ambition that all ranks and degrees of men seem to be on the point of being confounded'.[244] Vicesimus Knox described the detailed effects on fashion in 1782 as 'The lower ranks will imitate (the new modes) as soon as they have discovered the innovation. A hat, a coat, a shoe deemed fit to be worn only by a great grand-sire is no sooner put on by a dictator of fashion, than it ... is generally adopted from the first lord of the Treasury to the apprentice from Houndsditch.'[245]

Source after source informs us that the rural poor in 1782 'pant to imitate' the London fashions, that 'the girls in the country' were inspired in 1791 with 'the most longing desires' to participate in them; that 'the plough boys' and 'the cowherds ... desert their dirt and drudgery and swarm up to London (to) wear fine clothes', that 'the wives and daughters of low tradesmen are infected by the same rage of displaying ... absurd extravagance'.[246] Other sources spell out the fashionable consequences, marvelling at such 'poor, awkward, clumsy creatures' as *Nanny Ginger* being transformed by London fashions and appearing 'all bedizened over from top to toe with silks and sattins and laces, and fine cloaths, as grand I warrant you, as any princess in the land'.[247] As Soame Jenyns wryly put it 'the *valet de chambre* cannot be distinguished from his master, but by being better drest, and Joan, who used to be but *as good as my lady in the dark* is now by no means inferior to her in the daylight'.[248] As Von Archenholz wrote later in 1791, 'As to a *Lady's Maid*, the eye of the most skilful connoisseur can scarcely distinguish

---

[240] Davis, *Friendly Advice to Industrious and Frugal Persons,* (1817), p. 28.
[241] See J. J. Hecht, op. cit., p. 289.
[242] John Arbuthnot, *Inquiry into the ... Present Price of Provisions* (1773), p. 49; *London Chronicle* (1782) LII, 287a; *Manufacturers Improper Subjects of Taxation* (1785), p. 12.
[243] Henry Fielding, op. cit., p. 6.
[244] *London Chronicle* (1773), XXXIV, p. 213a.
[245] *The Works of Vicesimus Knox* (1824), I, p. 374.
[246] *London Chronicle* 1782, LII, 287a; Archenholz, op. cit., p. 19; Tobias Smollett, 'Humphry Clinker', *Works*, VII, pp. 108 and 41–2.
[247] *London Packet*, 31 January–2 February 1780, No. 1501.
[248] *London Chronicle* (1765), XVII, p. 300a.

her from the mistress. The appearance of a waiting woman is that of an opulent and fashionable person'.[249] The complaints about the disappearance of 'those becoming marks whereby the classes were formerly distinguished' were legion. Those looking back over the changes which had taken place in their lifetime almost invariably stressed the great change in fashionable consumption.[250]

The phenomenon was, of course, most marked and most noticed in London, and after London in the provincial towns, first the fashionable spas and then the rest, until it penetrated even into the villages and the farmhouses of Georgian Britain. The speed of the geographical spread of fashion, as well as its range, had increased dramatically. Whereas Addison could write in 1711 that 'the rural beaus are not yet out of the fashion that took place at the time of the Revolution', and that in the West Country 'the fashions of Charles II's reign were still worn', by the end of the eighteenth century the time-lag between London and the provinces was being measured in weeks and months rather than in decades. The excesses of fashionable behaviour were, of course, most spectacularly demonstrated by the rich, and after them by the middle class, but again I hope I have displayed enough evidence to show that it could penetrate even further than that. One does not have to believe that the costly perukes worn by even the meanest day labourers at their work, which so astonished the Swedish observer Pehr Kalm,[251] were common, or that most agricultural workers dressed like those portrayed by Stubbs, or that every 'man pushing a wheelbarrow ... has his white underclothing' and 'hardly a beggar can be espied who doesn't wear a clean shirt under his tatters' as Carl Moritz claimed in 1782,[252] to realize that the consumption of fashion had risen to quite unprecedented levels. The general evidence makes it difficult to ignore, the statistics of aggregate demand make it difficult to deny. The concern to explain it in terms of social emulation and class competition and emulative spending points persuasively towards the downwards spread of fashion and the social extension of the market. That much has been conceded. David Landes, as always in the vanguard of perceptive comment, said in 1969 of the imitation of city consumption habits by those in the country: 'This internal "demonstration effect" has been probably the most important factor—more important than the increase in income—in developing a market of high consumption ... that is a body able and willing to buy above the line of necessity'.[253] But his text is still dominated by the traditional preoccupation with the technological side of the Industrial Revolution.

---

[249] *Op. cit.*, p. 208.
[250] *The Memoirs of James Spershott,* ed. F. W. Steer (Chichester, 1962), p. 10.
[251] Pehr Kalm, *Account of his Visit to England ... in 1748* (1892).
[252] C. P. Moritz, *Journeys of a German in England in 1782* (trans. and ed. R. Nettel, 1965) pp. 33-4.
[253] D. S. Landes, *The Unbound Prometheus* (Cambridge, 1969), p. 243.

Many answers remain unsupplied to important problems in the nature of demand. Theories of demand routinely accept that 'consumer tastes are socially determined'.[254] Sociologists from Veblen onwards have long been eloquent on the significance of fashionable wants as an incentive to increased expenditure. But the traditional historical response is still to see the expansion of the market as little more than an automatic reflex action in response to the increase in supply. Historians have been far more interested in explaining how and why supply increased than in explaining how and why the products of that rising tide of industrial production were absorbed by the market. Preoccupied by the aggregate statistics they have given too little attention to the qualitative and behavioural changes which underlie them and indeed partly explain them. As Eric Jones has perceptively noted, 'Analytically there is no difference between income-induced and taste-induced increase in consumption; in either case the demand curve shifts outwards. Historically there is a world of difference; if changes in taste affected only the form or construction of commodities and not their value, they would still be crucial to understanding the configuration of economic history.'[255] If one believes, as I do, that the taste-induced changes provided a substantial boost to the size and value as well as the character of demand, then they assume an even greater significance.

Professor Jones poses a series of important unanswered questions in this field. 'Did demand *automatically* absorb all output with every rightward shift of the supply curve?' 'Did this taste for former inessentials prove ineradicably attractive so that they were built into the pattern of consumption?' 'Were manufacturers automata who kept on producing because output could always be sold at a profit and who needed to take no thought for sales promotion?' 'Could aggregate consumption be induced to grow by the manipulations of fashions?'[256] In deploying some of the detailed evidence of the commercial manipulation and exploitation of fashion in the eighteenth century I have tried to suggest some answers to these questions.

I have tried to show how inertia-selling campaigns created demand for English goods which would otherwise have remained unreachable; how new methods of display excited not only occasional impulse buying, but more sustained and regular buying than could possibly have occurred without them; how new methods of advertising excited a new eagerness to consume, and made known and desirable goods which would otherwise have languished unbought. I have tried to show how the manipulation of fashion made many consumer goods obsolete long before mere use would have made them so; how the exploitation of social competition created demands which would

---

[254] J. S. Dusenberry, 'Income Consumption Relations and the Implications', *Readings in Macroeconomics*, ed. M. G. Mueller (New York, 1967), p. 74. He sees consumer behaviour as 'a function of the ratio of his [the consumer's] expenditure to some weighted average of the expenditures of others with whom he comes into contact'.

[255] E. L. Jones, loc. cit., p. 200.

[256] Jones, loc. cit., p. 201.

otherwise have remained dormant; how new aggressive methods of selling penetrated into areas of demand previously untapped. I have tried to show how the many new places and agents of sale brought goods within the reach of classes never before offered such opportunities for buying, and made available a greater range of goods than ever before; how the manipulation of social emulation made men pursue 'luxuries' where they had previously bought 'decencies', and 'decencies' where they had previously bought only 'necessities'; how, in fact, fashion and its exploiters raised men's levels of 'pecuniary decency'.

The fashion doll, the fashion print, the fashion magazine, the fashion advertisement, the fashion shops, the great manufacturers making fashion goods and the hordes of those selling them were all agents in pursuit of new levels of consumption from an ever-widening market.

Those manufacturers who produced goods for mass consumption needed to reach markets never previously tapped. One must not forget that the prosperity of Lancashire cotton manufacturers, London brewers, Sheffield cutlers, Staffordshire potters, the toy makers of Birmingham—and the fortunes of the woollen, linen and silk industries—were based on sales to a mass market. Fashion was an essential, if not sufficient, key to open up the necessary access to that market. As such it deserves more detailed attention than economic historians have chosen to give it. As Braudel has realized, fashion is too important to be left to the antiquarians. 'Costume is a language. It is no more misleading than the graphs drawn by demographers and price historians'.[257]

If we follow Braudel's advice and see fashion as an important key to understanding both society and the economy, then a study of the tumult of fashion of late eighteenth-century England may help to unlock some of the mysteries still surrounding that period's remarkable economic growth. Certainly those concerned with selling and marketing and distributing their goods gave it their concerned and concentrated attention. 'Fashion' was seen by many of them as being 'far more important than merit'. So it commanded as much of their time and energy as did the traditional preoccupations with capital, labour and production. They were fully convinced of the commercial potential of fashion and they were determined to exploit it in their sales campaigns. Perhaps the only way fully to demonstrate the quality of those convictions and the quality of their commercial manipulation of fashion (and to demonstrate its economic importance in both the large-scale industrial concern and the small scale commercial one) is to examine in detail some individual case studies. In that way the general process of commercialization can be more precisely exemplified and explained, and the full flavour of the English experience of that process be appreciated.

At first sight Josiah Wedgwood and George Packwood could hardly be

---

[257] Fernand Braudel, *Capitalism and Material Life 1400–1800* (1973), p. 235.

more different in terms of the demands they have made on historian's time, but there are hidden similarities. For while Packwood's extraordinary advertising flair has been completely ignored, Wedgwood's extraordinary capacity as a salesman has also been neglected, even denied, by the traditional historiography. Yet they both provide wonderfully vivid illustrations of the commercialization of England in the late eighteenth century—as the next two chapters attempt to show.

By demonstrating the level of commercial skills involved in that process, and by exemplifying the eager and pervasive consumer response to those skills, their careers help to explain why Sir John Hawkins could write, of late eighteenth-century England, that 'a new fashion pervades the whole of this our island almost as instantaneously as a spark of fire illuminates a mass of gunpowder'.[258]

---

[258] Sir John Hawkins, *Life of Samuel Johnson* (1787), p. 262.

CHAPTER THREE

Josiah Wedgwood and the Commercialization of the Potteries

The demand for this s^d *Creamcolour,* alias *Queensware,* ... still increases. It is really amazing how rapidly the use of it has spread over the whole Globe, & how universally it is liked. How much of this general use, & estimation, is owing to the mode of its introduction & how much to its real utility & beauty? are questions in which we may be a good deal interested for the government of our future Conduct. The reasons are too obvious to be longer dwelt upon. For instance, if a Royal, or Noble Introduction be as necessary to the sale of an Article of Luxury, as real Elegance & beauty, then the Manufacturer, if he consults his own inter! will bestow as much pains, & expence too, if necessary, in gaining the former of these advantages, as he wo^d in bestowing the latter.

Josiah Wedgwood, 1767.

Fashion is infinitely superior to *merit* ... and it is plain from a thousand instances if you have a favourite child you wish the public to fondle and take notice of, you have only to make choice of proper sponcers.

Josiah Wedgwood, 1779.

It is difficult for twentieth-century man to understand the excitement that was generated by pottery and porcelain in the eighteenth century. To a society accustomed to regard crockery as a humble and ubiquitous accompaniment to everyday life, it is not easy to imagine the craving to possess it which gripped so many layers of eighteenth-century society. Most people know of the way in which the Dutch in the seventeenth century were caught in a fever of speculation over the possession and price of tulip bulbs, but very few are familiar with the far more important and far more pervasive china mania of the eighteenth century.

In the face of such ignorance, a consumer boom in pottery may seem an unlikely event. The aristocracy of England blocking the streets outside Wedgwood's London showrooms in their eagerness to buy his latest pottery; 'a violent vase madness breaking out amongst the Irish'; an 'epidemical' sickness to possess his wares amongst the upper and middling ranks; an extension of the market so profound that 'common Wedgwood' came within the reach of 'common people'[1]—such excitement strikes a surprising note to

---

[1] I am greatly indebted to Josiah Wedgwood and Sons Ltd. of Barlaston, Stoke-on-Trent, for permission to quote from the manuscripts in the Wedgwood Museum (subsequently referred to as WMSS). This chapter draws heavily on material previously used in my articles 'Josiah Wedgwood: An Eighteenth Century Entrepreneur in Salesmanship and Marketing Technique', *Economic History Review,* 2nd series, XII, No. 3 (April 1960), pp. 408-33; 'Josiah

a society so accustomed to the almost universal possession of ample crockery that a hunger to possess it, a compulsive need to own the latest fashions in it, is difficult to imagine.

In eighteenth-century England such excitement was less surprising. The simple fact that most people had possessed so little pottery—and were increasingly presented with both the ability to afford it[2] and ample opportunity to acquire it—offers some explanation of the depth to which the new consumer spending reached down the social scale. The very novelty of the consumer boom explains some of its hectic, hysterical nature, just as the eagerness to consume of previously deprived classes explains the mass nature of its ultimate market.

But novel and dramatic and far reaching as it was, the consumer boom in pottery was not entirely unheralded. The earlier excitement which had surrounded its up-market relative, porcelain, makes it easier to understand.

For by 1750 all Europe was already in the grip of a china fever. Royalty led the way. Augustus, King of Poland and Elector of Saxony, established Meissen in 1710; Louis XV of France sponsored the manufacture of china at Vincennes in 1747 and later in 1756 at Sèvres; the King of Naples set up a factory at Capo di Monte, and later at Buen Retiro near Madrid. The nobility were quick to follow the royal lead. 'A porcelain factory' said Karl Eugen, Duke of Württemberg, 'is an indispensable accompaniment of splendour and magnificence'.[3] He 'thought that no prince of his rank should be without one, a sentiment that was echoed throughout Germany in the 1750s. Four electors—Mainz, The Palatinate, Bavaria and Brandenburg—possessed flourishing factories, in output if not in profit, at Höchst, Frankenthal, Nymphenburg and Berlin ... elsewhere dukes, princes, bishops, *landgraves* and *margraves* were all in china, right down to the tiny principalities of Nassau-Saarbrücken and Pfalz-Zweibrücken'.[3] Few made any profit and most made considerable losses. But princely prestige demanded them, just as aristocratic prestige demanded that the aristocracy of Europe should purchase their products. They bought to such effect that, in J. H. Plumb's words, 'No mania for material objects had ever been so widespread, so general to the rich of all nations.'[4]

Wedgwood and Thomas Bentley: An Inventor-Entrepreneur Partnership in the Industrial Revolution', *Transactions of the Royal Historical Society*, vol. 14, (1964), pp. 1–33; and 'The World Market for Eighteenth Century Creamware', *Proceedings of the Wedgwood International Seminar* (1969), pp. 1–29. It is substantially extended, revised and reshaped and includes some new evidence relating to the size of Wedgwood's exports, taken from an article 'Home versus Foreign Demand in the Industrial Revolution: The "Myth" of the Wedgwood Exports'. This was accepted for publication by the *Economic History Review* but withheld for use elsewhere.

[2] Neil McKendrick, 'Home Demand and Economic Growth: A New View of the Role of Women and Children in the Industrial Revolution', *Historical Perspectives: Studies in English Thought and Society*, ed. Neil McKendrick (1974), pp. 152–210.
[3] J. H. Plumb, 'The Royal Porcelain Craze', *In the Light of History*, (1972), p. 57.
[4] Ibid., p. 58.

Conditions such as these provided entrepreneurs as perceptive as Wedgwood and Bentley with rich commercial opportunities to exploit. Wedgwood delighted in the compulsive pursuit of perfection in porcelain. He gloried in the astronomical prices charged by Louis XV at Sèvres. He heard with glee of the spectacular losses incurred and the royal subsidies which repaired those losses, because he realized that from such prices, such royal involvement, came prestige, a powerful social cachet, which could with skilful marketing be exploited to his own advantage and profit. Few men rode the currents of fashion more adroitly than Wedgwood and Bentley, and few realized more quickly what a powerful up-draft could come from a royal patron. Best of all was 'the fact that Louis XV, the arbiter of Europe's taste, had given the royal imprimatur to porcelain. Indeed Louis did more than this. He did not think it beneath his dignity to conduct personally an annual sale of his factory's products'.[5] The king himself was prepared to act as his salesman, to auction Sèvres himself. 'Nothing better indicates the reverence, the idolatry, that the European aristocracy lavished on china than that the Most Christian King, who could not socially meet a bourgeois, should have been willing to act as its huckster.'[5] The effects of such a royal patronage and promotion were not lost on the English. No English king founded a porcelain factory. But there was no lack of individual enterprise. For the English aristocracy wanted what their European cousins wanted, and many an eager entrepreneur rushed to take on the appalling costs of trying to satisfy their wants. For porcelain was highly valued by the fashionable world of mid-Georgian England. Fashionable women valued it, if not above all things, at least to quote Macaulay 'as much as they valued their monkeys, and much more than they valued their husbands.'[6] They were willing to pay handsomely for the pleasure of possessing it. Dr. Johnson and Boswell were not alone in commenting, after a visit to Derby, that 'the Derby China is very pretty, but ... so dear that perhaps silver vessels of the same capacity may be sometimes bought at the same price'.[7] Lesser factories such as those at Plymouth and Bristol offered tea-sets at '£7.0s.0d. to £12.12s.0d. and upward'[8] at a time when an average workman's wage would be substantially less than a pound a week. Yet such were production problems and such their costs that many porcelain factories faced great financial difficulties—Bow, Longton Hall and Chelsea had to close, Derby and Lowestoft came close to ruin, and many lesser factories went bankrupt.

The significance of such costly enthusiasms was not lost on Wedgwood. He realised that a powerful potential demand was there, that prices were

---

[5] Ibid., p. 63.
[6] It is no accident that this period saw the founding of so many of England's porcelain factories—Chelsea, Derby, Worcester and Bow, and a host of others.
[7] Samuel Johnson to Mrs. Thrale, 20 September 1777.
[8] Admittedly these were described as 'highly ornamented' and they offered other simple, less complex tea-sets at 'various prices as low as £2.2.0' but that was still three times an average workman's weekly wage.

high and the market was accustomed to paying them, that with skilful handling the market could be greatly extended. But more was needed than this to explain the consumer boom which followed. It required commercial and industrial skills of a very high order to take advantage of the market possibilities—to divert the enthusiasm from porcelain to pottery, from the aristocracy to the rest of society, from high prices that led to restricted sales and the bankruptcy court to high prices which attracted a mass market and bumper profits. It was Wedgwood's commercial triumph to turn that pursuit of ceramic luxury by the rich into the pursuit of useful (albeit fashionably desirable) pottery for the many. It required, in fact, one of the most brilliant and sustained campaigns in the history of consumer exploitation. To manipulate and to extend the market opportunities was not as simple as many historians have supposed.

* * *

When Josiah Wedgwood was born in 1730, the Staffordshire potters sold their wares almost solely in Staffordshire. Their goods found their sale in the local market towns,[9] and occasionally, carried by pedlars and hawkers or on the backs of the wretched packmen of the eighteenth century, they reached further afield[10]—to Leicester, Liverpool and Manchester. To sell in London in any quantity was rare,[11] to sell in Europe virtually unknown.[12] Yet by 1795 Wedgwood had broken through this local trade of fairs and pedlars to an international market based on elegant showrooms and ambassadorial connections; he had become the Queen's potter and sold to every regal house in Europe. His wares were known in China, India and America. Other potters had prospered but Wedgwood had flourished above all others. Born the twelfth son of a mediocre potter with only the promise—and a promise never fulfilled—of a £20 inheritance, he died in 1795 worth £500,000 and the owner of one of the finest industrial concerns in England. His name was known all over the world. It had become a force in industry, commerce, science and politics. It dominated the potting industry. Men no longer spoke of 'common pewter' but of 'common Wedgwood'.[13]

Such fabulous success is not easily explained. It certainly cannot be explained in terms of Wedgwood's gifts alone. For Wedgwood was fortunate

---

[9] Cf. Pitt Agric. Survey, pp. 2–3, 166, for list of the 24 markets.

[10] Cf. T. Whieldon: Memorandum Book. c. 1740-52, p. 78. An unusually distant order 'Mr. Green at Hovingham, Eylsham Norfolk. Aug. 11'.

[11] Ibid., p. 81. 'For Miss Ferney ... directed to Capt. Blake in Surrey St. in the Strand.' As Lorna Weatherill has shown, by the mid-1750s this had changed and John Wedgwood's Account Book records that most of his ware was sent to London, but this was a quarter of a century after Wedgwood was born. See L. Weatherill, *The Pottery Trade and North Staffordshire, 1660–1760* (1971), pp. 81–3.

[12] John Baddeley's records show that substantial quantities were sent to Alexander Parke of Amsterdam between 1753 and 1767 (see J. Mallet, John Baddeley of Shelton, part 1, *Transactions of the English Ceramic Circle* (1966), VI. pp. 126–7) but there is no evidence of such traffic in 1730.

[13] Cf. *The Black Dwarf*: 17 September 1817.

in the period in which he lived. Born poor into the squalor and dirt of a peasant industry,[14] one might have thought him unlucky. Superficially he was. The ware was still crude, the market still local, the roads almost impassable, and the workmen as likely to go drinking and wenching as to appear at work. Worse conditions for industrial expansion might seem difficult to imagine. But in all this were the signs of improvement. The technical discoveries of Astbury, Booth and Whieldon had opened up new opportunities for expansion and improvement; steam power was soon to open up more. Wesley was leading men to more methodical lives, Brindley and Bridgewater were building their canals, and agitation over the state of the roads had already started. By the 1750s the market had already grown: most of John Wedgwood's sales were to London and his account book shows that a far wider national market was now available than when Wedgwood was born a quarter of a century before. It was in this period—between 1739 and 1760—that the records of the Weaver Navigation show a six-fold increase in the carriage of pottery; and that the coastal trade in pottery grew in importance;[15] and the exports to the colonies took on a new significance. When Josiah was serving his apprenticeship, such movements were only in their infancy, but with each year they gathered strength and support. He still had to fight reaction. But in the 1760s he found allies he would have looked for in vain in the 1730s. Moreover the demand for earthenware was steadily growing. Tea-drinking—rapidly becoming a national characteristic—and beer drinking—already well established as such—were both increasing. These, and the more fashionable drinks of coffee and hot chocolate, greatly increased the demand. Further, the growth of incomes, the shift of tastes, particularly of the 'middle classes' and the expansion of overseas trade provided market opportunities in constantly mounting numbers.[16] But most important of all, the rise in population represented a vast and growing market with ever-expanding needs. It was Staffordshire that satisfied them. For plate was too expensive, pewter too scarce, and porcelain too fragile to compete with the versatile pot. In these conditions the potteries were bound to prosper.

The reasons why Wedgwood prospered above all others have proved more elusive. Most historians have argued that his discoveries—green glaze, creamware, jasper and black basalt—won him technical supremacy over his rivals; and that his factory organization and division of labour—his stated desire 'to make such machines of the Men as cannot err'[17]—confirmed his superior quality. But this alone is not sufficient to explain his supremacy. For his inventions were quickly copied and his quality easily reproduced.

[14] Josiah Wedgwood: *An Address to the Young Inhabitants of the Pottery:* Etruria. 27 March 1783, p. 21.
[15] T. S. Willan, *The English Coasting Trade, 1600-1750* (1938), and 'Weaver Navigation Records', Cheshire C.R.O., V. 1-6; see Weatherill, op. cit., pp. 80-1.
[16] Asa Briggs: *The Age of Improvement*, p. 28.
[17] WMSS. E.18265-25. J(osiah) W(edgwood) to T(homas B(entley), 9 Oct. (1769).

They won him immediate attention but they could not keep it unless he could afford to sell his ware more cheaply than his rivals. This historians have cheerfully assumed. The statement by Professor Ashton that 'it was by intensifying the division of labour that Wedgwood brought about the reduction of cost which enabled his pottery to find markets in all parts of Britain, and also of Europe and America'[18] is merely the most recent and most authoritative of a long line of such views—Meteyard,[19] Jewitt,[20] Church,[21] Smiles,[22] Burton,[23] and Trevelyan[24] all produce the same argument. They note the efficiency of Wedgwood's factory system, his avoidance of waste, the drop in breakages through the use of canals, the cheapening of transport charges because of canals and turnpike roads, and conclude that Wedgwood's wares were obviously cheaper than his rivals. Unfortunately they were not. His goods were always considerably more expensive than those of his fellow potters: he regularly sold his goods at double the normal prices,[25] not infrequently at three times as high, and he reduced them only when he wished to reap the rewards of bigger sales on a product that he had already made popular and fashionable at a high price,[26] or when he thought the margin between his prices and those of the rest of the pottery had become too great. In 1778, for instance, he introduced a cheaper teapot to cut down the huge price gap which had arisen between his prices and those of Palmer and Neale, a rival local firm, writing, 'Mr Palmer sells his three sizes of black fluted teapots at 18/- the long doz.^{ns} that is @ 9.^{d} 1/- & 18^d Per pot which we sell at 50 or 60/-!'[27]

There are ample reasons why the usual explanations did not apply. Canals, for instance, may have cheapened his goods, but they cheapened all other potters' goods as well; and though division of labour made for cheap production, the cost of experiments and the many failures they automatically entailed,[28] the expense of commissions to artists,[29] and the high wages that Wedgwood paid,[30] more than cancelled this out. But more important than this was Wedgwood's decision not to compete with his rivals in price. It was never his practice nor his intention to sell cheaply. As he wrote towards the

---

[18] T. S. Ashton: *The Industrial Revolution 1760–1830* (1948), p. 81.
[19] Eliza Meteyard; *The Life of Josiah Wedgwood*; 2 vols. (1865–66).
[20] Llewelyn Jewitt; *The Wedgwoods* (1865).
[21] A. H. Church; *Josiah Wedgwood* (1894).
[22] Samuel Smiles, *Life of Wedgwood* (1894).
[23] William Burton, *Josiah Wedgwood and his Pottery* (1922).
[24] G. M. Trevelyan, *The Social History of England*.
[25] WMSS. E.18457-25. JW to TB. 14 April 1773 & WMSS. Leith Hill Place MSS. JW to TB 21 & 22 April 1771.
[26] WMSS. E.18392-25. JW to TB. 23 Aug. 1772.
[27] WMSS. E.18814-25. JW to TB. 25 Feb. 1778.
[28] Wedgwood fired over 10,000 pieces of jasper before he achieved perfection.
[29] They included artists of the stature of John Flaxman, George Stubbs, and William Hackwood. Cf. Neil McKendrick: 'Josiah Wedgwood and George Stubbs', *History Today*, VII, No. 8. (August 1957), p. 514.
[30] To deal with this in detail is beyond the scope of this chapter.

end of his life, 'it has always been my aim to improve the quality of the articles of my manufacture, rather than to lower their price',[31] and, more important than his statements,[32] his price lists fully confirm this. His selling policy relied on quality and above all on fashionable appeal, and Wedgwood believed that high prices had an integral part to play in such a policy, writing 'a great price is at first necessary to make the vases esteemed *Ornaments for Palaces*'.[33] He did not charge his pottery at what it was worth (from the point of view of production costs) but at what the nobility would pay for it.[34]

Some idea of how this policy developed can be gained from a letter he wrote to his partner, Bentley, in 1771. Faced with a mounting stock he was overjoyed at the prospect of a large order[35] from Russia: 'This Russ.^{n} trade comes very opportunely for the useful ware, & may prevent me lower^g the prices here, though it may be expedient to lower the prices of the Tableplates to 4/- Per doz in London, as our people are lowering them to 2/3 or 2/- here. Mr Baddeley who makes the best ware of any of the Potters here, & an Ovenfull of it Per Diem has led the way, & the rest must follow, unless he can be prevail'd upon to raise it again, which is not at all probable, though we are to see him tomorrow, about a doz.^{n} of us, for that purpose ... Mr Baddeley has reduc'd the prices of the dishes to the prices of whitestone, ... In short the *General trade* seems to me to be going to ruin on the gallop—large stocks on hand both in London & the country, & little demand. The Potters seem sensible of their situation, & are quite in a Pannick for their trade, & indeed I think with great reason, for *low prices* must beget a *low quality* in the manufacture, which will beget *contempt,* which will beget *neglect,* & disuse, and there is an end of the trade. But if any one Warehouse, distinguish'd from the rest, will continue to keep up the quality of the Manufacture, or improve it, that House may perhaps *keep up its prices,*[36] & the *general evil,* will work a *particular* good to that house, & they may continue to sell *Queens ware at the usual prices,* when the rest of the trade can scarcely give it away. This seems to be all the chance we have, & we must double our dilligence here to give it effect. The same Idea may be applied to Ornaments, & the crisis in which a foreign vent for our goods will be the most singular service to us, is, whilst the General Manufacture is *degradeing,* the particular one *improving* 'till the difference is sufficiently apparent to strike the most common purchacers; & that crisis seems now to

[31] WMSS. E.8636-10. JW to Mr. Charles Twigg. 18 June 1787.
[32] The letter which he wrote to Lord Paget (E.18895-25, June 1, 1779) saying that he wished 'his profits rather to arise from a large consumption, than from a high price with diminished sale' which is quoted by Ralph M. Hower, *Journal of Economic and Business History*, vol. 4, no. 2, p. 306, is an exception which is not convincing in face of the mass of contradictory evidence in Wedgwood's letters to Bentley, e.g. E.18407-25, 19 Sept. 1772, and E.18770-25, 10 July '77.
[33] WMSS. E.18392-25. JW to TB. 23 Aug. 1772.
[34] WMSS. E.18307-25. JW to TB. 4 June (1770).
[35] It amounted to some £4,000.
[36] My italics.

be at hand, which I am very sorry for, but it seems to me inevitable; for I am certain the Potters cannot afford to work their goods in a Masterly manner, & sell them at the prices they now do, & they will probably go lower still.'[37] He held the same view in 1773 when 'the whole of the Pottery'[38] agreed to lower their prices a further 20 per cent. For though he anxiously asked, 'Do you think we can stand our ground in London @ 5/ P (doz) for plates, when everybody around us will be selling @ 2/6 & 3/-?',[38] and discussed the possibility of having two prices, he eventually decided against cuts of any kind, writing 'We must endeavour to make our goods better if possible—other people will be getting worse, and thereby our distinction will be more evident.'[38] And he took this decision despite the fact that other potters' prices were by now '1/3 of our price'.[38]

In taking this decision Wedgwood committed himself to new methods of selling his ware, for he not only decided on high prices, but also determined on large sales to a widespread market. He had quickly realized that at the prices he charged quality alone would be sufficient only to win for him a limited and specialized market, and to confine his sales to a small and exclusive class. Moreover in the eighteenth century his improvements and inventions did not remain his monopoly for long. They were copied and reproduced—cheaply and in quantity. Every new invention that Wedgwood produced—green glaze, creamware, black basalt and jasper—was quickly copied;[39] every new idea—jasper cameos, intaglios and seals, tea trays, snuffboxes and knifehandles—was eagerly taken up; every new design —Etruscan painting, the Portland Vase and Flaxman's modelling— was avidly reproduced. And in every case the reproductions were cheaper. Even William Adams, perhaps the finest potter amongst Wedgwood's rivals, whose products equalled if they did not surpass Josiah's,[40] could undercut his prices by 20 per cent.[41] The result was inevitable. Those customers who had been attracted by his novelty and his quality, reluctantly but nonetheless surely, left him for cheaper makers, writing like James Abernethy, 'I imagined that you was the only person that printed that sort of ware— but it seems that there are others that put up with smaller profits.'[42] Such comments occur over and over again in Wedgwood's early correspondence.

It was therefore not by novelty and originality alone that Wedgwood held his custom, nor was it solely by high quality. For his novelty did not survive

---

[37] WMSS. Leith Hill Place MS. JW to TB 21 & 22 April 1771.
[38] WMSS. E.18457-25. JW to TB. 14 April 1773.
[39] Creamware for instance—in its improved form virtually his own creation—was being made by 1784 by 25 potters in Burslem and Newcastle alone. Cf. Bailey's Western Dictionary for 1784. W. Mankowitz & R. G. Haggar, *Concise Encyclopaedia of English Pottery & Porcelain* (London, 1957), pp. 268-70.
[40] Ibid., p. 226, 'Turner's wares were "frequently equal in quality" to JW's', and W. B. Honey describes Adams' jasper as 'quite equal' to that of JW.
[41] Mankowitz & Haggar, op. cit., p. 4.
[42] WMSS. E.30554-5. J. Abernethy to JW, 2 Oct. 1763.

for long, and his high quality was not unrivalled. Both played an integral part in his sales policy, but they are not in themselves sufficient explanation of his success. He had the good sense to realize that he was not likely to invent pottery superior to his creamware, his black basalt, or his jasper. Having once achieved perfection in production, he must achieve perfection in sales and distribution. It was clear that Wedgwood must either cut his prices as his rivals did in the cut-throat race for the custom of an expanding market, or see some new distinction to mark off his wares from the rest of the pottery. He chose the latter course, and it is with these new methods that this chapter is mainly concerned: how Wedgwood won a world-wide demand, and how he invented the means of satisfying it.[43]

* * *

He did this partly by the capture of the world of fashion. For although Wedgwood had complete confidence in his wares—writing, 'wherever my wares find their way, they will command the first trade'—he also realized that '*Fashion* is infinitely superior to *merit* in many respects, and it is plain from a thousand instances that if you have a favourite child you wish the public to fondle & take notice of, you have only to make choice of proper sponcers [sic.].'[44] The sponsors he aimed to win for his pottery were the monarchy, the nobility, and the art connoisseurs—in fact, the leaders of fashion. He quickly realized that to make pots for the Queen of England was admirable advertisement. To become the Queen's Potter and to win the right to sell common earthenware as Queen's ware, was even better. As Wedgwood wrote: 'the demand for this s^d *Creamcolour*, alias, *Queensware*, ... still increases. It is really amazing how rapidly the use of it has spread over the whole Globe, & how universally it is liked. How much of this general use, & estimation, is owing to the mode of its introduction—& how much to its real utility & beauty ? are questions in which we may be a good deal interested for the government of our future Conduct. The reasons are too obvious to be longer dwelt upon. For instance, if a Royal, or Noble introduction be as necessary to the sale of an Article of Luxury, as real Elegance & beauty, then the Manufacturer, if he consults his own inter^t will bestow as much pains, & expence too, in gaining the former of these advantages, as he wo^d in bestowing the latter'.[45] Wedgwood was not a man to fail to consult his own interests. He took immediate action.

That Wedgwood sought such patronage has been categorically denied. Miss Meteyard for instance, wrote in tones of hushed approval, 'we have seen Mr. Wedgwood working silently onwards ... unsolicitous of patronage

---

[43] So that whatever the price merchants had to admit, as Boehler of Darmstadt did in 1789, that 'stamped with your name (your goods) will always find a ready sale anywhere'. And that is a single example from a chorus of such comments.
[44] WMSS. E.18898-26. JW to TB. 19 June 1779.
[45] WMSS. E.18167-25. JW to TB. (17 Sept. 1767).

... having laboured to invest the articles produced by his hand with an excellence and taste hitherto unknown, he left the natural results to their own time and place of fulfilment'.[46] She closes in defiance—and in capital letters—'IT WAS PATRONAGE WHICH SOUGHT THE GREAT POTTER: NOT THE GREAT POTTER PATRONAGE'.[47] It is an eloquent defence but unfortunately grossly untrue.[48] But in Miss Meteyard's *Life* eulogy strides across every page and criticism is scarcely allowed a footnote. And to her mind patronage-seeking was very definitely not praiseworthy. She was too well attuned to that attitude of her Victorian age which had condemned Millais and Frith for advertising soap,[49] to allow such methods to sully the name of her hero. She scarcely recognized that he had to market his goods at all. Only three pages out of some eleven hundred deal explicitly with how he sold and distributed his goods.

That Wedgwood did seek such patronage is indisputable. He went to endless trouble and expense to win the royal favour—the famous green and gold tea set was followed up by a box of patterns and a creamware dinner service, and by 1768 he was advertising his '*Royal Patronage*' in the *St. James's Chronicle* and 'in that morning paper which is mostly taken by the people of fashion'[50] to broadcast the opening of his new rooms. He did not let their support languish for want of attention, constantly urging Bentley, 'that a little push further might still be made with due decorum'.[51] In December 1770 Her Royal Highness the Princess Dowager was being waited upon,[52] and in 1771 he was scheming to become 'Potter to *His* Majesty' and 'Potter to the Prince of Wales'.[53] Nor did he neglect the younger members of the royal family, and by 1790 he had won the title of 'Potter to her Majesty & their Royal Highnesses the Duke of York & Albany & the Duke of Clarence'.[54] He did not hesitate to exploit it to the full, writing to congratulate his partner on his efforts with the Queen, 'you have sown the seeds of a plentiful & rich harvest, which we shall reap in due time ... Their majestys are very good indeed! I hope we shall not lose their favour, & promise ourselves the greatest advantage from such Royal Patronage, & the very peculiar attention they are pleased to bestow upon our productions.

[46] Eliza Meteyard, op. cit., I, pp. 368-9.
[47] Ditto.
[48] Apart from being untrue of the whole of JW's life, this statement also distorts the origins of the order for the Queen's tea-set. The order was offered to many potters before Wedgwood saw the potential value of accepting it.
[49] Marie Corelli in the *Sorrows of Satan* speaks of Millais as having 'degraded himself' when he painted 'the little green boy blowing bubbles of Pears' soap'. Cf. Neil McKendrick, 'Josiah Wedgwood and George Stubbs', loc. cit., p. 509.
[50] WMSS. L.17666-96. JW to Mr. Cox. 13 June 1768.
[51] WMSS. Leith Hill Place. JW to TB. 8 July 1771.
[52] WMSS. E.18334-25. JW to TB. 24 December 1770. Wedgwood was quite satisfied despite the small order because ''tis good to have an opening, & to be known, the former may increase [sic], & the latter cannot hurt us'.
[53] WMSS. Leith Hill Place. JW to TB. 8 July 1771.
[54] WMSS. E.1066-2. Printed Bill Head from Wedgwood. 24 Feb. 1790.

It was a good hint you gave them ... I hope it will work, & have its proper effect'.[55] On every bill head, every order form and every advertisement his titles were proudly displayed.[56] For he was confident that if he had the patronage of the great, he would have the custom of the world.

Having tapped or attempted to tap all the sources of royal patronage, he next broached the nobility and gentry. For he wished 'if possible (to) do in this as we have done in other things—begin at the *Head* first, & then proceed to the inferior members'.[57] Convinced of the value of a fashionable reception for his goods, he went to great trouble and expense to achieve it. Though he fully realized the cost, interruptions and poor immediate returns of special individual orders,[58] or 'Uniques'[59] as he called them, he willingly accepted expensive and difficult commissions. Other potters fought shy of such projects, Wedgwood and Bentley accepted every challenge. They welcomed commissions from Queen Charlotte for a specially designed tea-set which all potters had refused,[60] from George Stubbs for huge stoneware plaques of great technical difficulty,[61] and from Catherine the Great for a table service requiring 952 pieces and over a thousand original paintings.[62] Strictly uneconomical in themselves, the advertising value of these productions was huge.[63] In the same way, though on a lesser scale, he made pebbleware for Sir George Young,[64] cameo heads for the sons of Mrs. Crewe,[65] and printed ware for Lady Isabella Stanley.[66] For as Bentley wrote of the latter, 'Tho' this is trifling matter we must please these great Friends who are warm Patrons of this Manufacture'.[67] All of these orders were 'uniques'—they could never go into general production. They were made entirely for their advertising value, to win the patronage of the court and courtly circles; the friendship of the architects and the artistic world; the favour of the fashionable aristocracy and the gentry; and, of course, the future custom of them all.

By appealing to the fashionable cry for antiquities, by pandering to their requirements, by asking their advice and accepting their smallest orders, by flattery and attention, Wedgwood hoped to monopolize the aristocratic market, and thus win for his wares a special distinction, a social *cachet* which would filter through to all classes of society. Everything was done to attract

---

[55] WMSS. Leith Hill Place. JW to TB. 7 Sept. 1771.
[56] WMSS. E.18341-25. E.1066-2, E.18504-25, and many others.
[57] WMSS. Leith Hill Place MS. JW to TB. 2 Sept. 1771.
[58] WMSS. E.18283-25. JW to TB. 10 Jan. 1770. 'Defend me from particular orders'; also cf. WMSS. E.18269-25. JW to TB. 19 Nov. 1769.
[59] WMSS. Ditto.
[60] WMSS. E.18073-25. JW to John Wedgwood. Postmark 17 June (1765). He says he received the order 'because nobody else wo.^{d} undertake it'.
[61] WMSS. E.18785-25. JW to TB. 18 Oct. 1777 and many other references.
[62] WMSS. E.18450-25. JW to TB. Postmark 23 March (1773). Cf. Dr. G. C. Williamson.
[63] WMSS. E.18498-25. JW to TB. 14 Nov. 1773.
[64] WMSS. E.18269-25. JW to TB. 19 Nov. 1769.
[65] WMSS. Leith Hill Place MS. JW to TB. 2 Sept. 1771.
[66] WMSS. E.622-1. TB to JW. 21 June 1769.
[67] WMSS. E.622-1. TB to JW. 21 June 1769.

this aristocratic attention. A special display room was built[68] to beguile the fashionable company which Josiah drew after him to Etruria;[69] steps were taken to make the London showrooms attractive 'to the ladies',[70] and to keep the common folk out;[71] he was even prepared to adjust his prices downwards so that they could be paid genteely, writing to his partner, 'I think what you charge 34/- should ... be ... a Guinea & a half, 34 is so odd a sum there is no paying it *Genteely* ...'.[72] Once attracted everything was done to keep such attention. The good will of Wedgwood patrons never withered from neglect. Sir George Strickland was asked for advice on getting models from Rome;[73] Sir William Hamilton was asked for advice on gilding;[74] they were complimented by the reproduction of their country houses on the great Russian service;[75] and great care was taken to flatter them by giving them first sight of any new discovery.[76] The first Etruscan vases, for instance, were shown before they were put on sale to 'Sir Watkin Williams Wynn, Mrs Chetwynd,[77] Lord Bessborough, Earl of Stamford, Duke of Northumberland, Duke of Marlborough, Lord Percy, Lord Carlisle St James's Place, Earl of Dartmouth, Lord Clanbrazill, Lord Torrington, Mr Harbord Harbord'.[78] These were the nucleus of an aristocratic claque that did Wedgwood untold good. They praised his ware,[79] they advertised it,[80] they bought it,[81] and they took their friends to buy it.[82] Wedgwood had no scruples about exploiting their friendship and their praise. In 1776, for instance, by artful flattery he carefully prepared the ground for his new Bassrelief vases at the next season's sale, writing to Bentley, 'Sir William Hambleton, our very good Friend is in Town—Suppose you shew him some of the Vases, & a few other Connoisieurs [sic] not only to have their advice, but to have the advantage of their puffing them off against the next Spring, as they will, by being consulted, and flatter'd agreeably, as you know how, consider themselves as a sort of parties in the affair, & act accordingly.'[83] In the small, interconnected,

---

[68] WMSS. Leith Hill Place MS. (a fragment) JW to TB. 27 July 1771.
[69] WMSS. E.18878-26. 25 Feb. 1779. JW to TB.
[70] WMSS. E.18149-25. JW to TB. Postmark 1 June (1767).
[71] WMSS. Ditto. 'For you well know that ... my present sett of Customers ... will not mix with the rest of the World. ...'
[72] WMSS. E.18271-25. JW to TB. 1 Dec. 1769.
[73] WMSS. Leith Hill Place MS. JW to TB. 7 Sept. 1771.
[74] WMSS. E.18365-25. JW to TB. 11 April 1772.
[75] WMSS. E.18498-25. JW to TB. 14 Nov. 1773. An action designed to 'rivet them more firmly to our interests'. For list of views, cf. G. C. Williamson, op. cit., pp. 59-60.
[76] WMSS. E.18274-25. JW to TB. 9 Dec. 1769. Also E.18273-25. Sarah W. to JW, 6 Dec. 1769.
[77] Mrs. Chetwynd was their connection with the palace.
[78] WMSS. E.18274-25. JW to TB. 9 Dec. 1769.
[79] WMSS. Leith Hill Place MS. JW to TB. 7 Sept. 1771.
[80] WMSS. E.18367-25. JW to TB. 18 April 1772.
[81] WMSS. Innumerable examples, e.g. E.30857-5 and E.30859-5.
[82] WMSS. E.18505-25. JW to TB, 6 Dec. 1773. Lady Littleton, for example, makes a point of 'taking her friends to Wedgwood's showrooms.'
[83] WMSS. E.18693-25. JW to TB. 12 Sept. 1776.

gossip-ridden world of the English aristocracy in the eighteenth century, such introductions were vital, for even a very few sales could have an important effect.

For the lead of the aristocracy was quickly followed by other classes. Fashions spread rapidly and they spread downwards. But they needed a lead. As Wedgwood put it, 'Few ladies, you know, dare venture at anything out of the common stile [sic] 'till authoris'd by their betters—by the Ladies of superior spirit who set the ton'.[84] Wedgwood fully realized the value of such a lead, and made the most of it by giving his pottery the name of its patron; Queensware, Royal Pattern, Russian pattern, Bedford, Oxford and Chetwynd vases for instance. He went further than this with some. For he was not afraid to anticipate this patronage and to give his wares its beneficent sanction before it was bestowed. When he wished to give a new cheap line in flowerpots a good send off he wrote to Bentley, 'They want a name—a name has a wonderful effect I assure you—Suppose you present the Duchess of Devonshire with a Set & beg leave to call them Devonshire flowerpots. You smile—Well call them Mecklenberg[85]-or—or—what you please so you will but let them have a name'.[86] Once again Wedgwood is quite explicit about his expectations of the effect such names could have on the sales of his products. His repeated admission of the infallibly superior power of fashion over merit, of reputation over real utility or beauty contrasts starkly with the genteel position that Miss Meteyard paints. She admits the *fact* that Wedgwood gave his products the names of the rich, the royal and the influential, but her interpretation of the reasons for it is quite different: 'These were no vulgar appellations given to flatter a patron, or to insure sales; but simply showed[87] from whose possessions the vases had been modelled. Occasionally this was true, but even when it was, it was often merely the excuse for Wedgwood to gain for his product the selling power of the name involved, and often there was no such excuse. The cheap line in flowerpots had to be *found* a suitable patron—by Wedgwood presenting them to a suitably influential person such as the Duchess of Devonshire, or Queen Charlotte or her brother, Prince Ernst of Mecklenburg. Whether they owned the original or merely possessed a Wedgwood copy mattered little to Wedgwood's customers. The power of the association would be sufficient to boost sales.

Once committed to this policy of reliance on the support of the great, Wedgwood had to attend to every dictate of fashion. He could not afford to let Wedgwood ware become unfashionable. He combined with Matthew Boulton to satisfy the demand for ormolu-mounted pottery;[88] he banished gilding from his vases—and gilders from his workrooms—at the command

---

[84] WMSS. E.18766-25. JW to TB. 21 June 1777.
[85] The brother of Queen Charlotte.
[86] WMSS. E.18811-25. JW to TB. 9 Feb. 1778.
[87] E. Meteyard, op. cit., II, p. 68.
[88] WMSS. E.18193-25. JW to TB. 15 March 1768.

of Sir William Hamilton and an unresponsive market;[89] he made black teapots to show off to better advantage the current feminine vogue for bleached white hands; and when English society found the uncompromisingly naked figures of the classics 'too warm'[90] for their taste, and the ardour of the Greek gods too easily apparent, Wedgwood was quick to cloak their pagan immodesty—gowns for the girls and fig leaves for the gods were usually sufficient. But occasionally he had to go further. For as he wrote to Wright of Derby, 'fig leaves are not always enough,'[91] and in order to conceal 'that part which might give offence to our delicate Ladies' some figures were entirely redraped.

Some have assumed that since there was no apparent consistency to Wedgwood's draping—the Barberini vase still naked in 1795, while other designs were completely draped in the 1770s—then there could be no commercially purposeful thinking behind Wedgwood's policy. On the contrary, Wedgwood's policy on nudity provides a nice illustration of how he adapted his products to suit the market. The aristocracy could take their art largely unbowdlerized and Wedgwood was usually wholly faithful to the classical originals of his reproductions which were aimed at this market alone—as his immensely expensive reproductions of the Barberini Vase were in the 1790s. But when he aimed at the less tolerant middle-class market he was enthusiastically draping Greek originals in the 1770s. One can date the spread of the market, as well as the growth of prudery, from the different versions of some of Wedgwood's products. As the Dancing Hours went down market Hackwood had to redrape Flaxman's earlier version, and the Herm of Priapus had to be so heavily beflowered as to conceal his original purpose in life. Wedgwood was shrewd enough to realize that in some areas English prudery was even stronger than English snobbery. So he toned down the Greeks to maximise his sales. So long as they remained innocent of the generative powers he once symbolized, the genteel middle-class market would happily buy Priapus. They wanted a fashion symbol, not a fertility symbol. Authenticity alone would have disastrously limited Wedgwood's potential market. So Wedgwood used to the fullest extent the classical vocabulary of his day, and kept his more 'correct' interpretations of this classical grammar for his aristocratic customers.

Indeed his manipulation of the renewed classical enthusiasms of the late 1760s and early 1770s was of major importance to his sales promotion.

To the rage for antique and the excitement over Herculaneum Wedgwood gave special attention. It was vital that he should. For tired of the late

---

[89] WMSS. E.18365-25. JW to TB. 11 April 1772.
[90] WMSS. E.18278-25. JW to TB. 28 Dec. 1769, & E.18523-25. JW to TB. 13 March 1774.
[91] This correspondence often verged on broad comedy as Wright tried to meet Wedgwood's insistence on modesty without completely altering the composition of a picture. Cf. WMSS. E.672-1. Joseph Wright to JW and many others.

baroque and rococo extravagances of the middle decades of the century, the world of fashion had flocked to acclaim the new discoveries at Naples. The proliferating decoration, the exuberant colours, and the universal gilding of rococo were banished; the splendours of baroque became distasteful; the intricacies of *chinoiserie* lost their favour. The demand was for purity, simplicity and antiquity. The Grand Tour had done much to prepare the ground in England.[92] Familiarized with the ancients for the first time, hordes of English Milords[93] returned from the continent demanding the pure, the correct, the scientific art as they chose to call it. Before long the neo-classical reigned supreme, and a ready sale awaited the first potter to produce a pleasing neo-classical style. Here was the perfect market for Wedgwood to exploit. He was not the man to ignore it. He changed his style and became the prophet of the new art form. It was to this realization of the possibilities of neo-classicism,[94] whilst his rivals still busied themselves with what he called 'a dazzleing profusion of riches & ornament'[95] that Wedgwood owed much of his success. For it meant that he was fully established as the favourite of the world of fashion. He had first use of a market 'randy for antique'.[96]

Wedgwood did everything he could to promote and to serve the new fashion. He based his vases on the urns and amphorae of the ancients, he decorated them with classical swags and garlands, he reproduced their cameo medallions and reclining figures. He invented new glazes to suit these designs and revived encaustic painting to decorate them. He named his new factory 'Etruria' and inscribed on its first products the words 'Artes Etruriae Renascuntur'. To clinch his position as leader of the new fashion he sought out the famous Barberini vase as the final test of his technical skill. At first his efforts were in vain. Lady Portland, like an ecstatic squirrel with a unique nut, had secreted it away amongst her other treasures, and would show it to none but her closest friends. But her death gave Josiah his chance, and his reproduction of the vase caught the imagination of the whole continent. Every detail of the mythology behind the vase was eagerly discussed and Wedgwood's name circulated through every European court.

Moreover, Wedgwood wanted his wares to play the part in contemporary art that the statues and ceramics of the ancients had played in all previous centuries, to become in fact part of the works of art of the future. With this end in view he commissioned Wright of Derby to paint his ware,[97] and invited Romney to use his wares as background material when in want of

---

[92] It is interesting to note that JW's classical products did not sell well in Russia—beyond the reach of the Grand Tour and the new fashion.
[93] Gibbon was told that there were 40,000 Englishmen on the Continent in 1785.
[94] Cf. C. H. Wilson, The Entrepreneur in the Industrial Revolution in England, *Explorations in Entrepreneurial History*, V, p. 137.
[95] WMSS. E.18365-25. JW to TB. 11 April 1772.
[96] Cf. Philip Larkin, *The Less Deceived*, p. 27.
[97] WMSS. E.18834-25. JW to TB. Endorsed by TB. 'Should have been dated 5 May 1778'.

ornaments,[98] whilst in the family portrait by Stubbs, although most of the children are on horseback, and Wedgwood and his wife are sitting under a tree, a large Wedgwood and Bentley vase nevertheless found a place by Josiah's side. In encouraging this attitude Wedgwood discovered one of the most sophisticated advertising techniques of the century—for the fact that his wares alone appeared on the canvases of such famous artists was bound to excite attention[99]—especially amongst the fashionable connoisseurs who displayed their most favoured possessions in the same way. Zoffany's portrait of Lord Towneley surrounded by the spoils of the villa Hadrian, or Reynolds's portrait of Sir William Hamilton displaying his favourite antique vases were in the same tradition. The fact that the products of a contemporary factory could perform the same role and occupy the same place in paintings by Reynolds, Wright of Derby and Stubbs staked a powerful claim to status by association for Wedgwood and his pottery.

This kind of association also helped to win the favour and support of the artists and the connoisseurs. How highly Wedgwood rated this support can be seen from a discussion with 'Athenian' Stewart about whether they would gain or lose by competition with Matthew Boulton of Soho.[100] 'We agreed that those customers who were more fond of show & glitter, than fine forms, & the appearance of antiquity wo.d buy Soho Vases, and that all who could feel the effects of a fine outline & had any veneration for Antiquity wo.d be with us.—But these we are afraid wo.d be a minority; a third class we therefore call'd in to our aid, compos'd of such as wo.d *of themselves* choose shewy, rich & gawdy [sic] things, but who wo.d be *over ruled by their betters* in the choice of their ornaments as well as (in) other matters; who wo.d do as their *architects*, or whoever they depended upon in the matters of taste directed them; & with this reinforcement we thought Etruria stood a pretty good chance with any competitor.'[101] It would be difficult to find a more explicit statement of the importance to Wedgwood's sales of the influence of the legislators in taste; and it provides a nice example of Wedgwood's concern to make use of that influence, and of the pressure of his workload, that this long discussion of it should have been continued in a letter written over Christmas—one half on Christmas Eve, the second half on Boxing Day.

It was this belief in the selling power of fashion and the support of the art world which led Wedgwood to spend so much time in gaining the approbation of the connoisseurs, the artists and the architects. He had no intention of relying on merit alone to sell his goods, he sought out patrons and sponsors to reinforce that appeal. Just as he felt that his flowerpots would sell more if they were called 'duchess of Devonshire flowerpots', and

---

[98] Wedgwood Correspondence. John Rylands Library, Manchester, Vol. 10 (1110), p. 6.
[99] For more detailed discussion of this practice cf. Neil McKendrick: 'Josiah Wedgwood and George Stubbs', *History Today*, VII, No. 8 (August 1957), pp. 508-9.
[100] They were considering opening a London showroom in the Adelphi.
[101] WMSS. E.18335-25. JW to TB. 24 & 26 Dec. 1770.

his creamware more if called Queensware, so he longed for Brown,[102] Wyatt,[103] and the brothers Adam[104] to lead the architects in the use of his chimney pieces, and for Stubbs to lead the way in the use of Wedgwood plaques. And he was right to do so. He backed the leaders of fashion in the belief that the rest of society would follow—and they did. He was as aware as his contemporaries were of the power of class competition and the emulative spending which sprang from social emulation. He was aware of what Forster in 1767 called 'the perpetual restless ambition of each of the inferior ranks to raise themselves to the level of those immediately above them. In such a state as this fashion must have uncontrolled sway. And a fashionable luxury must spread through it like a contagion'.[105]

The struggle that Wedgwood had to sell his magnificent jasper tablets—generally accepted to be amongst the finest things he ever made, and now amongst the most expensive—illustrates the importance of this patronage. For the lack of it damned these tablets. Some were sold,[106] but they never sold well. For the fashionable architects refused to support them. Wedgwood and Bentley did everything they could to win them round: Wedgwood assiduously cultivated the friendship of 'Capability' Brown,[107] Bentley advocated their use to Adam,[108] and was urged by Wedgwood to call on Wyatt and 'try if it is not possible to root up his prejudices & make him a friend to our jaspers. If we could by any means gain over two or three of the *current architects* the business would be done'.[109] Once again Wedgwood is brutally frank. His admission of the importance to his sales of such a fashionable lead is once again quite explicit. He recognized very clearly that 'it is very much in Mr Adam's power to introduce our things into use'.[110] For he knew that their high quality alone could sell only a few. They needed proper sponsors. For 'If you are lucky in them no matter what the brat is, black, brown or fair, its fortune is made. We were really unfortunate in the introduction of our jasper into public notice, that we could not prevail upon the architects to be godfathers to our child. Instead of taking it by the hand, & giving it their benediction, they have cursed the poor infant by bell, book & candle, & must have a hard struggle to support itself, & rise from under their maledictions'.[111] For once Wedgwood and Bentley's marketing techniques had failed. Their salesmanship had drawn a blank.

---

[102] WMSS. E.18147-25. JW to TB. 23 May 1767. He wrote on meeting 'the famous Brown ... He may be of much service to me, & I shall not neglect what chance has thrown into my way'.
[103] WMSS. E.18855-26. JW to TB. 16 Oct. 1778.
[104] WMSS. E.18394-25. JW to TB. 30 Aug. 1772.
[105] N. Forster, *An Enquiry into the Present High Prices of Provisions* (1767), p. 41.
[106] Sir John Wrottesley, Sir Laurence Dundass and Lady Bagot bought them.
[107] WMSS. E.18853-26. JW to TB. 6 Oct. 1778.
[108] WMSS. E.18394-25. JW to TB. 30 Aug. 1772.
[109] WMSS. E.18855-26. JW to TB. 16 Oct. 1778.
[110] WMSS. E.18394-25. JW to TB. 30 Aug. 1772.
[111] WMSS. E.18898-26. JW to TB. 19 June 1779.

This was, however, an exception and serves only to illustrate the importance of Wedgwood's methods and the very real influence of that fashionable support which he so ardently courted. For by these methods Wedgwood had won the patronage of the court, the aristocracy, the artists and the *cognoscenti*. In doing so he had gained the favour of a powerful social catalyst. For in the smaller, more closely-knit society of the European nobility of the eighteenth century, these patrons, these *'lines, channels & connections'*[112] as Wedgwood called them, were of vital importance. They led the fashion. They encouraged imitation. They spread the Wedgwood name abroad and sent presents of his ware: Horace Walpole bought it[113] and wrote to his widely scattered friends about it;[114] Mrs. Crewe sent a desert service to the Countess of Zinzindorf in Vienna,[115] 'the Duke of Richmond ... made a present of a pair of vases ... to the Duke of Leinster who was in Raptures with them';[116] and so on. Wedgwood did not let the matter rest there. He had no hesitation in exploiting this patronage. When he heard of 'a violent *Vase madness* breaking out amongst'[117] the Irish, Wedgwood wrote in haste to Bentley: 'This disorder sho^d be cherish'd in some way or other, or our rivals may step in before us. We have many Irish friends who are both able & willing to help us, but they must be applied to for that purpose ... Ld. Bessboro' you know can do a great deal for us with his friends on the otherside (of) the Water by a letter of recommendation or otherwise as he may think proper. You are to visit him soon—the rest will occur to you. The Duke of Richmond has many & virtu-ous friends in Ireland. We are looking over the English Peerage to find out *lines, channels & connections*—will you look over the Irish Peerage with the same view—I need not tell you how much will depend upon a *proper* & *noble* introduction. This, with a fine assortment of Vases & a Trusty & *adequate* Agent will ensure us success in the conquest of our sister kingdom'.[118]

* * *

These were the more subtle advertising techniques of Josiah Wedgwood. They assured him a favourable reception for his wares in London and in the country houses of the rich. They stimulated interest and made his products known even in the provinces. They formed the basis of his sales policy—but only the basis. He had to use more direct methods to force home his advantage

---

[112] WMSS. E.18314–25. JW to TB. 2 Aug. 1770.
[113] *Catalogue of the Contents of Strawberry Hill,* 1842, pp. 130, 131, 179, 180, 181.
[114] *Letters of Horace Walpole,* ed. Toynbee, IX, p. 305; X, 282; XI, 172. Also cf. E. Meteyard, op. cit., II., p. 72. It must be admitted that Walpole was not always admiring.
[115] WMSS. E.18350–25. JW to TB. 17 Sept. 1771.
[116] WMSS. E.18314–25. JW to TB. 2 Aug. 1770.
[117] WMSS. Ditto.
[118] WMSS. E.18314–25. JW to TB. 2 Aug. 1770. Cf. E. Meteyard, op. cit., II, pp. 176–7.

and exploit the position he had won for himself. Warehouses, showrooms, exhibitions, trademarks, new standards of display, puffing articles, straightforward advertisement, free carriage, and travelling salesmen; all of these played their part in Wedgwood and Bentley's marketing campaign.

Wedgwood was quick to realize the value of a warehouse in London. For high-quality goods he needed a market accustomed to 'fine prices'. He was not likely to find it in the annual market fairs of Staffordshire—the time-honoured entrepôt of their county's pots—nor amongst the country folk who haggled over their wares straight from the crateman's back or the hawker's basket, and to whom expense was the controlling factor in deciding their custom. A London warehouse would give him direct access to the fashionable clientele he aimed at and an opening in what was still the major distributing centre for the wholesale trade of the country.[119]

He first opened a warehouse there as early as 1765 and it soon became an integral part of his sales organization. It gave him the opportunity to put into action some of his most creative ideas. For apart from its success in the wholesale trade,[120] Wedgwood quickly reinforced its position by developing a vigorous retail trade in London. In two years his trade had outgrown his rooms in Grosvenor Square, and he was writing to Bentley, 'We must have an Elegant, extensive & Conven(ien)t shewroom',[121] and discussing the merits of different sites. Pall Mall was thought to be too accessible to the common folk, for he wanted space for more exciting methods of display,[122] rather than for accommodation of the general public.[123] He planned to have a great display of his wares set out in services as for a meal 'in order to *do the needfull* with the Ladys in the neatest, genteelest, and best method. The same, or indeed a much greater variety of setts of Vases sho.^{d} decorate the Walls, & both these articles may, every few days be so alter'd, revers'd, & transform'd as to render the whole a new scene, Even to the same Company, every time they shall bring their friends to visit us.

'I need not tell you the many good effects this must produce, when business, & amusement can be made to go hand in hand. Every new show, Exhibition or rarity soon grows stale in London, & is no longer regarded, after the first sight, unless utility, or some such variety as I have hinted at above continues to recommend it to their notice ... I have done something of the sort since I came to Town & find the immediate good Effects of it. The first two days after the alteration we sold three complete setts of Vases at 2 & 3 Guineas

---

[119] C. R. Fay, *Great Britain: an economic and social survey*, p. 132.
[120] With the development of the canal system and the growth of turnpike trusts its importance to Wedgwood's wholesale trade naturally declined though it was still vital for foreign dealers.
[121] WMSS. E.18147-25. JW to TB. 23 May 1767.
[122] WMSS. E.18711-25. JW to TB. 4 Nov. 1776.
[123] WMSS. E.18149-25. JW to TB. Postmark 1 June (1767).

a sett, besides many pairs of them, *which Vases had been in my Rooms 6-8 and some of them 12 months & wanted nothing but arrang(e)ment to sell them'.*[124] (My italics.) It is clear from this that Wedgwood anticipated the most modern ideas of effective display—after nearly two hundred years retail potters use almost exactly the same layout to show off their wares.

He even anticipated a rudimentary self-service scheme—the pride of twentieth-century shopkeepers' ingenuity—for he planned to have his slightly inferior goods, priced according to their quality, and displayed 'in one of the best places of your lower Shop, where people can come at them, & *serve themselves'*.[125] (My italics.) Further he laid out his tiles in patterns to show their full variety;[126] he placed his cheap vases on a separate range of shelves;[127] and to give his customers a greater sense of the rarity of his goods, he strictly limited the number of jaspers on display in his rooms at any given time.[128] In the early 1770s when the fate of gilding was still in the balance, he proposed a temporary solution as a shield to the delicate sensibility of his patrons' tastes by proposing 'a Curtain immediately for your Pebble ware shelves, which you may open or shut, inlarge or diminish the shew of gilding as you find your customers affected . . . It wo.^{d} *moderate the shew* at the first enterance (sic)—hide the Gilding from those who think it a defect, & prevent the Gold from tarnishing'.[129] For their entertainment he provided pattern books in all his warehouses as 'they will be looked over by our customers here, & they will often get us orders, & be pretty amusem.^{t} for the Ladies when they are waiting, wh.^{ch} is often the case as there are som(e)times four or five diff.^{t} companys, & I need not tell you, that *it will be our interest to amuse, & divert, & please, and astonish, nay, & even to ravish the Ladies . . .*'[130]

His success was immediate. His account books, his list of visitors, and contemporary comment all record the constant streams of fashionable callers. As early as 1769 he was taking £100 a week[131] in cash sales at his London rooms alone, in addition to numerous orders which were often for even larger sums. His men had to work night and day[132] to satisfy the demand and the crowds of visitors showed no sign of abating.[133] Wedgwood's in fact had become one of the most fashionable meeting places in London. As Lord Townshend wrote of 'Squire Hanger', a beau and a macaroni,

---

[124] WMSS. E.18149-25. JW to TB. 1 June (1767).
[125] WMSS. E.17677-96. JW to William Cox. 7 April 1769.
[126] WMSS. E.18711-25. JW to TB. 4 Nov. 1776.
[127] WMSS. E.18364-25. JW to TB. 6 April (1772).
[128] WMSS. E.18802-25. JW to TB. 15 Dec. 1777.
[129] WMSS. E.18365-25. JW to TB. 11 April 1772.
[130] WMSS. E.18232-25. JW to TB. Feb. 1769. My italics.
[131] WMSS. E.30857-5 & E.30859-5. Peter Swift to JW 18 & 25 March, 1769.
[132] WMSS. E.18230-25. JW to TB. 15 Feb. 1769.
[133] WMSS. E.30857-5 & E.30859-5. Peter Swift to JW, 18 & 25 March, 1769.

> At Tattersall's,[134] Wedgwood's, and eke the Rehearsal,[135]
> Then straightway at Betty's[136] he's sure to converse all;
> At Arthur's[137] you meet him, and the mall in a sweat,
> At Kensington Garden's he's posted vidette.[138]

It is not surprising that Boulton and Fothergill in Pall Mall,[139] Josiah Spode in Fore Street, Cripplegate and then at the more genteel Portugal Street, Lincoln's Inn Fields,[140] and finally Minton[141] followed Wedgwood's lead and established warehouses in London. For a fashionable appeal in London had vital influence even in the depths of the provinces. The woman in Newcastle-upon-Tyne who insisted on a dinner service of 'Arabesque Border' before her local shopkeeper had even heard of it, wanted it because it was 'much used in Lond.º at present', and she steadfastly 'declin'd taking any till she had seen that pattern'.[142]

To encourage this outward spread of fashion and to speed it on its way, Wedgwood set up warehouses and showrooms at Bath,[143] Liverpool[144] and Dublin[145] in addition to the showrooms at Etruria[146] and Great Newport Street. The effect on the Liverpool potters of Wedgwood's competition can be seen from a contemporary's comment. The local historian Enfield wrote in 1774, 'English porcelain, in imitation of foreign China, has long been manufactured in this town; and formerly with success. But of late this branch has been much upon decline, partly because the Leverpool (sic) artists have not kept pace in the improvements with some others in the same way; but chiefly because the Staffordshire ware has had and still continues to have so general a demand, as almost to supersede the use of other porcelain. The great perfection to which this art, both in works of utility and of ornament and taste, is carried at the modern Etruria, under the direction of those ingenious artists, Messrs. Wedgwood & Bentley, at the same time that it is highly serviceable to the public and reflects great honour on our country,

---

[134] For sportsmen.
[135] Opera House, Haymarket.
[136] The famous fruit shop in St. James's St.
[137] Unknown.
[138] D. Marshall, *London & the Life of the Town*, in *Johnson's England*, ed. A. S. Turbeville, vol. I, p. 187.
[139] WMSS. E.18261-25. JW to TB. 27 Sept. 1769.
[140] Arthur Hayden: *Spode and his Successors*, pp. 20-2.
[141] Minton-Senhouse MS. & Minton Account Sales; cf. Dr. John Thomas: *The Economic Development of the North Staffordshire Potteries since 1730, with special reference to the Industrial Revolution*, p. 815. There had been other less successful attempts before Wedgwood to set up a fashionable warehouse in London. See L. Weatherill, op. cit., p. 88.
[142] WMSS. E.1192-2. Joseph Harris of Newcastle-upon-Tyne to JW. 1780. It was for this reason, too, that Wedgwood took such care to keep in step with London fashion, writing to Bentley on 17 Dec. 1777, 'if we should ever make this article in earnest you must furnish us with the fashion, shape, size & real model from the great City'.
[143] WMSS. Numerous letters to Mr. Ward from JW, e.g. E.4428-6 to E.4651-6.
[144] WMSS. Numerous letters to Mr. Boardman from JW, e.g. E. -8 and E. -9.
[145] WMSS. Numerous letters to Mr. Brock from JW, e.g. E.3880-5 to E.3908-5.
[146] WMSS. Leith Hill Place (a fragment). JW to TB. 27 July 1771.

must be unfavourable to other manufacturers of a similar kind'.[147] Many other were to suffer a similar fate.

It was on the London showrooms, however, that Wedgwood lavished most of his attention. By judicious use of shows and exhibitions he kept up his London sales[148] and advertised his more spectacular productions. These were carefully stage managed. Great care was taken in timing the openings,[149] and new goods were held back to increase their effect. As Wedgwood wrote to Bentley: 'Your shew will be vastly superior to anything your good Princes & Customers have hitherto seen. I am going upon a large scale with our Models &c which is one reason why you have so few new things just now, but I hope to bring the whole in compass for your next Winters shew and ASTONISH THE WORLD ALL AT ONCE, For I hate piddleing you know'.[150] Winter, summer, spring and autumn sales were bolstered up by the occasional exhibition. Anything they made for the Queen, for instance, was automatically exhibited[151] before it was delivered, with reproductions[152] on sale to press home their advantage after the show had ended. But the most influential exhibition of all was that of the Russian service for Catherine the Great in 1774. Its display, Wedgwood thought, 'would bring an *immence (sic) number of People of Fashion* into our Rooms—Wo.^{d} *fully complete our notoriety to the whole Island & help us greatly,* no doubt, *in the sale of our goods, both useful and ornamental*—It wo.^{d} *confirm the consequence we have attain'd, & increase* it, by *shewing that we are employ'd in a much higher scale* than *other Manufacturers.* We should shew that we have paid many comp.^{ts} to our Friends & Customers, & *thereby rivet them the more firmly to our interests . . .*'[153] The benefits which Wedgwood expected to flow from such fashionable 'notoriety' would be valuable both for his immediate sales and his future profits because it would help to boost his long term reputation on which he felt both ultimately rested.

Nothing was spared. For Wedgwood was determined to make the most of the opportunity. New rooms were taken;[154] the public—or rather the 'Nobility & Gentry'—informed that admittance was by ticket only;[155] and ample advertisement was planned.[156] The success of the show was certain.

---

[147] Dr. William Enfield, *A Hisotory of Liverpool,* 1774, p. 90, quoted in Knowles Boney, *Liverpool Porcelain of the 18th Century and its Makers* (1957), p. 7.
[148] WMSS. E.18853-26. JW to TB. 6 Oct. 1778.
[149] WMSS. E.18696-25. JW to (TB). (Sept. 1776.)
[150] WMSS. E.18614-25. JW to TB. 6 Aug. 1775.
[151] WMSS. E.18350-25. JW to TB. 17 Sept. 1771.
[152] WMSS. Uncatalogued. JW to TB. 17 Oct. 1771.
[153] WMSS. E.18498-25. JW to TB. 14 Nov. 1773. No. 2 (i.e. the second letter from JW to TB that day). My italics.
[154] Portland House, Greek Street, Soho. First mentioned as 'our new Rooms'.
[155] WMSS. Draft of advertisement. 30 May 1774. See C. C. Williamson, op. cit., p. 33.
[156] Ibid. Planned for the front page of Public Advertiser & Gazeteer (Miss Meteyard claims that it appeared in these and *St. James's Chronicle* but it can only be traced to *Public Advertiser* for 8 June 1774).

BIRTH OF A CONSUMER SOCIETY

Regarded as one of the most popular sights in London, it was visited by Queen Charlotte and by her brother His Royal Highness Prince Ernst of Mecklenburg,[157] and by the King and Queen of Sweden, and day after day for over a month the fashionable world thronged the rooms and blocked the street with their carriages.[158] Wedgwood had ensured its success by his choice of subject alone, for almost all of those whose country seats were represented on the service trekked from their distant homes to see the exhibition.[159] The last ounce of publicity was wrung out of it, by displaying duplicates of the service in the showroom at Etruria, and painting others 'without the Frog' for a continued display at Greek Street.[160] With this exhibition he had aroused and exploited the imagination of the fashionable world. He was equally capable of harnessing the emotion of the rest of society to serve his own ends.

No public event—Chatham dying,[161] Wesley preaching,[162] or Keppel pleading[163]—lacked its commerical opportunities for Wedgwood. As early as 1766 he wrote to Bentley, 'What do you think of sending Mr. Pitt upon Crockery ware to America. A Quantity might certainly be sold there now & some advantage made of the American prejudice in favour of that great Man'.[164] Similarly when Admiral Keppel was tried by court martial and, amidst great enthusiasm, acquitted, Wedgwood wrote at once for a picture to copy, regretting that he had not 'had it a month since, and advertis'd it for pictures, bracelets, rings, seals, &c.'[165] Exasperated by the delay he wrote that their travelling salesman 'says he could sell *thousands* of Keppels at any price. Oh Keppel Keppel—Why will not you send me a Keppel. I am perswaded (sic) if we had our wits about us as we ought to have had 2 or 3 months since we might have sold £1000 worth of this gentleman's head in various ways, & I am perswaded it would still be worth while to disperse them every way in our power'.[166] For the same purpose the rise of Methodism, the Slave Trade controversy, and the Peace with France were all given ceramic expression: Wesley, printed in black by Sadler and Green, on a Wedgwood teapot;[167] slavery on the famous jasper medallion of the kneeling slave, asking 'Am I not a man and a brother?';[168] the Peace treaty on a jasper plaque specially commissioned by Josiah from Flaxman.[169] Other contem-

[157] WMSS. E.18547-25. JW to TB 15 & 16 July 1774.
[158] *Diary of Mrs. Delaney.* 7 June 1774.
[159] Dr. G. C. Williamson, op. cit., The list of views (1282 in all), pp. 55-91.
[160] WMSS. E.18540-25. JW to TB. (20 June 1774).
[161] WMSS. E.18840-25. JW to TB. 30 June & 1 July 1778.
[162] Donald C. Towner, *English Cream Coloured Earthenware* (1957). Plate 85(b).
[163] Keppel had been accused by Sir Hugh Pallister, his second-in-command. He was acquitted on 11 February 1779 and received the thanks of both Houses of Parliament.
[164] WMSS. E.18123-25. JW to TB. 18 July 1766.
[165] WMSS. E.18878-26. JW to TB. 25 Feb. 1779.
[166] WMSS. E.18880-26. JW to TB. 1 March 1779.
[167] Donald C. Towner, op. cit. Plate 85(b).
[168] WMSS. E.19002-26. JW to Dr. Erasmus Darwin. (July 1789). A Copy.
[169] WMSS. E.30193-2. JW to John Flaxman. 2 Nov. 1786.

porary figures much in the public eye—Garrick, Dr. Johnson, Priestley, Mrs. Siddons, Captain Cook and many others[170]—joined Wedgwood's series of famous heads: Greeks, Romans, Poets, Painters, Scientists, Historians, Actors and Politicians.[171] Made up into 'Historical Cabinets'[172] these heads found a ready sale. One alone proved abortive—the Popes. They were tried but sold poorly. They lacked sales appeal, for as Wedgwood explained 'nobody now a days troubles their heads about his Holiness or his Predecessors'.[173] Not, at least, in England, but Wedgwood found an alternative use for him in his Catholic export trade.

Wedgwood also used newspaper advertisement—in London, provincial and even continental papers. This part of his marketing programme has received little attention; historians in general preferring to quote his occasional refusal rather than his more general acceptance of this medium. His remark, 'I would much rather not advertise at all if you think the sales are in such a way as to do without it . . .'[174] clearly indicates a certain reluctance. But this can be explained. It was due to his temporary fear of further attentions from 'Antipuffado'[175]—an anonymous opponent of 'that monstrous blast of puffery'[176] which eighteenth-century manufacturers used to advertise their goods. This method itself—articles pretending impartiality but in fact praising certain goods—seems to have grown out of the initial desire of some large firms to avoid direct advertisement. They shrank from what Wedgwood called 'blowing my own trumpet'[177] and preferred to get others to do it for them. The company they would have to keep must also at first have discouraged them, for many advertisements were from petty traders, hawkers, quacks, local shopkeepers, and other more dubious professions. The Queen's Potter was naturally not keen to share a column with battling women and fighting cocks; nor eager to offer his services alongside those of a prostitute or a gigolo, a wet nurse or a bug killer[178]—even though the latter claimed to serve the same monarch and be the oldest in the land. Wedgwood felt the same initial aversion to using travelling salesmen because it savoured of hawking.[179]

But whatever his feelings, a study of Wedgwood's letters and of contemporary newspapers makes it quite clear that he conquered them. Certain forms of advertisement he would never countenance. He banned his show-

---

[170] Wolf Mankowitz, *Wedgwood*, catalogues for 1779 and 1787, pp. 203-75.
[171] WMSS. E.18657-25. William Cox to TB. 24 Feb. 1776.
[172] WMSS. E.18433-5. JW to TB. 2 Jan. 1773.
[173] WMSS. ditto. Wedgwood was careful to avoid certain political implications, however, and refused to reproduce certain heads, e.g. E.18772-25. JW to TB. 19 July 1777.
[174] WMSS. Leith Hill Place. JW to TB. 13 Feb. 1771.
[175] WMSS. Leith Hill Place. JW to TB. 11 Feb. 1771.
[176] E. S. Turner, *The Shocking History of Advertisement*. Ch. II, *passim*.
[177] WMSS. E.19001-26. JW to Dr. Erasmus Darwin. Endorsed. 28 June 1789. Copy.
[178] Turner, op. cit., pp. 28-48 and *passim*. N. B. Turner makes no mention of Wedgwood and Bentley.
[179] WMSS. E.18827-25. JW to TB. 16 April 1778.

rooms from using handbills, writing 'We have hitherto appeared in a very different light to common Shopkeepers, but this step (in my opinion) will sink us exceedingly ... I own myself alarm'd ... it being a mode of advertisement I never approv'd of ...'[180] Wedgwood had to tread an especially careful path with regard to his advertisements. He had to make his goods widely known and yet avoid damaging beyond repair the special cachet he had won for his product as the prized possession of the fashionable and the great. To reach a very wide market and yet retain a fashionable reputation, indeed to use that fashionable reputation as an important part of his mass sales promotion, was not easy, but it was Wedgwood's distinctive achievement to do so. He could afford eventually to lose the hyper-fashionable (as he eventually lost the support of Horace Walpole) so long as his general reputation survived. He felt it would be damaged by association with those who used handbills. But there were many other forms, which, when his stock began to mount, he was quick to use, writing 'This seems to point out advertising ... All trifling objections vanish before a real necessity'.[181] His faith in the value of advertisement is further borne out by his belief that Cooper and Duburk failed in Amsterdam because they did not make 'a fair experiment what advertising &c would do'.[182] And it is conclusively proved by the numerous occasions on which he used it. He advertised his ware,[183] his warehouse,[184] and his agents;[185] he advertised his Royal patronage and the support of the nobility;[186] he marked his ware and he advertised that mark. As he wrote to Bentley in 1773, 'it will be absolutely necessary for us to mark them, and advertise that mark'.[187] He even organized the trial over encaustic painting in London for the sake of advertisement, writing to Bentley, 'May not this affair furnish us with a good excuse for advertising away at a great rate?'[188] Furthermore he proposed to publish prints of the pieces of furniture into which Wedgwood ware had been introduced in much the same way that Vincennes and Sèvres had long been used in French furniture. A step which he believed 'would give sanction, & notoriety to our productions to such a degree, perhaps, as we have at present no idea of. I would put these Nos. into the common mode of sale in all the shops, & in our own Warehouses every where'.[189] Here Wedgwood felt he was on sure ground. The association with fine furniture would reinforce his reputation with the fashionably elegant. The widespread demonstration of that con-

[180] WMSS. E.18427-25. JW to TB. 7 Dec. 1772.
[181] WMSS. Leith Hill Place MS. JW to TB. 16 Feb. 1771.
[182] WMSS. E.18616-25. JW to TB. 10 Aug. 1775.
[183] WMSS. E.18341-25. JW to TB. 17 Feb. (1771).
[184] WMSS. E.18563-25. JW to TB. 10 Nov. 1774.
[185] WMSS. E.18504-25. JW to TB. 2 Dec. 1773. In this case the agent was Brett.
[186] WMSS. Ditto.
[187] WMSS. E.18489-25. JW to TB. 7 June 1773.
[188] WMSS. E.18325-25. JW to TB. 13 October 1770.
[189] WMSS. E.18518-25. JW to TB. 20 Feb. 1774.

nection would make a wider market ever more eager to own those pieces of Wedgwood which they could afford. Those who could not afford the fine furniture embellished with Wedgwood plaques, could at least aspire to own the plaques, and could certainly afford to own the useful ware whose trade mark proclaimed its relationship with more exclusive and more expensive ornamental ware.

He did not neglect to keep up a steady stream of flattering articles in the press. Some of these occurred in the natural course of events. By its own fine quality and the judicious attention of its makers, Wedgwood's wares had many admirers amongst the literary connoisseurs and won periodic praise for them in the daily news-sheets. But Wedgwood did not rely on this alone. He speeded up the process and augmented it. Although, for instance, he received two unsolicited puffs[190] in August and September 1770, by October he was writing to Bentley, 'There is a most famous puff for Boulton & Fothergill in the St James's Chronicle of the 9th & for Mr Cox likewise, How the Author could have the assurance to leave us out I cannot conceive. Pray get another article in the next paper to complete the Triumverate.'[191] The attacks on this puffing technique, by Antipuffado, excited such attention that Wedgwood and Bentley discussed exploiting it for their own ends. For having realized that exaggerated abuse could be as effective in publicity as praise—one of the more advanced advertising ideas—they discussed methods of provoking their anonymous attacker to strike again: 'But should not we seem a little nettled & provoked to induce him to take up his pen again, for if he thinks his writing is of service to us, he will certainly be silent. You mention his letter as a foundation for my advertiseing—How wo^d you introduce the mention of it into an advertisement?'[192] After much discussion this idea was eventually rejected, but it shows an awareness of advertising techniques far ahead of their time. They were always conscious of the value of propaganda, and they were not above suggesting to the King and their customers that there was no hope of obtaining more of the vital ingredients for their jasper. 'This idea will give limits, a boundary to the quantity which your customers will be ready to conceive may be made of these bassreliefs, which otherwise would be gems indeed. They want nothing but *age & scarcity* to make them worth any price you could ask for them.'[193] He could not give them age but he did his best to imply that they were scarce. It is interesting to note that Wedgwood suggested to Bentley that he should burn this letter.

A study of their advertisements reveals a number of interesting develop-

---

[190] WMSS. E.18323-25. JW to TB. 1 Sept. 1770, one in the *Gazette* and another in *Lloyds*. Another in the *Daily Advertiser*. Leith Hill Place MS. JW to TB. 21 Jan. 1771.
[191] WMSS. E.18325-25. JW to TB. 13 Oct. 1770. Later JW denied that he ever advertised without affixing his name. L.H.P. MS, JW to TB. 11 Feb. 1771.
[192] WMSS. Leith Hill Place MS. JW to TB. 12 Feb. 1771.
[193] WMSS. E.18802-25. JW to TB. 15 Dec. 1777.

ments in the selling policy. From a copy of his first,[194] it is clear that he had decided to pay the cost of carriage on his goods to London, even though this would mean a loss of £500 a year in his profits.[195] Of even greater importance is the way this policy developed in the advertisement outlined to Bentley in 1771 when poor sales demanded 'that some additional mode of sale be thought of or our dead stock will soon grow enormous'.[196] In this,[197] free carriage to London is extended to part payment—and a very considerable part—to any place in England. In addition he offered the first recorded example of a satisfaction-or-money-back policy. Not only is this the first of its kind to be discovered in Europe or America but it antedates John Wanamaker—who is normally given the credit for this innovation—by nearly a century.[198]

Advertisement alone, however, was not sufficient fully to exploit the English market. As Wedgwood said, 'It seems absolutely necessary for the increase of our sales ... that some means must be unremittingly made use of to awake, and keep up the attention of the world to the fine things we are making & doing for them'.[199] He felt that his rival Voyez sold his wretched seals 'by mere dint of application to the buyers',[200] and so he went to work himself armed with pattern boxes, catalogues and samples. This was so successful that he extended it, and in 1777 he took the momentous decision to make his wares known throughout the country by personal introduction in the shape of travelling salesmen, and a crude and primitive version of the modern commercial traveller or sales representative can be seen in the proposals drawn up in October of that year between Wedgwood and John Brownbill.[201] Despite early difficulties Wedgwood persevered and by 1787 there were three such travellers on the road,[202] and by 1790 a book of rules and travellers' procedure, called the Travellers' Book,[203] had been drawn up. In it the record of their sales and their expenses bears ample testimony to their success.[204]

By such means Wedgwood broke through to a national market. By novelty, quality and fashionable appeal he won the favour of London and the notice of the provinces; with sales, exhibitions, and spectacular productions—all well advertised—he publicized this support; and with warehouses, salesmen

---

[194] WMSS. E.18230-25. JW to Sarah Wedgwood. (Feb. 1769).
[195] WMSS. E.18191-25. JW to TB. 3 March 1768.
[196] WMSS. E.18293-25. JW to TB. 18 April 1770.
[197] WMSS. E.18341-25. JW to TB. 17 Feb. (1771).
[198] Ralph M. Hower, 'The Wedgwoods—Ten Generations of Potters', *Journal of Economic and Business History*, vol. 4, No. 2, (1932), p. 305.
[199] WMSS. E.18880-26. JW to TB. 1 March 1779.
[200] WMSS. E.18507-25. JW to TB. 10 Dec. 1773.
[201] WMSS. E.18784-25. JW to TB. 17 Oct. 1777.
[202] WMSS. Byerley, Howorth and Brownbill.
[203] WMSS. L.23571. Travellers' Book, c. 1793.
[204] WMSS. ditto. In 10 days in June 1793, the expenses amounted to £2.9.10½ (added up wrongly by the traveller to £2.9.10) and the sales to £101.3.2.

and free carriages he invented the means of satisfying that demand. Having made his ware desirable, he had made it accessible.

* * *

The capture of the English market was not enough to satisfy Wedgwood. He longed to serve the whole world from Etruria, and constantly scanned the horizon for new markets. No country—Mexico, Turkey, not even China—was too distant for him to contemplate with excitement. No obstacle—Russia's taste, Spain's hostility, or Portugal's prohibition—was too great for him to hope to overcome it. Difficulties served only as a challenge to his ambition. France—home of European porcelain, centre of rococo elegance, and safe behind a high tariff wall—was the greatest challenge of all. Even the thought of it inspired Wedgwood, 'And do you really think we may make a *complete conquest* of France? Conquer France in Burslem? My blood moves quicker, I feel my strength increase for the contest—Assist me my friend, & the victory is our own ... we will fashion our porcelain after their own hearts, & captivate them with the elegance & simplicity of the ancients'.[205]

Necessity as well as ambition led Wedgwood and Bentley to seek new outlets for their products. They needed a larger market to move their stock, to exploit the capabilities of their production machine, and to swallow old lines which had exhausted their selling power in England. In the early seventies when sales were slack, Wedgwood wrote 'we must either find some new markets or ... turn off some of our hands'.[206] The stock was too large, '& nothing but a *foreign* market ... will ever keep it within any tolerable bounds'.[207] He determined that 'Every *Gentle* & *Decent* push should be made to have our things *seen* & *sold* at Foreign Markets. If we drop, or do not *hitt off* such opportunities our selves we cannot expect other People to be so (in)attentive to them, & our trade will decline & wither, or flourish & expand itself, in proportion as these little turns & opportunitys are neglected or made the most of'.[208]

Wedgwood seized on the slightest hint of an opening into a new market. Merely reading in Lady Mary Wortley Montague's *Letters* of the Turks' taste for pots of perfume in the numerous arches around their rooms, filled him with lust for the Turkish market. It was a purely ceramic lust, however, for he wrote, 'Let who will take the Sultanas if I could get at these delightful

---

[205] WMSS. E.18252–25. JW to TB. 13 Sept. 1769.
[206] WMSS. Leith Hill Place Ms. JW to TB. 10 April 1771.
[207] WMSS. Leith Hill Place Ms. JW to TB. 11 Feb. (postmark 14 March) 1771,.
[208] WMSS. E.18384–25. JW to TB. 5 Aug. 1772. Those, like Professor Payne, who see little evidence of any great pressure on Wedgwood to sell abroad [see P. L. Payne in *The Cambridge Economic History of Europe*, vol. VII, Part I, ed. P. Mathias and M. M. Postan (1978), p. 190] in 1771 and 1772 should take note of his expressed willingness to go 'to the utmost verge of prudence or rather beyond', and the quite exceptional risk of sending £20,000 worth of pottery to Europe in 1772 in his major inertia-selling campaign.

little niches, & furnish them, is all I covet in Turkey at present'.[209] This casual reference conjured up a whole range of commercial possibilities to Wedgwood and he was convinced that 'if we had a clever Ambassador there som(e)thing might be done'.[210] His desire for such a contact is easy to appreciate, for the diplomatic service—although this had remained largely unappreciated—had proved one of the most fruitful channels of entry into foreign trade.

It was yet another way in which he exploited the favour of the aristocracy and his connections with the Establishment. They had already ensured a favourable reception for his goods in England. Their influence was not unfelt even on the Continent, but it required something more than this to penetrate fully the European market. When offered on the open market through the normal channels of merchant and middleman, the high quality of Wedgwood's products earned them immediate attention, but their price worked against them. Many lay idle as dead stock, some were returned as too expensive. They required a 'proper & noble introduction' such as he had contrived for them in England to overcome this drawback. What better introduction to the heart of European courts and their fashionable attendants could be devised than through her Majesty's ambassadors?

Wedgwood realized that they were naturally keen to raise the prestige of their country, and by flattery and presents he rapidly won their allegiance. 'Suppose we were to make Sʳ Wᵐ Hamilton a present of an Etruscan tablet ... it would be the best introduction they could have in the country where he resides'.[211] His confidence in such introductions was such that he had once written, 'The Russians must have Etruscan, & Grecian vases about the 19th Century. I fear they will not be ripe for them much sooner, unless our good friend Sʳ Wm. Hamilton should go Ambassador thither & prepare a hot bed to bring these Northern plants to Maturity before their *natural* time'.[212] Many of his letters have survived as evidence of the care with which Wedgwood solicited such help. Bentley had done much of the original work in cultivating the diplomats,[213] but after his death Wedgwood took over and even as late as 1786 he still felt the need to prepare the ground carefully with the British ambassador in Vienna for the promotion of a new production (or rather a new application of his cameos):

> Sir, Encouraged by the many instances of your Excellency's condescension in giving my manufactures the honour of your patronage, and for which, I beg leave to assure you, Sir, I feel the most lively gratitude, I take the liberty to inclose to your Excellency specimens of a new production, or rather a new application of my Cameos of two colors to the purposes of buttons for Gentlemen's and Ladies' dresses, each button in a set having a different subject, principally from the

---

[209] WMSS. E.18407-25. JW to TB. 19 & 20 Sept. 1772.
[210] WMSS. ditto.
[211] WMSS. E.18855-26. JW to TB. 16 Oct. 1778.
[212] WMSS. E.18367-25. JW to TB. 18 April 1772.
[213] See Neil McKendrick, 'Josiah Wedgwood and Thomas Bentley', *Trans. Roy. Hist. Soc.* 14 (1964), p. 20.

antique. They have not yet been made public in this Kingdom, His Royal Highness The Prince of Wales only being in possession of a set of them. If these little things should appear to your Excellency likely to place the ingenuity of the manufacturers of this Kingdom in a favourable point of view to Foreigners, I shall not doubt your Excellency will do me the honor to take them under your patronage in the circle of your friends and I flatter myself, Sir, you will have the goodness to pardon the liberty which I thus most humbly presume to take. I have the honor to be, Sir, your Excellency's most obliged and most obedient humble Servant, Jos. Wedgwood.[214]

Everywhere such introductions proved invaluable, and through the agency of ambassadors, envoys, consuls and plenipotentiaries, Wedgwood's wares entered—with no trouble and little expense beyond the cost of the original presents to the diplomats—the courts of Russia, Poland, Portugal, Spain, Denmark, Sweden, the Netherlands, Turkey, Naples, Turin and even into China. Such a catalogue of services is impressive. But it is by no means complete. For these men were magnificent evangelising agents for Wedgwood's ware. Each representative did more than introduce Wedgwood into one country. Ambassadors are peripatetic beings and like malaria-carrying mosquitoes they carried Wedgwood's name abroad,[215] to convert the world to what Wedgwood called 'the true belief—(a belief) in our tablets'[216] vases and multifarious productions.

Wedgwood alone amongst the Staffordshire potters enjoyed these favours, and the honour of such attention was not lost on his customers. When the Portland vase was first successfully copied it was introduced to the courts of Europe in the finest possible style through Wedgwood's ambassadorial connections.[217]

Those connections were, however, only one of the methods used by Wedgwood to break through to an international market. In the export trade no less than in England, the process of marketing pottery underwent a great change. His general sales policy was the same. He was determined on superior quality rather than cheap production to sell his wares. He was also determined to keep his prices high. From the beginning, therefore, as in England he was committed to a policy of interesting the rich and exciting the favour of the fashionable. Once more he relied on court circles to publicize the unusual quality of his wares by buying the most outstanding pieces. He knew well enough that if it was bought by kings, it would be bought by their

---

[214] JW to Sir Robert Murray Keith, 1 March 1786. British Museum, Additional MSS. 35,536. f.118. I am indebted to Dr. T. C. W. Blanning for drawing my attention to this letter. Many similar ones could be cited.

[215] Men like Sir Robert Liston who bought over £238 worth of Wedgwood ware whilst he was at Madrid and Stockholm, and later visited Washington, Batavia and Constantinople on diplomatic missions, cf. D. B. Horn, *British Diplomatic Representatives 1689–1789*, pp. 138, 144, and *Concise D.N.B.*, p. 782(a).

[216] WMSS. E.18863-26. JW to TB. 22 Nov. 1778.

[217] WMSS. Moseley MSS. JW to T. Byerley, July 1790, containing a transcript of Lord Auckland's letter to Wedgwood.

courtiers, and once fashionable at court it would be bought by the gentry, and so on down the social scale. The ambassadors had set these wheels in motion. But more than this was required. For there were many competitors for the European market. Firms such as Boulton and Fothergill were as alive to the possibilities as Wedgwood and Bentley, and they were not squeamish in their compliments. Occasionally they stole a march even on Wedgwood. As in 1776, when Josiah wrote in anguish to Bentley, 'They are now preparing a complimentary Group with a proper Inscription, upon the death of the Grand Duchess. You see they have carried *into execution* what we have only *talked about,* and will proffit by it, so surely as Princes love flattery'.[218]

Moreover, they had to make their goods easily accessible to classes outside the county circles. There was no smooth ambassadorial introduction to the minor nobilities of Europe. They had to resort to cruder methods for them. One was the first recorded example of inertia selling on a significant scale by a major England exporter. For Wedgwood and Bentley proposed to send a thousand parcels containing £20,000 worth of pottery, to deluge Europe with earthenware, for it seemed 'the only mode in which our Goods can get into such Familys'.[219] As Wedgwood wrote excitedly to Bentley: 'This object is great indeed, and my general idea upon it is to close heartily with it *to the utmost verge of prudence* or *rather beyond*[220] ... I think we sho^d not sell all to Italy and neglect the other Princes in Germany & elsewhere who are waiting with so much impatience for their turns to be served with our fine things—unless you think it better to send all to one place at a time that one Agent may first do the business in Italy, then in Germany and so on to Spain, Mexico, Indostan, China, Nova Zembla and the L^d knows where.'[221] Germany was, in fact, the first to be tried. It was a great risk. But it came off.[222] Wedgwood did not propose to repeat it. Only rising stocks and the exhaustion of all other efforts to move them, justified such storm-trooper methods. It was an exceptional technique and similar only to Wedgwood's flooding of Frankfurt with specially prepared goods in 1790 at the coronation of Leopold as Emperor. The goods he prepared were in celebration of the coronation and of Leopold's life.[223] For such objects he could hope for only

---

[218] WMSS. E.18684–25. JW to TB. 14 July 1776.
[219] WMSS. Leith Hill Place MS. JW to TB. 2 Nov. 1771. When one realizes that the average workman's weekly wage is far more than one hundred times higher than its equivalent in the 1770s, it is not extravagant to see this as the equivalent of something approaching £2,000,000 in present day values. In fact the value was even higher, for the individual parcels actually sent cost far more than £20—those sent to Dukes and Princes averaged £35 each, those to Electors averaged £70.
[220] My italics.
[221] WMSS. Leith Hill Place MS. JW to TB. 26 Oct. 1771.
[222] By August 1773 eighteen of the projected customers had failed to pay up, but later accounts showed that the debtors finally dwindled to three.
[223] WMSS. E.19010–26. 'Invoice of the Ornamental Ware shipped by JW & Co, to Fran(c)furt S/M', 11 Sept. 1790.

a temporary sale, and his intention was to advertise as much as to sell. They were designed to display his goods in the most spectacular fashion to the great congregation of European nobility that gathered to watch the coronation, and to the huge crowds that swarmed in their wake, in the hope that 'the remembrance of fine things will be implanted with sufficient force upon their minds'[224] for them never to forget them. The Portland vase was displayed there for the same purpose. For it was not the Frankfurt market that Wedgwood was aiming at—he had harnessed that before—but at the market of the whole of Europe. This concentration of goods at Frankfurt was like throwing a pebble into a pond and Wedgwood was more interested in the ripples than the splash. For slowly the fashionable crowds would disperse and with them would go Wedgwood's cameos, carried as seals on the bellies of Polish noblemen like Prince Czartoriskie, or worn as lockets at the throats of Portuguese princesses like the Marchioness of Pombal to startle distant families by the brilliance of their colour and the sharpness of their modelling, and to win orders by their novelty from every corner of Europe.

Having won the notice and the custom of the nobility, Wedgwood wished to proceed lower in the social scale. 'The Great People have had these Vases in their Palaces long enough for them to be seen and admired by the Middling Class of People, which class we know are vastly, I had almost said, infinitely superior in number to the Great, and though *a great price* was, I believe, at first necessary to make the vases esteemed *Ornament for Palaces,* that reason no longer exists. Their character is established, and the middling People w.^{d} probably by (sic) quantitys of them at a reduced price.'[225] Simply by cheapening goods which he has already made fashionable Wedgwood immediately opened up a great new market. In years like 1771–72 and 1777–78 when home demand fell Wedgwood was more willing than usual to contemplate cutting his prices, writing uncharacteristically to Bentley on 17 December 1777 of pieces which he thought could attract very large 'foreign sales, if the price does not prevent it'. In his view the price 'should be lower'd very considerably ... A crown a piece for the largest wd. be quite enough to the merchants, & we had better sell five at 5/– each then two at 10/6. They are an excellent article to make in quantitys and we c.^{d} by any means find sale for them'.[226] But it was not a method which he relished, and his wares were still far from cheap. To win this class completely he had to appeal to the differences in interests as well as in its purse. It clearly required different marketing techniques from those used to seduce the upper classes.

---

[224] WMSS. Moseley MSS, JW to JW II, 3 Sept. 1790.
[225] WMSS. E.18392-25. JW to TB. 23 August 1772.
[226] WMSS. JW to TB, 17 Dec. 1777. This was a far cry from the impertinent pricing attitude developed in response to the rampant demand of the late 1760s;—'2 guineas is too little, but I am rather afraid of 5', but for all the subtle manipulation of his pricing policy Wedgwood ultimately always returned to his high price policy arguing that his goods were 'at least as much better as they were dearer'.

The mass of the population was socially inaccessible to ambassadors, too numerous for individual parcels, and too insignificant to be flattered by reproduction. But if Wedgwood could not appeal to their vanity, he found an admirable substitute in their loyalty. He made cameo medallions of their monarchs, writing to Bentley, 'I hope to make some ... use of his C(atholic) Majesty in the Spanish Trade—*if the subjects* are fond of their King[227] the Spanish trade will be ours.' He exploited not only their loyalty to the crown but their patriotism, their pride in their national heroes, writing, 'People will give more for *their own Heads,* or the *Heads in fashion,* than for any other subjects, & buy abundantly more of them ... We should select the proper Heads for the different European Markets ... and this Plan will certainly increase our wholesale business'.[228] Their faith was equally skilfully exploited: the Popes for Italy and Spain,[229] the saints for South America,[230] Mohammed or rather (as Wedgwood more precisely and more accurately phrased it) 'proper subjects for the Faithfull amongst the Musselmen' for Turkey.[231] Buddha alone of the better known gods seems to have been neglected—presumably for economic reasons.

To the varying fashions and different tastes of his foreign buyers he gave his detailed attention. For France, for instance, where the rococo wonders of the mid century were far from dead, Wedgwood produced ormolou-mounted pottery to meet the prevailing fashion.[232] Though in Russia he dumped his old goods 'much seen or blown upon', he also produced a special pot for them alone[233] and sent them 'shewy, tawdry, cheap things, cover'd all over with colors (sic)'[234] because they thought creamware ugly. For hot climates which shared this aversion, he made 'green & Gold ware'[234] [sic] 'because they do not like *pale, colourless* ware'.[235] To America, adjudged not ripe for expensive things at present he sent mainly cheap goods and seconds, whilst for Turkey he invented a whole new range of goods to suit its exotic fancy.[236] Nor did he neglect the minor details of national habit—cups in the Saxon fashion were made for Germany; and small coffee cups, as was their custom, for the Venetians.[237]

By these means Wedgwood had created an enormous demand for his ware both ornamental and useful. The upper classes bought both, but mainly the

[227] WMSS. E.18669-25. JW to TB. 15 May 1776.
[228] WMSS. E.18679-25. JW to TB. 2 July 1776.
[229] WMSS. L.10137-12. 'A List of orders for Mr. Walmesley, Deans Gate, Manchester.' 30 Jan. 1775. 'Saints &c may answer at this market, try to provide some ... & send a sett of the Popes ... or a few loose ones'.
[230] WMSS. E.18561-25. JW to TB. 5 Nov. 1774. '... some articles sho.d be made on purpose for this trade relative to their Religion ... Crucifixes, Saints.'
[231] WMSS. E.18522-25. JW to TB. 8 March 1774.
[232] WMSS. E.18193-25. JW to TB. 15 March 1786.
[233] The 'black & yellow'.
[234] WMSS. E.18487-25. JW to TB. 14 Aug. 1773.
[235] WMSS. E.18500-25. JW to TB, postmk 22 Nov. (1773).
[236] WMSS. E.18444-35. JW to TB. 4 & 6 March 1773.
[237] WMSS. E.31191-1. TB to JW. 18 Oct. 1776.

expensive ornamental wares, and in imitation of their social superiors the lower classes bought the useful. He had achieved this success by wide and sweeping changes in the potters' marketing techniques. He had, however, a further contribution to make. He radically altered their methods of distribution. He built canals, promoted turnpike trusts, and developed a sales organization of his own. His part in the promotion of turnpikes and canals was vital to the development of Staffordshire for 'they were the basis of the prosperity of the Potteries'.[238] This aspect of his work is too well known to require repetition here. His attempt to break away from the middleman in the distribution of his goods has, however, been only slightly touched upon by other historians.

He had dealt since 1769 through middlemen such as Boulton and Fothergill, Bentley and Boardman, Hume and Walmesley, Edmund Radcliffe and a host of others abroad. But, vital as their service was to most potters, Wedgwood was rapidly outgrowing his reliance upon them. More and more merchants, attracted by Wedgwood's name and reputation, were writing to him personally in order to get more favourable terms.[239] Naturally Wedgwood was keen to accept their advances and dispense with the middlemen and their profit-devouring commissions, and he knew that they would 'leave us whenever they can buy 6d P doz cheaper. I would therefore wish us to have a correspondence of our own, independent of any set of men whomsoever, both at home and abroad, with the Merch.ᵗˢ & with the Shops. We can make any quantity, & the only P(aten)t we can now have is to make them *perfect* & *disperse* them. The former shall have my best attention here & I shall lose no opportunity of assisting in the latter as occasions may offer',[240] a neat, in practice an almost too neat, definition of their respective roles in the partnership.

Although his reputation attracted many buyers, Wedgwood did not rely on his name alone to overcome the many difficulties—distance, language and tariff prohibitions—which foreign merchants had to face. He sought them out with pattern boxes,[241] and catalogues in translation;[242] tempted them with discounts, reductions and special terms for the first order;[243] and eased their problem of delivery by establishing foreign warehouses like those in Dublin,

---

[238] J. H. Plumb, *England in the Eighteenth Century* (London, 1950), p. 147.
[239] WMSS. E.5077-7. Conrad Wilhelm Krause of Brunswick ('Brounschwyk') to JW, 15 Feb. 1771. Krause has 'several Times received by Hands of my Friends Goods from your Fabric' but now he wished to 'Negotiate Direct'. There are many similar examples.
[240] WMSS. E.18473-25. JW to TB, postmark 21 June (1773).
[241] WMSS. E.18501-25. JW to TB. 21 Nov. 1773. 'We shall want some hundreds of small dishes to send abroad as patterns the next spring. . . .'
[242] First in French in 1773 (E.18501-25), then German and Italian in 1774 (E.18518-25 and E.18524-25), and finally Dutch and Russian in the same year (E.18527-25). They seem to have been a new idea, at least to the Potteries because incredibly elaborate steps were taken to keep the illustrated ones secret in order 'to get the start one season at least'.
[243] The elasticity of JW's attitude to discounts is fully illustrated in his dealings with Messrs. James Jackson & Co of St. Petersburg. L.H.P. 1771.

Paris and Amsterdam, and employing foreign agents like Veldhuyson and Perregaux. For the further comfort of his foreign buyers he employed French-, German-, Italian- and Dutch-speaking clerks and answered their letters in their native tongue. Ample testimony to his success and the increasing momentum of commercial development he brought about can be found in his account books. And an analysis of his foreign correspondence reveals the constant expansion of foreign orders. For although he only received his first order from abroad in 1764, by 1790 he had sold in every city in Europe. The spread of his foreign sales can be mapped out with considerable although not precise accuracy from the letters of foreign merchants buying direct from Wedgwood. Many more, buying through middlemen, would probably complicate the map of the evidence if their orders were available, but we know for certain that he had received orders from Amsterdam by 1764; from St Petersburg and Brunswick in 1769; from Dublin in 1771; from Naples in 1773; from Dessau, Leipzig and Paris in 1774; Bonn, Dresden, Dunkirk, Leghorn, Malaga, Rotterdam, Trieste and Venice in 1775; Goa in 1776; Moscow and Nice in 1777; Ostend, Rome and Vienna in 1781; Geneva in 1782; Antwerp, Brescia, Cadiz, Hamburg, Ratisbon and Stuttgart in 1783; Brussels, Genoa, Lisbon and Palermo in 1784; Dorpat, Marseilles, Stockholm, Strasbourg in 1785; Basle, Bilbao, Bologna and Madrid in 1786; Danzig, Rouen, Turin in 1787; Ancona, Berne, Oslo, Lübeck, Mittau, Nuremberg, Parma, Riga, Udine in 1788; Boulogne, Darmstadt, Douai, Mainz, Mannheim, Milan in 1789; Göttingen, Regensburg, Tournai in 1790; Ansbach and Copenhagen in 1791; Cologne and Memmingen in 1793.[244] This list is meant to give an impression of the rapid spread of Wedgwood's exports rather than to be a complete list. Many of the dates might well need to be adjusted forwards, and he is known to have been dealing with The Hague, Metz, Limoges, Zurich, Lausanne, Bordeaux, Épernay, Bayreuth, St. Amand, Florence, Gothenburg, Konigsberg, Oporto, Archangel, Warsaw, Brema and Messina by 1790, but it is not certain when the first order for these cities was received.

This list makes no mention either of his earlier colonial sales through Bentley and Boardman. The European market with a population of over 200 million (compared with a market of less than 3 million Americans or indeed a home market of less than 8 million) was increasingly after 1772, and dominatingly after 1784, to become Wedgwood's major outlet for his products, but in the 1760s his exports went primarily to the colonies. Wedgwood's hyperbole, the political intent of the letter, and the difficulties of judging the size of his sales through middlemen casts doubt on statements like the one to Sir William Meredith, M.P. for Liverpool in 1765 that 'the bulk of our particular manufacture is exported to home markets for our

[244] This list is culled from the whole range of WMSS. but more especially from E.609-1 to 30210-1; E.835-2 to 1954-2; E.2742-4 to 3282-4; E.3724-5 to 31090-5; E.4321-6 to 31129-6. Cf. Hower, op. cit., p. 309.

home consumption is very trifling in comparison with what is sent abroad, and the principal of these markets are the continent and islands of North America'.[245]

The detailed evidence for Wedgwood's exports is large in amount, varied in type and presents evidential difficulties of interpretation which make it impossible to examine in detail here. The list of direct evidence includes Wedgwood's claims, intentions and boasts, and Wedgwood's Books of Bad Debts, his lists of foreign orders, and his analysis of orders on hand at particular moments of time. But the indirect evidence requires one to take note also of the timing and distribution of Wedgwood's fakes, of Wedgwood's imitators, of foreign governments' protective tariffs, or even at times their total prohibition, of the activities of arcanists and foreign spies and the timing of Wedgwood's efforts to check the loss of industrial secrets to them, and of the times when Wedgwood actively smuggled his goods into foreign markets, not to mention the varied array of contemporary comment in letters, Board of Trade examinations, travellers' accounts and satirical cartoons.

In my view the contemporary values put on the size and importance of Wedgwood's exports are fully borne out by an examination of the detailed quantitative data. Those cartoonists who saw the figure of John Bull made up of British exports with English cotton as the main body, and English pottery as the unmistakable face, and Wedgwood's products as the jaunty hat with his name clearly stamped upon it, were right in both the relative proportions and the relative prominence they gave to Wedgwood. The cartoonist who presented John Bull as hurling the knives and forks of Sheffield cutlery, and skimming the plates of Wedgwood through the ranks of embattled French, whilst a frightened Napoleon crouched in terror at the effects of English exports used as guided weapons, was also right in spirit.

But if one eschews the more picturesque evidence and relies on hard statistics one can show from Wedgwood's lists of bad debts that approximately 10 per cent of them derived from exports in 1771, approximately 33 per cent in 1773 (when admittedly they were artificially swollen by the effects of his inertia selling campaign), and approximately 75 per cent in 1789. Now bad debts are not a direct and undeviating index to total sales, but in fact all the other evidence points in the same direction. A geographical analysis of his merchants' correspondence, a geographical analysis of the intended places of sale of unexecuted orders, a geographical analysis of actual individual orders (as well as the geographical analysis of bad debts), all point to substantial colonial demand in the 1760s, later dwarfed by sales to Europe. The significant change of gear in actively seeking foreign sales comes first in 1772, with a further sales effort in 1778, and unmistakable evidence that by 1784 Wedgwood was exporting nearly 80 per cent of his total produce. This is all the more significant because one can show that by 1785 the whole

[245] 'Home versus Foreign Demand: The Myth of Wedgwood's Exports'—see note 1.

of the Staffordshire potteries were exporting 84 per cent of their total produce abroad. I have discussed elsewhere the evidence which shows how the spread of individual orders matches this pattern. It shows that the spread of foreign factories set up specifically to rival Wedgwood's creamware matches it. It shows how the timing and intensity of foreign fakers, the peak activity, both by and against foreign industrial spies, the evidence of foreign observers, and the decline of foreign competition and the tariff activity to defend them, *all* fit in with this general pattern.[245]

One final point requires attention. For no account of Wedgwood's marketing activities would be complete without some mention of the part he played in organizing the potters, appealing to ambassadors and exploiting his noble connections to bring pressure to bear upon the formation of economic policy and the government's attitude to import restrictions and prohibitions. This aspect of his career is more germane to Wedgwood's political activities and as such is beyond the scope of this chapter, but it is necessary to point out here that by his action he influenced the Government in its formulation of the Irish Treaty of 1785, initiated an attempt to lift the Swedish prohibition on English earthenware in 1789, and led the potters in their efforts to secure favourable commercial treaties with Portugal in 1785, and, most important of all, with France in 1787. Some idea of the effects this could have on the official statistics, if not on the potter's actual sales, can be judged by a comparison of the earthenware exports to France in 1785 and 1789. In 1785 they totalled £641; four years later they amounted to £7,920.[246] Yet again Wedgwood had penetrated a market which had defied all previous English potters.

There are many reasons why the offical statistics are unreliable, and why, in my opinion, the reliance on Elizabeth Schumpeter's trade statistics is so misleading.[247] Too little allowance is made for smuggling (the fact that there were no export duties on pottery did not mean that there were not heavy import duties imposed by the governments of countries buying English pottery, and the cheerful assumption by historians that manufacturers like Wedgwood had no need to smuggle is not borne out by either the evidence that they did so, or the tariff barriers they were trying to avoid). Too little allowance is made for the effects of the rise of prices—not just the modest eighteenth-century inflation, but the decisive increase in the value of the goods manufactured by eighteenth-century entrepreneurs. Mrs. Schumpeter's statistics are based on a valuation for pottery of 5 shillings per hundred pieces—an adequate valuation when fixed, but absurdly inadequate for Wedgwood's products, or even those of his rivals who sold so much more cheaply than he did. If the value of six-tenths of one penny per piece of

---

[246] G. Villiers and John Baring, *Final Report of the Commercial Relations between France and Great Britain* (Parl. Report, 1834), p. 87.
[247] E. B. Schumpeter, *English Overseas Trade Statistics 1697–1808* (1960).

pottery exported[248] were to be raised to 3 pence per piece, the estimate that 16 per cent of total pottery manufactures were exported would rise to 80 per cent. When one realizes that the price per dozen of common Staffordshire creamware was 3 shillings a dozen—i.e. 3 pence each, the likelihood of this figure Mrs. Schumpeter relies on being correct can easily be judged.[249]

Such was his success that he had in the words of Faujas de Saint Fond, 'created a commerce so active and so universal, that in travelling from Paris to St Petersburg, from Amsterdam to the farthest point of Sweden, from Dunkirk to the southern extremity of France, one is served at every inn from English earthenware. The same fine article adorns the tables of Spain, Portugal, & Italy, and it provides the cargoes of ships to the East Indies, the West Indies and America'.[250] In Poland in 1783, it was announced that 'His Majesty (Stanislas Augustus) wishing to put an end to the considerable loss in currency caused by purchases of table-ware manufactured in England, has established ... at great expense, a pottery at the Belvedere palace'.[251] Even the great European factories—Sèvres, Meissen, Vienna, Fürstenberg, Paris and Doccia had to follow the humble Staffordshire potters and reproduce Wedgwood's designs.

If I have laboured this point it is to show to what lengths Wedgwood was prepared to go to sell his wares, to show what detailed attention he lavished on his customers' requirements and to show how misguided is the accepted and often repeated view that Wedgwood and Bentley 'were in fact too absorbed in the creation of beauty to be overmindful of the means and methods of its dissemination'.[252] Nothing could be further from the truth. In fact, far from such delightful indifference to sales and such unselfish devotion to beauty, Wedgwood was quite prepared to reproduce ugly objects if his customers wanted them, writing, 'I have a very small vase which was dug out of Herculaneum...I do not see any beauty in it but will make something of it'[253] if Sir William Farringdon wishes it. Moreover, when his orders exceeded his output, he answered the demand by supplying ware which he had bought from other potters—potters like Lowe, Astbury, Meir, Garner, Turner, Heath, Browne and Malkin and many others[254]—whose products were usually cheaper imitations of Wedgwood, often much below his standard

---

[248] i.e. 5 shillings or 60 pence divided by one hundred pieces equals 6/10ths.
[249] In fact if one painstakingly puts the known contemporary price to each piece ordered from abroad (and I have done so for many of Wedgwood's foreign orders) the average value per parcel is about 5 pence. Allowing for the margin between Wedgwood's prices and his rivals, one is not surprised when the average value of foreign orders for *their* products comes out at approximately three pence each piece.
[250] Faujas de st Fond: *Voyage en Angleterre, en Ecosse et aux Iles Hébrides*, vol. I, p. 112.
[251] Witola Kula, *Szkice o manufakturach w Polsce, XVIII wieku* (Warsaw, 1956) 1, 304; quoting from Pamiztnik... 1783 (ed. Switkowski). I am indebted to my colleague Professor L. R. Lewitter for this reference.
[252] Meteyard, op. cit., I, 368-9.
[253] WMSS. E.18271-25. JW to TB. 1 Dec. 1769.
[254] WMSS. E.4840-6 to 5062-6. And various other scattered references.

of production, which could never have sold in quantity without the aid of Wedgwood's marketing organization. In the 1780s when the supply constantly lagged behind the demand, Wedgwood was forced to buy in quantity from other potters—he bought £4,500's worth from George Neunburg alone in the first six months of 1784.[255] Nothing displays better the importance of Wedgwood's salesmanship than this period. For so fashionable had his name become and so popular his wares, that he could sell at a higher price what his rivals could not sell at all. His buyers complained bitterly when the pottery sent did not bear his name, but they usually accepted it—albeit reluctantly—so long as the pill was sweetened by a respectable amount of their orders being truly Wedgwood. The brand image was obviously of great importance to his buyers, and we know that many of their customers insisted that their purchases carried the Wedgwood trademark, but inevitably there was a less discerning market which would accept imitation Wedgwood.

Despite constant complaints of high prices, slow delivery, bad packing and inadequately made-up orders, the retail merchants had to deal with Wedgwood in preference to any other potter. For their customers—both foreign and English, both humble and aristocratic—knew of Wedgwood ware, knew that the English queen, the Russian empress and countless foreign and native aristocrats used it, and they were determined to have those pieces of Wedgwood which they could afford. Patterns seen in the London showrooms were insisted on by ambitious hostesses in the provinces; Catherine the Great's service seen in St Petersburg persuaded Muscovite nobles to order similar sets; heads of the Popes in jasper spread Wedgwood's name through Italy, Spain and South America; and the Queen of Portugal in cameo proved irresistible to the people of Lisbon. Medallions of the notables of Germany, Holland, France, Poland, America, Sweden, Denmark and Turkey served a similar purpose there. Once they reached these distant parts their excellence proved their own advertisement. It encapsulated all the virtues of the prevailing European taste for the neo-classics and when particular markets proved unresponsive to the current taste Wedgwood was always willing to adapt his designs to suit the market he was aiming at.

His customers also knew that his ware was easily available. For not only had he had to make his ware well known, he had also had to make it accessible to the world market whose attention he had won. The difficulties involved in buying from Etruria alone might have discouraged all but the most ardent. As Wedgwood rightly said, 'it will only be a few, who have the disorder very strong upon them who will be at the trouble of procuring them from such a distance'.[256] In fact the methods of distribution suited to the peasant craft stage of the potteries had proved totally inadequate to dispose of the growing production of Etruria. And Wedgwood had completely transformed them. The impact of the Industrial Revolution in the Potteries

[255] WMSS. L.1788 to 1789. Cf. Hower, op. cit., p. 301.
[256] WMSS. E.18318-25. JW to TB. 20 Aug. 1770.

had an inevitable effect on the attitude of the potters to marketing their goods. It called for new methods of salesmanship and new centres for display. Men with a specialized knowledge of commerce were needed as partners; foreign agents required to handle the European markets; and trained linguists were necessary to deal with the increasingly technical problems of foreign orders. To solve these problems Wedgwood set up salerooms in the provinces; experimented with travelling salesmen carrying pattern boxes for display; published catalogues with illustrations and in translation; employed foreign clerks to translate his orders from abroad; and took as his partner the Liverpool merchant Thomas Bentley.[257] He led the cry for canals and turnpike roads and petitioned the government on commercial treaties.

Dr. Thomas allows such changes to signify 'a commercial revolution in the disposal and dispersion of their goods as real and disturbing as the productive changes which occurred inside their industrial organizations and as far reaching as the Communication and Transport revolutions which occurred outside their factories',[258] and dates its completion as 1850. But although all the other potters did not experience such a revolution by that date, there can be little doubt that Wedgwood had initiated all the most important changes by 1790. Yet no aspect of Josiah Wedgwood's life has been so neglected as his impact on the commercial techniques of the eighteenth century. Few are more important.

For it was by such methods that a local craft became a national industry and served an international market. In 1775 Wedgwood had hoped to 'ASTONISH THE WORLD ALL AT ONCE'.[259] What he expressed as a hope in 1775 he had accomplished as a fact in 1795. His ware was in universal demand. Admired by the Emperors of China, Russia and Germany; praised by scientists of the calibre of Priestley, Watt and Black; and painted by artists as fashionable as Stubbs, Romney and Wright of Derby, it was acclaimed by art, science and society. And—which was more important for Wedgwood—it was equally acclaimed by the public. For it was from his huge sales of his common useful ware—seals, buttons, inkpots, tableware and the like—that Wedgwood drew his greatest reward from his commercial campaign. The servants' hall was quick to follow its mistress's lead, and Wedgwood's accounts consistently return a higher percentage of sales and takings in his useful ware than in his ornamental; even in fashionable Bath,

---

[257] Other potters teamed up with merchants—Josiah Spode II with William Copeland, the successful London tea merchant in 1824, Thomas Minton with William Pownall, the Liverpool merchant in 1793—but Wedgwood's association with Bentley which began in 1769 was one of the earliest and most successful of the great eighteenth-century 'inventor and entrepreneur' partnerships. Owing to the disappearance of all but fragments of Bentley's correspondence it is difficult to do full justice to his part in the partnership in this volume, but I have attempted to show elsewhere how important it was; see *Trans. Roy. Hist. Soc.* (1964).
[258] Dr. J. Thomas, op. cit., p. 771 *et seq.*
[259] WMSS. E.18614–25. JW to TB. 6 August 1775.

the proportion was 60 to 40.[260] It is therefore in the fading lists of outstanding accounts and amongst the neglected bundles of everyday orders that the true picture of Wedgwood's universal appeal and widespread success is to be found. They record ambitions of the chef of the Yacht Inn in Cheshire who hoped to found his gastronomic reputation on Wedgwood's creamware; the taste for Wedgwood shared by a German professor at Brunswick and a bachelor don at Cambridge; the popularity of Wedgwood in a lonely military garrison in Quebec; and the purchase of Wedgwood by Edward Gibbon whilst writing his great history in Lausanne. These and many others bought it: Spanish ambassadors, Indian colonists, Bohemian nobles, Bristol chemists, Oxford colleges, Lancashire merchants and Sicilian monarchs. By superb marketing methods and the exercise of his vivid entrepreneurial imagination, Josiah Wedgwood had achieved his purpose. He was what he wished to be: 'Vase Maker General to the Universe'.[261]

He had accomplished, in fact, the most spectacular example of a successful policy of product differentiation in the history of British pottery. He had played the dominant commercial role in helping to open up a world market for his new inventions, and then captured it for himself and his many Staffordshire competitors. Since he enjoyed no monopoly in the production, since he was not competitive in price, it required a remarkably effective marketing and sales campaign to achieve his success. As a sustained assault using such a variety of promotional ploys it was rivalled only by entrepreneurs of the calibre of Matthew Boulton,[262] but as I attempt to show below,[263] some of his commercial techniques were rivalled, and even surpassed, by many an unsung eighteenth-century businessman.

* * *

Josiah Wedgwood's career offers the perfect illustration of the most striking and characteristic features of the commercial and consumer revolution of the late eighteenth century. His marketing techniques might have been designed to demonstrate—although with an elegance and style and effectiveness which few of them can match—the concepts enshrined in such academic labels as the 'Veblen effect', the 'demonstration effect', the 'snob effect', the 'bandwagon effect' or the 'penetration effect'.[264] All these 'effects' were explicitly recognized by Wedgwood. Social emulation through emulative spending, the rich London market inspiring imitative behaviour in the provinces, the lead offered by the aristocratic few being aped by the socially aspiring many, the general clambering after the example provided by the

---

[260] WMSS. E.4428-6 to 4651-6. Returns to Wedgwood of the takings in the Bath salerooms.
[261] WMSS. E.18232-25; JW to TB, February 1769.
[262] Eric Robinson, 'Eighteenth Century Commerce and Fashion: Matthew Boulton's Marketing Techniques', *Economic History Review*, 2nd series, 16 (1963), pp. 39-60.
[263] See chapter 4.
[264] H. Leibenstein, 'Bandwagon, Snob and Veblen Effects in the Theory of Consumers' Demand, *Quarterly Journal of Economics* 64, (1950), pp. 183-88.

legislators of taste—all of these phenomena were thoroughly and efficiently exploited by Wedgwood.

His crisp and economical descriptions of current consumer behaviour and the action best suited to satisfy it—'Fashion is infinitely superior to *merit*', 'begin at the head first, and then proceed to the inferior members', 'Few ladies dare venture at anything out of the common stile 'till authorised by their betters', 'a *great price* was at first necessary to make the Vases esteemed *Ornaments for Palaces*', 'I need not tell you how much will depend upon a *proper & noble* introduction'[265]—often put to shame the jargon-ridden accounts of modern academic commentators. Indeed after examining the variety and ingenuity of his successful commercial techniques, one might feel that justice required that the creation and exploitation of this type of consumer demand should be labelled the Wedgwood effect, or more precisely the Wedgwood and Bentley effect.

Since modern academic convention (in modest acclaim of its own practitioners) attaches a nomenclature taken from those who first staked their claim to recognize a particular pattern of economic or social behaviour in the past, rather than giving the credit to those who recognised its contemporary importance and took commercially purposeful action, then Veblen is more likely to be honoured than Wedgwood or Bentley.

Yet few more deserve such recognition, for their partnership encapsulates a remarkable range of selling techniques—some revived and some original, some common to many of their competitors, others far ahead of their time. The full catalogue of their marketing techniques contains many ideas which seem startlingly novel and anachronistically modern. They used inertia-selling campaigns, product differentiation, market segmentation, detailed market research, embryonic self-service schemes, money-back-if-not-satisfied policies, free carriage, give away sales promotion, auctions, lotteries, catalogues (illustrated and in translation), advanced credit, three-tier discount schemes, including major discounts for first orders, and almost every form of advertisement, trade cards, shop signs, letterheads, bill heads, newspaper and magazine advertisment, fashion plates and fashion magazines, solicited puffs, organized propaganda campaigns, even false attacks organized to provide the opportunity to publicize the counter-attack (even the despised handbills were given a brief trial before they were banned). Some, like the self-service schemes, were of little significance; others, like the massive inertia selling campaign of 1771 were exceptional and born of the need for action up to 'the utmost verge of prudence or rather beyond'; but most were integral parts of an imaginative but consistently applied commercial policy which was designed to reach as wide a market as possible, even if different sections required very different approaches. There were campaigns specifically directed at the aristocratic market, the middling ranks and the mass market,

---

[265] All quoted above.

campaigns specifically aimed at different national markets, different religious faiths, and different aesthetic commitments. The range of goods which Wedgwood made allowed him to meet the needs of the kitchen, the dining room, and the drawing room; nor did he neglect the garden, the conservatory, or the dairy. With bin labels for the cellar, bidets for the bathroom, dog bowls for the kennels; with his chandeliers, crucifixes, water closets, fountains and plant pots, with his fonts for christening and funeral plaques for church memorials, he provided for most human needs from birth to death. Whether eating or excreting, whether drinking or washing, whether providing light for their homes, or playing chess, the eighteenth-century customer had a remarkable wide range of his consumer needs satisfied by the protean variety of Wedgwood's products. All this vast variety had to be directed at their appropriate buyers—and as a result there were campaigns aimed specifically at the male market, and, far more frequently, specifically at the female market—even the potential custom of children was not neglected. There were toys and miniatures directly aimed at the juvenile market, and, more obliquely, this particular consumer group were approached through the educational aspirations of their parents and the educational aids provided by their schools.

To all these different needs and different consumer groups Wedgwood gave his energetic attention. His commerical imagination missed few opportunities, and although he occasionally regrets a failure to satisfy a need (as with the demand for reproductions of Keppel's head), or concedes that Matthew Boulton has stolen a march in the art of strategic sycophancy ('and will proffit by it, so surely as Princes love flattery'), or bemoans his failure to win the support of the architects in the promotion of their large jasper plaques, his success rate was remarkably high and his attention to the market remarkably comprehensive.

In the history of such salesmanship it is natural to stress the landmarks in the history of entrepreneurial manipulation of the market. In the history of the Potteries (and Wedgwood's phenomenal personal success) it is necessary to stress the distinctive features which help to explain that success which so far exceeded most of his competitors. But if Wedgwood outshone all of his rival potters in this department as he did in so many others, it must not be forgotten that his promotional techniques and his sales organization helped to bring profits and prosperity—albeit of a lower order and to a lesser degree—to many of his fellow potters. Many rode to success on Wedgwood's commercial coat-tails, just as they clambered onto the classical bandwaggon he had set rolling, or copied his breakthroughs in technique, organization or invention. He, of course, enjoyed a considerable lead. The time lag between his introduction of new commercial ideas and the ability of the Staffordshire potters to respond to them was not always short. Some of the advantages Wedgwood won for himself were never accessible to his rivals, but the price of a 10 per cent commission to Wedgwood was often their route to markets opened up by Wedgwood. At the cost of lower profits—the result of their lower prices and his commission—they could absorb the custom of those beyond and below the reach of Wedgwood's price policy.

And just as canals and turnpikes promoted by Wedgwood opened up the national market for all the Staffordshire potters, just as the improvements and inventions made by Wedgwood extended the range of products for many of his rivals, just as the designs he paid famous artists to produce for him were soon the property of others, so this battery of commercial techniques benefited potters other than Wedgwood and Bentley. They benefited to a lesser degree, but by extending the market, by exciting new demand, and by commercializing his potteries, Wedgwood inevitably brought the advantages of an increased demand to the rest of his industry.

The growth of national aggregate demand was an inviting target for all. Existing demand levels—at the luxury end of the market and at the mass level—were all increasing. By so successfully exploiting that demand and by extending it further, by releasing latent demand, and by inducing new demand by exciting new wants, Wedgwood helped to create a host of new commerical opportunities from which others beside himself could benefit.

The response was inevitably varied and unequal. Eighteenth-century commercial techniques encompassed a world which still included the humble packman carrying his goods on his own back and peddling them in an area limited by his own stamina, by the often still execrable local roads, and by the poverty of many of his customers. But it also now encompassed world-famous companies using travelling salesmen equipped with illustrated bilingual catalogues, ambassadorial channels exploited for purely commercial purposes, elegant showrooms, foreign warehouses, royal patronage, international advertisement, all dependent on sophisticated pricing policies, effective market research, accurate cost accounting, skilled manipulation of fashion, and a whole battery of commercial techniques designed to make effective a carefully worked out marketing policy.

In one's immediate concern to stress the demand side of the equation one must not forget the supply side. Neither Wedgwood nor the rest of the Potteries would have flourished without new inventions, new methods of production and new standards of workmanship. Raising capital, collecting debts, costing accounts, recruiting and disciplining labour, controlling production, meeting wage bills—indeed the whole panoply of problems facing the businessman—had to be successfully solved in order to succeed.[266]

Here, however, the primary aim is to examine and explain his commercial skills. Having done so, it is difficult to deny that a quite new order of commercial sophistication had been introduced to the Potteries by Wedgwood. Of course new markets had been broached before, of course some Staffordshire potters had sold in London before Wedgwood, of course some had exported

---

[266] How Wedgwood met *these* challenges, and solved *these* problems is dealt with in detail in my forthcoming book *Josiah Wedgwood and the Industrial Revolution*.

their goods abroad—both to the colonies and to Europe—before Wedgwood. But the scale of their operations was dwarfed by his, just as the commercial skills of the pre-Wedgwood potteries were primitive compared with his.

By painstaking research one can establish that some of Wedgwood's techniques have an honourable pedigree before his day, just as by examining eighteenth-century rubbish tips[267] one can show that early Staffordshire slipware reached Chester, or infer that it reached Bristol,[268] or point out that some of the butterpots made for the local Uttoxeter market eventually reached London.[269] But after Wedgwood's commercial assault on the national and European markets the evidence of his success is overwhelming. The suggestion that 84 per cent of the total annual production of the Staffordshire potters (worth some £300,000 in eighteenth-century values, and approximately £30,000,000 at today's prices) was being exported by the late 1780s is difficult to avoid. The evidence of *how* Wedgwood achieved that commercial revolution is equally abundant.

Where else before the 1770s could one find such concentrated evidence of such an explicit awareness of the need for a varied commercial response to the needs of the market, such a variety of demand-enhancing commercial ploys, such an acceptance of the active promotional approach to salesmanship and marketing, as a single letter from Wedgwood to Bentley provides. It reveals a quite new intensity of concentration on commercial techniques compared with the pre-Wedgwood potteries:

'Wo^d you *advertise* the next season as the silk mercers in Pell mell do,—Or *deliver cards* at the houses of the Nobility & Gentry, & in the City,—Get leave to *make a shew* of his Majesty's Service for a month, & ornament the Dessert with Ornamental Ewers, flower baskets & Vases—Or have an *Auction* at Cobbs room of Statues, Bassrreliefs, Pictures, Tripods, Candelabrias, Lamps, Potpouris, Superb Ewers, Cisterns, Tablets Etruscan, Porphirys & other Articles not yet expos'd to sale. *Make a great route of advertising this Auction,* & at the same time mention our rooms in Newport St.—& have another Auction in the full season at Bath of such things as we have now on hand, just sprinkled over with a few new articles *to give them an air of novelty* to any of our customers who may see them there,—Or will you trust to a *new disposition of the Rooms* with the new articles we shall have to put into them & a few modest *puffs in the Papers* from some of our friends such as I am told there has been one lately in Lloyd's

---

[267] G. Webster and K. Barton, 'An eighteenth-century rubbish pit, Trinity Street, 1953', *Journal of the Chester and North Wales Architectural and Archaeological and Historical Society* (1957), XLIV, p. 19.

[268] Lorna Weatherill, op. cit., p. 80, argues that Staffordshire pottery of the pre-Wedgwood (i.e. pre-1730) period reached Bristol because of 'random finds of pieces which were *probably* not manufactured in Bristol and are *similar in style* to the Staffordshire pieces in the Victoria and Albert Museum.' My italics.

[269] Weatherill, op. cit., p. 77.

Chronicle,'[270]—but that surely is enough to give the flavour of the letter. Here auctions, exhibitions, visiting cards, straightforward advertisements, puffs, novelties and changes in the rooms are all considered in a single letter as 'new means of exciting attention to our vases'.[271]

The new levels of commercialization suggested by that single letter, are confirmed, reinforced and proved beyond reasonable doubt by the incomparable richness of the evidential resources of the rest of the Wedgwood archive.

[270] WMSS. E.18318–25. JW to TB. 20 Aug. 1770.
[271] Ibid.

CHAPTER FOUR

George Packwood and the Commercialization of Shaving
The Art of Eighteenth-century Advertising
or
'The Way to Get Money and be Happy'

'The trade of advertising is now so near perfection that it is not easy to propose any improvement.
Dr. Johnson, 1759.

THE NAKED TRUTH
Q. What was the original meaning and intent of *advertisements?*
A. To publish the truth.
Q. Where is the truth, that valuable jewel, to be met with?
A. Not only the truth, but the naked truth, is at this time copiously dealt out by PACKWOOD all over the land.
The Telegraph, 1795.

The choice of George Packwood to serve as my second main exemplar of the process of commercialization is a deliberate one. The contrast between Packwood, obscure to the point of anonymity even to eighteenth-century specialists, and Wedgwood, celebrated to the point of satiety to some of those same specialists, is also deliberate.

To some it may seem inappropriate to harness together, even if only in the process of explanation, men of such wholly different business stature. But Wedgwood, an entrepreneur of genius, the complete businessman who bequeathed a vast and multi-faceted business archive as evidence of his comprehensive business skills, and Packwood, the unknown small businessman, for whom evidence of only a *single* business skill has surfaced in the shape of his newspaper advertisements, were both significant parts of the same commercial revolution, both vital parts of the same entrepreneurial assault on the consumer market of the late eighteenth century.

In terms of their contribution to the economy Wedgwood and Packwood were, of course, of very different individual importance. In terms of their mastery of entrepreneurial technique Packwood and Wedgwood were completely different animals: they were as different as the hedgehog is from the fox. Wedgwood, like the fox, had mastered a remarkable variety of entrepreneurial skills and could respond imaginatively and creatively to a whole range of business problems; Packwood, like the hedgehog, relied above all on one particular skill, but his mastery of it made possible both his survival and his prosperity.

Both the hedgehog and the fox have their roles to play in the world of enterprise. By ignoring the hedgehogs historians diminish their understanding of the nature and variety of the business world. By ignoring men like Packwood, they diminish their understanding of the working of the economy in the late eighteenth century. There were after all many more Packwoods than Wedgwoods to be found then busily manipulating consumer demand, even if historians have largely chosen to ignore them.

But Packwood is more than a mere uncelebrated businessman. His significance lies also in the fact that he was a master of advertising. That is why the title of this chapter is deliberately reminiscent of an eighteenth century advertisement. Indeed part of it is taken from the cheerful slogans which announced George Packwood's own 'Account of his Diverting Advertisements'. It is also deliberately concerned with a minor aspect of the manipulation of consumer behaviour, for I wish to demonstrate that even in the lesser trades, like the selling of razor strops, the level of marketing skill, the ingenuity of salesmanship, the quality of promotional imagination could be remarkably impressive. Peripheral as shaving will always be in any history of the commercial revolution of eighteenth-century England, it is worth recalling how much advertising space and skill was, and still is, devoted to selling ways of removing men's facial hair. The techniques involved in promoting and selling the wherewithal with which to shave are far from irrelevant in any discussion of consumer behaviour and the methods used to manipulate it. They can serve as a significant pointer to prevailing advertising methods. One should not forget that Dr. Addison in the *Tatler* and Dr. Johnson in the *Idler*—those two authoritative voices on the life of Georgian England—both specifically singled out the promotional activities of the inventors of razor strops as being characteristic of current advertising practices.

By studying the advertisements of a single individual one can examine in detail the style, tone, variety and language used by eighteenth-century salesmen. Such minute dissection reveals much that is lost in the more general surveys. And such concern with a lesser tradesman not only illuminates areas usually wholly ignored by historians, but also illustrates how widespread advanced eighteenth-century commercial practices could be, and shows how far from the great centres of industry brilliant entrepreneurial endeavours can be found.

This is not, of course, to claim that Packwood was necessarily typical of the small anonymous men of business. His creative advertising skills do not prove the pervasive nature of the consumer revolution, do not prove that this commercializing process reached into every cranny of the eighteenth-century trading nation, do not prove that eighteenth-century advertisers were inventive, versatile, remarkably varied in their approach, and irresistibly persistent in their commercial intent; but they do prove that such things were possible, and that such skills were practised.

In demonstrating that they were both possible, and practised, by even the lesser breed of entrepreneur, they extend the boundary of debate and make a fresh look at eighteenth-century advertising both necessary and important. For advertisements provide the most obvious public evidence of how businessmen tried to manipulate consumer demand, provide the clearest public evidence of a businessman's persistence, inventiveness and commercial skill.

The image of his product which he tried to present to, and to imprint on, the public is most vividly revealed in his advertisements, along with the level and quality of the entrepreneurial imagination which had produced them.

That special skills *were* necessary for the eighteenth-century advertiser to flourish was clearly recognized by entrepreneurs. Dr. Johnson announced in 1761 that 'advertisements are now so numerous that they are very negligently perused, and it is therefore become necessary to gain attention by magnificence of promises and by eloquence sometimes sublime and sometimes pathetic'.[1] Sheridan was more specific and when he introduced Mr. Puff in *The Critic* as 'a practitioner in panegyric, or to speak more plainly a professor in the art of puffing, at your service—or anybody else's', he went on to recognize that 'puffing is of various sorts: the principals are the puff direct, the puff preliminary, the puff collateral, the puff collusive and the puff oblique, or the puff by implication'.[2]

By the turn of the century the art of puffing had reached such a pitch and commanded such a variety of techniques that a new vocabulary of description had been invented to do it justice. With what was to be called *The Language of the Walls* or *The Voice from the Shop Window* or *The Mirror of Commercial Roguery*,[3] consumers were being bullied and cajoled into buying by the insistent siren voices of advertisement. They demanded their attention from every direction, and in protean shape and variety. 'The newspaper press is the greatest lying and puffing machine in the world! Then comes the walls with their barefaced falsehoods and the shop windows with their gilded lies.'[4]

It was no longer enough to describe the way in which 'wives and daughters were puffed into fashionable dresses by puffing drapers', it was necessary to describe and identify and explain the techniques by which 'the Art of

---

[1] Dr. Johnson, *The Idler*, 20 January 1761.
[2] R. B. Sheridan, *The Critic* (1779).
[3] James Dawson Burn, *The Language of the Walls and the Voice from the Shop Window or the Mirror of Commercial Roguery* (1855). A history of the previous forty years' advertising.
[4] Ibid.

Persuasion',[5] to use Fielding's description, cunningly manipulated the custom of the world. It was increasingly recognized that when demand was in thrall to fashion successful manufacturers *needed* to puff their products and boost their sales through promotional publicity.[6] And by the end of the century mere recognition had been replaced by systematic diagnosis and detailed description.

There was by then a recognized hierarchy of puffs: amongst the 'puff genteel' and the 'polite puff' were 'the narrative, the poetical and the descriptive modes of puffing where the parties affirm no more than the truth'.[7] There was also the 'Puff Ostentatious', the 'Puff Concealed' ('so nicely veiled you do not know it is a puff until you have lost your money'), the 'Puff Boomerang' ('a weapon which when thrown in one direction, returns with greater force to hit the object in another'), the 'Puff Infantile', the 'Puff Interjectional', the 'Puff Admiring', the 'Puff by Reference', the 'Puff Authoritative' (Thomas Telford on the quality of a brand of cement), the 'Puff Classical', the 'Puff Economical', the 'Puff Boastful' ('better than any other offered for sale'), the 'Puff Superlative' ('the *best* in the world'). There were in addition the 'Puff by Emulation' ('By appointment to his, her or their majesties'), the 'Puff by Opposition' (inciting, even writing, scurrilous or exaggerated abuse in order to be able to reply, in a dignified and memorable way, which artificially created controversy and could offer, in Wedgwood's words, the opportunity 'of advertising away at a very great rate'[8]), the 'Puff Mendacious', the 'Swindling Puff', the 'Puff Familiar', the 'Puff Facetious', the 'Puff Beguiling' (the 'Sure Guide to Wealth and Prosperity' type, encouraging the purchase of Lottery tickets at 'the first office in CORNHILL ... distinguished by its extraordinary Luck in distributing more Capital Prizes, comparatively, than any other office'). There were 'Anecdotal Puffs', 'Adjectival Puffs', 'puffs aphoristic', puffs by proverb and example, puffs through song, verse and puzzles. There were aggressive puffs and defensive puffs. There were high-flown literary puffs and down-to-earth, demotic puffs.

By 1800 many writers admitted both the ubiquity of puffs—'we never know when and where we may be puffed upon'—and their effectiveness—'the fact is patent to everybody, that if the puff be properly manufactured, its success is only a question of time'.[9] They equated the Art of Puffing with the invention of printing, and saw its apotheosis in the England of George

---

[5] Henry Fielding, 19 December 1741, in a letter to *The Champion* signed Gustavus Puffendorf.
[6] Despite the attention of critics such as Anti-Puffado, who wrote in the 1770s, more and more manufacturers and tradesmen accepted the need to advertise and to advertise imaginatively. There had been previous attacks on the puffs from Lottery shops, and Fielding attacked the political propaganda published by Ralph Freeman in the *Daily Gazeteer* in the 1740s. See also Lawrence Lewis' *Advertisements of the Spectator* (1909).
[7] 'The Literature of Polite Puffing', in J. D. Burn, op. cit.
[8] See above in Chapter Three.
[9] *Puffs and Mysteries—the Romance of Advertising*. This was published in 1855 but was cast

III.[10] Certainly to judge from the performance of George Packwood, even an unknown and unremembered businessman could have mastered nearly every ingredient mentioned in the art of puffing by the end of the eighteenth century.

Yet historians have rarely chosen to examine individual businessmen's mastery of the art in any detail. Perhaps it is the sheer ubiquity of late eighteenth-century advertisements which has distracted them. Newspaper advertisements were, after all, easily capable of distracting one's attention. Their dazzling variety can blind the enquiring eye, their extravagant language can conceal their economic significance, and their sometimes unusual concerns can mislead historians from their serious commercial purpose. For few subjects were safe from advertisement in the late eighteenth century. Prostitutes, bug killers and wrestling women commonly offered their services in the pages of the popular press. Breast feeding, abortions and aphrodisiacs all attracted the promotional attentions of the advertiser: 'a fine young breast of milk willing to enter a gentleman's household' has a detached, slightly surrealist air today but appeared regularly in eighteenth-century newspaper advertisements; the advertisement reading, 'Any Lady whose situation may induce her to require a temporary retirement may be accommodated agreeable to her wishes in the house of a gentleman of eminence in the profession, whose honour and secrecy may be depended on, and where every vestige of pregnancy is obliterated',[11] appeared in the *Morning Post* in 1780; whilst in 1783 Dr. James Graham anticipated the most extravagant excesses of advertisers' copy when recommending his 'celestial, or medico, magnetico, musico, electrical bed'. If all other aphrodisiacs failed, claimed Dr. Graham, then his 'Grand Celestial State Bed ... twelve foot long by nine wide' with a dome 'very curiously inlaid or wholly covered on the underside with brilliant plates of looking-glass, so disposed as to reflect the various attractive charms of the happy recumbent couple, in the most flattering, most agreeable and most enchanting style' would surely 'improve, exalt, and invigorate the bodily ... faculties'. It is difficult to do justice to the bed's qualities by brief quotation, but some flavour of Dr. Graham's claims may be gathered from the following:

'In the celestial bed no feather is employed ... springy hair mattresses are used ... in order that I might have for the important purposes, the strongest and most

---

as the history of the previous forty years of advertising, and referred back to the turn of the century.

[10] In publications such as *La Belle Assemblée* or *'Bell's Court and Fashionable Magazine* addressed *particularly to the Ladies'*, or *Bell's Universal Advertiser*. In the latter, under the title 'Beneficial Advertising', John Bell announced that he had formed an original plan for advertising universally which will augment the revenue of the country and most essentially benefit every advertiser. Certainly the compendium of advertisements he published in *La Belle Assemblée* was remarkably advanced.

[11] This is the first recorded example of an abortion clinic: see Patrick Robertson, *The Shell Book of Firsts* (1977).

springy hair, I procured at vast expense, the tails of English stallions, which when twisted, baked and then untwisted and properly prepared, is elastic to the highest degree.

But the chief elastic principle of my celestial bed is produced by artificial lodestones. About fifteen hundred pounds' weight of artificial and compound magnets are so disposed and arranged as to be continually pouring forth in an ever-flowing circle inconceivable and irresistibly powerful tides of magnetic effluxion, which is well known to have a very strong affinity with the electric fire.

'Such a slight and inadequate sketch of the grand celestial bed, which being thus completely insulated—highly saturated with the most genial floods of electrical fire—fully impregnated moreover, with the balmly vivifying effluvia of restorative balsamic medicines . . . and moreover all the faculties of the soul being so fully expanded, and so highly illuminated, that it is impossible, in the nature of things, but that strong, beautiful, brilliant, nay double-distilled children . . . must infallibly be begotten.' For a mere £50 one could enjoy these life-giving benefits in the company of 'real living turtle-doves . . . on a little bed of roses' accompanied by 'a most elegant and sweet toned-organ' while 'at the head of the bed, in the full centre front, appears sparking with electrical fire, through a glory of burnished and effulgent gold, the great, first, ever operating commandment, BE FRUITFUL, MULTIPLY AND REPLENISH THE EARTH!'[12]

Such promotional literature very rarely graces the pages of economic history books. And it is, perhaps, as well that it does not. For although it provides authentic evidence of the range and ubiquity of eighteenth-century advertisement and gives some flavour of the language and nature of some of the more highly-coloured examples, it can, by stressing their engagingly specialist character, divert historians from the more serious economic intent, and the greater significance of those who persistently and regularly advertised their more mundane products in more prosaic language to a wider audience of consumers. Too many histories of advertising concentrate on such so-called 'picturesque' examples, and in doing so distract attention from the quantity and quality of straightforward advertising copy that filled so much newspaper space in the late eighteenth century.

Quoting the hyperbolic language of Dr. Graham makes it easier for historians to dismiss, as similar hyperbole, Dr. Johnson's claim that 'the trade of advertising is now so near perfection that it is not easy to propose any improvement'.[13] Greater familiarity with the advertising campaigns launched and successfully sustained by manufacturers and shopkeepers (of such modest renown that they rarely, if at all, trouble the indexes of even

---

[12] See for a full account of Dr. Graham's so-called 'sanitary lectures' John Davenport, *Aphrodisiacs and Anti-Aphrodisiacs* (1869).

[13] Dr. Johnson (1759). This is not, of course, to deny that much scurrilous and indecent material appeared in the advertisements of the mid-eighteenth century. *The Public Ledger* ran a whole paragraph in italics in January 1760 to say— 'Advertisements of an indecent nature are now become so common, that they are justly deemed a nuisance of the Press, and a Disgrace to the Papers in which they are inserted; it shall be our care, therefore, to guard against this abuse, and to spare the Blush of Modesty, by totally excluding all advertisements of an indelicate or immoral tendency . . .'

specialist historians of the period) makes Dr. Johnson's comment seem far less exaggerated, far less surprising. His failure in prediction (for, of course, later improvements were to be spectacular and of enormous importance) was not matched by a failure to recognize the remarkable developments and spread of commercial techniques which characterized the advertisements of late Georgian England. Dr. Johnson knew all too well the effectiveness of commercial techniques and the social pressures they exploited. 'He that has resolved to buy no more', he wrote, 'finds his constancy subdued ... he is attracted by rarity ... seduced by example and influenced by competition'.[14] Customers, he wrote, 'catch from example the contagion of desire',[15] and it was the skilful advertiser's aim to parade such contagious examples before his intended market.

The levels to which some eighteenth-century entrepreneurs carried their advertising campaigns have attracted far too little attention. Even real masters of the art of advertising have been almost wholly ignored. Such a man, one of those largely anonymous traders so often patronisingly dismissed as 'a plodding lesser man of business', was George Packwood who sold, and prospered on the sale of razor strops and his proprietary paste.

In an historiography dominated by attention to the supply side of the demand–supply equation, in a business-history tradition characterized by a concern with production rather than selling, in a period dominated by the great captains of industry at the cost of the lesser figures, it is scarcely surprising that a man whose claim to fame must rest more on marketing than manufacturing, on manipulating consumer demand rather than mastering new methods of production, and who sold a subject as humble as razor strops, has been comprehensively ignored by historians.

Yet in less than two years Packwood launched and sustained a quite remarkable advertising campaign in the newspapers of late eighteenth-century England. It was a campaign, which between October 1794 and July 1796, used advertisements of astonishing variety in type, language and appeal. Sixty separate Packwood advertisements, culled from twenty-six different newspapers in this short period, give a vivid demonstration of the enormous variety and vitality, and the imaginative quality, of late eighteenth-century salesmanship.

What first strikes one about Packwood's advertisements is the remorseless attempt to imprint the brand name on the public memory to ensure that they sought, and bought, indeed insisted on buying the right product. Repetitive imprinting remorselessly pursued was, and is, the hallmark of the successful advertiser. But repetition of commercial intent need not exclude variety, wit or the playful style which were also hall marks of Packwood's distinctive advertising campaign. Few modern copywriters can match the battery of

[14] Dr. Johnson, *Idler*, no. 56. See Neil McKendrick, 'Home Demand and Economic Growth' in *Historical Perspectives* (1974), ed. by N. McKendrick, pp. 195–203.
[15] Dr. Johnson, *Idler and Adventurer*, II, p. 463.

advertising gimmicks unleashed on the British public by this single entrepreneur in the space of less than two years.

For Packwood used riddles, proverbs, fables, slogans, jokes, jingles, anecdotes, facts, aphorisms, puns, poems, songs, nursery rhymes, parodies, pastiches, stories, dialogues, definitions, conundrums, letters and metaphors. He used advertisements disguised as 'sporting intelligence', 'electioneering intelligence', 'financial intelligence', 'farming intelligence', or trading information. He used advertisements disguised as law reports, as genealogies, as medical recipes ('taken externally any hour of the day, but the most proper reason is the first, second, or third thing done in a morning. N. B. One good Strop is a dose'), as miracle cures (with *Dr.* Packwood as the source of the cures), or as business history (naturally the history of his own business). He used advertisements aimed at men, women and children. The letters he published as advertisements appeared in the guise of letters to the editor, letters to himself, or letters between friends. His Dialogues were cast as conversations between Christian and Jew, between Merchant and Black Servant, between Welshman and Irishman, between English sailor and French barber, or simply between two friends. But they all resounded to the greater glory of Packwood. They all praised and promoted Packwood goods. They all underlined Packwood's special quality. They might be cast in the mould of a warning how not to misuse his goods and therefore blunt their distinctive qualities; they might be cast in the mould of knocking copy of rivals, or as warnings against deception and fakes; they might reveal the merits of his product by way of a discursive narrative, or simply draw attention to his existence by virtue of autobiographical reminiscence; they might embed the virtues of his wares in the middle of a parody of a soliloquy from *Hamlet,* or a well known nursery rhyme, or a popular song, or extempore verse; but whatever the approach they sought to engage the eager attention of the customer, attempted to cajole an initial trial, and once hooked they attempted to secure his lasting allegiance.

By the nature of the product the main market pursued was, of necessity, male, but Packwood did not neglect 'the Ladies'. The benefits of a smooth cheek in a lover, the benefit to a wife of a comfortable shave on the temper of a husband, the benefit of delighted gratitude extended both to a wife and a mistress who provided the wherewithal for such silken comforts, were emphatically spelled out to the female buyer.

Like so many eighteenth-century entrepreneurs Packwood aimed first at the market of London before seeking the custom of the whole country. His first advertisements were of the type designed to attract the attention of the coffee-house set and the London clubs, the leisured male market with time on its hands, money to spend, and always in search of novelty and diversion, and improvement.

Once London was captured, he sought the market of the rest of the country, although again significantly paying particular attention to the provincial capitals and places of fashion. From his advertisement, we can watch the ever widening provincial market he aimed for, and we can see how his advertising campaign was specifically aimed to draw attention to his chosen provincial outlets. Eventually he had established hundreds of 'places appointed for the sale' of his product, but what is especially interesting is to see how he sought to establish a common symbol for his outlets. We know from his advertisements that his goods were to be bought 'at the sign of the Naked Truth'. *The Naked Truth* was the name of Packwood's original outlet at No. 16 Gracechurch Street in London, and he had realized that his advertising campaign would pay greater commercial dividends if they were designed to plug not only a standard, easily recognized product, but also a name and a sign of a standard easily recognizable place of purchase. Much of his advertising was specifically designed to imprint the brand image of *The Naked Truth* on his readers and potential customers, just as it was designed to imprint the name Packwood indelibly on their memories. So by proverb and anecdote, by popular saying and popular song, 'the naked truth' was both the declared intent and the advertised place of sale which his advertisements proclaimed.

* * *

In a qualitative exercise of this kind in which the intent is to demonstrate the distinctive qualities of Packwood's advertising campaign, and, by so doing, to throw new light on the levels of commercial skill to be found even amongst the least celebrated eighteenth-century businessmen, the best method is, perhaps, to let a sample of Packwood's advertisements speak for themselves.

On October 15, 1794, Packwood opened his campaign in the *Times*. He used one of his favourite techniques for his longer advertisements—the dialogue. It read as follows:

A DIALOGUE BETWEEN TWO FRIENDS

B. GOOD MORROW, Friend; how do you do this morning?
A. How do I do! I have been shaving myself so uncomfortably this morning, my face smarts with pain.
B. And cannot you find out a better way, to shave yourself with more ease?
A. No; my razors I cannot get in order; I burn in torture now at this time, like a goblin grilled.
B. What do you use to sharpen your razor on?
A. A common strop that is generally used, but to very little advantage.
B. Ho! Ho! I find you are not in the secret then!
A. Pray what do you mean by the secret? Is there any good news this morning?
B. Yes, I find it will be good news; and my friendship leads me to inform you of something that will be as good to you as a small estate, towards the comfort of life.
A. I shall esteem your information a most singular favor.
B. Have you not heard of a strop that will take notches from razors, pen-knives, and surgeons' instruments, by way of polishing, and afterwards leave so smooth an edge as to shave yourself with that ease as is not to be described.

A. No, neither do I believe there is such a thing; you may as well tell me that this said strop would sharpen me into a razor.
B. Hold; do not be too positive, for if you will believe me, I know it true, and the Proprietor will give you ocular demonstration. He stropped a large notch from his own common sixpenny pen-knife (before he offered them to a generous public) and shaved himself dry therewith, although a hard beard, without a lather, much cleaner and smoother than he had done for many years before; he also considers that instrument for convenience in travelling preferable to a razor! After a pen-knife has been injured by cutting nails or pens, a few strokes on the *Superior Strop,* according to directions, will bring the edge to cut as smooth as before injured; he engages likewise to return the money (after trial) in one week, if not approved of; this he declares in a shop-bill, in which the strop is wrapped when sold, I know it to be a fact.
A. My dear Friend, this out-tops everthing I ever heard of; it puts me in mind of the Philosopher's stone; but, as you tell me so, I'll give you credit for it.
B. And what is a greater accquisition, he sells a paste to keep your Razor in good order, for years, in boxes, with directions, 2s. 6d. each. The Strops are sold for 3s. 6d.—5s.—and 10s. 6d. each A safe article for merchants to venture abroad.
A. This is good news indeed; pray where are they sold? I will have one of them, if it costs me a guinea.
B. They are vended, wholesale and retail, by the sole Proprietor, G. PACKWOOD, No. 16, Gracechurch Street, London: I likewise learn he is very desirous of being excused the postage of letters: the drawback is too much on his little profit.
A. My best friend and comforter, if I find it as true as you assert, I'll treat you with a bird and a bottle of the best.
B. A trial will convince; and, depend upon it, you will find what I say to be a fact.[16]

The essential information—the price, the sole place of purchase, the commodities themselves—are wrapped up in a natural conversation which allows the new 'secret' to be passed on, which allows personal conviction persuasively to answer understandable scepticism, which allows the advantage of a money-back-if-not-satisfied policy to be announced, and Packwood's own modest profit to be casually alluded to.

On November 5th, 1794, another dialogue was published in the *Morning Chronicle.* In this the dialogue has, as a coda, an easily-remembered jingle on the worth of Packwood's new invention, but the device is essentially the same as the *Times* advert of the month before—to engage the attention of the reader and painlessly to introduce the commercial message.[17]

A DIALOGUE BETWEEN A MERCHANT AND HIS BLACK SERVANT
M. Scipio.
S. What you please to ave, Massa?
M. Yesterday you did not perform your office properly, you tore the skin from my face; why do you not use hot water? I am convinced it would produce an alteration for the better.

---

[16] *Times,* 15 October 1794.
[17] It is interesting to note that in this one the Black Servant refers to *another* morning paper for the place of sale; and whereas the *Times* advertisement introduced the invention as 'a safe article for merchants to venture abroad', in the *Chronicle* advert the Merchant is shown as being instantly convinced that 'This will be a fine article to form part of my cargo in the next ship that goes out'.

S. Yes, Massa, I ave found hot water a very good ting, but Mr. Hone do not hit de method of putting your razors in good order.
M. Well, come and try and shave me better this morning; I declare my face is so tender, I can scarce undergo the operation.
S. Yes, Massa; I ave got good news dis morning, Massa.
M. Have you got that long looked-for letter from your father and mother?
S. No Massa; good to you, not to me Massa; I was no tinking of my fader nor moder.
M. Do you take off the beard, Scipio?
S. Yes, Massa; put you hand up to you face, and feel how smooth it is.
M. What razor are you shaving me with, Scipio, that makes such a difference? or is it the advantage of hot water?
S. I ave no hot water, Massa; dis is an old razor you trow away, Massa, about twelvemont ago, because was good for noting: I ave stropp'd it on de Butler's new Razor Strop, he bought dis morning, he say it would take out notches, he praise it so much, I taught me would try it on dis old razor, and I find it please you, Massa; dis is de good news, Massa.
M. Good news indeed, Scipio, for although my face was so tender, yet I could scarcely feel you; it was like as if the beard moved off with a touch; I never was shaved so nicely in all my life. (Aside) This will be a fine article to form a part of my cargo in the next ship that goes out. Do you know where they are sold, Scipio?
S. Look here, Massa, in dis morning paper de Butler shew me.
M. I shall reward you, Scipio, for your attention and fidelity.
S. A, Massa, if I am continued in your service, dat will be ample reward for Scipio; bring good news to you of Packwood's new invention dat will move tings with a touch.

> No wonder Packwood's Strops occasion a fuss,
> By their value, they are undersold;
> A most generous public acknowledges thus
> All their weight they are well worth in gold.[18]

By 18 December Packwood is already using an advertisement on 'the new Strop that is set forth to the public of late' without even mentioning his own name. Admittedly it too was published in the *Morning Chronicle,* and referred the reader to 'the Proprietor's shop bills and advertisements', but it shows a remarkable confidence that already his sales campaign had established a separate identity for his product.

> A remarkable circumstance took place a few days ago at a gentleman's house, a few miles from town—a question was put to a visitor, have you tried the new Strop that is set forth to the public of late, that will take notches from knives or razors?—the answer was, I give no credit to such puffing. Stop, says the gentleman, if you have got a knife in your pocket we will prove the effect, as I have had one of the Strops sent me on trial; a knife was produced, also two rusty razors, cast aside some years; thus the credulous were satisfied, for twelve or fifteen gentlemen were shaved with the instruments before mentioned, and all acknowledged what was set forth in the Proprietor's shop-bills and advertisements justly agreed with the Superior Razor Strop by virtue of the Paste it was composed of.[19]

[18] *Morning Chronicle,* 5 November 1794.
[19] *Morning Chronicle,* 18 December 1794.

In the *Sunday Monitor,* Packwood uses the fable as a vehicle in which to mount a defence of his claimed superiority—once again being sufficiently confident of the stir he has caused to leave out any mention of his own name:

A FABLE

Once upon a time it happened two slaves met together, the one named Common Strop, the other Superior Strop; Common Strop claimed preference of the other, and thus addressed him 'remember, Superior, you are but young in the world, and ought not to presume so much upon yourself. I have been useful to sharpen razors as a common strop for ages past, and lived in some credit before you came.' All this is self praise without foundation, answered Superior; but I understand the most you could ever do, with all your art and long experience, was only to smooth the edge of an instrument after the stone or barber's hone. Many a good razor has been cast aside for want of merit you now so much boast of: my superiority has already convinced the most credulous into surprize, that my power will remove notches from a razor or common knife, and give a delectable smooth edge to shave the hardest beard, and that to admiration.

THE MORAL
'Merit meets it's own reward on a fair trial.'[20]

By April 10, 1795, Packwood is printing congratulatory messages from 'a correspondent who has experienced . . . the NEW INVENTION' to the effect that 'the combined judgement of the first wise men of the age, could not have effected what Packwood has with such address accomplished: TO SHAVE THE NATION has hitherto been found a difficult matter, but Packwood has proved by a surprising effort of genius, and by the power of his Razor Strop, that nothing can be performed with greater ease'.[21] In the same month, he was even more self-congratulatory in the *True Briton,* and felt the need to offer no more than his address to identify himself and to warn the opposition.

The following whimsical, though ridiculous circumstance, took place a few days ago with one of honest John Bull's acquaintance. At the very instant he was laughing to scorn the wonderful wonder of wonders, he was struck with astonishment and surprize to see, at dinner time, a large notch entirely removed, as it were by magic, from a carving knife, by the power, I say, the uncommon power of an instrument, vulgarly called a Strap; but a high-flown gentleman, not a mile and a half from the corner of the Cross Keys, Gracechurch-street, seems to have defined this to the word strop, by the title or appellation of superior.—The cause of this phenomenon was a domestic, who dreaded a repetition of threats from his governor, recently had procured one of those magic strops to save the cutler the trouble of grinding. O grinders! O honers! O setters of razors! great will be the downfall thereof![22]

---

[20] *Sunday Monitor,* 22 February 1795. If Packwood had not laid proprietary claim to these anonymous advertisements the historian would have no certain proof that they were his.
[21] *Morning Chronicle,* 10 April 1795.
[22] *True Briton,* 27 April 1795.

BIRTH OF A CONSUMER SOCIETY

The late Spring of 1795 saw a further outbreak of so called 'impromptu' or 'extempore' praise presented as unsolicited puffs. In April, the *Sunday Monitor* carried the following advertisement:

EXTEMPORE
ON PACKWOOD'S RAZOR-STROPS

Sans doubte—Mr. Packwood, your elegant Strops
Are the best that e'er mortal invented,
We have nothing to do but to lather our chops,
The razor soon makes us contented.

Surely magic herself has been lending her aid,
To assist in the brilliant invention:
And the fam'd Composition you also have made,
Should assuredly gain you a pension.

SIR

My friend has experienced the salutary effects of your incomparable Razor Strops, &c.—In the effusion of gratitude, penned the preceding lines.

Your most cordial well-wisher,
STUBBORN ROUGHBEARD.[23]

In May the *Telegraph* carried another in similar vein.

IMPROMPTU
ON MR. PACKWOOD'S NEW-INVENTED RAZOR-STROP

In the compting-house the smart City blade,
Before he is dress'd for the shop,
The razor can flourish, what gives him the aid?
Why Packwood's ingenious Strop.

And see my lord's valet his shaving perform,
With a speed to astonish each gazer;
While his master is calm, his friends they all storm,
They are mad to possess such a razor.

Then to Packwood's repair, and your wishes possess,
And shave with a good inclination;
Your beards will come off with great ease and address,
Through the Strop that's the pride of the nation.[24]

And Packwood was not above planning, and then demonstrating, the good effects of using his products. On May 2nd he published what he called

ADVICE TO GENTLEMEN OF THE RAZOR

If to Packwood's you repair,
For his new-invented Strop,
Beards you'll shave with easy air,
Custom bring unto your shop.

[23] *Sunday Monitor*, 16 April 1795.
[24] *Telegraph*, 2 May 1795.

COMMERCIALIZATION OF SHAVING

> Be your Razors dull for use,
> This so fine an edge will give,
> All in praise will be profuse,
> And you'll midst commendations live.[25]

On 12 May he advertised the beneficial consequences of taking such advice—in the form of a letter of commendation based on the gratitude of one such gentleman of the razor:

> TO MR. PACKWOOD, No. 16 GRACECHURCH-
> STREET, LONDON
> *Proprietor of the New-invented Razor-Strop*
> SIR,
> Astonishment at having experienced a most agreeable sensation in the operating of shaving at a barber's, where I accidentally called for that purpose, I was induced to give the operator that praise which I conceived to be so justly due. But he, with a generosity highly commendable, replied, that the merit was not his; for that ease, with which my beard was taken away, entirely resulted from the virtue of PACKWOOD'S newly-invented Strops.[26]

On the same day he not altogether surprisingly felt the need to publish a self-justifying piece in the *Telegraph* on the meaning and intent of advertisements, entitled

> THE NAKED TRUTH
> A few reasonable questions may not be inapplicable to the present age.
> Q. What was the original meaning and intent of *advertisements?*
> A. To publish the truth.
> Q. Where is the truth, that valuable jewel, to be met with?
> A. Not only the truth, but the naked truth, is at this time copiously dealt out by PACKWOOD all over the land in his magic or powerful Strop, by whose means ease is given to the cheek, comfort to the upper lip, and an uncommon agreeable surprize to the bearded phiz. To convince those who are doubtful, PACKWOOD generously allows a week's trial, for this reason—before the Strop was proved, the world laughed at PACKWOOD, but afterwards astonishment took place of wonder, and PACKWOOD respectfully laughs in turn on the world; because he has the compliments and praises from his numerous friends and a generous public (which have been comforted); and another most powerful argument prevails, that is, he handles the chink.[27]

In this piece he takes the opportunity to congratulate himself on the results of his advertising, as well as to justify his methods, and explain his terms; and the title of the piece not only announced the contents but, of course, further advertised his shop sign.

Packwood rarely adopted a modest pose in his advertisements, and as his self-confidence mounted with his growing success, his self-praise reached new heights of hyperbole. In the *Telegraph* he published a seven-verse song

---

[25] *Star*, 2 May 1795.
[26] *Courier*, 12 May 1795.
[27] *Telegraph*, 12 May 1795.

in praise of his own achievement. A single verse will give its characteristic tone:

> A NEW SONG
> CALLED
> THE RAZOR STROP
> To the Tune of 'The golden days of good Queen Bess.'
>
> In this age of invention, improvement, and taste, sir,
> To the times greatest wonder, we'll immediately haste, sir;
> What is it preserves the most eminent station,
> But the new Razor Strop, the glory of the nation.
>   Thus happy such artists may now themselves confess,
>   As in the ancient golden days of good Queen Bess.[28]

And although each verse sings Packwood's praises, telling us his readers that

> 'From the bottom of the town, why even to the top, sir,
> All folks are delighted with this genius's Strop, sir,'[29]

or asking them

> 'Then what shall we say to this man of great fame, sir?
> Who by superior merit is the cock of the game, sir,'[30]

Packwood, like Schweppes in the twentieth century, has only to whisper his initial to identify himself. His name is never once spelled out in any one of the forty-two lines.

He is not always so reticent. In June in the *Oracle* he is lost in admiration at his own achievements:

> Rejoice! Rejoice! O ye mortals, at the good news of Packwood's new-invented superior Razor Strop! By its power it will remove notches, if required, from any small instrument; by its power it will give a most delectable smooth edge to a razor, inasmuch that before the strop is proved, this advertisement is treated with indifference; but after the trial, then what is the encomium? Why, that they are worth their weight in gold, that the Proprietor deserves our thanks for so much comfort we receive from his ingenuity, and we are lost in admiration![31]

In the *Public Ledger* he starts with a play on the word paste, and goes on to announce that

> Paste was never so much in fashion as since PACKWOOD has began to spread the Paste on his Razor Strops. By virtue of its uncommon power, it prevents ill humours in the matrimonial way, since gentlemen, by having their beards shaved with ease, sit down to breakfast with pleasure; and if they receive, or imagine they receive, (as is too common with both sexes), any provocation, they are in too good temper to retort. Oh ladies! ladies! what are you indebted to Packwood for producing such an invention? and can you, from an instinct of gratitude, do any

---

[28] *Telegraph*, 26 May 1795.
[29] Ibid.
[30] Ibid.
[31] *Oracle*, 11 June 1795.

less than send your husbands, lovers, brothers, fathers, grandfathers, and great-grandfathers, to the magazine appropriated for the sale of this super-superior Razor Strop.[32]

Two days later he continues with a further play on the same word, with the welcome addition of a little self-mockery

> There is a time and a season for all things, but now is the time for spreading: some spread manure on the land, others spread the linen; but the spreading of Paste, now is so much the rage, done by a whimsical mode of a whimsical fellow, that has given many persons the idea of bread and butter. This occasioned a remark from a facetious wag of the day that PACKWOOD (by spreading the Paste on his Razor Strops) had buttered his bread on both sides.[33]

The word play was continued in many advertisements, but Packwood rang the changes to avoid boring his readers. He could be brief:

> The epithet of a WHET is quite the rage: a most curious genius has so successfully WHETTED the inclinations of the people, that happy is the man now that can get a WHET at Packwood's new invention.[34]

He could be elaborately playful:

> A singular genius has proved himself an excellent arithmetician; he daily adds to his credit without subtracting from the merits of another; multiplies his celebrity, divides his ingenuity, among those who are best entitled to his gratitude; reduces the public opinion decidedly in his own favour, and by having a perfect knowledge of these rules, has become so competent a master of the rule of three, that his practice is the subject of universal admiration. He will never be at a loss while he has the heart of a customer to gain; his great knowledge of exchange has opened him an account current with the first personages in the kingdom; and he knows (by the power of his new-invented Razor Strop) to a fraction, what will suit the reigning taste of the age. A further discovery of those arts may be known by applying to Packwood himself.[35]

He could claim to have rendered some parts of the English language obsolete:

> The term 'good for nothing' is obsolete, and positively out of use. When a Surgeon had a dull instrument, his determination coincided with that of others—'it is good for nothing'. When a blade of the desk had a bad knife, the discussion was tantamount to the same purpose—'it will not mend a pen, it is good for nothing'. When a brother of the hone had a razor that left ruts in the chin, similar to those that are made by a broad-wheel waggon on a public road, the usual observation occurred—'it is good for nothing'. But since PACKWOOD has, by the discovery of his celebrated Paste, found a mode of successfully whetting the dullest of instruments, giving the smoothest edge to the worst of knives, and causing razors to perform their duty, as if by magic, does there remain a question, whether he is, or is not 'good for something', that can make so many good-for-nothings pleasing, useful, satisfactory, and agreeable.[36]

---

[32] *Public Ledger*, 26 June 1795.
[33] *Sunday Reformer*, 28 June 1795.
[34] *Norwich Mercury*, 11 July 1795.
[35] *Morning Chronicle*, 13 July 1795.
[36] *Morning Post* or *Fashionable World*, 24 September 1795.

He could be playful in verse—

> How great must P - - d's fortune be,
> All instruments to set, sir,
> And what may not be thought of he,
> Who gives the town a whet, sir:
> And still to add unto his fame,
> This daily is the case, sir;
> But if you think I jest or game
> He'll prove it to your face, sir.[37]

But whatever tone he adopted the commercial intent remained the same—to keep his wares fashionable, to keep the attention of as wide a public as possible, constantly to remind them of his name, indelibly to imprint the virtues of his product, its place of sale, its brand image.

Particular sections of the market received, from time to time, his special attention. In July 1795, he used a Bible story in the *Telegraph,* (and the history of women, complete with footnotes)[38] to explain why 'the ladies of this age . . .

> have come to this determination, to use every persuasive argument in their power to encourage their lovers and husbands to get possession, if possible, of one or more of Packwood's superior Razor Strops.[39]

A week later in the *Town and Country Herald,* he returned to the same theme.

> The nation is at this time in debt to a Worcestershire wag—200,800,000 thanks for the benefit derived from his ingenuity; but there is a great pleasure in informing the public, for their satisfaction, that the ladies have taken it in hand to pay off the interest by praises, and spreading his great fame and reputation, if possible, more and more, all over the land, in gratitude for the comfort they enjoy by their lovers and husbands beards being so closely shorn.[40]

Later under the title 'Better late than never' he archly reported to the readers of the *Oracle* that

> There is a current report spread abroad by persons (I do not say the ladies,) that are in possession of all the comforts of late recommended to mankind: but their extravagance cannot be accounted for in wishing Packwood had been dropped on earth half a century ago, for this reason, he might have contributed to the comfort of mankind in an earlier stage of life, as well as the present.[41]

If he lavished special attention on 'that half of humanity' who were likely to purchase his products but rarely use it, he did so because his stated intention was to be 'Razor Strop Maker to the Whole World'.[42] He lavished

---

[37] *Morning Chronicle,* 9 November 1795.
[38] 'Historical Sketches of the Fair Sex, chap. i, page 2. The original in the Universal History of All Nations, about the beginning of the 2d vol.' *Telegraph,* 17 July 1795.
[39] Ibid.
[40] *Town and Country Herald,* 25 July 1795.
[41] *Oracle,* 2 June 1796.
[42] *True Briton,* 9 November 1795 and many other sources.

even more attention on the market of the rest of Britain for the same reason. Indeed his assault on the provincial market alone would provide ample evidence to prove the fertility of his commercial imagination. Because while for the fashionable gossip-ridden world of London, where fresh wonders soon grew stale, it was *essential* to produce new promotional ideas to keep the capital's attention, the provinces might have been fobbed off with a more routine approach. But that was not Packwood's style. So Northampton was informed of Packwood's merits with the announcement:

> Good News for Northampton and it's environs, looked for upwards of one thousand years back, a method to get a comfortable shave, which now is happily discovered in the use of PACKWOOD's new invention.[43]

Gloucester was informed in Biblical style. There was no mention of the name of the true prophet, merely a direction to his leading convert.

> Brothers the Prophet.—Has he actually done more for us poor mortals than any other man?—There is a mortal now living in London, who does not stile himself a prophet, has a numerous body of converts, and all who follow him have a proof, they are in the straight road to present happiness, by virtue of his new-invented Superior Razor Strops. The leading convert is Mr. ADDIS of Gloucester.[44]

The Edinburgh market was informed of Packwood's arrival, appropriately enough in the language of the economist. Entitled 'WAYS AND MEANS', the advertisement stressed both the value and the trifling cost, saying:

> PACKWOOD is certainly a most capital financier.—His Budget (of Razor Strops and Paste) this season is opened at RAEBURN's Perfume Warehouse. No. 13, North Bridge-street, Edinburgh, with wonderful eclat; and he is determined that no beards in Scotland shall be taxed in future; a resolution which he has passed in every part of the kingdom. This determination will save government annually a revenue of torture, trouble, and anxiety; and is so adapted to essentially serve every individual, as well as the collective body of the people at large, as not to have met with a single dissentient voice. Even persons in opposition are not so opposite to their own interest as not to encourage what will secure them a surplus of satisfaction. Razor Strops, estimated in their value, to be worth their weight in gold, and sold only for a mere trifle.[45]

The approach to Cork also stressed economy.

> Experience has given rise to a curious acknowledgement in Great Britain, received from the county of Nottingham; that the first shave from the use of Packwood's Razor Strop is worth all the money paid for it. By this clear evidence, all the comfort received afterwards will be gratis.[46]

The approach to Dublin recognized that Packwood's triumphant march to ever-expanding sales was not achieved without opposition. One Dublin paper announced Packwood's defeat of his enemies:

---

[43] *Northampton Mercury*, 26 September 1795.
[44] *Gloucester Journal*, 25 January 1796. Mr. Addis was, of course, Packwood's chief outlet in Gloucester.
[45] *Caledonian Mercury*, 25 April 1796.
[46] *Cork Gazette and General Advertiser*, 1 June 1796.

> Packwood, like all men of sterling merit, has got a number of enemies, on account of that very useful invention, his incomparable RAZOR STROP. The good people in this city did not begin to shew their friendship until above 10,000 Razor Strops were sold by SIMMONS, in Capel-Street: To keep Razors in order was a pest, until these useful Strops were known, some drones in this city, appear to possess as much kindness as *utility,* and after dabbling in paste, for a long time, with a view to rival Packwood, his Razor Strops are still like a diamond of the first water.[47]

In another Dublin newspaper, Packwood recognized the existence of a prejudice against the exaggerated claims made in deceitful advertisements, but then offers an outrageously immodest puff of his own, disguised as an anecdote, to prove that the Packwood advertisements were the exception to this rule—modestly raising the value of his strop to twenty guineas, and offering it as the general opinion that he should be immortalized.

ANECDOTE

> Seeing is believing, but feeling is the naked truth.—Prejudiced as the public may be against the nostrums set forth in a flow of advertisements, merely to take the advantage of honest John Bull—yet there are some few exceptions allowed, and the merit due to PACKWOOD's superior Razor Strop is a proof to claim this exception;—the encomiums generally paid the proprietor are a little out of the common way, by those who have made trial of them—saying, if one could not be got for less—twenty guineas should not purchase the strop in their possession—others say, they are worth their weight in gold; and it is the general opinion the proprietor ought to be immortalized.[48]

It was typical of Packwood's approach to try to exploit an existing prejudice against him to his own advantage. For what distinguished Packwood's advertising campaign is not only its imaginative quality, and its sustained variety, but also his marked ability to profit from the slightest commercial opening that offered itself. He possessed the kind of entrepreneurial flair which could spot a business opportunity *and* exploit it before the opposition had done so. Any passing event could inspire a whole batch of advertisements on the same theme. In June 1796 he hit on the theme of the latest 'intelligence' whether farming, electioneering, sporting or legal and within a matter of days had turned to his own promotional advantage a whole series of events.

The fall in the price of wheat sparked off the first topical advertisement in *The Times.* It read—

On the great Fall of the Price of Wheat in the Spring of the Year 1796.

> Lately, a farmer chanc'd to pop
> His head into a barber's shop,
> Begg'd to be shav'd; it soon was done,
> When Strop (inclin'd oft times to fun.)
> Doubling the price he'd ask'd before,
> Instead of two-pence, made it four:

---

[47] *Dublin Public Register,* or *Freeman's Journal,* 26 April 1796.
[48] *Dublin Evening Post,* 21 May 1796.

COMMERCIALIZATION OF SHAVING

> The Farmer said, 'You sure must grant
> Your charge is most exorbitant:'
> No so (quoth STROP) I'm *right,* and you are *wrong,*
> For since wheat fell, *your face is twice as long.*
> Banbury, Oxfordshire, May 24, 1796.[49]

In the same lighthearted mood the *Telegraph* carried on the same day the following:

ELECTIONEERING INTELLIGENCE

George Packwood, we hear, is returned for the county of Strop, with very little opposition.[50]

A week later, an altogether more serious recent event inspired a variant on the theme:

LAW INTELLIGENCE

Last week was tried a cause of great importance to the commercial trade of this city, as well as to every individual at large. It was proved in clear evidence, by ocular demonstration, that a certain perfumer in credit, who had been looked up to with the greatest respectability in this city, did clandestinely and wilfully utter and sell a base counterfeit Razor Strop and a box of Paste, and imposed it upon his customers for the make of Packwood. After the Jury had examined the evidence, they viewed the article in question, found it a bad imitation, although it might deceive the unwary, and the label on the Strops marked with a pen and red ink, and the maker's name erased and torn off; the Paste on the counterfeit Strop and box of Paste when compared, are of a dirty brown colour, and Packwood's of a dark red colour; but what threw the greatest light on the deception that was working on the public credulity, the article in question was wrapped up with one of Packwood's bills, recently procured, with a few of Packwood's goods to carry on the deceit. The jury without hesitation, or going out of court, found a verdict for the plaintiff, with twenty pounds damages.[51]

Three days later Oxford was treated to another variation on the 'latest intelligence' theme, and although it was carried under the heading 'SPORTING INTELLIGENCE' it clearly referred to Packwood's recent success in

---

[49] *Times,* 1 June 1796. The previous autumn he had put to equally good promotional use, the news of the good harvest:

> The proof of the pudding is in the eating.—The oldest man acknowledges he does not remember a finer harvest; and happy are those who have embraced the golden opportunity; amongst whom is PACKWOOD, who need not dread the approach of winter, since his granaries are well filled with his celebrated RAZOR STROPS, to remove notches from hard steel, by way of polishing, and boxes of Paste to keep them in order. But what is still more to his credit, is, his resolution of dispensing the store among his brothers of the blade, who may take a whet any day at his hospitable board in Gracechurch Street.
> *Morning Post,* or *Fashionable World,* 21 November 1795.

[50] *Telegraph,* 1 June 1796.

[51] The events in London were used as a warning against counterfeit products as far away as Dublin. *The Hibernian Journal* of June 8th carried the advertisement with the additional words—

> And we hear Mr. Simmons of Capel-street, has authority to carry on prosecutions against others guilty of similar offences. It was observed in court, such a tradesman was dangerous to society.

165

the London courtroom. It was both an advertisement and a warning to the opposition.

SPORTING INTELLIGENCE

Packwood is a good shot, is evident from the excellence with which he always takes aim when practising his favourite diversion. The town has witnessed this on more accounts than one, but particularly when he takes his favourite piece (the Razor Strop) which brings down his game at a greater distance than can be imagined, and does such execution, that a whole covey falls into his possession by a single pull of the trigger. Read this, ye lovers of the sport, make sure of your bird, by taking Packwood's advice; a comfortable shave, such as is not to be gained but by virtue of his Razor Strop, which is to be disposed of at the sign of the Naked Truth.[52]

Interspersed with topical advertisements, provincial advertisements, advertisements devoted to shameless self-praise came a rising tide of one-off advertisements. 1796 saw a positive flood of them. The evidence of their mounting number alone suggests that Packwood grew increasingly to believe that his advertising yielded more than adequate commercial rewards. For where we have evidence for only approximately one advertisement a month in late 1794, we have proof of two a month for 1795, and over five a month for 1796. This record is not, of course, complete. These advertisements were chosen for their individual quality, designed to display Packwood's imaginative and inventive approach to sales promotion. A more exhaustive search for *all* of Packwood's advertisements would doubtless yield many repetitions. But in terms of individual invention each year produced a more abundant harvest. So although 1796 saw old favourites in new dress and many variants on old themes it saw even more new promotional ploys tried out.

Packwood's devotion to his old standby—the dialogue—never faltered, and in 1796 he published three new variants on this theme in the *Telegraph*. He seems to have had a high regard for the stamina and perseverance of *Telegraph* readers because these dialogues were, by a large margin, the longest type of advertisement he ever published. A mere excerpt will demonstrate the point:

A DIALOGUE
Between a JEW and a CHRISTIAN

Frolick. But Levi, I thought none of your tribe ever underwent the operation of shaving.

Levi. Dat depends upon shircumstances. I hope Maishter Frolick you do not forget in the grand history of de Vorld, dat ve ourselves vash de preshident to shaveing, for ve learn dat Joseph belonged to our tribe, de son of dat goot old Patriarch of old. He vas shav'd to appear before Pharo; by such examples we are taught cleanliness. But de most material invitation ish de comfort ve receive by de use of our goot friend PACKWOOD'S new-invented Rashor Strop, by which it sheems you have no knowledge of—by the appearance of your fashe, dat is torn and mandled in so treadful a manner, dat I tink you vill remember shaveing so long as you live.

[52] *Oxford Journal,* 11 June 1796.

Frolick. I must confess I have been too great a sufferer to trust to the same operator in future.

Levi. Ha! ha! a burnt childsh dredsh de fire; but you musht follow de example of our goot peoples, whom Maishter Packwood ish leading at dish time into de strait road of preshent happiness; he givish ease to de cheek, comfort to de upper lip, a pleasant familiarity to de shin, and an uncommon agreeable shurprishe to our bearded tribe, by virtue of hish incomparable Rashor Strop, vish sharpensh my rashor to so keen an edge, dat maketh my touch old beard come off so eashey, dat instead of de pain and torturesh I formerly endured, it sheems to put me in mind of a pleasant story given by Mishtresh Hazel, de Chrishten, of de feirsht part of matrimonish honey moonsh. O she vas very goot Voman.

Frolick. Mrs. Hazel's goodness, I suppose was like your shaving, it depended upon circumstances, ha, ha, ha.

Levi. Ah! maishter Frolick, don't you tink to laugh me out of Packwood's Rashor Strap, dat ish worth itsh weight in gold, and shold only for 3s. 6d. 5s. and 10s. 6d. ash you may she by de bills of his shop; and anoder goot ting, he shelh a box of paste for 2s. 6d. to keep de Strop in order for yearsh; and anoder goot ting, he takish dem back after a reasonable trial of a veek, if not approved of, eider for want of shugment in de use of it or odervise.

Frolick. You seem a great advocate for Packwood, and if what you say be true I have reason to rejoice too, for I do not know any thing more agreeable than a comfortable shave.

Levi. You have reashon to shay so, if you take my advish, and be particular when you buy. Shee dat Packwood;'s name ish on de Strop, and on de bills round de box of Paste, and a seal on with the impression of a bird, and the word FIDELLE, ash imposishions are libale (from de beginning of de vorld unto dish day) to be practised by humble immitations on all such valuable articles. Dere ish dat horrid monster, envy, still lives in de vorld, and has de modesty to offer a counterfeit instead of de real Strop. O, dat ish no goot—no goot by such proceedings. A generous public musht be very much injured, execpt dey vash as valuable in every respect but dere may be shome risk. O, it ish goot to be carefull.—Maishter Packwood vishes every honesht man a goot living by his trade (even in Razor Strops). But I vill tell you a story on dish business;—A shentleman, a few days ago, called on a shopkeeper, and gave him a verry shevere reprimand for imposing upon him one of dose pirated Strops, when he requested one of Packwood's. Do you know, shays the shentleman, dat you ansherable to your customers, for all such mal-practishes. Dose vilfull mishtakes, says the shentelman, are unparonable; I shall mark your shop in future. I hope dish vill be a varning to all de goot peoples, not to deceive deir goot customers. De shentlemens of descernmet, belonging to different laboratories, have paid Maishter Packwood verry high encomiums, on the excellent properties and fineness of de composition belonging to de Rashor Strop; vat it ish composed of, ish bet known to himself, ash he admits of no one being a partaker of dat grand shecret. De Strop acts vith great power, in as much ash it removish notches from a rashor or small knifesh, ash if by maggic. De ladish are very much pleashed such a man vash dropped into de vorld, to remove de scrubbing-brush from mansh beadrsh, it vould do you goot to shee de different fachesh come to maishter Packwood's shop, some smiling, some laughing, and some vith a broad grin; some to praise, and oders to buy. He shells goot rashors.

	He told me ash a shecret, that de virtue of de Strop makesh a small knifesh, or an old rashor cut so vell, dat it prevents the sale of many goot rashors.
Frolick.	Pray where does this wonderful, high-flying, miraculous, outlandish, never heard of before, uncommon Jew of ingenuity live.
Levi.	He ish ne shew—he ish a very friendly Christian—he vishes vell to all mankind, and he trusts all mankind vishes vell to him. He might have been a shew, if his relations had been of our tribe: but he ish very vell satisfied vith de shale of his Rashor Strops. He livesh in de great city of London, No. 16 Gracechurch-street. De Rashor Strops ish shold at de sign of de Naked Truth, in different parts of de three kingdoms.
Frolick.	Very comfortable information indeed.
Levi.	Oh, my very goot friend, your happiness ish to come if you takesh my advice, your shin vill not be put in purgatory any more. Farewell.
Frolick.	Farewell, Levi. I shall meet you upon 'Change.

> Now I'll to Packwood's with the greatest haste,
> To buy the Strop that whets the public taste;
> Though unbelievers will not think it true,
> A Christian may take pattern by a Jew.[53]

In his judgement even this did not daunt the appetite of the *Telegraph* readers for more. There was another mammoth dialogue in April, this time between 'a Welchman and an Irishman', containing much heavy handed humour particularly at the expense of the Irish. Interspersed amongst the jokes against the Irish and the Welsh, were repeated references to 'the great man... Packwood' who 'is appointed Razor Strop maker to the four quarters of the globe, and I find all the other quarters intend to encourage his wonderful art as soon as convenient'. A small sample will suffice to give the characteristic flavour of this dialogue:

> To be sure Packwood has had a fine leap at fame in Ireland since I came from there. Upon my honor, I believe he is a greater curiosity than the Colossus at Rhodes, for that, you see, only covers a little bit of dry water, whereas Packwood's fame and reputation has covered all the whole land of England, Ireland, Scotland, and all the continental islands in the Sea.[54]

In May 'an English Sailor and a French Barber' conspire to praise Packwood in suitable nautical and Gallic terms for the readers of the *Telegraph*, as they 'think on him whose sails being filled with ingenuity and invention, may ensure him a prosperous gale through life'. Packwood's appetite for self-praise through the dialogue of his chosen proxies is predictably gargantuan, but he makes sure that the main points of his marketing strategy emerge clearly enough.

[53] *Telegraph*, 4 February 1796.
[54] *Telegraph*, 25 April 1796. In this advertisement the Irishman proves his familiarity with Irish matters, and his Irishness, and his ability to see into the future by referring to 'the *Dublin Morning Chronicle*, dated 26 April 1796' which 'declares how highly the Strops are praised, and recommended by those WHO NEVER TRIED THEM; by this means I am likely to be converted'.

FRISEUR. Ce plaisir you receive belong to de merit of Mounsieur PACKWOOD, of No. 16, Gracechurch-street, proprietor of this new invented RAZOR STROP, la voila, (presenting the Strop) *ma foi.*
JACK RATLIN. Avast you lubber, let me try my knife; may I never cross the Line again if it does not take out the notches as if by magic. Mounsieur, are you sure it is not enchanted.
FRISEUR. It's most likely dat you will be enchanté with the excellence, comme tout le monde before you, as le noble, le marchande, le docteur, le cutler, le tonser, &c, &c, &c.
JACK RATLIN. Let me look: again strike my colours, if this is not the same Packwood that I see in all quarters. I have seen his name east, west, north, and south; and even in crossing the line, for his naked truth is lashed to our mainmast, as we had a heavy lading of his ware on board. But splice me to a worse mate than Bet Doxey at the Point, if I had the least knowledge what a valuable cargo we had on board till now.[55]

So convinced was Packwood of the *Telegraph* readers' unquenchable appetite for dialogues he even cast his serious defensive-instructive type advertisement in dialogue form for that newpaper.

A Dispute of a very serious nature was near upon taking place a few days ago, between a gentleman and a tradesman, I here give it verbatim question and answer, as it was:
GENT. Sir, I purchased an article some time ago, of your recommending; I find it does not answer my expectation, and I demand satisfaction.
TRAD. You shall have every satisfaction you require; but pray what article could that be, bought in my shop, as my goods are all warranted.
GENT. It is nothing less than one of Packwood's new-invented Razor Strops, to remove notches, here it is, look at it.
TRAD. Did you read the directions on the outside of the Strop?
GENT. No.
TRAD. Did you ever find it useful?
GENT. I cannot deny, at first, but it answered my most sanguine expectations; indeed I found my face smoother in the evening than with the use of other Strops, directly after shaving in the morning, but of late the Strop has fallen off very much.
TRAD. (Thus addressed him) So shall you and I fall off, if after breakfast we are not supplied with a dinner, and after that something on the next day; and this Strop is lost for want of a supply of Paste. Pray how long have you had it?
GENT. About three or four months.
TRAD. I see this Strop has attracted so much of the steel by application, as to prevent its use; and you confess you have neglected to read the red directions on the Strop, which runs thus, to spread on the paste, about once in two or three months, or oftener, if required. This keeps the Strop always in good order, and as good as new.
The consequence was, the gentleman bought a box of Paste, and the affair was happily adjusted, only he called again in a more calm manner to acknowledge his error, in not reading the label on the Strop, and left this advice for the future, never to sell a Strop without strongly recommending a box of Razor Paste with it, as one without the other, is like a flint without the steel.[56]

[55] *Telegraph,* 16 May 1796.
[56] *Telegraph,* 27 January 1796.

BIRTH OF A CONSUMER SOCIETY

Even the *Telegraph* advertisements in verse are characteristically lengthy. 'An unknown friend' felt moved to write to that newspaper a twenty-eight line poem as a New Year's gift addressed

>To Mr. G. PACKWOOD,
>*Superior Razor Strop Maker, Gracechurch-Street, London*
>Dear PACKWOOD, I now can no longer withstand,
>Giving praise to whom praises are due;
>As the finest invention on Britain's fair land,
>We owe, my dear fellow, to you.[57]

In view of 'many guineas a year' Packwood saved him; in view of 'the improvements [Packwood's] service has made to his life', it is not surprising that he felt that

>'Tis a duty we owe to the Public at large,
>To make known thy most useful invention:
>And the good we receive at so trifling a charge,
>Makes thy fame quite beyond all contention.[58]

Other newspapers were supplied with a very different diet. For the *Sun* he offered

>SMALL CHILDRENS AMUSEMENT; AND A COMFORT TO THOSE
>OF A LARGER GROWTH

This is the Strop that Packwood made.
This was the Paste that was spread on the Strop that Packwood made.
This is the Razor, that was whetted on the Paste, that is spread on the Strop that Packwood made.
These are the Notches, which are removed from the Razor, by whetting it on the Paste, that is spread on the Strop that Packwood made.
This is the Barber, that removed the notches from the Razor, by whetting it on the Paste, that is spread on the Strop that Packwood made.
This is the man that was shaved by the barber, that removed the notches from the Razor, by whetting it on the Paste, that is spread on the Strop that Packwood made.
>*This is the fair Damsel—see her pleasures increase;*
>*The rough beard is remov'd, left like down in its place;*
>*Great enjoyment she takes in her lover's smooth face.*
>*that was kissed by the man that was shav'd by the barber, that removed the notches from the Razor, by whetting it on the Paste, that is spread on the Strop that Packwood made.*[59]

True Briton readers also got lighter fare. On 10 March 1796 they were offered

>PACKWOOD'S NEW STRING OF CONUNDRUMS

Why is a dull Razor like a famished man?
>Because he wants whet.

[57] *Telegraph*, 1 January 1796.
[58] Ibid.
[59] *Sun*, 24 February 1796.

Why is Packwood's Paste unlike the stocks?
   Because it never falls, but always rises in the public opinion.
Why is Packwood's Strop unlike the present lottery?
   Because every purchaser draws a prize.
Why is a person that has been shaved with a blunt-edged razor like another on the brink of marriage?
   Because each wishes the business over.
And why is the inventor himself like a clergyman?
   Because he is never out of orders.[60]

A month later the same readership was offered verse in the form of
   A LESSON FOR LOVERS: OR THE VIRTUE OF THE RAZOR STROP.
Addressed to PACKWOOD'S Repository, No. 16, Grace church-street, London.
Half of the lesson should suffice to convey the message of 'the Porphian Queen' to the love-lorn swain.

> 'To Packwood, my agent, for comfort repair,
> 'He'll give you a face that shall soften your fair;
> 'His strop shall those bristles that fright me remove,
> 'And the maid shall exchange all her hatred to love.'
> The youth bow'd obedience, to Gracechurch-street went,
> And told Packwood the errand on which he was sent.
> Packwood smil'd, and display'd the best goods in his shop,
> His most fav'rite Paste—his most excellent Strop.
> The youth purchas'd both, since he each much approv'd,
> And obtain'd what he wanted the maid that he lov'd.
> Thus Venus with kind and ineffable grace,
> Has giv'n Packwood the means to improve on the face.[61]

For the readers of the *Town and Country* Packwood also offered light diversion. In April the 'Editor of the Country Herald' received a letter from 'A Fresh-stropp'd Razor' which took the form of the familiar narrative advertisement—a long discursive story loosely based on the necessity of memorizing vital numbers leading to the inevitable conclusion that

> But one of the most material numbers in life that draws my attention is in London; that is to say, in Gracechurch-street, No. 16; there a comfort for life is to be obtained at a very small expense, by virtue of Packwood's Razor Strops, acknowledged to be worth their weight in gold, and the naked truth given into the bargain.[62]

A month later these readers were offered a more literary advertisement, self-addressed to

---

[60] *True Briton*, 10 March 1796.
[61] *True Briton*, 13 April 1796.
[62] *Town and Country Herald*, 23 April 1796.

MR. PACKWOOD.

SIR
The celebrity of your New Invented Strops, induces me to send the following *Parody of Hamlet's Soliloquy*, which I trust you will think worth the postage.
'To shave, or not to shave? that is the question.'—Whether 'tis better for a man to suffer the grisly beard to grow upon his chin, or cut it off at once? To shave with ease, to clear the stubbled face—'tis a consummation devoutly to be wished.—To shave with ease; to shave! Perchance to tear; aye, there's the rub; for while we shave the thick rough hairs away, the razor's edge will pluck them by the roots, or checked turn inward on the tender flesh: then trickles down the blood, and the sharpe pain smarting the face, makes cowards of us all.—But who would bear these rubs and ghastly cuts, when he himself might his *quietus* make with PACKWOOD's New Invented Strop.—*Hail London Town! Hail Gracechurch-Street!* and No. 16, *hail!* That makes my healthful face both clean and fair.
DEVIZES, MAY 5, 1796.   A.S.[63]

The readers of the *Evening Star* were served much rougher fare. The only Shakespearian echo in their Packwood advertisement was the title of their ANECDOTE: 'All's well that ends well', but the tone was heavily rustic, the accent more heavily Somerset, the pun on the phrase 'Mark me well' even more heavily obvious. But nevertheless Packwood conveyed his essential message clearly enough, which was 'never buy a common Razor strop, when you can get one of Packwood's superior' kind. That sensible advice came from a country gentleman. That the lower orders could appreciate the sense of it (and the rewards it could bring) was spelt out by the country bumpkin: 'Aye, aye (says the boy) ... I know Will Thrush cou'dn't get Moll Skim with her hundred pounds' until he acquired the aid of Packwood's invention.

> To mov' the scrubbing-brush of Will's face, I vaith he sent all the way vor un to 16 Gracechurch-Street, Lunnon, and Will lends it my grandmother zometimes to shorpen her old knife to trim her whiskers, and cut her quirns, and the old woman is as pleased with it as punch.'[64]

The readers of the *Publican's Morning Advertiser* were offered an appropriately drunken set of 'CROSS READINGS' to puzzle over.

> Short crops are now in fashion all over the country—When his lordship ordered the price of bread to continue as before.
> Coals sold from forty-five to fifty shillings in the Pool—A number of villains was concerned in this *black* affair.
> On Wednesday last a young man cut his throat with a razor—This is the Strop that Packwood made.
> A tradesman's wife put an end to her existence—The lucky office is near Holborn Bars.
> Yesterday a gentleman shot himself at his house in Piccadilly—N.B. One small pill is a dose.[65]

---

[63] *Town and Country Herald,* 14 May 1796.
[64] *Evening Star,* 30 April 1796.
[65] *Publican's Morning Advertiser,* 9 May 1796.

But whatever the chosen literary form, the message was undeviatingly adhered to. When Packwood's strop played the central role as the schoolboy's friend in a narrative advertisement in the *Star,* not only is the story punctuated with lines such as 'Packwood for ever—my master likes to be in fashion', but the dénouement leads inevitably to a last act in which

> The master applied to PACKWOOD, Strop-maker to the whole World, No. 16, Gracechurch-Street, London, for a Strop, and a box of Paste to keep it in order. The fact being clearly proved, a free pardon was announced, and the youth now is the greatest favourite in the school.[66]

When *True Briton* readers are offered more praise of Packwood in verse, the verses are footnoted, and an asterisk leads one to the vital information—

> *PACKWOOD, Razor Strop Maker to the Whole World, No. 16 Gracechurch-Street, London.[67]

When the *Publican's Daily Advertiser* is offered 'A New Song on Razor Strops' to the rousing tune of 'Dicky Gossip' with an even more rousing chorus which culminates in the line

'Spread the fame of Packwood's Strops, he's your man'

repeated five times over, and extending Packwood's market range by including the tools of barbers, joiners, carpenters, tailors and doctors and anyone wanting an edge, the noisy tumult ends with firm directions to proceed

> To Mr. PACKWOOD, superior Razor Strop Maker to the Whole World, No. 16, Gracechurch-Street, London; and his Agents, at the sign of the Naked Truth, in different quarters of the globe.[68]

When on the rare occasion that Packwood was willing to indulge in mild self-mockery of his characteristic self praise and advertising hyperbole, as he did in the pages of the *London Chronicle,* he cannot resist a give-away reference to 'the Naked Truth' in an otherwise anonymous piece:

> Fame has been more liberal to one individual, than ever was expected could come to the share of any one man. I will give you one instance of her modest information: it was communicated to me in detailing the virtues of the new-invented Razor Strop: says she, the bashfulness of the Proprietor prevents him doing justice to himself, when he only speaks of its good effects, such as taking notches out of carving knives, &c. By keeping so much within the bounds of moderation, he has neglected to inform you of a gentleman, soon after he had purchased one of the superior Razor Strops; the gardener complaining his ragstone was insufficient to whet his scythe, the Strop was produced, and by giving it two or three touches, he not only found it cut the grass with facility, but he also cut down six elm trees that stood in his way. This was declared in the presence of the Naked Truth.[69]

For all the variety of his method, all customers were directed to 'the sign of the Naked Truth', all readers were reminded that Packwood was "the Razor

---

[66] *Star,* 22 October 1795. Wrongly dated in *Packwood's Whim* as 22 October 1796.
[67] *True Briton,* 9 November 1795.
[68] *Publican's Daily Advertiser,* 17 February 1796.
[69] *London Chronicle,* 17 May 1796.

Strop Maker to the Whole World;" all potential buyers instructed that '16 Gracechurch-Street' was the place to order from.

As to the value of his products he constantly hammered home the view that they were 'worth their weight in gold'. Whatever the chosen audience Packwood insisted on the same valuation. The readership of the *Times* was offered as

A FACT

The Public opinion on the power of Packwood's superior Razor Strop, agree that it is worth its weight in gold, and acknowledge their face to be cleaner in the evening (by the use of the Strop) than it used to be immediately after shaving in the morning.[70]

Overseas merchants were offered the following shipping intelligence in the

Bengal Shipping Intelligence to different parts of the Globe, as well as the East and West Indies, America.
Merchants, Captains of ships, and the different traders will find it a valuable acquisition to be put in mind of articles the most useful such as will tell to the best account, and take up little room in stowage. What say you for a venture of PACKWOOD's Paste and Razor Strops which are acknowledged to be worth their weight in gold.[71]

The nobility, gentry, and ladies in particular were offered, under the title 'Money Matters' in the *Sunday Monitor,* the fact that Packwood's products were 'acknowledged to be worth their weight in gold'.[72]

* * *

By 20 June 1796 Packwood had succeeded so triumphantly that he was not so much advertising his products, as advertising his own business history. In the *Telegraph* he related the story of his rapid success under the title

The GENEALOGY of the RAZOR STROPS

PACKWOOD first thought of this excellent invention in July; communicated his intentions to some intimate friends in August; received their decisive approbation in September; was determined in the object of his pursuit in October; purchased materials in November; set persons to work in December; made some promising experiments in January; founded the public inclination in February; found it would do in March; brought it to perfection in April; submitted it to public decision in May; and finally established it in June. This diary of a year, cannot fail of being highly satisfactory to all who are convinced that the discovery in question is one of the greatest comforts of the age.[73]

He wrote not only his own business history, but also his own autobiography in the form of an advertisement. Both were of necessity skeletal versions but the 'short sketch of my origins and present situation' ran to nearly 2,000 words. It is an extraordinary example of an advertisement disguised as, at

---

[70] *Times,* 5 February 1796.
[71] *Oracle,* 6 April 1796.
[72] *Sunday Monitor,* 14 February 1796.
[73] *Telegraph,* 20 June 1796.

once, a life story, a revelation of his own psychology, a diverting narrative, an extended proverb, a commentary on contemporary manners, a theatrical farce, and an essay on social behaviour and the consciousness of rank in eighteenth-century England. Only in the first sentence is there the slightest hint, and in the last sentence the final confirmation, that the whole elaborate performance is a dream.

The social nightmare takes the form of the humbly raised Packwood (apprenticed as a barber and for sixteen or seventeen years 'a knight of the comb or more vulgarly speaking a hair dresser') trying to overcome his appalling shyness and social gaucherie after he has risen in the world as a celebrated businessman. Despite lessons in deportment 'from a professor who teaches grown men to dance', his acceptance of a Baronet's invitation to dinner is a spectacular disaster: first he treads on the gouty toe of his host, then he inadvertently reveals that his host's learning is counterfeit, and in so doing pulls down a false set of sixteen volumes of Xenophon, which falls onto a Wedgwood inkstand, the ink from which streams from an inlaid table top onto a Turkey carpet with Packwood frantically but unavailingly mopping with his handkerchief. Disaster succeeds disaster. He bows so low that he spills scalding soup into his lap. He spills a sauce boat. He knocks down a salt cellar. Even worse is to follow. When asked to pass Miss Louisa Friendly a pigeon whilst holding a piece of pudding on his fork, poor Packwood 'in my haste, scarce knowing what I did, I whipped the pudding into my mouth hot as a burning coal, it was impossible to conceal my agony, my eyes were starting from their sockets; at last in spite of shame and resolution I was obliged to drop the cause of my torment on my plate'. Wine was advised to draw out the heat, but the butler gave him brandy 'with which I filled my mouth ... Totally unused to every kind of ardent spirits, with my tongue, throat, and palate, as raw as beef ... I could not swallow; and clapping my hands upon my mouth the liquor squirted through my nose and fingers, like a fountain over all the dishes'. To add absurdity to indignity he then wiped his face 'with the ill-fated handkerchief ... still wet from the consequence of the fall of Xenophon, and covered all my features with streaks of ink in every direction'. At this the scarcely suppressed hysteria of the company could be suppressed no longer, and Packwood fled the house to the sound of the whole household's laughter. His humiliation was complete, his lower parts 'almost boiled', his 'tongue and mouth grilled' and bearing 'the mark of Cain on his forehead' and covered in everlasting shame.

Any reader, whose enjoyment of the farce was being marred by the psychological cruelty of this social torture, was then instantly released from embarrassment by Packwood awaking from 'a vision of a dream' and finding himself safe, and successful and happy 'in the midst of my warehouse, famed for Razor Strops &c. at No. 16, Gracechurch-Street, London'.[74] The whole elaborate performance was merely the prelude to yet another advertisement.

[74] *Courier,* 16 April 1796.

It seems that there were no lengths to which Packwood was not willing to go 'to amuse and divert and astonish'[75] his readers and potential customers. A string of anecdotes in praise of Packwood's superiority kept his name in the papers, and, he hoped, his product in the news. Thirty year old rusty razors were so transformed by his incomparable razor strop that a village barber 'always saves one ... to shave Mr. Quiteright, the man-midwife, in cases of particular hurry'[76] Mr. Nimrod of Kent was in an even greater hurry. He 'had such a partiality for hunting he could scarce find time to have his beard taken off; by the use of the superior Razor Strop, he now shaves himself on horseback, full gallop, without the least fear, loss of time, or hindrance of business'. Dr. Packwood printed such 'well authenticated cases' (the result of 'the amazing powers of his antiobtuse Razor Strop') along with the expression of his 'extreme' pleasure 'in being the means of stopping the unnecessary effusion of human blood by the superlative power of his superior Razor Strop'.[77]

So proud indeed was Packwood of his 'Diverting Advertisements' that he could not bear that they disappear with the other ephemera in the daily press. He decided to re-use them, to squeeze further advertising value from them by republishing a collection of them. This publication is itself a milestone in the history of advertising. Newspaper advertisements were not always cheap. Daniel Stuart, whose brother bought the *Oracle* in 1795 and who together with his brother bought the *Morning Post* that year, (both papers used by Packwood), wrote that as 'advertisements flowed in beyond bounds, and each was desirous of having his cloud of advertisements inserted at once ... I charged enormously high ... when a long advertisement of a column or two came.'[78] So not surprisingly Packwood saw advantage in republishing his expensive long advertisements. There were other advantages too. Although each newspaper had its own class of readership and were known for their particular class of advertisements, such differences could be exaggerated and many of their readers enjoyed the chance to see another's papers' characteristic style.[79] Packwood's collection would give them the chance to do so. Some newspapers had a very select readership. In 1795, for instance, the daily circulation of the *Oracle* was a mere 800 and the *Morning Post* a mere 350 and although both then rose rapidly, these were too small to enjoy a monopoly of the advertisements Packwood placed in them. John Christie, the auctioneer, was sufficiently alive to the different audiences

---

[75] To adapt Wedgwood's description of his own commercial endeavours.
[76] *Telegraph*, 5 July 1796.
[77] *Telegraph*, 5 July 1796.
[78] Daniel Stuart, *The Gentleman's Magazine* (July 1838), quoted in B. B. Elliott, *A History of English Advertising* (1962), pp. 147-9.
[79] According to Daniel Stuart, ibid., 'The *Morning Post* was known for advertising horses and carriages. The *Public Ledger* shipping and sales of wholesale foreign merchandise; The *Morning Herald* and *Times*, auctioneers, *The Morning Chronicle*, books. All papers had all sorts of advertisements, it is true, but some were more remarkable than others for a particular class.'

reached by different newspapers, to go to the lengths of not only buying a part ownership in the Whig newspaper *The Morning Chronicle*, but also buying a part ownership of the Tory newspaper *The Morning Post* which started in 1772.

By republishing his advertisements Packwood could reach an audience unconfined to the special readership of particular newspapers. By ensuring that his own publication took advantage of every promotional trick he could think of, he made every effort to extend its sales. From title page to printers acknowledgements, Packwood's book of collected advertisements bristles with commercial intent.

Even the printer's postscript recognized the need to advertise—and to do so in an entertaining, eye-catching fashion. The acknowledgement to Walkinshaw, the printer, offers attractive confirmation of the commitment to the power of advertisement, of the belief in the need to capture a potential customer's attention, of the clear recognition that 'mere' information, routinely offered, risks being ignored. To make sure that the requisite facts were noticed, and to heighten the chances of their being absorbed and remembered, the usual acknowledgement to the printer employed several typical Packwood techniques—the question and answer format, the nursery rhyme jingle, the use of negro slang and rhyming doggerel:

'Who drew the Plate in the front of this book? I, says the Engraver. Who was the Engraver? I, says the Copper Plate Printer. Who was the Printer? I, says the—stop and read.

> Now critics, no doubt, will find out a flaw,
> A *juvenile* hand, nam'd *A. Walk-in-shaw*,
> In Finch and, Cornhill, he lives 'tis true,
> And will for *de pay*—do as much for you.
> FINIS.'[80]

Packwood's offering ended as it began with a deliberate effort to advertise through diverting and intriguing the reader. The title page of his booklet was characteristic of the whole. The title itself—*Packwood's Whim: The Goldfinch's Nest; or the Way to Get Money and Be Happy*—was a typical mixture of a prominent display of the Packwood name, an intriguing metaphor which echoed one of his standard advertising phrases, and the kind of promise exploited by contemporary 'How-to-succeed' literature.[81] 'The Way to Get Money' part of the title was an advertisement masquerading as financial advice: it consisted of no more than the caption 'THE WAY TO GET MONEY' in bold capitals, defined in the words—'is to sell a useful article that will do credit and sell to a good account, such as Packwood's Razor Strops and Paste; or his Goldfinch's Nest.'[82] Catching the reader's

---
[80] George Packwood, *Packwood's Whim* (1796), p. 48.
[81] See *The New Art of Thriving* (1798), or *The Pleasant Art of Money-Catching* (1800).
[82] *Packwood's Whim*, p. 8.

attention and imprinting the Packwood brand name were clearly valued far more than honouring the promise in any more than a token fashion.

To further incite customer interest the title page carried the following intriguing inducement to buy—'To *Make this Publication worth your Money, that there may be* NO GRUMBLING, AN HALF CROWN is placed in the Middle of it.' Since the price of the booklet was 'A GOOD TOWER SHILLING' the route to a quick profit beckoned as invitingly as Packwood's subtitle, and just as deceivingly. The promise *is* honoured, but only after the whimsical manner of the whole publication, by a story entitled 'AN HALF CROWN' placed as advertised in the middle of the book. It is a simple device and an old one. The deception, so quickly revealed as such, was clearly regarded as venial, and well justified by its advertising power. For even the morally improving fable that appeared under the half-crown caption included a hearty plug for Packwood—appropriately enough in a morality tale of this kind, this particular plug was for Packwood the benevolent employer,[83] but it did not fail to include a footnote pointing out what Packwood manufactured and where his products could be bought.

To complete the title pages there is a handsome engraving of Packwood himself surrounded by shelf upon shelf of his celebrated razor strops and pointing to the box of paste which gave rise to the distinctive brand image of *The Goldfinch's Nest*.

Further tricked out with a Latin tag from Horace, and the warning that 'when you have perused this Book and assert you were neither Excited to Cry, Laugh or Grin—you must not expect to be Ranked among the most Favourite Customers', the title page closes characteristically with a sample of outlets where the book could be obtained in London, Edinburgh and Dublin, and the advice that a further list would be found at the back of the book.

This longer list of suppliers is entitled 'A few of the Names among many hundreds appointed for the Sale of Packwood's Razor Strops and Paste and Goldfinch's Nest'. It includes fifteen separate outlets in London and six in the country. These are clearly Packwood's more important outlets. The London outlets include three 'Perfumers to the Prince of Wales', one 'Perfumer in ordinary to her Majesty', another 'famed for Restoring of Beauty' and there is even a cross reference complete with a page reference to the verses published in *Packwood's Whim* singing jointly the praises of 'Packwood's Razor Strops' and 'British Shaving Paste'. This joint advertisement, masquerading as 'Verses written extempore by a Gentleman immediately after Shaving' finished with the maxim

'If you would shave with ease and taste
Use PACKWOOD'S STROPS and BRITISH PASTE'.[84]

---

[83] Packwood appears as an employer who comes to the aid of a family in need, and he is described as keeping a number of such families 'in constant employment'.

[84] The two products are rather coyly anthropomorphized and announce themselves as 'Messrs

The provincial outlets listed are the ones which Packwood's provincial newspaper advertisements had introduced and backed. They too included a 'Perfumer to the Prince of Wales'—yet another instance of the eighteenth-century advertiser's reliance on social emulation and emulative spending—and Packwood reinforced his trademark by adding that his products 'may be had at the sign of the Naked Truth, in different parts of the three kingdoms'.

Packwood's Whim, in fact, ends as it began with its insistent advertising message. But the ending is factual and repetitive compared with the whimsical beginning. For *Packwood's Whim* is more than a mere collection of published advertisements. It is like a miniature monograph on the skill of late eighteenth-century advertisers, and the variety of ways in which they exercised that skill. It is also a self-congratulatory business history signalling unmistakably the particular commercial skill its founder wished to be remembered for.

The book opens with an extended allegory entitled 'THE GOLD-FINCH'S NEST, How discovered in the YEAR 1794'. Being intent on making his success story palatable to his readers, Packwood produced a most engaging piece of advertiser's copy masquerading as an historical account. Like a child's story, the narrative is simple, the events easily visualized and the chief characters (the commodities to be sold) are given the straightforward appeal of cartoon cut-outs, but the intention is plainly and insistently commercial. The economic intent may be playfully disguised, appealingly camouflaged, but only to the extent that a modern commercial uses animals to sugar its bid for the attention of its chosen market. The consumers are lulled into listening, amused into staying, cajoled into buying, and imprinted with an easily identifiable brand image so that they will buy and buy again. To help them remember the product and its image, its virtues and its distinctive character are repeated over and over again.

Because Packwood's circular boxes of razor paste, and the yellow balls of actual paste inside looked, as his illustrated frontispiece makes clear, like a nest of yellow eggs, Packwood based his introduction on the image of the goldfinch's nest. This allows him to advertise the site of the nest [his shop in Gracechurch Street, 'next door to the Cross Keys Inn',] allows him to date the arrival of his invention ['the first egg was deposited on the 23rd July 1794'], and allows him to describe its triumphant colonization of the market as a series of migrations: first to Brighton, then to London ['Mr. Love in the Haymarket'], then to Scotland and Ireland, and beyond. The method allows him to give a particular plug for his best provincial outlets, such as Mr. Raeburn of Edinburgh and Mr. Simmons of Dublin who 'particularly

---

RAZOR STROP and SHAVING PASTE' who 'beg leave to inform the public that they give constant attendance within, and will think themselves happy, either jointly or singly, to enter into any gentleman's service that shall please to employ them, not in the least doubting that they shall give the most compleat satisfaction'. *Packwood's Whim*, p. 22.

witnessed the attachment of these birds, the latter having acknowledged that he had disposed of ten thousand in ten months after he had taken a fancy to them'.[85]

The metaphor is further utilized to show how much they were valued, how universal was the spread of their sales, how their efficiency survived in different climates, how to sell them was to put oneself on a route to a rapid fortune, and of course where they could be bought from.

The introduction ends with the words: 'Indeed so much store was set by them, half a guinea has been known to be given for a single feather.[86] These birds can live in any part of the Universe, many of them having ventured as far as the East and West Indies, where they are in fine song and feather, notwithstanding the difference of the climate; such favorites [sic] are they in every part that those who take them under their care and will honourably return a part of the produce to the original Nest, may consider themselves on the eve of making a rapid fortune; such is the history of the discovery, rise, progress and present condition of the celebrated Goldfinch's Nest, the original of which may be seen to the entire satisfaction of the curious, at the sign of the Naked Truth, No. 16 Gracechurch-street London'.[87]

Tricked out with proverbs, anecdotes (improving, entertaining and defensive),[88] self-congratulatory verses, mocking stories told against himself[89] and detailed directions on how to get the best out of his product, *Packwood's Whim* ends with a further self-commendation—

> The Proprietor himself has stropped a notch out of his own common six-penny knife, and shaved himself dry (though a hard beard) without a lather, much cleaner and smoother than he had done for many years back.
> To give you a faint idea, permit the Proprietor to observe, that a diamond or flint will cut glass, and this Strop will have as powerful an effect on steel by way of polishing;

and then some final advice on further reading:

> Gentle Reader—if your patience is not exhausted in perusing the different serious and comic, prosaic, and poetic advertisements on the good properties of Razor Strops, and you have a desire for further information—by referring to the Tatler, by Isaac Bickerstaff, Esq. in 12mo. No. 224, there you may find Strops for Razors advertised with much more violence.[90]

Having published a book to advertise his advertisements, Packwood then published an advertisement to advertise further the book advertising those

---

[85] *Packwood's Whim*, p. 4. This particular triumph had been used in an advertisement in the *Dublin Register, or Freeman's Journal* of 26 April 1796.
[86] The Razor Strop.
[87] *Packwood's Whim*, p. 4.
[88] Defending him from the charge of having 'borrowed part of his materials from other foundations' with yet another negro slave story in which the slave gets the better of the white owner. *Packwood's Whim*, p. 8.
[89] Such as the story about the customer 'more elevated in the world than the generality of mankind' who turned out to have been 'gibbeted last Summer on Wimbledon Common.'
[90] *Packwood's Whim*, p. 47.

advertisements. To economize a little on his inventive powers, this last shot in this particular advertising campaign consisted of a single sheet of selected samples from the original advertisements which he had republished in *Packwood's Whim*.

It consisted of three dialogues and two songs celebrating Packwood's products, and was distributed under the following description:

> Just Published   Price 1s
> PACKWOOD'S WHIM: or the GOLDFINCH'S NEST
> Including his different Advertisements on his celebrated RAZOR STROPS and PASTE, sold WHOLESALE or RETAIL for the author G. PACKWOOD, 16 GRACECHURCH-STREET, LONDON, by Mr. SIMMONS, Perfumer No. 120 Capel St. DUBLIN, and Mr. RAEBURN, Perfumer to the Prince of Wales, No. 13, North Bridge Street, EDINBURGH; also may be had of the different News Carriers in Town and Country, and of the Shop keepers appointed for the Sale of his Razor Strops and Paste.[91]

It was the culmination of a remarkable advertising campaign. Packwood could congratulate himself on having won the market of fashionable London, of having extended it through Brighton, Bath, Bristol, Gloucester, Dublin, Oxford, Edinburgh, Norwich, Northampton and the rest of the provinces, of having reached as far afield as the East and the West Indies, and having sold as many as ten thousand of his products through a single outlet in ten months. Since each step of this campaign is recorded in his newspaper advertisements, since each provincial outlet is registered in the advertisements in the appropriate provincial newspaper, and since the remarkable variety of his promotional ploys have survived for posterity in the sixty different types of newspaper advertisements he used in less than two years, his publicity campaign is a remarkable testimony to the effectiveness of a planned commercial assault on the consumer market by one of those much derided 'lesser men of business' who operated so successfully in the late eighteenth-century economy, but who have failed so signally to be appreciated by twentieth-century historians. Packwood does not deserve the anonymity which has been thrust upon him.

His achievements as a writer of advertising copy were too memorable to merit being overlooked. For by selling under 'the sign of the Naked Truth', under the brand image of the 'Goldfinch's Nest', and backed by the insistent drum beat of the Packwood name repeated over and over again in his newspaper advertisements, Packwood succeeded in the twin aims of all advertisers—to hammer home his product's distinctive values and virtues, and its superiority over all rivals, and yet, by the novelty and invention with which essentially the same message was ceaselessly conveyed, to prevent interest in his product from flagging. So although the basic message remained

---

[91] I am indebted to Miss Ruth Rogers of the Kress Library, Harvard Business School, for knowledge of this single advertising sheet, which has recently been purchased for the Kress Library by Miss Rogers.

the same, this theme song was presented in almost endless variations. Interest was never allowed to grow stale, the campaign was never allowed to lose momentum.

As a result he could afford, in *Packwood's Whim*, a deserved note of self-congratulation. He published it deliberately on 23 July 1796—two years to the day since, as he whimsically described it, 'the first egg was deposited'.[92] To have so quickly and effectively, by his own estimation, captured a chosen market as a result of a deliberate advertising campaign is further evidence of the high levels of commercial skill being deployed by late eighteenth-century entrepreneurs. To demonstrate the case in all its depth and variety requires that the campaigns of individual businessmen be painstakingly picked out and collected from the advertising columns of eighteenth-century newspapers. For it must not be thought that Packwood did not have many rivals busily manipulating consumer demand in other fields. Many a Packwood lies undiscovered—or at least uncelebrated—in the advertising sheets of late Georgian England.

The self-congratulatory, whimsical tone of Packwood's advertisements invite the suspicion of an elaborate literary spoof on the advertisements of the day, but no such understandable suspicions can be cast on the welter of advertisements from a myriad other sources—many of them equally whimsical in tone, equally baroque in their use of imagery, equally ornate in their use of language, and undeniably serious in their commercial intent.

No more than an illustrative sample can be cited here but they should suffice to give some more general flavour of the nature of contemporary advertisements than Packwood alone can give. What his advertisements illustrate in detail about the process of commercialization is confirmed in general by the full range of products which were enthusiastically promoted in the newspapers and advertising sheets of the day.

Few experiences more vividly convey the sense of a consumer society than a sustained diet of late eighteenth-century advertisements. In content, in commodities promoted, even in psychological approach, sometimes even in style, and certainly in the human compulsions they pandered to, they remind one irresistibly of the rampant commercialism and the uninhibited materialism of American television advertising. Like present-day commercials, eighteenth-century advertisements were insistently preoccupied with food, drink and health, with fashion and cosmetics. Preserving one's health, improving one's appearance, and enhancing one's status and happiness through the acquisition of material possessions—these were, and indeed are, the obsessions which they exploited.

To complete the sense of *déjà vu* [or rather *déjà lu* in the case of the wordy advertisements of Georgian England], they were laced with lotteries offering golden prizes for the fortunate just as American television pro-

---

[92] *Packwood's Whim*, p. 3.

grammes are increasingly laced with panel games, the major interest of which lies in the cash prizes won, and the simple technique of which is little advanced on the lottery.

The language was inevitably slightly different—teeth were artificial rather than false, waves were not yet claimed to be permanent, hair was frankly dyed rather than genteely colour-rinsed. The dominant approach was still verbal rather than visual. The claims were unhindered by even the loosest code of advertising ethics—they were even less on oath than the authors of epitaphs, so superlatives abound and the most remarkable combinations of virtues co-exist in a single product. The knocking copy of rivals was more direct—usually straightforward warnings of deceit and commercial theft. But the similarities were greater than the differences. There was the same insistent propaganda, the same constant repetition of brand names, the same exploitation of snobbery and social emulation, the same use of the famous and the authoritative to promote their products—royalty used their hair dyes, doctors recommended their medicines, dentists sanctioned their tooth pastes, fashion leaders enthused over their new clothes styles. They even used eminent engineers to give authority to their cements and Parker and Company published in 1796 a long encomium by Thomas Telford, the famous engineer and road builder, in recommendation of their 'Roman Cement and Artificial Terras and Stucco'.[93]

Not all the recommendations were as dignified or as scientific as Telford's. Those urged to buy Prince's Cherry Lotion—the more firmly to secure their teeth—were assured that 'A Lady of Distinction has declar'd that most of her teeth became loose and some dropped out quite sound, but after using four bottles of Cherry Lotion the remainder of her Teeth became quite firm. Ask for Prince's Cherry Lotion. ½ a guinea a bottle, or one dozen bottles Five Pounds'.[94]

In a monthly publication such as *La Belle Assemblée* or *The Universal Advertising Sheet*—a magazine wholly devoted to advertisements—one gets a concentrated impression of the major products offered for sale through advertisement to the fashionable market of Georgian England. Where the provincial press carried a far higher proportion of lost and found advertisements, adverts for local schools and local sales, for flower seeds and vegetables, for wetnurses and flea-killers, *The Universal Advertising Sheet* was uninhibitedly up-market, designed for the capital and reflecting London taste. It was the original source of many of the advertisements for consumer products

---

[93] They published Telford's 'impartial and disinterested' report on their product as a separate pamphlet. It can still be seen in the Kress Library of Business History, the Baker Library, Harvard School of Business Administration, Cambridge, Boston, Massachusetts. See *Parker and Co: Roman Cement and Artificial Terras and Stones, examined and approved by Thomas Telford* (1796). Felton, the coachmaker also used advertisements disguised as technical treatises.

[94] *La Belle Assemblée* or *The Universal Advertising Sheet*—published monthly and begun in 1806.

that filtered rapidly through to the provinces by way of domestic servants' talk, by way of handbills, trade cards, provincial shops and warehouses, and of course, the provincial press which increasingly diluted its advertisements for pigs and poultry with the products most in demand in the capital.

But the overwhelming first impression which one gets from the pages of *The Universal Advertising Sheet* is of the dominant place occupied by face-creams, toothpastes, hair dyes, soaps and shampoos, by patent medicines and convenience foods, of hats and gloves, and corsets and dresses (indeed of the full panoply of female fashion). The major fare offered (as in present day advertisements whether in women's magazines or on television) was concerned with cleaning and beautifying the human body—in particular, the skin, the teeth and women's hair; and then in dressing it fashionably; and then in satisfying its appetites, and curing its ills. Furnishing the home with furniture, curtains, clocks, carpets, table clothing, pottery, cutlery and such like played a less prominent role than in the less grand publications.

Those unversed in late eighteenth-century commercial techniques are often surprised at the prominent place occupied by advertisement for convenience foods. Whereas in the 1720s separate books and pamphlets were written explaining in elaborate detail how to choose, store and prepare one's coffee—having first 'chosen your *Nuts*' and stored them in a garret (cellars were too damp, kitchens too warm) you were required to roast them slowly over a clear charcoal fire, then crush them between polished Porphyric stones acquired specially for that purpose;[95] by 1800 one was being offered instant coffee by Hawkins and Dunn. This advertisement under a banner headline 'COFFEE MADE IN ONE MINUTE' assured their customers that 'a small teaspoon full . . . put into . . . boiling water . . . instantly makes a cup of strong *clear* Coffee',[96] and pointed out that it was now distributed throughout the country and could be purchased from both 'Grocers and Chemists &c.'[97]

Other convenience foods figure prominently—such as 'Tomata (sic) Ketchups', 'Portable Soups and Gravies' and a whole battery of ready-made sauces. Under the title *SAUCE EPICURIENNE* Jasper Taylor tells us that his sauce is available in bottles in London, Kingston, Bath, Cambridge, Portsmouth, and Greenwich, and adds that

> The very high esteem in which this invaluable Sauce is held by the Nobility and Gentry, as well as for its exquisite flavour, as for its general application to all the purposes of Cookery, calls forth the grateful acknowledgement of *JASPER TAYLOR* and *SON*, the Inventors, for the liberal patronage afforded them; and

---

[95] See Humphrey Burton, *The Domestick Coffeeman* (London 1722). One is reminded of present-day American advertisement for Sanka brands by Burton's warning against coffee that 'In all Hot Constitutions, it is very hurtful, because it dries the nerves too much and is apt to make them Tremble, as in Palsies'.
[96] Most early issues of *La Belle Assemblée*.
[97] Ibid.; Hawkins and Dunn advertised widely and regularly.

induces them to take this public method of apprising such of their friends, and the Public in general, as have not yet had an opportunity of trying its unrivalled excellence, that it is the best Sauce for Steaks and Chops, Fish, Hashes, Ragouts, Soups, Hot and Cold Meats, ever invented, and is generally approved of in almost every preparation of the culinary art. And they have the further gratification to add, that it will keep good in any climate, and for any length of time.[98]

There was plenty of competition for this market. In the same periodical 'AVELING'S SAUCE A LA RUSSE' was advertised 'for Fish, Game, Steaks, Chops, Cutlets, Stews, Hashes, Harricoes (sic), Curries, Made Dishes, Cold Meats, or any Dish that requires a fine flavour'. Mr. Aveling cautioned his customers that 'the wellknown excellence and high estimation of the first Families and most curious in Fish Sauces in the Kingdom, with the increasing demands for Aveling's Sauce a la Russe, has induced many Shopkeepers to offer for sale a Composition of their own, under the same name. The Proprietor begs leave to caution the Public against such deception.'[99] [Such constant warnings give some impression of how quickly any fashionable product was copied and reproduced. It was a major preoccupation of every tradesman—whether a great manufacturer like Josiah Wedgwood or a modest purveyor of Razor-Strops like George Packwood.]

Other forerunners of modern products are provided by advertisements for such products as TRENTS DEPILATORY for the greater beauty of women's arms, or ATKINSON'S ORIGINAL CURLING FLUID ['a chemical article as innocent as new milk'], or MRS. SASS' FEMALE AGENCY ['even temporary assistants provided'], or WITMER'S SICILIAN BLOOM OR YOUTH BEAUTY, or John Ogilvy's POMMADE DIVINE, or TROTTER'S ORIENTAL DENTIFRICE, or PEAR'S TRANSPARENT SOAP, or the music publishers who produced their own lists of the current 'top twelve' songs with Miss Matthew's 'The Indian Maid' and 'The Nightingale's Club' occupying first and second place, and Miss Edgeworth's songs at three and four.

Less surprising is the welter of proprietary brand medicines, such as Dixon's Antibilious Pills, Dr. Fothergill's Female Pills, Godbold's Vegetable Balsam for Asthma, Butler's Restorative Tooth powder, Hackman's Pills for the Gravel and Stone. They were not modest in their claims. Dr. Fothergill's Nervous Cordial Drops were 'the most powerful Restorative both for preventing and curing all Cases of Lowness and Nervous Affections, Hypochondriacs, Hysterics, Spasms, Palsy, Apoplexy, loss of Appetite, Bilious Complaints, Convulsions and Fits attending Pregnancy, Stomach Complaints, Heartburn, Sick Headache, &c.'[100] In view of the range of

---

[98] *Bell's Monthly Compendium of Advertisements,* June 1813, p. 39.
[99] Aveling's Italian and Fish Sauce Warehouse at No. 63 Piccadilly, corner of Albemarle Street, also provided 'Somerset hares (twice a week during the Season), Prime Stilton Cheese in high perfection—new Sallad Oil, Macaroni, Parmesan Cheese, New Olives, Hams, Tongues, foreign and English Pickles, and all kinds of Fish Sauces.'
[100] For the rich or those in greatest need there was a bottle priced 22/-.

specific cures, not to mention the etcetera, the price at 4/6 a bottle could scarcely be held to be excessive, but if the drops were too specific in their cure or something less expensive was needed Dr. Fothergill's Female Pills offered a cheaper and more general palliative for the Ladies: 'We would beg leave to observe that Beauty loses its lustre without the possession of Health, and cannot be supplied by the roseate tint and artificial hue; on this account we would recommend to their attention DR. FOTHERGILL'S FEMALE PILLS, a medicine unparalleled in the cure of different Complaints incident to the Female Sex at particular periods of Life, and for preserving the Female Constitution at all times in a regular healthy condition, these Pills uniting the highest tonic and invigorating powers for only 2/9 a box.'[101]

Such advertisements for proprietary medicines have, of course, a long history and as early as 1710 Addison was complaining in *The Tatler* of the polemical advertisements of the several Proprietors of Dr. Anderson's Pills:[102] by 1730 the newspapers themselves were attacking the exaggerated claims of 'Prolifick Elixirs' (which cured 'barrenness in women, or imbecility in men', and 'even seems to keep back the effect of old age itself' by 'promoting the cheerfull curricle of the blood and juices', by 'raising all the fluids to one more florid and sparkling', by 'evidently replenishing the crispy fibres of the whole habit with a generous warmth and balmy moisture'),[103] saying of this remarkable piece of copy-writing 'The author of this great Secret means no more than by putting so many nonsensical phrases together, to make one Fool or another believe it is worth 5 shillings a bottle';[104] and by 1741 the *Publick Register* was self-righteously declaring that 'whereas one fourth part at least of all the Papers that are now extant, is filled with Quack advertisements; to prevent the like in this and to give room for matter of importance no Advertisements will be admitted, but such as relate to Books and Pamphlets.'[105]

Historians of advertising have understandably made good use of such quotable examples,[106] and it is important that we do not forget that advertisements for most products have a literary pedigree which reaches back far into the distant past. Graffiti on the wall of the Street of Abundance in the Pompeii of the first century A.D. have been listed in some histories of advertisement, and it is certainly not difficult to find examples of early commercialism in England before the eighteenth century.

An early, if rather primitive, form of 'product differentiation' can be seen in the same cloth being sold as 'durances, durettos, damazines and damazellas . . . as it is conceived the same might vent or sell the better' under different

---

[101] *La Belle Assemblée* (1808).
[102] Addison, *The Tatler*, 12 April 1710. In Addison's view 'above half the advertisements one meets with nowadays are purely polemical'.
[103] *The Evening Post*, 13 September 1730.
[104] *The Country Gentleman*, 30 September 1730.
[105] *The Publick Register or The Weekly Magazine* of January 1741.
[106] All the last four are quoted by B. B. Elliott, op. cit., pp. 102–8.

names.[107] And in Houghton's *Collections* at the beginning of the eighteenth century there are many examples which have an anachronistically modern ring to them. To cite, for instance, the description of 'a liquid soap ... which for its sweetness and delicacy in washing the finest laces, muslins, cambricks and other fine linens preserving their strength and beauty and making them curiously clear and white will be of great use and benefit to Your Majesty's subjects',[108] might seem to offer clear evidence of the soapmaker William Coupland effectively selling his liquid soap by advertisement. In fact he was seeking a patent for it, and the Commissioner of Excise heard the case in 1718 and turned Coupland down.

The early advertisers—John Houghton and his *Collections*, Edward Lloyd and *Lloyd's News* in the 1690s, and Charles Povey, *General Remark on Trade* of 1705, or *The General Advertiser* of 1707 or *the Useful Intelligence* of 1711—deserve to be remembered as pioneers, but their importance must not be overstated. Those who call Houghton the 'Father of Advertising' should make clear that although he may have sown a seed, his child was to require a healthy period of gestation before it was safely delivered and could announce its lusty presence in the eighteenth century. Houghton's *A Collection for Improvement of Husbandry and Trade* was only incidentally a vehicle for advertising—starting with his coy advertisement for his own chocolates in issue No. 12. Although he went on to 'advertise all sorts of things that are honourable', his papers remained essentially a useful means of spreading knowledge on husbandry to the farming community. In the same way *Lloyd's News* carried only the occasional advertisement, and, to judge from the few copies which have survived, Povey's advertising sheets were given away free like handbills and carried notices mainly about quack medicines.

They were part of the first stirring of the commercialization of the eighteenth century. They were the forerunners of the *Daily Advertiser* and the *London Advertiser* of 1731; the *General Advertiser* of 1744, the *Public Advertiser* of 1752, the *Morning Post and Daily Advertising Pamphlet* of 1772, and the *Morning Advertiser* of 1795. Many of those earlier titles are testimony to the short life and kaleidoscopic changes of title from which early eighteenth-century newspapers suffered. But some of the later ones showed an impressive ability to survive and prosper in the favourable demand conditions prevailing later in the century, and it is worth remembering how many famous and successful newspapers began their lives as advertising sheets or Trade organs in the reign of George III—the *Public Ledger* (1760), *The Morning Post* (1772), *The Times* (1785) and *The Morning Advertiser* (1795)—as indeed did famous auctioneers who advertised in them like

---

[107] K. J. Allison, 'The Norfolk Worsted Industry in the Sixteenth and Seventeenth Centuries, 2. The New Draperies', *Yorkshire Bulletin of Economic and Social Research*, 14 (1962), p. 69.
[108] John Houghton, *Collections*, vol. IX, no. 200.

BIRTH OF A CONSUMER SOCIETY

Christies and Tattersalls. They were part of the ever increasing tide of commercial activity. It was in the 1740s that Fielding wrote 'Totus mundus agit Pufstrionem', and although he was satirizing mainly politicians and writers ('the chief Art of Book-Puffing') he also noted as part of the pervasive puffery that ''tis this gave the Tradesmen the first notions of Signs, Handbills, fine shops . . . etc.'.[109] Certainly by mid-century the advertisements for 'ready made gowns', for pewter, copper, brass, silver and furniture and such like were beginning to rival the quack medicines in the largeness of their promise and the space they occupied in the press. By the 1770s 'the multitude of fine manufacturers and trinkets of which the shops are full', which according to Hanway provided so 'much entertainment and expense for the domestics', were announced widely in even provincial newspapers.[110] Since one third of many of those newspapers was given over to advertisements they had ample room in which to compete.

By the end of the century the spread of advertisements and the quality of some of the practitioners had developed to such a level that it is difficult to deny that in this aspect of marketing and salesmanship a commercial revolution had occurred in the course of the eighteenth century. England was increasingly taking on the appearance and the behaviour patterns of a consumer society. It was not, of course, a society of the high mass consumption type which prevails in so many countries today, but many of the infant features characteristic of those societies were unmistakably present in the world of newspaper advertisement. The consumer society conceived in the 1690s was certainly born by the 1790s, and the process of commercialization had penetrated an impressive array of consumer industries.

Those who looked back on this period from the mid-nineteenth century spoke of it as a period in which the British public developed 'a remarkable appetite for puffs and swallow[ed] them of all sorts and sizes, and in all sorts of places.'[111] For 'every new publication and newspaper, and the walls and windows of every city, town and village, teem with the multiplicity and variety of some of their advertisements'.[112] Not every one approved but the process of commercialization was widely recognized.[113]

One does not need to search to find illustrative advertising material by 1800. There is by then an embarrassment of riches and a remarkable range of products. In *Bell's Monthly Compendium of Advertisements* there were advertisements for Windsor Chairs, the *Encyclopaedia Britannica,* Handel's Vocal Works, Hogarth's complete works, and Vandyke's Portraits of Illustrious Persons. There were advertisements for periodicals such as *The*

---

[109] *The Champion,* 16 February 1740, and 19 December 1741.
[110] James Hanway, *Virtue in Humble Life* (1777), p. 294.
[111] *Puffs and Mysteries, or the Romance of Advertising* (1855), p. vi.
[112] *Hints on the Unlimited Diffusion of Useful Knowledge at No Expense to the Reader through the Medium of the Mercantile and Trading Classes* (Edinburgh, 1834), p. 6.
[113] *The Crying Frauds of the London Market.*

Repository of Arts with fifty-one plates which carried articles on 'Patterns of British Manufacture', 'Ladies Carriage Costumes, Ladies Morning Walking Dress, Ladies Opera Dress', 'the Comforts of Houses', and 'Cottage Ornée Styles'. Cooke's Elegant Editions offered selected poets, from Shakespeare at 2s. to Dryden at 6s. 6d.; selected novels (from *Zadig* for 1s., *Candide* for 1s. 6d. to *Tom Jones* at 8s., *Don Quixote* at 10s., and *Pamela* at 11s. 6d.); and a collection of British classics.

Instead of universal elixirs the market now carried specialists like Mr. Laidlaw the Chiropodist dealing with 'Corns, Callosities and Bunions', and Mr. Macarsie who dealt with 'the Diseases of the Female Organs' and 'never fail[ed] to impart the desired effect', and specialist products such as Mucillage of Marshmallows (a remedy for the Gravel), or CHING'S PATENT WORM LOZENGES for children (which carried the approving testimony of the Earl of Exeter, the Bishop of Carlisle, the Duchess of Leeds and Rutland, and four Countesses, and which could be bought in bulk 'for charitable purposes'), or 'BUTLER'S AROMATIC PECTORAL LOZENGES for Coughs'. Cures increasingly carried an impressive testimony of expert support: William Lewis who listed five London outlets for his Rheumatism Pills, and suppliers in twenty seven provincial towns (some of which, like Bath, needed four sellers to cope with the local demand), called on the support of 'the great Boerhaeve', the 'truly illustrious Cullen' and the writings of Bergius to 'sanction the propriety, safety and efficacy of the medicine now offered'. Mr. de Chamant's IMPROVED MINERAL TEETH carried an even more impressive list to prove 'the superiority of his teeth ... over those taken from dead bodies, or those fabricated of any other animal substances which are always corruptible and occasion a very offensive smell'. The mineral teeth carried 'the opprobation of all the learned societies of Europe and that of the most eminent Medical Gentlemen of Europe'. For those who needed more detail there was a list including Dr. Jenner, Dr. Reynolds, Dr. Baillie, Dr. Hooper, Sir Henry Halford, Bart., Sir G. Blane, Bart., Sir W. Farquhar, Bart., Sir James Earle, Ashley Cooper Esq., H. Clyne Esq., R. Keate Esq., J. Heaviside Esq., W. Blair, Esq.

Similar lists appeared in support of soothing syrups for gums, cures for teething babies, cures for ticklish coughs and troublesome colds. Improved dentifrices, better soaps, more effective hair shampoos or quicker-acting depilatories all received the support and recommendation of either the authoritative or the fashionable, the former dominating the advertisements for medicines, the latter presiding over the sales of cosmetics. The claim that 'Colley's depilatory' would 'remove superfluous hair from faces, necks and arms in 2 minutes', or that Mrs. Vincent's Gowland's Lotion for the Skin 'adds lustre to even the perfect beauty' and for the less fortunate 'cleanses the skin of all deformities' was often not enough to sell them without the additional facts that they were used by royal or aristocratic or at least fashionable women recognized and admired by their potential female markets.

There were specialist advertisements for 'Camphorated Matches for producing instantaneous Light': for 'Chapman's Patent Pocket Lanterns', for 'Hill's Permanent Ink for Marking Linen' and his rival Scott's for the same purpose, for 'Table Covers', 'Furniture Cloths', for 'Portable Shower Baths' (complete with curtains), for 'more Economical Air Stoves' ('may be seen constantly in use in Ludgate Hill'), for 'Henry Marriott's Improved Patent Kitchen Range', for 'Portable kitchens of various sizes convenient for Fishing, Sailing and Shooting Parties, and also for Camps, or to be used in the open Air', or even, at the extreme range of the market for portable objects, 'Small Portable Fire Engines'. Other specialists advertised their 'Treble distilled Lavender Water', or their 'Chronometers', their Snuff boxes, tooth picks and pencil cases, their opera glasses, their thimbles, combs, their 'egg spoons which do not lose their colour in the Eggs as Silver does', and all sorts of jewellery. Watches, any faults in which will 'be rectified free of expense during the course of a whole year' were sold by many advertisers. 'To All Who Value Their Sight' Bradbury's patent spectacles were strongly recommended

> 'The Sight of the Aged is restored
> The Weak Sight Strengthened
> And the Perfect Sight preserved
> Upon unerring principles'.

'Scott's Original Liquid Dyes' had not only been sold for thirty years, not only carried an impressive range of specialist colours which would 'dye any article of dress, as Silks, Muslins, Laces, Cottons, Linens, Feathers, Flowers &c.' but their advertisements kept the public informed of the rapidly changing fashions, and even specified which colour was in for what garment—'The Pink and Lilac are the present Fashionable colours for Silk Stockings'. Special Sales, Reductions in price, New Years Gifts, Special Autumn and Winter offers were all well advertised. New patents for anything from a new shape in a parasol or a new style in Ladies' Grecian stays received impressive promotional coverage. The examples are legion.

This sample is deliberately kaleidoscopic, and all these advertisements are deliberately chosen from a single source—*Bell's Monthly Compendium of Advertisements* in the first decade of the nineteenth century—to give a representative sample of the range of goods being assiduously and repetitively advertised by the turn of the century. But such advertisements were the satellites to the real stars of the fashion magazines—the silks, linens, cottons and all their fashionable concoctions provided by such as Mrs. Bell. The latest fashions from Paris, the latest colours, the latest designs were paraded each month before an expectant audience. Mrs. Bell was attentive to the needs of all ages. She was assiduous in solving the problems of the pregnant or the merely obese, she produced new inventions for the dress of nursing mothers; she invented her 'impervious Chapeau' as a substitute for the Parasol in March of one year and had 'the unequivocal approbation of all

Ladies of taste by September', and she promoted an endless stream of new ideas.[114]

Mrs. Bell was an advertiser of Packwood's quality in her perseverance, ingenuity and imagination. By tracing the full range of her advertisements one could build up a portfolio of promotional literature to match his. She too gave her inventions blanket coverage in order to ensure success.

But if George Packwood and Mrs. Bell were the stars of the advertising world there were many others recognized by their contemporaries as equally highly skilled and equally effective. The *English Review* of 1825 carried a retrospective piece entitled 'The Art of Advertising Made Easy' which singled out for praise *Lawton's Patent Lock* advertisement which offered 'one hundred guineas to any Artist who can pick it'; *Prince's Original Russia Oil*, a well advertised hair dye; and Rowland's Toilet preparations which were commended for the sheer persistence with which they were promoted. Other famous advertisements included Robert Warren's advertisement for boot blacking which not only carried a long poem in the Packwood style but carried a Cruickshank woodcut of a cat astonished by its own reflection in a boot polished with Warren's product—this single advertisement was credited with making Warren's fortune.[115]

* * *

This chapter has concerned itself with *one* aspect of the process of commercialization—the art of advertising. It has concerned itself particularly with *one* man's manipulation of consumer demand through *one* aspect of that art—namely newspaper advertisements. With a varied sample of contemporary advertisers drawn largely from *one* further source it has attempted to illustrate the extent of the commercializing process through the quality, the ubiquity, the variety and the pervasive nature of the advertisements with which so many entrepreneurs launched and sustained their assault on the new consumer market of Georgian England. To demonstrate how far the process had developed by the turn of the century, special attention has been focused on the years of the Napoleonic Wars.

By casting a wider net over the sales campaigns of *more* businessmen, by including the promotional techniques involved in *other* aspects of selling—auctions and shops and showrooms, markets and fairs, pedlars and travelling salesmen, loss leaders and inertia-selling campaigns (to mention only a sample); by choosing one's advertisements from *all* available newspapers; and by including the *whole* century within one's canvas, one could

---

[114] A typical example of her ability to create a constant stream of newly marketable ideas, and to create a specialist demand where none had been seen to exist before was 'the Ladies Bathing Preserver' invented by Mrs. Bell 'to relieve ladies of the nauseous idea of wearing the Bathing coverings furnished by women at the seaside from which dangerous and permanent illnesses have arisen, in consequence of their being worn by *all kinds* of persons however afflicted'.

[115] B. B. Elliott, op. cit., p. 158.

dramatically widen the evidential catchment area in support of the process of commercialization. But there are advantages to be found in the discipline of these self-imposed limits which would be lost by an historian trawling for evidence over a less restricted area and timespan.

By focusing on a single businessman one can demonstrate more conclusively just how advanced and varied, and how important to his business strategy, advertising in the late eighteenth century could be. By concentrating on an individual advertising campaign one can demonstrate in more convincing detail its characteristic quality. By limiting oneself to little more than a decade one can give a more concentrated flavour of the prevailing advertising practices. By eschewing the full range of newspapers one can show how wide and varied a diet of advertising copy could be directed at a single readership. By concentrating on Packwood and his advertisements, one can draw attention to the impressive extent to which a small businessman could master at least one aspect of business skills, and by implication draw attention to the hordes of contemporary small businessmen whose contribution to the process of commercialization has been ignored, or more likely, completely overlooked. .

In overlooking the collective importance of these forgotten men of business, historians all too often seriously distort the historical record, and greatly over-simplify the process of economic change.

All too often when one argues the case for a qualitative change in business practice and commercial techniques of eighteenth-century entrepreneurs, the standard rejoinder, from those who remain unimpressed, is that 'not every businessman was a Wedgwood'. Now few would wish to challenge such a view less than I would, but I *would* wish to take issue with some of the conclusions drawn from it. For all too often in conceding quite properly the primacy of the entrepreneurial giants, the sceptics (sceptical, that is, about the general level of business skills that prevailed in the Industrial Revolution) imply that the gifted few existed in lonely isolation, practising their highly developed, but atypical, business skills so far above and beyond the comprehension, and the practice, of the hordes of lesser businessmen that they should be regarded as the glamorous exceptions who prove the mediocre rule.

Paradoxically the importance of the few can be diminished rather than enlarged by their present isolation. For rather than being seen as the undoubted leaders in a surge of entrepreneurial energy, as part of a widespread change in commercial attitudes and technique, they can be presented as unrepresentative men of genius whose commercial brilliance helps to explain their own individual success but casts little light on the habits of their lesser business contemporaries, or on the general process of economic change. For if they can be established as atypical and unrepresentative, their achievements can be presented as of little general significance.

Professor Payne, writing of the entrepreneurs of the Industrial Revolution, states that 'the names which have become famous ... were not typical',[116] and goes on to say 'that it is not inconceivable that more representative were [those] whose concerns suffered from serious entrepreneurial shortcomings coupled with gross mismanagement'.[117] Clearly this is not inconceivable. But the choice of representative businessmen does not have to lie between the brilliant and the grossly incompetent. There are places on the spectrum of business skills for many more types than that. Many who would fail the requirements for the former category were very far from fitting into the latter. Many like Packwood might find that one commercial skill developed to a sufficient level was more than adequate to bring about and explain his distinctive achievements. After all if one posits a sufficiently exacting definition of entrepreneurial excellence, most businessmen will fail to meet it. According to J. K. Galbraith, Henry Ford had 'exceptionally comprehensive shortcomings as an entrepreneur'.[118] Looked at from a suitable eminence of individual achievement the lesser fellows inevitably look in Robert Owen's dismissive phrase like 'the plodding men of business'[119] that the great many clearly were. These men were not the human prototypes for Schumpeter's heroic definition of the entrepreneur as a creative destroyer, they were not entrepreneurial polymaths, but by their mastery of a single skill they could often make a significant contribution to rapid economic progress. If sufficient numbers practised that skill at a sufficiently high level, their collective importance could be as great as, or even greater than, the heroic individuals.

In the present state of entrepreneurial studies conclusive answers are not possible. One does not need to labour the point that the archives which have survived are few, that those which have been systematically and critically researched are even fewer, and that since business success *both* favoured archival survival *and* attracted historical attention, the favoured few consists largely of the great and the glamorous and the archivally well preserved. It is not the prominence of the great which should cause concern. That is inevitable and largely deserved. Our concern should be for the sea of ignorance over which their prominence looms, and the effects which this has on our judgement concerning the overall importance of their individual achievements.

For those who wish to present the Wedgwoods as unquestionably exceptional, and yet also as representative of a larger scale movement made up of countless imitators and, in some branches of business skill, emulators like Packwood, there is an evidential problem in the lack of supporting case studies.

---

[116] P. L. Payne in *The Cambridge Economic History of Europe*, vol. VII, Part I, ed. P. Mathias and M. M. Postan (1978), p. 187.
[117] See ibid., and P. L. Payne, *British Entrepreneurship in the Nineteenth Century* (1974), p. 34.
[118] J. K. Galbraith, *The Liberal Hour* (1960), pp. 141–63.
[119] Robert Owen, *Life of Robert Owen: Written by Himself,* (1857), p. 31.

This study of George Packwood is a modest attempt to start filling the evidential gap, to show that Packwood in his own more limited sphere was as alive and as responsive as Wedgwood was to the possibilities of manipulating and satisfying demand, and to demonstrate that in his own chosen speciality—the art of advertising—he far surpassed the great potter.

Packwood and his retailers selling his goods under the sign of the Naked Truth were essential agents in the process of commercialization. Such men provided the network of commercial outlets which helped to make possible the emergence of a consumer society. Without their assiduous advertising, without their persistent promotion of their product image, without their remorseless repetition of their brand names, aggregate home demand would have lost a vital sustaining element in its growth and its social and geographical diffusion. They spread both news of their products and the product themselves. They made them both fashionable and accessible. They made them both more desirable and more easily purchasable. They were, in H. G. Wells' phrase, the true 'propagandists of consumption'.[120]

For Packwood was but one of an unsung chorus of such men. They may be unsung and uncelebrated by historians today, but they certainly made their collective voice heard in their own society as they incessantly proclaimed their commercial message. Their advertisements were so ubiquitous and so insistent in late Georgian England that contemporaries complained that one could no more avoid their presence than one could resist the blatant appeal of their commercial promises. It was the commercial imagination and promotional creativity of Packwood and his like which help to explain why Flora Tristan wrote, after visiting England four times between 1826 and 1839, 'The puff is so much a part of English life that one encounters it everywhere'.[121]†

---

[120] H. G. Wells, *The Work, Wealth and Happiness of Mankind* (1932—new revised edition 1934) p. 225. Revealingly Wells used the phrase to describe the hordes of anonymous shopkeepers who 'taught people how to want things'.

[121] Flora Tristan, *Promenades dans Londres* (1842), translated by Jean Hawkes as *The London Journal of Flora Tristan: The Aristocracy and the Working Class of England* (1982), p. 295. See the chapter entitled 'The English Puff', pp. 295–301.

† I am grateful to the British Academy for a grant which supported my research in the Kress Library at Harvard Business School. This chapter is one of the by-products of my major research there into the changing social attitudes toward business and businessmen in the last two hundred years. Another related by-product—'Visible Heroes: The Commercialization of History for the Businessmen of Eighteenth Century England'—will appear elsewhere.

PART II

Commercialization and Politics

by

John Brewer

CHAPTER FIVE

Commercialization and Politics*

Eighteenth-century politics have traditionally been interpreted as the exclusive preserve of a patrician elite. Only the maiming of deer and the savage slaughter of the fox, it is argued, were a match for politics as the sport of gentlemen. Institutionalized politics, like game, was a highly prestigious, restricted multiple use-right. In a nation conveniently divided into the two classes of 'patricians' and 'plebeians', the former monopolized both the hunt and the benches of Parliament, while the latter were—with varying degrees of efficiency—excluded from both. To a remarkable degree Namier's view of Hanoverian society accords with that of recent social historians: we now have a peculiar consensus, uniting those whose political ideologies are often diametrically opposed, on the state of Hanoverian politics and society.

But the danger of this emerging orthodoxy is that it tends to ignore the considerable body of evidence for a growing group—the middling sort or bourgeoisie—who were numerous—as many as a million of the nation's nearly seven million citizens—and who began, during the course of the century, to distinguish themselves socially and politically from the patrician élite and the labouring poor. We should not regard these men of moveable property, members of professions, tradesmen and shopkeepers who inhabit the pages of the trade directories published in growing numbers from the 1760s onwards, as one-dimensional men. They were not simply a service sector for the aristocracy, a 'client economy' catering to the whims of the rich and helping them in their appropriation of the wealth of the poor. Though there were many such people amongst their number, ranging from the blind musicians who played at aristocratic orgies to the land stewards, lawyers and estate agents who frugally managed their masters' estates, not every member of the middle ranks of society was tied to the coat-tails of the aristocracy. Neither were they simply stout captains of industry and enterprise, ruthlessly intent upon opening up mass markets, a bourgeois vanguard striving through the ideology of entrepreneurship to produce the industrial revolution.

Yet these two types—the client of the aristocracy and the entrepreneur

---

*Research for this chapter was undertaken as part of a Social Sciences Research Council Project Grant. I would like to thank Joanna Innes, Edmund Morgan, John Styles, Peter Gay, Lawrence Stone and Susan Hewitt for their advice and criticism.

in the free market—are important expressions of a tension or duality that can be found within the eighteenth-century middling sort of people. There does seem to have been a first, measured move—led by sprinters such as Wedgwood and Boulton—away from the cosseted and constrained world of the client economy and towards the exploitation of a broadly based and socially heterogeneous market. Even the many, many small enterprises of the period felt this change. The broadening of the market involved a change in social and economic values; a transformation of the relationship between producers, distributors and consumers. Of course the patricians were still a vital part of the clientele—producers like Wedgwood were well aware of the value of a spectacular sale to a princeling, potentate or peer: those, after all, were the men who created 'fashion'—but, increasingly, the aristocracy constituted the top end of a large market rather than the market *tout court*.[1] They could no longer exercise such complete control or command through their purchasing power and patronage.

The problem, however, is to explain how this shift came about, Moreover, if, as seems probable, it was accompanied by a change in values, can we see any connection between this development and any particular eighteenth-century political viewpoint? I want to suggest a number of reasons why the client economy and the sort of politics that went with it should have seemed increasingly unattractive in the eighteenth century, and why a more broadly based market and a more equitably grounded politics should have been seen as desirable and mutually reinforcing replacements for the old order. The objections to the client economy were simple enough: the dependence of the tradesman on aristocratic patronage placed him in a highly vulnerable, occasionally humiliating and certainly weak position *vis-à-vis* his customer. The political influence that the patrician commanded either in the locality near his country seat or at court if he were in the metropolis could be used with crippling effect against the recalcitrant or uncooperative tradesman. Though Namier has reminded us that this iron fist was often clothed in a velvet glove, the mere prospect of retribution was often sufficient to enjoin deference. Clients in the client economy were not 'free' but tied, no matter how discreetly, to their patrons. Moreover the client economy compounded one of the greatest problems that faced the eighteenth-century tradesman, namely that of credit and debt. The patricians simply passed on their own indebtedness to the trader by taking credit and failing to pay their bills promptly, or, sometimes, not at all. No grievance was felt more strongly than this hidden subsidy to aristocratic wealth.

The client economy was an integral part of aristocratic and courtly politics.

---

[1] Neil McKendrick, 'Josiah Wedgwood: an eighteenth-century entrepreneur in salesmanship and marketing techniques', *Economic History Review*, 2nd ser., 12 (1960), pp. 410, 412–14; E.L. Jones, 'The Fashion manipulators: consumer tastes and British industries, 1660–1800', *Business Enterprise and Economic Change. Essays in Honour of Harold F. Williamson*, ed. L. P. Cain & P. J. Uselding (Kent State Univ. Press, 1973), pp. 217–20.

It formed one of the main buttresses of a political structure superintended with consummate skill by a succession of Whig oligarchs who established an efficient patronage system, a firm executive and a governmental financial structure based on deficit spending. Here again there was much to provoke the resentment and hostility of the tradesman, small merchant and shopkeeper. The *douceurs* of government—contracts to supply the armed forces, government loans—were not distributed liberally but reserved for the privileged few—the moneyed interest in the City and a few merchant fat-cats. As the century progressed, so it appeared that the middling sort were paying an increasingly large part of the tax burden that supported what they saw as a system of graft and corruption. Taxes on commodities—tea, sugar, tobacco, spirits, corn, beer, salt, glass—in the form of customs and excise duties subsidized, so it was claimed, the Hanoverian court, aristocratic pleasure-seekers and the venal transactions of stockjobbers and financiers. Indeed, the hostility to public credit was not an objection to credit *per se*—most bourgeois were all too familiar with the practical necessities of borrowing and lending—but to its *abuse* for the aggrandisement of unscrupulous and idle individuals through speculation, peculation and graft. (Beckford's language in a parliamentary speech of 1761 evokes this attitude: he criticized the aristocracy who 'receive more from the public than they pay to it. If you were to cast up all their accounts and fairly state the balance, they would turn out to be debtors to the public.')[2] This issue grew as a matter of public and especially bourgeois concern throughout the century as more and more traders were affected by fluctuations in national business confidence. Though there was not to be another disaster of the magnitude of the South Sea Bubble of 1720, the fear of an unsavoury *reprise* was never far from the tradesman's mind, and he was only too ready to blame the metropolitan financiers for the tremors that periodically shook the nation.

Many of the objections that tradesmen and urban groups made to the Whig patronage system and the client economy were, of course, shared by country gentlemen and Tories. But the bourgeois use of country ideology was highly selective, and its preoccupations were somewhat different from those of its allies. The urban element, dominated by the city of London, was much more likely to connect the problem of dismantling the spoils system with those regulating credit and of achieving independence from the client economy. The bourgeoisie's notion of independence reveals their difference from the country gentlemen. Traders and merchants saw independence not as freedom conferred by landed property but, as comments in the press show, as freedom from the economic political control of the patricians.

Yet before any alternative to clientage could be considered, and before the free market could even appear as a remotely attractive alternative, certain

---

[2] Quoted in Lucy Sutherland, 'The City of London in eighteenth-century politics', *Essays Presented to Sir Lewis Namier*, ed. Richard Pares and A. J. P. Taylor (London, 1956), p. 66.

conditions had to be fulfilled. Economic freedom was only possible if there were alternative resources: a change or shift in the structure of wealth was a necessary condition of such a social transformation or, at the very least, it involved the recognition that existing sources of wealth could be newly exploited. Bourgeois consumerism, the democratization of taste, the emergence of a more broadly-based market for goods and services were the preconditions. Without growing home demand the desire to escape the clientage system would remain a pipe-dream. But, of course, it did not. Eversley, John, Jones and McKendrick have provided a considerable body of evidence to show that a broadly-based home market burgeoned in the eighteenth century, even if the extent to which it touched the poorest members of society is still a matter of contention.[3] Though several explanations have been advanced to explain this development, we are still some way from understanding how and why it occurred. There were many major obstacles to overcome. Crucially, there was the question of credit in an era when the bulk of the assets of most enterprises was in circulating capital. How could you educate a populace which included aristocrats who found it insulting to have to pay bills promptly and a labouring poor trapped in an erratic seasonal pattern of borrowing and spending, to the difficult task of accepting a strictly regulated credit system? Much of the first section of this essay is devoted to this problem and to the expedients designed to overcome it. In particular I stress the importance of two developments: the growing amount of accurate information disseminated throughout England by the press, which made more precise calculations of business risk possible; and secondly, the emergence of voluntary associations—particularly masonic and pseudo-masonic orders—which cushioned the bourgeoisie against the difficulties associated with indebtedness and acted as vocal protagonists of values which would have regularized credit.

Clubs and lodges were also important in organizing subscriptions and raising capital for business ventures and civic improvements which furthered commercial interests. Collective action through voluntary associations conferred on these organizations a degree of power as well as financial and political independence which their members had not previously enjoyed. Association became a way of escaping economic clientage whilst providing protection against the vicissitudes of the open market; it also served to free citizens from the constraints of patrician political patronage and control. The opening up of politics and of enterprise went in tandem; in the eyes of

---

[3] D. E. C. Eversley, 'The home market and economic growth in England, 1750–80', *Land, Labour & Population in the Industial Revolution: Essays presented to J. D. Chambers,* ed. E. L. Jones & G. E. Mingay (London, 1967), pp. 206–59; E. L. Jones (ed.), *Agriculture and Economic Growth in England, 1650–1815* (London, 1967), intro., ch.7; E. L. Jones, *Agriculture and the Industrial Revolution* (Oxford, 1974), *passim;* Neil McKendrick, 'Home demand and economic growth: a new view of the role of women and children in the industrial revolution', *Historical Perspectives. Studies in English Thought and Society in Honour of J. H. Plumb,* ed. N. McKendrick (London, 1974), pp. 152–210.

predominantly urban and bourgeois groups, the two were seen as interconnected problems whose solution was mutually reinforcing.

This link is made quite explicit in the second part of the essay which focuses on a number of political and social aspirations associated with the career of the radical politician, John Wilkes.[4] The political issues raised by Wilkes—freedom of the press, the rights of electors, and the liberties of the subject—might seem to be only obliquely connected with the economic and social aims of the commercial classes. In many ways Wilkes was all things to all men, and he certainly enjoyed a heterogeneous following which included country squires and urban artisans as well as tradesmen, merchants and shopkeepers. But the impetus of the movement was very largely sustained by the middling sort, employing means that paralleled and, in some cases, overlapped the methods of voluntary associations. The clubs and lodges, originally established for convivial, commercial and civic purposes leapt to Wilkes's defence: they subscribed money for his cause, organized demonstrations in his favour, and raised a wide range of issues which, when aggregated, would have added up to the end of aristocratic clientage and its replacement by a social order whose values would have conferred considerable power and prestige on the men of moveable property.

I have chosen the Wilkite affair to illustrate the connections between commercialization and politics for several reasons. First, the events surrounding Wilkes's career were more than a single incident (such as the opposition to the Excise Bill of 1733) and were concerned with a wider range of issues than the (admittedly important) industrial lobbies like the General Chamber of Manufactures. In consequence, the movement was of sufficient duration and complexity to allow the radicals to articulate their views fully, and to elaborate their schemes for reform. Secondly, the *very same* clubs which pursued bourgeois social and economic aspirations turned to Wilkite politics: the link between radical politics and commercialization, forged by voluntary associations, could hardly have been stronger. Moreover, these clubs formed the nucleus of an expanding market for politics and political artifacts, a market of the sort which the associations themselves approved. The creation of a radical 'political culture' complete with its own forms of dress, types of food, and modes of celebration was not merely the creation of alternative means of political expression, but the expansion and diversification of a market for politics as a cultural commodity or product. This, in turn, was exploited by a number of occupational groups from amongst the men of moveable property—I have taken publicans, potters and printers as my three case studies—which helped generate and expand this market, by using marketing and advertising skills of remarkable ingenuity.

The question of the motives of these groups is a tricky one. It is most

---

[4] On Wilkes generally see George Rudé, *Wilkes and Liberty* (Oxford, 1962); Ian R. Christie, *Wilkes, Wyvill and Reform. The Parliamentary Reform Movement in British Politics, 1760-1785* (London, 1962).

clear-cut in the case of the printers where there is an undoubted connection between their radical politics, desire to reduce business risks, and their commitment to a broadly-based market. The experience of the publicans and potters is, however, somewhat more complicated. Though all three groups sought, in their different ways, to shape the market itself, there were powerful consumer pressures which the producers found very difficult to tame. Slowly but surely the constraints of the client economy were being replaced by the rather different controls of the open market. The producer and distributor found that they had a new and more impersonal master with whom to struggle for success.

CREDIT, CLUBS AND INDEPENDENCE

'Distressed tradesmen in general form a connection in keeping open their shops, by drawing bills upon one another, in being bail for each other, and having an attorney to defend all actions brought against them'.
(Edward Farley, *Imprisonment for Debt Unconstitutional and Oppressive* (London, 1788), p. 38.)

'Box and tradesmen's clubs which, according to their several conveniences, meet at taverns, inns, coffee and ale houses, wherein they have their respective orders for their better government, whereby during the times of their several meetings, virtue is not only promoted, and vice punished, but likewise a good correspondence cultivated, for the mutual improvement of their respective business, by dealing with one another' ... 'Though these societies consist of the meanest and rudest of the citizens, yet by their admirable regulations and constitutions (of their own making) they are kept in the best order and decorum.'
(William Maitland, *The History and Survey of London from its foundation ... to the present Time* (London, 1739), pp. 682-3.)

In the eighteenth century Britain's public indebtedness was put on a sound footing. The emergence of 'public credit', government deficit finance, a national market for securities, together with the birth of the Stock Exchange not only gave Britain a firm financial base, but facilitated political stability and enabled her to acquire the largest empire since the fall of Rome. In recent years, these crucial developments in the national economy have attracted historians as strongly as they fascinated—and sometimes repelled —Augustan Englishmen.[5] Private indebtedness, however, has received much less attention from historians despite the fact that it was a persistent and indeed ubiquitous source of anxiety in Hanoverian England. For the greatest weakness of private credit and debt was that the rules and conventions that governed their use were insufficiently clearly defined, and that the mechanisms that did exist for their regulation frequently exacerbated financial uncertainties rather than relieved them.

In part this was attributable to the burgeoning growth of new forms of borrowing and lending. Extending credit and obtaining loans had, of course, been an enduring characteristic of village life. Widows, 'kulak' peasants and local landlords had all lent to fellow parishioners, tenants, relatives, friends and neighbours. Indeed this 'face to face' credit persisted throughout the eighteenth century and, arguably, was the dominant credit relationship in the society at large.[6]

But we cannot afford to overlook a number of important developments that occurred even prior to the growth of provincial banking in the second half of the eighteenth century. The increased use of the mortgage—and the

---
[5] The classic study is P. G. M. Dickson, *The Financial Revolution in England* (London, 1967), *passim.*
[6] This I take to be the view of B. A. Holderness. See especially, 'Credit in a rural community, 1660-1800', *Midland History* III, 2 (1975), pp. 100-2, 111-12. Even in business enterprises kith and kin were usually the first source of a loan.

concomitant growth in property insurance—the rapid growth in the number of inland bills of exchange, and the widespread entanglement of almost all tradesmen in the snares of trade indebtedness not only facilitated business but created a new set of economic and social problems that had to be tackled if the merchant economy was to be put on a firm footing. As more and more men—even small producers—acquired credit, so the gravity of the problem increased. The ease with which credit in its different forms could be obtained exacerbated the situation.

Mortgages, for instance, were made more widely available. The growing mortgage market was not merely the way in which sybaritic aristocrats avoided the financially prohibitive consequences of dissipation but, rather more aptly, the means by which small masters such as builders, printers and cutlers obtained loans to expand and develop their businesses. Too often the mortgage has been portrayed as a safety-net for crashing landed fortunes. On occasion it certainly performed this function just as it served to raise capital for agricultural improvement. But more generally the mortgage was a highly flexible and widely used means of borrowing, often though not invariably superintended by the provincial attorney who would 'match up' those with idle savings and those needing ready capital. Borrowing was not difficult, as leasehold or personalty could act as collateral—a master might mortgage his tools, a printer his fonts of type—and loans may have been that much more attractive because legal process through the Court of Chancery against the mortgager could be tiresome, time-consuming and expensive for the mortgagee.[7]

The precise extent and importance of mortgaging through 'blind investment' via an attorney is a matter of some controversy.[8] But, as a result of the masterly researches of B. L. Anderson,[9] there can be very little doubt that, quite apart from the financial activities of the metropolis, there was an institutionalized regional credit market in such expanding areas as South Lancashire. There local attorneys ran a credit system in which, partly by dint of professional cooperation, they brought together creditors and debtors from throughout the area who were not previously acquainted. The specialized legal knowledge necessary to arrange a mortgage helped the attorney assume a financial role not unlike that of the later banker. Men such as Thomas Ball, attorney of Ormskirk, relied on a local reputation as a 'very

---

[7] Peter Mathias, 'Credit, capital and enterprise in the industrial revolution,' *Journal of European Economic History* 2 (1973), p. 138; B. L. Anderson, 'Provincial aspects of the financial revolution of the eighteenth century', *Business History* XI, 2 (1969), pp. 12-20; 'The Attorney and the Capital Market in Lancashire', *Capital Formation and the Industrial Revolution*, ed. F. Crouzet (London, 1972), pp. 227-8, 248. My debt to Anderson in the following discussion should be obvious.

[8] See Holderness's qualifications of Anderson in 'Elizabeth Parkin and her Investments, 1733-66, Aspects of the Sheffield money market in the eighteenth century', *Transactions of the Hunter Archaeological Society*, X, 2 (1973), p. 86.

[9] See fn. 7 above and 'Money and the structure of credit in the eighteenth century', *Business History*, XII, 2 (1970), pp. 87-100.

careful, substantial honest man' to obtain clients as both investors and borrowers. Regional webs of credit began to grow.[10]

These regional networks were interconnected through the widespread use of the negotiable instrument of inland bills of exchange. They were the customary means by which tradesmen, middlemen, manufacturers and shopkeepers paid for commodities, goods and raw materials, especially when they came from outside the region. They were certainly far more common, and generally treated as being far more reliable than the promissory notes which were also in use. A bill of exchange drawn on a third party was an order to pay off a debt at a certain future date. A provincial purchaser of London goods would draw the bill on a Londoner with whom he had credit; conversely, a metropolitan businessman buying from the provinces would draw his bill on a Liverpool, Leeds and Birmingham merchant with whom he did business. Because they were frequently not due for presentation for as long as forty or sixty days, bills could be remitted (after endorsement) and used as a medium of exchange. Most merchants seem to have stockpiled bills for this purpose. All endorsers were legally liable for the bill, and its reliability (and thus value) was affected by the number and quality of those who endorsed it. Not surprisingly a trade in the bills themselves developed and a discount market emerged centred on London. Like mortgages, bills were a highly flexible means of giving and obtaining credit: the laws governing their use were based on a series of *ad hoc* judicial decisions that sustained merchant custom, the number of bills in circulation varied according to the state of the economy, postponement of their payment was common, and they were sometimes drawn on those who were unaware of the transaction. Bills might even circulate before they were accepted by the drawee. Yet, despite this seemingly haphazard state of affairs, the bills usually served their purpose successfully.[11]

Bills of exchange, promissory notes, the mortgage, all of these credit mechanisms were not nearly as important as the trade debt or simple financial accommodation. Masters lent money to their apprentices so that they could establish themselves in an independent business; suppliers of raw materials gave credit to merchants and manufacturers who extended it to tradesmen who, in turn, gave credit to their customers; substantial merchants propped up their lesser brethren by providing them with loans. Producers, distributors and consumers were linked not only by the products of the market, but also by a highly elaborate (and extremely delicate) web of credit.[12]

[10] Anderson, 'Attorney and the capital market', *Capital Formation,* esp. pp. 233, 248–9.
[11] On domestic or inland bills see Anderson, 'Money and structure of credit', *Business History* (1970), pp. 90–4; T. S. Ashton, *An Economic History of England: the Eighteenth Century* (London, 1955); pp. 185–7; T. S. Ashton, *An Eighteenth-Century Industrialist* (Manchester, 1939), pp. 102–12.
[12] Anderson, 'Money and the structure of credit', *Business History* (1976), p. 95; A. H. John, 'Agricultural Productivity and Economic Growth in England, 1700–1760', *Agriculture and Economic Growth in England, 1650–1815,* ed. E. L. Jones (London, 1967), pp. 185–6.

Such a situation was almost inevitable in a society which suffered such an acute shortage of specie. On the one hand, the demand for cash was on the increase. Perks such as 'chips', 'sweepings' and 'gleaning' together with payments in kind slowly but inexorably gave way to cash assessments and wages.[13] Economic specialization, especially in the south of England, meant that subsistence production of such basic requirements as bread and simple clothing was being replaced by the purchase of these items. Money was needed to buy from the baker and shopkeeper what had formerly been cooked and crafted in the home. Overall, the number of cash transactions seems to have been on the increase.[14] Unfortunately, however, the supply of specie—especially in small denominations—was far from adequate. The decision to base the recoinage of 1696 on silver and not to reassess its value against gold meant that internationally British silver coin was grossly undervalued. As a result there was an extraordinary and rapid outflow of specie, particularly to the Orient but also to other European Countries. Good coin found its way into the melting pot and out of the country, leaving a residue of battered, clipped and worn currency. It was estimated that by 1762 total silver circulation was only £800,000. The exiguous remnant of silver coin was in such a sorry state that it was frequently valued by weight rather than denomination. Shop and innkeepers acquired scales to test the value of their customers' coins (both silver and gold), thereby defeating the very purpose for which a standardized currency was established. This situation was compounded by the Mint's failure to issue adequate amounts of coin. At no point prior to 1759 did the Mint issue more than £900,000 worth of gold coin per annum and the amount of silver minted was derisory. Moreover the mint paid its moneyers for the value and not the amount of coin that they produced. It was therefore far more profitable to manufacture coins of gold rather than silver and of high rather than low denomination.[15]

Copper coin was also in a terrible state, consisting of counterfeits, blanks and private issues of coin. A Mint inquiry in 1787 found that 43 per cent of all copper in circulation was 'blatantly inferior' to the King's coin, and that a further 37 per cent could only be described as 'trash'.[16] In sum, British coinage in the eighteenth century was a mess: overall, there was a specie shortage that led to such consequences as the extensive use of foreign coins—Portuguese moidores, for instance, were far more common in the West Country than were guineas—while the currency that did actually

---

[13] E. P. Thompson, 'Patrician Society, Plebeian Culture', *Journal of Social History* VII, (1974), p. 384; Peter Linebaugh, 'Eighteenth century crime, popular movements and social control', *Bulletin of Society for the Study of Labour History*, 25 (1972), p. 13.

[14] D. E. C. Eversley, 'The Home market and economic growth in England, 1750-80', *Land, Labour and Population in the Industrial Revolution: Essays presented to J. D. Chambers*, ed. E. L. Jones & G. E. Mingay (London, 1967), pp. 214-5.

[15] Ashton, *An Economic History of England*, pp. 167-73; Sir John Craig, *The Mint* (Cambridge, 1953), pp. 194, 214, Appendix I.

[16] Craig, *The Mint*, p. 253.

circulate was underweight and in appalling condition even when it was counterfeit—which was as often as not.[17]

The shortage of coin, especially small coin, had grave social consequences. Cash for wages, especially during harvest time when the demand for small coin for paying labourers was at its height, was hard to obtain. As a result employers paid their employees infrequently (and often irregularly) with coins of a high denomination. A number of men involved in piece-work might all be paid with a single, high-value coin or given a bill which needed to be discounted. One way of facilitating matters for the benefit of the employer was to deposit payments with a local innkeeper or tradesmen who then extended credit to the workforce. Labourers, however, would often have already contracted debts to such retailers precisely because of the infrequency of their wage payment. This, it would appear, was the origin of the egregious practice of 'truck'; it was also the way in which even the humblest of men found themselves enmeshed in the web of credit.[18]

Credit and debt, therefore, were almost universal. Local credit networks interlocked with those of a particular region, and regional credit, largely as a result of the financial activities of the middleman, merchant and shopkeeper overlapped with that of other regions. If for much of the eighteenth century Britain was a collection of regional economies, then one of the most important ways in which those economies were linked was through the circuit of credit—a route that was interregional even if its journey was often via the capital market and mercantile metropolis of London.

One example should make this point clear. Abraham Dent was a shopkeeper in Kirkby Stephen, a town perched on the edge of England in the county of Westmorland, halfway between Kendal and Barnard Castle. Not by the most extreme stretch of the imagination could Kirkby Stephen be described either as a throbbing urban centre or as a nodal point in the national economy, but Dent's activities linked the town to national circuits of credit. The wide variety of goods that passed over Dent's counter came from many parts of the country. Apart from Kendal, the most immediate source of most of his supplies, commodities came from Newcastle, Gateshead, Lancaster, Manchester, Leeds, Wakefield, Halifax, Norwich, Coventry and London. Most of these were paid for by bills of exchange, many drawn on Dent's London creditors. Local customers seem to have had little difficulty in obtaining credit from the shopkeeper, especially if they were reasonably respectable members of the community. About 50 per cent of Dent's sales

---

[17] Ashton, *An Economic History of England*, pp. 174–6; Craig, *Mint*, pp. 251–4; John Styles, 'Our traitorous money makers', *An Ungovernable People. The English and their law in the seventeenth and eighteenth centuries*, ed. John Brewer and John Styles (London, 1980), pp. 172–249.

[18] Anderson, 'Money and the structure of credit', *Business History* (1970), p. 98; Peter Linebaugh, *Tyburn. A Study of crime and the Labouring Poor in London during the first half of the eighteenth century* (Warwick Univ., unpub. Ph.D., 1975), pp. 132–3; Ashton, *An Economic History of England*, pp. 173–4.

were credit transactions, to a clientele that included parsons, schoolmasters, attorneys, doctors, an apothecary, innkeeper, tinker, tailor, mason and slater, carpenter and glazier, bleacher and dyer, and a carrier. Some customers' debts were still outstanding five years after the original purchase had been made. In addition, Dent supplied loans: his books reveal some forty-two in all, varying in amount from as little as one shilling to as much as seven guineas. Transactions were conducted in a bewildering variety of ways: apart from cash and bills of exchange, Dent used barter and bank notes on the Bank of England and northern country banks. Inextricably enmeshed in this network of credit, acting, as it were, as the spider at the centre of a complex web, he took full advantage of his situation, and eventually became a major discounter of bills.[19]

Clearly, the widespread and very largely informal credit system that existed throughout eighteenth-century England brought with it many advantages. It seems to have been relatively easy to borrow, and, because of the number of outlets and means of investment, savings, on the whole, do not seem to have lain idle. Provided an individual could demonstrate his probity, sobriety and reliability within a given community and as long as he had some assets to begin with, were they ever so small, he was generally deemed a sound risk. Equally the creditor had a considerable range of options open to him in investing savings. Indeed, a rich widow, such as Elizabeth Parkin of Sheffield, could play a considerable part in stimulating the local economy through her loans, mortgages and investments. For the purposes of most business enterprises—and most of them, it has to be remembered, were quite small—local or regional capital or credit of the sort provided by Elizabeth Parkin was more than sufficient. It was very unusual for any borrower to go further afield.[20] As the century progressed so, despite temporary fluctuations in the rate of interest, money became more readily available. Apart from those occasions when war drove up the cost of borrowing, the secular trend of interest rates was downwards: in 1700 one paid 6 per cent, in 1750 a mere 3½ per cent.[21]

The working debts of tradesmen, as opposed to the availability of capital through mortgage and the like for business expansion, was not so much advantageous as absolutely necessary. As Guy Green complained to Wedgwood: 'The very long credit taken by most of my customers, tho' contrary to agreement makes it difficult to fix a price where a profit will arise worth one's while—and without credit I am in doubt if any considerable business

---

[19] T. S. Willan, *An Eighteenth-century Shopkeeper. Abraham Dent of Kirkby Stephen* (Manchester, 1970), pp. 19–27, 29, 32–9, 42–9, 112–27.
[20] Holderness, 'Elizabeth Parkin and her Investments', *Trans. Hunter Arch. Soc.* (1973), p. 81 *seq.*
[21] Mathias, 'Capital, credit and enterprise', *J. Eur. Ec.H.* (1973), p. 124; L. S. Pressnell, 'The rate of interest in the eighteenth century', *Studies in the Industrial Revolution. Essays presented to T. S. Ashton*, ed. L. S. Pressnell (London, 1960), p. 179. But see Crouzet, *Capital Formation*, p. 32.

can be carried on'.[22] In the face of such a terrible cash shortage, commerce could probably not even have continued, much less prospered without working credit. Indeed, it has been suggested that the flexibility and ingenuity of credit arrangements in England is largely explicable in terms of the extraordinary difficulties created by the lack of specie.[23]

Yet, despite the obviously beneficial role played in the British economy by a very adaptive credit system, the means of borrowing and lending also served both to create and to exacerbate financial crises. A substantial proportion of the assets of nearly all eighteenth-century business enterprises, especially those of merchants, middlemen and retailers, was in the form of short-term credit which had been extended to customers and clients. Thus when Revel Humfray the printer went bankrupt, the bulk of his assets—84 per cent in fact—were out with other people.[24] Short term credit was often four or five times greater than fixed asset indebtedness or costs. As Peter Mathias has pointed out, 'the analyses of capital structure of firms ... show how small a proportion of their total assets, even for the most capital intensive business such as a large iron-works, a London porter brewery, lay in fixed assets'.[25] The firm of Truman, Hanbury and Buxton in Spitalfields with total assets of £130,000, had only £30,000 in fixed capital, but £74,000 in good trade debts and £24,000 in stocks of materials and beer in casks.[26] In both the humble printer's backroom shop and the large brewery short-term credit and debt were endemic.

Such a situation, the direct consequence of a shortage of cash, was perfectly tolerable as long as business and the market were buoyant, but any hint of individual financial insecurity and, *a fortiori*, the merest indication of a slump could bring the whole edifice crashing down. In good times credit was easy, there was a marked proclivity for holding goods and securities, and the number of bills drawn would multiply, thereby facilitating an increased volume of transactions. So-called bills of accommodation could be drawn to increase the funds available to an individual, commodities and securities would change hands as part of an accelerating speculative boom, and overall indebtedness would increase sharply. However, when the bubble burst—and it was almost certain to do so as long as there was a ceiling on interest rates, which meant an eventual check on credit of a rather unsatisfactory kind[27]—a major liquidity crisis ensued. Speculators, bankers, merchants and tradesmen alike, they all tried to realize their assets: to convert from commodities to

---

[22] Guy Green to Josiah Wedgwood, 2 April 1775, Keele University, Wedgwood-Etruria Mss. 5-3394-3663. I have to acknowledge the kind permission of the Wedgwood family and of the University of Keele to cite these manuscripts.
[23] Anderson, 'Money and the structure of credit', *Business History*, (1970), p. 100.
[24] Bill Noblett, *The Bankruptcy of Revel Humfray* (unpublished paper), p. 14. I am grateful to the author for being allowed to use this material.
[25] Mathias, 'Capital, credit and enterprise', *J. Eur. Ec.H.* (1973), p. 126.
[26] Peter Mathias, *The First Industrial Nation. An Economic History of Britain 1700-1914* (London, 1969), p. 148.
[27] T. S. Ashton, *Economic Fluctuations in England, 1700-1800* (Oxford, 1959), pp. 108-11.

cash, from bills to specie, and from trade credit to hard currency. Credit became almost impossible to obtain precisely when it was needed most. Cash, silver and gold were at a premium because of the sudden and substantial demand for them. Simultaneously nearly everyone was demanding payment of their outstanding bills and being asked to pay off their own extant debts.[28] As Anderson puts it: 'when expectations changed resort to liquidity was difficult in the short run, the way back from commitment was crowded with individuals of the same mind, crisis quickly followed'.[29] Such a sudden high liquidity preference might well be the death-knell of a small master's or shopkeeper's business, and could lead to insolvency and the debtors' prison. These crises were not entirely intrinsic or monetarist; they might be provoked by international speculation (the root cause of the South Sea Bubble), domestic conflicts such as the rebellion of 1745, or by the outbreak and fortunes of a foreign war.[30] Yet, whatever their cause, they were exacerbated by the credit system as it was constituted in the eighteenth century.

In other words the price that eighteenth-century Englishmen paid for easy credit and ready access to money was a concomitant insecurity which stemmed from the volatility of both business and the money market. Steeped in Victorian novels, we tend to think of indebtedness, the dark side of credit, as a Micawberesque, nineteenth-century phenomenon, but to the eighteenth-century shopkeeper and middleman it was no fiction but a daily threat to their livelihood. There is hardly a single account of a Georgian tradesman or merchant, and not very many that flowed from aristocratic and genteel pens that does not make reference to the frightful prospect of indebtedness. The bum-bailiff, the spunging-house (Francis Place's first home), Newgate, Marshalsea, and the King's Bench were the frightful prospect for the many unfortunates ensnared in the judicial process surrounding lending and borrowing. Casanova fled from England not, as we would like to think, because of some delicious sexual scandal, but because of some extremely shady financial dealings. His old mistress and mother of one of his children, Mme Cornellys, who, by all accounts, gave the most lavish parties and masques in the whole of London, junketings that were attended by princes and prime ministers, never went out, except on Sunday, because she feared arrest for debt.[31] Families upped stumps, packed their furniture in the middle of the night, and fled to the rules of the city's prisons in order to obtain immunity from arrest; others hastened to relatives in the country to win time to put their affairs in order.[32]

---

[28] Pressnell, 'The rate of interest', *Studies in the Industrial Revolution*, pp. 183, 197; Ashton, *An Economic History of England*, pp. 27–8.
[29] Anderson, 'Money and the structure of credit', *Business History* (1970), p. 100.
[30] Ashton, *Economic Fluctuations*, chs. 3, 5.
[31] *Memoirs of Jacques Casanova De Seingalt*, trans. A. Machen (6 vols, New York, 1959–60), V, pp. 186, 233, 429–30.
[32] See, as a typical example, *The Life of Thomas Gent, printer, of York, written by himself* (London, 1832), pp. 137–9.

The spectre of debt was all the more horrific because of its complex and highly unsatisfactory legal position. One could be arrested for debts of 40s. or more merely on the oath of the creditor. If the debt could not be paid immediately, or if there was not money forthcoming for bail, then the offender was imprisoned for a period that might be as long as twelve months before his trial.[33] In these circumstances the scope for malicious prosecution was considerable. To be in a man's debt was to be in his power, for it was he, in effect, who determined when the credit that he had extended transmuted itself into a debt for which one had legal liability. A rival, a disagreeable client, begrudging partner or personal enemy could all be hamstrung or even driven out of trade altogether by an action for debt. For even if the debtor could meet the immediate debt which he was legally required to pay, the news of his prosecution would, as often as not, bring all his other creditors rushing forward, clamouring for the payment of their bills and loans. The least hint of unreliability could produce a debtor's collapse as his creditors unceremoniously competed with one another to ensure the security of their assets. Thus in 1716 William Nost angered his fellow printers by leaking information to the Secretary of State; they, in turn, revenged themselves by burying him beneath an avalanche of actions for debt.[34] Mr. Micawber's 'vengeful bootmaker' had many eighteenth-century allies.

If the law was harsh on the debtor, it was hardly a great help to the creditor. While the debtor was in prison his creditors could not recover their money. Even if the appropriate writ of *fieri facias* was taken out by the lender, he could not seize freehold property, bills of exchange or notes to obtain satisfaction.[35] The situation was a stand off, which satisfied neither party. The creditor found it difficult to obtain financial redress, while the debtor languished in prison unless, somewhat improbably, he was able to find the requisite resources.

Imprisonment itself was a hazardous and expensive experience. Fever was rampant and life was only tolerable if one could pay for the necessities of life. Many found themselves even more deeply in debt because of the expenses incurred in gaol. Garnish, gaolers' fees and room rent all ate away the meagre resources of the unfortunate and the impecunious.[36] Such was the lot of debtors who made up the majority of prisoners in eighteenth-century gaols. Howard estimated that in 1776 there were 2,437 Englishmen in prison for debt,[37] and most of these were not rich merchants (who could use the more satisfactory procedure of bankruptcy) but tradesmen, shopkeepers, small masters and retailers: the men who stood at the centre of the web of credit and who, in a liquidity crisis, found it most difficult to realise their

---

[33] P. J. Lineham, *The Campaign to Abolish Imprisonment for Debt in England, 1750-1840* (unpublished M. A., University of Canterbury, N. Z., 1974), pp. 3-14.
[34] L. W. Hanson, *Government and the Press, 1695-1762* (Oxford, 1936), p. 39.
[35] Lineham, *Campaign to Abolish Imprisonment for Debt*, pp. 7-8.
[36] 'C. Telltruth', *Middlesex Journal*, 30 December 1769.
[37] Lineham, *Campaign to Abolish Imprisonment for Debt*, p. 56.

assets by cajoling their customers into paying their bills. This group bitterly resented the way in which gentlemen used their social standing to delay the payment of their debts. Much of the tradesman's wrath against the client economy was a direct consequence of the 'hidden' loans that they were forced to extend to their social superiors, and which often jeopardized an otherwise sound business venture.

A number of points need to be stressed about the tradesman's dilemma. First and foremost, eighteenth-century economic fluctuations, unlike their nineteenth-century counterparts, were not part of a regular, predictable cycle. Crises occurred with greater frequency than later, were usually shorter in duration, and might well end abruptly.[38] They seemed just as arbitrary and cruel as a death, flood or plague and, indeed, in some cases they were the direct consequence of such natural disasters. But slumps could not always be shrugged off with the sort of providential explanation that so frequently accompanied bad harvests, inclement weather or the outbreak of disease, for some of the nation's economic crises were clearly of human agency. Shopkeepers and tradesmen hated stockjobbers and speculators not merely because they were the *bêtes noires* of contemporary country ideology, but because they seemed to be directly responsible for the vicissitudes of the trader during a squeeze or liquidity crisis. Though a slump might be triggered by a bad harvest, a foreign war or foreign investors, it was thought—and often with good reason—that the speculator exacerbated the situation. His profit might well prove the trader's downfall, and it was for precisely this reason that the men of Change Alley were denounced with a passion that occasionally swelled to hysteria.[39] The effects of the South Sea Bubble were not felt solely by aristocratic and genteel investors in the metropolis who had their financial fingers burnt, but by provincial tradesmen and middlemen who were driven out of business by the sudden and catastrophic run on hard cash.

The victims of crises such as the Bubble were not necessarily those tradesmen who were careless in their business dealings or prodigal in their ways. Frugal, prudent retailers, as well as those who squandered their resources, were the likely or possible victims of such slumps for they were forced, whether they liked it or not, to extend credit and incur debts simply in order to carry on the day-to-day dealings of business. It was this which made such crises seem both exceptionally cruel and arbitrary. Of course the idle apprentice deserved his come-uppance: this was as it ought to be. But for the thrifty, the industrious and the sober to suffer was a threat to the very moral basis on which the work-ethic was built.

In fact traders of known probity enjoyed only one real and actually very slender advantage over their weaker brethren, namely their ability to maintain their credit-worthiness during a crisis. 'Local reputation', credit-worthiness, reliability: these were the vital if intangible bulwark against

[38] Ashton, *Economic Fluctuations*, p. 136.
[39] J. G. A. Pocock, *The Machiavellian Moment* (Princeton, 1975), ch. XIII.

financial disaster.[40] But, as Anderson has remarked, 'trade credit, depending in the end upon one man's measure of another's worth, was inherently unstable'.[41] There was no real guarantee, no formal process, that regulated the mechanisms of credit. Even good standing provided very little protection in the free-for-all of a financial crisis. In consequence the debtor was remarkably vulnerable and enormously dependent upon his creditors. One might assume that this would have led to a very cautious attitude towards business, but the exact opposite seems to have been the case. Precisely because of the difficulty of making accurate bets on the long-term future, and because of the ready availability of money, men tended to be daring, speculative and ambitious rather than prudent, penny-pinching and wise. Overall, the entire credit system engendered a highly speculative and volatile economy, full of enterprise and initiative, open to an extraordinary degree to the vagaries of fashion and fad, encouraging quick returns and setting a premium on highly flexible and imaginative business strategies.

Contemporaries were well aware of the gravity of this problem. Take, for example, the following extraordinary description of trade by that great *aficionado* of commerce, Daniel Defoe:[42]

> Trade is a Mystery, which will never be compleatly discover'd or understood; it has its Critical Junctures and Seasons, when acted by no visible Causes, it suffers Convulsion Fitts, hysterical Disorders, and most unaccountable Emotions—Sometimes it is acted by the evil Spirit of general Vogue, and like a meer Possession 'tis hurry'd out of all common Measures; today it obeys the Course of things, and submits to Causes and Consequences; tomorrow it suffers Violence from the Storms and Vapours of Human Fancy, operated by exotic Projects, and then runs counter, the Motions are excentrick, unnatural and unaccountable—A sort of Lunacy in Trade attends all its Circumstances, and no Man can give a rational Account of it.

The problem as envisaged by those such as Defoe was that trade depended on credit, and that credit was a *fickle* system, random in its operation. What was needed was a system for fixing and rationalizing it. In part this might be achieved by developing stronger bonds of trust and confidence between debtor and creditor, but, for this to occur, regularity and punctuality based on some fairly strictly defined set of conventions were absolutely necessary. (Credit, personified by Defoe as a fastidious but fickle woman, lost all good humour if she were not attended to punctiliously and promptly.[43]) But it was scarcely sufficient to regulate the credit nexus *internally* when the relationship was so frequently affected by developments beyond the immediate influence of debtor and creditor. The state of credit was a reflection of financial confidence, and this buoyancy depended, in turn, upon opinion, an ineffable

---

[40] On this all commentators agree: Pressnell, 'The rate of interest', *Studies in the Industrial Revolution*, p. 200; Mathias, 'Capital, credit and enterprise', *J. Eur. Ec.H.* (1973), p. 128.
[41] Anderson, 'Money and the structure of credit', *Business History* (1970), p. 95.
[42] Quoted in Pocock, *Machiavellian Moment*, pp. 452–3.
[43] Pocock, *Machiavellian Moment*, pp. 452–3.

and intangible notion that seemed, to many eighteenth-century Englishmen, to have a will and life of its own. As long as opinion was based on whim, hearsay, fantasy and rumour, it would exacerbate the capriciousness of credit; but, if it were founded on experience, intelligence and sound information, there was some hope of obtaining financial stability.[44] *Accurate* knowledge, it was recognized, was essential not only to prevent the system's abuse and exploitation by sharpers, tricksters, and con-men—the parasitic breed who lived off gentlemen, tradesmen and the poor alike—but also to avoid the absurd and highly unstable speculative frenzies that were so easily triggered by rumour and financial intrigue.

How, then, did eighteenth-century Englishmen deal with the difficulties engendered by indebtedness and a volatile economy? Clearly the problem was too generalized to admit of any single or simple solution. Contemporaries fumbled in their efforts to find an answer, and usually they came up with a series of expedients and accommodations rather than with any coherent or overall strategy. A number of these tactics need not detain us here though they are worthy of mention. It seems probable, for instance, that a concern for the credit-worthiness of oneself and of others affected the personal characteristics and qualities that one valued highly. Reliability—'to all his promises there needs no other bond but his word'—candour and affability—'piety, good humour . . . a plain dealer'—and, above all, fairness and generosity—'he is . . . so very generous to those that live in his debt, that none but a villain would wrong him': these were the qualities most highly valued. One needed to be or, at least, needed to appear to be a man with such characteristics in order to carry on trade: to 'keep up your reputation', 'preserve your integrity', 'maintain your credit'.[45] Whereas the language of personal trust had originally provided the metaphors for borrowing and lending, now, in a curious transposition, the language of finance was employed metaphorically to depict moral and social worth. Thus such phrases as 'to give a person credit for something' acquired their standard usage in the mid-eighteenth century. Presentation of self as sober, reliable, candid and constant was not merely a question of genteel manners, but a matter of economic survival.

The connection that eighteenth-century Englishmen so frequently made between commerce and civilization should, therefore, not surprise us. Foreign visitors to Hanoverian London remarked on the extraordinary civility of the shopkeepers and tradesmen; (they also, it must be conceded, were struck by the rude, undeferential independence of the labouring poor).[46] Affability, courtesy and reliability were all qualities that went to make up a business

[44] Cf. Pocock's remarks on public credit. (*Machiavellian Moment*, pp. 439-40, 452-3, 456, 459.)

[45] All of the quotations in this paragraph are terms used by John Dunton to describe his colleagues in the printing trade (Timperley, *Anecdotes*, pp. 630-3).

[46] P. J. Grosley, *A Tour to London; or New Observations on England and its Inhabitants* (2 vols, London, 1772), I, pp. 35-6, 62, 84, 88-9.

character and a trade ethic. Such attitudes oiled the wheels of commerce and enabled men to make greater profits: they had, in other words, their positive side. But they also served as a check or constraint, a means of ordering and regulating the trading community in such a way as to protect its members by reducing the risks involved in credit and debt. In sum, the mannerly conduct necessary to improve business and secure credit was as much a form of social discipline as those values connected with work itself. Indeed the middleman and retailer had a strong vested interest in persuading all those with whom he had dealings—and this included the aristocratic and gentleman customer of the client economy as well as fellow tradesmen and plebeian employees—of the values that underpinned prompt payment and regular transactions. This is a subject as yet unexplored, but it might well prove that the values espoused to obtain a creditworthy society may have had just as significant a social impact as those intended to secure an industrious and compliant labour force.

This subtle strategem—and its success, of course, is extremely difficult to estimate—was intended to rationalize the establishment and execution of credit transactions, but it did not deal with the equally tricky problem of the relationship between 'opinion' at large and the overall workings of credit. What did affect that relationship was the growth of the provincial newspaper, the first means by which regularly transmitted, reasonably reliable intelligence was disseminated throughout much of provincial England. It has always been something of a puzzle to scholars to explain why so much of the provincial newspaper was taken up with extremely detailed descriptions of wars and battles in far-away places, and with the minutiae of international treaties and diplomacy.

One explanation for the preponderance of foreign news is that their coverage was less hazardous for the printer than the controversial issues of domestic politics. It was unlikely that the description of a siege or a treaty, culled from that impeccable source, the *London Gazette*, would alienate or anger a particular section of the paper's readership, nor would it, in all probability, provoke legal action on the part of those in authority. In sum, the reporting of domestic politics was hazardous and difficult; the subject of foreign affairs was both safe and accessible.[47]

There is some truth in this view, but it fails to take into account the importance of war, diplomacy and foreign affairs for the provincial newsreader. All of these mattered to the local shopkeeper, like Abraham Dent,[48] because they affected business confidence and credit. No doubt there were patriotic souls in the provinces who were interested in international politics

---

[47] G. A. Cranfield, *The Development of the Provincial Newspaper 1700–1760* (Oxford, 1962), pp. 65–70.
[48] Willan, *An Eighteenth-century Shopkeeper*, pp. 72–81. Dent's interest in such matters as foreign affairs and wars would also have been heightened by his stocking contracts with the army.

for its own sake, and the concern with foreign affairs of an overseas merchant, an investor in stocks or the East India Company is perfectly understandable. But we must not omit that growing number of men who were involved in local business and whose interest in international diplomacy, colonial war and politics generally was stimulated by the realization that they affected their business interests in a direct way. As long as the prospect, outbreak and course of a war affected interest rates, the availability of credit, and the degree of confidence in the economy, there was good reason for the local trader to keep himself politically informed. Commercialization—especially the growth of credit—encouraged political involvement and gave political events an economic portentousness they had previously lacked. The newspaper catered to a curiosity that had already grasped that politics, commerce and credit were all part and parcel of the same problem.

The tradesmen and printers who set up and ran local papers had the same preoccupations and anxieties as their readers. They were middlemen and retailers themselves, not merely purveying news but also selling stationery, pamphlets and patent medicines to their readers. Like every other eighteenth-century tradesman, they extended credit to their customers, many of whom lived far away from the printer's shop. Printers had more than their share of tradesmen's misfortunes, many of them going bankrupt or spending time in debtor's prison. They understood only too well the worries about business confidence, credit-worthiness and reliable information. Papers like the *Northampton Mercury* prided themselves on their accuracy, the 'precisest exactness' of their commercial news. All aspects of the provincial newspapers' coverage improved as the century progressed. The growing concern in the society at large for specific, precise, weighed—often actually quantified—data was mirrored in the pages of the press. Even before the emergence in the middle of the century of such trades papers as *Williamson's Liverpool Advertiser* which was jam-packed with business information, the provincial press began to include shipping news, Lloyd's lists, import and export data, regional prices, and news of stocks and bankruptcies.[49]

Naturally not every newsreader was a trader or merchant, nor were all papers directed chiefly at a mercantile audience. Most provincial papers deliberately catered to gentlemen, merchants and traders alike. Though the first number of the *Liverpool Chronicle* not surprisingly gave pride of place to the reporting of commerce and navigation—'our interest as a commercial State, being so nearly and so importantly concern'd'—the proprietors did not neglect to ask 'gentlemen of learning and leisure' to contribute 'essays as have a tendency to extend and promote the improvement of Agriculture, Arts, Manufactures and Commerce, or the practice of the religious and moral Virtues'. In this way the editors hoped to provide news, serve as an

---

[49] For these aspects of the provincial paper see Cranfield, *Development of the Provincial Newspaper*, pp. 94–5, 96–8, 100, 228, 239–40, 253.

advertising medium, to entertain and instruct their readers, promote commerce, encourage conversation and, as was somewhat blasphemously suggested, to instil religiosity amongst the 'thousands of the people . . . ignorant of the discipline of the common-prayer book'.[50]

Though the proprietors of the provincial newspaper sought a heterogeneous audience, their papers were usually informed by a common outlook. In the paper politics, social morality and commerce were not seen as encapsulated entities. Diversions and entertainment, in the somewhat unexpected form of algebraic problems, sharpened the reader's mathematical skills; the moral instruction provided by the essayist had secular as well as spiritual purposes. Even the tales of crime and gore served their purpose by helping define conventional morality, and by sermonizing on the terrible fate of the deviant. The newspaper, therefore, served not only as a business seismograph, informing merchants, middlemen and traders of tremors that could lead to a financial earthquake, but also taught precisely those virtues and values which were necessary for survival in an economically expansive though debt-ridden society. Clearly, there existed even more compelling reasons than that of social emulation for thumbing eagerly through the news.

Accurate, regular and punctual news could at least forewarn those who were about to suffer financial misfortune, but such information could not, however, ward off disaster. Some rather stronger remedy or succour was necessary, and this many found in that most distinctive of eighteenth-century British institutions, the club. Dr. Johnson was not alone in noticing that almost every Englishman belonged to a society, lodge, fraternity or club, and that many of his fellow citizens belonged to several such voluntary associations. Today the term 'club' conjures up the impression of a venerable, neo-classical edifice filled with leather armchairs, musty volumes and antediluvian males. But in the eighteenth century the term 'club' was understood as a verb, rather than as a noun: *'to club together'* to pool one's financial resources for almost any collective activity, automatically created *a club*.

Some of these societies were as transitory as their definition suggests; many more, however, endured. There were clubs for every class of citizen: aristocratic clubs such as the Mohocks and Sublime Society of Beefsteaks, merchants' clubs such as the Half Moon Society, farmers' societies like the 'spending clubs' or 'drinking clubs' of the Hertfordshire market towns, and the 'Free and Easies' for the tradesmen and artisans of the cities. Every taste was catered for: societies were established for literati, the ugly, gamblers, politicians, homosexuals, rakes, singers, art collectors, and boating enthusiasts.[51]

---

[50] *Liverpool Chronicle*, 6 May 1757.
[51] John Timbs, *Club Life in London* (2 vols, London, 1866), *passim;* R. J. Allen, *The Clubs of Augustan London* (Cambridge, Mass., 1933); M. D. George, *London Life in the Eighteenth Century* (London, 1925), pp. 266-8; W. Branch Johnson, *The Carrington Diary 1797-1810* (London, 1956), p. 57.

These clubs were organized with varying degrees of formality. Often a club would be started merely because a group of sympathetic or like-minded men (there were few distinctively female societies) found themselves at the same tavern table. But others enjoyed a much greater degree of organization. This was the case with the burgeoning number of masonic lodges and pseudo-masonic societies. By 1768 291 British masonic lodges had been founded, including sixty-one abroad, several in the army and navy, and eighty-seven in London.[52] Though each lodge was a discrete entity, the Moderns and the schismatic Ancients both gave the masons a modicum of national coherence.[53] Formal constitutions were printed, and secret ceremonial became perhaps the best known masonic characteristic. The London Grand Lodges superintended the activities of the affiliated societies. Thus, when members of the Ship Lodge of St. Ives, Cornwall failed to contribute to the national Grand Fund of Charity organized by the London Grand Lodge, they were warned that their constitution was in jeopardy.[54] Equally well organized was the so-called Lumber Troop, for which Hogarth designed a coat of arms. It had between eight and nine thousand members in London and the Tyneside area.[55] Similarly the Bucks was a nationwide society, having thirteen lodges in London together with branches in Liverpool, Birmingham, Cambridge, Bath, Plymouth, the Isle of Man and (somewhat less predictably) Bombay.[56] These pseudo-masonic orders had regulations, constitutions, regalia and printed song books: they were well on the way to becoming established institutions.

Such societies may seem to have only the most oblique connection with the vicissitudes suffered as a consequence of a volatile economy. It is the colourful aspects of club life that are most striking and which have attracted historians in the past. The entertainment—gargantuan eating, drunken stupors—the ritual—epitomized by the arcane and inscrutable ceremonies of the masons—and the violence perpetrated by young, aristocratic rakes who slit watchmen's noses and rolled old ladies down hills in barrels full of nails: this is the stuff of which so many club and society histories are made. But there was a much more serious side to club activity for, though it is perfectly true that feasting, drinking and conviviality were central to every club's existence, the club also performed important social functions as a protection against adversity and as an elaborate system of reciprocal obligation. This was as true of the genteel societies and masonic lodges as of the more demotic organizations like the friendly society and the 'free and easy'. To a quite

[52] *A List of Regular Lodges according to their seniority and constitution* (London, 1763), *passim*.
[53] For the relationship between these orders see Bernard E. Jones, *Freemason's Guide and Compendium* (London, 1956), pp. 193-212.
[54] J. G. Osborn, *A History of Freemasonry in West Cornwall, 1765-1828* (Penzance, 1901), p. 18.
[55] *Notes and Queries* 9th Series X, p. 322; *Worcester Journal*, 5 January 1769.
[56] *Notes and Queries*, 1st Series, VII, p. 286; 2nd Series, V, p. 436; *Middlesex Journal*, 18 November 1769.

remarkable degree clubs drawn from all social groups—with the possible exception of the very rich—performed these apparently mundane but very necessary tasks.

Joining a club in eighteenth-century Britain often—though not always—involved the recognition and acceptance both of responsibilities towards fellow members, and of their reciprocal obligations. The resulting society often transcended traditional social, economic and religious boundaries. Although there were clubs comprised exclusively of a single class, or of only one occupational group, a large number of societies—and this was as true of the masons and pseudo-masonic societies as of some friendly societies—boasted of the way in which they united Anglicans and dissenters, men from different trades, merchants and gentlemen, whigs and tories, in a common association, promoting unanimity and harmony where only conflict had previously existed.[57]

Clearly, one could not, as it were, enter a club 'cold', adopting a 'take it or leave it' attitude. Clubs were a form of social bonding explicitly established to encourage 'mutual benevolence and friendship', 'union and friendly feeling', and the type of friendship and mutual aid dispensed within the society was often of a very tangible and direct sort.[58] The success, even the continued existence of the club depended to a very great extent on the willingness of members to participate to the full: only in this way could all those involved enjoy the society's benefits. Malingering could only encourage divisions.

What forms did this much vaunted 'mutual benevolence' take? First and foremost, it was a protection against adversity. Because of the arbitrary nature of misfortune—the way in which even the thrifty, sober and industrious as well as the prodigal, debauched and idle could suffer financial crisis and economic destitution—it was vital to establish some means of protection, some type of insurance, against unforeseen calamities. Equally, it was important to provide for the sick, the old and the unemployed. Many clubs, including the friendly societies so beloved of Sir William Eden, were explicitly established for this purpose. The society founded in Shrewsbury in 1768 was typical, both in its formation and in its functions. 'There is a clubb formed here', wrote one anxious onlooker,[59]

> among the lower sort of burgesses who meet every Wednesday night, their number does increase from time to time as they meet—They spend some money, & put some in a box which is gradually to raise a fund for relief and support of their bretheren when reduced and past labour, they give out that they will be unanimous in voting on all occasions.

---

[57] *Northampton Mercury*, 11 September 1732; *A Collection of Freemason's Songs* (London, 1904), pp. 30–2.

[58] [Cleland], *The Way to things by Words and to Words by Things. Also Two Essays, the one on the origin of the musical waits at Christmas. The other on the real secret of the Free masons* (London, 1766), pp. 110–11.

[59] John Oliver to Thomas Hill, 16 December 1767, Attingham Collection, Box 27, Salop R.O.

The format adopted by the citizens of Shrewsbury was the one employed almost everywhere. At a club gathering members contributed a fixed sum to a common pool or kitty which paid for the evening's entertainment of victuals or drink. The remaining cash, when the tariff had been paid, became part of the society's capital, available for whatever purpose the members thought fit. In many cases the money was deposited with the landlord of the hostelry where the club met. The large London brewers encouraged this activity by paying interest at 4 per cent on the sums so invested. In 1770 Samuel Whitbread was paying interest on what was, in effect, a loan of £3,135 from these tavern societies; Truman, in the same period, held sums between £1,000 and £6,000. These were a significant, because *regular* source of capital for the brewers, even though the contribution of individual societies might be as little as a few pounds. Such ale-house groups as 'the Sick Mans Friend', 'Thoughtful Sisters', 'Sons of Prudence', and 'General Funeral' not only served their members in ways which their names so vividly describe, but were also a means of mobilizing savings and providing some capital for one of the nation's most important industries.[60]

Masonic lodges and pseudo-masonic societies also helped cushion their members against indebtedness and social misfortune. The solid burghers and respectable tradesmen who made up the bulk of masonic membership had to protect themselves in ways similar to those used by the labouring poor, even if the reasons for mercantile adversity often differed from those that brought about the miseries of the day labourer and the apprentice. Masons would rally round a brother whose creditors threatened to foreclose on him. The knowledge that substantial friends, as well as kith and kin, would stand by a tradesman increased his creditworthiness and the confidence that both he himself and others had in his business. Sudden, short-term expenses could be met by a collection within the lodge or by drawing on the society's funds. Thus the Ship Lodge in St. Ives—consisting of some three hundred members—helped one of its brothers, a comedian, to pay off a creditor who was demanding immediate payment for a recently purchased suit of clothes.[61] The incident may seem inconsequential to us but for the hapless comedian masonic membership meant the difference between freedom and the horrors of the debtors' gaol. The advantages of being a mason, therefore, far exceeded the privilege of being initiated into a complex ritual and secret ceremonial, for it meant that the mason was cushioned, in a way that non-masons were not, against financial discomforture or even ruin. It was an essential part of the folklore about masons—appearing in their own songs as well as in the

---

[60] Peter Mathias, *The Brewing Industry in England 1700–1830* (Cambridge, 1959), pp. 264, 277–8. Money from the clubs constituted about 10 per cent of the liabilities of Truman, Hanbury & Buxton (Mathias, *Brewing Industry*, pp. 556–7).

[61] Osborn, *Freemasonry in West Cornwall*, pp. 14–17. Cf. Edward Farley, *Imprisonment for Debt Unconstitutional and Oppressive* (London, 1788), p. 38.

anti-masonic literature—that they stuck together through thick and thin.[62] And, although some unfortunate masons such as Mozart had reasons for regarding this tradition somewhat sceptically,[63] there is no doubt that it was one of the greatest attractions of masonic membership.

The selfsame functions were performed, of course, by trade and professional societies. Clubs of cordwainers, handkerchief makers, silk weavers, and coalheavers all helped accumulate savings for their members, just as the provincial law societies late in the century acted not merely as pressure groups for the profession, but gave charitable relief to lawyers' widows or to lapsed members of the profession such as John Moxen, attorney of Leeds, who found himself in the local workhouse in 1789.[64] Once money had been collected by a trade society, it conferred on members a degree of power and independence. 'Mutual benevolence' might well mean the funding of a strike as well as the paying of a widow's pension. Indeed, it seems to have been for this reason that employers were so reluctant to help their labourers establish any such society or club, and when they did so, like the Newcastle hostmen who established a society for the Tyneside keelmen, they fought tooth-and-nail to retain control of the funds.[65]

Similarly local electoral magnates frowned upon burgesses' clubs beyond their influence. They knew that the box clubs that emerged in such towns as Shrewsbury and Worcester in the 1760s and 1770s could be used to support independent political action, even to the extent of providing financial backing for an independent candidate. The parish clubs of Worcester that supported the radical candidacy of Sir Watkin Lewes tried to rely entirely on their own members. Two voters described how

> they belonged to a Club, at which a number of people subscribed according to their abilities, and that the men who attended (Lewes) in the Hall, and belonged to the Club, received two shillings each day out of the stock so subscribed; and Moore (a voter) declared, he had paid more money into the club than he ever received out.

The object of such societies, according to another of their members, was 'to support their independency'. Lewes himself, it was emphasized, never contributed money to the clubs, though he visited them as their guest.[66] A new type of relationship was deliberately fostered between the parliamentary candidate and his supporters. The usual treating was foregone to be replaced by entertainment and celebration which was funded by the voters themselves.

---

[62] *Masonry the Way to Hell. A Sermon* (2nd. ed., London, 1768), pp. 5-6, 29-30; *Collection of Freemason's Songs*, pp. 22-3, 45.

[63] E. Anderson & C. B. Oldman, *The Letters of Mozart and his Family* (3 vols, London, 1938), III, pp. 1360-5, 1383-7, 1391-1400, 1411-12, 1424.

[64] R. Robson, *The Attorney in Eighteenth-century England* (Cambridge, 1959), pp. 42-3; *Worcester Journal*, 2 February, 31 August 1769; Linebaugh, *Tyburn*, pp. 488, 514.

[65] E. Mackenzie, *A Descriptive and Historical Account of the town and county of Newcastle upon Tyne* (Newcastle, 1827), pp. 550-1; John Brand, *The History and Antiquities of Newcastle* (2 vols, London, 1789), I, pp. 451-4.

[66] See fn. 59 above and Foley Scrapbook vol. 3, pp. 87-90, 91, Worcester R. O.

In this way they established their independence of the traditional system of largesse and patronage: the voters—and their votes—were free. The Worcester clubs, therefore, helped liberate their members from traditional clientage—the political equivalent of the 'client economy'—just as the funds collected by the trades clubs strengthened their hand when dealing with employers and helped them counteract the influence of the rich. Such collective endeavours at self-support gave the employee, burgess and trader far greater power than they were capable of commanding individually.

Clubs and societies, then, were not merely defensive organizations, warding off the all-too-frequent social and economic ills of their members; they were also positive and constructive, seeking to improve the lot of their fraternity. At the most obvious level this included mutual benefits in trade. Societies that were not a single trade frequently contained the rule that no two persons of the same trade could be members of the same club. Joining the society would therefore give unrivalled access for each member to a substantial number of potential customers, especially as it was conventionally understood—and was sometimes included in the club rules—that trading would, in the first instance, be among members. Thus the *Spectator's* Twopenny Club included the rule that, 'None of the Club shall have his Cloathes and Shoes made or mended, but by a Brother Member.'[67] Rather more dramatically, the 45 Club that met in Temple Street, Bristol, dissolved in 1769 because of the animosities generated by one tradesman who refused to buy sugar from a fellow member in order to sweeten one of the club's feasts.[68] The same convention of society trading operated in the masonic lodges. Even the masons' most strident critics conceded that merchants and tradesmen at lodge meetings had the opportunity of winning aristocratic customers as well as of enjoying the social pleasures of rubbing shoulders with the rich.[69]

Much of the conviviality and junketing that took place in these societies had, therefore, a rather more serious and business-like purpose. Joining a club enabled the tradesman to extend the ambit of his acquaintance, to meet potential customers, creditors and partners in a highly convivial, amicable atmosphere. The backslapping bonhomie, the brimming glass, the boisterous songs and the roasted side of beef were all intended to promote unanimity, harmony and friendship, not only in the context of the club-room, but also in the commercial world outside. A regular gathering of the like-minded helped reinforce the values that they held; business could be conducted informally amongst friends; the bibulous atmosphere would encourage openheartedness, candour and honesty.

The time-honoured communal rituals of eating and drinking served to reinforce this camaraderie. As the *Spectator* pointed out: 'Our modern celebrated clubs are founded upon eating and drinking, which are points

[67] *The Spectator*, ed. D. F. Bond (5 vols, Oxford, 1965), I, p. 43.
[68] *Felix Farley's Bristol Journal*, 8 July 1769.
[69] *Masonry the Way to Hell*, pp. 27-8.

wherein most men agree, and in which the learned and the illiterate, the Dull and the Airy, the Philosopher and the Buffoon, can all of them bear a part'.[70] It was understood that all participated equally in what was essentially a group activity: drink was served from the communal punchbowl which so many societies purchased, the drinking vessels of the club were almost always of exactly the same size and shape, often decorated with a common symbol or inscription. It was the proud boast of many societies that the union that they encouraged helped commerce, industry and 'civilization'. The inscriptions on society medals and cups, together with the traditional club songs all attest to these exalted aspirations. 'Be merry and wise', urges the inscription on the mug produced by John Sadler for the Bucks, 'Industry produceth wealth, we obey Freedom with Innocence, Unanimity is the strength of society'.[71] Many of the clubs were, in effect, vehicles for the promotion of a morality and outlook conducive to successful trading.

It would, of course, be foolish to pretend that all clubs managed to conform to this exemplary model. There are plenty of examples of tavern discussions escalating into brawls and of club members being found in a gutter or a wayside ditch when alcoholic stupefaction successfully triumphed over their desire to return to house and home. The sad tale of the neglected wife and child appears too often in the anti-masonic literature for it to have been totally bereft of truth.[72] We are still in the age when drinking, at least of Portuguese wine and British beer, was a patriotic, convivial and socially desirable activity rather than the bane of nineteenth-century temperance societies or the evil spirit that haunts the novels of Emile Zola. Yet, despite the undeniable excesses, club life undoubtedly became less debauched and less vicious as the eighteenth century proceeded.[73] Indeed, in some cases it became increasingly difficult to differentiate a convivial club from an actual business partnership or association.

Such a development is hardly very surprising. Transactions amongst tradesmen were very often sealed over a mug of ale in the local tavern, and the clientele of a coffee house was frequently dominated by one particular trade or business. The tavern or coffee house served as a business address, a rendezvous for clinching deals, and as a place where the latest trade gossip and business information could be obtained. A group within the trade would meet and club together in order to raise money for a collective business enterprise. This was how the famous 'Chapter' of booksellers meeting at the Chapter Coffee House financed their more ambitious publishing enterprises. Later in the century James Lackington, that remarkable if somewhat ruthless

---

[70] *The Spectator*, ed. Bond, I, p. 42.
[71] E. Stanley Price, *John Sadler. A Liverpool Pottery Printer* (West Kirkby, 1948), p. 61; R. L. Hobson, *Catalogue of the Collection of English Porcelain in the British Museum* (London, 1905).
[72] *St. James's Chronicle*, 28 January 1769; *Masonry the Way to Hell*, p. 24.
[73] Even rake's clubs became more respectable. (L. C. Jones, *The Clubs of the Augustan Rakes* (New York, 1942), pp. 8-9).

founder of the London book emporium, belonged to a similar society called, in good Mandevillian fashion, the Busy Bees.[74] Money was sometimes raised through a subscription in an existing society, or the subscription itself gave birth to a new club. Thus the fishermen of Cromer formed themselves into an association and raised a fund in order to organize the marketing of their catch in London.[75]

The fund or, as it was more usually called, the *subscription* was probably the most common way of raising money for a particular project in eighteenth-century England, and, as often as not, it was organized by or centred on a club or society. To subscribe is, of course, to club together, and this is how contemporaries thought of subscriptions, even though there were a substantial number of occasions when a subscription was *public* and therefore did not necessarily involve the social and convivial aspects of clubbing.

The subscription has a great many advantages. It was a highly flexible form of fund raising which permitted the small saver to participate. Even the man with a few shillings or a pound or two would feel able to invest, and any given project was not dependent upon a large contribution from some enormously wealthy individual whose share in the enterprise would therefore be disproportionately grand. Though it is undeniable that aristocrats and men of considerable means were frequently members of a subscription, the typical investor or donor was far more likely to be a merchant, tradesman, tavern proprietor, or member of a profession. A tradesman with a relatively small sum of money to invest could nevertheless diversify his resources by making modest contributions to several subscriptions. And as these were frequently regarded as loans on which he would be paid interest, rather than as shares in a partnership, he was protected from the terrible responsibility that the absence of a law of limited liability put on the tradesman who combined with others in any business venture.[76]

The subscription, therefore, was primarily a tactic of the middling sort, that group whose incomes fell between approximately £50 and £400 per annum. It enabled them to exercise collectively an influence in the community far beyond that conferred by their individual incomes. Like the club, the subscription could liberate men from the client economy. There was less reason to turn to the local aristocrat or big wig for financial aid, charity or entertainment when a combination of local bourgeois could organize such projects for themselves, thereby acquiring not only local status but the pleasureable sensation of acting independently. The author who wanted money to publish a book and the builder who sought capital for constructing houses no longer needed to go cap in hand to a patron or sponsor, but could

---

[74] Marjorie Plant, *The English Book Trade. An Economic History of the Making and Sale of Books* (2nd. ed., London, 1965), pp. 162, 223.
[75] *Gloucester Journal*, 2 September 1771.
[76] Mathias, 'Capital, credit and enterprise', *J. Eur. Ec.H.* (1973), p. 134.

launch a public subscription through the newspaper. This did not mean, of course, that such men made an immediate leap from the client economy to the mass market, but the subscription helped facilitate the transition; it provided a degree of security in a period of change, enabling the small tradesman or producer to move outside the protected realm of patrician patronage without being totally at the mercy of the open market's vagaries and whims.

Much has been written in recent years of the importance of a middling-sort in stimulating home demand during the eighteenth century.[77] Perhaps rather more attention ought also to be addressed to the role of the small investor in stimulating the economy. The extraordinary number of subscriptions, many of them organized by clubs, lodges and societies, helped unlock the savings of merchants, tradesmen, and those in the professions, thereby ensuring their use not only in business projects but in the equally important spheres of charity and leisure.

For, although a great many subscriptions were used to fund entrepreneurial activities such as house-building, the sale of books and prints, and the erection of turnpikes,[78] even more frequently the subscription was employed to effect civic improvements and to provide community charity. Clubs and societies that had previously provided support and relief to their own members extended the ambit of their activities to those outside the charmed circle of club membership. The building of local assembly rooms and theatres, the erection of bridges where fords or a ferry had previously existed, the provision of street lighting and of night-watchmen, the opening of regional hospitals and the foundation of agricultural improvement societies were all effected through subscriptions.[79] In the forefront of this fund-raising were the masons. They seem to have been especially interested in the foundation of almshouses and hospitals, and it was because of their wide range of charitable activities that the Free and Accepted Masons sought legal incorporation in 1772.[80]

[77] See especially Eversley, 'Home Market and Economic Growth', *Land, Labour and Population*, pp. 206–59; A. H. John, 'Agricultural Productivity and Economic Growth', *Agriculture and Economic Growth*, pp. 173–93; Neil McKendrick, 'Home Demand and Economic Growth: A new view of the role of women and children in the Industrial Revolution', *Historical Perspectives. Studies in English Thought and Society in honour of J. H. Plumb* (London, 1974), pp. 152–210.
[78] William Albert, *The Turnpike Road System in England, 1663–1840* (Cambridge, 1972), pp. 100–3.
[79] J. H. Plumb, *The Commercialisation of Leisure in Eighteenth-Century England* (Reading, 1973), pp. 13, 18; *Northampton Mercury*, 27 December 1731 (bridge-lighting); *York Courant*, 5 October 1731 (assembly room), 22 August 1738 (infirmary); *Pope's Bath Chronicle*, 4 February 1768; *Farley's Bristol Journal*, 24 February, 13 October 1770 (hospitals); *Gloucester Journal*, 16 September 1771 (tavern), 20 April 1772 (agricultural improvement society); *Middlesex Journal*, 16 September 1769 (street lighting); *Newcastle Courant*, 21 May 1763 (lunatic asylum); *Western Flying Post*, 11 March 1771 (hotel and assembly room).
[80] *Felix Farley's Bristol Journal*, 29 February, 11 April, 10 October 1772; *Middlesex Journal*, 31 August 1769.

A certain amount of this charitable activity was carried out on an *ad hoc* basis. Thus the misfortunes of Pasquale Paoli and his fellow Corsicans at the hands of the French promoted English sympathizers to subscribe over £3,000 for their relief.[81] In 1731 the members of the Falcon Club in Cambridge organized a subscription for the victims of the terrible fire that ravaged the nearby village of Burwell.[82] Similarly, it seems to have been common practice to raise subscriptions for the relief of the poor during times of dearth. In Wisbech in 1740 and Bury St. Edmunds in 1772 there were subscriptions amongst the local traders to purchase grain for the country folks who had rioted about inadequate provision. These funds very often had a dual purpose: they were intended, in the first instance, to permit a magnanimous gesture that would encourage the voluntary restoration of order, but they could also be used to justify retributive action against the rioters if they were inappropriately ungrateful for the charity of the local burghers.[83] Some of these attempts to provide relief went to extraordinary lengths. In 1772 subscriptions to lower the price of meat and other foodstuffs were started by the booksellers of the Chapter Coffee House and London's silk weavers, at the New Lloyd's Coffee House and the King's Arms Tavern in Cornhill. Within a month nearly £7,000, it was claimed, had been collected, and, thanks to extensive publicity in the newspapers (many of which were owned by the booksellers), the scheme was copied in Bristol, Gloucester, Worcester, Leicester and Norwich. Subscribers either lent money free of interest for the purchase of meat, or tried to negotiate cheap, bulk orders from country butchers.[84] Such expendients were clearly necessary when economic fluctuations were so sharp and unpredictable, and when a bad harvest or prolonged period of bad weather could place the 30 per cent of the population which was 'at risk' below the poverty line.[85] The ease and rapidity with which a subscription could be raised made it an ideal means of providing some short-term response—no matter how unsatisfactory—to the spectre of extreme poverty.

Ad hoc charitable subscriptions sought to relieve or, at least, alleviate poverty and misfortune, but the majority of the enduring charitable societies sought to prevent them by providing schooling, employment and apprenticeship schemes. The Neptune Society of Liverpool, the Marine Society of London, the Naval Society, and Bristol's Anchor Society all provided training and relief for the children—often orphans—of men in the merchant marine,

---

[81] *Worcester Journal*, 10 November 1768, 5 January, 16 February, 18 May 1769; *Middlesex Journal*, 31 August 1769.
[82] *Northampton Mercury*, 11 October 1731.
[83] *Northampton Mercury*, 14 July 1740; *Felix Farley's Bristol Journal*, 25 April 1772.
[84] *Felix Farley's Bristol Journal*, 29 February, 7, 14, 28 March, 4 April, 9 May 1772; *Gloucester Journal*, 17 February, 2 March 1772.
[85] A. W. Coats, 'The relief of poverty, attitudes to labour, and economic change in England, 1660-1782', *International Review of Social History*, 21 (1976), pp. 101-2.

or took vagrant boys and prepared them for naval service.[86] A sizeable proportion of the nation's charity schools were organized and financed through subscriptions.[87] Most large towns seem to have had societies for apprenticing poor boys, such as that at Bristol, and the numerous county societies also paid for children from their locality to be trained in a particular trade. Thus the Gentlemen Natives of Hereford held monthly meetings in Bristol to raise money for the apprenticing of Hereford lads in that city, while in London the Gloucestershire society, with its annual subscription of 12s. a year, paid for the apprenticeship of 171 poor boys.[88] Such organizations linked the country and the city; young men who tramped their way to a regional centre or the metropolis could hope for the help of such a society in finding them employment in a strange town.

It should not be imagined that this charitable activity was totally selfless. As a great many critics of charitable activity, including the most acerbic of them all, Bernard Mandeville, pointed out, membership of a charitable society could confer considerable status on an individual. The organizers of charities, it was recognized, were often men of insufficient rank to occupy civic office but could nonetheless enjoy the sensations of power and control over others via the charity society. This opportunity to lord it over the unfortunate was all the greater because the charity dispensed was usually selective rather than indiscriminate. Unlike traditional forms of largesse such as the open house, common table or the tradition of throwing money or food to a scrambling crowd, club charity prided itself on its decorousness and chose its recipients carefully. They had to demonstrate that they were worthy of and justly entitled to relief, and were also compelled to show appropriate gratitude for the magnanimity shown towards them. On occasion a ticket system was employed whereby subscribers could dispense tickets redeemable on a tradesman or retailer (often a member of the society himself) to whoever they thought deserved relief.[89]

Power and status were not the only pay-offs. Charities and civic improvements meant jobs and patronage. A new bridge needed a tollmaster, schoolmasters were wanted for charitable educational establishments, a hospital had to be staffed by doctors and attendants. These were employment opportunities for precisely the social group which had funded the enterprise in the first place. Friends and relatives might be provided for, or appointments

---

[86] *Northampton Mercury*, 9 June 1733; *Liverpool Chronicle*, 27 May 1757; *Felix Farley's Bristol Journal*, 4 November 1769, 17 October 1772; *Gloucester Journal*, 14 December 1772.

[87] M. G. Jones, *The Charity School Movement; a study of eighteenth-century Puritanism in action* (Cambridge, 1938), p. 19.

[88] *Gloucester Journal*, 19 August, 14 October 1771; 'The Gloucestershire Society' in Glo. C. R. O., JX 113 (1-2).

[89] Bernard Mandeville, *The Fable of the Bees: or Private Vices, public benefits*, ed. F. B. Kaye (Oxford, 1924), pp. 253-332; *Masonry the Way to Hell*, pp. 27-8; *Crysal, or the Adventures of a Guinea* (London, 1760), I, p. 251.

dispensed as patronage. Just as the bridge provided income through its tolls, and the lighting schemes and watchmen protected tradesmen's property, so the charity schools and apprenticeship schemes provided their patrons with future servants and employees, educated in the appropriate values of industriousness, sobriety, thrift and punctuality.[90] No wonder subscribers so carefully attend the accounts of local improvements, and overlooked, with a zeal that surprised all but the cynical Mandeville, the individual progress of the students in their charity schools.

Clubs, lodges and subscriptions, therefore, brought many and considerable benefits to those who participated in them. Members were provided with a measure of security that was almost impossible to obtain outside the comforting confines of one's association. Trade and business were facilitated and made more reliable, for one came to know intimately the men with whom one was dealing. The club provided a cushion against a member's more aggressive creditors, made borrowing money much easier, and provided the organizational base from which to raise larger capital sums.

Clubs and societies were organizations which made men 'free': members were *'free* and easy' or *Free*masons. Free, of course, of the cares and worries that non-members suffered, but also free in the sense of being independent. Collectively the society determined its own activities; members governed themselves directly or through representatives who were regularly elected to offices that were usually rotated within the society. Within the group all were equal. Indeed, the eighteenth-century club closely approximated to the classical republican ideal so beloved of contemporaries yet so rarely realized in political society at large. Naturally oligarchs emerged in some clubs and lodges, just as they were apt to emerge at Westminster, but if a particular group in a club tried to monopolize power, the association tended to loose its unanimity, and to disintegrate.[91] Free and independent amongst themselves, club members were also free of others: they had the collective power and financial strength to *support themselves,* to avoid dependence on others. They could use this power, as I have argued, to free themselves from the constraints of the client economy and of the political control of their superiors.

Lodge and society membership also brought with it status and influence. Many clubs became powerful enough not only to aid themselves but to bring succour to others, though usually such help had its price. In order to enjoy the benefits offered by the burghers who ran clubs, subscriptions and charities, a man had to show that he was willing to embrace their tradesmen-like, bourgeois values. Charity was a means of converting the idle and unfortunate to the creed of industry; it acted as an evangelizing means of improving the

---

[90] Jones, *Charity School Movement*, p. 52; George Dyer, *A Dissertation on the Theory and Practice of Benevolence* (London, 1795), p. 31.
[91] See, for example, Osborn, *History of Freemasonry in West Cornwall*, pp. 26-8.

social environment, making it a better place in which to trade, sell, borrow and lend.

The benefits that accrued from club membership attracted so many applicants that the more prestigious societies grew increasingly selective. Since joining a lodge increased a new member's credit-worthiness, societies needed to be reasonably sure of the reliability of those they admitted. As one master put it, he accepted 'none but men of good principles and capable of acting upon the square, and living in obedience to the most excellent system of Morality and Good Fellowship delivered to us in the science of Freemasonry'.[92] A man's trade, his religious or political beliefs were not the relevant criteria for admission to a society—indeed, many clubs tried to overcome such distinctions—but an eager applicant would have to subscribe to the conventions, codes and practices of bourgeois probity and virtue.

Let us take stock of the argument so far. The problem of credit and debt operated at two levels in eighteenth-century society. First, changes in the scale of business, creating an extensive inter-regional credit structure centred on London, linked the fortunes of the local tradesman and of the London money market. The vicissitudes of the metropolis were now also the misfortunes of the commercial nation at large. The risks that the provincial businessman faced changed, altering in such a way as to increase his concern with events both in the metropolis and abroad. This, in turn, stimulated an interest in national politics. Reliable information from the centre was, of course, crucial, and was being provided with increasing exactitude by the provincial press, but a precise description of an incompetent policy, financial disaster or speculative mania was small compensation for those who had to suffer the consequences of political and economic policies whose formulation lay beyond their control. Hence the growing hostility towards a system of politics epitomized by the placeman and the stockjobber, and the desire to replace political clientage by a system that would give a greater say to men of moveable property.

Secondly, widespread credit and debt created comparable problems of regulation on a much more intimate scale. The relationship between borrower and lender was far more fraught, and a far more serious commitment than that between buyer and seller. The creditor's concern about the debtor extended far beyond the transaction of the loan itself. The fortunes of the lender were tied to those of the borrower: the debtor's indolence or adversity was the creditor's loss; the former had, quite literally, a vested interest in ensuring that the borrower conducted his business or employment precisely and successfully. Conversely, the debtor had to ensure the trust and confidence of the creditor, he had to accept that those who lent him money would make moral and social judgements about his worth over and beyond the immediate transaction. Otherwise it would be impossible to procure a loan, or the

[92] Osborn, *History of Freemasonry in West Cornwall*, p. 42.

creditor, if a loan was obtained, would foreclose. It is the on-going intensity of the credit nexus that made local borrowing and lending such an important issue and which encouraged regulation of the relationship.

Clubs and lodges—voluntary associations—were one short-term and frequently local means of regularizing credit arrangements. But the attempted regulation of credit which, given the universal practice of trade borrowing and lending, amounted to the regulation of business, was only a single aspect—though undoubtedly the most important one—of the efforts of voluntary associations and the social groups which they represented to establish their own, fairly complete control over their business activities. This aspiration must not be conceived of too narrowly. It was never simply a question of the internal ordering of trade and commerce. It involved the aggressive adoption of 'work ethic' values, attempts to enlarge the local power of mercantile groups through involvement in charitable projects and schemes for civic improvement, and a deliberate attack on the client economy and all it stood for. Reducing one's dependence on aristocratic clientage was analogous to escaping the impotent dependence that came from borrowing and lending. Naturally, neither could be entirely dispensed with, but both could be changed in such a way as to favour the tradesman and merchant: his direct control of the situation could be increased and, in consquence, his business risks reduced. But in order to bring this situation about, a number of important social and political changes had to be effected: the bonds between men had to be transformed, raising a major question about the exercise of power in the society.

Eventually the political issue had to be confronted, but it was not until the emergence of Wilkite radicalism that the clubs, lodges and societies firmly committed themselves to a political group or cause. It is the pseudo-Masonic societies, the lodges and trading clubs which link the economic and social to the political aspirations of the middling sort. For it was these voluntary associations which provided Wilkes with an aggressive and effective political organization, simply switching or extending already well-established economic activities into the political sphere. They were also the chief market for the many radical artifacts which were produced to exploit the emergence of John Wilkes as a shaper of fashion in the period. Voluntary associations lay at the heart of the Wilkite affair.

CLUBS, COMMERCIALIZATION AND POLITICS

Remember, that a free state is only a more numerous and more powerful club, and that he only is a free man, who is a member of such a state. ((Sir William Jones), *The Principles of Government; in a Dialogue between a scholar and a peasant, written by a Member of the Society for Constitutional Information* ((London), 1783), 14.)

> O all ye people praise ye WILKES, bless him,
> and huzza him for ever!
> O ye printers of the land, praise ye Wilkes,
> bless him, and huzza him for ever!
> O ye printers devils and your agents of
> whatsoever denomination, praise ye Wilkes,
> bless him, and huzza him for ever,
> O all ye booksellers, pamphlet stitchers, and
> bookbinders, praise ye Wilkes, bless him,
> and huzza him for ever...
> O ye glaziers of the city, praise ye Wilkes,
> bless him and huzza him for ever
> O ye chandlers of grease, praise ye Wilkes,
> bless him, and huzza him for ever...
> O ye ballad singers, hawkers and pedlars,
> praise ye Wilkes, bless him and huzza him
> for ever!
> Honour be to thee, O Wilkes!

(*Britannia's Intercession for the happy deliverance of John Wilkes, Esq* (London, 1768), 5.)

As we have seen, clubs, lodges and societies conferred on their members a whole series of economic benefits, including a degree of independence from the client economy, that was possible chiefly because of the power and financial strength derived from association. Such societies were a useful means of organizing men, accumulating savings and mobilizing wealth. These advantages of group organization were not lost on those eighteenth-century politicians who sought to mobilize political movements that did not depend on the traditional resources of clientage and patrician patronage. Political clubs, of course, were no new phenomena, especially in London where such societies had flourished at least since the Restoration.[93] But a distinction, albeit a rough and ready one, can be drawn between those societies like the Green Ribbon Club, or the Mug House clubs of the period of the Hanoverian succession, which were essentially extensions of a fairly well articulated party organization run by aristocrats,[94] and the sort of

---

[93] David Allen, 'Political Clubs in Restoration London', *Historical Journal*, XIX, 3 (1976), pp. 561-80; John Timbs, *Club Life in London* (2 vols, London, 1866), I, pp. 15-16.

[94] J. R. Jones, 'The Green Ribbon Club', *Durham University Journal* XVIII (1956), pp. 17-20; R. Chambers, *The Book of Days: A Miscellany of Popular Antiquities* (2 vols, London, 1868), II, pp. 109-12; Nicholas Rogers, 'Popular Protest in Early Hanoverian London', *Past and Present* 79 (1978), pp. 70-100; Linda Colley, 'The Loyal Brotherhood and the Cocoa Tree; The London Organization of the Tory Party, 1727-1760', *Historical Journal* 20, 1 (1977), pp. 77-95.

societies which could be found from the mid-eighteenth century and which tried to build an independent political movement, and express independent political initiative. Radical leaders such as John Wilkes cribbed from the tradesman's copybook, establishing societies, clubs and subscriptions whose organization was very largely derived from the example of bourgeois charities, lodges and trading associations. At the same time already existing voluntary associations of merchants, tradesmen and artisans leapt to Wilkes's support. The degree of unanimity these societies expressed is truly remarkable. There are almost no examples of clubs and societies which deliberately opposed Wilkes, and though many associations undoubtedly remained politically neutral throughout the Wilkes affair, there were nevertheless a substantial number of clubs which played an active role as Wilkite protagonists.

What united these societies with Wilkes was the notion of 'independence'. The autonomy and self-reliance sought by clubs of shopkeepers, retailers and tradesmen was readily expressed in the radicals' pursuit of freedom from clientage. The radical stereotype, as portrayed in their literature, makes this connection quite explicit, and self-consciously unites political independence with financial autonomy. As we have seen, this independence was not of the sort traditionally associated with the landed wealth of the gentleman. Rather it connoted freedom from the pressures that a patrician employer, patron or client could place on his workmen, tradesmen and creditors. Thus, when Wilkes was released from gaol in April 1770, the newspapers contrasted the joyous celebrations amongst the independent trading interest in the town of Gosport with the sullen silence of the local naval officers who were described as the kept, corrupt employees of the government, too fearful of their employer to express their honest political feelings.[95] Similarly, in radical propaganda, a distinction was always drawn between the intrepid, independently minded tradesman, like the poulterer William Edridge who defied the pressures of his aristocratic customers to support Wilkes, and such businessmen as the Westminster churchwarden who tried to prohibit Wilkite celebrations because he wanted to enjoy preferment and obtain aristocratic patronage of his grocery and small wares business.[96] Stories about independent yet poverty-stricken voters appeared repeatedly in the radical journals. The impecunious yet independent bricklayer, the decrepit, blind old man, the poor man from Brentford who shouted 'Let your duke bring a waggon load of money, we will throw him and all his money into the river': they were all vividly contrasted with the toadying footman, the venal customs official, the cruel bum-bailiff and the favour-seeking tradesman who were taken as stereotypical courtiers and conservatives.[97] When radical politicians com-

[95] *Middlesex Journal*, 23 April 1770.
[96] *Middlesex Journal*, 2 September 1769.
[97] *Middlesex Journal*, 18, 20 April, 7, 9 September 1769. The business of the engraver Grignon suffered because of his largely fortuitous association with Wilkes. (J. T. Smith, *Nollekens and his Times* (London, 1829), p. 103).

plained about corruption and patronage, they did not confine their criticisms to the presence of government employees in the legislature, or of tidewaiters and excise officers in the localities. They were fully aware of the extent of the client economy and how it could be used politically; indeed, they numbered it as one of the cardinal sins of the Hanoverian spoils system.[98]

The club members' desire for freedom from economic clientage went, therefore, hand-in-hand with a desire for political independence: the conditions necessary to obtain the one were also essential for the other. In consequence trading clubs and friendly societies very readily transmuted themselves into political associations. Of course a political crisis such as that surrounding the career of John Wilkes spawned many new clubs and societies, ranging from the rowdy and demotic Anti-Caledonian club in Wapping or the 'Free and Easy' under the Rose in Cursitor Street to the politically sophisticated and very orderly Retribution Club, Liberty Beefsteak Club, and Society of the Supporters of the Bill of Rights (SSBR).[99] But the majority of the clubs that did stalwart service for the Wilkite movement had existed prior to the emergence of the radical cause, and had deliberately decided to tack their colours to the mast of political independence. Wilkes himself did not choose to join many of the clubs; they determined to ally themselves with him. This was true of the Albions, the AntiGallicans, the Brethren of the Cheshire Cheese, the Bucks, the Colts of the City Lands, the First of August Society, the Hiccobites, the Leeches, the Free and Accepted Masons in their many branches, the Lumber Troop, the Mussel-Court Society and the Society of Old Souls.[100]

At first sight this support for Wilkes seems somewhat strange. Many of the societies which supported Wilkes stressed, as we have seen, the virtues of unanimity, harmony and good fellowship; they also professed to be above party squabbles and sordid politicking. This hardly seems to square with their support of one of the most notorious and controversial figures in eighteenth-century politics. But, for the clubs, masons and pseudo-masonic orders that backed Wilkes, their hero was above party and, in a sense, above politics. He was not obviously allied to any aristocratic group in parliament, and it was also apparent that his cause transcended the usual party boundaries. In fighting for liberty—or independence—Wilkes was pursuing a higher value; one that promised to create a commercially freer, politically self-reliant body politic which, in turn, would produce national unanimity, harmony and good feeling. Precisely because Wilkes promised to change the rules of politics in this way, he appealed to tradesmen, shopkeepers and members of the middling-sort. The numerous presents that Wilkes received

[98] Other examples, *Middlesex Journal*, 17 June, 30 September 1769.
[99] British Library, Add. Mss. 30867 f. 209; *Worcester Journal*, 27 February 1769.
[100] John Brewer, *Party Ideology and Popular Politics at the Accession of George III* (Cambridge, 1976), pp. 194–5; *Worcester Journal*, 5 January, 27 February, 9 March 1769; *Pope's Bath Chronicle*, 28 April 1768; *Felix Farley's Bristol Journal*, 30 July 1768; *Middlesex Journal*, 6 April, 18 May, 24 October 1769.

in gaol, so many of which were especially splendid examples of local industry or agriculture, as well as the frequently reiterated statements in radical meetings that only Wilkite success could restore the nation's commerce and wealth attest to the connection, firmly made in the minds of most of Wilkes's merchant and trading supporters, that right-thinking politics and prosperity were two sides of the same entrepreneurial coin.[101]

The support that the societies gave Wilkes was vital. Their experience in raising subscriptions, staging celebrations and co-ordinating political activity gave the radical movement a solid organizational base both in London and some of the larger provincial towns. Fund raising was probably their most important function. The Society of the Supporters of the Bill of Rights (SSBR) is usually portrayed as the first major extra-parliamentary political association—which it was—but it should not be forgotten that the society was originally established to handle the growing number of contributions which were pouring in from clubs and societies who wanted to give tangible proof of their political feelings. The SSBR, in other words, was at the top of a hierarchy of associations which supported Wilkes. Club subscriptions came from the West Indies and North America, Kent, Surrey, Sussex, Huntingdon, Worcestershire, Cornwall and Buckinghamshire, as well as the towns of Exeter, Oxford, Trowbridge and Bradford in Wiltshire, and Newcastle where several clubs combined their efforts.[102] In London, public house subscriptions were common. Even the poorer tavern associations of the East End managed to raise over £200 to help pay off Wilkes's debts just before his release from gaol. The Sons or Friends of Freedom who met at the Standard Tavern in Leicester Fields, and whose secretary Blair, was a haircutter, raised £150, while the Antigallicans, it was asserted, put up the enormous sum of £3,000 for Wilkes's election as sheriff.[103] Most of these societies used the traditional method of raising money: usually they held a dinner or feast and saved the remaining cash for 'Wilkes and Liberty'. This, indeed, was what the radical journals exhorted them to do. The *Middlesex Journal* in an open letter to 'the laudable Societies of Free and Accepted Masons, Antigallicans, and all *Independent* Societies and Public Meeting in the British dominions' (dominions because money was sent from North America and the West Indies) suggested that they 'provide immediately a box at each of your societies, with a slit in the top, to receive the free contributions of all the friends of liberty and the constitution'.[104] After a fixed period the money was to be counted and remitted to the SSBR in London.

[101] Brewer, *Party Ideology*, pp. 176-8.
[102] *Worcester Journal*, 26 March, 23 April 1768, 19 January, 27 February, 23 March, 15 June 1769; *Felix Farley's Bristol Journal*, 28 May 1768; *Farley's Bristol Journal*, 28 April 1770; *Newcastle Journal*, 4 March 1768, 21 April, 5, 26 May, 16 June, 1, 7 July 1770; *Gloucester Journal*, 6, 27 August 1770; *Middlesex Journal*, 23 May, 6 June 1769.
[103] *Worcester Journal*, 5 January 1769, 15 February, 15, 23 March, 19 April 1770; *Salisbury Journal*, 16 April 1770.
[104] *Middlesex Journal*, 17 June 1769.

Such strategies were clearly sufficiently successful to fund the many Middlesex elections and also to pay off the enormous debts that Wilkes had accrued.

Equally important was the organizational role that the clubs played during Wilkite demonstrations and festivities. They were responsible for renting rooms in taverns, buying butts of ale, and arranging firework displays, illuminations and celebratory music. The Forty-five Society and the Mussel-Court society staged elaborate celebrations for Wilkes's birthday, which the Standard Tavern society wanted to make into an annual jubilee. Wilkes's repeated re-elections for the county of Middlesex and his eventual release from the King's Bench Prison were marked by similar club festivities in Somerset, the North-East of England, and the environs of London. The Antigallicans at the Greyhound Inn in Greenwich, for example, commemorated Wilkes's release with fireworks, transparencies (very much a fad of the time), and rollicking music. In Newcastle the Cappadocians held a feast that was illuminated by a curious candle with 45 branches; they were sent Wilkite tobacco pipes by a local trader, and funded a special performance of Addison's *Cato* as a warning to those who had been responsible for Wilkes's confinement. Time and again we find local clubs and societies feasting and drinking on the dates of Wilkes's birth (28 October), his four re-elections to his Middlesex seat (16, 28 February, 16 March, 13 April), and his release from prison (23 April). Some even celebrated the twenty-eighth day of every month because so much of importance for the Wilkite movement happened on that day: it was Wilkes's birthday, the date of his entry into the King's Bench prison, and the occasion of one of his re-elections.[105]

Local societies had the expertise, experience, and could mobilize the funds to demonstrate their support for Wilkes on these occasions. They ensured that every Wilkite victory or radical triumph went off with a bang not a whimper. Sky-rockets, fire-crackers, bell-ringing, even gun salutes accompanied each celebration. The clubs quite literally kept the radical cause in the public eye, providing a powerful physical presence, a spectacle which reminded the public of the radicals' crusade. Yet in doing so they were drawing on techniques that had their roots in the social, economic and convivial traditions of the lodge, the trading club and the friendly society.

Not all club activity was so boisterous. Some societies were less centres of carousing and merry-making than places of political education and serious discussion. Many lodges held lectures before the drinking began. There was at least one London club whose members spent their time composing letters to the press exposing political and social evils.[106] And, of course, there were

---

[105] For clubs and calendrical celebrations see Brewer, *Party Ideology*, pp. 178, 195–6; *Worcester Journal*, 19 October 1769; *Leeds Mercury*, 18 April 1769; *Middlesex Journal*, 18 April, 24, 26 October 1769; *Western Flying Post*, 9 April 1770; John Sykes, *Local Records or Historical Records of Northumberland and Durham* (2 vols, Newcastle, 1866), I, p. 271.
[106] *Middlesex Journal*, 15 July 1769.

the debating societies. The Robin-hood society in Butcher Row, famous for its free-thinking religious views and candid discussion of the political issues of the day, raised such questions as 'what good has a certain popular gent. [Wilkes] done to his country?' and 'Can a people be free, whose representatives are nominated by representatives, instead of constituents?' Over in Newgate Street at the Queen's Arms similar issues were being publicly discussed. 'What', the members debated on 14 April 1769, 'is the proper definition of the word Liberty?'. The society concluded that liberty was 'the power of acting agreeable to laws which have the sanction of the people's consent'. The Middlesex elections, the administration of justice, and the value of instructions to MPs were all other topics of vociferous debate.[107]

Clubs and societies, therefore, were the foci of Wilkite organization: they were as prominent during the Middlesex elections where their banners led the serried ranks of radical supporters as in the King's Bench prison where masons, pseudo-masons and tradesmen's clubs gathered, bedecked in their society regalia, in order formally to elevate Wilkes into their fraternities.[108] They saw, with singular clarity, that Wilkes's politics coincided with theirs, and that it promised to achieve the economic and social goals that these societies had always pursued.

The symbiotic relationship between the radical politicans and the tradesmen's clubs created a powerful pressure group for improvement and reform which went to considerable lengths to expose the ills and inadequacies of court politics and the client economy. A fairly systematic muck-raking campaign was begun, spearheaded by the radical *Middlesex Journal*. The misuse of public funds, whether in parliament, a charitable bequest or at the parish officer's feast, was one of the paper's favourite grievances, as were trading malpractices of all kinds from selling short weight and measure to the speculative manipulation of commodity prices. The names of jurors in famous, especially political trials were printed in order to encourage public accountability, as were the names and addresses of those whom the paper regarded as especially miscreant and venal.[109]

The perennial question of indebtedness, so keenly felt by members of voluntary associations, was also taken up. Aristocratic and genteel customers of tradesmen were berated for failing to pay their bills promptly; bumbailiffs and spongers were attacked for the way in which they lived off the misfortunes of others; and the reform of the laws governing debt was often advocated. Writers in the *Middlesex Journal* complained of the ways in which the rich merchant could use bankruptcy to escape the full horrors of

---

[107] Debates at the Queens Arms, Newgate Street, were reported by the *Middlesex Journal* and occurred on 14, 21 April, 2, 5, 12, 19, 26 May, 2, 12, 17 June and 3 July 1769; at the Robin Hood Society the dates of the debates reported were 24 April, 8, 15, 22 May, 5, 12 June and 3 July.
[108] *Worcester Journal*, 9 March 1769; *Leeds Mercury*, 18 April 1769.
[109] *Middlesex Journal*, 22, 27 April, 2, 9, 27 May, 17 June, 27 July, 12 August, 2 September 1769.

indebtedness, while the smaller businessman—the shopkeeper or tradesman—had to languish in gaol. Such inequalities, together with the failure of the existing law to satisfy either creditor or debtor, were usually discussed specifically from the viewpoint of the retailer and small master.[110] There was even an advisory service for readers of the *Middlesex Journal* who had problems with debt and credit, run by the former turnkey of the King's Bench Prison, William Penrice.

Members of the SSBR such as Sir Watkin Lewes, Thomas Butterworth Bayley and George Grieve—the friend of both Franklin and Marat—were all involved in schemes for local improvement, including the building of hospitals and schools, the establishment of agricultural societies, and the introduction of street policing.[111] When the radicals had effectively established themselves in London's city government, they were similarly attentive to the interests of traders and shopkeepers. There was a serious attempt to keep hawkers off the streets, because they interfered with and undercut shopmen's trade, just as there was a campaign to remove the streetside fruitsellers (many of whom were prostitutes) who distracted potential shop customers near the Exchange and St. Pauls.[112] At the same time many radicals—especially the young lawyers such as Serjeant Glynn and John Reynolds—were concerned about anomalies in the law. Considerable attention was paid to the administration of justice which, broadly speaking, the radicals thought should be more equitable, even though rigorous.[113] Such sentiments certainly appealed to many of the middling sort who joined clubs and supported the radicals: they would have helped trade, institutionalized and regularized the retail business, helped reduce the theft that was so often directed against shopkeepers, and also furthered the trading interest in city government. Naturally enough, the apprentices and journeymen who bawled 'Wilkes and Liberty' on the streets and rioted in his favour did not have such reforms in mind; indeed, they would probably have resented them quite strongly. But the traders and merchants who were both the middle ranks of society and the middle ranks of the Wilkite movement looked upon such measures with heartfelt approval.

The Wilkites, therefore, united with trading clubs and societies, organizations that had originally been social and economic in intent and which had sought to foster commerce and the values compatible with good trading, and used them for political purposes. This never involved any abrupt transformation of purpose for these clubs because their politics and their economic concerns were inextricably linked. Such societies could hope to

---

[110] *Middlesex Journal*, 13 April, 10, 13, 17 June, 17 August, 25 November 1769.

[111] *Gloucester Journal*, 20 April, 21 September, 23 November 1772; [T. Percival], *Biographical Memoirs of the late Thomas Butterworth Bayley Esq. of Hope Hall near Manchester* (Manchester, 1802), pp. 4–8, 12; *Newcastle Journal*, 4 January 1772.

[112] *Middlesex Journal*, 22, 24 August 1769.

[113] See my essay, 'The Wilkite radicals and the law', *An Ungovernable People*, ed. Brewer and Styles, pp. 128–71.

benefit from the sort of reformist proposals that many of Wilkes's followers so ardently supported. But we must also recognize that politics, especially radical politics, was open to commercial development and exploitation. If the Wilkites used the techniques and methods of organization derived from the world of business, so the tradesman and entrepreneur treated politics as a commodity whose purchase could bring him profit.

Naturally, as we shall see in the ensuing discussion, those who engaged in the commercialization of politics sought to capture as broad a market as possible, to appeal to both the affluent and the humble; equally, they were never slow to exploit the transitory, calendrical occasions—the celebrations of victory and demonstrations of loyalty—which were such important expressions of political sentiment. But the centre, the hard core of the market for politics, and one which provided continuity between periodic expressions of jubilation which often proved enormously profitable to the potter, publican and printer, were the clubs and societies. These organizations were the chief purchasers of Wilkite commemoratives, of Wilkite ceramics for their club room, and of Wilkite regalia and bunting; they were the best customers of the publican, for not only did they meet, week after week, in the tavern upstairs or back room, storing their savings with the landlord, but they also organized and orchestrated the celebrations which involved the massive consumption of beer, the giving of gifts and public dinners.

Without the clubs there would have been no solid centre, no reliable, steady market for politics and political artifacts. Moreover, many clubs included in their fraternities the very producers of Wilkite artifacts. The concrete symbols of the Wilkite movement, therefore, were both instances of commercialization, and examples of the mutual support and club trading that were intrinsic to voluntary associations.

First and foremost among the Wilkite artifacts were the ceramics. Like nearly all Wilkite objects they ranged from the highly expensive to the relatively cheap, appealing to the entire range of radical supporters. The famous porcelain figure of Wilkes, usually ascribed to John Bacon, the Worcestershire porcelain tea-pot inscribed with the no. 45 under the spout, and the exquisite snuffboxes decorated either with portraits of Wilkes (taken from a contemporary engraving) or with the resplendent figure of Liberty were all well beyond the pocket of the patriot's humbler supporters.[114] Doubtless there would have been rather more purchasers of Wedgwood's creamware teapots—in both small and large sizes—which were transfer printed by John Sadler with a portait of 'John Wilkes, Esq. The Patriot', and of the very similar Leeds teapots inscribed on one side with 'Wilkes and Liberty' and, on the other, by the ubiquitous 'no. 45'.[115] Yet the great majority

---

[114] Arthur Lane, *English Porcelain Figures of Eighteenth-century London* (London, 1961), p. 55; *Wilkes and Liberty Catalogue, British Museum* (London, 1969).

[115] Price, *John Sadler*, pp. 23, 49; Donald C. Towner, *English Cream Coloured Earthenware* (London, 1957), p. 13; Stoke-on-Trent City Museum and Art Gallery.

of Wilkite ceramics were not even in the newly-fashionable creamware but in humble English delft. The typical Wilkite piece was the club mug, punchbowl or plate, usually decorated with a 'curtain' portrait of Wilkes, together with one of the political slogans of the day. 'Let not liberty be sold/ For Silver nor Gold/ Your votes freely give/ To the brave and the bold' is the motto of one such mug, while another has the rather more pithy inscription, 'Wilkes for ever'. The patriot and his enemies were regularly contrasted with one another in the delftware decoration: 'Wilkes & Liberty no Bu[te] 45' was easily transformed into 'Wilkes and Honest Juries No Ma[nsfiel]d 45'. Indeed one piece, a Chinese export bowl, actually reproduced a contemporary cartoon, 'The Arms of Liberty and Slavery' depicting the virtuous Wilkes and the heinous Lord Justice.[116]

Similar sentiments appeared on the large number of medals and medallets. These, like the ceramics, catered for those of all incomes. Many of the medals, including the most famous produced by James Kirk, the friend and drinking partner of the radical Thomas Hollis, were cast in gold, silver and base metal. The larger medals were for display at home or in the appropriate cabinet, while the medallets, like Masons' badges, were frequently worn around the neck as a token of allegiance to the radical cause.[117]

Equally popular was Wilkite clothing which enabled the radicals to display their political sentiments publicly. There were Wilkite coats with specially embroidered buttonholes, radical buttons, cuffs, rings and handkerchiefs, together with a Wilkite wig that had 45 curls.[118] Brooches or badges of the number 45 could be purchased in both gold and base metal. It was possible, if one so wished, to equip oneself almost entirely in Wilkite clothing and regalia, though few were as sartorially exuberant as Mr. Scott, 'the patriotic newscarrier', who wore a suit of blue and gold (the radical colours), a silver medal of Mr. Wilkes on his breast, and sleeve buttons and a breast buckle all marked with the number 45.[119]

There was virtually no end to the number of artifacts that were produced as Wilkite items, or transmuted through the addition of a symbol such as the number 45 into a pro-radical commodity. Tobacco pipes and papers, candlesticks and candles, pewter pots, flagons and tankards, cakes and confections were all tailored for the radical market.[120]

---

[116] Antony Ray, *English Delftware Pottery in the Robert Hall Warren Collection. Ashmolean Museum, Oxford* (London, 1968), pp. 126-7; Henry Housman, *Notes on the Willett Collection of Pottery in the Brighton Museum* (Brighton, 1893), p. 30.

[117] Batty, *Catalogue of the Copper Coinage of Great Britain* (4 vols, Manchester, 1868), nos. 4322, 5024, 4197; British Museum Department of Coins and Medals, Tray 145, M4734, 4740, 4741-4, 4749, English medal 215; Tray 147, Kirk medal; Tray 148, M4803, 4807. For later political medals and tokens, notably those of Thomas Spence, see J. R. S. Whiting, *Trade Tokens. A Social and Economic History* (Newton Abbot, 1971), pp.121-31.

[118] *Pope's Bath Chronicle,* 21 April 1768; *Salisbury Journal,* 8 January, 12 February 1770; *Worcester Journal,* 4 August 1768.

[119] *Middlesex Journal,* 13 May 1769.

[120] *Worcester Journal,* 14 July, 4 August 1768, 12 January 1769; *Pope's Bath Chronicle,* 21

BIRTH OF A CONSUMER SOCIETY

In exploiting the Wilkite phenomenon there seem to have been three particular tactics of note. The first was the use of the admittedly transient but very large market created by the Wilkite crowd. A tallow-chandler produced special blue candles in bundles of 45 for radical illuminations; over 3,000 blue cockades were sold to Wilkites by a city haberdasher; brewers cut the price of their ale on the days of Wilkite celebration; ballad singers were said to be making profits in the region of 18s. to 21s. a day on the occasions of radical demonstrations, using such ingenious ploys as selling blank sheets of paper, crying out 'Hallifax's speech' when the alderman failed to say anything on the platform of the 1772 mayoralty election.[121] The fate of the hats of Colonel Luttrell in 1769 and William Meredith in 1771 illustrate the extraordinary eye for the main chance that contemporaries had. Both were seized by the crowd and cut into pieces during Wilkite demonstrations. Almost immediately fragments appeared on the market, advertised as from the real hats of Luttrell or Meredith, and which could be purchased as radical trophies or souvenirs. A Luttrell hat button was said to fetch 2s. 6d., while Meredith's headwear was obviously less prestigious, costing only 6d. or 1s. a piece. As one wag remarked, there was almost as many pieces of Luttrell's hat in London as there were bits of the true cross in Rome.[122]

Entrepreneurs were equally adroit at changing their marketing techniques to exploit the Wilkes cult. Even the fair fruithawkers in the West End cried out that they were selling 'Wilkes's cherries', though it is hard to see how they would have tasted any different if they had been the fruit of King George and his ministers.[123] Cakes and confections, too, were simply 'radicalized' by marking with the number 45 or selling them in batches of that number.[124] Some such tactics were of remarkable ingenuity. John Sealy, for instance, inserted an advertisement in the *Middlesex Journal* 'To the Sons of Liberty and Encouragers of Penmanship'—not a connection that was immediately obvious even to his readers. But he offered them an engraving of the word Liberty 'in German text capitals carefully engraved ... from the design of John Sealy, writing master and accomptant, author of the Universal Tutor etc., and master of the academy in Bridgewater square, Barbican, where the curious may have them on plaister of Paris by paying the extra expense'. He had a plaster impression put up in the Royal Exchange on

---

April 1768; *Cambridge Chronicle*, 28 May 1768; Sykes, *Local Records of Northumberland and Durham*, I, p. 271.

[121] *Worcester Journal*, 20 April, 2 November 1769, 19 April 1770; *Boston Evening Post*, 4 April, 4 June 1770; *Gloucester Journal*, 23 April 1770, 12 October 1772; *General Evening Post*, 17 April 1770; *Middlesex Journal*, 13 April, 25 April 1769.

[122] *Boston Evening Post*, 12 June 1769; *Worcester Journal*, 20 April 1769; *Gloucester Journal*, 1 April 1771; *Middlesex Journal*, 15 April 1769.

[123] *Middlesex Journal*, 5 August 1769.

[124] *Worcester Journal*, 4 August 1768, 9 March 1769; *Middlesex Journal*, 22 April 1769; *Bristol Journal*, 26 August 1769; *Newcastle Journal*, 8 April 1769.

public view, and offered to send his clients 'Liberty' through the postal service.[125]

Another popular variant of this tactic was to obtain publicity and advertising for one's product by presenting Wilkes with an especially fine example of one's workmanship. This seems to have been at least part of the plan of the London sugar-baker who gave Wilkes a 45lb sugar loaf, and of the staymaker from Worcester who presented Polly, Wilkes's daughter, with stays 'of 45 pieces or quarters, . . . 45 holes and the no. 45 beautifully worked on the stomacher'. Even more improbably a 'mangle maker near Grosvenor Square' gave Wilkes 'an elegant mangle out of mahogany, on a construction entirely new, which, for its masterly and curious workmanship far exceeds anything of the kind that hath hitherto appeared before the public eye . . . in order to furnish him [Wilkes] with an article so necessary and useful for housekeeping'. Whether or not Wilkes was enamoured of this particular gift we do not know, but it served, as the language of the newspaper item vividly conveys, to publicize a product which claimed to be the very latest thing in household accoutrements. Joseph Leech of Romsey, Hampshire, used the same technique in advertising his wigs, including 'my new-invented Cork Peruke of 45 curls' which he had posted to Wilkes. His advertisement even included an ecstatic ode of his own composition which waxed lyrical on the patriot's pate and its elegant covering.[126]

Such tactics were widely used by all those who employed their entrepreneurial skills to commercialize politics. Three groups, however, stand out in their commercial involvement with Wilkes and the radicals of the clubs and they repay closer attention. Those involved in the drink trade—brewers, innkeepers and tavern proprietors—the manufacturers of ceramics, and the printers and booksellers who disseminated newspapers, pamphlets, songs, prints and cartoons all contributed towards the growth of a radical political style or culture centred on the club, tavern and coffeehouse while simultaneously reaping considerable, albeit short-term profits.

The tavern proprietor, the keepers of coaching inns and even the master of the public house were, of course, no strangers to the sort of organizing, entertaining, treating and celebrating that were an essential part of politics. No group had a stronger vested interest in encouraging a hotly contested election in which rival candidates would have to pour forth money to keep or win votes. The cash expended on the food and drink that was guzzled by greedy electors ended up in the pocket of the publican. In the Hertfordshire election of 1784, for instance, the Grimston interest paid out nearly £3,000 to 31 different taverns and inns, while Sir Beauchamp Proctor, in his efforts to defeat John Glynn at the Middlesex election of 1768, ran up bills totalling

---

[125] *Middlesex Journal*, 16 May 1769.
[126] *Middlesex Journal*, 16 May 1769; *Salisbury Journal*, 8 January 1770; *Bristol Journal*, 26 August 1769; *Worcester Journal*, 8 December 1768.

over £1,000 in the fifteen hostelries in Old and New Brentford that he patronized.[127]

Publicans knew perfectly well that contentious politics and heated debate meant bigger receipts and more custom. They made very little distinction between the crowds that they could draw on political occasions and those that congregated at the same hostelries for auctions, debates, florists' feasts, club meetings and concerts.[128] Doubtless the latter would often have been more respectable and more sober, but the profits from the former—provided no damage was done—would have been greater. All such activity was to be encouraged because of its commercial value to the tavern proprietor. Equally the experience that the innkeeper gained in organizing spectacles and public entertainments could be employed politically. The Southwark inns which staged the theatrical performances during the Southwark and Bartholomew fairs could readily switch their resources and expertise to more overt political activity.[129] Indeed, this is exactly what happened on 1 May 1769 in Lime Kiln Dock in Bristol, and on Whit Monday of the same year at St. George's Fields, where traditional May Day and Whitsuntide activities were transmuted into Wilkite fairs and festivities.[130]

Undoubtedly the clearest example, however, of the way in which publicans saw politics as a marketable commodity was in their extraordinary exploitation of the traditional election of the Mayor of Garret. Garret, a small community south of the Thames near Wandsworth, had elected a 'mayor' to lead their struggle to defend their local commons against encroachment and enclosure. A subscription—needless to say—was raised, a lawyer hired, and the case won. Thereafter a mayor was elected whenever a parliamentary election occurred. But the practice lapsed until it was revived by 'the publicans at Wandsworth, Tooting, Battersea, Clapham and Vauxhall' as a way of selling more ale. They put up the money for the candidates who were usually well-known figures of London low-life 'dressed like chimney-sweepers on May Day, or in the mock fashion of the period'. One of the earliest mayors so elected, a retailer of brick-dust, found that his success in the election helped stimulate his business. As a result, new candidates came forward, seeking to advertise their trades. In 1781, for instance, Mr. Cock, a basket-maker, appeared at the poll in a carriage made entirely of wicker. He was

---

[127] 'Hertford Bills paid by Mr. Hall by Order of the Committee', Grimston Papers, Herts. R. O.; 'The Honble Sir Wm Beauchamp Proctor Bart. Abstract of the Bills under the direction of Mr. John Janes, the following with respect to the Houses in Old & New Brentford being dissected', Proctor Papers, Ealing Borough Ref. Lib.
[128] For which see Plumb, *The Commercialisation of Leisure*, pp. 7, 18; Alan Everitt, 'The English Urban Inn, 1560-1760', *Perspectives in English Urban History*, ed. A. Everitt (London, 1973), pp. 114-9.
[129] Much of the material performed at these fairs was political in content, as is clear from many of the plays' titles cited in Sybil Rosenfeld, *The Theatre of the London Fairs in the Eighteenth Century* (Cambridge, 1960).
[130] *Western Flying Post*, 6 May 1769; *Middlesex Journal*, 18 May 1769.

accompanied by Thomas Cracknell, the proprietor of the Wilkes Head in Brentford, who played the handbells 'with an eye to business, as well as a disposition to waggery'. Other candidates included a seller of second-hand wigs, who was both witty and deformed, a Thames waterman, a muffin-seller and a carpenter. The victor in 1768, John Gardiner, was transported in 1769 for stealing lead coffins. During the 1760s the election became enormously popular: 'the road within a mile of Wandsworth was so blocked up with vehicles, that none could move backward or forward during many hours'. Booths and stalls were set up with entertainment and provisions. On one occasion there were so many visitors that 'all ordinary beverages [were] exhausted, and water was sold at twopence a glass'.[131]

Much of the popularity of the election was attributable to Foote's play *The Mayor of Garret* which was first performed in 1764 and which appeared regularly thereafter, usually being staged together with *The Beggar's Opera*. Foote fully recognized the motives that brought men to Garret. His characters range from a trading justice, who arrives with ready made-out warrants and mittimuses, hoping to make money from all the swearing that will occur, to 'Master Lint, the potter carrier' who wants to sell his services as a 'pharmacopolist' [sic] and 'chirurgon' together with patent medicines to those who are injured during the proceedings. It was asserted that Foote, together with Wilkes and Garrick, actually wrote some of the addresses for the candidates, including in the material popular and radical grievances. William Bingley, who published the later numbers of the *North Briton*, used an account of the election to moralize on the social and political ills of the nation.[132] The Garret election, therefore, was a manufactured political event, revived and revamped by members of the victualling trades to create the sort of market and trade that usually occurred only when a parliamentary election took place.

It therefore comes as no surprise to find that publicans were pivotal figures in the Wilkite movement. They sold cheaper beer on Wilkes's birthday—over a hundred public houses were open specially for the event in 1769—at the Middlesex elections, and on the occasion of Wilkes's release.[133] Publicans had their pots melted down and inscribed with the slogan 'Wilkes and Liberty' or purchased special cups and tankards to display to their cus-

---

[131] William Hone, *The Every-day Book* (2 vols, London, 1825-7), II, pp. 819-66; Sir Richard Phillips, *A Morning Walk from London to Kew* (London, 1820), pp. 78-82; *Worcester Journal*, 26 January 1769.
[132] R. Chambers, *The Book of Days. A Miscellany of Popular Antiquities* (London, 1868), pp. 659-61; *The Mayor of Garret. A Comedy in two acts, As it is performed at the Theatre Royal in Drury Lane. By Samuel Foote Esq* (London, 1764); *A Description of the Mock Election at Garret, on the Seventh of this Month. Wherein is given some Historical Account of its first Rise, the various Cavalcades of the different Candidates, the Speeches they made on the Hustings, the whimsical oath of Qualification, and an Authentic Copy of their several droll Printed Addresses* (London, 1768).
[133] See footnote 121.

tomers.[134] Mr. Ashley of the Marlborough Head, Bishopsgate, for example, had a gallon silver tankard made:

> Mr. Wilkes sits on the top of the lid, his right hand holds a staff with a cap of liberty on the top, and in the other, is a scroll with the inscription 'Liberty is the great Charter of the free born sons of Britannia.' On the front, is Britannia in the Temple of Liberty, ornamented with columns of the Ionick order enriched with a canopy over them. The handle is a cornucopia, with fruit and flowers flowing about the tankard.[135]

Not every proprietor was able to afford such an elaborate commemorative—Ashley paid £60 for it—but many publicans purchased similar artifacts in pewter or oak for the use of their regular customers and for the societies that meet in their taverns.

At the same time Wilkes Head hostelries sprang up in Brentford, the county town of Middlesex, in several provincial towns and in London at Kent Street, in Rotherhithe, Shoreditch and Shugg Lane. Wilkes's lawyer, John Glynn, gave his name to a public house near Holloway, and Wilkes, Glynn and Horne Tooke were the 'Three Johns' or the 'Three Patriots' who hung on the inn-signs of five London taverns. Equally famous was the 'Forty-Five Tavern' in Gray's Inn Passage, Bedford Row, Holborn. This hostelry was run by Mr. Keys, Beckford's former cook, and had a special illuminated sign at its door inscribed "The Arms of Freedom".[136]

The purpose of such signs was to attract custom. One West Country inn-keeper started life as the proprietor of the Nags Head. This sign he had changed to 'The Queen of Hungary' and then, following the diplomatic revolution, to 'The King of Prussia'. 'Every victory that was afterwards gained by that Prince gave an increase of custom to his house; his defeats were ever consoled over a pot of beer, and better success must be drunk to him another time.' With peace and increased beer prices, the publican's fortunes flagged, until 'by a little Alternation of the Drapery, and a cast given to one of his eyes, the Prussian monarch was converted into the Patriotic author of the North Briton'. Such a tactic not only restored the inn-keeper's custom, but increased his business to new heights.[137]

Taverns such as the Globe on Fleet Street, the Half Moon in Cheapside, the King's Arms in Cornhill, the London Tavern in Bishopsgate, the Prince of Orange in Jermyn Street, the Queen's Arms in St. Paul's Churchyard, the Standard Tavern in Leicester Fields, the Swan on Westminster Bridge and the Mermaid at Hackney were all essential parts of Wilkite radical organization. These houses were where the radicals met, plotted and planned. They were the homes of the clubs and societies which allied themselves with

---

[134] *Middlesex Journal*, 12 October 1769; *Worcester Journal*, 14 July 1768; *Cambridge Chronicle*, 28 May 1768.
[135] *Middlesex Journal*, 27 May 1769.
[136] Brewer, *Party Ideology*, pp. 185–6; *Middlesex Journal*, 20 April, 26, 31 August, 9 September 1769.
[137] *Worcester Journal*, 1 March 1770. Cf. Smith, *Nollekens and his Times*, pp. 22–4.

Wilkes, the centres of distribution and for advertisements for the *Middlesex Journal*, and the regular venue of public meetings of merchants, common councilmen, city companies and even the city livery.[138] But even as the taverns were important to the radicals, so the radical clubs were important to the taverns. They wanted the substantial trade and business that these groups brought.

In fact the position of the brewers and publicans vis-à-vis the radicals was a fairly complex one. For some reason there were persistent rumours when Wilkes was in gaol that he would set himself up as a brewer when he was released. The proprietor of the West Ham waterworks even offered to supply him if he did set up in trade.[139] Possibly this was a threat to undercut the main London brewers, for they had achieved a certain notoriety because of the first increase in the price of strong beer within living memory to 3½d. per pot. Though this was largely the consequence of increased taxation on beer, the measure had been concerted with the brewers, and had provoked considerable popular outcry.[140] It was still a sufficiently bitter grievance for publicans to make great play of their reduction of the price of beer on special Wilkite occasions to the traditional 3d. per pot. It is possible that some publicans—though not the brewers—were united with their customers in opposing the rise, and that they were using Wilkes to voice their objections to the tax. Some Wilkite medals seem to refer to this issue with their 'three pence' markings, and the giant vat built in Tooley Street was emblazoned with the slogan 'for beer at 3d. per pot' as well as with Wilkite inscriptions.[141] (Similar sentiments had been expressed about the cider tax in 1763. When Wilkes was in the Tower in that year he was sent a hamper of cider 'free from excise'.)[142] The landlords, therefore, may have been engaging in some politicking of their own, and they were supported by some of the radicals on the grounds that a direct tax on an essential commodity—such as beer—hurt the poor, while many of the (foreign) luxuries of the rich went unassessed.[143]

At the same time, landlords and brewers were under a certain amount of pressure from the radical societies to support the Wilkite cause. Thrale, the friend of Dr. Johnson and M.P. for Southwark, had voted against Wilkes in the Middlesex election and was in favour of his expulsion from the Commons. As a result, there were a number of attempts to persuade his landlords to change their brewery. Boycott was threatened if the proprietor failed to comply, and it is possible that there was also the threat of the removal of club savings from the brewer. This was a serious matter: loss of

---

[138] Brewer, *Party Ideology*, pp. 194–5.
[139] *Worcester Journal*, 26 January, 2, 28 February, 1 June 1769, 29 March 1770; *Bristol Journal*, 11 March 1769; *Middlesex Journal*, 27 May 1769.
[140] Mathias, *Brewing Industry*, pp. 112–3, 115.
[141] *Middlesex Journal*, 29 April 1769; B. M. Coins and Medals, Tray 145, M4749.
[142] *Newcastle Courant*, 21 May 1763.
[143] *Middlesex Journal*, 29 June 1769.

trade was bad enough, but withdrawal of society savings might run to hundreds of pounds. It is hardly suprising that Ben Truman was careful to let his signature of the Middlesex petition be known, and that he made a £50 donation to the SSBR.[144]

It is perfectly possible, of course, that Truman had radical sympathies. A great many publicans—though rather fewer brewers—seem to have been only too willing to take an active political role in the radical movement. Take 'Lord Mills', a publican in Fleet Market, for example. He attended the London parliamentary election of 1768 in the hackney carriage no.45 which he had hired especially for the occasion. In April 1769 he went to Brentford in a magnificent coach and six and paid for the transport of forty-five others to vote for Wilkes. In the following August at Barnet Races he put on a similar display arriving in a coach and four, on top of which 'sat a man with a blue flag in his hand, with "Magna Charta" and "The Bill of Rights" marked on it. On each of the four corners of the coach was a small blue flag with the same words, and on the front of the horses' head a blue paper was fixed with number 45 painted on it'.[145] These activities, of course, could simply have been a form of self-advertisement. But it was also 'Lord Mills' who, together with William Penrice, a former turnkey in the King's Bench, and landlord of the Surrey Tavern, rented the coffins which were used in the ceremonial execution on Tower Hill of effigies of the nation's political leaders on 1 April 1771.[146]

Nearly all publicans and vintners, regardless of their political affiliations, could see the manifest benefits that could be obtained by encouraging Wilkite celebrations and radical junketing. The landlord who sold 'Wilkes's eye-water'—so strong it made you cross-eyed—the tavern proprietor in Southampton who donated a bull for baiting at his door, and the publican who treated his regular customers to a side of beef on the occasion of Wilkes's release were all attempting to generate continued interest in their business and the radical cause.[147]

In some ways these efforts seem excessive: why try to exploit what was apparently a transitory phenomenon, likely to bring only short-term benefits? But the evanescent event, the special occasion, can, provided it is celebrated with sufficient panache, and made remarkable by its extravagance and pageantry, become a fixed addition to the calendar. The eighteenth-century market was not merely seasonal but *calendrical*. Holidays, as every publican, confectioner, baker, chapman, pedlar and hawker knew, were occasions of popular conspicuous consumption and traditional present giving. New Year's Day, for instance, was the date for giving books (usually almanacks), gloves,

[144] Brewer, *Party Ideology*, p. 197; *Middlesex Journal*, 18 May 1769.
[145] *Worcester Journal*, 20 April 1769; *Middlesex Journal*, 17 August 1769.
[146] *Middlesex Journal*, 2 November 1769; P. R. O., T. S./11/603/1972.
[147] *Salisbury Journal*, 16 April 1770; *Western Flying Post*, 16 April 1770; *Middlesex Journal*, 30 August 1769.

cakes and confections, pins, written verses and many sorts of produce.[148] Whit Monday and the dates of harvest festivals were important stimuli to popular spending. A special festival or celebration such as the Bicentennial of Shakespeare's birth organized by Garrick in Stratford in 1768 was very often justified in terms of the economic benefits it brought to local traders.[149]

In a similar fashion, politics was essentially a calendrical market. Far too little attention had been paid to the emergence during the eighteenth century of a Hanoverian political calendar, designed to inculcate loyal values in the populace, and to emphasize and encourage the growth of a national political consensus. Nearly every English market town celebrated the dates which were considered the important political landmarks of the nation. They can be found in most almanacks of the period, barely distinguishable from the time-honoured dates of May Day, Plough Monday, Twelfth Night, Shrove Tuesday and the like. The relevant dates were: the current monarch's birthday (28 May, 30 October, 24 May for the first three Georges); 29 May, Charles II's birthday, and the date of the Restoration, when it was customary to wear a sprig of oak on 'Oak Apple Day'; 1 August, the date of the Hanoverian succession (the First of August Society was one of the clubs which supported Wilkes); 4 November, William III's birthday and the occasion of his landing at Torbay; 5 November, Powder Plot; and finally, less frequently, Queen Elizabeth's Day, 17 November.[150]

In the early eighteenth century, these dates, together with the occasion of the Pretender's birthday, were occasions of conflict. The year of the Jacobite rebellion, 1715, was especially contentious, with Hanoverian Mug House clubs fighting it out in the streets with Jacobite apprentices and artisans. On October 30, frequenters of a Jacobite alehouse on Ludgate Hill were beaten up by members of the Loyal Society who were celebrating the birthday of the Prince of Wales, the future George II. A Jacobite attempt to burn William III in effigy on November 4 was thwarted by the same Whig clubmen who the next day tried to cremate effigies of the Pretender and his supporters. On 17 November further clashes ensued and two Jacobites were shot dead.[151]

By mid-century, however, these anniversaries were more commonly marked by the breaking open of a hogshead of beer then by the breaking of heads. Feasting, entertainment and present-giving replaced rapine and violence. Republican whigs continued to attend their Calves-Head feasts on 30 January and to drink to 'Old Noll' while the rest of the nation fasted, and

---

[148] A. R. Wright, *British Calendar Customs*, ed. T. F. Lones (3 vols, London, 1936-40), II, p. 26.

[149] L. Fox, 'A Splendid Occasion: the Stratford Jubilee of 1769', *Dugdale Society Occasional Papers* XX (1973); *Middlesex Journal*, 10 August 1769.

[150] Examples of such celebrations are almost too numerous to mention. The most perfunctory glance at an eighteenth-century newspaper reveals a vast body of evidence on these calendrical occasions.

[151] See footnote 94.

Jacobite drinking clubs persisted, but by mid-century unanimity seems to have emerged. The Hanoverian calendar was strongly monarchist and loyalist: hence its inclusion of the Restoration as well as the Hanoverian succession. Any indication that the calendar was declining provoked controversy and criticism. As was pointed out, if, through the decline of the festivals, the populace failed to realize where their true loyalty lay, the English political heritage would lapse together with its much vaunted liberties.[152] The Duke of Northumberland had the Prince of Wales's birthday celebrated in Alnwick by collecting together local children born in the same year as the Prince who were examined on their catechism. The most proficient youth was rewarded with a garland while the occasion concluded 'with such innocent rejoicings as may strongly impress their little minds, and inspire them with sentiments of loyalty, as it were, from the very cradle'. No wonder that Thomas Percy remarked, 'did all the nobility as strongly interest themselves in inspiring proper sentiments among their dependents as our good Duke and Duchess do, we should see a very different spirit prevail amongst the lower orders, from what we do at present'.[153]

Though they placed greater emphasis on the self-funding of independent celebrations and tried to avoid the treating and indiscriminate largesse of loyalist commemorations, the radical societies of the 1760s, in their turn, were implacably devoted to the establishment of a ritualized Wilkite calendar. Wilkes's birthday, the anniversary of the St. George's Fields Massacre, the numerous Middlesex elections, the release of Wilkes from the King's Bench, each of these occasions was feted not merely as a celebration but as a means of impinging upon the popular political conscience in a way that the government had employed for over a generation.[154]

For those who tried to commercialize politics the Wilkite calendar meant more than this: it provided them with an even greater number of celebratory occasions which could be transformed into profitable ventures. The activities of the pottery industry illustrate this admirably. Wilkes was not the first political figure, nor was the radical crisis of 1768–72 the first political upheaval that the potters had exploited. Ever since the Popish plot, when delftware tiles, based on a design taken from contemporary playing cards had been marketed in London,[155] there had been specialized political ceramics. These fell into a discernible pattern. Nearly all the cups, mugs, punchbowls and plates were designed either to commemorate a particular individual, or

---

[152] *Northampton Mercury*, 12 November 1733.
[153] Thomas Percy to Northumberland, 22 August 1768, Northumberland Papers, vol. 43/108.
[154] *Newcastle Journal*, 9, 23 April, 18 June 1768; *Norwich Mercury*, 4 November 1769; *Worcester Journal*, 7 April, 4 November 1768, 23 February, 16 March, 2 November 1769; *Pope's Bath Chronicle*, 7 April 1768; *Felix Farley's Bristol Journal*, 2 April 1768; *Bristol Journal*, 4 March 1769; *Cambridge Chronicle*, 18 June 1768; *Gloucester Journal*, 18 April 1768; *Oxford Magazine* (1768), p. 163; *Middlesex Journal*, 18 April, 23 September, 26, 31 October, 7 November 1769; *Newcastle Chronicle*, 4 November 1769, 14 April 1770; *Newcastle Journal*, 4 March 1769, 28 April 1770; Brewer, *Party Ideology*, pp. 178–9.
[155] Antony Ray, *English Delftware Tiles* (London, 1973), pp. 114–5.

to celebrate a particular occasion—whether it be an election, a royal birthday or a military victory—or as a special order for a club or society. The individuals were frequently opposition heroes: clearly the category in which Wilkes belonged, but which also included Sacheverell—portrayed on delftware plates—the elder Pitt and Admiral Vernon. Vernon, of course, was celebrated not simply because of his politics but because of his victories against the Spanish. Together with Cumberland, Wolfe and Frederick the Great he occupied the ceramic pantheon of military heroes. Monarchs, including the Pretender, were also strongly in evidence. The occasions celebrated by ceramics closely paralleled the heroes that were portrayed. Royal birthdays, weddings and coronations were all represented, together with the Hanoverian political calendar and military victories such as Portobello, Culloden and Quebec. The Popish Plot, the Act of Union, the Excise Crisis, the 1745 Rebellion, and a great many elections (a speciality of West Country potters) were similarly commemorated. Finally, there were the clubs: the innumberable masonic lodges with their insignia, drinkingware and badges decorated with the arms of the order; the pseudomasonic Bucks, AntiGallicans and Albions; charity and reforming associations such as the Marine Society and the Abolitionist Society; and the tavern clubs—some of them Jacobite—that met in hostelries like the Butcher's Arms in Hereford or the appropriately named Royal Oak.[156]

What exactly are we to make of this phenomenon? The parallels between Wilkes and some of the other individuals are clear enough: they were popular heroes who enjoyed an enormous amount of publicity and who provided a short-term opportunity to sell ceramic wares. (It is noticeable how many of the standard products of potters were either painted over or transfer printed to cater for these temporary novelties, though not all potters were as cynical as those in early nineteenth-century Liverpool who produced a 'Hunt and Liberty Cup' by printing the slogan over one of their standard pictures of American naval heroes.)[157]

The careers of Sacheverell, Vernon, Pitt and even Frederick the Great prefigure the experience of Wilkes. Sacheverell was the proximate cause of rioting, had confections, fighting cocks and children named after him: exactly the same was true of Wilkes.[158] There were commemorative medals struck to celebrate Vernon's victories, he gave his name to the prize flower at a florists' feast, his birthday and the anniversary of his victories were all

[156] Ray, *English Delftware Pottery*, pp. 115-8; R. L. Hobson, *Catalogue of the Collection of English Pottery in the British Museum*, (London, 1905), pp. 136, 142-4, 148, 160, 179, 182, 185, 187-9, 196, 198, 201; B. Watney, *English Blue and White Porcelain* (London, 1973), pp. 48, 52; Lane, *English Porcelain Figures*, p. 54; William Turner, *Transfer Printing* (London, 1907), p. 69.

[157] J. & J. May, *Commemorative Pottery, 1780-1900. A Guide for Collectors* (London, 1972), p. 136.

[158] Geoffrey Holmes, *The Trial of Doctor Sacheverell* (London, 1973), pp. 156-76, 233-6, 240-1, 244-8, 254.

occasions of jubilation, and his praises were sung in many contemporary ballads and broadsides. There was even an *Admiral Vernon's Weekly Journal*.[159] Pitt, of course, enjoyed a comparable popularity, while Frederick the Great—the first political figure to be commemorated on a transfer printed ceramic[160]—enjoyed quite extraordinary notoriety. As Horace Walpole remarked:[161]

> All England kept his birthday: it has taken its place in our calendar next to Admiral Vernon's ... the people I believe think that Prussia is a part of Old England.... It is incredible how popular he is here: except a few who take him for the same person as Mr. Pitt, the lowest of the people are perfectly acquainted with him: as I was walking by the river the other night, a bargeman asked me for something to drink the King of Prussia's health.

In fact both Frederick and William, Duke of Cumberland were celebrated in more ceramic pieces than was Wilkes.

In dealing with heroes, celebrations and clubs, the potters had isolated a rather more complicated market than might at first appear. The ceramics that were decorated with the features of individuals or slogans in their favour were also those used on special occasions. A mug with the portrait of the Duke of Cumberland would be purchased for the special celebration and subsequent anniversaries of the victory of Culloden. Patriot whigs could toast the Duke and heap imprecations on the hapless Pretender and his Scottish allies. Thus one such vessel reads 'In remembrance of the Glorious Victory of Culleaen [sic] April 16 1746' while another punchbowl declares 'Confusion to the Pretender 1746'.[162] Ceramics of Vernon frequently include the actual date of his triumph at Portobello, reminding their purchasers of the appropriate date to celebrate his patriotic victory.[163] Royal ceramics were used for royal birthdays. The medium was the message: one punchbowl reads, 'Now friends are mett/Lets drink and sing/A health to George/Our British King'.[164] Rather more fancy wares were produced for royal coronations or weddings, because they could be given as gifts to friends as part of the celebrations associated with such special occasions.[165] The potters were exploiting the Hanoverian calendar—and some dissident variants of it—in precisely the same manner as the brewers and publicans.

---

[159] George Watson (ed.), *The New Cambridge Bibliography of English Literature*, vol. 2. *1660–1800* (Cambridge, 1971), p. 1331; B. Watney, *English Blue and White Porcelain*, p. 18; Bernard Rackham, *Catalogue of the Glaisher Collection* (2 vols. Cambridge, 1935) I, p. 79; Nick Rogers, 'Aristocratic Clientage, Trade and Independency', *Past and Present* 61 (1973), p. 96; *Northampton Mercury*, 23 March, 14 April, 23 August 1740.

[160] Price, *Sadler*, p. 21; *Gentleman's Magazine* (1757), p. 564.

[161] Walpole to Mann, 9 February 1758, *The Yale Correspondence of Horace Walpole* (37 vols. to date, New Haven, 1937–), XXI, p. 171.

[162] Hobson, *Catalogue of Pottery*, pp. 136, 144, 148; Ray, *English Delftware Pottery*, pp. 117, 125.

[163] Hobson, *Catalogue of Pottery*, pp. 182, 188; Housman, *Notes on the Willett Collection*.

[164] Ray, *English Delftware Pottery*, p. 117.

[165] Housman, *Notes on the Willett Collection*.

Ceramics made for special occasions were, in turn, used for club feasts and to vaunt the praises of specific individuals. Electoral pottery, such as that produced in Bristol for elections in Devonshire, Tewkesbury, Taunton, Barnstaple, Wooton Bassett and Bristol itself, very often served this purpose. At the Taunton election of 1754 Sir John Pole held an electoral feast at which the guests ate off plates inscribed 'Sir Jno Pole for ever', and which they were allowed to take home with them to commemorate the occasion.[166] Club ceramics were also produced to praise their heroes: Jacobite clubs bought punchbowls of the Pretender or of the famous Oak Tree—used to celebrate the Restoration and the Pretender's birthday—while John Sadler, the transfer printer, decorated an entire series of masonic mugs with the mason's arms flanked by William Pitt and the Marquis of Granby.[167]

But perhaps the best example of the interlocking nature of this market was the relationship between Frederick the Great and the Bucks. The famous transfer of Frederick, produced by John Sadler, taken from a contemporary engraving, and loudly praised in rather bad verse in the *Gentleman's Magazine,* was probably produced to celebrate Frederick's birthday. But the King of Prussia, as Sadler's own paper, the *Liverpool Chronicle,* reminded its readers, was not only a brave soldier, a patriot and a friend to Britain, but also a brother freemason. For all of these reasons, lodges of the Bucks and masons regularly celebrated Frederick's birthday, just as they celebrated that of the English king. Though it is not possible to demonstrate conclusively that the Bucks and masons were the first or chief purchasers of the transfer artifacts of Frederick, it is clear that they were the customers that Sadler had in mind. They had organized celebrations, saluted Frederick as their hero, were numerous and had the wealth and wherewithal to guarantee Sadler a reasonable sale. They were not, in any sense, a mass market, but as a group they offered a larger potential sale for customized items than any individual. So that, when Sadler advertised an enamelled portrait of Frederick in the *Liverpool Chronicle,* he was also careful to include an announcement about the production of his latest Bucks' and Freemasons' medals.[168]

It was Sadler who really developed the transfer printing which was such an enormous boon to the production of custom-made ceramics. Transferring was both far quicker and far cheaper than hand-painting as a means of producing distinctive items, and it meant that bulk orders could be handled more easily. The finished artifact was often more finely executed than by the craftsman's brush and produced a more standardized product. And, undoubtedly, one of the most important of Sadler's markets for transfer-printed wares were the masons and pseudo-masonic societies. Transfer-printed items for the Bucks included membership medals on enamel, tiles, mugs, jugs,

---

[166] Hobson, *Catalogue of Pottery,* p. 144; Ray, *English Delftware Pottery,* pp. 127–8.
[167] Price, *Sadler,* p. 48; Hobson, *Catalogue of Pottery,* p. 142.
[168] Price, *Sadler,* p. 80; *Liverpool Chronicle,* 20 January, 10 November, 15 December 1758.

teapots and bowls, all decorated with the society's arms. The patriotic Anti-Gallicans also ordered transfer mugs and badges. Quart, pint and half-pint mugs decorated with masonic symbols were a staple part of the trade of Sadler and his partner, Green, for well over a decade. They wrote regularly to Wedgwood requesting pottery ranging from coffee cups to milk jugs which they inscribed for their masonic customers.[169]

For the politician the ceramics played an important part in the expression and development of a political culture. For men like Wilkes, they were a vital prop in the ritual performances of political allegiance and solidarity, giving forceful expression to political sentiment. Their inscriptions were often the actual toasts of those who drank from them and they thus acted both as a slogan-bearer and a prompt sheet. Ceramics were, in a very real sense, *cartes d'identité*. The Mug House Clubs at the Hanoverian succession were so called because of the drinking vessels that were hung in the taverns which they frequented. The traditional convivial sentiments associated with drinking—'Fill me Full of Licker that is Seet for/ for it is Good when friends do met'—were given political meaning. Thus a white earthenware jug of 1807 declares on its side: 'He that calls here/ Shall have this full of beer/ That gave Milton/ a Plumper'.[170] The suitably inscribed drinking vessel was just as much a part of the political proceedings as casting one's vote or burning Lord Bute or Don Blass (the stereotypical Spaniard) in effigy. Political allegiance, equality and unity were given tangible expression by the pottery itself: supporters all drank from the same punchbowl—they shared it communally—mugs and drinking vessels were usually of equal size and bore the same inscriptions. Just as the club ceramics expressed the bonds within their society, so did the pottery produced for a special celebratory occasion.

For the potter, however, the political artifact represented a means of diversifying his product—a move greatly facilitated by the development of transfer printing—as well as a way of exploiting temporary fads. Like the publicans, they saw the chances created by this calendrical market and, in doing so, made an important contribution to the evolution of distinctive political styles. We should not, of course, exaggerate the importance of political pottery and commemoratives for the trade as a whole. They might serve, as no doubt Sadler hoped, to draw attention to particular businesses and to advertise relatively new processes. But the marketing of potters and transfer printers does illustrate, once again, the power of the lodge and club. Groups of men, not individuals—except for the occasional aristocrat, were the predominant purchasers of political artifacts in pottery.

The contribution that publicans and potters made to the Wilkite movement

[169] Price, *Sadler*, pp. 21, 48-9, 61, 80; Guy Green to Wedgwood, 22 July 1771, Wedgwood/Etruria Mss 5-3394-3663; ibid. [January 1781?], Wedgwood/Etruria Mss 5-30475-30478.
[170] Rackham, *Catalogue of the Glaisher Collection*.

was enormously facilitated by the activities of the most important entrepreneurial group to the radicals, namely the printers and booksellers who published and sold newspapers and political propaganda. By the 1760s London had four daily papers, five or six tri-weekly evening papers—which circulated extensively in the provinces—and innumerable evanescent weekly and fortnightly political essay papers.[171] The Metropolis lay at the centre of a large information network which reached out through most of provincial England. Each week thirty-five provincial papers, in locations as diverse as Newcastle and Sherborne, crammed their pages with news gleaned from the London tri-weeklies which arrived with the posts.[172] The press—newspaper and pamphlet, cartoon and song—put Wilkes and his followers on the national political map. Newspaper readers throughout the nation learnt not only about Wilkes's activities in London, but of the demonstrations in his favour in cities and market towns as far apart as Berwick-on-Tweed and Penzance. Radicals such as Sir Watkin Lewes and John Glynn were welcomed in the provinces because of the news coverage of their strenuous efforts in the cause of liberty.[173] At the same time, the press gave the congeries of grievances that made up the radical cause a coherence and unity that it would otherwise have lacked. Local grievances were compared and seen as part of a national problem. But, above all else, the press shaped and moulded the radical political culture. It was the advertising medium for Wilkite artifacts and, by reporting the highly elaborate radical demonstrations, as well as devoting considerable space to the enormous number of gifts that were sent to Wilkes in gaol, it encouraged others to emulate these expressions of support. Without the press Wilkes and his followers would never have achieved notoriety, nor have become more than a metropolitan phenomenon.

The printers and booksellers who directly supported Wilkes were not a cross-section of the publishing world, nor a haphazard collection of printers; they were a clearly defined group. Such coherence was symptomatic of the organization of a publishing industry which had reached a high degree of specialization by the accession of George III. Individuals, partnerships and collectives—known as congers—each developed their own area of expertise: the partnership of J. Cooke and J. Coote, for example, concentrated on jest books and chronicles of crime; Johnson and Payne, on the other hand, tended to publish religious and theological works, especially those that appealed to dissenters.[174] Not surprisingly, therefore, Wilkes's allies in the printing trade were usually specialists in the field of polemical political literature, and many of them—such as Isaac Fell and Meres, the proprietor of the fiercely

---

[171] Brewer, *Party Ideology*, p. 142.
[172] Brewer, *Party Ideology*, pp. 142-3.
[173] Lewes stood as a radical candidate for Worcester in the 1773 by-election. Glynn defended the burgesses of Newcastle in their fight with the corporation over the Town Moor.
[174] H. R. Plomer, G. H. Bushnell & E. R. McC. Dix, *A Dictionary of the Printers and Booksellers who were at work. 1726 to 1776* (Oxford, 1932), pp. 60-1, 141.

anti-government *London Evening Post*[175]—had been leading luminaries of the opposition press long before Wilkes became a *cause célèbre*.

Very few of the printers and booksellers who published Wilkite propaganda seem to have been members of the most powerful group in the trade, the Chapter Coffee House 'Chapter' which published such works as Gibbon, Hume and Dr. Johnson. Most of this establishment group were at best lukewarm and more usually overtly hostile to Wilkes. Strahan, with an income of about £10,000 a year, and the post of royal printer, was part proprietor of the *London Chronicle,* one of the very few papers which tended to favour the government. His close friend and partner, Andrew Millar, refused to publish the *North Briton* when asked to by Wilkes, while Millar's successor, Cadell, marketed anti-radical material including Dr. Johnson's acerbic *False Alarm*. W. Nicoll, another member of this group, was one of the chief publishers of pro-government pamphlets in the early years of George III's reign.[176] Only Henry Sampson Woodfall was a member both of this powerful group and of the coterie of radical printers. Of course, many of these important booksellers held shares in newspapers in which they had invested to facilitate the marketing of their books, periodicals and pamphlets, together with the patent medicines which were such a lucrative sideline of the publishing business.[177] But even if for political reasons they had wanted to exclude Wilkes from the newspapers, they knew that to do so would have been commercial suicide. They were therefore grudgingly instrumental in reporting Wilkite activities, even though they failed to lend active support to the movement.

The most ardent protagonists of the Wilkite cause were not, therefore, at the pinnacle of the publishing trade, though they were the most experienced publishers of oppositionist propaganda, specializing in the hazardous but very profitable enterprise of vilifying the all-too-vulnerable patricians who ran the nation. Many were old acquaintances, drinking partners and dining companions of Wilkes. John Almon had been one of Wilkes's chief contacts in London while he had been in exile and had plied him with advice and (rather more reluctantly) with money. T. Baldwin and the Davises—father and son—were Wilkes's dining companions. T. Becket's premises were used by Wilkes as a mailing address and he kept the patriot supplied with the latest political magazines and journals. Meres, in turn, had his house at the Old Bailey consigned to Wilkes so that he could qualify for the aldermanic

---

[175] For which see G. A. Cranfield, 'The *London Evening Post* and the Jew Bill of 1753', *Historical Journal* VIII (1965), pp. 16–30.

[176] Plant, *The English Book Trade*, p. 223; Steve Botein, ' "Meer Mechanics" and an open press: business and political strategies of the colonial American printers', *Perspectives in American History* IX (1975), p. 141; J. A. Cochrane, *Dr. Johnson's Printer: the Life of William Strahan* (London, 1964), pp. 170–1.

[177] M. R. A. Harris, The London Newspaper c.1725–1746 (unpub. Ph.D., Univ. of London, 1974), pp. 96–8.

election of Farringdon Without. Several of these printers and booksellers extended their radical activities beyond the press and the pamphlet shop. Almon proposed the vote of thanks after the pro-Wilkite Westminster petition was drafted in August 1769 and lashed out at those who claimed that the likes of mean booksellers should stick to their trade and keep their noses out of politics. The Davises were both active members of the SSBR. Dryden Leach, one of the original printers of the *North Briton*, used his influence in the ward of Farringdon Without to increase Wilkes's power in the City. Oppositionist printers did not hesitate to come forward for Wilkes's cause.[178]

This was also the group that displayed the greatest ingenuity in marketing pro-Wilkite printed material. John Williams, the bookseller who published many Wilkite tracts and cartoons and who had stood in the pillory for publishing the *North Briton*, was the inspiration behind *English Liberty Established*, the most remarkable of a number of single sheets and handbills dedicated to Wilkes. Each of these had its individual selling point: one would include Wilkes's speeches, another a miniaturized portrait of him which could be cut out and used 'for a Watch Paper'.[179] But *English Liberty Established* was the most elaborate of them all. It displayed on one sheet a portrait of Wilkes holding the Bill of Rights, a portrayal of his interrogation by the Secretaries of State, a depiction of his carriage being dragged through the streets by a joyous mob, an extract from his letter to the Duke of Grafton, his speech in favour of liberty in the Court of Common Pleas, an address to the Middlesex freeholders, and a speech in the Court of King's Bench. A tidy encapsulation of the whole radical cause, and all this for 6d., though it 'would not, according to the usual Custom of Trade, be fixed at less than a shilling, but the price is put low, so that every one who has a regard for Mr. Wilkes may purchase it'. The print was advertised in a great many provincial newspapers. Readers were urged to buy quickly in order to get a copy of the first impression. Every patriot, the *Worcester Journal* urged, ought to have one in his home. The *Newcastle Journal* advertisement was accompanied by a story designed to win the sixpences of even the humblest of men:

> The following, which is a real matter of fact, may serve as one instance to shew the prodigious regard the populace have for Mr. Wilkes—One of them passing by a shop, where the print of Mr. Wilkes entitled, *English Liberty Established*, hung up in the window, ey'd it attentively for some time, and then going into the shop purchased it; on which a gentleman that happened to be in the shop said, I imagine you are a Wilkite; that I am, replied the other, and perhaps more than you; for this is the only six-pence I have in the world, and it shall go for this Print: Will you do as much for the cause?

---

[178] *Worcester Journal*, 19 October 1769; Brewer, *Party Ideology*, p. 174; Heaton Wilkes to John Wilkes, B. L. Add. Mss 30869 f.154; Diary, 3 December 1774, B. L. Add. Mss 30866.

[179] Brewer, *Party Ideology*, pp. 172-3.

It was this sort of appeal and the careful distribution of the print which accompanied it which explains why Williams and the printer Lee were so successful with this enormously popular item.[180]

Old acquaintances and allies of Wilkes were behind the serial publication of his works and correspondence. These 'part books', sold a few pages at a time, were, of course, a very popular technique for a whole range of publications from the Bible to medical and gardening dictionaries, but their first use for political literature seems to have been during the Wilkes affair. John Baskerville, japanner, freethinker and friend of Wilkes, printed a serial edition of Wilkes's works, with subscriptions in seventeen different locations in the Midlands as well as in London. Baldwin and Woodgate also published serials of Wilkes's works, promising that 'In the last number will be given a beautiful engraved frontispiece of Mr. Wilkes's Head; a view of the Massacre of St. George's Fields; the murder of Clarke by Balfe and Macquirk at Brentford ... with a complete index and patriotic dedication'. Another serial appeared in 45 parts, stitched in blue paper (the Wilkite colour), and was distributed throughout the nation together with the tri-weekly papers. Its first number could be had on loan for two days for those who were interested: surely one of the earliest examples of inertia selling.[181]

One of the chief characteristics of Wilkite publications was their broad appeal: they were tailored to attract all those interested in politics, whether rich or poor. One of Woodgate's other projects illustrates this admirably. He produced the *New Form of Prayer and Thanksgiving for the Happy Deliverance of John Wilkes*. This blasphemous rendition of the creed went through nine editions in a year, became a popular street song and was established on both sides of the Atlantic. It appeared in three different versions: one, in chapbook form, was intended for the poorest of Wilkes's supporters, while the quarto and folio editions catered to bourgeois and genteel taste.[182]

The printers and booksellers who were most imaginative in their selling techniques were often the most radical in their politics. Quite possibly their political ardour led them to feats of greater ingenuity and to take greater risks than was customary. A number or radicals even risked starting new publications. Almon established the *Political Register,* the most sophisticated radical periodical, and one that invariably included its own political cartoons and prints. William Bingley began the *Freeholders Magazine* and the short-lived *Independent Chronicle*, while Fell became the first printer of the radical tri-weekly, the *Middlesex Journal*. These papers and journals all began with the most pious of sentiments: 'we undertake to vindicate the cause of depressed liberty, by exhibiting, in full view of the people, every measure

[180] On *English Liberty* see *Pope's Bath Chronicle*, 19 May 1768; *Felix Farley's Bristol Journal*, 28 May, 16 July 1768; *Cambridge Chronicle*, 4 June, 30 July 1768; *Worcester Journal*, 21 July 1768; *Newcastle Journal*, 28 May, 9 July 1769.
[181] On Wilkite serials see Brewer, *Party Ideology*, p. 172; *Worcester Journal*, 6 April, 18 May, 1769, 22 November 1770; *Middlesex Journal*, 11 April, 6 May 1769.
[182] Brewer, *Party Ideology*, p. 173.

that has already been taken ... upon that great charter of our laws, the Palladium of English liberty', promised the *Middlesex Journal*.[183] The *Freeholders Magazine* and the *Independent Chronicle* began in the same vein. 'Deprived of freedome, for contributing my Mite to the great cause of Liberty', read Bingley's advertisements, 'the only service that I can perform for my Country whose welfare I prefer to my own, is to introduce to the public the sentiments of those bold and intrepid patriots, who are determined to oppose the torrent of arbitrary power and corruption'.[184] The *Middlesex Journal*, indeed, became the English muckraker and constitutional watchdog *par excellence*: sexual malpractice amongst the aristocracy (the Cumberland/Grosvenor correspondence, Luttrell's illicit affair with Miss Bolton—both of which were announced in the best 'shock! horror!' fashion), abuses of the client economy, bakers who sold underweight, crooked lawyers and trading justices, malicious prosecutions were all exposed in the paper which issued dire warnings to the transgressors.[185] Such copy was very popular. Though the *Middlesex Journal* was accused by its critics of riding a political wave and of being a party paper—and both accusations were correct—it was also a huge success. Copies of the first number of the paper were reprinted again and again, and back numbers were sold in the form of complete sets.[186] Bingley, however, was rather less fortunate. He tried to titillate his audience with engraved heads of Wilkes (by this time a *must* for every self-respecting radical paper), Sawbridge, Glynn and Horne Tooke in the *Freeholders Magazine*, but by the third number he was forced to announce that, 'In compliance with the request of many of our customers, the political part of our Magazine shall, for the future, be confined to a certain quantity; and the rest be devoted to miscellaneous articles for general instruction and amusement'. His fellow proprietors as well as the readers could not stomach so much political stodge.[187]

Bingley, no doubt, had overreached himself: he went bankrupt in 1771 when the schism that developed within the SSBR led his creditors to foreclose on him. But the efforts of zealots such as he, Almon and Fell, together with Wilkes's own activities generated a 'bandwagon effect'. So much controversy, so much polemic led others with less idealistic motives to try to exploit the burgeoning interest in politics. The period 1768–74 saw a tremendous growth not only in the volume of the press, but also in the number of new publications trying to seize the opportunity created by the radicals. The *London Packet*, the *London Museum*, the *Gentleman's Museum*, the *Cambridge Magazine*, the *Court Miscellany*, the *Patriot*, and the *British Oracle* all appeared for

[183] *Middlesex Journal*, 4 April 1769.
[184] *Felix Farley's Bristol Journal*, 23 September, 7 October 1769; *Worcester Journal*, 21 September 1769.
[185] *Middlesex Journal*, 4 April, 27 May, 3 June 1769; *Farley's Bristol Journal*, 7 July 1770; *Newcastle Journal*, 8 April 1769; *Worcester Journal*, 13 April 1769.
[186] *Middlesex Journal*, 15, 27 April, 6 May 1769.
[187] *Worcester Journal*, 7 December 1769; *North Briton* CLXVI.

the first (and often the last) time in these years. As J. Bell, the proprietor of the famous circulating library in the Strand, put it: 'It is no less surprising than true, that the Vegetation of Newspapers within the last six months has been of the mushroom kind; and many of them, no doubt enjoy full as precarious an existence'. Yet Bell, like others, was not averse to leaping on the bandwagon himself. Some of the essays in these papers, he argued, were worth preserving, and for this reason he planned a serial compendium of the the best materials.[188]

Even the traditional press had to respond to the craze for politics. In 1769 and 1770 joke books, an enduring and profitable *genre* in the publishing industry, had to have political titles or, at least, certain political jokes. Wilkes's *Jest Book* or *Jemmy Twitcher's Jests* were the wit and wisdom of the hour. Similarly the well-established magazines had to pander to the new, radical sensibility. The *London Magazine,* still eager to outstrip its indubitably superior rival, the *Gentleman's Magazine,* ran engravings of Catharine Macaulay, the radical historian, Junius, who naturally presented no problems of representational accuracy, Pasquale Paoli, the Corsican Patriot, and Wilkes himself. The last engraving, it was claimed, was more valuable than the cost of the magazine itself. The same sort of tactics were adopted by the *Oxford Magazine.* Even the shadiest of publishing ventures acquired a radical tinge. *Memoirs of the Amours of the Duke of Grafton* succeeded, in five numbers and a copper plate, in combining sexual prurience with political moralism.[189]

Most these projects were symptomatic of the printers' and booksellers' eagerness to seize the main chance, and to respond swiftly to changes in taste and fashion. Politics was popular, the order of the day, and was therefore provided. Indeed, frequently there seems to have been little concern with the actual content of the material, very little sense of the message conveyed. Those who leapt on the radical bandwagon, as opposed to the identifiably radical printers themselves, were simply out to make a quick buck, though not all were as transparent about their intentions as Pine and Roberts, the proprietors of the new tri-weekly *London Packet.* Their advertisement is worth quoting in full as an attempt to justify the founding of a new paper for no higher motive than sheer profit:[190]

> Nothing is more customary with the Proprietors of newspapers, at their first setting out, than Professions of Candour, Integrity and Benevolence. *Their* works are not undertaken with any sordid view of private gain, but established wholely from the most exalted desire of public benefit. *They* have no *despicable* self interest to advance, but are stimulated *entirely* by a generous solicitude for the welfare of their fellow citizens; besides these arguments *they* always find auxiliary reasons for troubling the world with a new paper in the dulness or partiality of their rival news writers.

[188] *Felix Farley's Bristol Journal,* 23 December 1769.
[189] *Worcester Journal,* 23 June, 11, 31 August 1769; *Felix Farley's Bristol Journal,* 28 April 1768; *Farley's Bristol Journal,* 3 March, 14 July 1770.
[190] *Felix Farley's Bristol Journal,* 4 November 1769.

The proprietors of the LONDON PACKET, however, neither pique themselves on their disinterestedness, nor presumptously sit down to censure the productions of their neighbours: so far from being without their lucrative ends on this occasion, they candidly confess that their chief, nay their only, Inducement, is a hope of profiting by the Success of the Work.

But the payoff for the radical printers who supported Wilkes was never simply pecuniary. They engaged in a business that had always involved considerable risks. In particular, there were the hazards of the libel laws and state prosecution. The legal armoury available to the Attorney-General for combating the excesses of the press was truly formidable. He could use general warrants as a catch-all means of arresting those suspected of involvement in some libel. In 1728, for example, twenty-two people were taken into custody for a libel in *Mist's Weekly Journal*.[191] Printers were roughly tumbled out of bed, frog-marched away, locked up and often eventually released (there were many more warrants than persons brought to trial) without ever knowing why they had been apprehended in the first place.[192] If the Attorney-General applied for an *ex officio* information he could, in effect, have a printer incarcerated or bound over without trial. Sureties for good behaviour were often deliberately punitive: in 1723 Mist paid over £1,400, a crippling sum.[193] And once in court the cards were stacked against the accused for it was not the jury—usually, though not always sympathetic—but the judge who determined whether or not the material was libellous. In short, the laws governing libel, especially libel against the state or government, were severe to the point of being draconian, a situation attributed by contemporaries to their derivation from the practice of Star Chamber.[194] The law was a serious business risk for those who specialized in oppositionist publishing, especially as a prosecution often provoked the creditors of a printer to demand immediate payment of their bills.[195]

The debt the printers owed Wilkes, therefore, was not simply a financial one, for he showed the booksellers and publishers of papers a legal means of striking back at the government and of diminishing the threat of prosecution. Wilkes and his lawyer allies such as Serjeant Glynn were the inspiration behind a series of prosecutions brought against the government officials who had apprehended those suspected of involvement in the *North Briton* no.45. The decisions in *Leach* v. *Money*, *Wilkes* v. *Wood*, and *Entick* v. *Carrington* effectively put an end to general warrants and were a sharp reminder to the Secretary of State and the Attorney-General that the courts

---

[191] Hanson, *Government and the Press*, pp. 46–7.
[192] *The Life of Thomas Gent*, pp. 122–4.
[193] Hanson, *Government and the Press*, p. 54.
[194] Hanson, *Government and the Press*, p. 19.
[195] The experience of Kearsley in 1764. (Kearsley to Wilkes, [October 1764?], B. L. Add. Mss 30868 f.129).

of law could be used against them.[196] This lesson was not lost on printers and booksellers. William Bingley, for example, launched an attack on all of the special powers used by the Attorney-General and, when prosecuted, steadfastly refused to recognize the legality of interrogatories upon attachment.[197] The nub of the radicals' case was that libel cases should be treated like all others and proceed via the Grand Jury to a petty jury trial in which the twelve citizens rather than the judge decided whether there had been a breach of the law. Such arguments had been used in *Rex* v. *Almon* in 1765 and were the entire tenor of Glynn's impassioned appeal to the juries involved in the trial of the printers and publishers of Junius's Letter to the King. The tactic was an enormous success: of the defendants in the Junius trials only Almon was found guilty, because the juries, reminded so forcefully by Glynn of their supposed rights, refused to convict.[198] The effective power of the court was diminished.

Similar gains for the radical printers were achieved over the publication of parliamentary debates. Once again Wilkes and his lawyers were the inspiration behind the printers' defiance of authority. They used the jurisdictional and judicial power of the City of London to oppose the privileges of the Commons. When the lower House tried to take action against Wheble—the printer of the *Middlesex Journal*—and R. Thompson, the newspapermen failed to appear before the Bar of the House. Attempts to apprehend them only resulted in the arrest of a Commons' messenger, who was promptly charged before the city magistrates with assault and false imprisonment. It became impossible for the Commons to take retributive action against those who published their proceedings.[199]

This particular radical conspiracy, hatched at the Queen's Arms Tavern in St. Paul's Churchyard, vividly demonstrates the common interests of radicals and printers. The radical politicians wanted parliamentary reporting and a free press because they wished to ensure the accountability of the representative of the people; they sought a means of keeping the public informed so that the idea of on-going consent in government could be realized. For the printer the removal of legal constraints or, at least, a drastic reduction in their effectiveness made the task of reporting much easier and reduced the risks involved. By 1770 the public's demand for parliamentary news was such that the newspaper printers could ill-afford to omit reports of debates; failure to do so could effect sales adversely. There was clearly a growing market for such political news. If the printers were to exploit this successfully, and at minimum cost to themselves, they needed the help of the radicals who were the body most likely to protect and succour them.

[196] Hanson, *Government and the Press*, pp. 31-2.
[197] *North Briton*, LXIII-IV, LXXV, XCI, CLXXV.
[198] See Robert R. Rea, *The English Press in Politics, 1760-1774* (Lincoln, Neb., 1963), pp. 174-87.
[199] Rea, *The English Press in Politics*, pp. 201-11.

The commercial exploitation of the Wilkite agitation, and the commercial pressures that the movement put on such producers as newspaper printers and proprietors, touches upon one of the paradoxes or ambiguities that was never truly resolved by the radicals. Many of the calendrical celebrations and much of the feasting designed to publicize the radical cause and to demonstrate its hold on the nation at large was very much in the mould of traditional politics. True, there was greater emphasis on self-support and less on largesse, but all too often work came to a stop on a Wilkite holiday or election, and the populace gormandized and drank themselves into a stupor. The very potters who produced the custom-made electoral ware—punchbowls, mugs and the like—also complained bitterly of the difficulties they had in getting their employees to work while the rest of the community was out junketing. The paradox—that of using old methods for a new cause, one of whose aspirations was to undermine and destroy the old methods—was never really resolved, though a rough and ready compromise was worked out. The celebrations and demonstrations continued, but more and more emphasis was placed on the orderliness, discipline and self-control of the participants. Independent men, made free through association, and educated through the rules, ritual and constitutions of their own clubs and societies, sought to control their more enthusiastic and frequently more disruptive associates.

This tension reflected a basic difference within the radical movement. Wilkes and his immediate circle of friends were little concerned with effecting the basic social changes that were so strongly supported by the clubs and lodges. They saw the value (and profit) of using recently refined marketing and advertising techniques to publicize their cause, and perceived how the interests of the politicians could be harmonized with those of certain commercial groups. The use of a large carrot (profits) and the very occasional threat of a big stick (tavern boycotting by clubs, for example) kept the radicals and producers (when they were not one and the same person) working together. But the question was, 'working for what?'. Was the Wilkite movement to be merely a brilliantly orchestrated and skilfully advertised radical soap-opera (only one remove from the election of the Mayor of Garret), or did it have a coherent set of social and political objectives over and beyond the furtherance of John Wilkes's career? The Wilkite movement, of course, was many different things to different men: the views of the country gentlemen who signed the county petitions, and of the artisans, day-labourers and wage earners who rioted and demonstrated were a far cry from the opinions of the mercantile and trading supporters of Wilkes. Yet within this last group there was a hard core of radicals—centred on the clubs—who saw radical politics as a vehicle for creating a polity in which moveable property would play a new and more powerful role. Parliamentary reform, including a redistribution of seats based on all tax payments (not just the land tax), the increased enfranchisement of moveable property, the removal of placemen from the Commons, the introduction of the secret ballot (a stab at the heart of the client economy), together with legal and moral reforms would have changed British politics—and the distribution of power within the society—quite fundamentally.

The political culture from which these aspirations emanated deserves closer investigation. Can we, for example, find a comparable interest in mutual benefit and voluntary association amongst later radical groups? Do the issues of indebtedness, credit and reciprocal trading recur? Can it be argued that commercialization and a certain type of politics continued to work in tandem? Such questions must at present remain open and unresolved, though there is much suggestive evidence that could be elaborated. In the 1832 general election, for example, Acland, the radical candidate for Hull, opened a shop, the Anticorporative Castle, where he sold Anticorporate tea, public opinion coffee and Radical tobacco.[200] Other continuities can be found amongst the Chartists. As Gammage remarked, 'The members of the National Charter Association were ... to earnestly recommend each other, by precept and example, to the practice of temperance and uprightness, to cultivate the intellect and moral feelings, to fulfil the golden maxim, 'Do unto others as ye would they should do unto you', to trade with each other, and to assist each other in case of sickness or distress, and in finding employment'.[201] The precepts, attitudes and organizing principles of Wilkite radicalism undoubtedly endured well into the nineteenth century.

---

[200] *Victoria County History, the East Riding of Yorkshire*, p. 200.
[201] R. G. Gammage, *History of the Chartist Movement* (Newcastle, 1894), p.245.

PART III

Commercialization and Society

by

J. H. Plumb

CHAPTER SIX

The Commercialization of Leisure in Eighteenth-century England

Leisure is commonly purposeful and usually it requires the expenditure of money as well as time. Indeed, leisure is at present one of the greatest industries in the world, employing millions of workers and involving immense capital resources. It is surprising that both economic historians and social historians have scarcely paid attention to the early history of commercialized leisure. And yet one of the distinguishing features of capitalistic development in the West during the last two and a half centuries has been not only accumulation, which has received more than its fair share of attention, but also consumer expenditure. To spend has been the rising chord of Western European capitalism; saving has increasingly meant delayed expenditure. However, it is not my concern to stumble blindly into the arcane problems of economic growth or to get entangled in the economic and social problems of emerging industrial society, or even to attempt to tilt the balance between home and foreign demand. Here, I hope to draw attention to what seems to me to be one of the incontestable signs of growing affluence in eighteenth-century British society—the commercialization of leisure. This can be discerned in the 1690s, and by 1750 and 1760 leisure was becoming an industry with great potentiality for growth.[1]

Our own experience should teach us a little about the social signs of affluence—increased consumption of food, particularly beef, increased expenditure on houses, increased pre-occupation with fashion, a boom in books, music, entertainment and holidays: and the rapid growth of leisure towns. There are, of course, far more, but these are clear and obvious. The acquisition of increased leisure, combined with a modest affluence in a rising social class, has usually led to a desire for self-improvement. The emergence of the lower-middle class in our own day is reflected both in the pressure for increased education and in the demand for books, which has been met by the paperback revolution, as well as in the sale of recorded music and the astonishing growth in visiting country houses and museums. In any con-

---

[1] Like all great wars, those of William III and Anne had a profound effect, almost all to the good, on the economic and social life of Great Britain. Apart from P. G. M. Dickson, *The Financial Revolution in England* (1967) and one or two perceptive articles by K. G. Davies and D. C. Coleman, there is little yet of value on the economic surge and social dislocation caused by twenty years of war.

sideration of leisure it would be quite wrong not to put cultural pursuits in the foreground.

I do not wish to discuss the complex class stratification of the late seventeenth and early eighteenth-century English society, which undoubtedly helped to foster social emulation, or the economic structure that encouraged upward moblity; I assume we all accept that these conditions existed. I do want, however, to draw attention to one aspect of what one might term intellectual technology which is rarely stressed. Two inventions—printing combined with the alphabet—possessed explosive social possibilities that only began to be exploited to their fullest extent in the eighteenth century, firstly in the Netherlands, then in England and to a lesser extent elsewhere.

The Chinese had, of course, invented printing long before Europe either learned the technique or discovered it anew; but the effects on Chinese society were limited. Printing obviously made the examination system, although already established, more sophisticated and its application to a wider segment of the Chinese gentry possible; it created paper money, rendered taxation more systematic and indeed eased administration in every way. But outside the scholar-gentry it did not increase literacy very much. For this reason. To be literate in Chinese one must learn at least 4,000 characters; to be able to read the sophisticated literature of the classics, far, far more, which requires prolonged education and ample leisure. Although there was, it seems, some literacy outside the scholar-gentry class, it was never widespread. Elementary literacy led to very little in China because the complexity of the written language was so great. Leisure could not be used for self-improvement in the same say as in Europe.[2]

However, the Western alphabet made a perfect marriage with print. Print provided the possibility of a large audience; the simplicity of the alphabet made learning to read easy. Also, once reading was mastered, the whole of literature in the language read was open, or at least potentially open, to anyone with reasonable intellectual energy and dedication. Also the alphabet had this further advantage, it allowed for a very easy systematization of knowledge in dictionaries, encyclopaedias, gazetteers and the like, again aiding self-education. Once the tools were available, anyone sufficiently dedicated could teach himself to read and write: those who had been given modest schooling to the age of nine or ten could build easily on the foundations which they possessed, had they the will to do so. It is no surprise to us that Josiah Wedgwood, who left school at ten, was reading Voltaire and Rousseau in middle age. But it should amaze us. This could rarely have happened outside the Western World. There was very little possibility of any Chinese manufacturer or craftsman teaching himself to read, to write and to study the classics. From the Renaissance onwards, as soon as the elementary primers and simple dictionaries were available, there could always be the

[2] See J. H. Plumb, Introduction to Raymond Dawson, *Imperial China* (1972), p. 13.

possibility of self-education. *Leisure could be turned to profit.* And, indeed, we find this where we should expect to find it first—in religion. Printing combined with our alphabet system made self-education possible, making therefore, as never before in the world's history, for a steady cultural seepage: ideas adumbrated in narrow élitist groups might, and often did, permeate society.[3] No knowledge was necessarily the arcane possession of a limited class once printing and publishing had got into their stride and—*most important of all, once the lower classes were in a position to purchase cheap books*. And the growth of the market in printed materials is the first aspect of the commercialization of leisure with which I want to deal, for reading implies time to spare and money to spend.

The full exploitation of printing was curiously slow, largely because in the sixteenth century the books that were produced were mainly theological or classical, usually if not uniformly printed in large folios or quartos, and the books were expensive and so bought mainly by lawyers, clergymen, gentry or prosperous merchants. Only in the great upheavals of the 1640s and 1650s did printed materials—pamphlets, ballads, handbills and the like—begin to reach anything approaching a large audience in London: nor should we exaggerate its size; editions were extremely small.[4] However, in spite of the attempt of Charles II to suppress political comment, this pamphleteering never quite died out and, of course, revived sharply at moments of national crisis—the Popish Plot and Exclusion Crisis and the Revolution of 1688, all produced outbursts of ephemeral political literature. The importance of this for my theme of leisure is secondary, but important. It helped to create the conditions by which freedom of the press was won in the 1690s and without such freedom, combined with moderate affluence, the full extension of the possibilities of printing would not have happened. One has only to contrast England with France.

Let us glance at the London of Pepys, which I shall be taking as my base for comparison with the 1760s and 1770s.[5] There was only one daily newspaper—*The London Gazette*—which contained official matters relating

---

[3] This view is substantiated in a series of important articles by Elizabeth Eisenstein: 'Some Conjectures about the impact of Printing on Western Society and Thought: A Preliminary Report', *Journal of Modern History*, xl (1968), pp. 1-56; 'The Advent of Printing and the Problem of the Renaissance', *Past and Present*, xlv (1969), pp. 18-89; 'The Advent of Printing in Current Historical Literature: Notes and Comments on an Elusive Transformation', *American Historical Review*, lxv (1970), pp. 727-43. To some extent Professor Eisenstein's case suffers a little from over-emphasis. See the doubts raised by T. K. Rabb in *Past and Present*, lii (1971), pp. 135-40. See also Eisenstein's reply, ibid., pp. 140-4. However, neither Miss Eisenstein nor T. K. Rabb stresses the value of the alphabet combined with printing.

[4] See Bernard Bronson, 'The Writer', in *Man versus Society in Eighteenth Century Britain*, ed. James L. Clifford (Cambridge 1968), p. 106.

[5] For the London of Pepys see the new edition of *The Diary of Samuel Pepys* (ed. R. C. Latham and W. Matthews), 7 vols. to date (1970-). Also J. H. Plumb, 'The Public and Private Pepys', *The Saturday Review*, New York, 24 October, 1970, pp. 29-31, 71. Reprinted in Plumb, *In the Light of History* (1972), pp. 225-32.

to the Court—proclamations, decrees, promotions and the like, and a little very stale foreign news. Pepys had to go, and almost every day he went, to the Royal Exchange to pick up gossip from foreign merchants to learn what was happening in Europe. Similarly he would spend half an hour or so at Westminster Hall in search of news of the happenings at Court or in Parliament. He haunted taverns, not only because he loved wine, but also because he was avid for news which was often to be found there. If you happened to live out of London, of course, the situation was worse. A rich man, such as Simon Le Fleming, could subscribe to a manuscript newsletter sent to him by a journalist who, like Pepys, did the rounds and then summarized what he learned for his country correspondents.[6] In consequence, it was a world of surprising ignorance, alive with rumours, wonders and marvels. For Pepys, as for most of his dilettante friends, books were semi-precious objects as much as they were tools—carefully and beautifully bound, they were stored in handsome locked bookcases. Still, books were available; large libraries, such as the Earl of Sunderland's, not uncommon, and reading as a pastime, as well as a scholarly pursuit, was well established—but confined largely to the affluent. Even if one had the leisure to read a newspaper, only the *Gazette* was regularly available.

Also the dissemination of printed materials was equally backward. There were no circulating libraries, very, very few public libraries, no book clubs, no specialized publishers in music, which indeed was not frequently printed; no magazines, no books designed to attract children, and few elementary or cheap dictionaries for self-education, although a few dealing with book-keeping, surveying, arithmetic and navigation were beginning to appear in the 1660s and 1670s, but in not very significant quantities. Engravings and prints were produced in very small editions, often for subscribers; usually the prints were of the Court. There were very few satirical prints except those directed against the Pope during the hectic days of the Plot. There were some ballads and handbills, but as many circulated in manuscript as in print.[7] The bulk of publishing indeed was still theological or classical and was still enshrined in massive and expensive folios and quartos.

A hundred years later this had totally changed and print had been exploited in all its possibilities and was reaching out and responding to an ever widening market and in so doing was, as we shall see, constantly stimulating the market in leisure.

Accelerating growth, never even surely, began in the 1690s. In that decade the first two London non-official newspapers were successfully

---

[6] For a typical newsletter see *Historical Manuscripts Commission, 12th Report, Appendix, Part VII:* S. H. Le Fleming MSS (1890), pp. 305-7. For two official newsletter series see Peter Fraser, *The Intelligence of the Secretaries of State and Their Monopoly of Licensed News, 1660-88* (Cambridge, 1956), pp. 147-52.

[7] *Poems on Affairs of State*, ii, pp. 1678-81, ed. Elias F. Mengel, Jr., (New Haven and London, 1965), p. 511.

established—the *Post Boy* and *Post Man*: in 1702 the *Daily Courant* gave London its first daily newspaper. There were frequent attempts to start magazines—one of the most successful for a time was the *Athenian Mercury*, which invited 'customer participation'. But it was only in Queen Anne's reign that the magazine, which consisted entirely of essays on manners, social morality and self-improvement, found the right mixture for the new and growing middle-class audience. *The Spectator* was a triumph. It had subscribers in Sumatra as well as New England and was a *daily* magazine.[8] The most important aspect of *The Spectator* is that it found the market and taught others how to exploit it. Addison and Steele discovered the new and growing middle-class audience, an audience which longed to be modish, to be aware of the fashion yet wary of its excess, to participate in the world of the great yet be free from its anxieties, to feel smug and superior to provincial rusticity and old world manners, above all to be deeply respectful of the world of commerce: an audience in which a hunger for culture could easily be induced and one which had both the leisure and the affluence to indulge it.

The size of the audience must not be exaggerated. No more than 3,000 copies of *The Spectator* were ever printed.[9] The *Craftsman* at the height of its popular attacks on Sir Robert Walpole rarely reached 10,000[10]—the same figure given by Dr. Johnson for the most successful of all eighteenth-century magazines—the *Gentleman's Magazine*. We know too that newspaper editions, both London and provincial, were quite small, but by 1760 the whole country was covered in a network of newspaper distribution;[11] furthermore, new institutions had developed to give these editions an even wider distribution. Coffee houses and taverns kept racks of newspapers and pamphlets and sometimes ballads for their customers—and there were 2,000

---

[8] See Donald F. Bond's excellent and definitive edition of *The Spectator*, 5 vols., (Oxford, 1965), i, pp. lxxxv–lxxxvi. Also *Studies in the Early English Periodical*, ed. Richmond P. Bond (Chapel Hill, 1957). For the proliferation of newspapers after 1695, see *British Mercury*, 2 August 1712, 'About 1695 the press was again set to work, and such a furious itch of novelty has ever since been the epidemical distemper, that it has proved fatal to many families, the meanest of shopkeepers and handicrafts spending whole days in coffee houses to hear news and talk politics, whilst their wives and children wanted bread at home, and their business being neglected, they were themselves thrust into gaols or forced to take sanctuary in the army. Hence sprang that inundation of *Postmen, Postboys, Evening Posts, Supplements, Daily Courants* and *Protestant Post Boys*, amounting to twenty-one every week, besides many more which have not survived to this time, and besides the *Gazette*, which has the sanction of public authority'. Quoted in G. A. Cranfield, *The Development of the Provincial Newspaper, 1700-60* (Oxford, 1962), pp. 9–10.

[9] Bond, op. cit., i, pp. xxv–xxvii.

[10] J. H. Plumb, *Sir Robert Walpole*, 2 vols. (1956 and 1961), ii, 'The King's Minister', pp. 141-3, 179–82.

[11] For Dr. Johnson's estimate of the *Gentleman's Magazine* see Ian Watt, *The Rise of the Novel* (Los Angeles, 1967), p. 51. For the circulation of newspapers and periodicals in general see James R. Sutherland, 'The Circulation of Newspapers and Literary Periodicals, 1700-30', *The Library*, series iv, no. 15, 1935, pp. 110–24. Cranfield, op. cit., pp. 168–89.

coffee houses in London by the reign of Queen Anne.[12] By 1700, there were newsrooms in London where newspapers could be read for a fee or borrowed for an hour or two by depositing the full price. Circulating libraries, in which bound volumes of magazines prominently figured, were established in the provinces and in London by 1720. George Barton was running three circulating libraries at his shops in St. Ives, St. Neots and Peterborough in 1718. By 1750, circulating libraries were established in a considerable number of provincial towns (119 towns in 37 counties for the eighteenth century as a whole) and London, of course, possessed many, some of them, like Fancourt's, running to thousands of volumes, and requiring therefore a considerable capital investment. Fancourt was a dissenter and a close friend of Isaac Watts. His venture was strongly opposed by London publishers who placed an embargo on Fancourt's attempts to advertise his library in the newspapers which they controlled. Fiction, often trashy and ephemeral, was borrowed more frequently than any other subject, but all libraries in London had 80 per cent non-fiction on their shelves, even though they were borrowed less frequently. They consisted of a wide variety of literature, including often the Philosophical Transactions of the Royal Society, as well as dictionaries and grammars of foreign languages. They possessed considerable holdings in science and the useful arts. But even the trashiest fiction had its economic and social uses in stimulating appetite for the fashionable.[13] As well as circulating libraries, there were private subscription book clubs about which we know too little. Tamworth, which cannot have had a population of more than 2,000, if that, had several by the 1770s, mainly associated with the local taverns. All of these devices extended the market and indicated a considerable audience with leisure to read.[14]

[12] Also there is evidence that some government servants organized clubs for the reading of newspapers and discussions of news in their homes: *The Verney Letters of the Eighteenth Century*, ed. Margaret Maria, Lady Verney (1930), i. p. 308. 'Have been severall times at Westminster since Parliament met, with design to speake to your Lordsp. that you would be favourable and kind to send the Votes, the Post Boy and Post Man to Sherrington, at the Crown in Chesham, Postmaster, as your Lordsp. did last Session of Parliament. He has a Club of your friends meet every Friday at his house, who will desiert for want of hearing from their friends. Sir Edmund Denton furnisht another house most plentifully, out of Parliament as well as in during all last Summer.' Viscount Cheyne to Lord Fermanagh, 18 Dec., 1711; and ibid., p. 318.
[13] Paul Kaufman, 'The Community Library: A Chapter in English Social History', *Transactions of the American Philosophical Society*, lvii, Part 7 (Philadelphia, 1967), pp. 50–3. George Barton of Huntingdon was advertising his circulating library in the St. Ives, St. Neots and Peterborough newspapers in 1718: ibid., pp. 8–9. Also J. H. Plumb, 'Reason and Unreason in the Eighteenth Century: The English Experience', *William Andrews Clark Memorial Lecture* (University of California, Los Angeles, 1971), p. 15.
[14] John Money, 'Taverns, Coffee Houses and Clubs: Local Politics and Popular Articulacy in the Birmingham Area in the Age of the American Revolution', *Historical Journal*, xiv, no. 1, 1971, pp. 15–47. For book clubs see Kaufman, op. cit., pp. 26–8. Also Paul Kaufman, 'English Book Clubs and Their Role in Social History', *Libri*, xiv, pp. 1–31. 'It is reasonably certain that, as the reading public swelled to take in lower social levels, the size of books tended generally likewise to descend, resulting at the end of the century in the publica-

But with the entrepreneurial ingenuity which is such a hallmark of eighteenth-century commerce, printers and publishers pushed their wares to the very limit of the market. They devised the 'part-book'—a device which has had a renewed vogue in Britain these last five or six years. The part-book has two great advantages. The price of a bit of a book can be kept within the means of the poorest section of the market. On the other hand, the profit is enormous, for the total cost of the book soars well beyond what it would be if sold in a single volume, (often as much as 1,000 per cent profit). In a desultory way, it had been tried for ballads and poems in Queen Anne's day (a dreadful poem entitled 'A Journey to Hell' had struggled through three parts in 1705); but the boom time came in the twenties and thirties when histories, encyclopaedias, gazetteers and even the Bible were produced in penny and twopenny parts.[15] The avidity for knowledge to which this was the commercial response caught the eye of the provincial newspapers which were being established at this time and more often than not at their wit's end for material—and they too started serial publication of useful knowledge.

The diffusion of printed material was combined with a much more sophisticated publisher's knowledge of the market. New interests were rapidly catered for. For example, before 1700 cook-books were comparatively rare and usually they were of a quasi-medieval nature: the books being a hotch-potch of household recipes from soap-making to simples. The eighteenth century saw the cook-book as we know it, many of them ran through several editions and even regional cook-books appeared: in 1758, Thacker, the Dean of Durham's cook, produced the *Art of Cookery, principally for the Northern Counties*.[16] The boom in gardening produced a spate of gardening books and gardening journals.[17] Publishers who limited their production to musical scores and books kept pace with the increased delight in music. Again the 1690s is the watershed, when Thomas Cross, John Hare and John Walsh applied high pressure methods to the publication of musical scores—large cheap editions, wide-scale advertisement and considerable surreptitious puffing in the newspapers. In twenty-five years Walsh produced over 600 musical works. Between 1740 and 1800 over four hundred publishers

---

tion—disregarding issues de luxe—of far fewer folios and quartos than at the commencement, and of many more octavos and duodecimos'. Bertrand H. Bronson, *Printing as an Index of Taste in Eighteenth Century England* (New York Public Library, 1963), p. 11.

[15] R. M. Wiles, *Serial Publication in England before 1750* (Cambridge, 1957), pp. 133-94.
[16] A. W. Oxford, *English Cookery Books to the Year 1850* (Oxford, 1913), p. 88.
[17] John H. Harvey, *Early Gardening Catalogues* (Chichester, 1972), particularly pp. 24-34. Blanche Henrey, *A History and Bibliography of British Botanical and Horticultural Books up to 1800* (Oxford 1976). George W. Johnson, *A History of English Gardening* (1829), pp. 147-222. Flower shows with prizes, organized by societies of florists, were established by the mid-eighteenth century. In 1759 prizes were given for auriculas and polyanthus in April, and carnations 'Picattee and Whole Blower' in August, *Leicester Journal*, 31 March and 21 July 1759.

are known to have been involved in musical publication.[18] And, of course, the eighteenth century witnessed not only the rapid growth of fiction but also of theatrical publications, which were second only to novels in the demands made on the circulating libraries. All of these things are, of course, associated closely with other leisure activities which were absorbing more and more capital and to which I must shortly turn. But there are two other features of publishing which also need stressing—one of the growth of the primer, the educational aid, whether it is the exceptionally valuable encyclopaedia, such as Harris's *Lexicon Technicum*, or the simple books on arithmetic, geometry or the art of writing which were produced in very considerable quantities at increasingly modest prices—enabling any earnest apprentice to struggle up the ladder of self-education in his leisure hours.[19] More important, perhaps, was the development of specialized children's literature. Indeed middle-class children themselves became leisure objects in eighteenth-century England. More money is poured on their schooling and on their social accomplishments and their health.[20] They began to develop distinctive clothing; often they are put in semi-fancy dress as sailors, soldiers, highlanders or even gardeners—on the way to specialized children's clothes. Toys are mass-produced for the first time—dolls with interchangeable clothes, doll's houses and, of course, forts and soldiers (the latter, as one might expect, not an English but a German invention—otherwise England led the way in toy manufacture).[21] But the changing attitude to children arises because parents had more leisure and more money to spend on them, as well as a stronger desire for social emulation. However, that is by the way. The production of children's books is a reflection of the growing sophistication of publishing and it began with a singularly adroit entrepreneur: John Newbery, who had launched himself by marrying his employer's widow, obtained thereby the direction of the *Reading Journal:* naturally he started a circulating library. With an eye to the main chance he bought a half share in Dr. James's fever powders which, of course, he puffed in his children's books. The first of these, *A Pretty Little Pocket Book*, was designed to teach the alphabet. It was beautifully produced and illustrated and as a sales gimmick, for an extra twopence you could buy a pincushion for your

---

[18] Charles Humphries and William C. Smith, *Music Publishers in the British Isles* (1954), pp. 14, 17-19.

[19] For example, see Augustus de Morgan, *Arithmetical Books from the Invention of Printing to the Present Time* (1847).

[20] One sharp-eyed tradesman introduced to London 'Anodyne Necklaces', a new style teething ring as used by the 'Princess of France' in January 1731; to help sell it, he gave away a pamphlet on the necklace, a guide to all symptoms of secret diseases and a gleet! The cost was 5s. per necklace and his success was considerable, enough for him to advertise regularly throughout 1731, and maybe beyond as *Read's Weekly Journal* was only easily available for me for 1731. The upper classes, of course, used more expensive teething rings, a silver-mounted piece of coral, decorated with little silver bells. The 'Anodyne Necklace' was aimed at a much wider market.

[21] Lady Antonia Fraser, *A History of Toys* (1967); Karl Groeber, *Children's Toys of Bygone Days* (1928); Flora Gill Jacobs, *A History of Dolls' Houses* (1954).

daughter or a ball for your son. The book was 6d. Newbery was good at sales gimmicks. He gave books away free—so long as you bought the binding. Nevertheless, the *Pocket Book* enjoyed a prodigious success—the *Art of Writing* and the *Art of Arithmetic* soon followed. He tried a children's magazine—*The Lilliputian,* but that failed. This specialized publication indicates a large growing class of people with leisure to buy and money to spend.[22]

The most important function of print, however, in the sophisticated exploitation of leisure was, almost certainly, in the advertisement and information carried in the newspaper. Very early, by the 1720s if not earlier, horse-races were advertised, cricket followed soon after; naturally theatres and concerts were prominent in criticism as well as advertisement. The presence of London salesmen—particularly of fashionable London goods—was always well reported in the press. Naturally, too, balls, assemblies, routs and pleasure gardens used the local press increasingly. At the beginning of the century advertisements in newspapers rarely contained more than the books and articles the publisher himself sold. By the middle of the century, advertisements had become exceptionally diversified and there was scarcely a leisure activity, apart from fox-hunting and yacht-racing, which was not widely advertised. And it must be stressed that every aspect of leisure that I touch upon in the rest of this chapter is aided in its development and commercial organization by print, whether it is the circus or landscape gardening, horse-racing or concert-going.[23]

I do not have sufficient time to discuss the increasing professionalism, the increasing commercialization of leisure in all its manifestations. I intend, for example, to ignore the mania for gardening and planting which affected the middle-class city merchant—indeed special gardening manuals were written for him—as much as it did the country gentleman or the stimulus this gave to horticulturists, seedsmen and nurserymen.[24] Indeed I must leave to another occasion what is perhaps the most seductive of all leisure activities—casual shopping, for which the eighteenth-century tradesman devised the bow-window and the display cabinet.[25] Nor have I time to deal with the growth

---

[22] For John Newbery, see William Noblett, 'John Newbery, Publisher Extraordinary', *History Today,* xxii, April 1972, pp. 265-71; Charles Welsh, *A Bookseller of the Last Century, Being some Account of the life of John Newbery and the Books he published with a notice of the later Newbery's* (1863), pp. 40-51; F. J. H. Darton, *Children's Books in England* (2nd ed., 1958), pp- 122-40. Later in the century, there was a bookshop in New Bond Street which specialized in children's books. Sir Ambrose Heath, *London Tradesman's Cards of the XVIII Century* (New York, 1968), p. 28.

[23] G. A. Cranfield, op. cit., pp. 207-23; also Carroll Romer, 'Eighteenth Century Advertisements', *The Nineteenth Century and After,* cvi (1929), pp. 124-32; Frank Prestbery, *The History and Development of Advertising* (New York, 1929).

[24] See for city gardening, Thomas Fairchild, *The City Gardener* (1722).

[25] The style of shops changed dramatically in the early eighteenth century. Defoe satirized the gaudy embellishments of pastry-cook shops and toy shops. The first well-known architect to design shops as such appears to have been George Dance. See H. Kalman 'The Architecture of Mercantilism', in *The Triumph of Culture, Eighteenth Century Perspectives,* ed. Paul

of interest in the visual aesthetic experience from the highly profitable print shops on which Hogarth, that great entrepreneur, had so remarkable an effect,[26] to the organized viewing of country house collections of new and old masters. At some famous houses, such as Holkham, it was not unusual to queue for an hour before being shown the house.[27] I must ignore, alas, many sports—social activities of great importance that still wait an historian of merit; but developments in fishing, in yacht-racing, in prize-fighting all fit the pattern of increasing systematization, more exact rules and greater participation, and in prize-fighting, as with horse-racing, the development of a paying audience.[28] Perhaps even more regrettable, because totally ignored, I have not time to discuss what can only be described as the pet-industry—the commercialization not only of dog-breeding, which became highly specialized, but also of bird-breeding—canaries, finches and racing pigeons, which became well-established and widespread in eighteenth-century England, beginning, as with so many commercialized aspects of leisure, about London and rapidly spreading to the provinces.[29] However, I will confine myself to the theatre, to music and to horse-racing,[30] all of which

---

Fritz and David Williams (Toronto, 1972), pp. 69-83. Also Dorothy Stroud, *George Dance Architect 1741-85* (1971). The term bow-window was first used in 1753.

[26] For Hogarth see Ronald Paulson, *Hogarth: His Life, Art and Times*, 2 vols. (New Haven, 1971). Also J. H. Plumb, 'Hogarth's Progress', *The New York Review of Books*, xvii, no. 10, December 16, 1971, pp. 27-8.

[27] See Esther Moir, *The Discovery of Britain: The English Tourists 1540-1840* (1964), p. 61; R. W. Ketton Cremer, *Norfolk Assembly* (1957), p. 194.

[28] For Cricket, H. S. Altham, *A History of Cricket* (1962); for prize-fighting, Pierce Egan, *Boxiana: or Studies of Ancient and Modern Pugilism* (1812), i, p. 7; Henry Downes Miles, *Pugilistica: The History of British Boxing*, 3 vols. (Edinburgh, 1906).

[29] So far I have discovered little written on this subject and most of my information is derived from newspaper advertisements. However, goldfish were introduced into England in c. 1705, see G. F. Hervey and J. Hems, *The Goldfish* (2nd edn., 1868), pp. 79-80. They rapidly became popular. Horace Walpole, who had a goldfish pond at Strawberry Hill, often gave them away as presents. The possession of aviaries or 'vollerys', as they were called, was very fashionable amongst the rich in the early eighteenth century. Lady Walpole possessed one at her Chelsea home, and the Duke of Chandos had a large one full of exotic birds at Cannons, where he kept storks, ostriches, flamingoes, mocking birds, blue macaws, etc., etc: J. H. Plumb, *Walpole*, i, p. 206; C. H. Collins Baker and Muriel Baker, *The Life and Circumstances of James Brydges, First Duke of Chandos* (Oxford, 1949), p. 185. Birds in the home were popular, particularly parrots: some were kept in exquisite and elaborate cages. By 1771, small cage birds were very popular indeed, with the middle classes, and were widely advertised, for example 'About twenty-three pairs of exceeding well-bred Canary birds of the Fancy Sort. The owner spared no Expense in procuring some of the best in Town. Also about Twenty Pairing-Cages with all Partitions', *Daily Advertiser*, 25 February 1771. They were to be sold at auction. Canaries had, of course, reached England in 1576, but they seem to have been comparatively rare until the late seventeenth century. A bird market was held on Sunday mornings in Covent Garden by the 1720s, Ronalley Weber, *The Early Horticulturists* (Newton Abbot, 1968), pp. 81-2.

[30] For a brief treatment of the mushrooming of the trade in prints in the eighteenth century, which I hope shortly to deal with more extensively, see J. H. Plumb, 'The Public, Literature and the Arts' in *The Triumph of Culture, Eighteenth Century Perspectives*, ed. Paul Fritz and David Williams (Toronto, 1972), pp. 38-9.

underwent dramatic development between 1670 and 1770, and to what can only be described as festivals of leisure, which brought all of these activities together in the county towns.

Although quite popular, the restored theatre of Charles II was poverty-stricken—indeed there were only two good theatres—Drury Lane, rebuilt in 1673 for the modest cost of £4,000 and the Duke of York's in Lincoln's Inn Fields,[31] and afterwards in Dorset Gardens. New plays were rare, most were badly acted and vilely produced. Addicted as Pepys was to the theatre, he was rarely pleased by what he saw.[32] As with literature, there was a steady expansion of the audience after 1689: theatres became more numerous and old theatres were improved or rebuilt. At the Drury Lane, which was entirely rebuilt in 1673, there were alterations and improvements in 1715, 1762, 1765 and 1775. By 1762 the box office potential had risen to £354 per performance and in 1780, further improvements provided an audience capacity of 2,000. In 1792 the old theatre was pulled down and a new one designed by Henry Holland, with a capacity of 3,611, was built at a cost of £150,000—a very considerable capital investment. Also the average audience per performance doubled as did the takings in the same period.[33] Taken with

[31] For the theatre, the most valuable bibliography is *Restoration and Eighteenth Century Theatre Research. A Bibliographical Guide 1900-1968*, ed. Carl J. Stratman, David G. Spencer and Mary Elizabeth Devine (Carbondale: Southern Illinois University Press, 1971). Equally important are *The Theatre Notebook*, which incorporates the *Bulletin of the Society of Theatre Research*, and all the critical introductions to the volumes of the magnificent series, edited by George Winchester Stone, *The London Stage 1660-1800*, published by the Southern Illinois Press at Carbondale. It is important to stress here that I am not unaware that drama, like music, had both an audience and considerable publication before the end of the seventeenth century. My contention is, however, that this audience was small, largely confined to London, and that the eighteenth century unleashed a great and rapid expansion of the audience and a greater sophistication and professionalism in the presentation of both drama and music to the public. This development was even more marked in the provinces. I am aware, of course, that there were commercially-minded men in the Elizabehtan theatre who made fortunes and that professional musicians existed in Elizabethan England and earned a living—sometimes a good one. These caveats are necessary because in a short chapter it is necessary to stress the explosive growth rather than seedtime and germination which will be corrected when this chapter is expanded to book length. The first Drury Lane only cost £1,500. *The London Stage 1660-1800*, pt. 1660-1700, ed. William Ven Lennap (Carbondale, 1965), pp. xxxvi-vii.
[32] See Latham and Mathews, op. cit., i, pp. 309-10, 5 December 1660: 'I dined at home and after dinner went to the New Theatre and there I saw *The Merry Wifes of Windsor* acted. The humours of the country gentlemen and the French Doctor very well done: but the rest poorly and Sir J. Falstaffe as bad as any.' ii, p. 175, 9 September 1661: '... thence to Salisbury Court play-house, where was acted the first time *Tis Pitty shee's a Whore*—a simple play and ill acted.' p. 202, 20 October 1661: '... I to the Theatre and there saw *The Country Captaine*, the first time that it hath been acted this 25 years—a play of my Lord Newcastles, but so silly a play as in all my life I never saw, and the first that ever I was weary of in my life.' p. 223, 29 November 1661: '... I to the Theatre ... and there saw *Love at first sight*, a play by Mr. Killigrew, and the first time that it hath been acted since before the troubles: and great expectations there was, but I find the play to be a poor thing; and so I perceive everybody elso do.'
[33] Alwin Thaler, *Shakespeare to Sheridan* (New York, 1963), pp. 214-5; Percy Fitzgerald, *A New History of the English Stage* (1882), ii, pp. 234, 309-19, 339; Quentin Skinner, 'Sheridan and Whitbread at Drury Lane 1809-15', *Theatre Notebook*, xvii (1962-3), p. 41.

Covent Garden the audience capacity steadily grew from 14,016 a week in 1732 to 22,182 in 1762.[34] As with publishers, theatre managers discerned that there was an audience for their plays amongst the lower-paid workers, so they put on 'after-hour' performances at cheaper rates at the end of the regular performance and the Covent Garden account book shows that this development was very successful, earning the theatre an extra £200–£300 a week.[35] Minor theatres, such as the Theatrical Booth in Southwark, began to accommodate themselves entirely to this type of audience, not opening their doors until 6 pm.–usual performances began at 5 pm.–and promising to conclude by 9 pm., which suited better the working hours of the lower-paid audience.[36] This ever expanding passion for the theatre is further reflected in the number of new plays written between 1700 and 1800: in the first half of the century 1,095 new plays were produced: in the second half 2,117, more than one a week during the theatrical season.[37] As well as straight theatre, the eighteenth century witnessed the establishment of pantomime under Rich in the 1720s, comic opera begins with Gay's *Beggar's Opera* in 1728; ballet and mime and puppet theatres were all well supported by the 1720s.[38] Philip Astley established his equestrian circus at the foot of Westminster Bridge in 1770. He quickly added wild-animal trainers, conjurers, jugglers and trapeze artists and indeed began the professionalization and stabilization of the individual performers who had wandered about London and the provinces, picking up what contribution they could from their audiences—often performing in the street, or in an inn yard or between plays at the theatre. Astley was a brilliant entrepreneur. He started the circus parade through the streets to attract audiences: indeed he was never at a loss for a gimmick. He himself was a brilliant trainer, teaching his horses, much to Horace Walpole's amazement, to dance the horn-pipe: perhaps more astonishing was his favourite horse's trick of making tea—the horse lifting the kettle with his teeth from the blazing fire.[39]

---

[34] H. W. Pedicord, *The Theatrical Public in the Time of Garrick* (New York, 1954), pp. 3–4, 15.

[35] Ibid., pp. 36–9, 183–5.

[36] Ibid., p. 39.

[37] Allardyce Nicoll, *A History of Early Eighteenth Century Drama, 1700–50* (2nd ed. Cambridge, 1929), pp. 293–387. Allardyce Nicoll, *A History of Late Eighteenth Century Drama 1750–1800* (Cambridge, 1927), pp. 232–348. Also *The London Stage 1660–1700*, pt. 2, ed. Emmett L. Avery; pt. 3, ed. Arthur H. Scouten; pt. 4, ed. George Winchester Stone Jr.; pt. 5, ed. Charles Beecher Hogan (Carbondale, Illinois, 1965–8).

[38] See George Speaight, *The History of the English Puppet Theatre* (1955)—an excellent survey of the rise and fall of the eighteenth-century puppet theatre. By 1731, Rich, who introduced pantomime, had made so much money and was so popular that he was able to build Covent Garden Theatre: a subscription of £6,000 was quickly raised. See Thaler, op. cit., p. 213.

[39] The literature on the circus is very extensive, see R. Toole-Stott, *Bibliography of Circus History* (New York). For Astley see Willson Disher, *The Greatest Show on Earth* (1937); Joan Selby Lowndes, *The First Circus: The Story of Philip Astley* (1957); *Astley's Royal*

In Pepys's day there had been no provincial theatres of any kind. A band of players obtained a royal licence and then wandered from town to town setting up their stage in inn yards or in barns to astound the yokels with melodrama or acrobats.[40] A hundred years later, every town of any pretension had a well-built theatre, a regular company and often enjoyed the visits of the best London companies during the summer when the theatre was closed in London. A theatre was built in Bath by subscription in 1705: by 1730 York had a modest repertory company which, instead of sharing the profits, was employed on a salary basis—a revolutionary development that was to spread and, of course, to give increased profits to managers and shareholders. The theatre established at the county-town usually served by the middle of the century the surrounding area. Norwich had a well-established theatre by the 1740s (a large new theatre was built in 1758) and a resident company. They played in Norwich from January to May and returned for three weeks during the assizes in July and August. They performed usually five times a week, but only three in Lent, but outside Norwich they cut their performances to three times a week, but added others for special requests. In June they were in Dereham, in July Ipswich, in August Beccles; they spent two months in Bury (September, October) largely for the fair (later in the century Bury established a very fine theatre of its own) and for the last three months of the year (October to December) they played at Colchester. In addition to the straight theatre at Norwich, there was also a puppet theatre and a theatre of varieties—the ancestor of the Victorian music hall. These were filled by touring companies which, at times, drew very large audiences indeed.[41] Nor was Norwich exceptional. During the eighteenth century fourteen theatres were established in Lincolnshire, usually regarded as one of the backward rural areas, in Alford, Boston, Bourne, Brigg, Gainsborough, Grantham,

---

Amphitheatre, a scrapbook on Astley by an unknown compiler is in the British Museum (TC 35-37). Horace Walpole wrote, on 12 September 1783, to the Earl of Stratford 'I could find nothing at all to do so went to Astley's, which indeed was much beyond my expectation. I do not wonder any longer that Darius was chosen King by the instructions he gave to his horse; nor that Caligula made his consul. Astley can make his dance minuets and hornpipes.' John Astley, Philip Astley's son, was the first performer to dance on the back of a horse as it charged round the circus. *Letters of Horace Walpole*, ed. Mrs. Paget-Toynbee (Oxford, 1903), xiii, 54-5.

[40] Sybil Rosenfeld, *Strolling Players and Drama in the Provinces 1660-1765* (Cambridge 1939), p. 5. Before 1737 strolling players needed a licence from the master of the Revels or the Lord Chamberlain or Letters Patent. After 1737, the Justice of the Peace licensed, ibid., p. 6.

[41] The literature on the development of the provincial theatre in the eighteenth century is very extensive. For Bath, see Arnold Hare, *The Georgian Theatre in Wessex* (1957), pp. 14-19. For York, Rosenfeld, op. cit., pp. 136-67. For Norwich, T. L. G. Burley, *Playhouses and Players of East Anglia* (Norwich, 1928); Rosenfeld, op. cit., pp. 61-95. Other excellent studies of local theatrical development are J. E. Cunningham, *Theatre Royal, the History of the Theatre Royal, Birmingham* (1950); K. Barker, *The Theatre Royal, Bristol: the First Seventy Years;* Historical Association Bristol Branch, Pamphlet no. 3 (1961); H. Sargeant, *A History of Portsmouth Theatres:* The Portsmouth Papers, no. 13 (Portsmouth, 1971).

Grimsby, Horncastle, Lincoln, Louth, Market Deeping, Market Rasen, Spalding and Stamford: one or two were small and attached to inns, for some of these market towns were little more than villages, but most were long-lasting.[42] This does, however, illustrate not only the passion for the theatre, but also the entrepreneurial excitement which it attracted. By 1770 England was better equipped with theatres than it is today. (Even Wisbech had a theatre.)[43] In London and the main provincial centres, capital investment was considerable and profits in general good, if very liable to be dissipated by an over-ambitious manager. The shareholders of the Theatre Royal, Liverpool, drew a regular 5 per cent interest and saw the capital value of their shares steadily, if not dramatically, rise.[44]

As with the theatre, so with music. In Pepys's day London was full of musicians—mainly amateur, although of course there were professional performers and teachers. There was good Church music, occasionally there were fine musical interludes at the theatre, and Matthew Locke provided some excellent incidental music for *Macbeth, The Tempest* and Shadwell's *Psyche*.[45] For those who were lucky enough to have the entrée to the Royal Palace, Charles II kept a French orchestra, having found the English band unsatisfactory.[46] Those not so lucky had to go to a tavern or coffee house where there might be a girl with a good voice singing ballads or traditional songs, and some inns employed a fiddler from time to time. The provinces were, of course, worse off as far as secular music was concerned. Either one made it oneself or waited, as Sir Robert Walpole's father did, for the visit of a strolling fiddler.[47] Sometimes for a dance it was possible to hire the

[42] Alfred Welby, 'Lincolnshire Play Houses in the Eighteenth Century', *Lincolnshire Notes and Queries*, xxii, pp. 69–70; additional notes by J. B. King, ibid., pp. 104–7: xxii, pp. 19–20.

[43] Richard Southern, 'The Theatre Remains at Wisbech', *Theatre Notebook* (1949), iv, pp. 21–3.

[44] Arthur C. Wardle, 'Liverpool's First Theatre Royal,' *Transactions of the Historical Society of Lancashire and Cheshire for the Year 1938* (1939), xc, pp. 207–9. Also R. J. Broadbent, *Annals of the Liverpool Stage* (Liverpool, 1908).

[45] The bibliography of music is as extensive as that of the theatre. Of particular value have been Charles Burney, *A General History of Music*, with critical and historical notes by F. Mercer (1935); Sir John Hawkins, *A General History of the Science and Practice of Music*; introduction by Charles Cudworth (New York, 1963), 2 vols.; *Grove's Dictionary of Music and Musicians*, ed. Eric Blom, 5th ed. (1954); *The Oxford Companion to Music*, ed. Percy Scholes, 9th ed. (1955); John Harley, *Music in Purcell's London: The Social Background* (1968); Charles Humphreys and William C. Smith, *Music Publishing in the British Isles from the earliest times to the Middle of the Eighteenth Century* (1954); Eric David Mackerness, *A Social History of Music* (1964); Stanley Sadie, 'Concert Life in Eighteenth Century England', *Royal Musical Association Proceedings* 85th Session (1954); J. L. Hodgkinson and Rex Pogson, *The Early Manchester Theatre* (1960), pp. 17–30; Paul Henry Lang, *George Frideric Handel* (1966). Like the theatre, music had achieved a public audience before 1689, particularly in London, and this audience was serviced by teachers, instrument makers and publishers, but it was small-scale.

[46] Tom Killigrew, a boon companion of Charles II, was passionately keen on Italian opera, but he found it impossible to get opera thoroughly supported; for his and the King's orchestra see *The Diary of Samuel Pepys*, ed. Henry B. Wheatley, vi, pp. 162–3 (12 February 1667).

[47] J. H. Plumb, 'The Walpoles, Father and Son', in *Men and Places* (1962), p. 130.

services of a local amateur. And, of course, music lovers got together and made music, and this audience, modest in London and small in the provinces, was catered for by the publication of song books such as Playford's.

But in the 1660s there was no true opera, no ballet, no musical festivals, no specially designed concert halls of any kind, although John Bannister the violinist gave a few public performances between 1673 and 1676 in London.[48] Again by 1760 all was changed, aided of course by the rapid increase after 1690 of musical publication, in which primers for teaching were very prominent. Blow produced his primer for the harpsichord in 1704. The first primer for the flute was printed in 1721, both published by Walsh, who specialized entirely in music. Indeed, he started the first specialized monthly magazine, *The Monthly Mask of Vocal Music*, which ran from 1702 to 1724.[49] Equally important was the rapid development and specialization of musical-instrument makers to meet the ever-increasing demand. The development of musical entertainment both amateur and professional was extremely rapid, ranging from the greatest Italian, German and English composers to popular music of the most traditional kinds. The Three Choirs Festival, which linked Hereford, Gloucester and Worcester Cathedral choirs in a yearly fiesta of music which drew large audiences from the West Midlands, was inaugurated about 1713.[50] Indeed, so large were the crowds that gathered for this festival that the Bath theatre company usually played at the cathedral town where the Festival was being held: much, of course, to the delight of the tradesmen and inn-keepers. Public concert halls became well established at the turn of the century. A primitive one was started in the 1670s by Thomas Britton—a musical coal merchant who cleared out the loft of his warehouse and organized concerts, at first free, but afterwards at 10s. a year, including coffee. He was one of the first to introduce Corelli and Vivaldi to the London public. As Sir John Hawkins loftily wrote in his *History of Music*, 'This mansion, despicable as it may seem, attracted to it as polite an audience as ever the opera did!'[51] More important, however, was

---

[48] John Bannister called these concerts his 'Public Musicales' and he gave them at his Music School, a room over the George Tavern in Whitefriars: *The London Stage*, pt. 1, ed. William Van Lennap (Carbondale, 1965), p. cxix. Also Roger North, *Memoirs of Musick*, ed. E. Rimbault (1846), p. 111.

[49] Charles Humphries and Charles C. Smith, *Music Publishing in the British Isles* (1964), pp. 17-19; Eric D. Mackerness, *A Social History of English Music* (1964), p. 107. Again it must be stressed that primers for seventeenth century musical instruments had been published before Walsh, but he published larger and cheaper editions of primers and was quick to seize the opportunity of new fashions in instruments, that is, he was highly market-conscious.

[50] Watkins Shaw, *The Three Choirs Festival* (Worcester, 1954).

[51] William Van Lennap, op. cit., p. cxix. Britton's loft was in Aylesbury Street, between Clerkenwell Green and St. John's Street. He had a Five-stop organ and a Ruckers virginal. The concerts began in 1677-8. By 1700 the York Buildings had become the great concert centre, ibid., p. xxviii. Also, Sir John Hawkins, *A General History of the Science and Practice of Music* (New York, 1963), p. 790 for quotations. On pp. 792-3 Hawkins prints the catalogue of music, which was extremely extensive and catholic, prepared for the sale at Thomas Britton's death.

the opening of Thomas Hickford's rooms in St. James's Street, Piccadilly, in 1713 which, after a move to Brewer Street, lasted until 1779. For over sixty years brilliant concerts by leading English and continental musicians were given there.[52] Hickford was overshadowed in 1775 by the opening of the Hanover Square Rooms where Bach, Mozart and Haydn were first performed in England. Many inns, particularly the very large Crown and Anchor in the Strand, not wishing to lose custom, built or set aside a concert room, where usually a wide variety of music was to be heard, traditional as well as modern.[53] Much to the horror of a foreign visitor sacred music was also played and indeed one tavern set up a church organ.[54] The Crown and Anchor was also the home of the Academy of Ancient Music which ran from 1726 to 1792, a club for the study and practice of vocal and instrumental harmony.[55] As with the theatre, concert-going spread rapidly in the provinces. Manchester had a series of subscription concerts in 1744 which were suspected of being a cover for secret Jacobite sympathizers.[56] According to Paul Henry Lang, 'toward the middle of the century almost every town, castle, University and Church had its orchestra and many musical associations gathered for weekly musical exercises'.[57] Just as they could not possibly collect Old Masters, but had to content themselves with prints, so too the middle class could not behave like the Duke of Chandos and keep a full scale orchestra at Cannons, along with a resident composer such as Handel or Pepusch.

Neither could the middle class afford to run a racehorse or to support a cricket team, but both games fascinated them for they provided excellent opportunities for gambling. All societies gamble, but affluent societies gamble most. Football pools, bingo halls, betting shops are a clear indication of the affluence of the working class of the middle decades of the twentieth century—the development of horse-racing which became an industry in the eighteenth century similarly points to the affluence of both the gentry, the pseudo-gentry and the upper middle class.[58]

Some regulation and order had taken place in racing in the reigns of Charles II and James II: rules for particular races such as the Town Plate

---

[52] Percy M. Young, *The Concert Tradition* (1965).
[53] Stanley Sadie, 'Concert Life in Eighteenth Century England', *Royal Musical Association Proceedings*, lxxv (1959), pp. 17–30; *Grove's Dictionary of Music and Musicians*, ed. Eric Blom (1954), p. 391; *Oxford Companion of Music*, ed. Percy Scholes, 9th ed. (1955), pp. 227, 517–729. Hawkins, op. cit., p. 762.
[54] Young, op. cit., p. 34.
[55] Young, op. cit., p. 74. Dr. Johnstone of Reading University informs me that the first meeting of the Academy was on 7 January 1726.
[56] Young, op. cit., p. 101.
[57] Paul Henry Lang, *Music in Western Civilisation* (1942), p. 724.
[58] There is no scholarly history of games for the eighteenth century; no work by a professional historian on horse-racing, or indeed on horses, vitally important as they are to the economic and social life of the time. I am particularly indebted in this section to my research assistant, William Noblett, whose help for the chapter as a whole was invaluable.

at Newmarket had been laid down, and professional jockeys were permitted for the first time in the reign of James II and the first professional trainer, Tregonwell Frampton, was employed at Newmarket by William III and later by Queen Anne and the first two Hanoverians.[59] But by the standards of 1750, horse-racing in 1700 was still rather primitive—there were conventions rather than rules, the man who owned the horse usually rode it and, more often than not, races were between two horses for a wager between the owners. And there was little control of the jockeys when employed. There was a very rough programme of meetings—conventional times at Newmarket and Doncaster and at some of the large county towns which organized races to coincide with their assizes.[60] The courses were traditional or arranged on the spot.

Changes began, however, early in the century and the newspapers played a vital part in the development of racing. Very early indeed race meetings were advertised,[61] and by the 1750s London newspapers were carrying advertisements of all the major meetings in the country and often too carrying news of the results. By 1722, 112 cities and towns in England were holding race meetings.[62] Indeed the spread of racing for small stakes led to Parliament attempting to regulate the sport in 1711 and again in 1740—they tried to check the growing demand.[63] The introduction of Arabian bloodstock by Lord Godolphin improved breeding dramatically and involved greater expenditure: and the more spirited and nervous horses required more professional skill in training and riding. The establishement of the Racing Calendar in 1727 helped not only to regulate meetings but also to increase both competitors and attendance.[64] No longer was it merely a matter of owners, their followers and friends and a few neighbouring gentlemen farmers, but crowds were gathering at all race courses. Indeed the population of the sport became so great that more and more race-courses were specially laid out for racing. At Richmond in Yorkshire the city fathers laid out a new course near the town (formerly races had been held on a wind-swept plateau some fives miles from the town) and they built what may have been the first grandstand for which a charge was made for seats.[65] The Jockey Club, established by 1725, quickly brought order into the betting and began to reform the rules of racing.[66] By the 1770s Tattersalls had come into existence and betting no

---

[59] J. P. Hore, *The History of Newmarket and the Annals of the Turf* (1886), iii, p. 194.
[60] Andrea T. Cook, *A History of the English Turf* (1901-5), i, p. 160.
[61] Ibid., i, p. 192. For an excellent example of the elaborate nature of these advertisements by the 1730s, see *Read's Weekly Journal*, 27 February, 1731, for a 'List of the Horse Matches to be run at Newmarket in March, April and May 1731', where owners, horses, weights, miles, wagers and forfeits are all listed—twenty-one races had been arranged, the majority were between ten horses. Results were being printed in *Read's Weekly Journal* in 1731.
[62] Cook, op. cit., i, p. 199.
[63] 9 Anne, c. 14; 13 George II, c. 19.
[64] C. M. Prior, *The History of the Racing Calendar and the Stud Book* (1926), p. 93.
[65] J. Fairfax-Blakeborough, *Northern Turf History* (1949).
[66] Roger Mortimer, *The Jockey Club* (1958), p. 10.

longer had to be man to man.[67] Steadily the important race meetings began to distinguish themselves and draw enormous crowds. The St. Leger was founded in 1776, the Oaks in 1779 and the Derby in 1780, the 2,000 Guineas just after the turn of the century in 1809.[68] By then racing was a complex industry involving thousands of workers and an investment that ran into hundreds of thousands of pounds.[69] England exported the industry, first to France and then to America. Racing was the first sport to become a highly organized, nationwide social activity, run as much for profit as for fun. But other sports were not far behind. Cricket had developed to the full elaboration of its rules by the end of the century and had also become stabilized in special grounds which charged admission, again drawing large crowds, both for the betting and the sport.[70]

Theatre, music, dancing, sport—these were the cultural pastimes for which the prosperous gentry and the new leisured middle class hungered. But their houses were not large enough for private theatres, for private orchestras and private concerts, nor had they money to lavish on such conspicuous aristocratic consumption as a string of racehorses. And so it is not surprising that market towns began to build subscription Assembly Rooms, where the social élite of the county and the county town could meet for balls, for music, for improving lectures and, of course, for dramatic performances. Some Assembly Rooms, such as those at York, designed by the Earl of Burlington and paid for by public subscription, were magnificent in conception and design; others were one or two great rooms attached to the leading inn and could double up on occasion for Masonic meetings. Often the subscription was quite high, which at least kept out the minor shopkeepers and traders.[71] These Assembly Rooms mark the transitional stage between

---

[67] Robert Black, *Horse Racing in England* (1893), pp. 85-6.
[68] Ibid., pp. 59-60.
[69] On the economics of horse-breeding, training and racing there is nothing, but some light is shed by the stud book (1716-52) of Cuthbert Routh, a well-known Yorkshire breeder and trainer. In 1752, ten horses, one pregnant, and one foal were worth £1,640. See C. M. Prior, *Early Records of the Thoroughbred Horse* (1925), pp. 54-5.
[70] There is no better game than cricket for continuous betting between spectators. For the history of cricket see H. S. Altham, *A History of Cricket* (1962). The literature of cricket is very large but almost entirely antiquarian.

A similar professionalization also takes place in boxing, cock-fighting and fox-hunting. For boxing see Paul Magriel, *A Bibliography of Boxing: A Chronological Check List of Books in English published before 1900* (New York Public Library, 1948). John Broughton printed the rules of boxing in 1743; amphitheatres were opened in London by Figgin in 1719 (afterwards Taylor's). Broughton's opened in 1743 and he became the first manager, taking thirty per cent of his boxers' earnings. Mendoza undertook exhibition tours throughout the provinces. At 21 Mendoza made £1,000 out of a fight with Martin the Butcher: see Pierce Egan, *Boxiana* (1812), i, pp. 16-59. *The Memoirs of the Life of Daniel Mendoza*, ed. Paul Magriel (1951), pp. 5, 54, 64, 68-9, 94, 98. For cock-fighting, G. R. Scott, *The History of Cockfighting* (1957). For fox-hunting, C. D. B. Ellis 'Hunting' in *Victoria County History of Leicestershire*, iii, pp. 269-81; Henry Higginson, *Two Centuries of Foxhunting* (1946). Again the laws seem to have been promulgated in the mid-eighteenth century, ibid., pp. 61-2.
[71] This, of course, was a concomitant of the entire leisure situation. Although the audience or

private and fully public entertainment. As culture seeped through to the masses, and so became more commercially viable, these subscription rooms fell into desuetude. Many, however, remain to remind us of the elegance and sophistication of upper class provincial life in eighteenth-century England.[72] They were, of course, the provincial equivalent of those two wonders of London—Vauxhall and Ranelagh Gardens, where one could, dine, listen to music, look at excellent pictures—indeed buy them—and of course dance (sometimes masked, sometimes not), and above all partake in that favourite eighteenth-century sport of sauntering to ogle the girls.[73]

A similar transitional stage can be seen in the growth of towns dedicated entirely to leisure or retirement—a phenomenon which is now so commonplace in the western world that it is difficult to remind oneself how recent and how significant this development is. Like the readers of *The Spectator* or *Pamela,* eighteenth-century men and women, eager for a holiday, liked to have a sound moral excuse for their enjoyment. And so the first holiday centres grew up at Spas—Bath and Tunbridge Wells, quickly followed by Scarborough, Bristol Hot Springs, Cheltenham, Harrogate, Matlock and the rest. Brighton, where one took the sea water internally as well as externally, got off to a slow start, but roared ahead under the patronage of the Prince Regent towards the end of the century, when the spas themselves began slowly to decline and men and women began to accept frankly the idea of a holiday for holiday's sake.[74] Also men and women may have become healthier as personal and social hygiene improved, for there can be no doubt that the majority of those who went to the spas in the middle of the century usually had some ailment, major or minor, frequently due to over-eating and

---

market expands, attempts were always being made to try and make the leisure activity exclusive. The creation of grandstands, the fencing of race-courses, the prevention of small races amongst farmers, similarly attempted to keep out the lower orders. The formation of clubs for fox-hunting, the Quorn, the Belvoir, the Fernie and the like is a similar development. Mostly these efforts proved unsuccessful as affluence spread. There was also an attempt to restrict leisure activities to the middle and upper middle classes, not only by making such activities both expensive and exclusive, but also by suppressing the riotous and vulgar entertainments of the not so prosperous—the fairs, church-ales, wakes and the like, which were regarded more as a licence to sin than a means of self-improvement. Both of these subjects will be dealt with more extensively in my book on *The Growth of Leisure, 1660-1830.*

[72] Typical small town assembly rooms, both beautiful eighteenth-century buildings, are those at Bury St. Edmunds and Leicester. For Leicester see Jack Simmons, 'A Leicester Architect, 1752-1814' in *Parish and Empire: Studies and Sketches* (1952), which deals with John Johnson. The Lion Hotel, Cambridge, possessed a brilliant eighteenth-century assembly room, now demolished, that doubled as a Masonic Lodge. The early assembly room at Brighton is attached to the Old Ship Hotel.

[73] For the Vauxhall Gardens see Millie Sands, 'Music not too refined', *Musical Times,* xli (1950), pp. 11-15. See also Percy M. Young, op. cit., p. 138. For the Ranelagh Gardens see ibid., p. 140. See also E. D. Mackerness, op. cit., pp. 104-5. It was, of course, Hogarth's idea that Vauxhall Gardens should display contemporary paintings: he never missed a chance of exploiting the market; see Paulson, op. cit., i, pp. 347-8.

[74] For Brighton, see Osbert Sitwell and Margaret Barton, *Brighton* (1935); also J. H. Plumb, 'The Brighton Pavilion', in *Men and Places,* pp. 80-97.

drinking, which they hoped the hideous waters might cure. But the main business of spas was amusement—dancing, theatre, music and reading and, of course, flirting and making love, just as it was a little lower down the social scale at Islington or Sadlers Wells, the spas nearest to London to which the townsmen flocked.

Islington had been languishing until the proprietor secured the visit of two young princesses (Caroline and Amelia). Takings then shot up and Pinchbeck, whose entrepreneurial eye glinted as sharply as John Newbery's or Josiah Wedgwood's, produced a medallion of the occasion in the base metal, faked to look like gold, to which he gave his name.[75]

All the activities that I have so far described point to the growth of a middle-class audience—not a mass audience by our standards, but so large and so growing that its commercial exploitation was becoming an important industry, involving considerable capital. It was also a market that had enormous potentiality for growth.

The middle-class culture which this commercialization of leisure brought about expanded greatly in the nineteenth century, modified maybe, but not essentially changed, and lasted until our own time. The collected *Spectator*, for example, was reprinted over and over again, and Addison was the model essayist in thought as well as style when I was a boy at school; equally persistent were the 'tea-gardens' modelled on Islington or Sadlers Wells. Although the growth of this leisure industry has had considerable economic effects, these were partly the result of social effects equally profound.

In the early eighteenth century, culture and sport slowly ceased to be élitist and private and became increasingly public. The more public cultural and sporting activity becomes, the more it provokes social emulation—one has only to think of Covent Garden, the Private View at the Academy or Ascot to realize how socially competitive human beings may become—even in their pleasures. And social emulation usually leads to increasing consumption and expenditure. And it encourages the entrepreneur to exploit and extend his market. Furthermore, the media of communication of the eighteenth century—literature, particularly the novel, the theatre, and the opera—all helped to diffuse, in a way never before experienced by Englishmen, social attitudes and social criticism—that seepage of ideas which is the distinguishing mark of leisure in western society.

And, finally, to be a little reckless. It has always been my view that the situation which gives rise to the early beginnings of the industrial revolution arose from an affluent society wanting more goods than the labour force, as then organized, could produce. After all, the new industrial methods began in the consumer industries—textiles, pottery, the buttons, buckles and pins of Boulton and Watt. And I hope this all too rapid survey of leisure, its increasing professionalization and commercialization between 1670 and 1770

[75] William B. Boulton, *The Amusements of Old London* (1901), i, p. 48.

points to an affluent and growing middle class which was willing to spend for the sake, not only of prestige, but also for enjoyment and self-improvement: neither, may I add, necessarily uncomplementary.

I have only had time to skid across the surface and I am indebted to a host of admirable antiquarians and a few literary historians of distinction, but I have been surprised to find so little good professional economic and social history written on these topics. There is no good history of any sport, other then cricket. Excellent histories of the Crocus and the species Dianthus, but no history of horticulture.[76] One useful book on toys by Lady Antonia Fraser. No history of meat or of food in general, apart from Sir Jack Drummond's, which is superficial.[77] No professional economic and social history of Bath or any other leisure town. Although nearly seven thousand books and articles were written on the theatre from the Restoration to 1800 between 1900 and 1968, they are almost entirely antiquarian, literary or factory-made Ph.D. exercises.[78] We have the Jew in Eighteenth-century Theatre, the Quaker, the Rake, the Reformed Rake, the Cuckold and a host of other stock figures analysed at length in thesis after thesis, but there are only a few chapters in one short monograph that deal adequately with the theatre's economic history.[79] These and many other subjects await the attention of trained professional historians.

And yet the way man enjoys himself and the way his enjoyments are exploited—surely both are of considerable importance for economic as well as social history.

---

[76] George Maw, *The Genus Crocus* (1886); Ernest Thomas Cook, *Carnations, Picotees and the Wild and Garden Pinks: a History of the Genus Dianthus* (1905).

[77] J. C. Drummond and Anne Wilbraham, *The Englishman's Food: A History of Five Centuries of English Diet* (1939). It is worth noting that Richard Leveridge, a powerful bass singer, made 'The Roast Beef of Old England' the popular hit of the 1720s. See Grove, *Dictionary of Music and Musicians*, ed. Eric Blom (5th ed. 1954), v, pp. 152-3.

[78] See *Restoration and Eighteenth Century Theatre Research: Bibliographical Guide, 1900–1968*, ed. Carl J. Stratman, David G. Spencer and Mary Elizabeth Devine (Carbondale, 1971), *passim*.

[79] Van der Veen and R. S. Harm, *Jewish Characters in Eighteenth Century English Fiction and Drama* (Groningen, 1935). Ezra Kempten Maxfield, 'The Quakers in English Stage Plays before 1800', *Publications of the Modern Languages Association*, xl (1925), pp. 874-80. Donald Clark Wall, *The Restoration Rake in Life and Comedy*, unpubl. Ph.D. thesis, University of Florida (1962); Lemiel N. Norell, *The Cuckold in Restoration Comedy*, unpubl. Ph.d. thesis, University of Florida (1962). The volume in question is Harry W. Pedicord, *The Theatrical Public in the Time of Garrick* (New York, 1954). There are also some perceptive paragraphs in the introductions to *The London Stage* (Carbondale, 1965-8).

CHAPTER SEVEN

The New World of Children in Eighteenth-century England

The new wave of historians of childhood[1] have not yet examined the role of children as consumers but the lives of children were influenced by the growth of a consumer economy as much as were gardens or politics or women or fashion. They became a sales target—their toys, their books, their clothes and even their education. Social envy, social pride expressed either in possessions or services enjoyed were easy to stimulate for commercial profit. For the last two hundred and fifty years one of the easiest routes to a middle-class man or woman's pocket has been through his children. But before the full economic exploitation of children could develop, it was very necessary to change attitudes towards them. This happened partly consciously and partly unconsciously. To spend more money on children required not only greater surplus income but also a preoccupation with the child's future and his or her standing in society. Before 1700, the dominant social attitude towards middle-class children had been more concerned with their relation with God, to their salvation, than with their social accomplishments, and the catechism had been one of the corner-stones of their education. Socialization rather than salvation became the new aim of education. Yet as fundamental as this change of attitude was an alteration in the demography of children.

In the seventeenth century the births of children had been deliberately limited and when born their life expectancy was low, so low that many parents, though not all, could not bear to burden themselves with an emotional commitment to a life that might be so very transient. In the eighteenth century, however, small-pox, one of the great killers, was slowly mastered, the plague died out, but more important still, people began to marry earlier. The easing economic climate, the greater opportunities for work and success, perhaps even better food, all worked towards the increase

---

[1] Philippe Ariès, *Centuries of Childhood: A Social History of Family Life* (London, 1962). See also John C. Sommerville, 'Towards a History of Childhood and Youth', *Jl. Interdisciplinary History*, iii (1972), pp. 438–47. Particularly valuable are the following: Peter Coveney, *The Image of Childhood: The Individual and Society. A Study of the Theme in English Literature* (Baltimore, 1967); David Hunt, *Parents and Children in History* (New York, 1970); Lloyd de Mause (ed.) *The History of Childhood* (New York, 1974); Peter Laslett, *The World We Have Lost* (London, 1965); John Demos, *A Little Commonwealth: Family Life in Plymouth Colony* (New York, 1970); Ivy Pinchbeck and Margaret Hewitt, *Children in English Society*, 2 vols. (London 1969–73); Alan Macfarlane, *The Family Life of Ralph Josselin* (Cambridge, 1970).

in the number of children born and to a somewhat greater rate of survival. Hence parents, although still frequently forced to face the tragedy of a child's death, had an increasing expectation that they might live: hence, in economic and social terms, a less risky vehicle for capital investment.

In the late seventeenth century we can discern a new social attitude towards children developing, and it was this attitude which John Locke gave literary force and substance in what was to prove as influential as any work that he produced, his *Some Thoughts Concerning Education,* published in 1693.[2] The dominant attitude towards children in the seventeenth century had been autocratic, indeed ferocious. 'The new borne babe', wrote Richard Allestree in 1658, 'is full of the stains and pollutions of sin which it inherits from our first parents through our loins.'[3] From birth English children were constrained. They spent their first months, sometimes a year, bound tightly in swaddling bands. Their common lot was fierce parental discipline, even a man of a warm and kindly nature such as Samuel Pepys thought nothing of beating his fifteen-year-old maid with a broomstick, and locking her up for the night in his cellar, or whipping his boy-servant, or even boxing his clerk's ears.[4] Samuel Byrd, of Virginia, who rebuked his wife for severity towards a servant, could make a young dependant of his, Eugene, drink, according to Byrd's diary, 'a pint of piss' as a punishment for bed-wetting. A fortnight later the same punishment was inflicted, apparently with success, because some weeks later Eugene, according to the diary, was flogged just 'for nothing'.[5] Lloyd de Mause reports that 'the earliest lives I have found of children who may not have been beaten at all date from 1690'.[6] And of two hundred counsels of advice on child-rearing prior to 1700, only three, Plutarch, Palmieri and Sadoleto, failed to recommend that fathers beat their children.[7]

Subservience was expected from children, and sometimes the autocratic power of the father was enforced by law. It was a crime in New England, punishable by death, for a child of sixteen to curse or strike a parent.[8] Harsh

---

[2] *The Educational Writings of John Locke,* ed. James L. Axtell (Cambridge, 1965), is the best edition of *Some Thoughts.* It also contains an admirable introduction. For Rousseau, see Henri Roddier, *Rousseau en Angleterre* (Paris, 1950); W. A. C. Stewart and W. P. McCann, *The Educational Innovators, 1750-1800* (London, 1967), pp. 23-35; A. A. Evans, 'The Impact of Rousseau on English Education', *Researches and Studies,* University of Leeds, Institute of Education, no. 11 (Leeds, 1955), pp. 15-25.
[3] Richard Allestree, *The Whole Duty of Man* (London, 1658), p. 20.
[4] *Diary of Samuel Pepys,* ed. Robert Latham and William Mathews, i-viii (London, 1970-74), *passim.*
[5] *The Secret Diary of William Byrd of Westover 1709-12,* ed. Louis B. Wright and Marion Tinling (Richmond, 1941), quoted in John F. Walzer, 'A Period of Ambivalence', in de Mause (ed.), *The History of Childhood,* p. 369.
[6] Lloyd de Mause, 'The Evolution of Childhood', ibid., p. 42.
[7] Ibid., p. 40.
[8] Demos, op. cit., p. 100. No case of a child being executed is known, but they were publicly flogged for the offence.

discipline was the child's lot, and they were often terrorized deliberately and, not infrequently, sexually abused.[9] Their toys were few, often homemade, and, except for the very rich, their pets were usually purposeful—a pony for riding, a dog for shooting and hunting.[10] Much of their education was devoted to religion and to the catechism. Naturally, there were many exceptions to this dark picture—parents who doted on their children, and who played with them; they were a minority, for most of the upper and middle classes rarely had their children at home. If they had children in the house, they were more often than not other people's, and therefore more likely to be ill-treated.[11] The typical childhood of an upper-class English boy of the late seventeenth century was Sir Robert Walpole's, who was born in 1676. Almost immediately after birth he was sent out to a wet-nurse at the nearby village of Syderstone, where he remained until he was weaned, at about eighteen months. At six he was dispatched to a school at Great Dunham kept by the rector, Richard Ransome, where he remained, enjoying only very brief holidays, until he went to Eton; nor did he go home for all of his holidays. Often he stayed with Townshend relations nearby. Indeed, until he was summoned home from King's College, Cambridge, in 1698, after the death of his elder brother, Walpole had rarely spent more than a few weeks at his Norfolk home in any year since he was six.[12] Not all families, however, sent their children away from home so early, or for so long. The Ishams were kept at home by Sir Justinian, their father, and taught by a tutor who lived at Lamport.[13] Some others, however, like the Earl of Sandwich, sent their sons in the first instance to the local grammar school.[14] We need a far more systematic study of the education of the gentry and aristocracy then we have, but the impression is that the Ishams and Sandwiches were a minority, and most gentry families acted like the Walpoles. This meant that children and parents shared few pursuits together, and the art of the seventeenth century would seem to bear this out. Up to about 1730 family portraits are formally posed groups; increasingly, however, after 1730 children are shown playing or reading or sketching or fishing or picnicking with their parents—family scenes of mutual pleasure and enjoyment, and ones which the parents wanted recorded. One has only to compare Michael

[9] *Diary of Samuel Pepys*, viii, pp. 276, 280, 451 ff. Pepys frequently abused his female servants—references are scattered throughout the diary, and on occasion the maid lost her post because of the jealousy of Pepys's wife.

[10] Toys were available at country fairs, but in 1700 there was no shop, not even in London, specializing in children's toys.

[11] For treatment of apprentices, see Steven R. Smith, 'The London Apprentices as Seventeenth-Century Adolescents', *Past and Present*, no. 61 (Nov. 1973), pp. 152-3, where he quotes a number of horrifying cases which came before the Middlesex Quarter Sessions. It required considerable courage, or neighbourly assistance, for a boy or girl of thirteen or fourteen to sue a master. Much brutality went unchecked.

[12] J. H. Plumb, *Sir Robert Walpole, The Making of a Statesman* (London, 1956), pp. 87-8.

[13] The Diary of Thomas Isham of Lamport 1671-73, ed. Sir Giles Isham (Farnborough, 1971).

[14] *The Diary of Samuel Pepys*, viii, p. 472.

Wright's 'Sir Robert Vyner and Family' (1673) with David Allan's 'Family of Sir J. Hunter Blair, Bt.'.[15] Also, portraits of individual children are far more common in the eighteenth century than in the seventeenth, again arguing both for a change in fashionable attitudes, and also, may be, for a greater emotional investment in children by parents.

There had been, however, towards the end of the seventeenth century, a perceptible new attitude—John Evelyn, long before Locke, had practised many of the Lockeian ideas on education on his own son, preferring a system of rewards, provocations, emulation and self-discipline to physical punishment or verbal chastisement. His whimsical friend, Aubrey, was also strongly against corporal punishment, although he allowed the use of thumbscrews as a last resort.[16] Indeed, Locke's book encapsulates what was clearly a new and growing attitude towards child-rearing and education which was to improve the lot of the child in the eighteenth century.

Locke, although not opposed to corporal punishment as a final sanction, nor indeed for very young children of an age too tender to be reasoned with, in order to instil the necessary fear and awe that a child should have for an adult, strongly disapproved of beating once formal education had begun, just as he was equally opposed to bribing the child to work through material rewards.

> The *Rewards* and *Punishments* then, whereby we should keep children in order, *are* quite of another kind; and of that force, that when we can get them once to work, the Business, I think, is done, and the Difficulty is over. *Esteem* and *Disgrace* are, of all others, the most powerful Incentives to the Mind, when once it is brought to relish them. If you can once get into Children a Love of Credit, and an Apprehension of Shame and Disgrace, you have put into them the true principle...[17]

As well as arguing for a more liberal attitude towards the child, Locke also pleaded for a broader curriculum. He believed education should fit man for society, as well as equipping him with learning, hence he pressed not only for lessons in drawing, but also in French. Indeed, he opposed rigid grounding in English grammar and urged that Latin be taught by the direct method, as it would have been had it been a living language.[18]

---

[15] Michael Wright's 'Sir Robert Vyner and Family' is illustrated, plate 67, in Ellis K. Waterhouse, *Painting in Britain 1530–1740* (London, 1953); see ibid., plate 191(A), for 'Family of Sir J. Hunter Blair, Bt.' For Wheatley's 'Browne Family', see *Painting in England 1700–1850. Collection of Mr. and Mrs. Paul Mellon* (Richmond, Virginia, 1963), p. 207.

[16] *Aubrey's Brief Lives*, ed. Oliver Lawson Dick, 3rd edn. (London, 1958), pp. xc-cxl. Like Locke, Aubrey believed in practical and modern subjects, but, as might be expected, his choice was odder, if sensible. 'Cookery, Chemistry, Cards (They might have a Banke for wine, of the money that is wonne at play every night). Merchants Accounts, the Mathematicks, and Dancing.' He believed that 'a Schoole should be indeed the house of play and pleasure.' See *Aubrey On Education*, ed. J. E. Stephens (London, 1972), p. 38.

[17] *The Educational Writings of John Locke*, ed. Axtell, pp. 152–3. Also p. 183: 'But, as I said before, *Beating* is the worst, and therefore the last Means to be used in the Correction of Children'.

[18] Ibid. pp. 267 ff.

Locke's attitude to child-rearing was as modern as his view of education. In his letters he encouraged breast-feeding by the mother, and was concerned with early toilet-training—indeed, his attitude towards the child was ahead of his time, but in no way original.[19] There had been a current of antipathy to the strict Calvinist view of the child throughout the seventeenth century; and the concept that, given the right environment and the proper course of education, compassion and benevolence, the essential goodness of the child would triumph over its propensity for evil, already had a longish history.

John Earle, as early as 1628, likens the child to Adam before the Fall—all innocence which time destroys, for experience corrupts; yet the original nature of the child is pure.[20] However, this thin stream that stems from earlier generations becomes a broad river in the generations that follow Locke.

After Locke the education of the child increasingly becomes social rather than religious. Morality is still uppermost, but it is a social morality with which parents and teachers are concerned, not the repression of old Adam, the suppression of evil, or the breaking of the will, and, in consequence, the view that a proper submissiveness in the child can only be achieved by harsh discipline weakens, at least for a time.[21] The birch existed, particularly in the older public and grammar schools, nor was it absent from some of the newer schools, if the denunciations of some publicists are to be believed.[22] Nevertheless, no one can read through the hundreds of advertisements in the provincial press for private schools, or the numerous handbooks on the care and education of children, or the occasional prospectuses of academies that have survived, without realizing that the emphasis on education had changed. Its aim was social, to equip the child with accomplishments that would secure for it gainful employment, and this, doubtless, was a major inducement for parents to spend money; but every advertisemet boasts that the school will instil those virtues—sobriety, obedience, industry, thrift, benevolence

---

[19] Joseph E. Illick, 'Child-Rearing in Seventeenth Century England and America', in de Mause (ed.), *A History of Childhood*, pp. 318-20 and 341, footnotes 68 and 69, and the sources there quoted.

[20] John Earle, *Micro-cosmographie* (London, 1628: S.T.C. 7439; 5th edn., London 1629: S.T.C. 7442), pp. 1-2: 'A child is a man in a small letter, yet the best copy of Adam before he tasted of Eve or the apple; and he is happy, whose small practice in the world can only write his Character. He is nature's fresh picture newly drawn in oil, which time, and much handling, dims and defaces. His Soul is yet a white paper unscribbled with observations of the world, wherewith, at length it comes a blurr'd note-book. He is purely happy, because he knows no evil....' However, Earle also believed in the rod. His attitude, although shared by a few, was less widely held then Allestree's. See George Boas, *The Cult of Childhood* (Studies of the Warburg Institute, xxix, London 1966), pp. 42-3.

[21] *Some Thoughts on Education* exercised immense influence from the moment it was published. It was reprinted nineteen times before 1761, and during the same period there were thirteen editions in French and five in Italian. See Axtell, op. cit., pp. 98-103.

[22] *Boswell's Life of Johnson*, ed. G. B. Hill, revised and enlarged edition by L. F. Powell (Oxford, 1934), ii, p. 407. 'There is less flogging in our great schools than formerly, but there is less learned there.' Dr. Johnson believed firmly in the educative powers of the rod: ibid., i, pp. 45-6.

and compassion—that educationalists regarded as the virtues of a successful social man. And the best way of achieving these ends was through developing the child's sense of emulation and shame. The true aim of education, according to the author of the *Dialogues on the Passions, Habits, Appetites and Affections etc., Peculiar to Children,* was not to teach bad Latin, harsh French, as if the children were 'a parcel of Parrots or Magpies', but 'to teach them the Government of themselves, their Passions and Appetites'. Better an increase of virtue than 'their abounding in human literature'. And teaching should be quite natural and the pupils free to speak as they wished before their masters. Indeed, the author was against all restrictions. Children should never realize that they are on a curb or under its direction. They must be taught through benevolence and sympathy; when the necessity arises shame may be used, but fear only in the last extremity, and then 'with such delicacy that if possible that habit may not gather strength by the use you are constrained to make of it'.[23] This, indeed, is a far cry from Sam Byrd's 'pint of piss' or beating his boy Eugene 'for nothing'. The attitude to children had radically changed. True, there were still plenty of pockets of sadism where the whip and the birch were freely used.[24] Not all fathers or mothers were converted so easily from tyranny to benevolence, but, by the 1740s, a new attitude to children was spreading steadily among the middle and upper classes. By 1780 John Browne could make one of the principal virtues of the expensive academy for gentlemen's sons that he proposed to set up a total absence of corporal punishment.[25] This gentle and more sensitive aproach to chidren was but a part of a wider change in social attitudes; a part of that belief that nature was inherently good, not evil, and what evil there was derived from man and his institutions; an attitude which was also reflected among a growing élite in a greater sensitivity towards women, slaves and animals.

Not only did this new attitude towards children begin to emerge among educationalists in the middle decades of the eighteenth century, but we can deduce also from the success of small private academies, from the development of a new kind of children's literature, and from the vastly increased expen-

---

[23] Anon., *Dialogues on the Passions, Habits, Appetites and Affections, etc., Peculiar to Children* (London, 1748), viii, pp. 8, 17-18.

[24] A very popular chap-book, sold for a penny, was titled *The Rod:* in lachrymose prose, a sermon by a Sunday-school mistress on the virtues of the birch rod. There is no Rousseauism here. 'Foolishness and bad passions are found in the heart of a child, and unless they are corrected and restrained, they grow stronger and stronger.' Victor E. Neuberg, *The Penny Histories* (Oxford, 1968), pp. 202-3. Corporal punishment was certainly widely used, and one must not exaggereate the prevalence of opposition to it.

[25] Brit. Lib., Sir Ambrose Heal's Collection of Trade Cards, *Proposals for Instituting and Establishing an Academy* by John Browne (London, 1780), p. 4: 'It is the opinion of the proposer that Chastisement should only be called in, when Emulation, and the rewards attending laudable endeavours in study and modest demeanour have failed'. And later, p. 8: 'Blows and all sorts of mean and slavish treatment are to be excluded this institution'. No teacher is to be allowed to punish any pupil in any way, punishment is reserved entirely to the Headmaster.

diture on the amusements and pleasures of children, that parents, too, were no longer regarding their children as sprigs of old Adam whose wills had to be broken. Many had come to look upon their children as vehicles of social emulation; hence they began to project their own social attitudes as the moral imperatives of childhood. And so education for society became paramount. Owing to the growth of economic opportunity and social mobility, it was now less necessary to make a child accept its calling as a dictate of God. Locke's attitudes were replacing those of the catechism.

The repercussions on the world of children were very great. Society required accomplishment, and accomplishment required expenditure. The children's new world became a market that could be exploited. Few desires will empty a pocket quicker than social aspiration—and the main route was, then as now, through education, which combined social adornment with the opportunity of a more financially rewarding career for children.

From 1700 to 1770 there was a steady growth in England of educational facilities, especially for the commercial classes, and probably for the skilled artisan; after 1770 this growth became very rapid indeed. About provision for the poor, except for charity schools, we know very little. Many villages had dame schools, and in most major towns evening classes could be very cheap.[26] Some aristocrats, such as the Marquis of Rockingham, provided a school on their estates, supporting the schoolmaster and buying the books.[27] Sunday schools were more concerned with religious indoctrination and social conformity than education, and only a few encouraged reading. Many of the patriarchally minded founding fathers of the Industrial Revolution ran schools, as Robert Owen did at New Lanark, or provided a craft teaching, as did Josiah Wedgwood, or supported schools, as did Jedediah Strutt and Richard Arkwright.[28] The variety of educational opportunity increased

[26] N. Hans, *New Trends in Education in the Eighteenth Century* (London, 1951), pp. 87-92. For village schools and dame schools, see *Archbishop Herring's Visitation Returns, 1743,* ed. S. L. Ollard and P. C. Walker (Yorks. Arch. Soc., lxxi, lxxii, lxxv, lxxvii, lxxix, 1928-31). Herring's third question 'Is there a Public or Charity School?' revealed that out of 645 returns, 266 parishes did not have a school of any kind. The worst-provided area was the East Riding. In many places the parish clerk has a few shillings of endowment to teach reading and the principles of the Christian religion. Very little but reading was taught in most parish schools; their aim was to inculcate obedience. Often parents, as at Barnborough, had to rely on 'an useful person to teach such children as they send to him, to read English, and some of them to write, they paying for those they send to him'. For the parish schools in Cheshire, see Robson, *Education in Cheshire*, pp. 11-43. Also M. G. Jones, *The Charity School Movement in the Eighteenth Century* (Cambridge, 1938). Evening classes were to be found in any town of consequence by 1770.

[27] Sheffield City Library, Wentworth Woodhouse Muniments, A. 1099, General Ledger 1765-70. The Marquis of Rockingham paid small salaries for schoolmasters in seven of his villages, and provided books. As the highest salary was £6, the schoolmasters were probably parish clerks who taught reading and 'the principles of the Christian religion'. Sir Griffith Boyston paid £5 a year at Barneston (Yorks) for twenty children to be taught the catechism. Lady Malton, however, kept a schoolmaster at Hoyland to teach both boys and girls English and writing. *Archbishop Herring's Visitation*, i, p. 109; ii, p. 65.

[28] R. S. Fitton and A. P. Wadsworth, *The Strutts and the Arkwrights* (Manchester, 1958), pp. 102-3; pp. 254-6.

considerably after 1750, whatever may have been happening at the universities and the more ancient grammar and so-called public schools.

The greatest surge in education took place in the small private schools and academies, most of which provided an education that was modern in outlook and socially orientated. The lifetime of these schools was often short, no longer than the working life of the school-master or mistress who started them. Indeed, frequently less, for many rapidly failed. The competition was intense and almost anyone with a little education felt that the teaching profession was an open road to financial security. Sometimes, however, the school rooted itself in a house and was sold, and so remained a school sometimes for decades, like Mrs. Barbauld's famous school at Palgrave, or the even more famous school at Cheam which still exists, as fashionable today as it was when it first started in 1752.[29]

The only source which gives an idea of the range of these small schools are advertisements in local newspapers which can be supplemented by town and country directories of the late eighteenth century, and occasionally by trade cards and handbills. Almost no county or district has yet been studied with the thoroughness which the subject deserves.[30] The size of these schools varied considerably, and so did the age of the pupils. Most were single-sex schools, but not all, and one ingenious schoolmaster took both sexes, but segregated them for teaching by placing his usher in a booth in the middle of the partition which kept them apart.[31] The subjects varied from the three R's for infants to navigation, fortification, trigonometry, surveying, merchants' accounts, and almost every European language. Music, art, dancing and fencing were the common extras. The emphasis, however, was overwhelmingly on commercial subjects for boys and social deportment for girls.[32]

---

[29] Stewart and McCann, *The Educational Innovators*, pp. 3-13.

[30] The major exceptions are: Robson, op. cit., which, however, is not strong on private schools; he lists twenty for the entire century which, compared with other districts, seems very small. Also Zena Crook and Brian Simon, 'Private Schools in Leicester and the County 1780-1840', in *Education in Leicestershire 1540-1940*. This, however, only deals with the last two decades of the century.

[31] *Ispwich Jl.*, 2 June 1744.

[32] The advertisements occur almost daily in every provincial newspaper from the 1760s onwards, and also many schools advertised by handbills and tradesmen's cards, which are to be found in the Sir Ambrose Heal Collection and the Banks Collection at the British Library, and among the collections at local record offices. A typical advertisement of the most enterprising schools is to be found in the *Leeds Mercury*, 2 February 1773:

At Eland near Halifax
Young Gentlemen are genteely boarded on EASY, MODERATE TERMS, and accurately instructed in the GREEK, LATIN, FRENCH AND ENGLISH LANGUAGES. They are also taught WRITING in an elegant manner: Arithmetic, in several Branches: BOOK KEEPING: the Elements of GEOMETRY and TRIGONOMETRY: ALGEBRA: NAVIGATION: MENSURATION of Superficies and Solids: GEOGRAPHY and the Use of Globes: the general PRINCIPLES OF NATURAL PHILOSOPHY and ASTRONOMY etc.

The greatest Attention is paid to their Improvement in MORALS as well as KNOWLEDGE: and nothing omitted that may be likely to render them useful Members of Society and happy in themselves.

What, perhaps, is most surprising, is that these schools were to be found more frequently in the old country towns, and the surrounding districts, than in the new manufacturing towns. The *Leeds Mecury* advertises surprisingly few schools, whereas the newspapers of Northampton, York, Norwich, Ispwich and similar towns are full of them. G. A. Cranfield counted one hundred schools advertised in the *Northampton Mercury* between 1720 and 1760, and sixty-three in the *Norwich Mercury* between 1749 and 1759.[33] Ipswich, however, provides a fascinating example, for the *Ipswich Journal* throughout the eighteenth century carried more advertisements than most provincial newspapers.[34] Between 1743 and 1747 the *Ipswich Journal* carried thirty-five advertisements for schools, of which ten were situated in Norfolk (one at North Walsham, seven at Norwich and two at Great Yarmouth), and three in Essex (Colchester, Great Baddow and Dedham).[35] Between 1783 and 1787 ninety-one schools advertised, and a further ten are mentioned through the individual advertisements of dancing masters. The geographical range is somewhat wider, for there are single advertisements for a school in Yorkshire, at Catterick, another in London, and one in Cambridgeshire, but the overwhelming majority are situated in west Suffolk—only two Norwich schools advertised in this period, and one of these is for a new headmaster, and not to solicit pupils. From this list it is clear that every town in Suffolk, no matter how small—for example Debenham, Needham Market, Boxford, Woodbridge, Lavenham or Long Melford—had their schools. But so did many villages, villages as small as Wyverstone, Walsham-le-Willows, Fornham St. Martin or Stonham Aspal. Ipswich, apart of course from its Grammar and Charity schools, schools which did not advertise, had eight such schools and four more were in villages in the immediate vicinity, two at Tuddenham, one at Claydon, and one at Hintelsham.[36]

As many of these schools were located in villages, one might expect that the overwhelming majority of schoolmasters would be clergymen. Not so. Only fourteen schools were run by the clergy; of the rest seventeen were run

---

[33] G. A. Cranfield, *The Development of the Provincial Newspaper,* 1700–1760 (Oxford, 1962), p. 215.
[34] Ibid., pp. 209–10. Only the *Newcastle Jl.* and *York Courant* surpassed the *Ipswich Jl.* in number of advertisements printed in the 1750s. Both average above 2,000 per year, Newcastle, indeed, topping 3,000 in 1753.
[35] I am indebted to my research assistants, David Vincent and Andrew Parkinson, for help with the material about Suffolk. From 1740 to 1744 23 schools advertised in the *Newcastle Jl.* In 1767, the *Liverpool Directory* lists 24 schoolmasters—two were teachers of French, two were dancing masters, and two masters at the Charity (Blue Coat) School, two were women who kept boarding schools. There were still 25 when the Fourth Directory was printed in 1773, but in 1774 (Fifth Directory) the number had jumped to 29, and included a lecturer in philosophy, appropriately living at Newton's Head, 17 Pool Lane. In Bristol in *Matthew's Directory* for 1793/4 there are listed 55 educational establishments and 57 people concerned with education. By any standards, these figures are very impressive.
[36] *Ipswich Jl.* 1783–7, *passim.*

by women, one by a man and wife, and the remainder by men.[37] This should, perhaps, not be surprising, as the subjects taught were largely those for which clergymen had not been trained—for the education offered was more frequently commercial and social, and less frequently classical and mathematical. The curriculum of most schools was very varied, and although all schools do not advertise their wares, many do, either in the newspapers, or by prospectuses and handbills, or by both. In the 1780s only five schools advertised the teaching of reading, which would imply that almost all schools expected that the child would have been taught to read at home, even though schools offered to take boys of six.[38] The availability of attractive primers for small children had made the teaching of reading in the home much easier. The most popular subjects were writing, which almost certainly implies the hands required by clerks, either legal or mercantile (thirty-four advertisements), arithmetic (twenty-nine), English (twenty-two), drawing (nineteen), dancing (sixteen), and music (twelve). Other subjects offered were French, Latin, mathematics, mensuration, accounts, navigation, surveying, needlework, and one school taught experimental philosophy.[39]

The size of the school is less easy to discover than the subjects taught; a very fashionable school such as Cheam has a limit of eighty pupils, but this was exceptional for this type of school.[40] The author of the *Dialogues on the Passions, Habits, Appetites and Affections, etc., Peculiar to Children* thought that twenty boys ought to be a full complement.[41] Occasionally a school advertisement gives a precise figure: John Smith of Bury St. Edmunds starting a new school in 1786 had room for six boarders and twenty day-boys.[42] The Barbaulds at Palgrave in Norfolk, just over the border from Suffolk, limited their boarders to thirty.[43] The Rev. J. Holmes of Stoke-by-Clare, who concentrated on a mathematical and classical education to prepare boys for Cambridge, took thirty-five pupils.[44] When Mrs. Dawson opened a Ladies' Boarding School in Park Row, Leeds, she advertised for twenty boarders.[45] A very cheap day-school in the same town advertised that

---

[37] The Schools run by clergy were at Stonham Aspal, Lavenham, Dedham, Needham Market (2), Palgrave, Bury, Wyverstone, Benthall, Ditchingham, Norwich, Stoke by Clare, Boxford. Girls' boarding schools were located at Ipswich (3), Thetford, Beccles, Norwich, Manningtree, Bury (2), Harleston, Diss (3), Hadleigh, Long Melford (2), Swaffham.

[38] They were at Yarmouth (Southtown), a very cheap school indeed—only 4s. a quarter for reading; at the Misses Brands at Norwich; and schools at Claydon, St. Osyth and Earl Soham.

[39] As might be expected from friends of Joseph Priestly, Palgrave was the school that taught experimental philosophy.

[40] For Cheam, see Stewart and McCann, op. cit., p. 5. Bradford Grammar School, a flourishing eighteenth-century school, had 60 pupils in 1743: *Archbishop Herring's Visitation Returns*, 1743, i, p. 59.

[41] *Dialogues on the Passions, Habits, Appetites and Affections, etc., Peculiar to Children*, p. 6.

[42] *Ipswich Jl.*, 23 December 1786.

[43] Eric Pursehouse, *Waveney Valley Studies* (Diss, n.d.), p. 123.

[44] *Ipswich Jl.*, 22 December 1787.

[45] *Leeds Intelligencer*, 21 March 1780.

it would not take more than twenty.[46] A smart and very expensive Ladies' Academy at Clifton, near Bristol, took only twelve girls,[47] and Mr. Moor of Sidmouth, also expensive, permitted himself only eight pupils, but he could boast that each pupil had his own bed, and those who bathed were attended by a servant.[48] It would seem that one schoolmaster, perhaps with help from wife, daughter, or son, could manage twenty boarders but, above that number, an assistant might be needed. Even small schools were dependent on itinerant teachers of music, dancing, drawing, and sometimes fencing, for which the pupils usually paid extra—typical charges being two to six guineas for these subjects. John White and his sons taught dancing over a wide area of East Anglia, covering most of north Essex and west Suffolk; they claimed to be teaching in nineteen schools at one time, and they must have spent a great deal of their lives on horseback;[49] Harrington, a dancing master, not quite so peripatetic, nevertheless serviced several schools around Ipswich.[50] Bonington, the famous painter's father, was a drawing master in Nottingham, but he rode over to Sheffield, some thirty miles away, to take weekly classes.[51] The age of pupils was as varied as their numbers. Some specialized in very young children—Mrs. Rowe and Miss Whitman of Bristol took boys from three to ten in their boarding school;[52] five to six, however, was a more usual age. Terminal ages varied from eight to sixteen, or possibly later, as the information given by advertisements is not very exact. Almost certainly, however, the leaving age for most pupils was late adolescence for the commercially orientated schools and girls' schools, and early adolescence for the classical preparatory schools whose pupils either went on to a public school or, if exceptionally bright, to the university or one of the Dissenting academies.

The cost of school varied from the very expensive, such as Bristol Ladies' Academy, at £50 a year plus extras, to the exceedingly cheap, such as Mr. Wray, who had a room in Mr. Tinsdale's Yard in Briggate, Leeds, who charged 7s. 6d. per quarter for reading, and 10s. 6d. for grammar. As the room limited him to twenty scholars, his total earnings were unlikely to be

---

[46] Ibid., 2 January 1781.
[47] *Felix Farley's Bristol Jl.*, 9 March 1805.
[48] Ibid., 13 and 20 July 1805.
[49] *Ipswich Jl.*, 3 July 1784. They claimed to teach at Ipswich and the following schools: Bury, Walsham-le-Willows, Mendlesham, Lavenham, Long Melford, Cavendish, Timworth, Linton, Saffron Walden, Old Samford, Thaxted, Little Writtle, Danbury, Southminster, Maldon, Witham, South Halsted and Colchester.
[50] Ibid., 27 December 1783.
[51] *The Encyclopaedia of World Art* (New York, 1960), ii, pp. 545-6. Also W. A. Noblett, 'Printing and the Book Trade in Sheffield in the Latter Half of the Eighteenth Century' (Univ. of Sheffield, School of Librarianship, M. A. thesis, 1974), p. 68. Bonington gave lessons at Jennings Circulating Library.

I am greatly indebted to William Noblett for a great deal of research as well as criticism in the writing of this chapter.

[52] *Felix Farley's Bristol Jl.*, 19 January 1805.

more than £40—£50 per annum gross, if he filled his room and survived.[53] Some schoolmasters, of course, did not. How many failed we shall never know, but James Leathhead, a Newcastle schoolmaster, was reduced to coining and absconded;[54] Mary Wollstonecraft struggled hard for a few years at Stoke Newington, but finally failed financially, as well as becoming bored with the project—a fate which one suspects overtook many hopefuls.[55] It was often difficult, owing to intense competition, for the less successful, and they tried to survive by developing ancillary occupations. John Richardson, who ran a school in Paradise Square, Sheffield, combined it with a circulating library which opened before school, during the two-hour dinner break, and again when school closed. If not enough, he also gave evening classes for aspiring apprentices and free Sunday school for poor widows' children. And his wife also ran a girls' school.[56] Another schoolmaster in Newcastle sold ink as a sideline;[57] another, this time at Darlington, went in for haberdashery.[58] Others survived by giving evening lectures in science, popular in Leeds and Newcastle;[59] others taught evening classes to 'young gentlemen', presumably apprentices or shop-assistants who had done a day's work.[60] It was obviously difficult for some schoolmasters to make an adequate living from the fees of their pupils, probably because intense competition by the 1780s had overcrowded the profession. This may also be the reason for the modesty of the average charges. The usual fees in the 1780s for the more expensive and well-established schools were, for full boarders, sometimes known as parlour boarders, about £20 to £25 per year, usually excluding washing; day-boarders, presumably those children who went home on Saturday and Sunday, thirteen to eighteen guineas; day-scholars, two to four guineas. Schools tended to be somewhat cheaper in the north than the south of England.[61] Children under ten were usually boarded more cheaply.[62] These costs are also substantiated by a number of school bills and it is

---

[53] *Leeds Intelligencer*, 2 January 1781.
[54] *Newcastle Jl.*, 12 November 1743. Leathhead had run a school in Westgate Street, Newcastle, and specialized in lectures on geography: ibid., 19 March 1743.
[55] Claire Tomalin, *The Life and Death of Mary Wollstonecraft* (London, 1974), pp. 29-44.
[56] See Noblett, op. cit., pp. 62-3.
[57] *Newcastle Jl.*, 1 August 1741; 12 May 1743. He ran a school at the Hen and Chickens, Groat Market, Newcastle, removed in 1742 to the Queen's Head.
[58] Ibid., 14 May 1743. Joseph Foster advertised that he was a haberdasher of hats as well as a schoolmaster, willing to teach anything from Latin to navigation.
[59] Ibid., 11 August 1744; *Leeds Mercury*, 13 February 1739; 1 July 1773; 28 March 1780.
[60] A typical example is F. Coulton, who taught, in North Street, York, young ladies from 5.00 to 7.00 p.m. for writing and arithmetic at 5s. per quarter and young gentlemen from 7.00 to 9.00 p.m. writing and arithmetic at 5s. per quarter and mathematics and book-keeping for 7s. 6d. He charged 7s. 6d. entrance. *York Courant*, 23 May 1780. Such classes were a commonplace of any town of modest size by the 1780s.
[61] However, it was quite easy in most areas to find a good school for 14 guineas for boys and 12 guineas for girls, plus the usual entrance fee and extras. University preparation—classics and mathematics—was always more expensive than commercial subjects.
[62] For example, Miss Cole, who taught, in Tower Churchyard, Ipswich, boys from 3 to 6 years, charged £10 plus half a guinea entrance: *Ipswich Jl.*, 21 February 1795.

obvious from these that schoolmasters made a shilling whenever they could by charging for laundry, mending and hair-cutting. A year's education of a son of a Mr. Bennet cost £31 7s. 6d. and this included everything—transport to the school, pocket-money, books, pens, ink, laundry, mending shirts, hair-cutting, postage, indeed every possible expenditure.[63]

Considering that these children were at school often for ten months of the year, the prices were remarkably low. Most schools charged a modest entrance fee, which would suggest that the drop-out rate may have been high, or that, among the day-scholars, fees might be hard to collect, for the entrance fee for these pupils was high, usually a guinea, half of their yearly fee. Two guineas for a year's schooling was not, in terms of a family budget, beyond the means of eighteenth-century shopkeepers, small farmers, tenant farmers, or, indeed, skilled artisans for that matter. Whether or not classes as low in the social scale as artisans sent their children to school is almost impossible to discover. Probably not, but who supported these schools is unlikely to be known. Small squires, farmers, tradesmen, merchants, shopkeepers and clerks most certainly, but there are, so far as I know, few lists, except for schools of great distinction, such as Cheam or Mrs. Barbauld's at Palgrave. The best schools are likely to have been those run by the clergy and the letters of the young Macaulay give one an insight into the high quality of teaching and care that such a school might provide.[64] Most were commercial, profit-orientated enterprises, battening on the social emulation that parents were increasingly focusing on their children.

Many schoolmasters, as the author of the *Dialogues* wrote, crammed as

---

[63] Brit. Lib., Ambrose Heal Coll.; one of the half-yearly bills is worth quoting in full:
Mr. Chas. Bennet Dr. To John Williams
1755

For a Years boarding and schooling due at Midsummer	£10. 10. -
Coach downe	- 3. -
2 writing books & 1 slate	- 3. 6
Whole Duty of Man	- 3. -
Caesar's Commentaries	- 6. -
Letters	- 1. 6
Cutting & curling hair	- 1. -
Ribbon & Worsted	- 3. -
Pens Ink & Paper	- 3. -
3 shirts mended	- 1. 6
Weekly allowance	- 9. -
Mending cloaths	- 8. -
Shoemakers bills	- 6. 2
Coach to London	- 3. -
Set of Merchants Accounts	- 10. 6
Dancing	1. 1. -
	£14. 12. 9

[64] *The Letters of Macaulay*, ed. Thomas Pinney (Cambridge, 1974), p. 1, *passim*. A list has been discovered of Fairbank's School, Sheffield, which may make some identification possible: T. Warner Hall, *The Fairbanks of Sheffield, 1688 to 1848* (Sheffield, 1932), pp. 6-7 (*ex inf*. W. A. Noblett).

many children as they could into a large house in order to compensate for the smallness of their fees, and then taught them 'like a parcel of Parrots or Magpies'.[65] This might do for the cheap end of the market, but competition was fierce and so entrepreneurial vigour was no more absent in schools than it was in selling children's literature. After all, parents had to be *attracted* to schools. The obvious method was to provide subjects which appeared useful for a career, or to add, especially with girls, to social graces. Some schools, with the army in mind, provided military education, others provided for law, for professional estate management, and for the life of a merchant.[66] These were obvious means of attracting clients. As all the advertisements puff the services of dancing masters, these extra-curricular subjects obviously had great appeal. However, many schools felt more was needed; and then, as now, headmasters set out to create school loyalty by annual reunions, probably copied from Eton and Oxford and Cambridge Colleges.[67] Old Johnians (Cambridge) in Yorkshire were holding annual, sometimes bi-annual feasts by the 1750s; Old Etonian reunions in London were common in the 1730s.[68] School balls in which the pupils could show off their social graces to the town were a commonplace of the Assembly Rooms, and widely advertised; plays and charades and musical evenings also helped to establish the social superiority of a school. At least one school held a yearly exhibition of calligraphy and in the early nineteenth century the headmaster of a commercial school at Diss in Norfolk held the yearly examinations before an audience of parents and patrons.[69] I have not, however, among these schools, traced any competitive games in the eighteenth century. Indeed, games are never mentioned, one alone boasted of a gymnasium.[70] Commodious playgrounds are sometimes advertised, frequently a large library, and even more often opportunities for playing music (and one for using scientific

---

[65] *Dialogues on the Passions*..., p. viii.
[66] Brit. Lib. Banks Coll., handbill advertisements for 'The Naval, Military and Mercantile Academy' at Rotherhithe. Fencing, music, drawing and dancing were offered as extras, taught by visiting masters. A similar institution existed, not surprisingly, at Cold Harbour, Gosport: *Salisbury and Wilts. Jl.* 2 January 1797. *The Bury Post*, 13 March 1799, for a school kept by a land-surveyor. Also *Leeds Mercury*, 20 July 1773. See also Appendix.
[67] Palgrave School, Norfolk, held regular reunions; so did the school at Wyverstone, a very small Suffolk village: *Ipswich Jl.*, 7 August 1795; ibid., 21 August 1789. It was indeed the most common method used for breeding school loyalty. Wakefield School prudently held its reunion in race-week: *York Courant*, 30 July 1754.
[68] *Leeds Mercury*, 1 May 1750. From the style of the advertisement—both stewards had been appointed—it would seem that meetings of Old Johnians at the White Hart, Wakefield, were well established. There were 18 advertisements for Old Etonians' meetings in the *Daily Advertiser* for 1731.
[69] School balls: *Salisbury and Wilts. Jl.*, 10 May 1797; *York Courant*, 30 April 1759; *Leeds Mercury* 23 November, 28 September 1773. Plays, concerts and charades: *Suffolk Mercury*, 28 October, 1734. Calligraphy and public examinations: Pursehouse, *Waveney Valley Studies*, p. 73; *Salisbury and Wilts. Jl.*, 5 June 1797.
[70] *York Courant*, 12 September 1780. S. Morny, headmaster of Kirkleatham Grammar School, advertised his gymnasium. He was an ardent follower of the educational innovator, David Williams.

apparatus).[71] Some schools, following the best of all entrepreneurial precepts, charged extravagant fees; nothing is more ostentatious, nothing more likely to create envy in those who would, but could not, emulate, and so some schools boasted of their high fees and tiny numbers. Although there is a great deal of uncertainty, one can be sure that the lower middle class were spending far more on their children's education than this class had ever done before. We could be more certain of this if we knew more about day-scholars whose fees might be very low indeed. Children had become counters in the parents' social aspirations; their son's or daughter's education reflected status. And the image of the child which the schools, as well as children's literature projected was the image of an ideal parent's child—industrious, obedient, constantly respectful; and indeed a pet, never too spoilt, but occasionally indulged as a reward for virtue. Reality was, of course, harsher, but you do not sell much except through hope and illusion—at least educationally.

Parents were commercial targets through their children—they could, through the best of motives, be made to spend money on schools which they could scarcely afford, but there were other ways to the parents' pocket-books: educational games and instructional toys, which became increasingly available as the century progressed.

Books by which children could be taught had existed from the first days of printing—alphabets, grammars, and the like—but few, if any, were designed specifically for children. Authors and publishers made very little attempt to entice the young mind. Fairy stories, ballads, riddles and fables were intended as much for adults as for children. Indeed, Aesop was not specifically adapted for children until 1692, when Roger l'Estrange produced his edition.[72]

As with so many cultural developments, the late seventeenth and early eighteenth centuries saw the beginnings of a changed attitude towards children's literature and methods of learning to read. In 1694 'J. G.' published 'A Play-book for children to allure them to read as soon as possible. Composed of small pages on purpose not to tire children and printed with a fair and pleasant letter. The matter and method plain and easier than any yet extant', which was, for once, a true statement in a blurb. The book has wide margins, large type; its language simple and concrete and mostly within the compass of a child's experience. The author states in his preface that he

---

[71] *Felix Farley's Bristol Jl.*, 12 January 1805 (playground). *Ipswich Jl.*, 24 June 1786; ibid., 14 January 1775 (library). Brit. Lib., Banks Coll., handbill for J. Sharp's School in Warwick: 'Such young Gentlemen who are of an age, and have Genius and Inclination to improve by Reading and Experiments, will have free Access to the Library, furnished with the best initiating Authors in the Arts and Sciences, and a proper Apparatus of Mathematical and Philosophical Instruments' (c 1775). *Newcastle Jl.*, 16 May 1741.

[72] John Locke was strongly in favour of using a simplified version of Aesop, with woodcuts and interlinear translation. His edition appeared in 1703. Axtell, op. cit., p. 271, n. 2.

wished 'to decoy Children in to reading'.[73] It did well enough to be reprinted in 1703, by which time a few other authors—notably William Ronksley—were attempting to find methods and materials more suitable for very young children. He believed in teaching by verse according to the metre of the Psalms—first week, words of one syllable, the next week words of two syllables, and so on. And he used jokes, riddles and proverbs to sugar his pills.[74] Even so, his and other innovative children's books of Queen Anne's reign were designed, quite obviously, to be chanted, to be learnt by the ear, rather than by the eye. They were more for teachers and parents to teach with than books meant for a child's own enjoyment. Similar books were slow to appear and it is not until the 1740s that the change in style of children's literature becomes very marked. The entrepreneurial noses of Thomas Boreman and John Newbery twitched and scented a market for books that would be simple in production, enticing to the eye, and written specifically for children. Of course, it was not quite as simple as that. Children do not buy books, adults do.

So the new children's literature was designed to attract adults, to project an image of those virtues which parents wished to inculcate in their offspring, as well as to beguile the child. These alphabet and reading books, by their simplicity, also strengthened the confidence of parents in their ability to teach their children to read in the home. The new children's literature was aimed at the young, but only through the refraction of the parental eye.

By the 1740s and '50s, as in so many aspects of English life, the market was there, ready to be exploited, and no man was quicker to seize the opportunity than John Newbery, whose *Pretty Little Pocket Book,* in 1742, captured the public imagination. Until the early nineteenth century Newbery's family produced vast quantities of children's literature.[75] Each decade the number of titles grew, and the most popular books were reprinted over and over again. His range was exceptional—from simple books for reading, writing and arithmetic, to Sir Isaac Newton's philosophy digested for young minds by Tom Telescope.[76] This book—*The Newtonian System of Philosophy adapted to the Capacities of Young Gentlemen and Ladies,* to give it its full title—is one of the most remarkable children's books printed in the eighteenth century—its authorship, alas, is problematic; it may be by Oliver Goldsmith,

---

[73] William Sloane, *Children's Books in England and America in the Seventeenth Century* (New York, 1955), p. 211.

[74] Ibid., pp. 225-7.

[75] For Newbery and his family, see S. Roscoe, *John Newbery and his Successors, 1740-1814; a Bibliography* (Wormley, Herts., 1973); Charles Welsh, *A Bookseller in the Last Century* (London, 1885); William Noblett, 'John Newbery, Publisher Extraordinary', *History Today,* xxii (April 1972), pp. 265-71. *A Pretty Little Pocket Book,* ed. M. F. Thwaite (Oxford, 1966).

[76] Roscoe, op. cit., pp. 252-3. 'Tom Telescope' may have been a pseudonym for Newbery himself. First published in 1761, there were nine editions by the end of the century.

it could have been written by John Newbery himself. It is crystal-clear, the examples exceptionally apposite, and its attitude to the universe, to philosophy, to humanity, and to the natural sciences would have drawn prolonged cheers from the Encyclopaedists. Hence it is not only a brilliantly produced book for adolescent children, but it also gives a novel insight in how the ideas of the Enlightenment were being disseminated through society. The way ideas become social attitudes is one of the most complex problems that face a social historian, and almost all have neglected the influence of children's literature in changing the climate of ideas. Therefore Tom Telescope deserves a closer study.

There are six lectures. The first is on matter and motion, quite brilliantly explained. The second deals with the universe, particularly the solar system, and also with the velocity of light. Tom Telescope then moves on to atmosphere and meteors, and so to mountains, particularly volcanoes, and earthquakes, and so to rivers and the sea. Minerals, vegetables, and animals follow, and the final lecture is on the natural philosophy of man—his senses, the nature of his understanding, and the origin of ideas, with a great deal on optics, including the prism; Tom also deals with pleasure and pain. The book is relatively brief—only 126 pages—nevertheless it is wide-ranging, giving a simple outline of the most advanced attitude to the universe and to man's place in it. God is present, but only as divine wisdom which reason will, if pursued, ultimately reveal to mankind.

The philosophic attitude is purely Lockeian, as the science is entirely Newtonian. 'All our ideas, therefore,' says Tom Telescope, 'are obtained either by *sensation* or *reflection*, that is to say, by means of our five senses, as *seeing, hearing, smelling, tasting,* and *touching,* or by the *operations of the mind* [upon them].' Although packed with lucid scientific information, the book has many asides, allegories, and stories that plead for a compassionate humanity, particularly toward animals. Cruelty to animals is improper, although cruelty between animals is necessary to sustain the life of the animal creation; hence cruelty, in this aspect, is a part of divine wisdom, but such necessity alone permits cruelty in the shape of killing and eating. Wanton cruelty is reprehensible, particularly to young animals and, above all, young birds. Most detestable of all is cruelty to a mother bird by the taking or destruction of eggs. (This is an exceptionally common theme in children's books.) Tom has no patience, however, with those who put kindness to animals before that to their fellow men. Tom's lecture reminds his hostess, Lady Caroline, of one of her neighbours, Sir Thomas, whom young Tom has seen treat animals well if they please, 'but rave, at the same time, in a merciless manner, at poor children who were shivering at his gate, and send them away empty handed.' Another neighbour, Sir William, 'is also of the same disposition; he will not sell a horse, that is declining, for fear he should fall into the hands of a master who might treat him with cruelty; but he is largely concerned in the slave trade (which, I think, is carried on by none but *we good Christians,* to the dishonour of our *celestial Master*) and makes no difficulty of separating the husband from the wife, the parents from the children, and all of them ... from their native country, to be sold in a foreign market, like so many horses, and often to the most merciless of the human race.' Kindness to animals, yes, but greater kindness to human beings is the burden of Tom's final lecture.

Hence, perhaps, we may discern one way by which ideas became social attitudes, that is, through the education of young and impressionable minds. For Tom's book, I would say, was aimed to be read in the home—it was partly directed, like many children's books, in its sentiments to mothers (this is very marked in the passage about animals, cruelty to birds, and the like)—and read, I would have thought, to, or by, children between twelve and fourteen, the impressionable years. Certainly it had an extraordinary success. Within a few weeks of publication in 1761, it was on sale in Norwich and was being advertised there in the newspapers. A new edition was required in 1761, a third edition in 1766, and a fourth in 1770. Altogether there were at least ten editions by 1800. It is difficult to be in any way certain of the size of the edition of Newbery's books. He printed 1,500 copies of his juvenile edition of Dr. Johnson's *Idler*; but editions of 10,000 were made of his very popular *Pretty Little Pocket-Book.* Doubtless the editions of *Tom Telescope* varied, the second probably being much larger than the first, which, following Newbery's usual practice, would be small to test the market. A conservative estimate would be that the book enjoyed a sale of 25,000 to 30,000 copies between 1760 and 1800, but the number could be far higher. Hence Lockeian and Newtonian ideas, combined with a compassionate humanity, were being widely disseminated amongst the middle-class young, and must have influenced their attitude to life.

And it must be stressed that *Tom Telescope* was not a unique book. For example, *A Museum,* published probably for the first time in 1750 or earlier, contained essays on the solar system, on volcanoes and earthquakes, and on natural history. This work was aimed at a somewhat younger audience than *Tom Telescope,* but it was equally successful, running to fifteen editions by 1800, and nineteen in all. *A Museum* also contained, very much in the spirit of the *Encyclopaedia,* a description of the manners, customs, and habits of foreign countries.

Newbery and *Tom Telescope*'s success, naturally, did not go unnoticed, and the range of cheap books on science, designed for children, grew. The Reverend Samuel Ward produced twelve such volumes on *The Modern System of Natural History* in 1776. In the same year *Mr. Telltruth's Natural History of Birds and of Animals* was written for very young children—but again it was full of the reasonableness of nature. And it cost only sixpence. In 1800 one publisher, not Newbery, advertised thirty-eight books for children, covering the arts and sciences; of these, fifteen were scientific and only two dealt with religion. Geography, history and the classics were adapted to the juvenile readers, and so was a great deal of natural history.[77] Newbery also produced quantities of morality tales, more beloved, one suspects, by the parents than by the children. Through Edward Augustus Kendall, the Newberys produced new types of fable, derived from the ballad of Cock Robin, in which birds develop human attributes, converse freely among themselves, and offer their own criticisms of human failure and shortcomings. Kendall wrote *The Swallow, The Crested Wren, The Canary Bird, The Sparrow:* and their themes are simple—cruelty to birds, taking eggs, breaking up nests, caging finches, is the mark of an evil boy.[78] Cruelty is wicked, humane behaviour entirely laudable. Charity and benevolence will not only make a child happy, but bring him the proper social rewards. A similar burden is echoed in the potted biographies of eminent children or in the examples of historic characters held up for the edification of youth.[79] There is no time to investigate them in detail, but the themes of most of them are avoidance of cruelty, violence, brutality, and the development of innocent virtues which are obedience, sensitivity, a love of nature, and therefore of reason, which naturally leads to industry, benevolence and compassion.

---

[77] Ibid., p. 183; for example, *The Menagerie,* OR *A Peep at the Quadruped Race,* with 110 copperplates.

[78] Roscoe, op. cit., pp. 157–60. *The Crested Wren* (London, 1799); *The Canary Bird* (London, 1799); *The Sparrow* (London, 1798); *The Swallow* (London, 1800). The new sensitivity to birds and animals is best conveyed in the Robin Redbreast's song in *The Swallow,* pp. 140–1:

>Here, if heedless childhood plays,
>Here, if truant schoolboy strays,
>Let him, ere he hie along,
>Stop, and here the Robin's song!
>To please *his* ears, I'll frame my lays,
>Deeds of ruthless sport to praise;
>I'll Chuse the theme his heart approves;
>I'll sing the joys that most he loves;
>Bliss to the wild unthinking bands
>Who nobly seize, with eager hands,
>The downy nest, in gallant train,
>And triumph in a parent's pain.
>May thread-strung eggs still swell your store!
>Deride, as ever, pity's lore!
>For plunder, still, thro' spring-time rove,
>And revel in the pangs of love!
>Or, snare the bird, and starve its nest,
>Nor care what anguish rends its breast! . . .
>Ah! stay, forgive, thou peaceful shade!
>That these rude notes your bow're invade!
>And, schoolboy! If you dare refuse
>A cruel sport, yet want excuse,
>Stop, when you're ask'd to hie along,
>and say: 'I've heard the Robin's song!'

[79] Particularly, Augustus Louis Josse, *Juvenile Biography* (London, 1801); also William Dodd, *The Beauties of History* (London, 1795).

Nothing was regarded as more edifying than the death of a model child.[80] Between 1780 and 1800, the moral note gets stronger. Mrs. Trimmer dominates, and Mrs. Trimmer was not light of heart. There had always been a savage, macabre streak in the attitude to children. Corpse-viewing—practised at Wesley's school at Kingswood—had been thought of as salutary. Before Mrs. Trimmer, the desire to entertain, delight and instruct children had disguised, if not obliterated, much of the heavy moralizing. The Evangelical Revival, however, made a great deal of children's literature darker and gloomier as the century drew to a close.

However, I am less concerned with the content than with the availability of children's books, and with the problem of who could and did afford to buy them.

The contrast of, say, 1780 and 1680 in the range of what was available for children is vivid. By 1780 there was no subject, scientific or literary, that had not its specialized literature designed for children—often beautifully and realistically illustrated. The simpler textbooks—for reading, arithmetic and writing—were carefully designed, with large lettering, appropriate illustration with a small amount of print on a large page; that is as well as books for children there were books for very young children.[81] Novels specifically written about children for children began with *Sandford and Merton,* by Thomas Day.[82] And the arts, as well as letters, were catered for—Master Michael Angelo's *The Drawing School for Little Masters and Misses* appeared in 1773, and there are books designed to teach children the first steps in music.[83] And, as with adult books, less prosperous children could buy their books a part at a time.[84] Nor was it necessary to buy the books, they could be borrowed. By 1810 there was a well-established juvenile library at 157 New Bond Street, run by Tabart. Some owners of circulating libraries kept a special juvenile section.[85]

---

[80] Augustus Francis Emilian, perhaps the most nauseating boy in all children's literature, takes twelve pages to die in *Juvenile Biography,* pp. 271–83. After being on the point of death for over thirty-six hours, Emilian rallies sufficiently at the last moment to say (although with painful effort), 'What grieves me most is to quit you Mamma, as well as not to have lived long enough to be useful to my country'. Not surprisingly, 'At these immortal words a rattling in the throat stifled the half-articulate words'. However, death did not come for another page and a half.

[81] For example, *A Little Lottery-Book for Children* (London, 1756) and *A Pretty Plaything for Children* (London, n.d., but *c.* 1760), at 3d. This market continued to grow and shortly after the turn of the century there were beautifully boxed small libraries for infants, published in large editions, and occasionally translated into French. See S. Roscoe, 'Some Uncollected Authors. John Marshall and the Infant's Library'; *The Book Collector,* iv (1955), pp. 148–55.

[82] First published London 1783. For Thomas Day, see G. W. Gignilliat, *The Author of Sandford and Merton* (New York, 1932).

[83] Roscoe, *John Newbery,* p. 47.

[84] ibid., p. 218.

[85] Brit. Lib., Ambrose Heal Coll.; Noblett, 'Printing and the Book Trade in Sheffield', p. 64. James Woolleen's circulating library in Sheffield had, in 1806, a section entitled 'Children's Library' which contained 84 volumes.

And children's books, as well as becoming far more plentiful, also became cheaper. John Newbery had used every type of gimmick to extend his market. With the *Pretty Little Pocket Book* he had offered—for an extra twopence—a ball for the son or a pincushion for the daughter. He had used new types of binding that did not stain, and he had even tried giving a book away so long as the purchaser bought the binding. He advertised his books in every possible way—rarely did a parent finish one of his books without finding in the text a recommendation of others. He sensed that there was a huge market ready for exploitation.[86] He was right. Within twenty years, children's books were a thriving part of the Newcastle printer's trade;[87] indeed, educational books attracted a very large number of provincial printers in the late eighteenth century, for they were well aware of the hunger of shopkeepers, tradesmen and artisans, such as weavers, for education, not only for themselves, but also, and most emphatically, for their children. By 1800, children's books at 1d. were plentiful and this was a time when books in general, because of inflation, had increased in price by 25 per cent. Nevertheless, Oliver and Boyd of Edinburgh turned them out by the score, under the title of *Jack Dandy's Delights*. They published forty at sixpence, twenty-six at twopence, forty at one penny, and ninety at a halfpenny.[88] The penny books were well printed and delightfully illustrated. Only the very poorest families of unskilled labourers could not afford a halfpenny. Like Tom Paine's *Rights of Man,* children's literature was within the range of the industrious working class, and particularly of those families where social ambition had been stirred by the growing opportunities of a new industrializing society—more and more clerical jobs were available, and more and more parents were willing to make sacrifices to secure them for their children.

Education was public as well as private, and there was far more entertainment designed both to amuse and instruct, to which parents were encouraged to take their children by sharply reduced prices for them. Children were expected to be companions of their parents in ways which would have been impossible in the seventeenth century, because the attractions did not then exist. Exhibitions of curiosities; museums; zoos; puppet shows;

[86] Noblett, 'John Newbery: Publisher Extraordinary'. The success of the Newberys may be judged by numbers of children's books published per decade from 1742 to 1800.
  1742–50: 18   1771–80 : 129
  1751–60: 47   1781–90 : 167
  1761–70: 111   1791–1800: 218
(Figures kindly supplied by William Noblett, abstracted from Roscoe, *John Newbery,* but these figures apply only to datable editions; the figures for complete publication would very likely be more striking.)

[87] Thomas Saint, the proprietor of *Newcastle Courant,* published a considerable number of children's books, some of them illustrated by Thomas Bewick. *Memoir of Thomas Bewick written by himself* (London, 1925), p. 52. See also, R. Welford, 'Early Newcastle Typography, 1639–1800', *Archaeologia Aeliana,* 3rd ser., iii (1906), pp. 1–134.

[88] Lists of advertisements printed with copies of *Jack Dandy's Delights.* Lumsden of Glasgow were also publishing very cheap literature for children by the early nineteenth century: Roscoe, *John Newbery,* p. 33.

circuses; lectures on science; panoramas of European cities; automata; horseless carriages; even human and animal monstrosities were available in provincial cities as well as in London. Sir Ashton Levers's Museum of Natural History at Leicester House, a typical eighteenth-century hotchpotch, advertised family tickets. A yearly season ticket for the entire family was quite expensive at five guineas, but it included both the tutor and the governess, and so was aimed at the rich.[89] In April 1773 families of Leeds were regaled by Mr. Manuel of Turin with his display of automata which, as well as having an Indian lady in her chariot moving around the table at ten miles an hour, also contained the 'Grand Turk, in the Seraglio dress, who walks about the table smoking his pipe in a surprising manner'. All, of course, to the accompaniment of mechanical musical instruments. The prices were cheap enough, 1s. front seats, 6d. back, and servants at 4d. Mr. Manuel also sold fireworks as a sideline. After Mr. Manuel, Mr. Pitt, arrived with his principal marvel, a self-moving phaeton which travelled at six miles an hour, climbed hills, and started and stopped with the touch of a finger. He also brought along his electrifying machine, his camera obscura, his miraculous door which opened inside, outside, left or right by the turn of a key. All for one shilling. The phaeton either wore out, broke down, or at five hundredweight proved too expensive to move, for it was dropped by Pitt, who continued for some years to travel the Midland circuit, Nottingham, Coventry, and so on, but only with his scientific apparatus. Quite obviously he made a tolerable living.[90]

On 10th August the attraction at Leeds was geographical rather than mechanical, when the model of the city and suburbs of Paris arrived at the Town Hall. It was extremely elaborate and eighteen feet square. Viewing started at 9.00 in the morning and closed at 8.00 in the evening, price, as usual, one shilling. In September a spectacular, double-column advertisement with woodcuts announced the arrival of Astley's circus, prices as usual a shilling for front seats, sixpence back, but Astley warned that boys trying to climb in would be taken care of by guards. He now also brought along with him his famous 'Chronoscope': an apparatus for measuring the velocity of projectiles.[91]

The emphasis was on marvels, curiosities that were new and remarkable, and usually mechanical or optical; hence many children were given a keen sense of a new and developing and changing world in which mechanical ingenuity, electricity and science in general played an active part—a totally different cultural atmosphere from that in which their grandfathers had lived. Their cultural horizons, too, were widened by the availability of music

---

[89] Brit. Lib., Ambrose Heal Coll. See also *Dict. Nat. Biog., sub* Sir Ashton Lever. The museum lasted from 1774 to 1788.
[90] *Leeds Mercury*, 13 Apr. 1773 (Manuel); ibid., 15 June 1773 (Pitt); *Leicester and Nottinghamshire Jl.*, 15 May 1779.
[91] *Leeds Mercury*, 10 Aug. 1773 (Paris panorama); ibid., 21 Sept. 1773 (Astley).

to listen to in festivals and concerts, the cheapness of musical instruments, and the plentiful supply of music teachers; the same is true of art.[92] Art materials were to be found in every provincial town, and so were drawing masters, who taught in the home as well as in the school.[93] Prints of old masters and modern artists were a commonplace of provincial as well as London life. Visually it was a far more exciting age for children than ever before.[94] And they could travel. By the end of the century middle-class families were on the move, visiting country houses and ancient ruins, viewing the industrial wonders of Boulton and Watt, Wedgwood, Arkwright, and braving the dangers and dirt of coal-mines, sailing in splendid barges along the new canals, going off to the sea—to take the water externally and internally—an outburst of travel that is recorded in hundreds of illustrated books which depict children with their parents, enjoying, as they themselves enjoyed, the wonders of their world.[95] The intellectual and cultural horizons of the middle-class child, and indeed of the lower middle-class child, had broadened vastly between 1680 and 1780, and this change was gathering momentum. Parents, more often than not, wanted their children with them, not only in the home but on holidays.

However, through most of the amusements ran the theme of self-improvement and self-education. The same is true of indoor games, as well as outdoor excursions. Playing cards had long been used to inculcate knowledge—largely geographical, historical or classical. One of the earliest packs of about 1700 taught carving lessons—hearts for joints of meat, diamonds for poultry, clubs for fish and spades for meat pies.[96] But more often than not these were importations, usually from France. The eighteenth century witnessed a rapid increase in English educational playing cards, so that almost every variety of knowledge or educational entertainment could be found imprinted on their faces.[97] The majority of booksellers, provincial as well as metropolitan,

---

[92] Some pictures went on a provincial circuit, for example, Robert Kee Porter's 'Storming of Seringapatam' (2,550 square feet of canvas) was on view, 1s. admission, in the circus in Gibraltar St., Sheffield (c. 1800): Sheffield City Lib., Misc. Papers, 26 S.

[93] R. B. Harraden was a drawing master at Cambridge.

[94] Some of the excitement of the new world of science and technology that fascinated children is beautifully realized by Joseph Wright of Derby's 'An Experiment with the Air-Pump', and 'the Orrery'.

[95] Esther Moir, *The Discovery of Britain* (London, 1964), pp. 77–107. Children were having sea-side holidays with their parents by 1780. At Bridlington, William Taylor charged 9s. per week for children. *York Courant*, 4 July 1780.

[96] Catalogue of exhibition of *The Art of the Playing Card* (Yale Univ., New Haven, 1973).

[97] John Locke had advocated simple games for teaching, and by the 1730s and '40s educational games were being manufactured and sold, some claiming to be on his principles. *Ipswich Jl.*, 12 July 1746, advertised 'a set of 56 square, with cuts upon a plan of Mr. Locke'. On 30 Dec. 1774, *Etherington's York Chronicle* carried an advertisement for 'Price only one shilling, a new and handsome edition, beautifully coloured, of Riley's Royal Spelling Cards. Adorned with Cuts, and Verses under each, with their emphasis properly marked, and the words divided so as to prevent false pronunciation. On the top of the cards is the Alphabet, displayed in large and small Letters, so contrived as to cut off at Pleasure, without injuring the Beauty of the Devices; by which Infants may very soon be taught to compose their Names, Words, Dates, etc.' Discount was allowed for purchases by boarding schools.

stocked them. Some cards were designed for the education of adults, or at least adolescents, but there were packs, very simply designed, for young children to play with and learn at the same time. One pack taught the first steps in music.[98]

After playing cards, one of the earliest educational games to be developed was the jig-saw puzzle, seemingly an English invention by the printer-bookseller John Spilsbury, a young entrepreneur of twenty-three who, in 1762, produced dissected maps for the teaching of geography.[99] These enjoyed an immediate, perhaps a phenomenal success, and by the mid-1760s he had thirty different maps in jig-saw form for sale. His entrepreneurial appetite may be judged by the fact that he also printed his maps on silk kerchiefs—whether these were sold as a gimmick with the puzzle is not known. Unfortunately Spilsbury died young—but what he had launched quickly proliferated not only in the teaching of history, geography, classics or morals, but also purely for fun, though even these tended to have a moral overtone. The principal publisher of educational games became John Wallis, whose firm began to flourish in the 1780s, and lasted until 1847, during which time, with the Dartons, it led the field of educational games, some of which were extremely complex.[100] All such games were not jig-saws. In the seventeenth century, Pierre du Val had used the painted-board, dice-gambling games for teaching geography and history, indeed it has been said that Louis XIV learnt his lessons in this way, for the French court and aristocracy of the seventeenth century had no inhibitions about children gambling.[101] The first dice game in England played on a painted board for instruction seems to have been invented by John Jeffreys in 1759. His game was called 'A Journey through Europe or the Play of Geography', and the players moved along a marked route according to the throw of their dice.[102] This proved very popular, and spawned a host of similar games, some of extreme complexity, such as Walker's 'Geographical Pastime exhibiting a Complete Voyage Round the World in Two Hemispheres', which must have taken hours to play.[103] As well as board games, there were card games—often employing the rebus, which were extremely popular for teaching spelling and extending the vocabulary, as well as quickening wits, similar to scrabble.[104] By the early nineteenth century, in spite of the fulminations of Maria Edgeworth about the uselessness of these toys,[105] there were almost as many educational toys available as there are today. For boys, there were complex

---

[98] *The Suffolk Mercury*, 13 Dec. 1725. They were published by Cluer and Creek of Bow Church Yard, London.
[99] Linda Hannas, *The English Jigsaw Puzzle 1760–1890* (London, 1972), pp. 15–20.
[100] Ibid., pp. 28–35.
[101] Ibid., p. 13.
[102] Ibid., p. 13.
[103] An example is in the Paul Mellon Collection, Oak Springs, Virginia.
[104] *The Art of the Playing Card*, p. 19.
[105] Maria Edgeworth, *Practical Education* (London, 1798), pp. 2–5.

mechanical toys—water-mills, looms, miniature printing presses and so on, which could be assembled and made to work; there were also cheap inflatable globes, complicated perspective views and toy theatres with movable scenery and actors, on which whole plays could be acted and reacted from the scripts provided, and there were scientific toys, camera obscuras and the like, made cheaply for children. And by that time too there were large quantities of toys on the market whose educational value was present, if secondary—Noah's Arks, Animal Farms, soldiers and forts of every variety for the potential soldier, and, of course, dolls' houses and dolls. These varied from the extremely cheap—cut-outs in paper with brightly coloured interchangeable clothes—to elaborate models with wax or earthenware faces, jointed bodies, and elaborate wardrobes.[106] And in London there were, by 1800 at least, two shops that specialized in making rocking-horses.[107] In 1730 there were no specialized toyshops of any kind, whereas by 1780 toyshops everywhere abounded, and by 1820 the trade in toys, as in children's literature, had become very large indeed.[108]

Children, in a sense, had become luxury objects upon which their mothers and fathers were willing to spend larger and larger sums of money, not only for their education, but also for their entertainment and amusement. In a sense they had become superior pets—sometimes spoilt excessively like Charles James Fox, sometimes treated with indifference or even brutality, but usually, as with pets, betwixt and between. Whatever the attitude of parents, children had become a trade, a field of commercial enterprise for the sharp-eyed entrepreneur. Nor was education and amusement the only field in which children had become a market. The eighteenth century was exceptionally dress- and fashion-conscious; indeed, fashions in textiles had begun to change every year. And naturally parents who were sufficiently affluent began to spend more and more money on the clothes of their children and they were increasingly induced to do so by tailors and milliners who

---

[106] Karl Groebner, *Children's Toys of Bygone Days* (London, 1928), pp. 38-9, for dolls with interchangeable clothes, first advertised in 1791. Vivien Greene, *English Dolls' Houses* (London, 1955); Mary Hillier, *Dolls and Dollmakers* (London, 1968); and *Pageant of Toys* (London, 1965), pp. 43 ff., for Noah's Arks. F. Nevill Jackson, *Toys of Other Days* (London, 1907). Lady Antonia Fraser, *A History of Toys* (London, 1967). John G. Garratt, *Model Soldiers: A Collector's Guide* (London, 1959). A Chapuis and E. Droz, *Les Automates* (Neuchatel, 1949). George Speaight, *Juvenile Drama: A History of the English Toy Theatre* (London, 1946). William Hooper, *Rational Recreations* (London, 1774). Toy farm animals were sold to Lord Winterton by Willerton and Roberts of Old Bond St., *c.* 1760; he paid 5s. for a stable of horses, 5s. 6d. for a musical farmhouse, 1s. for a pig and 1s. for a fowl: Brit. Lib., Ambrose Heal Coll., 122.39. E. G. Green in Crooked Lane sold 'Bristol Toys in General, such as Coaches, Wagons, etc.', 1d. and 2d. He also sold cattle, milkmaids and armies in boxes as well as 'babies dressed or undressed, jointed, wax or common'; indeed by 1784 he sold little else but toys. Brit. Lib., Ambrose Heal Coll.
[107] Rocking-horse makers were: Edward Benton, near Elephant Stairs, Rotherhithe (oddly enough he was also a butcher); and Taylors of Black Street, who seem to have specialized entirely in making rocking-horses. Ibid.
[108] Hannas, op. cit., pp. 54-7.

specialized in making clothes for children. And not only children, but also babies; infant materials which the seventeenth century had produced in the home were now sold wholesale in London—diapers, cradles, cradle blankets, Moses baskets, satin coverlets, baby clothes of all kinds were being produced for bulk sale. Although children were still dressed as miniature adults, towards the end of the century it became fashionable to dress children up as soldiers, sailors, highlanders, milkmaids or gardeners. Dress for children became lighter and freer, and it was quite customary for boys to wear open-necked shirts. A number of tailors and haberdashers found it profitable to specialize entirely in children's clothing.[109] Clothes-consciousness, also, among children and adolescents became quite strong, particularly among adolescents, and working-class adolescents at that. Sheffield, in spite of its dark satanic mills of the Industrial Revolution, possessed plenty of working-class gaiety. There were dress shops where the young cutlers' apprentices and their shop-assistant girl-friends could hire their finery for Saturday night—dresses for the girls, suits for the boys, so that they could go decked out like the middle-class to their penny or threepenny dances or 'hops' as they were known, then, as now.[110]

A hundred years had brought about a remarkable change in the lives of middle- and lower middle-class children, and indeed of the aristocracy as well. From Locke onwards there had been a greater preoccupation with educational ideas; indeed, in the second half of the eighteenth century, stimulated by Rousseau, the advanced radicals—the Burghs, the Days, the Edgeworths, and the rest—had been deeply concerned. Many, particularly the Edgeworths, disapproved of the growing indulgence of parents towards their children, particularly the waste of money on useless toys. Maria Edgeworth denounced dolls and dolls' houses, had no use for rocking-horses, and strongly disapproved of baa-lambs, squeaky pigs and cuckoos, and all simple action toys. She was for a pencil and plain paper, toys which led to physical exercise—hoops, tops, battledores and a pair of scissors and paper for a girl to cut out her fancies; later boys should be given models of instruments used by manufacturers—spinning-wheels, looms, paper-mills, water-mills which, as I have said, were readily available.[111] Maria Edgeworth resonates with modernity, but the interest in her long discussion of toys lies in the huge variety which obviously abounded in the 1790s—a variety not

---

[109] Brit. Lib., Ambrose Heal Coll.; ibid., Banks Coll. Specialization in children's clothing and baby clothes came quite early. S. Underwood, for example, in 1746 in Ludgate Hill, specialized in making children's coats, stays and babies' baskets, but also maintained a considerable adult trade as well, whereas Monk and Bennett, of Tavistock St., Covent Garden, and Ann Bentley of the same street specialized in the 1760s almost entirely in children's and babies clothes and requirements, including diapers, satin baskets, cradles, etc. There were, of course, many other shops by 1800 selling similar goods.
[110] *Advice of An Overseer of the Industrious Poor of Sheffield* (Sheffield, n.d., but c. 1790–1800). Sheffield City Lib., Misc. Papers 416 M.
[111] Edgeworth, *Practical Education*, pp. 23–6.

as extensive, of course, as today, but reflecting our world rather than that of seventeenth-century England. Indeed, wherever we turn in the world of children—clothes, pets, toys, education, sport, music and art, their world was richer, more varied, more intellectually and emotionally exciting than it had been in earlier generations.

And yet all was not gain. One must not paint too radiant a picture, too exciting a world. Mrs. Trimmer was there, so was Hannah More. One must remember the Fairchild family trooping off to view the corpse decomposing on the gibbet, the frightful treatment of William Cowper at Westminster, the horrors of Harrow and Eton and Winchester that drew boys into violent rebellion. Nor should we forget the dangers to children in the growing sentimentality about the innocence of the child which needed to be protected at all costs, nor the dangerous intellectual concept that regards each human life as recapitulating that of the human race, which firmly placed the child in Eden, but surrounded by serpents and cluttered with apples.[112]

As a richer life in material objects became available to children, so did their private lives, in some aspects, become more rigidly disciplined. The world of sex was to become, in the eighteenth century, a world of terror for children, and one which was to create appalling guilt and anxiety. We know little about the history of sexual attitudes. In eighteenth-century children's literature, adultery is mentioned, not approvingly, of course, but as a fact of life. In some tales for children men and women were discovered in bed together.[113] This certainly would not have been allowed in Victorian literature for children. And such references were few, and vanish after the 1780s. In another respect, at least, there had been a disastrous development. In the sixteenth century Fallopius had encouraged masturbation in boys as a method of enlarging the penis,[114] and Pepys, who had considerable guilt and shame about his fumbling of women, took masturbation in his stride, and indeed mentions with considerable pride that he had managed it without using his hand and with his eyes wide open. He did, it is true, wish it had not happened at midnight mass in the Chapel Royal, but that was his sole reaction.[115] The early eighteenth century witnesses a total change of attitude, if Pepys and Fallopius are at all typical. The publication, probably around 1710, of *Onania: Or, The Heinous Sin of Self Pollution, and all its frightful Consequences in both Sexes considered with spiritual and Physical Advice to those who have already injur'd themselves by this abominable Practise*, unleashed a deluge of denunciation about masturbation. By 1727, this book had reached twelve editions, with fatter and fatter supplements of horrifying and lurid letters of saved sinners. This book was advertised extremely extensively in the provincial as well as the London press, and it proved a

[112] Boas, *The Cult of Childhood*, pp. 60 ff.
[113] For example, William Dodd, *The Beauties of History* (London, 1800 edn.), p. 249.
[114] De Mause, 'The Evolution of Childhood', p. 48.
[115] *Diary of Samuel Pepys*, viii, p. 588.

best-seller for decades, and gradually accumulated about it a horrific literature that attributed every disease and inadequacy to self-abuse. The medical quacks rapidly got on to the band-wagon, and many pamphlets were merely puffs for curative medicines or restrictive machines.[116] And by 1800 crimes of unbelievable cruelty were being practised on young boys in order to cure them, such as circumcision without, of course, anaesthetic.[117] This development was not an English phenomenon. Dr. Tissot produced an equally alarming and equally popular book in Switzerland and France in 1760.[118] And Kant denounces the practice with intense moral fervour in his *Über Pädagogik* (1803).[119]

Chastity and abstinence, however, were imposed with an increasing verbal and, at times, physical violence on the growing boy and girl. The practical results of this campaign were probably minimal, but the psychological danger to the sensitive was considerable, as we may see from the diaries of men so different in temperament as Samuel Johnson and William Ewart Gladstone. Childhood had become more radiant, but there were dark and lowering clouds. Children, in fact, had become objects: violence and noise, natural to children, were deplored, so was greed for food as well as lust. Obedience, sweetness, honesty, self-control were the qualities desired and inculcated. They were to stay firmly in Eden with their hands off the apples and deaf to the serpents. Fortunately the images that society creates for children rarely reflect the truth of actual life. If we turn from theory, from projected literary images, to the artefacts of childhood, then we can rest assured that children, both girls and boys, had, so long as they were middle-class, entered a far richer world. They had more to stimulate the eye, the ear and the mind, and that was pure gain.

Appendix

The most comprehensive description that I have come across of the specialized curricula offered for particular professions is the following, which is to be found in Sheffield City Library, Misc. Papers:

[116] Cranfield, *The Development of the Provincial Newspaper, 1700–1760*, pp. 222–3.
[117] De Mause, op. cit., pp. 48–9, and references there cited.
[118] Simon Tissot, *L'Onanisme: Dissertation sur les Maladies Produites par la Masturbation* (Lausanne, 1764). For the bibliography of masturbation, see René A. Spitz, 'Authority and Masturbation. Some Remarks on a Bibliographical Investigation', *The Psychoanalytical Quarterly*, xxi (1952), pp. 490–527. See also P. Lejeune, 'Le "dangereux supplément": lecture d'un aveu de Rousseau', *Annales*. E. S. C., xxix (1974), pp. 1,009–22. Tissot's book sold 100,000 copies 1760–1856.
[119] E. Kant, *On Education* [Über Pädagogik], trans. Annette Churton (London 1899), p. 116: 'Nothing weakens the mind as well as the body so much as the kind of lust which is directed towards themselves, and it is entirely at variance with the nature of man. But this also must not be concealed from the youth. We must place it before him in all its horribleness, telling him that in this way he will become useless for the propagation of the race, that his bodily strength will be ruined by this vice more than by anything else, that he will bring on himself premature old age, and that his intellect will be very much weakened, and so on.
I owe this reference to the kindness of Professor Bernard Williams.

AT WAKEFIELD

YOUNG GENTLEMEN are Boarded, and Taught all the Varieties of MODERN PENMANSHIP, and the several Branches of the MATHEMATICS and ACCOMPTS, requisite to Qualify them for the Counting-House or Trade, the Law or a Stewardship, the Army or Navy.

By Robert Nicholson

For the COUNTING-HOUSE or TRADE:

1. WRITING, in a free, mercantile Manner.
2 ARITHMETIC, Vulgar and Decimal.
3. The *Computation of Exchange.*
4. MERCHANT'S ACCOMPTS, or, the *Italian Method of Book-Keeping.*
5. *The Italian Method* applied, in keeping *Tradesmen's Books,* in the wholesale or retail way.
6. GEOGRAPHY, and the *Use* of the *Terrestrial Globe* and *Maps.*

For the LAW or a STEWARDSHIP:

1. THE LAW HANDS.
2. *Vulgar* and *Decimal* ARITHMETIC.
3. The Extraction of the Roots, with their Use.
4. GEOMETRY in *Theory* and *Practice.*
5. MENSURATION of *Surfaces* and *Solids* ... also *Artificer's Works,* with a new method of measuring *Standing Timber.*
6. SURVEYING and *Mapping Estates.*
7. STEWARD'S ACCOMPTS, or *Book-Keeping* adapted to this Class.
8. INTEREST, SIMPLE AND COMPOUND, with the Manner of *Purchasing Annuities, Reversions, Real* and *Life Estates,* renewing of *Leases, Fines, &c.*
9. The USE of the *Terrestrial Globe and Maps.*

For the ARMY

1. ARITHMETIC, Vulgar and Decimal.
2. The *Extraction* of the *Roots* and their uses in the Computation of *Balls, Shells, Charges, &c.*
3. The first Principles of ALGEBRA.
4. PRACTICAL GEOMETRY, with the Demonstration of some necessary Theorems.
5. MENSURATION of *Plains,* and certain *Solids.*
6. TRIGONOMETRY PLAIN, with its Application to *Altimetry* and *Longimetry.*

7. SURVEYING and PLANNING, or the Method of laying down any Parcel of Ground.
8. GUNNERY, or the Doctrine of *Projectiles*.
9. FORTIFICATION, or *Military Architecture,* laid down according to *Vauban, Coehorn, Muller, &c.*
10. The Method of *Attack* and *Defence.*

For the NAVY:

1. ARITHMETIC, *Vulgar* and *Decimal.*
2. The *Extraction* of the *Roots,* with their Application to various Purposes in the *Mathematics.*
3. GEOMETRY PRACTICAL, with some necessary *Theorems* demonstrated.
4. MENSURATION, and *Cask Gauging.*
5. TRIGONOMETRY PLAIN, with its application to the measuring of *Heights, Depths, Distances, &c.*
6. NAVIGATION, in all its *Parts,* with an exact Method of keeping a *Journal.*
7. *Surveying* and *Planning* of *Harbours.*
8. The USE of the *Globes, Maps, Charts* and *Nautical Instruments.*
9. *Spheric Geometry,* with the *Projection* of the *Sphere.*
10. SPHERIC TRIGONOMETRY, with its Application to *Practical Astronomy;* also Variety of Methods for determining the *Latitude* at *Sea.*

Also the USE of the GLOBES, MAPS, CHARTS, and other Mathematical Instruments.

CHAPTER EIGHT

The Acceptance of Modernity[1]

During the eighteenth century extraordinary economic and social changes swept through Britain and brought into being the first society dedicated to ever-expanding consumption based on industrial production. For this to succeed required men and women to believe in growth, in change, in modernity; to believe that the future was bright, far brighter than the past; to believe, also, that what was new was desirable, whether it was the cut of a dress, the ascent of a balloon, or a new variety of auricula. Novelty, newfangledness, must be matters of excitement for an aggressive commercial and capitalist world: ever-increasing profit is not made in a world of traditional crafts and stable fashions. Appetite for the new and the different, for fresh experience and novel excitements, for the getting and spending of money, for aggressive consumption lies at the heart of successful bourgeois society. These must be its dominant moods. They will not, naturally enough, be the only social attitudes. The minds of men can carry contradictory ideas, even contradictory hopes, with consummate ease. The acceptance of modernity does not imply the rejection of all tradition; the growth of scientific ideas, of deliberately-sought technological change, does not mean the expulsion of religious fervour any more than a hatred of slavery leads to a desire for social justice either for the blacks or for poverty-stricken whites. Similarly the gullibility of so many educated men and women of the eighteenth century who accepted Caligostro, Swedenborg or Casanova does not negate the spread of scientific intellectual enquiry beyond the confines of educated élites or widespread acceptance in quite humble circumstances of the motto of the seventeenth-century intelligentsia—*sapere aude*.[2]

What I wish to trace is how quite humble men and women, innocent of philosophical theory, began to be fascinated not only by nature but also by the manipulation of nature; how even their hobbies or their pets might lead them to accept, perhaps unconsciously, the modernity of their world, and to

---

[1] Some of the material used in this chapter is also to be found in Chapter Six 'The Commercialization of Leisure in the Eighteenth Century' and Chapter Seven 'The New World of Children in the Eighteenth Century,' but it is used to argue a different, if complementary, thesis.

[2] See J. H. Plumb, 'Reason and Unreason in the Eighteenth Century' in *In the Light of History* (1972), pp. 3–24; Franco Venturi, *Utopia and Reform in the Enlightenment* (Cambridge, 1971), pp. 7–8.

relish change and novelty and to look with more expectancy towards the future. They did not reject tradition or the past; many, very much in tune with the new scientific and technological developments of the age, could still believe in the literal interpretation of the Bible and had a splendid time fitting the Flood into more accurate geological observation.[3] Likewise religion. It was not rejected but reduced as a vehicle of explanation of phenomena either human or material. God's creation, in a sense, became divorced at one remove from God and so explainable by man.

Before 1700 there had been a growth and seepage of curiosity about the material world. The stimulus of the great discoveries in the East as well as the West during the sixteenth century had excited the imagination and created a sense of a knowable unknown. When the first rhinoceros reached Portugal it drew huge crowds: the courtiers of Charles V gaped at the Indians brought back by Columbus and the Conquistadors. The brilliant works of Aztec art deeply moved Dürer when he saw them at Brussels; but even so these stimuli were intermittent and often confined to very specific geographical or social situations and to a handful of men and women. Except for plants: seeds were easy to transport and by 1600 there was a discernible flow of new shrubs and trees as well as flowers from the Middle East and beyond as well as some from North America into Europe.

There was a steady growth of literature during the seventeenth century about the wonders of the New World and a constantly thickening corpus of scientific or quasi-scientific information, a continuing refinement of scientific instruments, particularly the telescope and the microscope that revealed world upon world hitherto hidden. There can be no doubt that there was a mounting excitement about the novelty of discovery, a growing desire to know. This attitude, however, was mainly confined to sections of the intellectual élite, to the small but closely knit republic of letters;[4] it still had to seep through to the lives of ordinary men and women. We may regard the growth of enquiry as a small and winding stream in the sixteenth century, that swells to a river in the seventeenth century and reaches, about 1680, its delta, a complex web of channels and streams that ultimately flow into the sea—the mass of society—in the eighteenth and nineteenth centuries. It is some of the channels and streams of this delta which I wish to explore.

The history of animals has largely been confined to agriculture: no serious historian that I know of has paid any attention to pets—particularly to

---

[3] R. S. Porter, *The Making of Geology: earth science in Britain 1660–1815* (Cambridge, 1977) and J. W. Burrow, 'The Flood', *Horizon*, 1972.
[4] This is clearly shown by the correspondence of John Locke who exchanged new knowledge of exotics and curiosities with a wide range of friends and scholars in England, France, the Netherlands and elsewhere. Having tasted red cabbage salad for the first time in 1687 in Holland, he immediately acquired the seed and sent it to friends in Somerset to grow. *The Correspondence of John Locke*, E. S. de Beer (Oxford, 1978), iii, p. 508. We can follow similar activities in the letters of Oldenburgh, see *The Correspondence of Henry Oldenburgh* (ed. A. R. and M. B. Hall (Madison, Wisconsin, 1965-), i-xi, *passim*.

canaries, pigeons, dogs or goldfish: or indeed to the impact of animals, not on the feelings and affections of men or women, or to changed relationships with them, but on what we may term 'social knowledge'—the unquestioning acceptance of ideas.

Before the eighteenth century selective breeding of a kind had been practised for time out of mind, but it had largely been casual and intermittent. A fine stallion, a powerful bull, a strong ram or boar, or animals possessing highly desirable qualities, such as fine milk yields, had been sought after in their localities, but there had been no widespread, deliberate, long term, selective breeding geared to the production of an animal with highly defined and very specific qualities. This was the achievement of men such as Robert Bakewell, Hugo Meynell, George Culley in the middle decades of the eighteenth century, but they themselves—particularly Bakewell, a comparatively unlettered farmer—were not giants of invention but men who applied successfully and specifically the new attitudes towards breeding that were already being widely accepted in eighteenth-century England.[5]

Both the growth of horse-racing and the improvements in transport which led to the widespread use of coaches that required an increased performance in speed and stamina of horses, stimulated selective horse-breeding between 1680 and 1750.[6] The purchase of Arabian stallions, and afterwards of Arabian brood mares, by Lord Godolphin and others received wide publicity.[7] The value of this strain for improving the speed and stamina of the race horse was known in racing circles: the presence of some Arab blood in a stallion was used to advertise it for stud purposes and it also put up its price. By the 1720s careful and detailed records were being kept of the performance of individual horses—indeed the results of races were published in the provincial press from its inception, and the Racing Calendar, begun in 1727 by John Cheney, systematized this knowledge. Individual owners naturally kept their own stud books. When on 20 November 1739, Mr. Henry Ibbotson advertised the sale by auction of his stud on his farm near Knaresborough, he offered to produce the pedigree of all of his horses, if required; but he did not feel—quite clearly—that the publication of any of the pedigrees would necessarily boost the sales.[8] In the early decades of the provincial press—that is from 1705-40—advertisements are comparatively rare for stallions stand-

---

[5] R. Trow Smith, *A History of British Livestock Husbandry, 1700-1910* (1959); Juliet Clutton Brock, 'Garrads Livestock Models', *The Agricultural History Review* (Reading, 1976), xxiv; H. Cecil Pawson, *Robert Bakewell, Pioneer Lifestock Breeder* (1957).

[6] Daphne Machin Goodhall, *A History of Horse Breeding* (1977).

[7] Rather like Lord Townshend and the turnip, Lord Godolphin was giving publicity to a well-established development, although his Arabian, imported in 1728, was an outstanding horse, several hundred had been imported by that date—the Byerly Turk in 1689, the Darby Arabian in 1705 and many others in the last decades of the seventeenth century. See *The Diary of John Evelyn* (ed. E. S. de Beer, Oxford 1955), iv. pp. 398-9 for three Arabians captured at Siege of Vienna. Daphne Machin Goodhall, op. cit., p. 238.

[8] *Leeds Mercury*, 20 November 1739, 4. He was prepared to give twelve months' credit to the buyers.

ing at stud at inns: pedigrees are given only occasionally and the bait usually is that the horse had belonged to a nobleman.[9] From 1740 onwards there is a marked change; advertisements became extremely numerous. A very large number of inns of market towns had stallions stabled there for many weeks, sometimes months, ready to cover mares for fees that range from half a guinea to five or even ten guineas for horses with long pedigrees in which there was both Arabian blood and one or two well-known and successful racehorses.[10] Famous horses such as Eclipse, his father Marske and his rival Herod, who proved to be an even finer stud horse than Eclipse, commanded exceptional fees—100 guineas, for example, for Marske, a prodigious fee in terms of Hanoverian gold. This selective breeding was very widely discussed in the press and doubtless by word of mouth at race-meetings and discussions and arguments over a drink on market days.[11] It spread the acceptance of the idea that men could improve nature and create different and more highly specialized animals.

Nor was it merely racehorses and hunters that were being carefully and deliberately bred and their breeding meticulously recorded. There were, of course, regional breeds of horses long before the eighteenth century—the Clydesdale, the Cleveland, the Black Horse of the Fens, the Suffolk and others—but these breeds were not so sharply differentiated in 1700 as they were to become by 1800 after several generations of careful inbreeding combined with deliberate crosses to enhance their specialized qualities. The Norfolk Hackney, the best of all trotting horses produced in England, emerges in what is essentially its present form in Norfolk in the 1740s as the result of careful and very selective breeding. Similarly the Suffolk Punch, which developed around Woodbridge, achieved in 1774 the characteristics which made it, and still make, it, famous as a heavy draught horse. All present day Suffolks are derived from a great and extremely active stallion of that date. An even better example is the Cleveland bay—which combined speed and stamina and became the ideal coach horse for its ability to cover a stage of twenty miles quickly with a fully loaded coach. They were so well suited by their careful breeding for this task that they were exported in very

---

[9] *The Post Man*, 22-4 March 1705. Two horses belonging to the late Earl of Stanford.

[10] *York Courant*, 26 February 1754. Regulus, son of Godolphin Arabian was priced at five guineas 'a leap' and half a crown for the groom. He was also advertised as having won eight Royal Plates at 100 guineas each. A half brother of Regulus, Whitemore, was also priced at five guineas, whereas a descendant of the Darby Arabian only cost a guinea. On 5 March, Shock was advertised at ten guineas in the *York Courant*. He was so famous that no pedigree or achievements were given.

[11] Theodore Andrea Cook, *Eclipse and O'Kelly* (1907), 72. Eclipse covered for fifty guineas, ibid, pp. 86-7. See also, Peter Willett, *An Introduction to the Thoroughbred* (1966). In September 1743 233 gentlemen sat down for dinner at Lichfield races: it would have been odd if horses, performances and pedigrees were not discussed. Ann J. Kettle, 'Lichfield Races', *Trans. Lichfield and South Staffordshire Archaeological Society* (Walsall 1966), vi, p. 39.

large numbers.[12] It has long been thought that Robert Bakewell, who improved the breed of the black Shire horse, was an innovator and the first man to rent his stallions for specific periods. But this is not so; he was following a well-established habit. By the 1750s, the newspapers—particularly those of York, Hull, Norwich, Stamford, which were close to good horse breeding country—are full of advertisements for stallions standing at stud in the inns of market towns for months on end.[13] By 1800, the horse had been deliberately bred with specialized capacities to meet life's necessities, whether of sport or of work.

Nor was this done without overcoming traditional prejudice. As George Culley wrote in 1786 in his *Observations on Life Stock*, which dealt with cattle, sheep and pigs as well as horses, 'The great obstacle to the improvement of domestic animals seems to have arisen from a common and prevailing idea amongst breeders that no bulls should be used in the same stock more than three years, and no tups more than two. Otherwise the breed will be too near of kin'. And he added, 'Some have imbibed the prejudice so far as to think it irreligious'—that is, such inbreeding was a deliberate encouragement and exploitation of incest; therefore a flouting of God's ordnances.[14] Nevertheless, anyone who was born in 1710 and died in 1780 could not have failed to notice the vast improvement in every type of horse and the way that they had been carefully bred to their specialized purposes—and not only horses, but also cattle, sheep, pigs[15] and dogs—particularly foxhounds. The great foxhound breeder was Hugo Meynell, the Master of the Quorn Hunt and the friend of Robert Bakewell, who may well have learned practical lessons of careful inbreeding from Meynell. Meynell had used his inbreeding method extensively to develop his packs of foxhounds for stamina, speed, and keenness

---

[12] See Robert Trow Smith, *A History of British Livestock Husbandry, 1700-1900* (1959) 42-4; 158-62: Daphne Machin Goodall, *A History of Horse Breeding* (1977), 216.

[13] For example *York Courant,* 19 March 174? when 31 horses at stud were advertised: 26 March there were 32: 2 April, 19: 9 April, 20 and so on: on 9 April 1760, Young Samson was advertised in the *Ipswich Journal*. His owner was taking him around the East Suffolk market towns.

[14] George Culley, *Observations on Life Stock, containing Hints for choosing and importing the Best Breeds of the most Useful Kinds of Domestic Animals* (1786): For the Culleys see D. J. Rowe, 'The Culleys, Northumberland Farmers', *The Agricultural History Review* (1971), xix, pp. 156-74.

[15] One of the most spectacular improvements was in pig-breeding. 'Chinese, Siamese and Neapolitan pigs were probably brought into Britain continuously from 1770 onwards. They were small, fat, hairless pigs ... and so characteristic of all present days pigs.' Juliet Clutton Brock. 'Garrods Livestock Models', *Agricultural History Review* (Reading, 1976), xxiv, p. 21. Also W. Youatt, *The Pig* (1847).

Exotic bulls and cows from India and Ceylon were also cross-bred with less success. Cross-breeding—particularly between Flemish and British cattle had been practised occasionally for a very long time. John Locke, for example, sent sheep from Holland to Somerset (*The Correspondence of John Locke*, ed. E. S. de Beer (1977), iii, p. 322). But from the 1760s cross-breeding was far, far more widespread, more carefully planned, carefully observed and carefully recorded and with more deliberate and specific ends—for example the gentry led the fashion in breeding cattle for beef rather than milk.

of scent as well as breeding out tendencies to riot or reluctance to work in a pack. But is was not only Meynell who was concerned to produce a well-defined, highly specialized breed of dog.[16] Dog fanciers of all kinds—aristocrats such as George, Earl of Orford and the coal miners of Newcastle and Durham—were experimenting with dogs. Coursing became a fashionable and popular pastime, involving organized meetings and extensive betting so that owners were very preoccupied with the qualities of their greyhounds and whippets. Lord Orford tried to improve the stamina and aggression of his breed of greyhound by deliberately making a cross with a bulldog, it itself a highly specialized animal.[17] Gun dogs also became an object of careful attention and of deliberate experiment so that varieties in breeds such as spaniel and the retriever became thoroughbred. Similarly lap dogs of very specialized types became more popular—partly through the pug introduced into England probably, by Queen Mary II. By 1800, breeds of dogs had become far more strictly defined and the variety of breeds had mulitiplied considerably.[18] Furthermore, there was now a very active trade in dogs, both for sport, for pets and for protection.

Most of the experimentation with animals, apart from whippets, bulldogs and greyhounds, was largely conducted by the gentry and prosperous farmers such as the Culleys and Bakewell but by 1780 this development was being institutionalized in local agricultural societies, specialized publications and competitive agricultural shows. Further propaganda was made by exhibitions (such as the Durham Ox), by models of famous animals, and by prints. And one further point should be stressed—much of this new livestock farming was also associated with new mechanical devices—such as the turnip slicer which produced feed quickly for winter cattle. Those farmers or landowners who were open to the new experimentation in breeding were also sympathetic to new agricultural machinery. They accepted the concept of change and improvement. However, breeding for improvement went deeper into the population than landowners and farmers.

Urban dwellers too were engaged in breeding song birds, pigeons, and ornamental fish. Canaries had been on sale in London from the sixteenth century, but the growth in the trade was not very rapid until after 1700. In the early eighteenth century families were encouraged to buy nesting boxes

---

[16] 'A vast amount of experimental breeding went on throughout the century with squires and lords corresponding and exchanging hounds from one end of England to the other.' Raymond Carr, *English Fox Hunting* (1976), p. 37. Also Collin D. B. Ellis, 'Hunting' *The Victoria County History of Leicestershire* (1955), pp. 269-74. Also Ellis's *Leicestershire and the Quorn Hunt* (Leicester 1952). A. Henry Higginson, *Two Centuries of Fox Hunting* (1946). T. F. Dale, *The History of the Belvoir Hunt* (1899).
[17] For George, 3rd Earl of Orford, see R. W. Ketton-Cremer, *Norfolk Gallery* (1948), pp. 162-87.
[18] The Hon. Mrs. Lyttleton, *Toy Dogs and Their Ancestors* (1911), pp. 6-8. E. C. Ash, *Dogs, their History and Development* (1927), 2 vols. H. Dalziel, *British Dogs, Their Varieties, History and Characteristics, Breeding, etc.* (1856). For the pug, Henri and Barbara van der Zee, *William and Mary* (1973), p. 291, and W. H. Goodger, *The Pug Handbook* (1959).

to try and breed their own outstanding songsters.[19] The variety of birds for sale constantly expanded, and novelties were eagerly sought. Parrots and cockatoos, the pets of the aristocracy of the sixteenth and seventeenth centuries, now adorned the parlours of shopkeepers and artisans. So popular were unusual birds that the owners of pleasure gardens around London and the provincial towns set up aviaries in order to attract customers. Again it was novelty, a sense of new experience, that drew families and their children either to breed their own birds or to spend money to look at them. Perhaps, however, one of the most striking developments in the eighteenth century was the breeding of homing pigeons and the beginnings of pigeon racing, a sport which, according to the book devoted to pigeons—John Moore's *Columbarium or The Pigeon House,* published in 1735—brought the artisan and the gentry together. The pouter pigeons 'were a bird more peculiarly suited to watch makers, cobblers and weavers and such trades only as worked in the same room where they were kept, that the lower class of fancier may converse and familiarize with them, without lavishing that time that should be occupied in providing for their families'.[20] John Moore was so certain that semi-literate people would buy his book that he published a glossary of difficult words. The breeding of these pigeons was undoubtedly widespread and the improvements made were commensurate with those made by Bakewell or Meynell. Moore mentions in 1735 men such as Sir Richard Atherton who died in 1726, who had purchased exceptional birds and experimented with them. Moore lists twenty-eight breeds of pigeon that were being cultivated in England in the 1730s, some were ornamental, some were for the table, and two varieties which were being used as letter carriers and for racing. The Horseman (*Columba Tabelleria Minor*) was regarded as the best pigeon for over ten miles, the Dragoon (*Columba Tabelleria Minima*) as faster under that distance, but by 1765, the stamina of the Dragoon had been improved for in his second edition Moore reports the flight of a Dragoon from Bury St. Edmunds to Bishopsgate, London, seventy-two miles in two hours and a half. There were, of course, pigeon shows for tumblers as well as very widespread racing of pigeons. But, unlike horses or cattle, the

---

[19] Eleazor Albin, *A National History of English Song-Birds* (1738), 84–94. Albin lists twenty-two British song-birds that could be purchased and which were bred in captivity and he devotes a section of his book to each bird. By 1779 there were four editions of this book and two pirated. Advertisements for canaries, song-birds, cages and nesting boxes were common in both the London and provincial newspapers from 1700, e.g. *The Post Man,* 29 March 1705: For Nicholas Heath's shop near the Monument whose sign was 'Old Black Joe the German Bird Man'. 'Choice Parakeets, Talking Parrots, the finest Cockatoo that was ever seen in England, choice Canary Birds, Muscovy Ducks' etc. etc. were being sold by David Randall in Westminster. *The Post Man,* 1 December 1705. An itinerant birdseller, Joseph Salus, visited Suffolk in March 1726. *The Suffolk Mercury,* 28 March 1725/6. For parrots, see Edward J. Boosey, *Parrots, Cockatoos and Macaws* (1956), pp. 14–15. Breeds of game cocks were also improved, see George Ryley Smith, *The History of Cockfighting* (1957): Herbert Atkinson, *Cockfighting and the Game Fowl* (Bath, 1958).

[20] Daniel Girton, *The New and Complete Pigeon Fancier* (1785), p. 19. This book, like most books on pigeons, is based on John Moore's book.

breeding of birds, whether song birds or pigeons, permeated more deeply into the population. Highly specialized books devoted to the breeding of cage birds as well as pigeons were first published in the 1730s and had become both numerous and cheap by 1800 when the canary had reached the humblest cottage. The same experimentation had taken place with ornamental fish, particularly the goldfish, an aristocratic marvel in the 1730s which had become a plebeian decoration before the end of the century.[21] The importance of these activities lies in the fact that in every town and in many villages, adults, and even children, were attempting to improve nature, indeed to control it, to attempt deliberately to breed a better songster, a faster homing pigeon, a more variegated fish. The idea of experiment, of changing nature, was no longer a philosophic concept but a widespread practical art. And a novel one. Such activities stimulated curiosity and helped to generate the feeling among men and women that they belonged to a changing and exciting world. The sense of novelty was also strengthened by the famous animal and bird museum of Piddocks at the Exeter Exchange where they could watch crocodiles, ostriches, kangaroos, elephants, rhinoceroses, toucans and birds of paradise amongst the more mundane collection of monkeys. And travelling circuses were increasingly exploiting wild animals. The new and the rare were being constantly displayed, exciting the imagination and helping to create a sense of a novel world.[22]

What is true of animal creation is also true of vegetable creation. It was probably in Restoration England that the first societies of gentlemen florists began to meet in the provinces to exchange information and to exhibit to each other their specimens. The influx of new plants, new trees, new flowers, particularly from America and the Near East, was greatly encouraged by Henry Compton, Bishop of London, whose garden at Fulham became a sort of experimental seed station. He was also Bishop for America and so made certain that the Anglican priests he despatched there were as ardent for botany as for Christ.[23] In the world of botany there was a sense of endless riches to be discovered. But there was more than mere discovery. The influence of the Dutch and their passionate attachment to the tulip had spread to England where amateurs like Nicholas Blundell were eagerly attempting to find new hybrids. He, searching like so many for the elusive

---

[21] G. F. Hervey and J. Hems, *The Goldfish* (2nd edn., 1968), pp. 79-80. In 1774 Gough and Co. had a large collection of 'gold and silver fishes' at the warehouse at Holborn Hill, London, with a very large variety of ornamental birds—parrots, pheasants, peacocks, ducks in every variety—song birds, fighting cocks, squirrels and monkeys. *British Library*. Sir Ambrose Heal's Collection of Trade Cards.

[22] One cannot, of course, pretend that this type of display was in any way scientific any more than the display of animals and human freaks which had gone on for centuries at fairs: but the variety of creatures must have seemed almost endless as the new and the rare poured into England. For shows and much else, see Richard D. Altick, *The Shows of London* (1978).

[23] Alice M. Coats 'The Hon. and Rev. Henry Compton, Bishop of London', *Garden History*, iv, (no. 3), pp. 14-19: J. H. Harvey 'Turkey as a Source of Garden Plants', ibid., pp. 21-26.

black tulip, soaked his bulbs in black ink—naturally to no avail.[24] But tulip growing and breeding was very widespread, and by 1776 choice bulbs were regularly auctioned at Christie's.[25] Bulbs of hyacinth as well as the tulip were often the targets of thieves who preyed on the specialist gardeners. A prize tulip bulb called 'Georgie' was stolen from Samuel Sicklemore at Ipswich in June 1760 and the local Society of Florists offered a reward of three guineas for the capture and conviction of the thief so the bulb was probably valued at between £30 and £50.[26] Even so the prices were low by the standards of the Dutch tulipmania.

By the middle of the century the hyacinth, particularly the double hyacinth, had equalled, if not surpassed, the tulip as a cult for connoisseurs. One of the greatest hyacinth breeders was Sir James Justice, Bt, the Scottish botanist and horticulturist, who produced the *Scots Gardeners' Directory* and was an indefatigable experimenter not only in hybridization but also in the experimentation of microclimates and heating appliances. He was in close touch with the great Dutch firm, *Voorhelms of Harlem*, and by 1755 he was growing eighty-six varieties of hyacinth. This, however, appears to be a modest number when compared with Philip Miller who claims to have grown two thousand varieties. Not surprising a treatise on the hyacinth appeared in 1743.[27] But tulip and hyacinth breeding pales into insignificance compared with the popularity of the auricula and the carnation. It would not be in any way rash to say that by 1750 every market town—towns as small as Newport Pagnell or Atherstone—possessed a Society of Florists, or Sons of Flora as they were usually called.[28] It was customary throughout England for these societies to hold two exhibitions a year—one usually in April for auriculas, the other late July or early August for carnations, at which several prizes of a modest kind were awarded—usually 10s. 6d., 7s. 6d., 5s.—for the best flowers of a stated variety or for a novel seedling. The Sons of Flora were bent not only on improvement but also on innovation. There were some highly skilled growers, such as Mr. Brewin of Leicester, who won a large number of prizes throughout the West Midlands for a decade, or John and Henry Stow, millers of Lexden near Colchester, who

---

[24] *Blundell's Diary and Letter Book 1702-28*, ed. Margaret Blundell (Liverpool, 1952), p. 55 'I helped to set some Tulip Roots as were dressed with Ink after different manners and some as were ordered other wayes in hopes to change their colour but to no good effect'. Blundell bought tulips, anemones, ranunculuses in Flanders during a visit there and spent hours in his garden planting and grafting.

[25] 'A choice collection of Flower Roots, particularly Tulips and Hyacinths remarkably Fine', Christie's *Auction Catalogue*, 30 September 1773.

[26] *Ipswich Journal*, 5 July 1760.

[27] For Sir James Justice, Bt, see four admirable articles by Priscilla King in *Garden History*, i, (no. 2), pp. 41-63; ii (no. 2), pp. 51-65; iii (no. 2), pp. 37-59 (this is particularly valuable for it deals with the Dutch bulb trade and Justice's work with tulips and hyacinths); iv (no. 2), pp. 57-68.

[28] For Newport Pagnell, *Northampton Mercury*, 27 July 1730: a prize of 40s. for the best bunch of twelve different varieties of carnation. Atherstone, *Leicester Journal*, 10 April 1789.

grew an auricula with one hundred and twenty-three blossoms on one stem. Henry was also a tulip specialist. Doubtless some Sons of Flora were gardeners on the estates of the gentry, but not all—too many of these societies were located in London and other large towns, and they were far too numerous to consist of professional gardeners only. Towns such as Leicester or Norwich had several societies. Often their shows were sponsored by innkeepers who provided the room, took the entrance money and supplied the exhibitors with a cheap ordinary.[29] This manipulation of nature brought anxiety to some about the propriety of interfering with God's creation. Thomas Fairchild (1666-1729) who produced a cross between the carnation and the sweet william, 'Fairchild's Mule Pink' had serious moral scruples about what he was doing.[30] By 1750 such fears had vanished and by 1800 the Sons of Flora with their carnations and auriculas had been joined by gooseberry lovers and melon and cucumber buffs. There was scarcely a flower or a vegetable that lacked enthusiasts.[31]

This amateur activity, however, was as nothing compared with the professional activity of horticulturists. Before 1700 some localized varieties of vegetables had developed but, owing to the absence of catalogues, we know very little about them. It would seem, however, that varieties of peas, beans cabbages and the like were very limited, although some early peas such as Hotspur had been developed. Good seed shops existed in London but probably nowhere else. In the provinces friends and professional gardeners exchanged what they considered fine specimens.[32]

By the second half of the eighteenth century the seed trade had been completely transformed. Any town of moderate size, such as Leicester, had at least one shop, often more, that specialized entirely in the sale of seeds, shrubs, bulbs and garden equipment, but the amazing fact is the extent of specialized varieties offered in their catalogues. William Johnson was a well-established seedsman who kept a shop in the upper end of the Market Place at Leicester—convenient for the gentry, farmers and villagers who drove in for the weekly market. In March 1789 he published an enormous and expensive advertisement in the *Leicester and Nottingham Journal*.[33] He

---

[29] John Harvey, *Early Nurserymen* (1974), 71; *Leicester and Nottingham Journal*, 20 July 1779: 24 July 1779, one Society met at the Three Cranes, the other at the Lion and Lamb. *The Norwich Gazette*, 13 July 1741: 25 July 1741 (another Society).

[30] Harvey, op. cit., 76.

[31] Winchester had a well-established cucumber feast by 1797—*Salisbury and Wiltshire Journal*, 9 January 1797. The oldest Florist Societies with a continuous history appear to be The Paisley Florist Society (1782) in Scotland. Ex. inf. Henry Button: and the Ancient Society of York Florists (1768) in England, Harvey, op. cit., but very little work has been done on these societies and there may be many older. Certainly they were widespread through the British Isles long before 1780.

[32] There may have been a few seed shops and nurseries in the provinces in the late seventeenth century but the evidence is obscure. See Harvey, op cit., pp. 39-58. See also Harvey, *Early Gardening Catalogues* (1972). However fresh catalogues and long lists printed as advertisements in provincial newspapers are constantly coming to light.

[33] *Leicester and Nottingham Journal*, 13 March 1789.

was offering not only large quantities of asparagus plants but also forced asparagus ready to eat. His range of potatoes, peas, beans, onions, etc. outdistanced even modern seed catalogues; for example, he had sixteen varieties of peas for sale from very early frame peas to regular and late croppers and his list included a *mangetout*. There were thirteen varieties of bean, nineteen different herbs, fifty-six varieties of annual flowers; more remarkable still, he offered aubergine seed. Almost all of his flowers and vegetables were available in a large number of varieties.[34] Such an astonishing array of vegetable seeds had been made possible by the very active breeding and cross-breeding of stocks; from the early decades of the eighteenth century seedsmen sought for specialized characteristics such as early or heavy cropping. In the 1720s Mr. Knight of Bedfordshire had made a speciality of peas—collecting all the known varieties and making detailed experiments to improve them or to find new varieties.[35] William Johnson's catalogue was nothing untoward by the 1780s. Thomas Whaley of Liverpool, Thomas Barnes of Leeds, the Telfords of York and the Perfects of Pontefract and dozens of other seedsmen and nurserymen could have given their customers an even greater choice. As with plants and flowers, so with trees and shrubs, the varieties available were light years away from what had been available in the late seventeenth century, both in species and in quantities. By 1839 18,000 species of cultivated plants were listed by Loudon. It is thought that there were only two hundred cultivated in the middle of the sixteenth century. The bulk of the new species and their innumerable varieties were introduced after 1680. Tens of thousands of men and women, probably hundreds of thousands, were actively concerned in horticulture, eager for novelty and determined on improvement. The importance of this was the sense of modernity and novelty generated by this widespread activity, bent on changing nature. People no longer expected flowers, vegetables or trees to be static objects in the field of creation, but constantly changing, constantly improving, the change and the improvement due to the experimental activity of man. They also expected the variety of nature to be infinite.

It may be objected that this activity of breeding, either of pets or flowers, was limited to a small section of the population. This is true in the sense that the very poor, who were still the bulk of the population, certainly could not afford seeds, but the poor do not create social attitudes except towards poverty and crime. Even so the different varieties of vegetables—including the spread of the potato adapted to different climatic conditions—brought improvement, at least, to the diet of the poor. Also there was a conscious effort to bring the new knowledge to the poorest members of society. Loudon, the editor and

---

[34] Johnson also ran a coach hire service: he had eighteen horses, a chariot, a horse chariot and a stage coach which ran once a week to Birmingham. However opposition forced the stage coach out of business, see *Leicester and Nottingham Journal*, 27 February 1779; 9 October 1779.

[35] Harvey, op. cit., p. 82.

proprietor of the *Gardeners' Magazine,* wrote in his letter of intent in 1826: 'We hope not to forget the horticultural comforts of the poor. We shall endeavour to promote a taste for arts among country labourers and draw the attention of every cottager who has a garden to the profit and enjoyment that he may derive from its improved cultivation.'[36] He was as good as his word and all the early volumes of the magazine possess articles on the running of cottage gardens or on potato and cottage vegetable production.[37] Furthermore there was a consistent effort at education by setting up village libraries as at Carcolston, Nottingham and Newcastle on Tyne. East Lothian went one better and set up mobile libraries or 'Itinerating Libraries' which were started in 1824. Samuel Brown wrote to Loudon on 16 January 1828 that 'Every year's experience convinced me that the itinerating library is the cheapest plan for diffusing knowledge, where there is a reading population, that has been adopted since the invention of printing. At Haddington, North Berwick, and some other stations almost the whole books on general subjects have been in constant circulation.'[38] In addition to libraries Loudon and his supporters wanted lectures, a village museum of dried specimens and displays of new materials. Nor were they narrowly horticultural, they also urged music and dances for villagers, indeed they were ardent missionaries for civility as well as professional education. Nevertheless it was the levels of society above that of the indigent poor to whom a vision of a new and changing future of development and improvement and modernity was important. Such men and women had to get and spend money, to be willing to pay for novelty, to want passionately to add to their wordly goods, to develop indeed the appetite of a consumer without which the Industrial Revolution would have been stillborn.

I do not, of course, suggest that these activities made people think philosophically about science. What it did was to make a considerable number of people receptive of scientific activity, of technological change, of modern as against traditional methods.

Between 1700 and 1770 the visual world in which these generations of English men and women were living was changing too: the accelerating rate of enclosure was altering the face of the traditional landscape. It is very difficult for us to realize that in 1700 England looked totally different, except in a few small areas, from what it did in 1800: As well as enclosure there were other vital and very visible changes, all novel, all speaking of modernity: roads, increasingly rapid transit between towns; the beginnings of an elaborate canal system; widespread provincial newspapers (that too was a novelty), and the increasing range of cultural and intellectual entertainment; all of

---

[36] *Loudon's Gardeners' Magazine,* (1826), i, p. 7.
[37] Ibid., a series of articles by John H. Moggridge on 'Some Account of the Progress of an Experiment going on in Monmouthshire for bettering the condition of the Labouring Classes' ibid., iv, p.. 533-8; W. Wilson 'On Improving the Gardens of Cottages' ibid., ii, p. 271.
[38] *Loudon's Gardeners' Magazine,* 1829, pt. II, p. 95.

these helped to create a belief, perhaps not yet profound nor accepted even by the majority of society, that there was virtue in modernity and change. New social attitudes permeate very slowly in society and they require diverse and complex channels to do so. Often they operate most effectively when unaccompanied with the panoply of overt propaganda.

This was true, or partly true, of the diffusion of science in eighteenth-century England. The scientific and philosophical societies that developed in Europe in the second half of the seventeenth century played a part; so did the increasing body of published scientific literature. Equally important in diffusing scientific attitudes, however, was lecturing in science for its entertainment value. This was an eighteenth-century phenomenon. Scientific lecturers, such as Hawksbee, Whiston, Jurin and Desaguiliers, were making a satisfactory living early in the century based principally on London and Bath and considerable provincial capitals such as Newcastle. By 1770 the profession was almost overcrowded.[39] Throughout the year there were courses, often of eight weeks, in all the principal towns of Britain —Birmingham, Liverpool, Manchester, Leeds, Newcastle, Bristol, Norwich—in the lesser market towns, Leicester, Bury, Nottingham, Stafford, Halifax, and in the spas—Bath, Tunbridge Wells, Cheltenham.[40] Indeed it would be no exaggeration to say that lectures about natural philosophy were available to the entire urban population, generously interpreted. We do not know a great deal of the content of these lectures, apart from their titles and occasionally the apparatus used in demonstration. They were principally concerned with the wonders of nature, displayed through the use of telescopes, orrerys, microscopes, air pumps, and simple but dramatic electrical experiments, such as drawing sparks from a spectator. They brought to their audiences the sense of recent discovery and of things yet to be discovered.[41] And there can be no doubt that this sense of discovery, of technical and

---

[39] See Margaret Rowbottom 'The Teaching of Experimental Philosophy in England, 1700-30'. *Actes du Congrès International d'Histoire des Sciences Varsovie-Cracovie 24-31 Aôut 1965* (Warsaw 1968), iv, pp. 46-53. Margaret Rowbottom 'John Theophilus Desaguiliers (1683-1744), *Proceedings of the Huguenot Society of London,* xxi (1968) pp. 196-218. By 1724 Desaguiliers had conducted 121 courses of experimental philosophy before a variety of amateurs, including George I and the court.

[40] One of the earliest itinerant lecturers was Benjamin Martin who maintains that so backward was provincial society that even in the 1740s he was taken for a magician and so aroused the rabble. However, itinerant lecturers were not all that uncommon. Griffiths and Demainbray had given courses at Leeds in 1739 and 1750, Booth and Jurin at Newcastle-on-Tyne. Martin does, however, appear to be the first lecturer to have worked the smaller towns. In 1748 he was advertising courses from Bewdley, Kidderminster, Leominster, Bridgwater, Ludlow. (*The Gloucester Journal,* 24 May 1748). See John R. Millburn, *Benjamin Martin, Author, Instrument Maker and Country Showman* (Leyden 1976), pp. 41-3, 61. Also *Leeds Mercury,* 13 and 20 February 1739: 17 April 1750. See also P. J. G. Robinson 'A Philosophic War: An Episode in eighteenth-century scientific lecturing in North East England', *Trans. of the Anth. and Archeological Soc. of Durham and Northumberland* (Newcastle 1925), ii, pp. 105-7.

[41] The courses were long—often 40 lectures; five times a week for eight weeks but directed at the leisured classes (including clergymen) for they might take place at noon.

scientific achievement, created very widespread interest. Two of Wright of Derby's most popular prints were of his paintings of the air-pump and of the orrery. Again, the Darby iron works and the iron bridge at Coalbrookdale brought hundreds of visitors every year and large prints of the bridge and the iron works sold briskly. We have grown so blasé about science and discovery that we cannot imagine that coloured prints of nuclear reactors or of cyclotrons would have much of a sale today. Technological advance and new industrial processes fired the imagination of many educated and semi-educated men and women of the eighteenth century. Some doubtless attended lectures or made visits to industrial sites because others did and were as unmoved by what they saw as many of the crowds that troop through great country houses are by their works of art. Nevertheless even these could not avoid realizing that they lived in a world of growth and change. Perhaps even to the majority the entertainment was of greater importance than the knowledge, but most important of all was the novelty of what was taught.

Much of the visiting and lecture-going was deliberately educational, for parents were concerned to bring these new excitements, these new stimuli, to the imagination of their children. From 1750, the acceptance of novelty, of the sense of belonging to a new world, began to be an increasingly important aspect of the experience of the eighteenth-century child.[42] This did not mean, however, that traditional attitudes were thrown overboard lock, stock and barrel.

Children's literature is full of ancient tales, whether from Plutarch or mediaeval folk lore. *The Seven Wonders of the World* and *The Seven Champions of Christendom* along with *Tom Thumb, Valentine and Orsin, Robin Hood, Babes in the Wood* and the rest were re-hashed and re-illustrated; sometimes brilliantly, as by Bewick; sometimes hideously in cheap woodcuts. Children's literature of the eighteenth century devoted to religion and morality is immensely large and often nauseating to read. After a long conversation conducted by a twelve-year old boy with a girl of six and a boy of eight about the wickedness and unchristianity of slavery, in *The Happy Family: or Winter Evenings' employment. Consisting of readings and conversations in seven parts. By a friend of youth* (1801), they all settled down to hours of instruction on Intemperance and Dissipation, Sincerity and Truth, on the Choice of Company, the Employment of Time and the Public Worship of God. The twelve-year old did the preaching and the tots listened to his dreary mixture of evangelical religion and bourgeois morality. Between 1760 and 1820, and for long afterwards, such books poured from the presses and sold in astonishing quantities—Miss Elizabeth Sandham's *The twin*

---

[42] See J. H. Plumb, 'The New World of Children in Eighteenth-Century England' above pp. 286–313. All titles given below in the text were published in London unless otherwise stated. Footnotes are not repeated here.

sisters; or, The advantages of religion (1805) over 12,000 in its first edition.[43] Other books were concerned to impart bourgeois morality without much addition of evangelical religion, either in bad verse, such as:

> If you wish for the pleasures that riches impart
> You must first learn these tables correctly by heart
> Rise early, live temperate, be just and have care
> And out of your income save at least a third share.

or heavy-footed prose.[44]

But embedded in this mass of moralistic, cautionary or traditional stories was a growing body of literature that was designed to instruct the young about the expanding world of knowledge. And authors were showing an extremely lively interest in the best ways of making knowledge attractive and easy to assimilate. Mrs. Barbauld, for example, addressed herself to the problem of teaching infants and produced *Lessons for Children,* of which Part I was for two to three year olds. She admitted in her preface that 'a grave remark, a connected story, however simple, is above his capacity, and nonsense is always below it for folly is wiser than ignorance'.[45] She was concerned not only about content but also about the infant's eye which 'cannot catch, as ours can, a small, obscure, ill-formed word amidst a number of others all equally unknown to him'. So she devised very large clear type on good white paper and stuck to the alphabet adorned with 'talk that is humble but not mean'. Another educator, this time a German, B. H. Blasche, invented *Papyro-plastics, or, the art of modelling in paper* (1820) because he felt that young children learned more quickly through shape and touch. Hence he produced models that could be handled and put together as triangles and quadrangles and could be used to create house or furniture, a type of primitive Lego. There was also considerable debate at this time as to what age children should be taught science. When the memorable book *The Newtonian System of the Universe Digested for Young Minds* by Tom Telescope appeared in 1761, the age of the children, although not stated, is, by inference, about 14-15. In 1800 the Reverend Jeremiah Joyce in his *Scientific dialogues, intended for the instruction and entertainment of Young People* (1807) assumed that he had found 'so familiar and easy a method' that science was well within the capacities of a child of ten or eleven, and that this was 'no means too early to induce in children habits of scientific reasoning'—an attitude that must have been widely accepted, for publishers advertisements, from 1760 onwards, list ever-increasing numbers of books on science, history, geography aimed at attracting young children to seek knowledge as well as instructing them in it. And these books, too, which had

---

[43] *The Osborne Collection of Early Children's Books 1476–1910,* (Toronto 1975), ii, p. 933. There were twenty-two editions by 1884.

[44] Ibid; 725. Quoted from *New Arithmetical Tables for the use of schools, enlarged and improved* (Exeter *c.* 1825).

[45] Anna Laetitia Barbauld, *Lesons for Children,* 2 parts, (1779).

in their early days been somewhat crudely illustrated, from 1780 onwards appeared with complicated pictures and diagrams, often of exceptional beauty. And yet, because, presumably, of very large sales, the price, even when very heavily illustrated, like Joyce's *Dialogues on the Microscope* (1812) in 2 vols, was rarely more than half a guinea. There were plenty of small books available on all scientific subjects for sixpence—or, after 1810, for less. In the prefaces and advertisements for these books one theme is repeated again and again, best perhaps expressed by the author of *The Lilliputian Magazine* (1752) 'Had nobody deviated from the beaten path, we should have had no improvements in the sciences, nor even in the common business of life: and have enjoyed our forefathers ignorance and bigotry'. Books for children and young people on science certainly led to an appreciation of the Creator through the wonders of His universe. They also fortunately led, according to their authors, to knowledge, modernity and profit.

There are two further points to make about children's literature in creating a sense both of belonging to a fresh exciting world, a natural, yet complex, world that could be intellectually explored. This first is easier to identify—illustrations and diagrams, often of the highest merit and of a visually exciting kind, surged like a flood into children's literature between 1780 and 1830. These illustrations, particularly in those dealing with the natural world, either the microcosmic world or the macrocosmic world of the stars, spoke of worlds beyond worlds, but ever knowable worlds that man could investigate. That is, they encouraged a belief in a new, progressive and developing knowledge of the Universe. Equally important was the fact that children's books were consumed, edition after edition, new books followed new books; and although the same stories might persist, novelty was constantly sought in their presentation. We know that many children's books had very large sales—editions of 10,000 to 15,000 were not uncommon, and some books ran through twenty or thirty editions, often with new material or new illustrations. And yet, as every bibliography of children's books demonstrates many editions have completely disappeared, others frequently remain in single copies. The importance of this very quick turnover of children's literature—instructional literature as well as mere entertainment—implies that parents wanted the latest, the most up-to-date, for their children and were prepared to regard children's books as a constant item of their family expenditure. An astonishing change in the social attitudes in perhaps three generations.

Quite as important as the enormous expansion of children's literature is the growth in the availability of children's toys between 1750 and 1830. Their range is very extensive. Instructional board games, such as *Pleasures of Astronomy* or *Natural Philosophy* and games of moral improvement, such as *The Road to the Temple of Honour and Fame* were very popular indeed between 1790 and 1830.[46] Card games to teach spelling, arithmetic, music,

[46] *The Osborne Collection of Early Children's Books* (Toronto 1975), ii, pp. 844-56.

historical and classical knowledge—along with jig-saws (an invention of the 1760s)—became increasingly available from 1730 onwards and were to be found in most provincial bookshops by 1800. More important still, I think, were the industrial and scientific toys such as the world had never seen before. Miniature printing presses, cheap microscopes, cheap telescopes, looms that took to pieces but also worked when assembled—likewise coaches and wagons, zoos and aviaries with foreign animals—giraffes, ostriches, elephants; all of these brought a sense of novelty and change to the eighteenth-century children. Few of us realize the range of such toys or their availability. *Benison of Margate* in 1800 had more than two hundred varieties of toys for sale from simple dolls to microscopes and camera obscura.[47] Again the contrast between one or two generations is very great.

And the advertisements for these toys stress frequently their novelty, their modernity, as well as their instructional value: a microscope will teach a child the inexhaustible wonder of God's creation, that is of the reality of the world about him. There may be mysteries in God's creation but such mysteries may also be explicable. The world in which the middle class child now lives is more exciting, full of wonder, discovery and change—far different than 'the bigotted age of our forefathers'. If we add to these toys, the visits to museums and zoos—both institutions of great novelty in 1800—and the scientific lecturers with their mechanical as well as their rather alarming electrical apparatus, we should be able to imagine both the excitement of parents and children in the last quarter of the eighteenth century and the early decades of the nineteenth, when *both* parents and children were having novel experiences together, and the children were acquiring objects such as their parents had never possessed. It is, of course, impossible to cover all the novelties that abounded at this time, and one more must suffice—the balloon, for example: for the first time man conquered travel in the air in the 1780s, and for the eighteenth century this was equivalent to setting foot on the moon.[48]

'Improvement' was the most over-used word of eighteenth-century England—landscapes, gardens, agriculture, science, manufacture, music, art, literature, instruction both secular and religious, were constantly described as improved. Advertisements use the word to the point of boredom: after 'improvement', the phrase in which salesmen put their faith was 'new method', after that 'latest fashion'. This is true of dresses, hair arrangements, children's clothes or furniture or china or prints. The middle and lower middle classes, not only in England but increasingly too in Western Europe, particularly the Netherlands, had been taught to buy, to expect novelty, to relish change. Not all were happy about it, many feared that it would create greed and excess. Hence the constant iteration in the sale of any amusement that it would be instructive either in knowledge or in moral improvement.

[47] *British Library.* See Sir Ambrose Heal's Trade Cards.
[48] See L. T. C. Rolt, *The Aeronauts, A History of Ballooning, 1783-1903* (1966).

This ever-expanding world of knowledge and of things led, or helped to lead, to the acceptance of modernity—of the replacement of the Providence-dominated world of early modern and mediaeval Europe by the world of expanding knowledge and science, of discoverable nature and rational exploration. In the middle ages, the peasant knew nothing of the elaborate theological arguments of the doctrine of the Reservoir of Grace. Nor could he have explained the nature of the Trinity or the Holy Ghost, but he accepted without question that the Church held the key to the understanding of his world. He knew that the forces of Satan could be active in his farmyard, that Providence was there to be invoked to save him from disaster. God was certainly not abolished from the life of eighteenth-century society. Even though He was not then controlling every event of daily life, the living world was still His creation. Yet it was a rational creation whose mysteries could be penetrated by the mind of man. Amongst the intellectual elite God was retreating to more strictly defined areas—of personal life and commitment or to a shadowy existence at the boundaries of knowledge. A rational explanation increasingly carried more weight than a theological or biblical one. The great intellectual change from a providential to a scientific world was under way, and, by 1800, could not be reversed. The difference in intellectual climate between 1700 and 1800 was therefore qualitative. An intellectual attitude of scientific rationalism was acquiring greater social acceptance. The modern factory worker knows nothing of the Quantum Theory or the Double Helix but he believes without question that scientists do and can explain the natural world.

This change cannot be explained by the scientific revolution of the seventeenth century or the discovery, before that, of the new world of flora and fauna in America which so stimulated Europe's imagination, although they were strong contributory streams. To change the attitudes of men, the ideas of intellectual élites must be socially accepted. It is my belief that quite humble activities played their part in the acceptance of modernity and of science: growing auriculas or cucumbers, crossing greyhounds with bulldogs, giving a child a microscope or a pack of geographical playing cards, taking it to look at the first kangaroo seen in England or to watch a balloon rise in the skies did much to create one of the greatest revolutions in human life. These were the tiny channels and rivulets by which the main stream of élitist thought reached the mass of the people.

And often there were sandbanks which blocked the way for such changes brought fear as well as excitement. Men like Dr. Johnson felt that society might be overwhelmed by a cheap and vulgar culture. And that foundation of society in which he so deeply believed—subordination— would be sapped beyond repair. Traditional arts and crafts suffered severely; agricultural labourers were brought near to starvation. The Luddites were a violent reaction to the new emerging technology but, bleak though it may seem to say so, the Luddites were doomed to be losers. Traditional craftsmen and peasants were not in 1810 a revolutionary force, merely a reactionary one. As Marx realized, the revolutionaries in 1800 were the bourgeoisie and most of these believed, as they had to, in modernity. No consumer society can exist or expand without such a belief.

PART IV

The Commercialization of Leisure
Botany, Gardening and the Birth of a Consumer Society

by

Neil McKendrick

CHAPTER NINE

The Commercialization of Leisure: Botany, Gardening and the Birth of a Consumer Society

In the amiable exchange of insults between historians and economists the most common interchange of accusations is that historians are innumerate and economists illiterate. These friendly libels are now so well used that they are encapsulated in the international folklore and anecdotes of everyday academic life. If a donnish figure in a supermarket in Boston tries to take a loaded basket of consumables through a check-out limited to five items or less, he is likely to be rebuked (according to the David Landes version) with the words "You must be from Harvard and can't count; or from MIT and can't read". In the Cambridge (England) version you substitute History faculty for Harvard and Economics faculty for MIT, but the message remains the same.

The retelling of the tale is all the more acceptable now since today *most* historians think that they are numerate; *some* economists think that they are literate; and *all* economic historians think that they are both. The insult is rendered harmless by being self-evidently untrue.

Let me add a new accusation, which may prove more painful by being more pertinent, and more annoying by being aimed at both disciplines.

I want to suggest that the academic walking confidently through the check-out is delinquent not because he cannot read or because he cannot count, but because he cannot see. Before the restraining injunction can work it has to be seen, and selective blindness, expressed as an inability to see certain kinds of obvious visual evidence, seems in some branches of our profession to have grown from being an occupational hazard to become a characteristic industrial injury.

My accusation is general as well as specific. It is aimed at all those historians and economists who think that they have abolished the industrial revolution because their inadequate cliometry does not prove its existence. At the command of their incomplete aggregate statistics, they happily overlook the obvious visual manifestations of dramatic regional and sectoral change. Having subjected themselves to trial by simple arithmetic, they cease to be able to see the factories, the furnaces and the kilns; the roads, the canals and the railways; the harbours, the bridges and the viaducts;

the towns, the cities and the industrial conurbations. They can no longer see their revolutionary products either. Manchester cotton, Birmingham metals, Staffordshire pottery, Sheffield cutlery – all have become less visible as their significance has been steadily demoted.

If the vivid prints of Coalbrookedale, Soho, Carron and Etruria cease to signify; if the town-plans of the industrial cities cease to impress; if the paintings of Ironbridge cease to thrill; if Wright of Derby's canvases count for nought; if mules and jennies and frames and steam engines are robbed of their industrial significance, and if models of great industrial inventions are rendered puny at the behest of selective use of computer-friendly data, then there can be little hope for the less obvious signs of rapid change during the early industrial revolution.

Given the revisionists' inability to see (or given at the very least their ability to overlook or be blind to the significance of) the great traditional symbols of industrial change – the factories, the workmen and the machinery – it is hardly likely that they will be impressed (as evidence of a consumer revolution) by the importance of fashion so vividly etched into Hogarth's prints, so colourfully recorded in Wedgwood & Bentley's pattern books, so richly exemplified in Boulton & Fothergill's advertisements, so indelibly captured in the directories of Chippendale, Sheraton and Hepplewhite, so ecstatically chorused in the eye-witness accounts of Pehr Kahn from Sweden, Faujas de St Fond from France, Karamzin from Russia, von Archenholz from Prussia, Count Pecchio from Italy, de Saussure from Switzerland and a whole host of other international commentators such as Sophie von la Roche, Professor Lichtenberg, Carl Moritz and François de La Rochefoucauld.

Visual and material evidence of what they saw has survived in abundance. But the brass, the copper, the pewter and the plate; the pottery and the glass; the knives, forks and spoons; the tables and chairs; the carpets and clocks and watches; the cottons, the calicos, the linens, the wools, and the silks; the fans and the wigs and the boots and the shoes and the hats and the handbags; the glittering shop windows and the highly-coloured fashion prints; the illustrated fashion magazines and the English fashion dolls; indeed all the rich paraphernalia of the fashion world, to which the international observers recorded their amazed responses, are dismissed as appealing trivia by the currently dominant revisionist orthodoxy, in favour of gradualism and the absence of any marked, discontinuity in eighteenth-century England.

For the revisionists cannot see marked change in either the supply side or the demand side of the equation. Shops have become invisible as well as factories; customers have disappeared along with workers; advertisements have faded into insignificance along with inventions. The transport revolution, the retailing revolution, the advertising revolution; the revolutions in production, distribution and exports have all been de-emphasized at the stroke of the revisionists' pen.

If historians can become blind to the visual evidence of the world of production and consumption, how much more can they be blind to the visual evidence of the world of leisure. If they cannot see the significance of the blazing inferno of Phillippe de Loutherbourg's *Coalbrookedale at Night* of 1801, what hope is there of their realising the import of de Loutherbourg's earning £500 per annum for his spectacular stage sets at Drury Lane; or, indeed, what hope is there of their recognizing the significance of the startling botanical drama played out in Thornton's *Temple of Flora?*

This is where my accusation becomes more specific.

For although the commercialization of leisure in the hundred and fifty years before 1800 allows one to make use of a remarkable wealth of evidence, it is largely overlooked by most historians. For all the importance of leisure in the history of human society a curious myopia has seemed to afflict our profession when faced with evidence as vivid as that offered by the highly-coloured prints of the Montgolfiers' air balloons or the dashing representions of racehorses; evidence as solid as the theatres, the assembly rooms, the concert rooms and the lecture rooms of post – Restoration England; evidence as memorable as Wright of Derby's *Orrery* and his *Experiment on a Bird in an Air Pump;* evidence as nostalgia-filled as jigsaw puzzles and all the other childhood toys spawned during the birth of a consumer society; evidence as colourful as the reproductions of pigeons, canaries; gold-fish, and all the vast array of different breeds of dog which flourished for the first time in the eighteenth century.

Specialists have not, of course, ignored this evidence. There are marvellous antiquarian seams of expert knowledge to quarry. Popular histories have been happy to pick on the more picturesque and appealing tit-bits to illustrate their texts. Only rarely, however, have academic historians explored the evidence of the growth of leisure in detail or seen its significance as part of the growing prosperity of the early modem period, as part of the purposeful entrepreneurial response to the commercial opportunities offered by it, as part of the commercialization of Georgian England and, indeed, as part of the birth of a consumer society.

This is where my accusation becomes highly specific.

It would require a substantial volume to do justice to the commercialisation of music and the theatre in eighteenth century England, to deal with the commercialisation of sport, to see how breeders with no sense of the Plenitude of Nature happily and purposefully pursued new and exotique shapes, sizes and colours in the world of pets, to explore the commercialisation of print with the explosion in book production, to trace the commercialisation of the world of toys and games (more than two hundred varieties of toys were offered for sale by a single shop in provincial England in 1800), to examine the way in which the growing need to possess (what eighteenth century commentators called this epidemic of getting and spending, this infection, this disorder, this contagion, this mania, this spreading plague, this new disease of consumption) was so effectively cosseted by advertisers and marketing men that it bred its own self-sustaining cure, a kind of retail therapy which turned shopping (both window-shopping and actual purchasing) into a new kind of leisure activity.

Lacking such enticing space I shall confine myself to examining the way in which gardening, that most common and ubiquitous form of leisure, and botany (what one might call cerebral gardening) were commercialized in eighteenth century England.

In *The Birth of a Consumer Society: The Commercialization of Eighteenth Century England* I pointed out that "Even flowers had to submit to the tyranny of fashion. Nature itself had to conform to the lust for novelty". As early as 1723, Bernard Mandeville with his gift for happy hyperbole, wrote "How Whimsical is the Florist in his Choice! Sometimes the Tulip, sometimes the Auricula, and at other times the Carnation shall engross his Esteems, and every Year a new Flower in his Judgement beats all the old ones, tho' it is much inferior to them both in Colour and Shape".

I also pointed out that this fashionable enthusiasm did not go commercially unnoticed. Indeed it enjoyed a fervent entrepreneurial response. The "disorder", to quote Wedgwood, was "cherished" so effectively by the trade that it developed into the flower mania of the late eighteenth century, infecting grand aristocratic patrons and influential academic promoters, and spreading its benign contagion down through the social ranks to flourish in provincial societies, clubs and public houses. Some of the latter were even rechristened as "The Flowerpot", "The Sons of Flora", and "The Nurseryman" in honour of the new craze for gardening. As with other aspects of the arrival of a consumer society in England, the rich may have led the way, with the middle classes hot on their heels, but there can be no doubt that the commercialization of gardening reached clearly and significantly into the ranks of the working classes.

By the end of the eighteenth century the seedsmen, the nurserymen and the bulb growers had harnessed a vast range of novel techniques with which to promote and advertise and sell their products. They successfully adapted the commercial techniques of other salesmen to the needs of flowers and bulbs and seeds and shrubs and trees. They also built up a national chain of retail outlets to meet the needs of a growing market of gardeners eager to acquire the latest varieties, the latest fashions, the newest exotiques from abroad.

In gardening, as in so many other leisure activities, the process of commercialization embraced an impressive range of marketing techniques. The introduction of new plants such as the camellia and the fuchsia were as carefully and as artfully stage-managed as Matthew Boulton's ormolu or Josiah Wedgwood's jasper. Indeed the pricing of the fuchsia followed a very similar strategy to the pricing of Wedgwood's pottery: with first a very high price to catch those rich enough to be able to indulge in the exclusiveness of rarity (the London nurseryman, James Lee, offered rooted cuttings at £20 a time in 1788), then a reduced price to widen the market catchment area, and finally cheap offers to take advantage of the fact that the fuchsia, for all its exotic appeal and its initial reputation of being rare and difficult, is one of the easiest plants to propagate and to mass produce. As Robin Lane Fox has written" Around ... 1788, the Fuchsia was set on the path of big business".

In the version of the story dignified by an entry in the *Dictionary of National Biography*, Lee heard tell of a remarkable plant flowering in the window of a sailor's wife in Wapping, found the plant, bought it for the money he had in his pocket, broke up the plant and propagated it so successfully that by the next season he had three hundred plants for sale. Such was their appeal that "new chariots flew to the gates of old Lee's nursery grounds" and society's horses "smoked off to the suburbs" to buy it. This colourful version first appeared in the *Lincoln Herald* of 3 November 1831 but other authorities have questioned it. As Alice M. Coats concluded, "The only facts which emerge beyond "all possible, probable shadow of doubt" are that in the year 1793 Lee did sell a large number of fuchsia plants at a handsome profit – all accounts agree about this". In marketing the exotic new plant he had triumphed. In a history of the commercialization of gardening that is the most significant point of the episode. It is also entirely characteristic of James Lee's successful promotion of new plants. The first Rugosa roses arrived in England from Japan and China in 1784, and Lee marketed them so effectively that by the end of the century they were widely planted throughout the country and had been successfully exported to the newly independent America. In McMahon's basic list of *Hardy and Deciduous Trees and Shrubs* one could find "*Rosa rugosa*, the wrinkled leave rose" offered for sale in 1806. The Banksia Rose, the Tea Rose and the multifloras also arrived in this period, and by 1826 a leading nurseryman was listing over 1,400 different species and varieties of the rose.

In the public promotion of the camellia, the French outdid the English. The story includes the French novelist and dramatist, Alexandre Dumas, the Hungarian pianist and composer Franz Liszt, the Italian composer Giuseppe Verdi and the Parisian seamstress, Alphonsine Plessis, who slept with two of them and inspired all three. Her trademark was the white camellia she invariably wore, except for the five days a month on which she wore a red one as an unusual horticultural signal to her admirers that she was temporarily sexually off-limits. The cultural spin-off includes the younger Dumas's *La Dame aux Camélias*, Verdi's *La Traviata* and the French rage to possess the latest variety of camellia. Dumas's *La Dame aux Camélias* was as much a dramatic tribute to the Parisian camellia mania of the nineteenth century as his father's *The Black Tulip* was a fictional tribute to the Dutch tulip mania of the seventeenth century.

Indeed the Dutch were also involved with the commercial promotion of the camellia. They held lotteries and auctions to promote the sales of the plants, just as the French later flamboyantly stage-managed new introductions with exhibitions in the Champs Elysees, complete with bands playing themes from *La Traviata*. But one should not forget that the camellia was introduced into England far earlier, in 1739, and English growers were the first to popularize it. Indeed it was an English grower from Bromley who supplied, at a very great price, the first red and white striped camellia which caused such a sensation in Paris. It was named Queen Victoria and was merely the latest in the royal dynasty of a long succession of successful English-bred camellias. The English growers had been growing and hybridizing and selling camellias long before the nineteenth-century excitement on the Continent.

In fact, if less spectacular than the Dutch tulipomania and less culturally celebrated than the French camellia craze, the English commitment to gardening was more popular, more persistent and more pervasive than either. Dutch tulip mania was a brief financial frenzy between 1634 and 1637; the French fling with camellias was a Paris-based phenomenon with neither the social depth nor the geographical spread nor the institutional underpinning of the commercialization process that occurred in eighteenth-century England. The English gardening experience mirrored in a nationally distinctive way not only the commercialization of leisure in general but the whole consumer revolution.

Indeed the pattern and the timing and the techniques involved in the process of commercializing gardening for leisure in England were remarkably similar to the marketing methods used by the great manufacturers of the early industrial revolution. Even the social motivations appealed to were strikingly similar. They were also strikingly successful.

It was Dr. Johnson's view that by 1759, "The trade of advertising is now so near perfection that it is not easy to propose any improvement". He was all too well aware of how customers "catch from example the contagion of desire". In his view even "he that has resolved to buy no more finds his constancy subdued". In his explanation the reluctant buyer "is attracted by rarity", is "seduced by example", and is "influenced 'by competition". The marketing of plants fully lives up to both Dr. Johnson's verdict and his explanation. Class competition, social emulation, and emulative spending – all played their part in the commercialization of gardening. And all were amply cherished by creative entrepreneurs, eagerly encouraged by advertising men and readily supplied by a growing army of retailers.

Indeed some promotional campaigns, such as Thornton's *Temple of Flora*, surpassed even Johnson's flattering judgement on the quality of contemporary marketing endeavour. It is perhaps the most vivid single piece of the surviving visual evidence of sales promotion and commercial flamboyance in the whole history of entrepreneurial activity in Georgian

England. It is also the most beautiful.

Thornton was promoting academic botany as much as simple gardening. Botany was the intellectual underpinning of the eighteenth-century flower mania. Botany was a major leisure pursuit of the fashionable upper classes and the educated middle classes. It reached its peak in the late eighteenth century. Its skilful promotion by enthusiasts such as Thornton played a very important part in sustaining the growth of commercial gardening. It publicized the latest imports. It advertised the latest varieties. It dramatized the scientific advances. It encouraged the hybridizers. It promoted plant collecting. It sponsored foreign expeditions. It enveloped the whole gardening world in the excitements of academic controversy. It gave intellectual respectability to a hobby.

It also added the improbable spice of sexual scandal to the demure world of gardening. It is often forgotten that the title of Thornton's most famous publication, of which the *Temple of Flora* was merely a part, was *A New Illustration of the Sexual System of Carolus von Linnaeus*. The adjective "new" was there to distinguish it from other botanical publications busily cashing in on the popularization of the Linnaean system of plant classification, and the controversies which surrounded it. Botanical scholarship might seem an unlikely source for a vigorous moral debate, but the reactions to Linnaeus's sexual system for the classification of plants were frequently violently hostile.

The grounds for concern were initially moral rather than scientific. Botanists as well as moralists rushed into print to express their outrage on behalf of the sensibilities of young women, their disgust that Providence should be presented as producing such a promiscuous plant world, their alarm at the sexual metaphors used to describe the loves of the plants, and their horror at the frank vocabulary employed to do so (even if it was cloaked in the decent obscurity of a learned language). At first commentators contented themselves with the thought that few botanists "will follow (the) lewd method" of Dr Linnaeus. Others, more alarmed at "such loathsome harlotry" being imputed to flowers and plants, questioned whether God would ever have sanctioned "so licentious a method" of reproduction as one which required several males to service a single female.

Perhaps some of the protests owed more to personal pique than to outraged morality. One of the most vociferous early opponents to Linnaeus was the St. Petersburg academician Johann Siegesbeck, who may well have been less than flattered to discover that the plant to which Linnaeus attached the name *Siegesbeckia* was "an unpleasant small-flowered weed".

But more powerful and more influential guns were being trained on Linnaeus, and in 1768 the first edition of the *Encyclopedia Britannica* fired a thunderous salvo. It was a double-barrelled attack. It dismissed the scientific basis of the Linnaean system and it denounced the sexual analogy on which it was based. It cast doubt on both his motives and his taste, not to say his sense of decency. "One would be tempted to think", thundered the *Britannica*, "that the author had more reasons than one for relishing this analogy so highly. In many parts of this treatise, there is such a degree of indelicacy in the expression as cannot be exceeded in the most obscene romance writer." To hammer home the message, telling examples of Linnaean prose were quoted ("the calix is the bride chamber in which the *stamina* and *pistilla* solemnize their nuptials") and damaging examples of his vocabulary were cited (for example a Latin passage containing the words "CUNNUS", in capitals, "*labia*", "*genitalia*", "*nymphae*", "*vasa spermatica*", "TESTICULI", this in smaller capitals, "*vulva*", "*vagina*", "*tubae Fallopianae*" and other words and phrases "impossible to do justice to in translation". Surely, concluded the *Britannica* "a man would not naturally expect to meet with disgusting strokes of obscenity in a system of botany. But it is a certain fact, that obscenity is the very basis of the Linnaean system. The names of his classes, orders, etc., convey often the vilest and most unnatural ideas. For example, *diandria*, the name of his second class, is thus explained by Linnaeus ... i.e. one female married to two males...The number of males goes on increasing till the 13th class, the plants belonging to which are said to have from 20 to 1,000 husbands to one wife!".

Rarely had the quiet academic backwaters of botany enjoyed such scandal and notoriety. It did no harm at all to its popularity. For it was a controversy which was to run and run. Forty years after the *Britannica* article and seventy-three years after Linnaeus first published his ideas in 1735, Sir James Edward Smith, who founded the Linnean Society, was still being rebuked by the future Bishop of Carlisle, and reminded that "To tell you that nothing could equal the gross prurience of Linnaeus's mind is perfectly needless. A literal translation of the first principles of Linnaean botany is enough to shock female modesty. It is possible that many virtuous students might not be able to make out the similitude of *Clitoria*." Even Goethe weighed in with a condemnation of the effect that the Linnaean "dogma of sexuality" might have on innocent young minds, especially young female minds. Many seemed "to long for a more innocent form of reproduction, such as that which Erasmus Darwin's poetry offered in the lines "Unknown to sex, the pregnant oyster swells".

Even Darwin could be playful about the loves of the plants. He wrote, for instance, of the female campion (*Lychnis coronaria*) behaving with a saucy, if improbable, abandon; as she –

> "*In gay undress displays her rival charms,*
> *And calls her wondering lovers to her arms.*"

Indeed Darwin's *Loves of the Plants* in his famous poem *The Botanic Garden* was, in some ways, the literary counter-part of Thornton's *Temple of Flora*. His poetry struck a resounding and popular chord with the aspiring gardeners and educated botanists of his day. As Desmond King-Hele has written of

Darwin's botanical writings: "Science, so pleasantly presented, was much to the taste of the leisured reading public." In the 1780s Darwin had spent seven years on two lengthy translations of Linnaeus, the *System of Vegetables* and the *Families of Plants.* In the 1790s he completed *The Botanic Garden*, publishing the first volume, *The Loves of the Plants*, in 1789, and the second, *The Economy of Vegetation*, in 1799. It was a remarkable achievement. As L.T.C.Rolt said of it, Darwin performed "the astonishing feat of rendering in imaginative terms which any literate man could then appreciate the sum of human knowledge at that time. It was an achievement which was never repeated or even attempted." It was certainly very popular. Those of us reared on the mockery of Darwin by the Anti-Jacobins often forget how highly he was once rated. In the 1860s Craik's popular *History of English Literature* still gave him as much space as Shakespeare and six times as much as Byron. In the eighteenth century his standing was even higher. Even the fashionable, cosmopolitan London critics applauded, writing like Horace Walpole, "Dr. Darwin has destroyed my admiration for any poetry but his own." The reading public responded eagerly to the sex lives of plants presented in such accessible poetry. Vegetable sexuality in rhyming couplets meant that one could enjoy the illicit thrills of Linnaean theories in apparent innocence.

Such literary accessibility and scientific controversy served only to heighten interest and to keep botany at the forefront of fashionable concern. In fact female enthusiasts proved more robust in their response to Linnaeus than those male writers who protested on their behalf. Indeed Thornton deliberately targeted the leisure time of women with the *Temple of Flora*, writing in 1799 to recommend "a study of the Science of Botany ... as an elegant pursuit for ladies"; and urging them to seek enlightenment in his pages, where

"...*In bright leaves, the sexual pleasures dwell*".

But there were many other factors at work to keep an interest in botany alive, and to make gardening and a love of plants a popular recreation for all classes.

The most obvious stimulus came from the continuous stream of new species which flowed into Britain as a result of the work of the plant collectors and their botanically minded patrons and sponsors. This "boom in exotics" provided the life models for the flood of coloured plates which whetted the buying public's appetites for the new species. Since 1759, when the Royal Botanic gardens at Kew were founded, the flow of imports had sustained interest in botanical innovations at an extraordinary high level. Even for most of the Napoleonic war years, in which Thornton was publishing *The Temple of Flora*, the flow of botanical novelties continued to create a climate of constant excitement and rarely disappointed expectation. In 1796 there were, according to the second edition of William Townsend Aiton's *Hortus*

Kewensis, 141 new species introduced into Britain. In 1797 when France unleashed a predatory pack of privateers which captured three hundred American ships in retaliation for the closure of the American ports to French shipping, the figure fell to 22, the lowest figure since 1759. But the figures quickly picked up and in the five years between 1798 and 1802 Aiton recorded an average of 98 new species arriving in Britain each year, and after the Peace of Amiens in 1802 the restrictive dam created by the war gave way completely (if briefly) and 210 new species flooded in.

How much the fashion for botany relied on the continuous refreshment of interest provided by these new plants can clearly be seen when the tide turned. When in 1807 the figure dropped down to 14, and in 1811 down to 3, the consequences for botany and for Thornton were to prove dire, as we shall see.

But when Thornton first planned his great work, botany and the biological sciences were still "in the ascendant". The excitement over Linnaeus was far from dead; the Linnean Society had only recently been founded; and a flood of botanical publications responded to and further stimulated public interest. Amongst all the botanical ephemera, some major works appeared; such as Curtis's *Flora Londinensis* (1777–87), Smith and Sowerby's *English Botany* (1790–1814), and, of course, all of Erasmus Darwin's *The Botanic Garden*. Of even greater long term significance was William Curtis's production, in 1786, of the first issue of the *Botanical Magazine*. Curtis found the market sufficiently responsive to publish drawings of flowers from fifteen different London nurserymen and florists between 1786 and 1800, his magazine serving both an educational and an advertising function. Customers for the new varieties were told how to grow them and where to buy them from.

Against such a background of botanical publication Thornton felt confident that the gardening enthusiasm of the leisured classes would respond warmly to his own great work.

It was certainly a most ambitious project and even when judged against the clamouring opposition of rival botanical publications it stands supreme. As Erasmus Darwin said of it, it had "no equal". Even now, nearly two hundred years after its inception, Geoffrey Grigson can still write, "No other book of English flower illustrations has quite the celebrity of the *Temple of Flora*". Thornton was its inspiration, its promoter, its author, its editor, its banker and in part its illustrator.

Thornton is a perfect exemplar of the eighteenth-century cult of botany in its extreme form. Educated for the Church at Cambridge (the Master of Trinity College thought that he would shine in the pulpit), he later trained for medicine, took his Cambridge M.B., proceeded to Guy's and studied abroad before setting up practice in London. But his leisure time from youth to old age was dominated by botany and gardening. At school he kept a small botanic garden and an aviary containing every species of

English hawk. According to the *European Magazine* of 1803, as a child "all his weekly allowance went to maintain his garden and menagerie".

His life-long obsession with flowers and plants led to a remarkable list of botanical publications. He wrote on politics – *The Politician's Creed* (1795–9), and *The Philosophy of Politics* (1799); he wrote on medicine – *The Philosophy of Medicine* (1796–1813) and the vindication of vaccination, *Vaccinae Vindicae* (1806); he wrote on religion – *The Lords Prayer* (1827); and he wrote on the classics – mainly Vergil; but his major subject was botany. Apart from his magnum opus on *A New Illustration of the Sexual System of Carolus von Linnaeus* which he published in many parts between 1799 and 1807 and which included *The Temple of Flora*, or *Garden of Nature*, he also published his "Account of Dr Thornton's exhibition of botanical paintings" (1804), a "Sketch of the Life and Writings of William Curtis" (1805), *Practical Botany* (1808), *Botanical Extracts, or the Philosophy of Botany* (1810), "Elementary Botanical Plates to illustrate Botanical Extracts" (1810), *Alpha Botanica* (1810), *A New Family Herbal* (1810), *A Grammar of Botany* (1811), *The British Flora* (1812), *Elementary Botany* (1812), *Outline of Botany* (1812), *Temple of Flora* (1812), *Juvenile Botany* (1818), *The Greenhouse Companion* (1824) and even *The Religious Use of Botany* (1824).

These lesser works all played their part in the popularization of gardening and botany. They fostered the growth of gardening as an informed leisure pursuit, they publicized the art and mysteries of plant growing, they illustrated new plants, they introduced children and beginners to botany and the delights of the garden. They were all the more influential in that they came after the publicity which surrounded the launch of Thornton's great work. But it was Thornton's *Temple of Flora, or Garden of Nature* which stands out not only as a supreme example of the illustration of plants, but also as the supreme example in this field of the commercialization of gardening publications. It employed a whole battery of promotional devices. For all its sumptuous luxury, for all its extravagance, for all its overweening ambition, it was always commercially purposeful. It was always intended to sell. And Thornton went to enormous lengths to try to do so.

It was published in parts. It was published whole. It was republished in different forms. It was advertised. It was exhibited in New Bond Street. It was the subject of a royally sanctioned lottery. It was sold with free gifts, with prizes and at different prices. It was reproduced in folio editions and quarto editions. Its illustrations could be bought singly or jointly. It contained work by major artists and major poets and major botanists. Such was the level of royal patronage sought that Thornton proclaimed the support of one royal duke, several royal daughters, the Prince Regent and both the King and the Queen: Queen Charlotte, addressed as "the Bright Example of Conjugal Fidelity and Maternal Tenderness" as well as "Patroness of Botany", was particularly honoured, with an exciting and dramatic new species being labelled simply "the Queen", and then "the Queen Flower", and, in Latin,

Strelitzia reginae after her maiden name. Such was the level of advertising sophistication that it contained self-referential jokes for the cognoscenti – the eggs that nestled in the folio plates of "A Group of Roses" had hatched out into appealing fledgelings in the later Lottery edition. Such was the attention to eye-catching detail that the exhibition of original paintings in New Bond Street took place complete with clouds of exotic butterflies and flocks of English and foreign birds to complement the exotic plants and to dramatize the event.

As an example of ambitious sales promotion and marketing it ranks alongside those other three great eighteenth-century marketing campaigns, Wedgwood's promotion of his jasper to replace marble in Georgian interiors, Boydell's great Shakespeare gallery to promote his edition of Shakespeare, and Fuseli's corresponding effort on behalf of the work of Milton. Like them it failed – at least in the short run. Like them it failed financially, but triumphed artistically. Like them it triumphed in terms of its ambitions, in terms of its promotional techniques, and in terms of its lasting fame. Like them in the long run its glorious failure was transmuted into a lasting success. The permanence of the success lies in what was being promoted and what we still have. Its contemporary importance lies in its intentions – what it tried to do and how magnificently it tried to do it. Its commercial significance lies in the level of its entrepreneurial ambition and the level of the promotional skills which it demonstrated.

The failure of Thornton's great enterprise, like the failures of Wedgwood, Boydell and Fuseli, does not rob it of significance. For like them it was the flawed jewel in the otherwise immensely successful campaign of commercialization. That the jewel itself did not lead to immediate profit for the individual promoter, did not mean that the commercialization of pottery or print or gardening did not gain immensely from the publicity involved in its aspirations.

It is difficult now given our familiarity with plants such as the cyclamen, the strelitzia, the passion flower, the rhododendron, the kalmia, the Venus fly-trap, the sensitive plant or the begonia, to realise how exciting their first introduction must have been for those who had never seen them before. Thornton's plates had for many the impact of revelation. And the shock of the new has rarely been more beautifully or dramatically exploited. Not that Thornton's prints relied purely on novelty to make an impression. His portrayals of such familiar flowers as tulips, carnations, roses, auriculas, and lilies could attract attention by their sheer beauty, and have continued to do so to the present day. But he rarely missed a chance to make a commercially purposeful botanical point. Characteristically his plate of the madonna lily – one of the best-known and best-loved plants of antiquity – presented the golden variegated form to take advantage of the contemporary fashion for variegated plants. But many of his plates went much further in order to exploit attention and create sensation. His melodramatic representations of the night-flowering Cereus, the funereal dragon Arum or the maggot bearing Stapelia, would have done justice to a Gothic horror novel and could make both the familiar and the strange seem startlingly arresting.

The presentation could be disarmingly simple. What could be more appealingly straight-forward than Thornton's group of Auriculas? It consisted of just four plants each with a single stem set against a mountainous background – a purple flower called "Redman's Metropolitan", a yellow one called the "Egyptian", and two others looking at first sight very similar to the untrained eye, one called "Cockup's Eclipse" and the other "Grime's Privateer". It is a compellingly beautiful print, painted by Peter Henderson and engraved in aquatint, stipple and line by two engravers, Lewis and Hopwood. But Thornton was not satisfied and had a second plate made, banishing the two easily distinguishable auriculas into the distant background, so banished indeed that many authorities wrongly describe this plate as containing only "Cockup's Eclipse" and "Grime's Privateer". It is another beautiful plate (painted by Philip Reinagle and excellently engraved by Sutherland), but by containing only the two very similar plants in close-up it allowed Thornton to highlight, but not exaggerate, the most subtle differences – the more emarginate petals of the "Privateer" and the more completely circular flower of the "Eclipse". In his text Thornton spelled out the differences in precise detail (the edge of apple green which identified Cockup's flower justified that grower's claims to fame) and added a note to explain exactly what qualities a new variety of auricula must possess to be considered fine.

The auricula had achieved such a cult status in eighteenth-century England that such tiny differences were of crucial importance to plant enthusiasts. Introduced by Huguenot weavers in 1575, the auricula had achieved a remarkable position in the gardening world of Georgian England. In 1792 the Sons of Flora concentrated on the eight classic florists' flowers – the auricula, the anemone, the hyacinth, the tulip, the ranunculus, the carnation, the polyanthus and the pink. These eight were the workingmen's flowers, later joined by the Sweet William and the pansy. Up to fifty shows a year were held in eighteenth-century Yorkshire and Lancashire for auriculas alone. Prizes were eagerly competed for and usually won by the artisan competitors. In 1770 William Hanbury's important *A Complete Body of Planting and Gardening* offered the following solace to the professional gardener defeated by the auriculas of a mere working man: "At these feasts", he wrote, "let not the Gardeners be dejected if a weaver run away with the prize, as is often done; for the many articles he (the gardener) has to manage demand his attention in many places. A very small shower, which may come unexpectedly, when he is engaged in other necessary work at a distance, will take off the elegance of a prize auricula or carnation; whereas your tradesman, who makes pretensions to a show, will ever be at hand; can help his pots into the sun, and again into the shade; can refresh them with air, or cover them at the least appearance of a black cloud; and this will be an ease and a pleasure to him, and enable him to go to work with more alacrity". Whatever the reasons, Lancashire weavers were famed for their show auriculas, Staffordshire potters for their polyanthus, and the workers at Paisley for their laced pinks.

To these enthusiasts news of new varieties and improvements on the old was constantly sought. Sensational blooms such as John and Henry Stow's auricula which bore 133 blooms on a single stem were eagerly reported in the general press, and the trade press carried news of colour breakthroughs and novelties. It was a world of rapid and bewildering change. By 1770 there were over 1,000 named ranunculuses, and more than two hundred double hyacinths; in 1798 there were 117 varieties of *purple* ranunculus alone, and a single grower might have a thousand different polyanthus for sale.

Specialist auricula growers needed continuously to re-new their stock with the latest fashionable varieties, and specialist buyers needed precise and accurate information which the botanical magazine and botanical plates alone could provide. Thornton was only one source of such information, but his high-profile, up-market promotional campaign made auricula-growing even more popular, firstly by making it fashionable amongst the rich and then, by a process of social emulation and imitation, giving a further boost to the rest of society. Many have seen the *Temple of Flora* as the catalyst which led to the auricula becoming "the pet plant of polite society" between 1811 and 1820. It was in these years that the "auricula theatres" flourished.

Such theatres flourished, of course, only for the rich. Black velvet draped over shelves or tiers provided the flattering background, ornate mirrors at the back and sides of the staging provided the sophisticated reflections, candle-lit chandeliers provided the dramatic lighting for evening performances. Owners of such theatres were the audience who could afford to buy the complete Thornton collection of *The Temple of Flora*. It was a restricted market. Only about 800 volumes were sold before the plates were destroyed after the lottery, which partially explains their current high value. Rarity added to beauty is rarely resistible in the world of antiques.

If the rich were the target for Thornton's beautiful plates, it was not only as patrons of the fine arts that they were targeted but also as botanical enthusiasts. Flowers as familiar as the rose, the carnation, the tulip and the hyacinth were not only beautifully illustrated, but they were also accurately presented with name and provenance and special characteristics precisely delineated and described. Although prices of hyacinths never matched those paid for tulips, a single bulb of the variety "Rouge eblouissante" fetched £83 at the time of Thornton's endeavours, and the five different varieties he chose to depict were highly prized and for once Thornton chose a professional botanical artist to paint them. Significantly he chose

Sydenham Teak Edwards who did much of the finest work in the early years of Curtis's *Botanical Magazine*.

With his "Tulips", perhaps along with the auriculas the most simply satisfying portraits, of them all, Thornton not only names the seven different blooms, but tells us that the Louis "sells for forty guineas and the "Washington" for ten!". The names of the bulbs are as revealing as the prices about the market whose patronage was being signalled. They were "Louis XVI", "La Triomphe Royale", "La Majestueuse", the "Duchess of Devonshire", the "Earl Spencer", "Gloria Mundi" and "General Washington". The Duchess of Devonshire and the Earl Spenser were raised by Davey and Masson and deliberately and specifically named by Thornton in recognition of their namesakes' role as patrons of his enterprise. Shades of Josiah Wedgwood naming his cheap flower pots "Duchess of Devonshire flowerpots" in 1786 on the ground "they want a name – a name has a wonderful effect" on sales "I assure you". Shades of George Stubbs changing the hats worn in the latest version of the *Haymakers* because Gainsborough's portrait of the Duchess of Devonshire had made enormous picture hats fashionable in the mid-1790s. Shades of women wearing "false fronts" in 1783 because the Duchess of Devonshire had made pregnancy fashionable in that year. The power of patronage, its impact on sales, the need to seek it and to advertise it, was as well understood in the commercialization of gardening as it was in the world of manufacturing and marketing more obvious consumer items. The Duchess of Devonshire was not alone in serving such purposes. The Countess of Bective was used in exactly the same way by Foster to give snob appeal to his carpets. All fashion goods used the same technique.

With his "Carnations" the six different blooms are chosen to illustrate the precise standards laid down by the Sons of Flora for the competitions, two "Flakes" (flowers with broad stripes of one colour), two "Bizarres" (flowers with stripes of two or three colours) and two "Piquettes" (flowers with toothed or coloured edges to the petals). The names honoured either growers or patrons and often both – "Palmer's Duchess of Dorset", "Caustin's British Monarch", "Midwinter's Duchess of Wurtemburg", "Davey's Defiance" and Palmer's Defiance". He included no "Painted Ladies", the second of the four divisions recognised by the strict rules of the Florists, but in tune with the spirit of commerce, which was such a distinctive part of his work, he added that "these carnations are all of them copied, of the exact size of Nature, from out of the choice collection of Mr Davey, of the King's Road, Chelsea, as were the Tulips from that of Mr Mason, certainly the first florists in the world, and gentlemen extremely desirous of giving every information and encouragement to the botanist." Growers such as Davey were well known to gardeners of the day – indeed they were continuously advertised by the flowers which bore their names. Thomas Davey moved to Chelsea in 1798 and rose to great fame as a breeder of carnations, tulips and pinks, but his father, who lived to be ninety, had been a successful nurseryman before him for most of the eighteenth century.

If these beautiful plates give us an accurate impression of Thornton's appeal to eighteenth-century gardeners, they do not perhaps catch the extra excitement that much of his work produced. That came from his presentation of the new imports. Here Thornton's plates conveyed not only the sheer novelty of plants, often never seen before, but also some sense of their exotic origins. The Strelitzia known as the "Bird of Paradise Flower" (when not carrying its royal labels) was so exotic-looking that it hardly needed the parakeet which accompanied it in Plate II or the palms and mountains that more discreetly backed it in Plate XI. It had been introduced by Sir Joseph Banks with flamboyant publicity in the 1780s and its bizarrely-shaped blooms, "quite unlike anything known at that time", created their own sensation.

With the "Limodoron", introduced more discreetly by Dr Fothergill in 1778 from China and grown in his 260 foot-long greenhouse at his house in Essex, the flower could stand alone because exotic orchids were scarcely known in Europe at the time. The flowers alone caused great excitement. The same was true of the "Oblique Leaved Begonia" (*Begonia nitida*) from Jamaica (another Banks introduction); and of the Winged Passion Flower introduced from Peru in the late eighteenth century; and of another hothouse sensation, the "Nodding Renealmia" introduced from Japan in 1792, again by Banks. But with the "Indian Reed" Thornton provided a pagoda to underline the exoticism of the *canna indica*; with the "Sacred Egyptian Bean" he provided the pyramids; with the Persian Cyclamen he provided an oriental temple; with the poisonous Kalmia he provided snow-capped mountains as a background and lines from Dr George Shaw of the British Museum as back-up

"High rise the cloud-capped hills where Kalmia glows
With dazzling beauty, 'mid a waste of snows...";

with the "Large Flowering Sensitive Plant" he provided humming birds and a negro to underline its Jamaican origins; while with the "Blue Egyptian Water-Lily" he provided "a distant view of Aboukir and the waters of the Nile" complete with palm trees, a mosque and a minaret, to take advantage of the contemporary excitement over Nelson's triumph over Napoleon's fleet in the Battle of the Nile. Indeed more of the text is concerned with Nelson's triumph than with the botanical introduction – another sign of Thornton's desire to take advantage of any helpful current association, just as Josiah Wedgwood and George Packwood and Matthew Boulton did in their remarkable marketing campaigns.

The Water Lily offers us a specific visual reminder of the Thornton-Darwin-Wedgwood link in industrial operation. For the Wedgwood factory exploited the waterlily at much the same time by producing the well-known brown Water-Lily Plates for the Darwins. The idea and the order came from the Darwins, but the design struck a sufficient chord with contemporary interest to be reproduced in different colours to satisfy a more general public demand. The original plates ordered by Dr. Robert Waring Darwin in 1807 and delivered on 29 March 1808 can still be seen in the Fitzwilliam Museum along with later copies. The design includes three different plants from the species *Nymphaeceae* – *Nymphaea stellata, Nymphaea lotus,* and *Nelumbium speciosum* (*Nelumbium nucifera*). They were taken from engravings in the *Botanist's Repository* for October 1803 and September 1804, and the *Botanical Magazine* for December 1804 and February 1806. They, and the many other botanical plates produced at Etruria at this time, offer further visual evidence of the taste for botany and its commercial exploitation in late Georgian England which Thornton both symbolised and helped to create.

Even more dramatic was Thornton's presentation of the more sinister oddities of the plant world. With the "Pitcher Plant" (so named "because small birds repair to it and drink out of the hollow leaf"), the "Venus Fly-Trap", the "Dragon Arum", the "Maggot-bearing Stapelia", and the "Night-Blowing Cereus", he encouraged his painters to allow their creative imaginations free play. They responded eagerly. In these plates Thornton offered us in Geoffrey Grigson's words "Romanticism, neoclassic, oriental and Gothic – romanticism of sentiment and romanticism of horror."

With the innocuous arum Thornton exploited to the full the theatrical possibilities offered by its funereal colour, its purple spike and its unpleasant smell. As Ronald King has written of this plate, "Thornton gives full sway to these horrific properties ... knowing that his audience, spellbound by the fashionable Gothic novel, loved the delicious thrill of romantic horror which the plant could unleash. Peter Henderson does his best to convey the feeling in his picture, in which black and threatening clouds brood over the hills and, mountains while the dark and noisome plant thrusts its un-wholesome menace up from below." To reinforce the effect Thornton added his own prose poem. "This extremely foetid poisonous plant will not admit sober description. Let us therefore personify it. She came peeping from her purple crest with mischief fraught: from her green covert projects a horrid spear of darkest jet, which she brandishes aloft: issuing from her nostrils flies a noisome vapour infecting the ambient air; her hundred arms are interspersed with white, as in the garments of the inquisition; and on her swollen trunk are observed the speckles of a mighty dragon: her sex is strangely intermingled with the opposite! confusion dire – all framed in horror." In the even more sensational plate prepared for the Lottery edition, flashes of lightning add a further, quite superfluous, theatrical touch. This was pure melodrama. We are a very long way from the sober, cool, scientific tone of academic botany here.

Botany as a leisure pursuit was being presented as exciting, dramatic, and accessible. It is a vivid example of the higher popularization of the currently most fashionable up-market leisure activity in Georgian London. By publishing in parts, Thornton offered a succession of new delights and new botanical surprises to the gardening enthusiasts. By stage managing their presentation he added to the excitement. By dramatizing their contents he made his products even more alluring.

His presentation of his chosen plants could be unashamedly sensational. The language he used to introduce the Venus Fly-Trap was blatantly melodramatic and, as we now know, botanically incorrect, but it not unnaturally intrigued his readers. He described the Venus Fly-Trap as being "exactly similar in shape and contrivance to our rat-trap, with spikes in the centre and teeth around, also baited from glands which distil honey. No sooner does a deluded insect touch this honey, than the trap instantly closes, and with such softness, as never to miss its prey, and with such a spring as to defy all exertions to escape, and opens only when the insect is dead, when it expands again for fresh murders." It is a very disappointing print, but like the pitcher plant and the stapelia it demonstrated a triumph of the plant world which was very much to the taste of contemporary botanical enthusiasts. In Thornton's words, it showed "the vegetable... deceiving and overcoming the animal creation".

Such rare examples of horticulture rampant were not to be wasted. The pitcher plant's ability to delude and then consume insects led to its appearing in two plates, but the maggot-bearing stapelias received even more loving and detailed attention. It was justifiably presented in the company of blowflies since it had "so strong a scent, resembling carrion, that blowflies in abundance hover round it, and mistaking the corolla for flesh, deposit there their eggs, which are soon converted into real maggots, adding to the horror of the scene, some being seen writhing among the purple hairs of the flower, and others are already dead for want of food". To add a further sinister touch a malevolent-looking snake glides under the leaves. It is another aesthetically disappointing plate. The macabre proved no substitute for beauty, but its purpose was to intrigue as much as to please, and it undoubtedly generated much contemporary interest. Once again its publication was timed to take advantage of the current botanical news. As Ronald King has written, "*Stapeliae* were in the news." Francis Masson, the famous plant collector, had returned from South Africa with thirty-eight new species to add to the previously known two and had published *Stapeliae Novae* to publicize the fact. Characteristically, Thornton cashed in on the short-lived attention – not even the most obsessed botanist could be expected to remain interested in the *stapelia* for long. The brief commercial opportunity had to be exploited quickly or not at all.

Much more successful was the "Night-Blowing Cereus". Indeed so effective was this plate that Thornton had two virtually identical plates made. In them Thornton combined a striking looking flower (in his own words, "equally grotesque as terrific"), the botanical interest of a plant which bloomed at night for pollination by night-flying insects, and, despite its Cuban and Jamaican background, an English church at dead of night with the moonlight revealing that the clock stood at 12.03 to high-light this nocturnal behaviour. Since the opening hours of botanical gardens could not accommodate this flowering timetable, botanists and flower lovers alike were encouraged to arrange evening parties during which the flower of the Moon Cactus, as it was also called, could dramatically unfold around midnight. It provided a theatrical climax to botanical evening meetings. (They still happen. I have attended such a meeting in Caius College, Cambridge.)

It was also the dramatic flowering habit of the aloe or American Century Plant which made Thornton publish his version of it so illogically early. A supposedly seventy year old *Agave americana* had flowered in September 1790 and Thornton could not resist taking early advantage of the publicity which surrounded the event. Such a flowering had never occurred before in Britain, and turned out to be as impressive as it was unique. In Thornton's word, its flower "trunk" grew "with astonishing rapidity, until it reached the height of nearly 30 feet, resembling the mast of a ship". As if this was not enough to excite the botanical world, it then "projected from its summit...13 great branches, at each of whose extremities were found from 80 to 100 flowers, on proper peduncles, or flower-stalks, of different lengths, that each flower might have its due position as to light and heat, exciting in each beholder the idea of a vast chandelier." Little wonder that the world of botany wished to see and read about such a marvel. (The original plate of 1 May 1798 had to be replaced because of wear on 1 May 1807 and the new plate was more correctly labelled "The American Aloe").Little wonder, too, that such marvels added to the pleasure and kudos of owning a glass-house. Such houses were necessary to grow many of the tender exotics illustrated by Thornton and this one had the added excitement of requiring panes to be removed from the roof to allow the flower to reach its full height. Little wonder that the Russian traveller Karamzin was able to report in 1790 that "attached to each house are vast greenhouses, where fruits and plants have been gathered from all parts of the world", and that La Rochefoucauld could write in 1784 "heated glass-houses ... are common in England ... I've seen them in the majority of town gardens". Karamzin was talking of country houses and la Rochefoucauld was talking of the gentry, but the fashion spread downwards and wonders like Thornton's flowering century plant produced an added sensation which further fuelled the desire to own one.

Other sources of wonder were also exploited. With the passion-flower plates, for instance, one once again feels that the value of the story attached to the plant was as important as its botanical interest. It is true that the blue passion flower from Brazil and Peru was the first of its genus to prove hardy in Europe but it had been known since 1699. It is true, too; that the Winged Passion Flower had only been known for thirty years, but to include them both and the Quadrangular Passion Flower as well (three out of only thirty-seven plates completed and seventy planned) suggests something more than simple botanical interest. The answer lay in its religious symbolism. Here was yet another seam of interest to be mined by Thornton. It allowed him to supplement sex and science with religion.

As he wrote of the Blue Passion Flower: "It was discovered in the Brazils, and its wonders were soon proclaimed to Christian Kingdoms as representing the Passion of Our Lord, whence its present appellation." Thornton then proceeded to spell out the full symbolic import of the passion flower for Christian iconography. "The leaves were said exactly to resemble the spear that pierced our Saviour's side; the tendrils, the cords that bound his hands, or the whips that scourged him; the ten petals the apostles, Judas having betrayed and Peter deserted; the pillar in the centre was the cross or tree; the *stamina*, the hammers; the styles, the nails; the inner circle about the central pillar, the crown of thorns; the radiance, the glory; the white in the flower, the emblem of purity; and the blue, the type of heaven. On one of the species, the *Passiflora alata*, even drops of blood were seen upon the cross or tree. The flower was three days open, and then disappeared, denoting the resurrection."

As if beauty, novelty, poetry, art, exoticism, horror, romanticism, sexual controversy, scientific discovery, royal and even imperial support and religious symbolism were not enough, Thornton even offered botanists the excitements of the chase. One of his plates is an exciting seascape entitled "The Pursuit of the Ship containing the Linnaean Collection by order of the King of Sweden." It was Thornton's way of dramatizing the purchase of the Linnaean collection by Sir James Edward Smith, around which the Linnaean Society was set up. The Swedes had no sooner agreed to the sale that they started to regret it. By order of the king a ship was sent in hot, but vain, pursuit of the vessel bringing the collection to England. How flattering for botanists to see a European monarch in frustrated pursuit of what they now possessed. What greater recognition of the importance of their hobby could they want?

This was the leisured world of rich fashionable enthusiasts enjoying having their hobby of gardening publicized, dramatized, romanticized, immortalized, sensationalized, sexualized, botanized, commercialized and intellectualized. It was even academicized. For one must not forget that *The Temple of Flora* came with a host of academic authorities to give it their beneficent authority and approval. Of the thirty-one portraits published in *The Temple of Flora* most were of eminent botanists. Thornton not unreasonably quoted their praise of his work as a sign of its accuracy, just as he cited royal or even imperial approval as a sign of his public standing. He knew as well as the great eighteenth-century manufacturers how much royal sanction could help with sales, and he was just as quick as they were to seek it. In 1805 he issued an engraving called "The Imperial Jatropha", a tropical South American shrub" and dedicated it to "the wise, magnanimous and munificent Alexander, Emperor of Russia." His Imperial Majesty promptly and generously responded to the flattery, sending "a Ring (an Emerald set round with diamonds) as a mark of his Majesty's approbation of your elaborate and most elegant Botanical works, *The Temple of Flora* and the *New Illustration.*"

Not wishing to waste such praise, Thornton immodestly advertised it to his potential readership, justifying publishing the praise of himself by trying to turn it into flattery of all Englishmen. "This public approbation of *The Temple of Flora* and *New Illustration* …to Dr Thornton, who is a stranger in Russia, from a foreign and most powerful monarch, with the testimony borne to these works from the President of a learned Society, like our Royal Society, is a proof of the high estimation in which they are held on the Continent, and must be very flattering to an Englishman." Transforming vanity into patriotism was a common promotional device of marketing men. Advertising royal support was an even commoner one, and was usually highly effective. Thornton sought the patronage and support on the Wedgwood principle that he would benefit from it "as surely as princes love flattery". The simple fact that the Queen and the princesses "cultivate the Science of Botany" added social kudos to it. If, in response to Thornton's sycophantic assertion that they "have obtained a proficiency in this science, such as none, that I know of, in the inferior ranks have equalled", they agreed to visit his exhibitions and publicly praised his endeavours, then so much the better.

Alas this, and all Thornton's other promotional techniques, were suddenly battling against the tide. They had to compete with war, war-time inflation, war-time taxation and a recession in trade. To make matters worse, they had to compete with a sudden change in taste in the leisure pursuits of the educated, intellectually-aspiring, wealthy and fashionable clientele which made up Thornton's prime market.

Thornton blamed the war. "It was my original idea, had the times been propitious", he wrote, "to have greatly enlarged this part of the work, and present to the world…seventy Picturesque Botanical Coloured Plates, in which case another distribution of them would have been made, and every class illustrated by select examples of the most interesting flowers, accurately described and immortalised by poetry: but during the progress of this expensive work, with the exception of a few months respite, infuriate war has constantly and violently raged: commerce, agriculture and the Arts, all the sources of public prosperity and private happiness, are dried up and annihilated. The once moderately rich very justly now complain that they are exhausted through taxes laid on them to pay armed men to diffuse rapine, fire and murder over civilised Europe."

With the interruptions in trade came the disastrous depression year of 1811, with the interruption of shipping came the all-time low in the import of new species (only three in 1811), without the stimulus of new plants to keep their interest alive the fashionable elite started looking elsewhere for new interests. The decline in public favour of botany was led by the royal family. They ceased to visit Kew after 1805, and soon even Sir Joseph Banks, the doyen of English botanists, was starting to admit defeat. Chemistry had become the new scientific fashion of the moment – the excitement generated by Sir Humphrey Davy was starting to make botany seem rather *passé*. The lectures given by the young self-taught Cornish chemist were 'creating a sensation in fashionable London. "The enthusiastic admiration which his lectures obtained in this period is scarcely to be imagined", wrote his biographer, "Men of the first rate and talent, the literary and the scientific, the practical, the theoretical, blue stockings and women of fashion, the old, the young, all eagerly crowded, into the lecture room." For botany as a popular leisure pursuit this new rival presented a serious challenge. As Banks conceded, when writing to the Australian plant collector, George Caley, in 1808: "I cannot say that Botany continues to be quite so fashionable as it used to be". By 1811 matters seemed even worse.

Thornton's response to a threat to his project was as always positive. In 1804 (when he had completed only 20 colour engravings and 20 portrait engravings of botanists) he had responded to an earlier dip in interest by organising his exhibition of all the original paintings in New Bond Street to boost fashionable support. It was called Dr Thornton's "Linnaean Gallery" and was designed to act as a permanent advertisement for his great work. The catalogue for the exhibition, priced at one shilling, went into four editions, and Thornton felt sufficiently rejuvenated to produce seven more coloured plates in a single year. The price per part publication was doubled from 12 shillings and 6 pence to 25 shillings, and Thornton's promotional flamboyance seemed to be both refreshed and successful. The exhibition of 1804 had allowed Thornton to seek and receive a whole new round of flattering attention from academic botanists, and botanically minded poets, and allowed him to make further efforts to stimulate royal patronage. It was no accident that the Queen flower (*Strelitzia reginae*) was launched in 1804. It was no accident that his portrait of Lord Bute, entitled "The Maecenas of Botany" appeared soon after. It was no accident that his approach to the Russian emperor occurred at this stage too.

But in 1811 the problems were more serious. The costs of Thornton's ambitions were mounting seriously. Each plate required an original painting, an engraving often by several hands and in several versions, and often an original poem commissioned for the purpose. Thornton's perfectionism meant that slight defects (such as the ghostly second crane which continued to appear after the engraver's attempts to remove it on the first plate of the Pitcher plant) meant further plates, further expense and an obvious loss of profit. Without continued enthusiastic support from the fashionable elite, the project was doomed.

Urgent action was required and urgent promotional and marketing action was taken. Nothing demonstrates better the process of the commercialization of botany than what followed. After years of skilful sales promotion, of academic and aristocratic commendation,. of melodramtic art-work and of sugary poetry

> *"With honey'd lips enamoured Woodbines meet,*
> *Clasp with fond arms, and mix their kisses sweet",*

there came the concentrated hard sell.

In May 1811 Thornton received the Royal Assent for "The Botanical Lottery, for the Promotion and Encouragement of Science". A lottery prospectus was published in 1812 proudly emblazoned as "A Royal Botanical Lottery" with the intention of raising £42,000 by selling 20,000 tickets at two guineas each. The largest type advertised "10,000 PRIZES!", and it was stressed that the price of a ticket which could win you a prize of over £5,000, was "ONLY TWO GUINEAS".

It was an extremely bold move on Thornton's part. He was willing to put up all his original paintings, the whole Linnaean Gallery, to produce a first prize worth £5080; he had reprinted 400 sets of folio sized plates of *The Temple of Flora* to be given away as capital prizes; he had six hundred quarto sized plates of *The Temple of Flora* printed to be given away as more modest prizes; there were a further 2,000 prizes, each consisting of the five volumes of *The Flora of the United Kingdom* with 400 descriptive plates; and finally there were 7,000 prizes, each consisting of two volumes of *The Elements of Botany* containing 200 plates. In all he was offering 10,000 prizes worth £67,000.

The advertising was intense as Thornton concocted one promotional device after another. There were free gifts for everyone who bought a lottery ticket – the gift was a print of the Emperor Alexander (very much the hero of the moment after Napoleon's retreat from Moscow in 1812), who was described by Thornton not only as "the brave Cossack!", but also as "the illustrious Patron of Dr Thornton's works".

Thornton did everything he could to pump up interest. The public were urged to support the lottery on patriotic grounds ("Britons! join Hands and Heart in promoting the Arts and sciences of your Country, by the Immediate Purchase of a Lottery Ticket"); on grounds of not missing a profit ("All the PLATES are to be DESTROYED" declared one advertisement on 1 May, so that the prizes "will rise considerably in value"); on grounds of not missing a bargain (the tickets were "ONLY TWO GUINEAS BUT EXPECTED SHORTLY TO BEAR A HIGH PREMIUM"); on grounds of not missing their chance (the tickets, it was falsely claimed, were going fast such was "the present generous patronage the Public has already exhibited").

On the day before the draw, the Linnaean Gallery was opened and free admission was offered to "all properly dressed persons", so that the spectacular prizes could be seen. On the evening before the draw, Thornton gave a botanical lecture, advertised as for "the Benefit of the Sufferers in Russia", but clearly a last desperate effort to whip up interest and support. In a style described as "grandiloquent", Thornton offered to "expatiate on the great merits of Linnaeus, explain his System, and exhibit the choicest Flowers of Europe, Asia, Africa, and America, and discourse on them, and display a light obtained from Plants, equal to that of the Sun".

He went down with all promotional guns blazing, but his great scheme had foundered. He had overspent and not even his dramatic presentational skills could bring him the public triumph he sought. He had achieved a certain recognition (even a contemporary notoriety) but not the financial reward which he felt his work deserved. Immortalised by Keats as the "folio-sized physician", less kindly remembered by a vengeful Blake whose designs Thornton had used, with the imprudent apology that they "display less of art than of genius, and are much admired by some eminent painters", Thornton had to wait for posterity for *The Temple of Flora* to achieve its due in terms of lasting fame and popularity.

Thornton continued to promote botany, he continued to publish botanical books, but he had missed his moment commercially. His plans had begun in 1791, and he did not admit defeat until 1813, but by that date the successful promotion of gardening and botany had passed on to other hands, the national network of nurserymen who were satisfying the demand for new plants which Thornton had done so much to publicize.

It is difficult for many gardeners to imagine a world in which so many of our ubiquitous favourites were not available, or in many cases not even known. It is often not realised how late many of these plants arrived in England: what we know as the chrysanthemum did not arrive until 1793, the zinnia not until 1796, the geranium (perlargonium quinquevulnerum) not until 1796, the dahlia not until 1798. It was a similar story in the world of shrubs: the first camellia in 1739, the first buddleia in 1774, the first fuchsia in 1788, the first hydrangea macrophylla in 1789, the first tree paeony in 1789, the first Japanese quince in 1796, the first double camellia in 1792. Some which had arrived earlier in the eighteenth century, such as the camellia in 1739, the magnolia grandiflora in 1737 and the rhododendron in 1736 were slow to be made available. The rhododendron did not flower until twenty years after its introduction; most of the magnolia grandifloras were killed in the notorious winter of 1739 and the plant remained rare until the middle of the century; and the first camellias were famously killed by kindness in Lord Petre's stove house.

Botanical prints played a vitally important role in making these novelties known to the gardening world. If there were space available I would show in detail how these new arrivals were presented visually, how their numbers built up to a climax at the turn of the century, and how they were made increasingly available in the second half of the eighteenth century. Thornton was appealing more to botany as a leisure pursuit of the educated middle and upper classes than to the vast and growing army of humbler gardeners. Other illustrators aimed for and reached a far wider audience. The farmer's wife who was described in Mary Mitford's *Our Village* in 1824 was specifically identified as the (unfortunate) product of such botanical fashion and the over-refined taste of the florists and those who illustrated the latest so-called advances. She was, we are told, "a real genuine florist: valued pinks, tulips and auriculas for certain qualities of shape and colour, with which beauty has nothing to do; preferred black ranunculuses, and gave in to all those obliquities of a triple refined taste by which the professed florist contrives to keep pace with the vagaries of the bibliomaniacs. Of all odd fashions, that of dark, gloomy, dingy flowers appears to me the oddest. Your true connoisseur now shall prefer a deep puce hollyhock to the gay pink blossoms which cluster round that splendid plant like a pyramid of roses!". Thornton and his many rivals were obviously influencing gardeners even in deepest Hampshire.

But without catalogues to indicate the plants' characteristics and price, without newspapers to advertise their virtues and place of sale, and without a national network of nurserymen to make them available and easily accessible, then all the publicity of *The Temple of Flora* and the more populist rival illustrators would have counted for little for most of the country's gardeners. Without suitable services to transmute the promise of the botanical engraving into the performance of the delivered plant, even Thornton's promotional work would have been of little commercial significance. Fortunately gardening was provided with the institutional underpinning it needed to succeed as a popular leisure activity. It was provided by those wishing to profit from it commercially. The half century before Thornton began his great work had seen a remarkable revolution in the marketing and advertising of plants and seeds.

So if *The Temple of Flora* marks the pinnacle of promotional endeavour and beauty (if not success), it should not distract us entirely from the road which led through the interesting foothills towards it. Gardening has a very long history as a leisure activity as well as part of human subsistence. The record of trade in seeds can be easily pushed back to the beginnings of the period which interests the Datini Institute. Waiter of Henley, writing about 1250, observed that "seed grown on other ground will bring more profit than that which is grown on your own", and warned the husbandman against the false economy of using seed "which you have grown" rather than "seed which is bought". The records from the great garden of the Earl of Lincoln at Holborn, show that seeds and bulbs and plants (slips of grapevines and named varieties of pears) could be bought in London in 1295–96.

Although English gardening history can yield at least seven hundred years of recorded trade (painstakingly researched by scholars such as John Harvey in *Early Nurserymen* and *Early Gardening Catalogues*) the evidence is surprisingly meagre before Restoration England and almost embarrassingly abundant for the following one hundred and fifty years. The eighteenth century provides a gold mine of evidence for those in search of evidence of the commercialization of leisure.

If there were space available to do so one could trace in detail the way in which a national network of nurseries spread across Britain in the eighteenth century. The growth in numbers was dramatic, especially in the second half of the century, as a detailed chronology clearly shows. The growth from three major firms of seedsmen in London in 1688, to five commercial nurseries in London in 1691, to fifteen in greater London by 1700, marks a significant starting point to the commercial development of gardening, but there were still no significant nurseries in the provinces. By 1730 the number of nurseries in and around London had swollen to thirty, plus five substantial firms of seedsmen, by 1760 it had risen to forty, by 1786 it had reached eighty-four. The growth in the provinces was even more dramatic, from none in 1700 to one hundred and fifty firms of some substance in 1800, with hundreds of market gardeners and corn chandlers who acted as seed merchants and seedsmen as a profitable sideline. Even antiquarian specialists, scrupulously recording every herbal and every minute change in gardening history, allow themselves a certain excitement over such dramatic change. Chapters headed "A century of Expansion" and "Nurseries Galore", and triumphant verdicts (such as "The year 1760, with the accession of George Ill, was one of the great turning points in history...in the nursery trade", or "this major climacteric") underline the perceived decisiveness of the change. Some have risked hyperbole, calling "the tremendous development of plant nurseries...a miracle of organisation...an accompanying and parallel development...(to) the Industrial Revolution".

If there were space available to do so one could describe in detail the range of new marketing techniques that these nurserymen used. Some were startlingly, even anachronistically, modern. Christopher Gray of Fulham was admittedly a leading figure in the world of commercial gardening. He claimed in his 1755 catalogue that "there are a greater Variety of Trees, Shrubs, Plants and Flowers, cultivated in *Mr. Grays's* Nursery, than can perhaps be found in any other Garden, for Sale, not only in England, but also in any Part of Europe". It was this Christopher Gray who provided most of the trees and shrubs which Horace Walpole planted at Strawberry Hill and Walpole was clearly an admirer. In 1755 Walpole wrote to commend Gray and his plants to a friend, saying *en passant* "I mentioned cedars first, because they are the most beautiful of the evergreen race, and because they are the dearest; half a guinea apiece *in baskets*. The arbutus are scarce, and a crown apiece...Gray...sells cypresses *in pots* at half a crown apiece; *you turn them out of the pot with all their mould, and they never fail*" (my italics). Here in the mid-eighteenth century was a nurseryman employing one of the pride of the late twentieth-century nurseryman's selling techniques – the containerized tree or shrub.

There is evidence of commercial tact as well as innovation in marketing; Thomas Ashe, nurseryman to Alexander Pope and to Horace Walpole, knew how to handle the needs of such writers, replying to Walpole's request for a particular pattern of planting for his trees, "Yes, Sir, I understand; you would have them hang down somewhat poetical".

If there were space available to do so one could show how the history of early gardening catalogues matches the timing, and confirms the geographical spread, of the commercial revolution that took place in gardening in the eighteenth century. Christopher Gray was for long famous in gardening history for publishing a catalogue in 1740 under the mistaken impression that it was the first of its kind. It is now known that Robert Furber sold *A Catalogue of English and Foreign Trees and A Catalogue of Fruit Trees* at his nursery in Kensington in 1727. The detailed work of John Harvey (confirmed by Blanche Henrey in *A History and Bibliography of British Botanical and Horticultural Books up to 1800*) shows, however, that the history of garden catalogues reinforces the evidence in favour of a new intensity of commercial change in the second half of the eighteenth century. The first catalogue to include prices (added to the printed plant list in ink) is dated 1754. The first catalogues of a truly botanical character were those produced by Gordon about 1770 and by Lee in 1774. The first botanical catalogue produced in the provinces was that produced in Birmingham by John Brunton in 1774. The first with printed prices appeared in 1775. The first multi-lingual one appeared in 1777. "It was, then", in John Harvey's words, "about the 1770's that the modern era of horticulture began, firmly based on scientific nomenclature, and offering clearly marked", and clearly priced, "goods to the public". They had even introduced the modern method of code letters and serial numbers for ease of ordering.

From such rich evidential sources one can trace the spread of new introductions and the drop in prices as a wider and wider market was sought. The evidence confirms what eye-witnesses described. In the first half of the eighteenth century, the nurserymen carried huge stocks of a relatively limited range. Tree nurseries could supply holly, box and yew in bulk; and specialist hedging suppliers (such as the firm of Wood at Huntingdon and Brampton) could supply as many "slips and shoots" as an enclosing landlord could wish for. As Per Kalm, the Swedish visitor, wrote in 1748, "In England there is the advantage that nearly in every town and large village there is one or more nurseryman, whose principal occupation is to sow and plant the seeds, of a number of different trees...so that they can sell a number of all kinds...for a reasonable price... When a farmer wishes to lay down a new hedge, he goes…and buys of him as many 1,000 shoots as he requires."

If there were space available one could trace in detail the widening market for the plants newly made accessible by the "boom in exotics", the boom in retail outlets and the boom in sales occasioned by the falling prices recorded in the printed catalogues. Suffice it to say that during the second half of the eighteenth century the nurserymen's stocks changed dramatically in range and variety. The process showed how exclusive rarities became affordable novelties and finally cheap, routine "necessities" for the keen gardener. In mid-century a typical order from the mother of George III to the nurseryman. John Cree shows the taste for new introductions. Out of twenty three items, seventeen were for new plants (some apparently not even yet named): "Three new andromedas, nine plants unknown, one new rudbeckia, two new Helianthus's, one Hopea a new Genus, two new laurel leav'd Olives, a new climbing plant, two new Eupatoriums, two new shrubby Vacciniums, two new Asters, two new Agaves, two new Carolina Smilaxes, a new Styrax tree, a new Toothach tree, two new Hedysarums, a new Sideroxyllon, a new Sassafras tree". The social élite could afford to pay for such novelty and rarity, but for plants which proved their garden worth, their ease of propagation and their general appeal, the transformation from being regarded as a desirable rarity to becoming a flower for everyman could be surprisingly fast. Prices could fall very quickly indeed. Francis Masson introduced the African geranium (Pelargonium) and the heath (erica) from South Africa late in the century, but from being initially the exclusive plaything of the rich they rapidly spread down the social scale. By 1819 Sir James Edward Smith could happily recollect "the novel sight of an African geranium (Pelargonium), in Yorkshire and Norfolk, about forty years ago. Now every garret and cottage-window is filled with numerous species of that beautiful tribe, and every greenhouse, glows with the innumerable bulbous plants and splendid heaths of the Cape." A few years later one cottage gardener was writing in ecstatic self-congratulation of her "splendid pyramid of geraniums. Such geraniums! It does not become poor mortals to be vain – but, really, my geraniums!".

The dahlia was also quickly popularised and "improved". The dahlia was, even cited to disprove Rousseau's assertion that all things degenerated in the hands of man. It certainly multiplied. By 1826 there were 60 varieties known ill England; fifteen years later there were 1,200. The fuchsia followed a very similar rapid social and geographical spread, as did countless breakthroughs in the Florists' flowers. Their novel characteristics were quickly and efficiently advertised through the competitions of the Sons of Flora. Some like the Pontic Rhododendron proudly flaunting its beauty in Thornton's *Temple of Flora* proved so rampant a coloniser as to entirely lose its reputation (if not its looks) and was rapidly reduced to being regarded as a despised weed on many country estates. Self-advertisement on that scale was clearly a disaster. Other forms of self-advertisement were commercially more effective.

If there were space available one could show in detail how the nurserymen of the early eighteenth century advertised their wares in an increasingly purposeful way as the century wore on. Some advertisements were simple and direct: Mr Malcolm's nursery near Kensington very successfully promoted the sales of *Hibiscus syriacus* by "having selected", in Cobbett's words, "a patch of it to plant just by the side of the Turnpike road, to attract the attention of lovers of shrubs". Many advertisements were initially disguised as botanical information and advice. Robert Furber published the earliest book form catalogue-cum-advertisement in 1727, followed by *Twelve Months of Flowers* with splendid illustrations in 1730 and *A Short Introduction to Gardening* in 1733. Other publications such as Loddiges's *The Botanical Cabinet* (1777) and John Kennedy's *A Treatise upon Planting, Gardening and the Management of the Hot-House* (1776) or James Lee's *Introduction to Botany* (1760) were published by nurserymen at least in part as advertisement. The major nurseries such as Telfords of York, Perfects of Pontefract, Barnes & Callender of Leeds, Popes and Bruntons, both of Birmingham, (with their "lists of plants botanically arranged according to the system of Linnaeus, most of which are cultivated and sold by" the nurseryman publishing the list) happily combined the botanical education of the public and advertisement of their wares.

From the second quarter of the eighteenth century onwards they increasingly used the more obvious method of newspaper advertisements. Newspapers such as the *York Courant*, the *Leeds Mercury*, the *Northampton Mercury*, the *Leicester Journal*, the *Norwich Gazette*, the *Ipswich Journal*, the *Salisbury and Winchester Journal* and many others carried the news of the arrival of the latest plants to the provinces, and advertised the place of sale and the prices of those who could supply them. None of these provincial nurseries were in the George Packwood class for promotional innovation and inventiveness, but then, as Mrs Packwood said when asked to explain the remarkable literary quality of her husband's advertising campaign, "Why, Bless you Sir, we keep a poet for it". But their newspaper advertisements bear comparison with those of such contemporary entrepreneurial giants as Josiah Wedgwood and Matthew Boulton.

From 1725 onwards most of England began to be served first by weekly and then by daily newspapers. Commercial advertisements were their stock in trade – between a third and the whole of most papers being occupied by commercial intelligence of one sort or another. As John Harvey said, "It is worth noting that this development almost exactly coincided with the first period of the founding of the greater provincial nurseries". The national spread of nurseries also coincides with the canal development, with the spread of retail shops recently described by the Muis, and with the birth of a consumer society in general.

The features, the timing, the regional distribution and the social motives exploited by the promoters of the consumer revolution of the eighteenth century fit the commercialization of botany and gardening very well. The areas of most rapid economic growth – London, Lancashire, Yorkshire and the industrializing Midlands – were the areas where the commercialization of horticulture was most obvious, and where the process reached furthest down the social scale. Just as the democratization of consumption in general was initially a regional rather than a national phenomenon, so the democratization of gardening was most obvious in the working class enthusiasts of Lancashire, Yorkshire and the Midlands. As with consumption in general London was the heart of the whole process – the sales promotion almost invariably required a lead from the capital, just as the process of social emulation required a lead from the aristocracy or royalty.

Fashion played as vital role in the commercialization of gardening as it did in the pottery trades of Staffordshire, in the metal trades of Birmingham, and in the textile trades all over the country. The importance of a fashionable lead has been demonstrated in furniture, in carpets, in silver, in wallpapers, in hats, in wigs, in shoes, in handbags and indeed in the whole spectrum of domestic consumer spending. It was just as important in gardening.

Robert Thornton's high-profile campaign allows us to savour in detail the flavour of an eighteenth-century sales promotion and marketing campaign which lasted over a quarter of century. It allows us to examine the variety of promotional ploys available to the salesmen of Georgian England. It permits one to demonstrate beyond reasonable doubt that the commercial development of botany and gardening produced in Robert Thornton an individual to rank alongside Josiah Wedgwood, Matthew Boulton and George Packwood in the commercialization of their own particular sector of the economy. The careers of Henry Wise, Christopher Gray, James Gordon, James Lee, and William Curtis demonstrate that he was far from being alone amongst gardeners as a skilful marketing man.

Indeed the biographical case studies, the case studies of individual firms, the statistical data, and the eye-witness accounts all point in the same direction – as do the botanical histories, the history of gardening catalogues, the history of the distribution of plants and the history of gardening advertisement. The leisure potential of this most popular hobby was being transformed. This particular leisure industry was undergoing a commercial revolution. As in many other industries, the significant technological changes came after the commercial ones. There *were* major technical innovations. J.C. Loudon's thin iron glazing bars, which were introduced in 1816, "changed the face of Victorian gardening" and "heralded a golden era in conservatory building". E. B. Budding's first mechanical lawn mower, introduced in 1830, and the first powered ones, driven by steam, were to revolutionize the maintenance of the centrepiece of English gardening. But dramatic changes had already occurred by then, long before these and other technological innovations first made their mark on English leisure.

By the end of the eighteenth century the evidence that in gardening the commercializing process was well under way is undeniable. A horticulture of aristocratic ostentation had developed to such an extent that it now encompassed the leisure time of the middle classes and the hobbies of working men and women. Gardening had been democratized as well as commercialized. The evidence exists in an encouraging variety of types. The most convincing, to those raised in a cliometric era, may well be the remorseless spread across the face of England of substantial well-stocked nurseries and successful nurserymen. Their numbers rose from 3 significant firms in 1688 to 234 major firms a hundred years later, plus hundreds of smaller satellite suppliers as well.

Even more dramatic are the figures for what they had to sell. In the middle of the sixteenth century there were 200 cultivated plants known in England, by 1839 Loudon listed 18,000 species cultivated in Britain; and more to the point, by 1800 there were nurseries "making a serious effort to supply everything worth while in all categories". The number of different varieties of a single species offered for sale showed the massive scale of eighteenth-century planting. Cobbett planted out "not much short of a million of trees" on 4 December 1827, heeling them into trenches so that they could be quickly got up for sale as the orders came in. The professional nurserymen carried far larger stocks.

But the most memorable evidence is surely provided by the visual record. One can choose such vivid evidence from such an astonishing variety of sources. There is the visual record of the spectacular number of new species introduced in the eighteenth century which every historical border in university botanic gardens still makes so charmingly obvious. There is the visual evidence preserved in the plans for the famous newly-laid gardens of eighteenth century England and the planting schemes that went with them. There are the palatial park-lands laid down for posterity and the now majestic trees which still stand as visual proof of the major tree planting that accompanied the wave of neo-classical buildings in the 1760s and 1770s. There is less obviously the visual evidence provided by Thomas Milne's maps of 1795 to 1799 which surveyed every field and plot of land in the London area and distinguished with different letters and colours every nursery, orchard, park and market garden and, in doing so, identified the forty-five significant nurseries in an area measuring eighteen miles by fourteen. There is the pictorial impact provided by paintings such as Henry Danckerts's picture of John Rose, gardener to the king, presenting the first pineapple raised in England to Charles II (a painting which belonged significantly to the London nurseryman George London, the partner of Henry Wise, before it was given to Horace Walpole in

1780). There is also the less well-known evidence such as the engraving of *Banksia serrata*, the first Australian plant raised in Britain by James Lee at the Vineyard Nursery, Hammersmith in 1788. There are the influential impressions provided by the *Botanical Magazine*, such as the *erica ampullacea* raised from seed from South Africa in 1780 and first flowered in 1784, or the *Chrysanthemum indicum* which first flowered in Britain in November 1795 at the Chelsea Nursery of James Colvill or the *Azalea pontica* (now *Rhododendron Luteum*) which first, flowered in Britain in 1798 at the Islington Nursery of Thomas Watson, or the geranium (now *Pelargonium*) introduced from South Africa in 1796 by John Armstrong of the North Warnborough Nursery. There are the illustrations to poems such as Darwin's *Botanic Garden*. There is the ceramic evidence provided by the famous Chelsea botanical plates, and by the wide market for cachepots, jardinieres and cheap flower pots illustrated in Josiah Wedgwood's catalogues and those of his Staffordshire rivals. There are the surviving public houses still proudly bearing the title *Florist, Flowerpot, Nurseryman* and *Sons of Flora* and the vivid painted pub signs which illustrated the botanical enthusiasm they once served. There are, of course, the coloured botanical prints of which Thornton's are merely the most famous.

Such paintings, portraits, pictures, palaces, pineapples, pelargoniums, plates, plants, park-lands, poems, pubs, pub signs, pots, plans and maps provide a rich alliterative sample of the varied visual evidence still available for the historian willing to see it and willing to use it. The botanical books, the business directories of seed merchants and nurserymen and florists, the seed and bulb and plant catalogues, the newspaper advertisements, strongly reinforce the impression of gardening as a leisure activity being systematically and successfully commercialized.

The rich potential of a single source or a single garden accessory could yield enough evidence for a separate article. The fierce competition between Josiah Wedgwood, Matthew Boulton and the manufacturers of artificial Bath stone to supply garden urns for the new gardening enthusiasts shows how eagerly that market was fought over. The fact that every potter and porcelain maker in the second half of the eighteenth century included *pot-pourris* in his catalogues shows how large the market was thought to be for this minor spin-off of the enthusiasm for gardening. The markets for terracotta pots, for garden seats, for garden trellises, for glass-houses, for garden aquatics – all supply evidence of burgeoning demand.

If there were space available one could demonstrate the commercialisation of botany from the ceramic evidence alone. The ceramic exploitation of flowers as a decorative device is, of course, an ancient one, but in the eighteenth century it took on a novel botanical precision and accuracy which was characteristic of its day. It is no accident that the use of botanical flowers is associated originally with Meissen, a Royal pottery of the eighteenth century. It is no accident that its popularity spread in eighteenth-century England, first with Sir Hans Sloane's plants on Chelsea porcelain taken from engravings in Philip Miller's *The Gardener's Dictionary* (1724), and later with William Pegg's work at Derby, William Absolon's work at Yarmouth, and Thomas Pardoe's paintings at Swansea. It is no accident that the turn of the century saw the peak of botanical enthusiasm in English pottery and porcelain.

It was no accident either that the exploitation of this new enthusiasm proceeded down the social scale, from the exclusive clientele of the royal factories to the popular audience reached by the Staffordshire potteries. The close connection between the Wedgwoods and the Darwins ensured that Wedgwood would respond to the Darwins' enthusiasm for the Water Lily pattern. But John Wedgwood's own botanical interests ensured the response would be a warm and commercially purposeful and a continuing one. John Wedgwood was to chair the meeting at which the Royal Horticultural Society was founded in 1804, and he showed a greater enthusiasm for his gardening than he did for his pottery. When he could combine his hobby with his inheritance, however, the results were significant in the popularization of botany.

Between 1806 and 1811 the Wedgwood factory produced five botanical patterns – "Hibiscus", "Peony", "Water Lily", "Chrysanthemum" and "Blue Botanical Flowers". Because cobalt was so "very scarce & dear" during the war, the "Water Lily" and the "Chrysanthemum" were first produced in a rather disappointing and unsuccessful brown, but sold better later in red versions, blue versions and in combinations of blue, yellow, green and mauve. Of greater significance were the "Blue Botanical Flowers" first introduced in 1808–9. There were forty-seven different plants each numbered to correlate with a printed list of their names. They were taken from Curtis's *Botanical Magazine*, Sowerby's *English Botany* and Salisbury's *Paradisus Londinensis*. Later versions in red, and in naturalistic colours, followed, with examples such as "no. 492, Botanical Flowers" giving some idea of the range. Number 492 carried the names "ochna squarrosa" and "epigenea repens" enamelled alongside the impressed Wedgwood mark.

Other potters rode the same botanical band-waggon. They responded eagerly to the growing demand for accurate representation of both traditional plants and the latest botanical discoveries. They painted them with scrupulous precision. They painted them as isolated specimens the better to reveal their distinctive characteristics. They labelled them with their common English names and their correct botanical names. They sold in very significant numbers. This was not simply the traditional use of flowers as a decorative device. This was a direct response to the current popularity of botany, and a further contribution to it.

With the porcelain makers, as with Wedgwood, the first few years after 1800 saw a new burst of enthusiasm. But by this time the interest had reached the provincial makers. Thomas Pardoe, a flower painter, who worked at Derby, Worcester, Swansea, Bristol and Nantgarw, is a prime example, His most important productions came from his period at Swansea from 1797 to 1809, and his pieces in the Swansea museum carry such revealing botanical titles as the "Ash leav'd Trumpet flower", the "one flower'd Diosma", the "Bladder Hibiscus", the "Two leav'd Lady's slipper", the "Herbaceaous Heath", the "Asiatic Globe Flower", the Narrow Leav'd Willow Herb", the "Eastern Poppy", the "Rose Cistus", the "Cobweb Houseleek" and many, many more – traceable as always to the most accurate current botanical sources. These paintings were not just randomly picked decorative flowers. They were deliberately chosen and then precisely aimed, addressed and advertised for botanical enthusiasts. The target audience consisted of informed and enthusiastic gardeners, By 1800 one could display one's hobby at both the tea table and the dinner table, one could exhibit one's leisure interests from breakfast to dessert with beautiful and botanically accurate depictions of one's favourite plant and one's latest acquisitions in the garden. The potters marketed their goods as knowledgeably and as purposefully as did the nurserymen. They were part of the same commercial revolution. They have left a marvellous visual heritage as proof of their endeavours. It is a pity economic and social historians have been so blind to their significance in the spread and commercialization of leisure.

If potters provide a wealth of under-used evidence as to the individual plants which commercially prospered in Georgian England – one could illustrate a whole book from ceramic sources alone – they rarely illustrate the gardens that those plants did so much to create and adorn. For the complete gardening environment one has to turn to a higher form of the graphic arts. One has to turn to those painters who recorded in detail the changing face of eighteenth-century gardening and the way the commercial revolution made many of those changes possible.

Even restricting oneself simply to well-known paintings of gardens would yield a rich evidential return. If one chose the top of the social scale and examined Leonard Knyff's great panoramic view of Hampton Court in 1702 one would find its details of the planting scheme adopted for William III so accurate that they can be used as a reference plan for the current restoration work. To use a garden which was successively replanned and replanted for Cardinal Wolsey, Henry VIII, Charles I, Oliver Cromwell, Charles II and William and Mary would scarcely be socially typical, although it is not without significance that the finest version was the eighteenth century garden created for William. It was the product of an era of box, yew, holly and pleached limes and avenues of elms, and was the outcome, and the explanation for, a nursery trade which carried huge numbers of a limited range of plants. Nothing shows better that in the early eighteenth-century nurserymen were building up their stocks to serve a market of parklands and pleasure grounds. They were not yet carrying the range of plants to suit more modest gardens and a far greater social range which was to be the mark of the trade by the end of the century. Plant inventories made for probate and nursery stock lists can be very revealing. The fact that the great nursery at Brompton was said to have ten million plants in 1705, that William Cox of Kew had over 30,000 plants in a small nursery at Kew in 1722, and that Peter Mason of Isleworth had over 115,000 at his death in 1730, needs to be qualified by the knowledge that of Mason's stock, 15,690 were elms (8,000 English, 6,000 Dutch, 1,670 Wych and 20 "yellow"), 13,000 were yew, 2,500 were hollies, 5,000 Scotch fir, 5,000 spruce and 2,700 Silver fir, and the rest were dominated by forest trees or hedging material.

If one looked at the paintings of aristocratic gardens one would find an even richer source. Here evidence of England's great contribution to the history of garden design – the natural landscape garden – finds its finest expression. William Kent may not have "leaped the fence and seen all nature as a garden", as Horace Walpole so famously put it, but by adopting Bridgeman's device of the ha-ha he certainly banished the apparent barrier between garden and countryside, and paintings of his gardens at Stowe, at Chiswick and at Rousham faithfully record the results.

Kent's declared intent was to recreate around Georgian buildings

"Whate'er Lorrain light touched with softening hue
Or savage Rosa dashed or learned Poussin drew",

and artists returned the compliment by painting his gardens for posterity. Economic historians would find as much to interest them as art historians in these portraits of aristocratic leisure spending. Paintings of the work of Kent, Brown and Repton faithfully record the changing commercial importance of hedges, trees and newly introduced plants.

Hedges, the characteristic symbol of the English countryside, flourished spectacularly in the eighteenth century as a result of the enclosure movement – as the contents of the nurserymen's lists confirm. Trees, the characteristic symbol of English parklands, flourished as never before as a result of the "explosion" of the landscape movement – as the nurserymen's catalogues confirm. "Exploded" is no piece of anachronistic historical hyperbole, it was the phrase used in the eighteenth century by the grave Dr. Hunter, who edited Evelyn. Previously unknown plants, the characteristic symbol of Georgian gardening, also flourished as never before. Horace Walpole was so impressed with his own country's gardening efforts that he dismissed the hanging gardens of Babylon as "trifling" and "of no extent" – Pliny, he wrote, "delighted in what the mob now scarce admire in a college garden". Others recognized that instead of "the same tiresome and returning uniformity" of even noblemen's gardens in 1700, one could find a riot of novelty, rarity and exoticism in 1800. The stovehouses, the hot-houses, the glass-houses and the conservatories of the rich accommodated an unprecedented array of plants. The "personal botanical paradise" was now a legitimate aspiration for the English aristocracy. For many it was an achieved ambition. In Howitt's words, "Nothing could be more delicious than the paradises which now surround our country houses". Commercial expertise and botanical enterprise had made possible what previous generations could merely have dreamed of. A leisure activity of the rich had been transformed into an important signal of social accomplishment. An aristocratic hobby had become a significant status symbol for the socially aspiring of all classes.

If one moves further down the scale one can find the product of a banker's gardening enthusiasm at Stourhead. This genuine masterpiece of European gardening was created by the financier Henry Hoare who inherited the property in 1741 and spent the next thirty years incorporating all the ingredients of eighteenth-century landscape gardening into his great design – a temple, a grotto, a lake, a bridge, a hermitage and majestic trees and shrubs. They are still there as visible evidence of leisure in the form of conspicuous consumption and of the ability of eighteenth-century garden suppliers to indulge it. The change in the botanical palette which Hoare could paint from in the third quarter of the eighteenth century is a striking confirmation of both botanical and commercial progress.

More representative of the effects of the late eighteenth-century commercialization of leisure can be found in the illustration of a middle-class garden. The changes depicted in the view, before and after "improvement", from the Essex cottage of the famous landscape gardener, Humphry Repton, show the original pair of ancient trees joined, after Repton's improvements, by climbing roses, standard roses and pillar roses in profusion; by beds of annuals, herbaceous beds, and shrub beds; by a rich array of specimen plantings; and by a sample of gardening accessories, a garden seat, a watering can, iron work supports for the climbing roses, and a wooden trellis for further climbing plants; all standing on a newly-laid lawn and enclosed by a neatly-clipped hedge. It was enough to make a nurseryman's mouth drool in anticipation of the sales potential offered by the chance to provide the goods necessary to effect such improvements. That they took advantage of their chances can be judged from the outraged critics of the over-commercialised *cottage orné* of the early nineteenth century "tricked out with conservatories, roseries, pond, rustic seats, Gothic dairies and all the other fripperies" and the botanical vagaries of the latest "bible" of garden fashion.

Paintings again can vividly recall how well the gardening trade exploited those chances. One can effectively illustrate this even if one confines oneself to paintings of artists' own family gardens. Paul Sandby painted his own garden at Englefield Green in Surrey in 1746, and the portrait of his wife and daughter tenderly watering the row of ten terracotta pots, each containing a different choice plant, is testimony to the growing enthusiasm for middle-class gardening, quite apart from the rest of the garden richly planted with shrubs, trees and flower beds. By 1815 when John Constable offered us such splendidly detailed evidence of his father's enthusiasm for gardening, the number of varieties of garden plants made available by the nursery trade had multiplied spectacularly. *Golding Constable's Kitchen Garden*, painted in July 1815, and *Golding Constable's Flower Garden*, painted in August of that year, offer us a wonderfully memorable tribute to that change.

Even paintings of the plantings in workmen's cottages gardens show how far this process reached down the social scale. Some historians have been reluctant to accept this evidence, arguing that the aesthetic conventions of the day, the romantic expectations and the preference of the middle-class market (which bought the paintings and the prints taken from them) for prosperous peasants set in an Arcadian idyll explain these well-flowered gardens of the labouring classes.

One needs to remember that there is also a tendency in the opposite direction. Some historians and some literary observers have preferred misery to proletarian prosperity. Some like Mrs Oliphant's Miss Marjoribanks are "exhilarated" by poverty and like to turn their backs on such potent expressions of working-class comfort and working-class leisure as well-stocked and well-tended gardens: "If it had been a model village, with prize-flower gardens and clean as Arcadia, the thought of it would not have given Miss Marjoribanks half so much pleasure" was Mrs Oliphant's ironic comment on such preferences. George Eliot was 'equally ironic about Dorothea Brooke's similar dismay at finding in pre-Reform England "not a cottager in those double cottages at a low rent but kept a pig, and the strips of garden well tended…She felt some disappointment, of which she was yet ashamed, that there was nothing for her at Lowick…she would have preferred (to find) that her home…had a larger share of the world's misery".

There was plenty of authentic misery and squalor without denying the benefits and consolations which industrialisation brought in its train for many members of the working class. Fortunately there were other observers who recognized this and took delight in working-class gardens. La Rochefoucauld described the neat houses, each "brightened by a flower garden", of the "peasants" of Suffolk in 1784 and revealingly connected such pleasures and other indulgences ("the furniture was in good order and in each of them we saw a good clock – a luxury peasants now enjoy") to the fact that both wives and children worked in industry. The earnings of women and children swelled the family unit income of many working-class families and significantly increased the surplus left over after the purchase of "necessities". That surplus could be spent on "decencies" and "luxuries". Spending on gardening was one of those "luxuries" which increasingly came to be regarded as well within the reach of many of the more prosperous workers. Contemporary writers increasingly recognised that gardening for pleasure had become "a mere decency" to which many could reasonably aspire.

The social and horticultural consequences did not go uncelebrated. "You see", wrote Cobbett in 1822, "in almost every part of England, that most interesting of all objects, that which is such an honour to England, and that which distinguishes it from all the rest of the world, namely, *those neatly kept and productive little gardens round the labourers' houses*, which are seldom unornamented with more or less of flowers." The flowers were the same as those identified by Mary Russell Mitford: a mixture of traditional cottage garden favourites, and only recently introduced exotics such as dahlias and chrysanthemums and the ubiquitoue geranium – "the casements full of geraniums" all through the year.

Some observers were revealingly specific about the pleasures of working-class leisure spent in gardening. William Howitt in *The Rural Life of England* wrote ecstatically of idyllic cottages in Hampshire "almost buried in the midst of their orchard trees...little paradises of cultivated life", and wrote approvingly of the 5,000 allotment gardens about a quarter of an acre in size, rented by mechanics on the outskirts of Nottingham. These were scarcely less idyllic. That they were designed for pleasure and for leisure, as well as for food, is made clear by Howitt's description of the huts on these allotments: "Every garden has its summer-house; and these are of all scales and grades, from the erection of a few tub-staves, with an attempt to train a pumpkin or a wild-hop over it, to substantial brick-house with glass windows, good cellars for a deposit of choice wines, a kitchen and all necessary apparatus, and a good pump to supply them with water. Many are very picturesque rustic huts, built with great taste, and hidden by tall hedges in a perfect little paradise of lawn and shrubbery". Clearly some of those who rented these allotments must have been substantial tradespeople rather than working men, but Howitt is adamant that most were operatives who found solace in spending their leisure time in these little gardening oases: "Many of the mechanics have very excellent summer houses, and there they delight to go, and smoke a solitary pipe with a friend, or spend a Sunday afternoon, or a summer evening, with their families". Little wonder that he thought that "the advantage of these gardens to the working-class of a manufacturing town is beyond calculation".

Little wonder too that official reports spoke approvingly of working-class cottages "with a neat and civilized garden, in which the leisure hours of the husband are profitably employed". Other contemporaries spelled out in detail what plants there were in these gardens. Mitford's *Our Village* describes in detail the cottage garden of Three Mile Cross in late Georgian England, taking delight in the mason's wife's prize dahlias and chrysanthemums, the rat-catcher's climber-strewn garden, and the arrival of "gorgeous exotics" in their cottage gardens.

Even those who disapproved added their confirmation of the existence of the democratization of gardening. Even those who thought it was "downright wicked" for working men to spend their leisure time in the pursuit of beauty rather than utility confirmed how they actually did so. The Victorian George Glenny looking back at late Georgian England supplied his own disapproving negative answer to his title "Ought Cottagers to grow Flowers?". "The idea", he wrote, "of tempting poor men to grow Pansies, and Pinks, and Carnations, by awarding them prizes, seems to us downright wicked...Half a dozen pair of pinks...would require more time and attention than a rod of cabbages, potatoes, turnips or carrots". Disapprove of the process as he obviously did, the title of his book *Gardening for the Million* offers its own eloquent recognition of what had happened. Gardening for leisure and gardening for pleasure – even gardening for sheer indulgence – was now within the reach of some of the working classes.

Working-class literary observers have lyrically described the same process. Even the poet-labourer, John Clare, who reacted so sharply against the idealization inherent in so much of the pastoral tradition, sang without a trace of irony of the pleasures of the cottage garden:

> *"Where rustic taste at leisure trimly weaves*
> *The rose and straggling woodbine to the eaves,*
> *And on the crowded spot that pales enclose*
> *The white and scarlet daisy rears in rows,*
> *Training the trailing peas in bunches neat,*
> *Perfuming evening with a luscious sweet,*
> *And sun-flowers planted for their gilded show*
> *That scale the window's lattice ere they blow."*

Clare wrote lovingly of flowers which were "each cottage garden's fond adopted child". They were what he called "the best flowers". They were "not those of wood and fields",

> *"But such as every farmer's gardens yields –*
> *Fine cabbage-rose, painted like her face,*
> *The shining pansy, trimm'd with golden lace,*
> *The tall-topped larkheels, feather'd thick with flowers*
> *The woodbine, climbing o'er the door in bowers,*
> *The London tufts, of many a mottled hue,*
> *The pale pink pea, and monkshead darkly blue,*
> *The white and purple gilliflowers, that stay*
> *Ling'ring, in blosson, summer half away."*

These were, in Clare's words, "the flowers which housewives love so well". The show auriculas of the Lancashire weavers, the laced pinks of Paisley, the polyanthus of Staffordshire, along with such other show flowers of the Sons of Flora – the carnations, the ranunculus, the hyacinths – were regarded as largely a male preserve. They were the subject of fierce competition at spring and summer shows and their credentials as part of working-class leisure are well established and well recorded. We even have engravings of the flower competitions and the ideal shapes their flowers should achieve as further visual evidence.

If there were space available one could show that by 1800 prize-show vegetables and fruits had joined flowers as part of the working man's leisure-time activities. Once again newspaper advertisements reveal an astonishing range and variety of seeds. William Johnson, who kept a shop in the market place in Leicester, advertised in 1789 sixteen varieties of peas, thirteen varieties of bean, nineteen different herbs, along with fifty-six different varieties of annual flowers. His list went far beyond the mere quotidian: his vegetables included such luxuries as asparagus and aubergine and *mangetout*. He satisfied needs that went far beyond mere utility: he and his like were supplying a highly competitive market. Esteem was at stake as well as mere eating, pride as well as mere produce. The latest varieties of the heaviest cropping seed were urgently sought for competition purposes. For as Sir John Plumb has written, by 1800 there was "scarcely a flower or a vegetable that lacked enthusiasts". The Sons of Flora had been "joined by gooseberry lovers and melon and cucumber buffs".

Clubs sprang up to serve these *aficionados* of fruit and vegetables. Competitions were held. Prizes were won. Winchester had a well-established cucumber feast by 1797, and provincial newspapers advertised the competitions and published the prize-winners – much to the gratification of the seedsmen who supplied their ever-more demanding and more sophisticated needs.

Perhaps the most serious horticultural rival to the florists' flowers for working men's leisure time was the gooseberry. Records of the gooseberry shows in Lancashire, Staffordshire, Yorkshire, Derbyshire and Nottinghamshire survive from 1809 onwards. The prizes – usually teapots and copper kettles – survive too, as do the illustrations of the most popular varieties. Their names – Sportsmen, Huntsman, Yaxley hero, Foxhunter, Wonderful, Ringer, Leveller and London, and, much later, Garibaldi – properly suggest more proletarian heroes than those carried by most plants; the competitions were held at local pubs, the most obvious popular meeting place; and the whole ceremony (complete with singing, solemn measuring and weighing, refreshments, prizes, competitions between parishes as well as individuals, and bands playing the *Gooseberry Growers' Anthem* to the tune of "With Wellington, We'll Go, We'll Go") seem redolent of ancient folk festivals. But the new commercial element was clearly there, with nurserymen advertising their wares and boasting of the girth and weight achieved by berries produced from their plants. The berries came in four colours – red, yellow, green and white – but the number of named varieties for sale was huge. For the frustrated cliometricians there are even records of weights achieved by the prizewinners for them to measure, but more persuasive evidence of the gooseberries' popular appeal can be found in glowing contemporary illustrations, such as Mrs Augusta Withers portrait of "Compton's Sheba's Queen" published in *Drawings of Fruit* by William Hooker et al. in 1825.

In fact the visual record alone presents an embarrassment of riches with which to illustrate and to explain the commercialization of this most popular form of leisure. The print evidence is admittedly the most ubiquitous visual record of all. But it is not just the sumptuous flower prints and botanical plates which are of interest to the historian of leisure. The cheap everyday prints and cartoons are not be despised. For these recorded, almost incidentally, both sides of the commercialization of gardening – the contented customers inspecting the ever-widening choice of plants with which to indulge their gardening interests and fill their leisure time; and the happy salesmen reaping the benefits from the growing consumer response to the ubiquitous advertising of their new varieties and their new methods of selling.

A print published by Bowles & Carver of 60 St. Paul's Church Yard on 17 January 1806 nicely captures the happy symbiosis of the leisured gardener and the profit-seeking (and profit-achieving) nurseryman. Three elegant customers, dressed in the latest fashions (high-waisted, high-bosomed, long-legged, and all wearing hats and shoes in the latest style), beam expectantly at the spade-carrying, waistcoated tradesman in his gardener's apron standing proudly in front of his containerized plants, his terracotta pots and his greenhouses bursting with figs and grapes and tender exotic flowers.

The text that accompanies the print is a light-hearted hymn to horticultural felicity, justifying the gardener's trade, the gardener's business and the gardener's rewards (his profit is stressed quite as much as his contentment).

"A Lady once requested me
Some Reasons good to state,
Why I esteem'd the Gard'ner's Trade
Above all others great

Because (said I) no Man on Earth
More Bus'ness does transact'
Whate'er I do, I always have
Good Ground *whereon to act;*

I'm always Master of the Mint;
My Thyme's *my own, 'tis clear,*
The Penny-royal *I can touch,*
And Celery *ev'ry Year;*

That Season's bad that brings me not
More Plums *than two or three,*
Nor does a Minister of State
Meet with more Boughs *than me;*

Than any Prince more Beds *I make,*
More Painted Ladies *keep,*
And from my Raking, *strange to say!*
Both Health and profit reap;

Lads-Love *and* Hearts-ease *for my Wife*
I always will provide,
And tho' a Man of Humble State
I have some London Pride;

I have more Bleeding-Hearts *than e'er*
Your Lady ship can boast,
More Laurels *than Lord Nelson won*
In Honours dang'rous Post;

But 'tis My Happiness, and what
An envious World must tease,
That I (so absolute's my Will)
Can have Yew *when I please."*

The title of the print is nicely ambiguous. It does justice to the rewards of gardening as both a pastime and a trade. Happily combining both the business and the leisure aspects of gardening it neatly symbolizes the commercialization of this form of leisure. It manages to include the herbs, the fruit, the vegetables, the shrubs, the herbaceous plants, the evergreens (even the pots in which they were sold) which formed the staple sales of the nurserymen; it also manages to paint a picture of the pleasure such purchasers offered to the leisured customer in Georgian England. As such it might serve as the last word on the interaction of commerce and leisure in the birth of a consumer society in the late eighteenth century. It is called "THE HAPPY GARDENER".

Neil McKendrick, "The Commercialization of Leisure: Botany, Gardening and the Birth of a Consumer Society" (delivered as a paper On 22 April 1994 at the Instituto Internazionale di Storia Economica "F.Datini" Prato), and first published in "IL TEMPO LIBERO ECONOMICA E SOCIETA (Loisirs, Leisure, Tiempo Libre, Freizeit), SECC. XIII-XVIII", a cara di Simonetta Cavaciocchio, (1995), pp.567–614.

Note: 'Introduction to 2018 edition' and 'Part IV, Ch. 9, The Commercialization of Leisure: Botany, Gardening and the Birth of a Consumer Society', do not appear in the Index.

Index

ACLAND, Sir T. D., 262
Adam, Robert, and brothers, 10,12,116
Adams, William, potter, 107, 107n
Addison, Dr. Joseph, 11, 44, 44n, 84, 95, 147, 186, 186n, 235, 269, 284
advertisements, propaganda, puffs, 1, 2, 6, 11, 13, 22–3, 31, 41, 44, 47–8, 54, 57, 64–5, 72–6, 82–5, 88, 90, 92–4, 97–8, 108–10, 111, 115, 117–8, 121, 123–6, 131, 141, 143–5, Ch 4, 146–194 passim, 201, 240–1, 251, 257, 271–3, 281, 290, 293–6, 299, 299n, 303, 306–7, 312, 318–20, 325, 330–2
aggressive selling, 63, 67, 76, 85, 97
Alexander, Dr. David, 94, 94n
Allestree, Richard, 287, 287n
Almon, John, 254–7, 260
America, 35, 67–8, 103, 105, 122, 126, 132, 134–5, 137–8, 182, 234, 249, 270n, 282, 317, 323, 333
Amsterdam, 21, 124, 134, 137
Anderson, B. L., 204, 204n, 205n, 209n, 210, 210n, 213, 213n
Anne, Queen, 265n, 269–71, 281, 301
Appleby, Joyce, 5n, 14n, 15–16, 15n-16n, 19n
Archenholz, J. W. von, 10, 10n, 55, 55n, 57, 58n, 94, 94n
Arkwright, Richard, 292, 292n, 308
Ashton, T. S., 24n, 31–2, 32n, 105, 105n, 205n, 207n, 209–10n, 212n
Astley, Philip, 276, 276n, 277n, 307
'Athenian' Stewart, 57–8, 71, 115
Aubrey, John, 289, 289n
Augustus, King of Poland, establishes Meissen factory, 101
auriculas, 66, 271n, 316, 324–5, 333
Austen, Jane, 41, 41n, 92

BACH, Johann Sebastian, 280
Bacon, Sir Edmund, 37
Bakewell, Robert, 318, 320, 321–2
bakers, 206, 246, 257
Baldwin & Woodgate, publishers, 254, 256
Bamford, Samuel, 88, 88n
bankruptcy, 15, 32, 102, 209, 211, 216, 236, 257
Bannister, John, 279, 279n
Barbauld, Mrs. Anna Laetitia, 293, 295, 330, 330n
barbers, 168, 170, 173, 175, 234
Barbon, N., 15, 15n
Barnes, Thomas, 326
Barton, George, 270, 270n
Baskerville, John, friend and publisher of Wilkes, 256
Bateman, Hester, 10
Beckford, William, Lord Mayor of London, 199
Beckford, William, son of above, has Fonthill rebuilt, 12
Bective, Countess of, 28
beer and brewers, 23, 29, 53,. 98, 104, 199, 209, 220, 223, 235, 238, 240–1, 243–7,250,252
Bell, John, 150n, 185n, 188, 190–91, 258
Bell, Mary Ann, 48–9,190,191, 191n
Bentley, Thomas, 73, 73n, 75–6, 75n-6n, 90, 93, 101n, 102, 106, 106n-8n, 109–12, 109–14n, 115–8, 116n-33n, 120–22, 124–34, 137, 137n-40n, 139, 141,143,144, 145n
Berrill, K., 30, 30n
Bewick, Thomas, 329
Bierce, Ambrose, 39, 39n
Bill of Rights, The, and Society of Supporters of, 233–4, 237, 246, 255
bills of exchange, 203, 205, 207–11
Bingley, William, 243, 256, 257, 260

379

Birmingham, 31, 50, 53, 66–70, 67n-8n, 70, 75, 98, 205, 218, 270n, 328
black basalt (Wedgwood), 76,104,107–8
Blake, William, 12, 62, 62n
Blasche, B. H., German educator, 330
Blow, John, writes primer for harpsichord, 279
Blundell, Nicholas, gardener, 323, 324n
Bonnington, drawing master, the famous painter's father, 296, 296n
books, 54, 65, 84, 178–9, 184, 186, 188, 224–6, 231, 241, 246, 253n, 253–6, 258–60, 265–8, 270–3, 270n-4n, 279, 286, 292, 298, 300–3, 305–6, 305n, 308–9, 312, 322–3, 329–31
'bosom bottles', 92
'bosom friends', 82
Boswell, James, 102, 290n
Botero, Giovanni, 22, 22n
Boulton, Matthew, 10,32, 42n, 48, 48n, 66, 69–77, 70n-7n, 112, 115, 125, 130, 133, 140, 140n, 142, 198, 284, 308
Boulton and Fothergill, 71, 72n-3n, 73, 120,125,130,133
Brainiff, Eleanor, 'Bugg destroyer to His Majesty, 84
Bramah, Joseph, locksmith, 32
brass and braziers, facing p.1, 12, 23, 26–7, 31, 67–9, 79, 84, 87
Braudel, Fernand, 31n, 33, 33n, 34–5, 35n-6n, 65, 65n, 98, 98n
Brewer, John, 207n, 233n, 234n, 237n, 244n, 245n, 246n, 253n, 255n,256n
Brewin, of Leicester, florist, 324
Britton, Thomas, musical coal merchant, 279, 279n
Brown, 'Capability', 116, 116n
Brown, John, poet, 16, 16n
Brown, Samuel, introduced itinerating libraries, 327
Browne, John, opposed to corporal punishment in schools, 291, 291n
Browns of Chester, 91, 93n
breeding, of livestock, 10, 318–23
Brummel, Beau, 56
buckles, 23, 29, 31–2, 53, 57, 59, 67, 70–2, 92, 239, 284
Burlington, Earl of, 282
Burton, Robert, *The Anatomy of Melancholy* by, 39, 39n
Burton, William, 105, 105n
Butchell, Martin von, 93

buttons, 10, 12, 23, 29, 31–2, 37, 53, 58, 67,69–72, 74, 92, 129, 139, 239, 284
Byrd, Samuel, 287, 291
Byrd, William of Westover, 287n

CALDWELL, engraver, 58
Campbell, Richard, 49–50, 49n-50n, 94, 94n
carnations, 66, 324–5
carpenters and joiners, 28, 173, 208, 243
Casanova, 210, 316
Catherine the Great, 110, 121, 138
Chambers, Sir William, King's architect, 71
Chandos, Duke of 274n, 280
charitable activities, 22, 224, 225–8, 232, 236
Charlemagne, 4
Charles 11, 95, 267, 275, 278, 280
Charles V, Emperor, 317
Charlotte, Queen, wife of George III, 82, 110, 112, 122
Chartists, 262
Chaucer, Geoffrey, 35
Chelsea porcelain, 10, 102, 102n
Cheney, John, 318
Chesterfield, Lord, 39, 39n
Chetwynd, Mrs, 111, 111n, 112
China, 12, 36–7, 103, 127, 129–30, 139, 239, 266, 266n, 320
chinoiserie, 12, 114
Chippendale, Thomas, 10, 42
Christie, John, auctioneer, 72, 176, 188, 324, 324n, 327, 327n
Church, A. H., 105, 105n
Cibber, Colley, 39, 39n
Claremont, Lady, 72
class distinctions, 9–10, 16, 20, 22–4, 28, 35, 53–4, 59–61, 95, 101, 104, 115–6, 130–31, 133, 141, 197, 266, 280, 283n
client economy, 197–201, 212, 215, 222, 224–5, 231–3, 257
clocks, clockmakers and watches, 12, 27, 71, 75, 79, 82, 184, 190, 322
clothes, dress and dressmakers, 1, 2, 8, 11–12, 15, 17–21, 23, 26, 28, 31, 35–9, 44–5, 47, 49–61, 66, 72, 74, 79–80, 82, 91–2, 94–5, 98, 183–4, 188–90, 206; 222, 239, 272, 286, 310–2, 316, 332
clubs, societies, lodges and fraternities, 200–1, 203, 217–44 passim, 270, 270n, 282

380

INDEX

Cobbett, William, 27–8, 28n
Cock, Mr, basketmaker, 242
coinage and specie, shortage of, 206–7, 209
Cole, Miss, 297
colourists, of fashion plates, 48
Colquhoun, Patrick, 20
Colton, Charles Caleb, 39, 39n
Columbus, Christopher, 317
commercial revolution, 3, 3n, 4, 5n, 69, 79, 139, 140, 144, 146–7, 188
Compton, Henry, Bishop of London, botanist, 323, 323n
Connoisseur, The, 74
consumer behaviour, 2, 3, 5, 10, 13, 21–2, 27, 39, 141, 147, 188
consumer boom, 2, 9, 13, 19, 100, 101, 103
consumer revolution, 1, 5, 5n, 9, 13–4, 29–30, 69–70, 140, 147
consumer society, 2, 3, 5, 5n, 6, 13, 21, 29, 31, 33, 83, 182, 188, 334
consumption, conspicuous, 2, 10, 15n, 18, 21–2, 37, 41, 52, 86, 246, 282
consumption, democratization of, 16, 23, 25, 29
consumption patterns, 5, 9, 10, 12–5, 19–24, 26–9, 41, 66, 96–7, 112, 114
convenience foods, 184
Corelli, Marie, 109n, 279
Cornellys, Mme, mistress of Casanova, 210
corporal punishment 287, 291
Cortes, Father de la, painter, 36
Coulton, F., 297
country houses, viewing their collections, 265, 274, 308
coursing, 321
Covent Garden, theatre, 276, 276n, 284
Cracknell, Thomas, 243
Cranfield, G. A., 215n, 216n, 269n, 273n, 294, 294n, 313n
creamware or Queensware (Wedgwood), 59, 61, 100, 104, 106–9, 107n, 112, 116, 132, 136–7, 140, 238–9
credit, credit-worthiness, 2, 86, 88, 141, 198, 200, 203n, 203–5, 207–16, 220, 222, 228–30, 232, 237, 259, 262, 318n
Crewe, Mrs., 1) 0, 117
Critic, The, 148
Cross, Thomas, music publisher, 271
Culley, George, 318, 320, 320n, 321
Cumberland, Duke of, 249–50
Cunnington, C. W. and P., 40n, 42n, 53–9n, 54–5, 64n, 75n, 91n-3n

cutlery, 10, 23, 27–8, 31–2, 53, 72, 84, 98, 135, 205, 312
Czartoriskie, Prince, 131

DAILY COURANT, first daily newspaper in London, 269
Dance, George, architect, 85, 85n, 273n, 274n
Darton, devised educational games, 309
Davis, Dorothy, 42n, 86, 86n-7n, 87, 89n, 91, 91n
Davis, *Friendly advice to Industrious and Frugal persons*, by, 54, 88n-9n, 94n, 95
Davis, father and son, friends of Wilkes, 254–5
Dawson, Mrs., 295
Day, Thomas, 305
Deane, P., and Cole, W. A., 29, 29n
debt, debtors, 32, 91, 130n, 135, 143, 198–9, 203–5, 207–14, 216–7, 220, 220n, 229–30, 236–7, 259, 262
Defoe, Daniel, 52n, 59, 59n, 94, 213, 273n
Demos, John, 27, 27n, 286n-7n
Dennis, John, 17, 17n, 19n
Dent, Abraham, 207–8, 208n, 215, 215n
Desaguiliers, scientist, 328, 328n
Devonshire, Duchess of, 28, 62, 82, 112, 115
Dibden, 9, 53, 53n
division of labour, 69, 104–5
doctors, 2, 173, 183, 189, 208, 227
Donne, John, 38, 38n, 69
Dopsch, Alfons, 3n, 4
Drummond, Sir Jack, 285, 285n
Drury Lane, theatre, 243, 275, 275n
dumping, 75
Dürer, Albrecht, 317

EARLE, John, 290, 290n
East India Co., 14, 216
Easter sales, 74
Eclipse, stallion, 319, 319n
Edgeworth, Maria, 309, 309n, 311, 311n
Edridge, William, poulterer, 232
Enfield, William, 120–21, 121n
entertainments, marvels, curiosities, 210, 217–8, 220–1, 224, 235, 243, 247, 274–5, 279, 283–4, 306–7, 310, 323, 329
emulation, social emulation and social pride, economic advantages of, 11, 14–5, 18, 20–2, 25, 28, 34, 43, 52, 56, 71–2, 74, 77, 95, 98, 116, 140, 149, 266, 272,

381

284, 286, 289, 292, 298, 300
Etruria, 69, 75–7, 111, 114–5, 120, 122, 127, 138
Evelyn, John, 289, 318n
Eversley, D. E. C., 5n, 23n-4n, 26n, 29, 59n, 200, 200n, 206, 225n
Excise Bill 1733, 201
Exclusion crisis, 267

FAIRCHILD, Thomas, florist, 273n, 325
fairs, 1, 33, 59, 89, 102, 117, 191, 242, 242n, 283, 288n
Fallopius, attitude to masturbation, 312
Fancourt, Samuel, pioneer of circulating libraries, 270
Farley, Edward, 203, 203n, 220
fashion, 1, 2, 10–5, 20–2, 25, 27, 34–6, 38–71, 74–80, 82–4, 86, 88, 90–3, 95–8, 100–106, 108–12, 114–9, 121–2, 124–6, 128–32, 138–9, 141, 143, 148–9, 154, 161–3, 165n, 172–3, 178, 182–5, 189–90, 198, 230, 239, 242, 258, 265, 269–70, 273, 274n, 286, 289, 293, 295, 310, 321, 332
fashion dolls, 1, 43–6, 48–9, 84, 98
fashion magazines, list of, 47
fashion prints, 1, 47–9, 54, 84, 98
Fell, Isaac, 253, 256–7
Fielding, Henry, 24–5, 24n-5n, 54–5, 55n, 149, 149n, 188
Flaxman, John, 105n, 107, 113, 123n
Fleming, Simon H. Le, 268, 268n
florists, gardeners, horticulturists, nurserymen, seedsmen, 66, 242, 249, 272–3, 323–6, 311
Foote, Samuel, *The Mayor of Garret* by, 243, 243n
Ford, Henry, 193
foreign and colonial trade, 24, 67–8, 71, 104, 127–9, 131–2, 134–7, 139, 144, 267
Forster, N, 11, 11n, 34, 38n, 116, 116n
Fortnum & Mason, 86
Foster, John, carpet maker, 28
Fox, Charles James, 310
Frampton, Tregonwell, first professional horse trainer, 281
France, facing 1, 4, 17, 20–1, 25, 41, 44–8, 67–8, 122, 124, 127, 132, 134, 136, 137, 138, 153, 168, 267, 278, 282, 289, 291, 293, 295, 308–9, 313
Fraser, Lady Antonia, book on toys, 44n, 46n, 272n, 285, 310n

Frederick the Great, 249–51
Frith, W. P., 109
furniture, facing 1, 9, 10, 12, 17, 19, 23, 25–8, 42, 70, 124–5, 184, 188, 332

GAINSBOROUGH, Thomas, 62
Galbraith, J. K., 193, 193n
Gammage, R. G., 262, 262n
Gardiner, John, transported for stealing lead coffins, 243
Garrick, David, 123, 243, 247, 276n
Gaskell, Mrs., 92
Gay, John, *The Beggar's Opera*, by 276
Gentleman's Magazine, The, 32, 72, 176n, 251, 258, 269, 269n
George I, 42, 247
George II, 42, 54, 247, 281n
George III, 51, 54, 149–50, 187, 240, 247, 250, 253–4
Germany, 45, 67
Gibbon, Edward, 3–4, 114n, 140, 254
Gilboy, Elizabeth W., 5n, 23, 23n
Gillows of Lancaster, furniture made and sold, 28
Gillray, James, engraver, 57, 57n
Gimblett, John, 70, 71
Gladstone, W. E., 313
glass shop windows, 78–9, 148, 273
Glynn, John, Wilkes's lawyer, 237, 241, 244, 253, 257, 259, 260
Godolphin, Lord, horsebreeder, 281, 318n, 318n
Goldfinch's Nest, The, 177–81
Goldsmith, Oliver, 301
Graham, James, 150, 151, 151n
Green, Guy, 208, 209n, 252, 252n
green glaze, (Wedgwood), 104, 107, 109, 132
Gregory of Tours, 4

HACKWOOD, William, potter, 105n, 113
Haedo, Father, 36
hair, hairdressing, wigs, pernwlgs and perukes, 11–2, 31, 37, 45, 49–50, 55–9 (where 'bag'='wig'), 62–4, 81–2, 84, 95, 175, 239; cork peruke, 241, 332
Hamilton, Sir William, 71, 75, 77n, 111, 113, 115, 128
Hamilton, Lady, 77
handbags, 65
Handel, George Frideric, 188, 278n, 280

INDEX

Hanway, James, 188, 188n
Hanway, Jonas, 28, 29n, 53, 53n
hats, hatters, bonnets, 11, 12, 32, 45, 47, 48, 56, 58, 60–2, 68, 80, 82, 92, 135, 184, 190
Hare, John, music publisher, 271
Harrington, dancing master, 296
Harris, *Lexicon Technicum* by, 272
Harris, Joseph, 20, 20n
hawkers, 13, 77, 103, 118, 123, 231, 237, 240, 246
Hawkins, Sir John, *History of Music* by 279, 279n
Hawksbee, F., scientist, 328
Haydn, Joseph, 280
Hazlitt, William, 39, 39n
Heal's, 86
Heideloff, Nicolaus von, *The Gallery of Fashion* by 48, 48n
Henry VII, 40
Hepplewhite, G., 10, 42
Hickford, Thomas, 280
Hobbes, Thomas, 16
Hogarth, William, 57, 83, 93, 188, 218, 274, 274n, 275, 283n
Holbein, Hans, 42
Holland, Henry, designed Drury Lane theatre of 1792, 275
Holland, Vyvyan, 48
Hollis, Thomas, 239
Holmes, J., Reverend, 295
Homer, 35
Horace, 178
horse-racing, 246, 273–4, 280–1, 280n, 281n, 318–9
Hoskins, W. G., 26n, 87
Houghton, John, 15, 15n, 187, 187n
Howard, John, prison reformer, 211
Hume, David, 254
Humfray, Revel, printer, 209
Hunter Blair, Sir John, 289, 289n
Hutton, William, *History of Birmingham* by, 66, 66n, 67, 68, 68n
hyacinths, 324

IBBOTSON, Henry, 318
Idler, The, 146, 147n, 151n, 303
import restrictions, 136
'improvement', 332
impulse buying, 79, 85, 97
Industrial Revolution, 3, 5, 5n, 9, 9n, 13, 22, 24, 30–2, 43, 53, 66, 69, 70, 96, 101n, 114n, 120n, 138, 143n, 192, 197, 200n, 213n, 284, 292, 311, 327
inertia selling, 94, 96, 130, 135, 141, 191, 256
investors, importance of small, 225
Isham, Sir Justinian, 288
Isham, Thomas, diarist, 288n
Isham, Sir Giles, editor of Thomas Isham's diary, 288n

'J. G.', *A playbook for children* by, 300
Jack Dandy's Delights, series of children's books, 306, 306n
James I, 22
James II, 280–1
jasper, (Wedgwood), 42, 66, 104, 107–8, 116, 119, 122–3, 125, 138, 142
Jeffreys, John, educational games, 309
Jeffries, Nathaniel, King's cutler, 72
Jewitt, Llewelyn, 105, 105n
jigsaw puzzles, 81, 309, 332
John Bull, 135, 157, 164
John, A. H., 5n, 23, 23n, 24n, 200, 205, 225n
Jones, Eric L., 5n, 24n, 26n, 30n, 89, 90n, 96, 96n, 190, 198n, 200, 200n, 206n
Jones, Inigo, 85, 85n
Jones, Sir William, 231
Johnson, William, seedsman, 325–6, 326n
Johnson, Dr. Samuel, and Boswell, 10, 25, 25n, 85, 85n, 101, 102n, 123, 146–8, 148n, 151, 151n, 152, 152n, 217, 245, 253–4, 269, 269n, 290n, 303, 313, 333
Joyce, Jeremiah, Reverend, 330
Junius, 258, 260
Jurin, scientist, 328
Justice, Sir James, 324, 324n

KALM, Pehr, 28, 28n, 62n, 95, 95n
Kant, Emanuel, 313, 313n
Karamzin, Nikolai Mikhailovitch, 10, 10n, 79, 79n, 80, 80n
Kendall, Edward Augustus, 304
Mr. Keys, landlord of 'Forty-five' tavern, 244
King, Gregory, 20
Kirk, James 238
Knight, Mr., seedsman specializing in peas, 326
Knoutschoffierwitz, Ivan Peter Alexis, hairdresser, 64

383

LACKINGTON, James, founder of London book emporium, 85, 86, 86n, 223–4
Landa, Louis, 52, 52n
Landes, David, 95–6, 96n
Lang, Paul Henry, 280, 280n
Latouche, Robert, 3n, 4, 4n
lectures on science, for entertainment, 306, 328–9
Leech, Joseph, wigmaker, 241
L'Estrange, Roger, adapted Aesop for children, 300
Levers, Sir Ashton, 307, 307n
Lewes, Sir Watkin, 221, 237, 253, 253n
libraries, circulating, and 'itinerating', 268, 270, 272, 327
Lichtenberg, G. C., Professor, 10, 10n
Lind, Dr., physician to George III, 72
Linnel, mirror maker, 10
Locke, John, 287, 287n, 289–90, 289n, 292, 300n, 302, 303, 308n, 311, 317n, 320
London, 1, 10, 21, 21n, 22, 33, 37, 41, 44, 49–51, 58–60, 64, 68, 71–4, 76, 77–9, 80–1, 80n, 83, 86, 88–95, 98, 100, 103, 104, 106, 107, 111, 115, 117–24, 126, 138, 139n, 143–4, 153–5, 159, 163, 165n, 166, 170–71, 172, 175, 178–9, 181, 182, 182n, 189, 199, 205, 207, 209–10, 214, 218, 220, 224, 227, 229, 231, 235, 237, 240–2, 242n, 244, 248, 253, 256, 260–1, 267–70, 267n, 273–4, 275n-6n, 276–9, 281, 283–4, 284n, 288n, 294, 299, 307–8, 310–1, 313, 322, 325, 328
'Lord Mills', Wilkes supporter, 246
loss leaders, 94–5, 190
Loudon, editor *Gardener's Magazine*, 326, 327, 327n
Louis XIV, 309
Louis XV of France, establishes Sèvres factory, 101, 102
Lot, Ferdinand, 3n, 4
Lowe, Roger, 90, 90n, 91
Lloyd, Edward, 187
Luddites, 30n, 333
Luttrell, Colonel, 240, 257
luxuries, luxury, 1, 8, 9, 10–1, 14–20, 17n, 24–5, 28, 30, 31, 34, 50, 52, 60, 65, 70, 80, 89, 94, 98, 100, 103, 108, 116, 143, 245, 310

MACAULAY, Lord, 102, 298, 298n
Macaulay, Catherine, radical historian, 258
McGuffog, Mrs, Stamford shopkeeper, 90, 91
Machiavelli, Niccoó, 16
McKendrick, Neil, 7, 9n, 23n, 30n, 33n, 36n, 42n, 55n, 61n, 101n, 105n, 115n, 128n, 152n, 198, 200, 200n, 225n
Macpherson, David, *Annals of Commerce*, 24, 24n
Magna Charta, 246
Maitland, William, 203
Malthus, T. R., 20, 20n
Malynes, 14
Mandeville, Bernard, *Fable of the Bees* by, 8, 15, 16–7, 16n-8n, 25, 51–3, 51n-2n, 66n, 224, 227–8, 227n
Manchester Men, 41, 86, 88, 89n
Manuel, Mr of Turin, exhibits automata, 307
Marx, Karl, 334
Masons, Freemasons and masonic lodges, 200, 218, 219–20, 225, 228, 230, 236, 251, 252
mass market, 10, 20, 22–3, 31, 43, 53, 56, 65, 66, 70–1, 73–5, 77, 98, 103, 124, 141, 143, 197, 225, 251
Mathias, Professor Peter, 5n, 28, 29, 29n, 53n, 127n, 204n, 208n-9n, 209, 213, 220n, 225, 245n
Mause, Lloyd de, 286–7n, 287, 290n, 312n, 313n
Meissen, porcelain factory, 101, 137
mercantilism, 13
Meredith, Sir William, M. P., 134, 240
Meres, John, publisher, 253, 254
Meteren, Emmanual von, 39–40, 40n
Meteyard, Eliza, 105, 105n, 108–9, 109n, 112, 112n, 117n, 121n-2n, 137n
Mexico, 127, 130
Meynell, Hugo, 318, 320, 322
middlemen, 133–4, 205, 207, 209–10, 215, 216–7
Millais, Sir John; 109, 109n
Miller, Philip, bulb grower, 324
milliner, 21, 48–9, 90, 92, 310
Mint, The, 206
Minton, Thomas, potter, 120, 120n, 139n
mirrors, 10, 28
Misselden, Edward, economic writer, 14
Mitchell, B. R., and Deane, P., 29, 29n
'money back if not satisfied' policies, 83, 94, 126, 141, 155
Montgolfier brothers, 63

384

BIRTH OF A CONSUMER SOCIETY

INDEX

Montagu, Lady Mary Wortley, 127
Montague, Mrs E., 70-1, 70n-1n
Montague, Viscount, 37
Moore, Doris Langley, 47n-8n, 48, 56n
More, Hannah, 63, 312
Moritz, C. P., 60, 60n, 95
mortgages, 203-5, 208
Moxen, John, 221
Mozart, Wolfgang Amadeus, 221, 221n, 280
Mun, Thomas, economic writer, 14
music, 185, 197, 222, 235, 241, 253, 265, 271, 272-3, 272n, 274, 275, 278-80, 278n-80n, 282-4, 283n, 285n, 293, 295-6, 299, 305, 307-9, 312, 327, 331-2

'NAKED TRUTH', sign of the, 84, 154, 166, 173, 179-81
naked truth, the, 146, 154, 159, 164, 168, 169, 171, 173
Namier, Sir L., 197, 198, 199n
Napoleon, S, 46, 135
Naples, King of, establishes China factories, 101
neo-classical style, 12, 59, 62, 114, 138
neolithic revolution, 9
Netherlands, Holland, Dutch, 41, 67-8, 99, 129, 133-4, 138, 266, 332
Newbery, John, begins publishing for children with *A pretty little pocket book*, 272-3, 273n, 281, 284, 301, 301n, 302-4, 305n-6n, 306
newspapers, see under names or in footnotes, also 91 (list of), 215-7, 253, 267, 269-70, 273, 281
Newton, Sir Isaac, 301-3
nobility, gentry and aristocracy, 2, 4, 12, 20, 22, 24-6, 33, 37-8, 43, 50, 55, 64, 68, 71-5, 77, 91, 100-3, 106, 108, 110, 114, 117, 121, 124, 128, 130-1, 138, 140-1, 144, 174, 184-5, 189, 197-9, 204, 212, 215, 217-8, 222, 224, 231-3, 236, 248, 252, 257, 266-7, 280, 282, 288, 292, 309, 311, 319, 321-3, 325
North, Sir Dudley, 15, 15n
North Briton, The, 243-4, 254-5, 259
Northumberland, Duke of, 111, 248
Nost, William, printer, 211
novels, 272, 305

OIL LAMPS, and (1792) gas in Oxford St., 78-80
Oliver and Boyd, 306

Oracle, The, 160, 160n, 162, 162n, 174, 176
orerry, (clockwork model of planetary system), 308n, 328-9
ormolu, 66, 71, 72, 112, 132
ornament, 70-1, 73, 106, 114-5, 120, 125, 130, 131-3, 141, 144
Ovid, 34
Owen, Robert, 91, 91n, 193, 193n, 292
Oxford, Lord, 321

PACKWOOD, George, 48, 48n, 84, 90, 93n, 98, 146-7, 150, 152-82, 157n, 163n, 165n, 173n, 177-80, 182n, 185, 191-3, 194
Packwood's Whim, 173n, 177n, 179-80, 179n-80n, 181-2, 182n
Paine, Tom, *The Rights of Man* by, 306
Palmer & Neale, 105
Paoli, Pasquale, 226, 258
Paris, 21, 43-4, 50, 79-80, 134, 137, 190, 307
Parkin, Elizabeth, 208, 208n
patronage, 48, 71-2, 76, 84, 93, 102, 109-10, 115-7, 119, 124, 128, 143, 184, 198-9, 200, 224-5, 227, 228, 232-3, 283
pattern books, 67-8, 70, 75, 119
pattern cards, 67-8
Payne, Professor, P. L., 126n, 192-3, 193n
pedlars, 1, 13, 33, 41, 77, 86-8, 89, 103, 143, 191, 231, 246
Penrice, William, landlord of the Surrey Tavern, 246
Pepusch, J. C., musician, 280
Pepys, Samuel, 267, 267n, 268, 275, 277, 278, 287, 287n-8n, 312, 312n
Percy, Thomas, 248, 248n
Perfects of Pontefract, seedsmen, 326
Perkin, Harold, 20, 20n
pets, 10, 274, 288, 310, 312, 317-8, 321-2, 326
pigeons, 318, 321-3
Pilkington, glass manufacturer, 32
Pinchbeck, Christopher, clockmaker and metalworker, 284
pinchbeck, alloy called after above, 71, 77
Pine and Roberts, founded *The London Packet,* 258
pins, 31, 247, 284
Pirenne, Henri, 3n, 4
Pitt, William, 249, 250, 251
Pitt, Mr, proprietor of mechanical marvels, 307

385

Playford, John, musician and publisher, 279
playing cards, 308–9, 333
Plumb, Professor, J. H., 11n, 37, 37n-8n, 66n, 101, 101n-2n, 133n, 200n, 225n, 242n, 264, 266n-7n, 269n-70n, 274n, 278n, 283n, 288n, 316n, 329n
pockets, 65, 92
Pole, Sir John, 251
Pombal, Marchioness of, 131
Pompeii, 186
Pope, Alexander, 52
Popish Plot, The, 267
Portland, Duchess of, 73n, 114
Portugal, 67, 127, 129, 131, 134, 136, 206, 223, 317
Post Man, The, and *The Post Boy*, first two non-official newspapers, 269, 269n, 270n, 319n
pottery, porcelain and ceramics, 10, 12, 23, 27–9, 31–2, 42, 53, 59, 62, 69, 72, 75–6, 80, 83, 100–145 passim, 184, 201–2, 238–9, 241, 248–52, 249n, 251n, 260, 332
poverty, and the poor, 2, facing 9, 10, 14, 17, 19, 25–8, 30–1, 35–6, 62, 80, 104, 143, 197, 200, 220, 226, 226n, 232, 311n, 316, 326–7
prelapsarian myth, 30
Prévost, Abbé, 44
prices and price policy, 12, 23, 47, 53, 66, 73–5, 79, 83, 86–88, 90, 94, 102, 105–7, 111, 119, 126, 128–9, 131, 136–8, 141–3, 151, 155, 167, 172, 186, 189, 219, 222, 240, 244–5, 266, 268, 271–3, 296–8, 300, 307, 318–9, 324, 331
Priestley, Joseph, 123, 139, 295n
print shops, 274
printers, printing, booksellers, 32, 53, 81, 157, 177, 201–2, 204, 209, 211, 215–6, 230–1, 238, 241, 253, 253n, 254, 256, 258, 259–60, 266–8, 267n, 271–3, 272n, 300, 305, 306, 309–10, 327
prisons (gaols, including Fleet, King's Bench, Newgate, Marshalsea), 210–11, 216, 220, 235–7, 245–6
Proctor, Sir Beauchamp, 241, 242n
product differentiation, 186
production loan, oldest form of, 4
proprietary brand medicines, 185–6
publicans, profit from Wilkite clubs, 201, 202, 238, 241–6, 250, 252

QUANT, Mary, 64

RABONE, 71
Ransome, Reverend Richard, schoolmaster, 288
razor strop, Packwood's, 146–94 passim
Rembrandt, H. van Ryn, 38
Revolution of 1688, 267
Reynolds, John, lawyer, 237
Reynolds, Sir Joshua, 115
Rich, John, established pantomime, 276, 276n
rich, the, facing p. 9, 10–2, 14, 15, 17, 25, 29, 56–7, 64, 80–1, 95, 103, 112, 117, 129, 185n, 197, 245, 274n, 288, 307
Richardson, John, 297
Riem, Andreas, Prussian preacher, wrote *Travels*, 81
Robinson, D. E., 42, 70, 70n-4n, 77n, 140
Roche, Sophie von la, 79, 79n, 80, 81n, 85
Rockingham, Marquis of, 292, 292n
Romney, George, 114, 139
Ronskley, William, 301
Rousseau, Jean-Jacques, 287n, 311
Rowe, Mrs, runs boarding school, 296
Rowlandson, Thomas, 62
Russia, 106, 111–2, 114n, 121, 127–9, 132, 133n, 134, 137–9, 191

SACHEVERELL, Dr., 249, 249n
Sadler, John, 223, 223n, 238, 238n, 251, 251n, 252, 252n
Saint Fond, Faujas de, 137, 137n
sales, policy and technique, 2, 4, 5–6, 9, 11–3, 22–3, 33, 43, 62, 67–9, 70n, 71–3, 76–7, 84–5, 87–8, 90, 93–4, 96–100, 102–4, 107–9, 112–3, 116–9, 122–4, 126–31, 133–5, 137–48, 154, 177, 188, 191
salesman, travelling, 67, 86–7, 89–90, 118, 122, 123, 126, 139, 143–4, 191
Sandby, Paul, 83
Sandwich, Earl of, 288
schools, small private 290, location 294; increase in numbers of 293; reunions 299, books 300–6
Scotch Drapers, 13, 41, 86–9
Scotch Hawkers, 41, 86, 88
Schumpeter, Mrs. Elizabeth B., 5n, 29n, 136, 136n, 193
Seally, John, writing master, 240
Seddon and Son, furnishers, 28

386

INDEX

self-education, 266–8, 272, 308
self-service, 33, 94, 119, 141
servants, maids, 21–3,38,49,57–60,62, 74, 80, 94–5, 139, 153, 155–7, 184, 228, 307
Sèvres, 101, 102, 124, 137
Shakespeare, William, 35, 88, 247, 275n
Shaw, George Bernard, 39, 39n
Sheffield, 10, 31, 50, 53, 98, 135, 204n, 208, 296–7, 305n, 311, 311n, 313
Sheraton, Thomas, 10, 42, 83
Sheridan, R. B., 148, 148n, 275n
shoes and shoemakers, 11, 18, 31–2, 41, 57, 63, 68, 72, 79, 84, 89, 92, 222
shops and shopkeepers, 1, 4, 4n, 6, 13, 21, 30, 33, 41, 49–50, 59, 71, 77–9, 82–3, 87, 90–4, 98, 119–20, 123–4, 133, 141, 148, 151, 155–7, 158–9, 167, 169, 171, 181, 184–5, 188, 191, 197, 199, 201, 203, 205–7, 210–2, 214–5, 233, 237, 255, 269, 270, 273, 273n, 280, 282, 298, 306, 310–1, 322, 325, 325n
silver, 10, 12, 42, 56, 64, 71, 79, 90, 188, 190, 206, 210, 239, 244
Smiles, Samuel, 105, 105n
Smith, Adam, *The Wealth of Nations* by 15, 15n, 19–20, 20n, 31
Smith, John, schoolmaster, 295
Smith, Sydney, 89
snobbery, 28, 71,140
social mobility, 11, 16, 20, 22, 25, 36, 292
Sommerville, T., 54, 54n, 95, 95n
South Sea Bubble, 199, 210,212
Southey, Robert, 78, 78n, 85
Spain, 127, 129, 130–32, 134, 137–8, 140, 249, 252, 284
spas, 283–4, 320
spectacles, 190
Spectator, The, 222, 222n, 223n, 269, 269n, 283–4
Spershott, James, 95, 95n
Spilsbury, John, 81, 309
Spode, Josiah, sets up warehouse in London, 120, 120n; son teams up with William Copeland, 139n
Staffordshire, 31, 69, 97, 103–4, 118, 120, 129, 133, 136–7, 140, 142–4, 144n
Stanley, Lady Isabella, 110
Steele, Sir Richard, 55, 269
Stout, William, Quaker grocer, 90, 91n
Strahan, William, royal printer and Dr. Johnson's printer, 254, 254n
Strickland, Sir George, 110

Strutt, Jedediah, 292, 292n
Stubbs, George, 12,60–2,95, 105n, 110, 115–6, 115n, 139
Stubbs, Philip, 38
Stubs, Peter, nailmaker, 31
sugar, as a loss leader, 94, 199
sugar-baker, honours Wilkes, 241
sumptuary laws, 2,19,37,40
Sunderland, Earl of, 268
Swan and Edgar, 86
Swift, Jonathan, 19, 19n

TABART, ran juvenile library, 305
tailors (taylors), 18, 21, 49, 82, 173, 208, 310–1
Tatler, The, 147, 180, 186, 186n
Tattersall, Richard, horse auctioneer, 120, 188, 281
Tattersalls, 120
taverns, inns and coffee houses, 153, 203, 206–8, 218, 223–4, 226, 234–6, 236n, 238, 241–2, 244–6, 249, 252, 260, 268–70, 269n, 279–80, 279n, 282, 325, 325n
Taylor, John, 67n, 68, 68n, 70–1
tea,28, 29, 81, 104, 108, 139n, 199, 262, 276
Telescope, Tom, pen-name of children's writer, 301, 301n, 302–3, 330
Telford, Thomas, engineer, 149, 183, 183n
Telfords of York, seedsmen and nurserymen, 326
Thacker, Dean of Durham's cook, *Art of Cookery* by, 271
theatres, See also (,Covent Garden' and 'Drury Lane'), 225, 242, 242n, 273–6, 275n, 275–8, 282, 284–5, 285n
The Times, 65, 92, 154–5, 155n, 164, 165n, 174, 174n, 176n, 187
The way to get money, 146, 177
Thirsk, Joan, 5n, 26n, 38, 38n
Thomas, Dr. J., 120n; 139, 139n
Thompson, R., radical printer, 260
Thrale, Henry, friend of Dr. Johnson, 245
Timmins, Samuel, 67, 67n
Tissot, Dr. Simon, 313, 313n
Towsey, Elizabeth, Chester milliner and haberdasher, 90, 92–3
Townshend, Lord, 119–20, 119n, 318
toys and games, 74, 81, 97, 142, 272, 273n, 286, 288; 300, 308–12, 331–2
'toys' (small brass articles) 68–70

387

trade cards, 32, 41, 65,81–5, 93, 141, 184, 293, 323, 332n
Trevelyan, G. M., 105, 105n
Trimmer, Mrs, 305, 312
'truck', origin of, 207
True Briton, 157, 157n, 162n, 170n, 171, 171n, 173, 173n
Truman, Ben, of following firm, Wilkite, 246
Truman, Hanbury & Buxton, London brewers, 89, 209, 220, 220n, 246
Truslet, John, 29n, 50, 50n-1n
Tucker, Josiah, facing p. 1, 25–6, 26n, 53, 53n
tulips and tulipmania, 64, 66,100, 323–4
Turkey, 127–9, 132, 138, 323n
Turner, Thomas, 90, 90n

VAL, Pierre, du, 309
Vaughan, William, 14,38
Veblen, Thorstein, and 'Veblen effect', 15, 38, 52–3, 52n-3n, 58, 58n, 96, 140, 140n, 141
vegetables, as hair accessories, 63
Vernon, Admiral, 249–50
Vichert, Gordon, Professor 15n 52 52n
Vincennes, original location of Sèvres porcelain factory, 124
Vivaldi, Antonio, 279
Vyner, Sir Robert and family, 289, 289n

WAGES, 19, 23–4, 40, 59, 130n, 143, 206–7,224
Walkinshaw, printer, 177
Wallis, John, publisher of educational games, 309
Walpole, Horace, 117, 117n, 124, 250, 250n, 274n, 276, 277n
Walpole, Sir Robert, 269, 269n, 288, 288n
Walpole, Robert, father of Sir Robert, 278
Walsh, John, music publisher, 271, 279, 279n
Wanamaker, John, satisfaction-or-money-back policy, 126
Ward, manufacturer, 71, 120n

Watt, James, 77, 77n, 139, 284, 308
Watt, John, proprietor of Manchester Bazaar, 90
Watts, Isaac, 17n, 270
Wedgwood, John, 103n, 104, 110n
Wedgwood, Josiah, 10, 23n, 28, 32, 33n, 42–3, 42n, 48, 48n, 59, 65–6, 69, 71–3, 72n-3n, 75–7, 75n-6n, 80 83, 90, 93, 100, 100n-1n, 102–105, 102n-133n, 135n, 137n-140n, 143–5, 145–7, 149, 175, 176n, 185, 192–3, 198, 198n, 208, 238, 252, 252n, 266, 284, 292, 308
Wenderborne, F. A., 55, 55n-6n
Wesley, John, 16, 16n, 122
Wilkes, John, 201, 201n, 230–50, 232n, 252–6, 255n-6n, 258–61, 259n
Wheble, printer of *Middlesex Journal*, 260
Whiston, Rev. William scientist 328
Whit bread, Samuel, 89: 220 '
White, John, dancing teacher, 296
William Ill, 247, 265n, 281.
Williams, John, Wilkite bookseller and publisher, 255, 256
Wolfe, General James, 249
Wollstonecraft, Mary, 297, 297n
Wood, Ralph, 62
Woodgate, Wilkite printer, 256
Woodward, engraver, 57
'work ethic', 230
Wright, Joseph, of Derby, 113–5, 113n, 139, 308n, 329
Wright, Michael, 289, 289n
Wright, Thomas, King's clockmaker, 71
Wrigley, Professor, E. A., 5n, 21, 21n, 22
Würtemberg, Duke of, establishes porcelain factory, 101
Wyatt, James, architect, 116

YOUNG, Arthur, 9, 20, 20n
Young, Sir George, 110

ZOFFANY, John, painter, 115
Zola, Emile, 223
zoos and 'animal and bird museum', 10, 306, 323, 332

Lightning Source UK Ltd.
Milton Keynes UK
UKHW020431300520
364119UK00005B/355